The Almanac *of* State Legislatures

The Almanac *of* State Legislatures

Changing Patterns, 1990–1997
Second Edition

William Lilley III

Laurence J. DeFranco

Mark F. Bernstein

 CONGRESSIONAL QUARTERLY INC.
Washington, D.C.

A Note from the Publisher

The Almanac of State Legislatures, Second Edition, is the fourth in a series of unique reference works published in the 1990s by Congressional Quarterly Books. It provides a detailed socioeconomic snapshot of the nation's 6,744 state legislative districts. Although many of these newly apportioned slices of geopolitical terrain are small in land mass, they are nevertheless large in their political importance. The almanac presents critical baseline data against which trends in legislative district demographics can be measured.

This book could not have been done without sophisticated computer software that made it possible to juxtapose massive amounts of electoral, demographic, and socioeconomic data with an equally massive database of 6,744 state legislative districts. Through these techniques new references based on additional economic and demographic measures will be possible. Further manipulation and elaboration of the data make possible district rankings showing who speaks for the rich and who speaks for the poor, who speaks for the most educated and who speaks for the least educated, and so on. With a continued emphasis on state and local politics, the almanac and the material that underlies it represent an unusually rich lode of information for scholars, legislators, and others.

Copyright © 1998 Congressional Quarterly Inc.
1414 22nd Street, N.W., Washington, D.C. 20037
(202) 822-1475; (800) 638-1710

http://books.cq.com

Library of Congress Cataloging-in-Publication Data

Lilley, William.
    The almanac of state legislatures : changing patterns 1990–1997 /
William Lilley III, Laurence J. DeFranco, Mark F. Bernstein. — 2nd
ed.
        p.   cm.
    ISBN 1-56802-434-7
    1. United States—Administrative and political divisions—Maps.
2. Election districts—United States—Maps. 3. United States—
Statistics, Vital—Maps. 4. United States—Economic
conditions—1981– —Maps. 5. United States—Social
conditions—1980– —Maps. 6. Election districts—United States—
Statistics. I. DeFranco, Laurence J. II. Bernstein, Mark F.
III. Title.
G1201.F7 L5 1998 <G&M>
912.73—DC21
                                              98-47468
                                                 CIP
                                                MAPS

CONTENTS

PREFACE

The Almanac of State Legislatures: Changing Patterns, 1990–1997, Second Edition, is a thorough revision, expansion, and update of the three previous books published in this series of analyses of American state legislatures: *The Almanac of State Legislatures* (1994), *The State Atlas of Political and Cultural Diversity* (1997), and *State Legislative Elections* (1998, written with Michael Barone). Whereas the socioeconomic data underpinning those three books relied heavily on the 1990 census, this fourth volume relies almost entirely on 1997 data charting how much each of the 6,744 districts has changed during the 1990s. This volume captures alterations in each district's population, wealth, and racial composition for the period 1990–1997. The changes in many cases are large; hence this book provides an end-of-the-century snapshot of what the redistricters in each of the fifty states will face early in the coming decade.

The introduction to the volume summarizes the major trends at work in all fifty states. State-by-state analyses and data follow. Each state profile includes an essay analyzing the major changes that are taking place; two-color maps showing how much population each legislative district has gained or lost during the 1990s; and statistical tables showing population change, income change, and racial/ethnic change for each district during the decade. The data are juxtaposed with the district's geodemographic status (urban, suburban, or rural) according to 1990 census data. The state-by-state data enable the reader to make informed judgments about how a state's legislative composition will change in the next decade.

Methodology

Two basic methodological components underlie the information in this volume, and both reflect refinements and expansions of methodologies used in the previous three volumes. The meshing of the two creates the book's added value.

The first component is the boundaries of each of the 6,744 state legislative districts. Just as in the three previous books in this series, the basic building block was the digitized state legislative boundaries. Before publication of the 1994 almanac, no single volume contained all of the precise geographical boundaries of every state senate and house district in the country. These boundaries have been re-created for this volume and include revisions made by the states during the decade. The methods used to determine each state's boundaries were described in detail in the prefaces of the earlier volumes. Suffice it to say that no state's districting process is the same as any other state's, and thus determining the boundaries and maintaining their accuracy is a complex task.

The second component is the state-by-state data sets for population, income, racial/ethnic composition, education, and unemployment for 1997 and 1990–1997 growth rates—both provided by Claritas Demographics Inc. Claritas collected the data from a number of official government and commercial sources, then disaggregated these data to census block groups—an official government geographic definition. InContext then, as it did in the previous volumes, aggregated the census block group data to the legislative district level.

The authors are fully aware that there are many legitimate and sophisticated debates in the country as to the ways the Census Bureau and other official government entities collect data. In *The State Atlas of Political and Cultural Diversity,* we noted that the Census Bureau has long been challenged on how it defines racial and ethnic groups and how it collects racial/ethnic data, but we used the Census Bureau data because they are the best available. This volume used the most reliable and comprehensive estimating counts taken during the decade. These include the biennial Census Bureau population estimates for the nation's 35,298 Minor Civil Division levels of government, the combined Bureau of Labor Statistics and Census Bureau annual population surveys of 60,000 households, and the Bureau of Economic Affairs' annual surveys of county income levels. These counts are all mandated by federal statutes. Claritas supplemented the federally collected data with population estimates taken during the decade by the 1,600 local governments that also mandate mid-decade estimating. Like the decennial census, all of these estimates are open to challenge. Finally, Claritas supplements its information with commercially available data and its own research. We rely on these data because they are official, they are numerous, they are inherently cross-checking, and they are collected on an ongoing basis during the decade. They are the best available.

A final methodological note: This volume identifies each district's geodemographic status—urban, suburban, or rural—based on 1990 census data and the district's current geographic boundaries. That geodemographic identification, so critical to a district's potential political leanings, will change after redistricting early in the next decade.

Acknowledgments

This volume in the series, like the ones before it, owes much to InContext's ability to maintain, manipulate, and merge complex databases and equally to the ability of

InContext to create two-color maps based on merges of geopolitical data. Of the many people who have helped us nurture and enhance these abilities, fourteen have been especially helpful over the years. We take this opportunity to thank Robert T. Blau, Walter P. Czarnecki, Derek L. Crawford, John R. Dunham, Alfredo Filippone, David I. Greenberg, David G. Laufer, Michael H. Moskow, Frances M. Norris, John Roberts, Joshua J. Slavitt, Ronald F. Stowe, William A. Testa, and Wayne H. Winegarden. We had the good fortune to continue our multivolume partnership with two key people at Congressional Quarterly Books—Nancy A. Lammers and David R. Tarr. As in the previous volumes, the heavy lifting in the critical computer mapping and tabular areas was done by InContext's Peter W. Fleury, and, as before, Diane I. Ching DeFranco, vice chair and cofounder of InContext, was responsible for much of the book's design, formatting, and production in computerized files.

William Lilley III
Laurence J. DeFranco
Mark F. Bernstein

INTRODUCTION

In 1910, Lord Bryce, whose assessments of the United States were usually right on the money, wrote in the last chapter of *The American Commonwealth,* "To make rural life more attractive and so check the inflow to the cities, is one of the chief tasks of American statesmanship today." Bryce would have been surprised to learn that the rural exodus never really stopped. That many rural counties in this decade have halted their decline or even posted modest population gains reflects not so much a return to the land as the continuing spread of the suburbs.

Cities have been shrinking and suburbs growing since the 1920s. Those trends have accelerated in the 1990s. In region after region, a pattern repeats itself: a central city losing population is surrounded by close-in suburbs of modest growth, which are themselves surrounded by more far-flung suburbs of much faster growth, with growth often spreading into rural districts once considered to be outside the metropolitan area.

Of the fifty fastest-growing state house districts in the United States, twenty-eight are suburban, fifteen are rural, six are urban, and one is of mixed use. (The six rapidly growing urban districts are all in booming Arizona and Nevada.) Of the country's fifty fastest-shrinking state house districts, twenty-nine are urban, thirteen are rural, seven are suburban, and one is of mixed use.

This change in residential patterns has produced what is sometimes called the "metropolitan doughnut": a situation in which people are simultaneously pushing out from the city center and rushing in from the countryside, creating an ever-widening circle of suburbs. This process has also been called the "rural rebound," but that is something of a misnomer. The rural areas that are growing fastest are those that are most rapidly losing their character as rural. People are not moving to places like Roseville, California, or Schaumburg, Illinois, to live the country life but to live the suburban life no longer possible in many crowded, older suburbs. Such rural districts will be under enormous pressure in the coming years to provide the suburban services—schools, roads, shopping—that wealthy new arrivals will demand.

Beyond the metropolitan doughnut, rural districts still based on farming or mining have either lost population or have posted only modest gains. In Pennsylvania, for example, rural house districts between Philadelphia, Harrisburg, and Reading have done well since 1990, but rural districts in the coal counties have grown much less rapidly, if at all. Isolated rural areas that cater to recreation, such as Myrtle Beach, South Carolina, or to retirees, such as the new communities around Branson, Missouri, have fared much better.

Tables 1 through 4 provide examples from four cities—Chicago, Los Angeles, Philadelphia, and St. Louis—that illustrate the metropolitan doughnut. In each table, the first line is a district close to the center of the city, the last line a rural or suburban district on the fast-growing fringe of population growth. In between are districts moving geographically from the city's edge to older suburbs to newer ones. It is worth noting that the wealthier districts are often those closer to the cities. Many families leapfrog to distant suburbs because they cannot afford to buy in the established suburbs.

For the second decade in a row, most of the fastest-growing states are in the Mountain time zone. A broad line drawn diagonally from Seattle to Houston would cross them all except Georgia—Washington, Oregon, Idaho, Utah, Nevada, Colorado, Arizona, New Mexico, and Texas. Almost all of the slowest-growing states are in the Northeast, areas that have lost their industrial base and continue to struggle with overcrowding, high taxes, and crime.

Another demographic phenomenon of the 1990s has been the steady increase in the number of Hispanics. The Census Bureau estimates that within the next ten years, Hispanics will overtake African Americans as the country's largest racial or ethnic group. Because of a steady stream of immigration, Hispanics in this decade have already surpassed the number of blacks in two of the four largest states: Florida and New York. By 2030, the Census Bureau estimates that whites will account for less than half of the country's population.

Although a great deal of ink has been spilled during the decade about the need for black-majority legislative districts, it is apparent that many of the residents of those districts do not want to live there. Of 339 black-majority state house districts in the United States, 210 have lost population since 1990. Only one black-majority urban district outside the old Confederacy has grown by more than 4 percent, and only two black-majority districts anywhere in the United States (in Atlanta and Charlotte) have enjoyed double-digit growth.

The opposite is true of Hispanic-majority districts. Of 113 Hispanic-majority districts, 86 have gained population, although their rate of growth is slow except along the southern border. What is also striking is that there are exactly three times as many black-majority districts in the country as there are Hispanic-majority districts, despite the fact that blacks now only barely outnumber Hispanics. The political considerations that have created this imbalance may come under attack as Hispanics assume more political power.

The third phenomenon is age. It is well known that the nation is growing older. In many places, however, the two fastest-growing age categories are senior citizens and children; these areas, in other words, are growing both older *and* younger. Less well appreciated is the way in which age and race sometimes intersect. It is estimated that by 2010, more than two-thirds of California's school children will be Hispanic, Asian, or African American, while the population over age fifty will remain mostly white.

We can only guess at the social and political implications of these figures as whites, with fewer children and living ever farther from the cities, are asked to provide social services to growing numbers of urban minorities, and as shrinking cities seek more assistance from state government but have less political clout with which to get it.

The state legislatures will remain the field on which many of the nation's most important battles are fought.

Table 1 Selected Chicago-area House Districts

State average household income: $54,426
Racial/ethnic composition: 72% white, 15% black, 3% Asian, 10% Hispanic
State population growth, 1990–1997: 4%

District	Type	Racial/Ethnic Composition	Population Growth, 1990–1997	Average Household Income, 1997
10	Older residential, northwest side	5% white 80% black 1% Asian 14% Hispanic	–10	$31,160
8	Residential urban, inside South Tollway	22% white 70% black 1% Asian 6% Hispanic	–6	$49,429
77	Close-in suburbs	76% white 4% black 2% Asian 17% Hispanic	–1	$58,368
46	Close-in suburbs	80% white 1% black 5% Asian 14% Hispanic	0	$ 61,724
45	Rural, just inside I-290	82% white 3% black 9% Asian 6% Hispanic	+8	$ 68,405
49	Suburban Schaumburg	79% white 4% black 9% Asian 8% Hispanic	+21	$ 69,497
50	Rural, Cook/DuPage County line	86% white 1% black 4% Asian 8% Hispanic	+23	$ 77,923

Table 2 Selected Los Angeles-area House Districts

State average household income: $57,083
Racial/ethnic composition: 52% white, 7% black, 11% Asian, 30% Hispanic
State population growth, 1990–1997: 8%

District	Type	Racial/Ethnic Composition	Population Growth, 1990–1997	Average Household Income, 1997
46	Urban Los Angeles	3% white 7% black 14% Asian 75% Hispanic	−13	$26,835
45	Urban E. Los Angeles	8% white 3% black 21% Asian 68% Hispanic	−16	$ 35,290
44	Urban San Gabriel	50% white 12% black 13% Asian 24% Hispanic	+7	$ 65,731
59	Suburban Pasadena	54% white 6% black 11% Asian 28% Hispanic	+11	$ 61,145
36	Suburban San Gabriel Mtns., Lancaster	65% white 5 % black 5% Asian 24% Hispanic	+29	$ 55,287
34	Rural Mojave Desert	70% white 5% black 3% Asian 20% Hispanic	+18	$ 41,860

Table 3 Selected Philadelphia-area House Districts

State average household income: $48,834
Racial/ethnic composition: 87% white; 9% black; 1% Asian; 2% Hispanic
State population growth, 1990–1997: 1%

District	Type	Racial/Ethnic Composition	Population Growth, 1990–1997	Average Household Income, 1997
198	Germantown and East Mt. Airy, older residential	31% white 66% black 1% Asian 2% Hispanic	–7	$49,862
200	Residential urban	26% white 71% black 1% Asian 1% Hispanic	–7	$ 52,535
154	Close-in suburbs	82% white 12% black 4% Asian 1% Hispanic	–2	$ 79,360
148	Close-in suburbs	93% white 3% black 3% Asian 1% Hispanic	+1	$110,681
61	Norristown suburbs	88% white 4% black 6% Asian 1% Hispanic	+10	$ 86,643

Table 4 Selected St. Louis-area House Districts

State average household income: $44,506
Racial/ethnic composition: 86% white, 11% black, 1% Asian, 1% Hispanic
State population growth, 1990–1997: 5%

District	Type	Racial/Ethnic Composition	Population Growth, 1990–1997	Average Household Income, 1997
67	Central urban	66% white 29% black 3% Asian 2% Hispanic	−16	$32,983
65	Urban residential, near Forest Park	88% white 9% black 1% Asian 2% Hispanic	−7	$ 43,987
84	Close suburbs inside I-170	79% white 15% black 4% Asian 2% Hispanic	0	$ 60,225
87	Middle suburbs around Clayton, Ladue	87% white 8% black 4% Asian 1% Hispanic	−2	$117,225
86	Middle suburbs around Chesterfield	90% white 2% black 6% Asian 1% Hispanic	−2	$106,631
89	Distant suburbs	93% white 4% black 2% Asian 1% Hispanic	+22	$ 92,260
13	Rural St. Charles County	92% white 5% black 1% Asian 2% Hispanic	+21	$ 56,433

About the Authors

The Almanac of State Legislatures: Changing Patterns 1990–1997 was prepared by **InContext** Inc., an international information company based at 1615 L Street, N.W., Suite 650, Washington, D.C. 20036 (phone, 202-659-1023, fax, 202-293-9236). InContext specializes in political-economic analyses that juxtapose economic data (such as the numbers of jobs in specific types of local businesses) with geographic areas defined by a political jurisdiction (such as a state assembly district or city council district), an economic service jurisdiction (such as a daily newspaper service area, a local gas utility service area, or a Yellow Pages market area), or a local or regional market area affected by a major entertainment or sports event.

William Lilley III, chairman and cofounder of InContext, is an economic historian with experience in the private and public sectors. Lilley was a senior corporate official of CBS Inc. in New York. Previously, he served as director of the U.S. Council on Wage and Price Stability and as staff director of the Budget Committee of the U.S. House of Representatives. He received his Ph.D. from Yale University, taught at Yale, and has written widely on the effects of government policies on local economic activity, the economics of professional sports, and the social-economic makeup of state and local political constituencies.

Laurence J. DeFranco, president and cofounder of InContext, is an expert in the new field of geoeconomics, which merges the disciplines of economics, geography, and computer science. DeFranco has coauthored many studies on the effects of economic policy on businesses. He has provided expert testimony and addressed industry leaders on economic policy. He is also president of Program Flow, Inc., a research and consulting firm in McLean, Virginia. Previously, he worked for CBS Inc.

Mark F. Bernstein is a writer and lawyer whose work has appeared in the *Public Interest,* the *New Republic,* and the *Wall Street Journal.* Previously, he was a law clerk for a judge on the U.S. Court of Appeals, a legislative aide to Rep. Richard J. Durbin, D-Ill., and a research assistant to Sen. Daniel Patrick Moynihan, D-N.Y. Bernstein graduated from Princeton University and received his law degree from the University of Virginia, where he was an editor of the law review.

ALABAMA

As it does all southern states, the Voting Rights Act prohibits Alabama from redrawing its electoral districts without prior approval from the Justice Department. This legacy of segregation unavoidably complicates the state's redistricting process, though with good reason.

Alabama has had, to put it mildly, a colorful history of reapportionment. As late as the early 1960s, Alabama still apportioned its legislative districts according to the *1900* census, despite a provision of the state constitution requiring that districts be redrawn every ten years. Some districts had forty times as many people as others. It was a challenge to those boundaries in 1964 that led the Supreme Court to issue its famous "one person, one vote" decision in *Reynolds v. Sims.* The Court in *Reynolds* required that electoral districts in both houses of bicameral state legislatures be equally populated

It is worth noting that the plaintiffs in *Reynolds* were white. As C. Vann Woodward and others have noted, because hardly any blacks in Alabama could vote before 1964, such gerrymandering was intended to disenfranchise poor white voters, especially those in industrial Birmingham, who might support more radical Democrats. Race baiting was then a tactic of the white establishment to prevent poor whites and poor blacks from finding common cause. No one today would fear that those groups would form a political coalition. Alabama, like most southern states, is sharply divided between white Republicans and black Democrats.

One key to understanding Alabama is the extent to which its racial divisions are geographic. The northern counties along the Tennessee and Coosa Rivers remain overwhelmingly white, while the black population (the smallest by percentage, incidentally, of any deep southern state except Florida) remains concentrated in the rich cotton lands of central and southern Alabama. Residential separation translates into political separation. Twenty-three northern Alabama house districts are more than 90 percent white, while another fifteen districts, all in central Birmingham and the southern counties, are more than two-thirds black.

Blacks have gained the franchise in Alabama, but they make up a much smaller share of the state than they once

did. In 1870 blacks constituted 47 percent of the state's population. By 1910 it had dropped to 42.5 percent. Today it is barely 26 percent.

In order to maximize black voting districts in Birmingham after the 1990 census, the state engaged in racial gerrymandering, which has had the unintended consequence (though some argue it was deliberate) of leaving the areas surrounding those black-majority districts with more white, conservative voters. Certainly it has cost Alabama Democrats dearly. Over the last six years, the party has lost three U.S. House seats, as well as four in the state senate and another ten in the house. Statewide, they have also lost the governor's mansion and both U.S. Senate seats.

Furthermore, the growing areas of the state are almost all white—the suburbs across Mobile Bay, suburban Huntsville in the far north, and suburban Birmingham in the mid-state.

Politically, the growth in the predominantly white suburbs may have great implications. Despite their losses, Democrats still control the state house of representatives, 71–34, and the senate, 22–12. But nine of the ten fastest-growing house districts and seven of the ten fastest-growing senate districts are held by Republicans. Then too, nine of the ten slowest-growing house and senate districts, and twenty-one of the twenty-three Alabama districts that have lost population during the 1990s, are held by Democrats. In order to preserve seats African Americans can win, it may be necessary to pull black voters from surrounding districts that currently have a white majority, thus reducing the supply of reliable Democratic votes in those surrounding districts and perhaps starting another electoral chain reaction.

Thus, the partisan gap in the Alabama legislature could close considerably over the next several years, and if Republicans can keep the governorship for the next round of reapportionment, what was once one of the nation's most Democratic states could surrender entirely to the GOP early in the next century.

ALABAMA
State Senate Districts

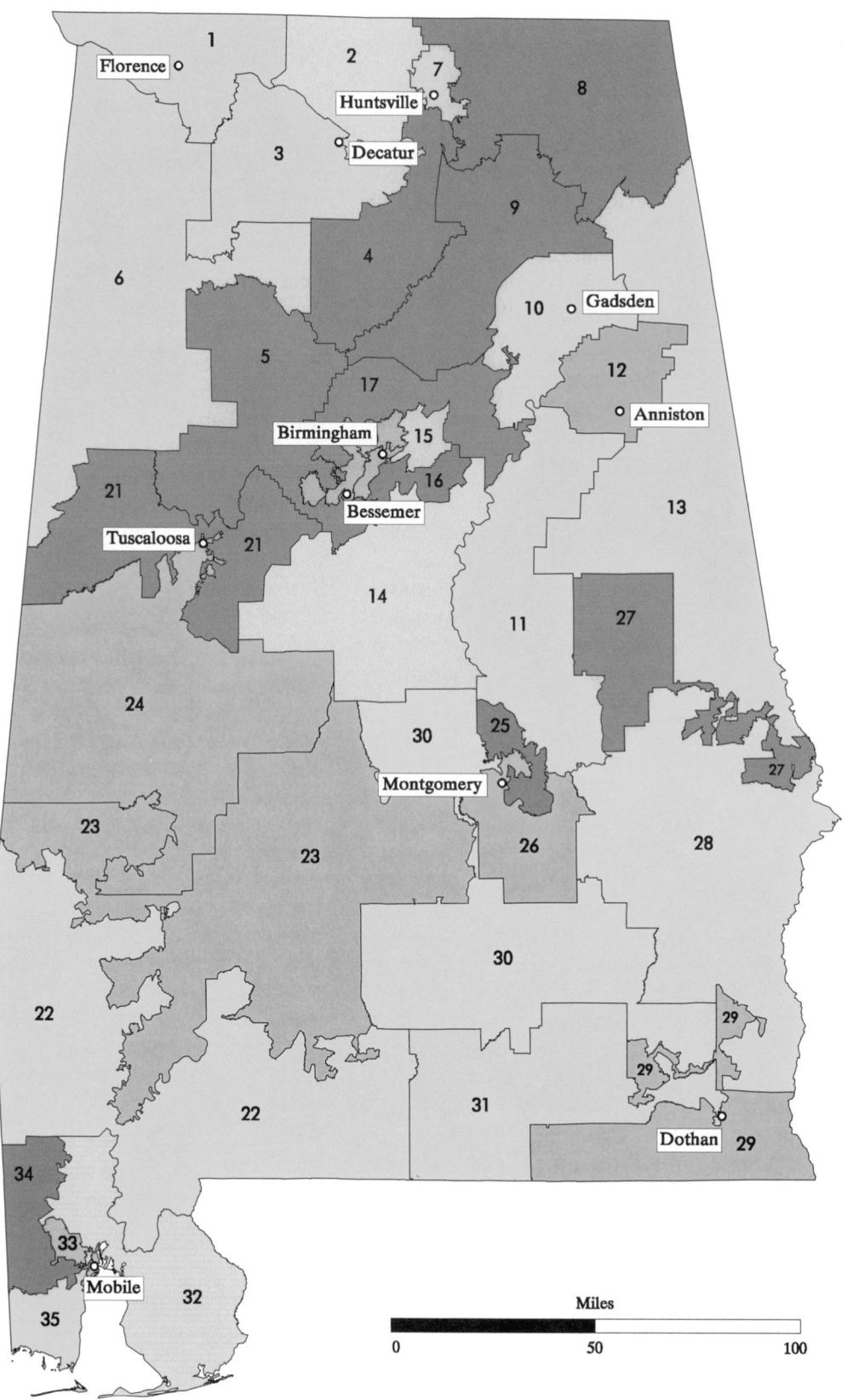

Population Growth   ☐ -5% to 1%   ☐ 3% to 7%   ☐ 8% to 14%   ☐ 22% to 24%

BIRMINGHAM

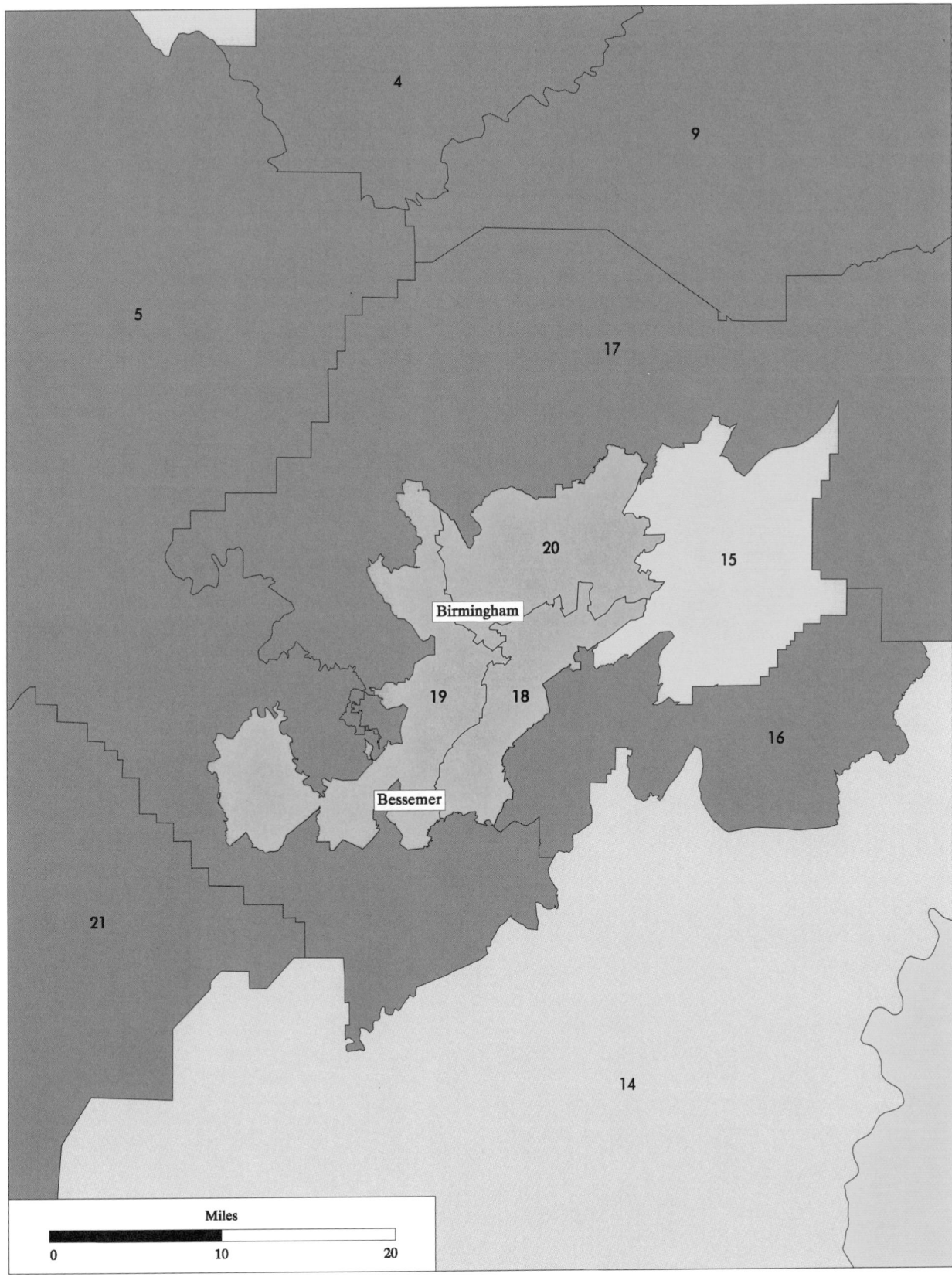

Population Growth   ▢ -5% to 1%   ▢ 3% to 7%   ▢ 8% to 14%   ▢ 22% to 24%

Alabama State Senate Districts: Demographic Data

Senate District	Population		Average HH Income		District Type	Unempl. Rate	College Educ.	White (non-Hispanic)		African American		Asian American		Hispanic American	
	1997	+/-	($)	+/-		(%)	(%)	(%)	+/-	(%)	+/-	(%)	+/-	(%)	+/-
Alabama	4,298,323	6	41,710	37	M	7	30	72	5	26	8	1	34	1	47
1	124,809	4	41,987	40	M	6	29	86	3	13	9	0	26	1	46
2	140,362	23	51,797	36	M	5	43	82	19	15	36	1	78	1	87
3	128,369	7	41,830	37	M	6	25	84	6	13	12	0	29	1	53
4	128,200	8	44,907	32	R	5	37	94	6	3	21	2	47	2	58
5	138,107	10	43,994	36	M	6	25	92	8	7	24	0	38	0	52
6	120,938	3	35,305	43	R	8	15	92	3	8	7	0	-28	0	33
7	123,552	3	48,344	25	U	6	44	64	-2	32	11	2	36	1	34
8	130,553	13	38,248	38	R	6	20	94	12	4	30	0	31	1	50
9	134,397	12	37,053	38	R	7	21	97	11	2	18	0	14	1	67
10	117,984	4	37,777	36	M	7	23	85	3	14	8	0	8	1	63
11	118,469	7	35,061	29	R	7	22	69	6	30	11	0	30	1	38
12	113,567	-2	37,081	32	S	8	29	78	-4	19	2	1	25	2	39
13	122,066	4	34,816	32	R	6	17	79	3	21	6	0	7	0	26
14	148,076	24	47,542	38	R	4	30	87	23	12	29	0	66	1	82
15	117,759	4	59,671	39	S	4	42	88	1	10	33	1	36	1	54
16	125,082	9	78,451	38	S	3	64	93	7	4	37	2	47	1	72
17	132,477	14	46,638	41	S	5	22	92	12	8	44	0	30	0	25
18	111,751	1	34,773	43	U	9	38	30	-6	68	4	1	23	1	37
19	104,447	-5	31,228	34	U	9	21	32	-18	67	3	0	-24	0	-20
20	104,117	-4	32,368	36	U	10	21	33	-12	66	0	0	-12	0	12
21	123,674	8	43,296	39	M	6	36	77	5	22	20	1	31	1	48
22	119,673	3	35,278	40	R	9	19	68	2	29	8	0	-24	1	23
23	111,829	-1	31,746	38	R	11	21	38	-4	62	1	0	-3	0	-2
24	113,992	-1	30,132	35	R	9	24	36	-5	63	2	0	17	0	15
25	134,109	13	56,257	35	U	3	49	82	8	16	35	1	45	1	63
26	106,237	-3	30,620	27	U	11	27	25	-16	73	2	0	-5	1	17
27	125,357	9	37,101	28	R	6	35	78	7	20	17	1	38	1	57
28	122,333	3	32,981	36	R	10	24	39	-1	60	5	0	22	1	16
29	113,820	1	37,583	33	R	5	26	73	0	24	3	1	25	2	38
30	119,834	7	36,988	38	R	8	24	71	6	28	10	0	24	1	42
31	118,709	4	37,291	31	R	6	29	81	2	16	11	1	32	1	46
32	144,784	22	45,778	42	S	5	31	85	21	13	32	0	36	1	77
33	108,213	-1	27,873	32	U	14	23	32	-9	67	2	0	13	1	29
34	131,996	10	55,488	39	U	5	44	85	6	11	39	2	40	2	64
35	119,032	6	38,569	34	M	9	26	68	3	29	10	1	30	1	39

Note: U=urban, S=suburban, R=rural, M=mixed, HH=households.

ALABAMA
State House Districts

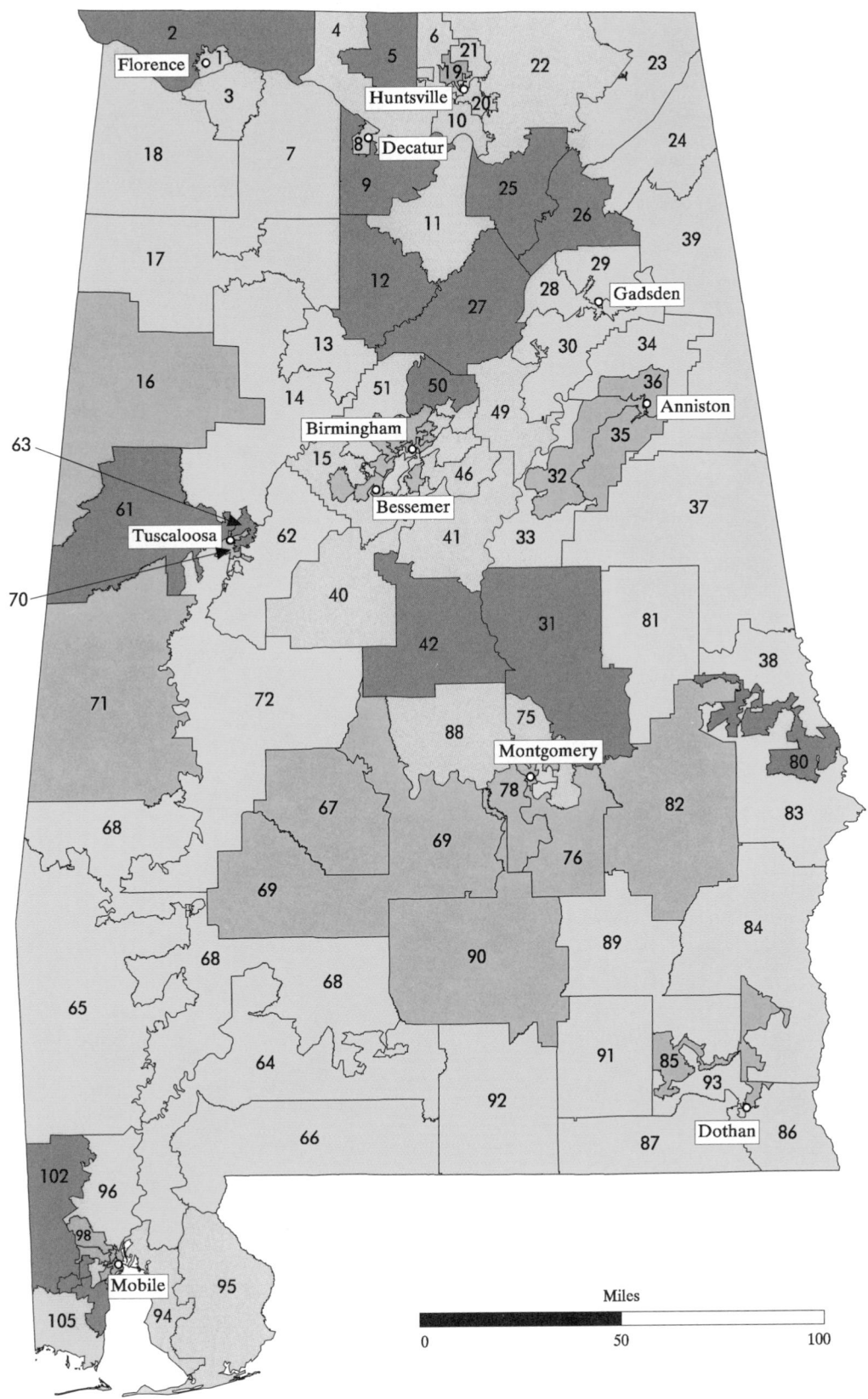

Florence
2
1
4
6
21
22
23
19
3
5
Huntsville
20
7
10
24
18
8
Decatur
9
25
26
11
39
17
29
12
28
Gadsden
30
34
13
27
16
14
51
50
49
36
Anniston
Birmingham
35
63
15
46
32
37
Bessemer
41
33
61
62
Tuscaloosa
70
40
42
31
81
71
72
88
75
38
67
Montgomery
80
68
78
82
69
76
83
69
90
89
84
68
68
65
91
85
64
92
93
66
87
Dothan
86
102
96
98
105
Mobile
95
94

| Population Growth | -8% to 0% | 1% to 8% | 9% to 16% | 20% to 32% |

BIRMINGHAM

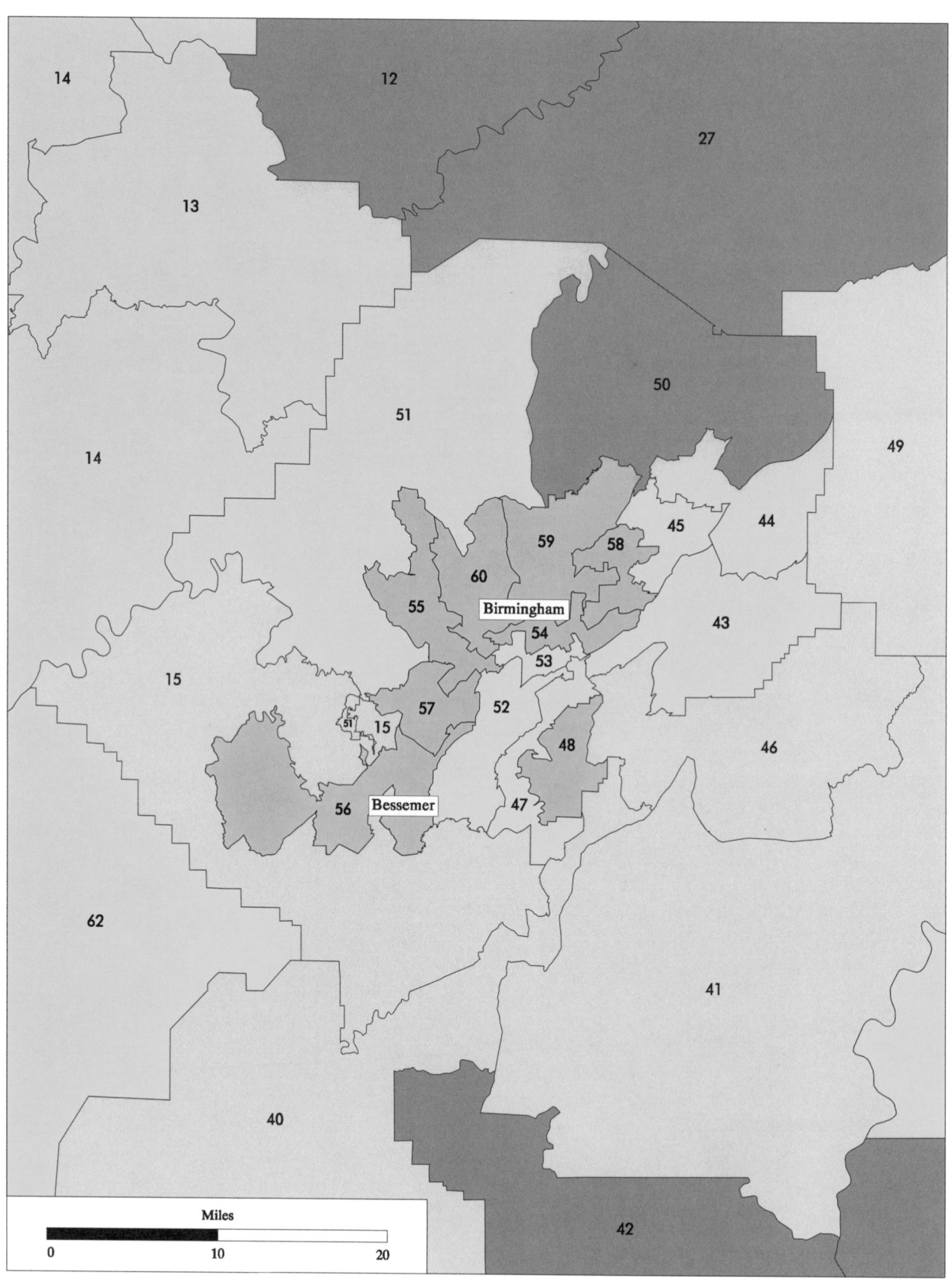

Population Growth   █ -8% to 0%   ☐ 1% to 8%   █ 9% to 16%   ☐ 20% to 32%

MONTGOMERY

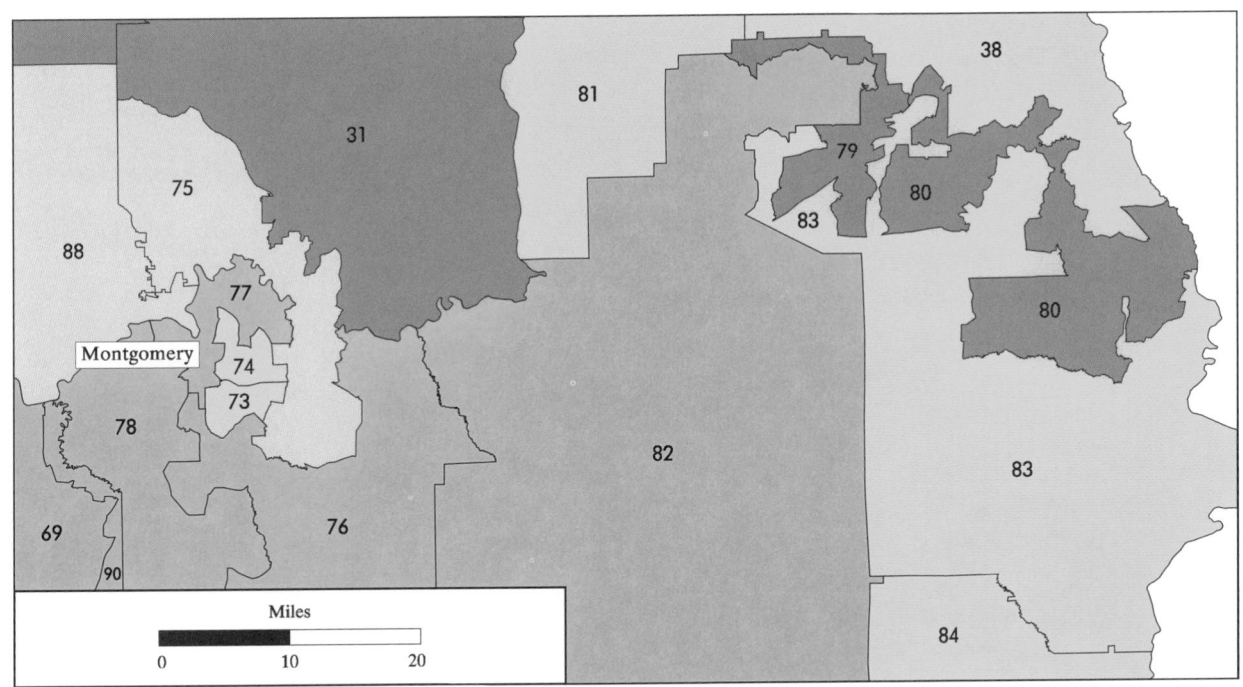

MOBILE

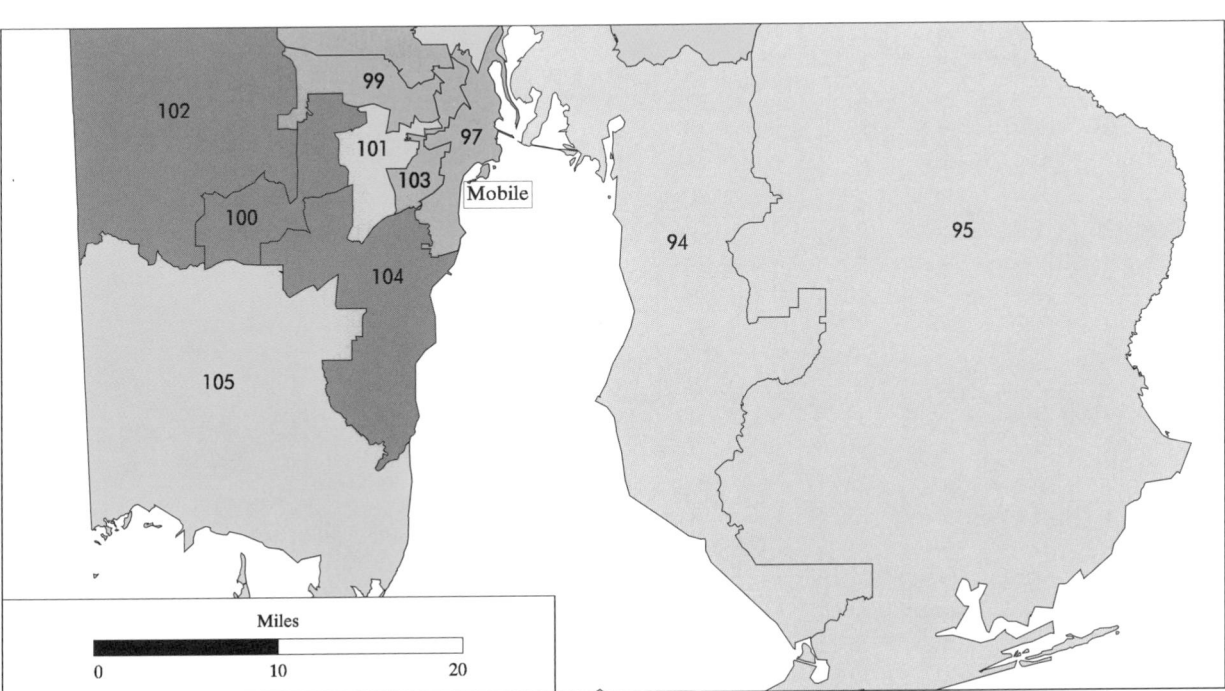

Population Growth   -8% to 0%   1% to 8%   9% to 16%   20% to 32%

Alabama State House Districts: Demographic Data

House District	Population 1997	+/-	Average HH Income ($)	+/-	District Type	Unempl. Rate (%)	College Educ. (%)	White (non-Hispanic) (%)	+/-	African American (%)	+/-	Asian American (%)	+/-	Hispanic American (%)	+/-
Alabama	4,298,323	6	41,710	37	M	7	30	72	5	26	8	1	34	1	47
1	38,867	1	41,358	40	U	7	36	81	-1	17	8	0	31	1	60
2	45,148	9	40,788	35	S	5	24	95	9	4	26	0	25	0	32
3	40,802	2	43,878	47	S	7	27	79	1	20	7	0	19	1	42
4	48,209	25	54,430	34	M	5	47	81	20	15	45	2	92	2	112
5	44,281	14	41,992	33	R	6	28	86	12	12	22	0	42	1	57
6	47,838	30	57,562	39	S	5	52	79	27	16	39	2	77	2	80
7	42,106	5	37,288	42	R	7	15	82	5	13	13	0	-53	0	40
8	34,203	4	44,109	36	U	6	32	80	2	18	9	1	39	1	66
9	52,070	11	43,981	34	S	5	27	89	10	9	18	0	37	1	47
10	41,847	5	58,145	24	U	3	63	84	1	7	21	5	49	4	58
11	40,386	2	39,328	40	R	5	23	99	2	0	27	0	-14	0	28
12	45,972	15	37,868	39	R	6	21	97	15	1	17	0	50	1	82
13	41,713	5	37,769	32	R	7	21	91	5	8	9	0	19	0	59
14	44,466	4	37,328	33	R	7	18	94	3	5	16	0	5	1	50
15	51,883	20	55,352	37	S	5	35	90	17	9	42	0	68	0	48
16	36,945	0	34,493	35	R	7	16	83	-1	16	5	0	-33	1	24
17	42,813	6	35,662	46	R	9	13	97	6	3	10	0	-43	0	30
18	41,175	4	35,647	47	R	7	16	93	3	6	10	0	-8	0	44
19	38,951	-1	39,871	23	U	9	39	31	-15	67	7	1	20	1	31
20	42,341	2	64,721	27	U	4	57	87	0	8	18	3	42	1	33
21	42,174	8	37,830	26	U	6	33	71	3	25	20	2	33	1	35
22	49,253	27	39,863	32	S	6	22	92	26	6	48	0	77	1	54
23	38,879	6	39,962	45	R	7	21	93	6	5	12	0	13	1	52
24	42,393	6	34,882	37	R	5	17	97	5	1	11	0	4	0	40
25	44,436	9	37,760	36	R	8	25	97	8	2	21	0	27	0	37
26	45,987	15	35,241	36	R	7	20	98	14	1	15	0	28	1	92
27	43,973	12	38,311	41	R	5	17	97	12	1	13	0	-33	1	64
28	39,986	6	35,533	35	M	8	21	83	5	15	7	1	17	1	61
29	37,796	2	33,137	35	U	8	21	77	0	22	8	0	-11	0	37
30	40,205	3	45,024	37	S	7	26	95	3	4	14	0	-7	1	79
31	41,855	16	37,276	33	R	6	22	74	14	26	20	0	51	0	31
32	36,173	-4	26,891	25	R	13	16	35	-11	63	0	0	14	2	59
33	39,589	6	35,043	29	R	7	22	74	4	25	11	0	16	0	-28
34	41,207	5	37,215	31	S	7	31	88	3	10	21	1	35	1	66
35	37,205	-1	35,780	29	S	7	23	88	-3	11	11	0	17	0	28
36	35,969	-6	43,306	32	S	7	36	81	-9	14	2	2	24	3	30
37	43,401	1	34,062	36	R	6	17	72	-1	28	5	0	-17	0	14
38	38,994	3	35,061	23	R	7	21	72	2	27	6	0	26	0	28
39	39,651	8	35,397	39	R	7	14	93	7	7	15	0	-14	0	34
40	52,070	30	57,639	37	R	4	43	88	30	10	24	1	84	1	108
41	52,724	28	46,251	34	R	4	28	86	27	12	38	0	61	1	86
42	43,274	14	37,664	42	R	6	17	85	12	14	25	0	14	1	45
43	40,347	6	70,702	34	S	3	54	85	3	13	34	1	43	1	63
44	38,321	3	57,837	43	S	4	36	94	2	5	36	0	34	1	29
45	39,106	2	50,241	39	U	4	36	86	-2	12	32	1	30	1	65
46	47,285	21	93,375	37	S	3	65	96	20	2	41	1	63	1	67
47	38,104	6	68,209	39	S	3	63	91	3	6	35	2	44	1	66
48	39,681	0	71,552	34	S	3	64	92	-2	4	37	2	40	2	80
49	44,750	24	43,916	40	S	5	21	89	23	10	31	0	32	0	36
50	43,982	16	51,307	44	S	4	27	94	14	6	53	0	32	0	21

Note: U=urban, S=suburban, R=rural, M=mixed, HH=households.

Alabama State House Districts: Demographic Data (cont.)

House District	Population 1997	+/-	Average HH Income ($)	+/-	District Type	Unempl. Rate (%)	College Educ. (%)	White (non-Hispanic) (%)	+/-	African American (%)	+/-	Asian American (%)	+/-	Hispanic American (%)	+/-
Alabama	4,298,323	6	41,710	37	M	7	30	72	5	26	8	1	34	1	47
51	43,730	3	44,740	39	S	5	18	92	1	7	57	0	14	0	21
52	37,289	4	36,457	39	U	8	39	28	-7	70	8	1	42	1	36
53	37,979	2	33,456	45	U	9	42	30	-4	67	5	2	18	1	54
54	36,420	-3	34,567	44	U	11	33	32	-7	67	0	0	16	1	19
55	35,029	-3	29,232	30	U	9	22	32	-20	68	8	0	-32	0	-31
56	33,026	-8	29,186	39	U	11	16	35	-16	64	-3	0	-50	0	-26
57	36,367	-4	35,181	33	S	8	25	30	-19	69	4	0	-13	0	-6
58	33,132	-7	28,206	34	U	11	18	35	-17	64	-1	0	-9	1	28
59	35,756	-3	32,733	42	U	9	16	35	-6	65	-1	0	-19	0	16
60	35,192	-2	36,132	32	U	10	28	30	-13	70	3	0	-13	0	-20
61	41,475	10	38,703	36	R	7	28	71	7	27	15	0	41	1	51
62	38,565	7	42,513	30	M	5	32	84	4	15	27	0	20	1	46
63	43,613	9	47,747	48	U	6	47	75	4	22	24	2	31	1	49
64	40,880	7	37,451	45	R	9	20	68	4	30	12	0	-1	1	23
65	38,486	2	36,277	42	R	9	19	67	0	30	6	0	-68	0	15
66	40,311	2	32,168	32	R	10	18	70	0	26	4	0	-23	1	27
67	35,187	-1	31,551	43	R	12	24	35	-3	64	0	0	12	0	11
68	39,184	1	33,744	38	R	10	19	41	-3	58	3	0	-45	0	-14
69	37,456	-1	29,779	32	R	11	21	36	-5	64	1	0	-9	0	2
70	37,085	-4	27,958	32	U	9	30	38	-10	60	-1	1	23	1	23
71	37,121	0	30,766	35	R	9	22	33	-3	67	1	0	-9	0	0
72	39,691	2	31,586	37	R	8	20	38	-2	62	5	0	-26	0	14
73	41,972	7	65,475	33	U	4	58	84	3	13	32	1	36	1	70
74	42,076	5	44,907	30	U	3	43	87	2	10	39	1	34	1	45
75	50,065	26	58,158	43	S	3	46	75	22	22	35	1	63	1	73
76	34,903	-3	35,119	23	U	7	33	29	-16	70	3	0	-6	1	4
77	34,871	-5	27,471	31	U	14	25	24	-20	75	0	0	-10	1	-10
78	36,345	-1	29,355	26	U	13	25	23	-13	75	3	0	1	1	42
79	39,563	11	33,790	29	R	6	62	82	8	12	24	4	40	1	72
80	45,915	13	40,042	25	S	6	24	80	10	19	26	1	34	1	52
81	39,907	3	37,291	30	R	5	23	72	1	27	7	0	-22	0	13
82	41,458	-2	30,221	35	R	11	32	25	-4	74	-2	1	17	1	12
83	43,550	8	31,384	29	R	11	17	37	0	62	12	1	36	1	25
84	37,324	3	37,794	44	R	7	22	58	0	41	7	0	2	1	11
85	32,808	-7	29,885	30	R	8	24	47	-14	47	-3	1	17	3	31
86	40,801	3	39,624	31	U	5	25	79	0	19	13	1	22	1	42
87	40,242	8	41,229	34	R	5	29	88	7	10	12	0	48	1	62
88	46,432	20	43,599	35	S	5	29	78	18	21	25	0	56	1	66
89	37,502	2	35,143	35	R	7	24	69	0	30	8	0	-3	1	24
90	35,899	-2	30,895	38	R	12	17	63	-3	36	2	0	-48	0	6
91	42,049	4	39,720	34	R	6	32	79	3	18	9	1	34	2	49
92	37,346	2	32,185	37	R	5	20	85	1	14	7	0	-21	0	33
93	39,335	5	39,628	24	M	6	33	80	1	16	17	2	36	2	46
94	52,552	30	53,721	43	S	4	42	84	29	14	32	0	54	1	92
95	54,155	32	40,793	40	R	5	26	88	30	9	42	0	34	2	88
96	38,062	4	41,488	40	S	7	19	81	1	17	26	0	9	1	19
97	35,939	-1	26,420	32	U	16	25	31	-9	68	2	0	11	1	36
98	35,408	-3	27,756	38	S	14	17	34	-5	65	-2	0	0	0	15
99	36,797	0	29,471	28	U	12	26	31	-12	68	6	0	15	1	26
100	44,956	13	63,568	45	U	5	55	84	8	11	38	3	43	2	71

Note: U=urban, S=suburban, R=rural, M=mixed, HH=households.

Alabama State House Districts: Demographic Data (cont.)

House District	Population		Average HH Income		District Type	Unempl. Rate	College Educ.	White (non-Hispanic)		African American		Asian American		Hispanic American	
	1997	+/-	($)	+/-		(%)	(%)	(%)	+/-	(%)	+/-	(%)	+/-	(%)	+/-
Alabama	4,298,323	6	41,710	37	M	7	30	72	5	26	8	1	34	1	47
101	40,956	2	56,516	38	U	5	47	79	-4	16	31	2	37	2	67
102	45,975	15	45,409	35	S	6	28	91	12	7	56	0	45	1	46
103	34,419	-5	28,783	31	U	13	24	30	-15	68	1	0	-4	1	17
104	43,064	13	49,788	35	U	6	35	88	10	10	51	1	44	1	57
105	41,565	8	34,801	28	S	8	17	80	3	15	36	3	31	1	37

Note: U=urban, S=suburban, R=rural, M=mixed, HH=households.

ALASKA

Alaska celebrates the fortieth anniversary of statehood in 1999 as one of the youngest places in a young nation. Yet it remains an alien place to most Americans and largely inaccessible even to its own citizens.

To put its age in some perspective, the state of Alaska is younger than Madonna, Katie Couric, or Disneyland. Alaskans themselves are young; only 12 percent of the population is over age fifty-five, by far the lowest percentage in the country. They are also wealthier and better educated than most other Americans. Alaska has the fourth-highest average household income and the eleventh-highest percentage of college graduates, despite having no nationally known university. White Alaskans still tend to come from elsewhere. Neither Alaska's governor nor any of its current congressional representatives was born in the state.

Although the state known as the Last Frontier covers a land area almost half the size of the lower forty-eight states, more than half its population lives in and around the city of Anchorage, which accordingly dominates the state legislature. Another third lives in and around Fairbanks and Juneau. The vast balance of the state remains sparsely populated, much of it—including the capital city of Juneau—still reachable only by airplane.

None of this appears to have changed much during the 1990s. Suburban sprawl has come to Anchorage as people have moved to outlying areas around and across Cook Inlet. All ten of the fastest-growing state house districts are located in and around the city—the Twenty-sixth, Twenty-seventh, and Twenty-eighth Districts in particular—while most of the state's population loss has occurred downtown, in the Fourteenth, Fifteenth, and Twenty-third Districts. It is no longer far-fetched for Anchorage, which now has almost as many people as Newark, New Jersey, to bid for the Winter Olympics, as it did for the 2002 Games, and may again. Alaska is projected to be one of the fastest-growing states over the next quarter century, rising from forty-eighth in population today to forty-fifth by 2025.

One particularly interesting place is the Fortieth House District, which extends out from the mainland to cover all of the Aleutian Island chain. The area was hit hard when the Adak Naval Air Station was closed. The district lost fully 35 percent of its population, the second-largest population loss of any state house district in the United States, and the county in which it sits was the nation's fastest-shrinking county. Yet many of the military jobs lost did not pay well, so average income in the Fortieth is actually up almost one-third during that time, and the unemployment rate remains below the state and national averages. This is a phenomenon one can see in several other parts of the country as well.

Politically, Alaska is a Republican state. The Democrats have strongholds in the Panhandle, the Bush, and parts of downtown Anchorage. Republicans are strong almost everywhere else. As they do in the rest of the country, Democrats fare well among minority groups (here Aleuts comprise the largest minority group) and the elderly. Seven of Alaska's ten oldest districts have Democratic state legislators; eight of the ten youngest have Republican.

Unfortunately for Alaska Democrats, all ten of the fastest-growing districts in the state are currently represented by Republicans, while seven of the ten slowest-growing districts are represented by Democrats, who also represent most of the poorest Alaska house districts. This may have significance in the next round of redistricting. Alaska is one of only two states (Maryland is the other) that places responsibility for reapportionment entirely in the hands of the governor, although there is a referendum on the November 1998 ballot to change that system. Alaska's governor is currently a Democrat, up for reelection in 1998. If he is defeated, his Republican successor will oversee reapportionment and may be able to help his party pad its lead in the state legislature. The demographic trends appear to be pointing the Republicans' way.

ALASKA
State Senate Districts

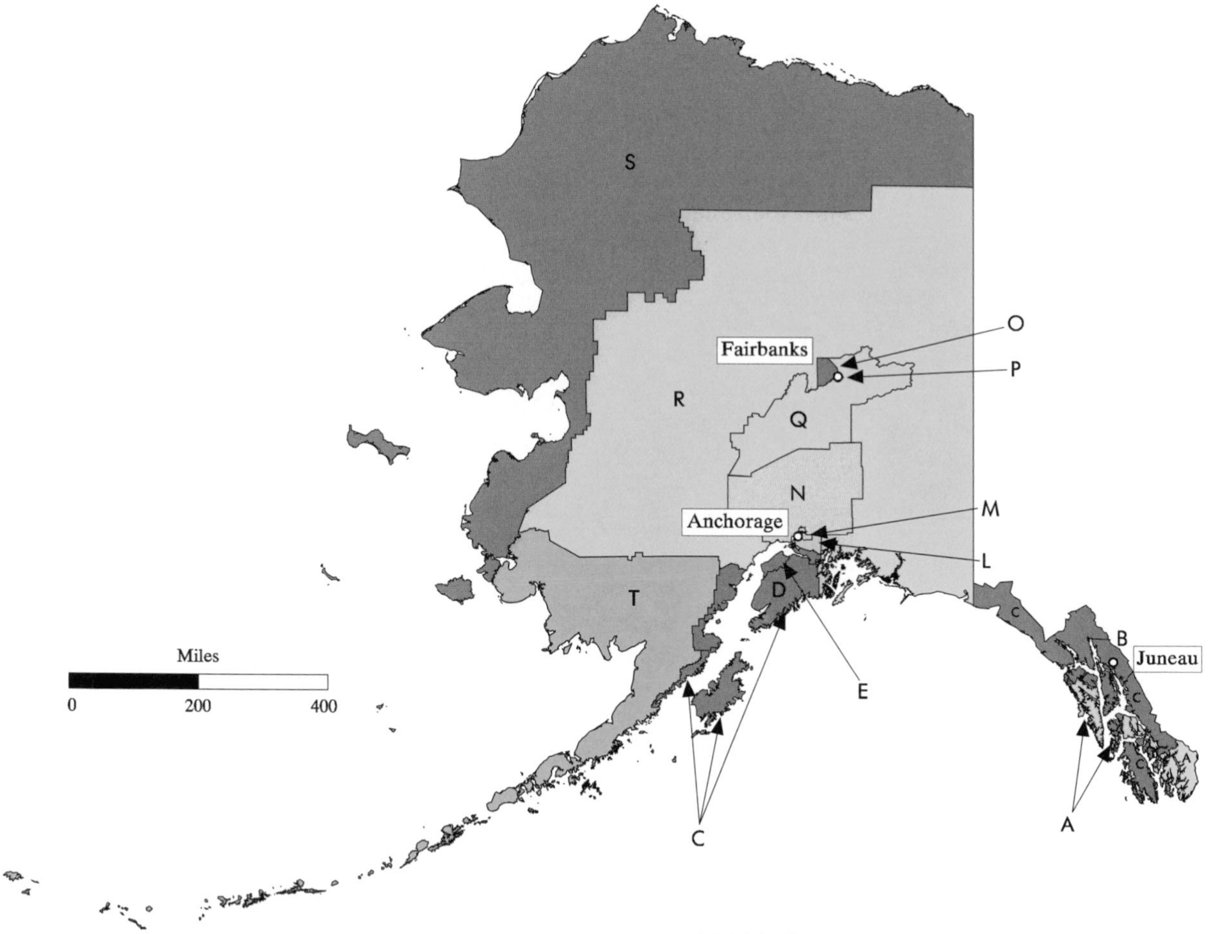

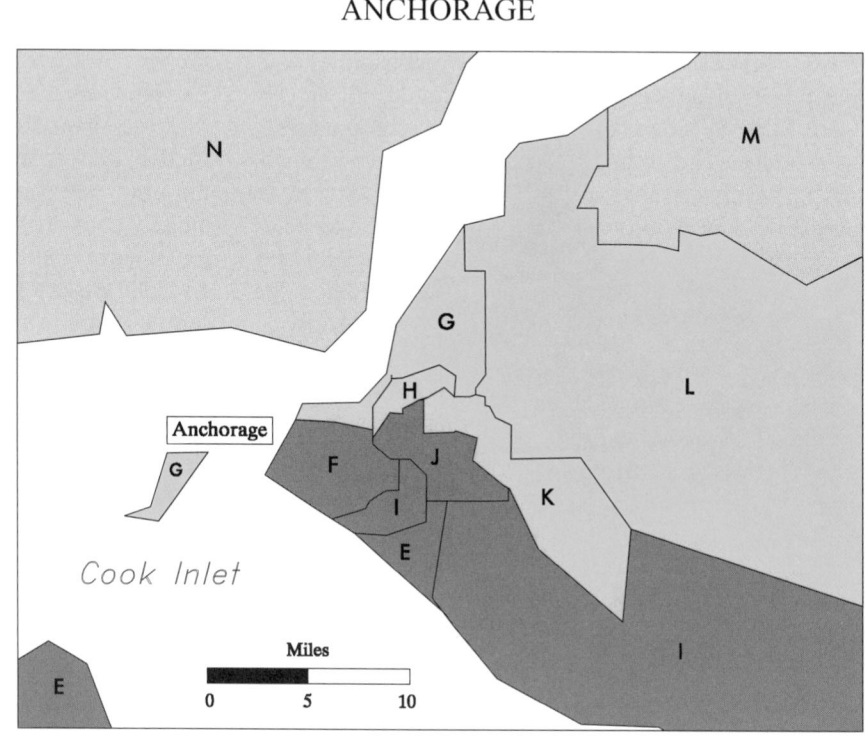

S

R

Q

Fairbanks

O

P

N

Anchorage

M

L

T

D

E

C

B

Juneau

C

A

C

Miles

0   200   400

ANCHORAGE

N

M

G

H

L

Anchorage

G

F

J

K

I

E

E

I

Cook Inlet

Miles

0   5   10

Population Growth   -9%   -1% to 6%   10% to 23%   31% to 37%

Alaska State Senate Districts: Demographic Data

Senate District	Population		Average HH Income		District Type	Unempl. Rate	College Educ.	White (non-Hispanic)		African American		Asian American		Hispanic American	
	1997	+/-	($)	+/-		(%)	(%)	(%)	+/-	(%)	+/-	(%)	+/-	(%)	+/-
Alaska	609,288	11	62,525	26	R	9	43	73	10	4	12	4	24	4	32
A	29,258	3	64,191	27	R	7	39	78	2	0	-8	3	18	2	15
B	30,136	12	68,721	29	R	5	49	79	12	1	10	5	33	3	24
C	29,364	12	56,646	10	R	9	36	64	10	0	3	7	36	3	20
D	32,042	19	63,592	24	R	10	40	89	18	0	4	1	34	2	48
E	32,208	17	79,804	28	U	8	48	88	15	1	31	3	39	3	60
F	31,511	15	71,206	25	U	6	47	79	11	4	31	8	37	4	38
G	28,057	0	65,643	29	U	6	47	74	-4	8	10	7	22	5	25
H	28,283	-1	41,266	17	U	12	36	57	-8	10	10	9	19	8	26
I	32,196	23	87,522	31	U	6	55	85	21	3	38	4	45	3	55
J	33,270	14	66,557	26	U	7	48	76	11	6	28	6	35	5	50
K	29,634	6	72,132	25	U	5	50	75	3	9	19	5	23	5	38
L	30,274	3	59,416	29	U	7	42	76	2	11	0	3	17	6	24
M	32,804	31	66,863	27	U	8	45	90	29	2	52	2	55	3	70
N	42,473	37	57,865	25	R	12	39	91	36	1	51	1	46	2	78
O	30,266	10	57,936	18	R	9	53	81	9	5	15	3	20	4	40
P	26,963	13	53,328	21	R	11	36	77	11	7	20	2	29	4	37
Q	30,497	6	51,667	26	R	11	39	78	4	9	3	3	13	6	34
R	24,491	-1	53,635	22	R	15	33	58	-2	1	-10	2	13	2	16
S	30,114	13	49,428	22	R	19	24	16	11	0	-12	2	21	1	17
T	25,447	-9	51,776	25	R	9	29	29	-28	1	-47	3	-31	2	-35

Note: U=urban, S=suburban, R=rural, M=mixed, HH=households.

ALASKA
State House Districts

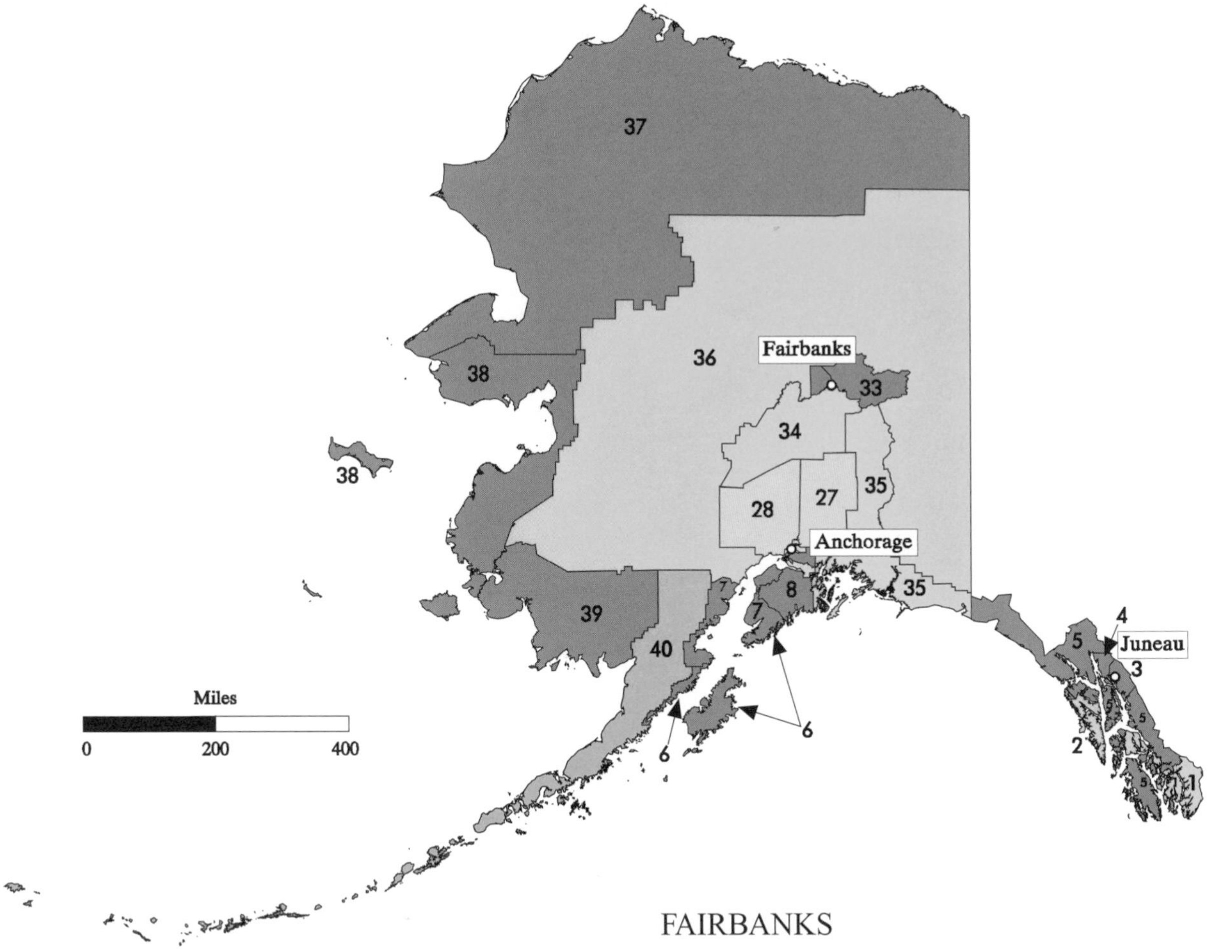

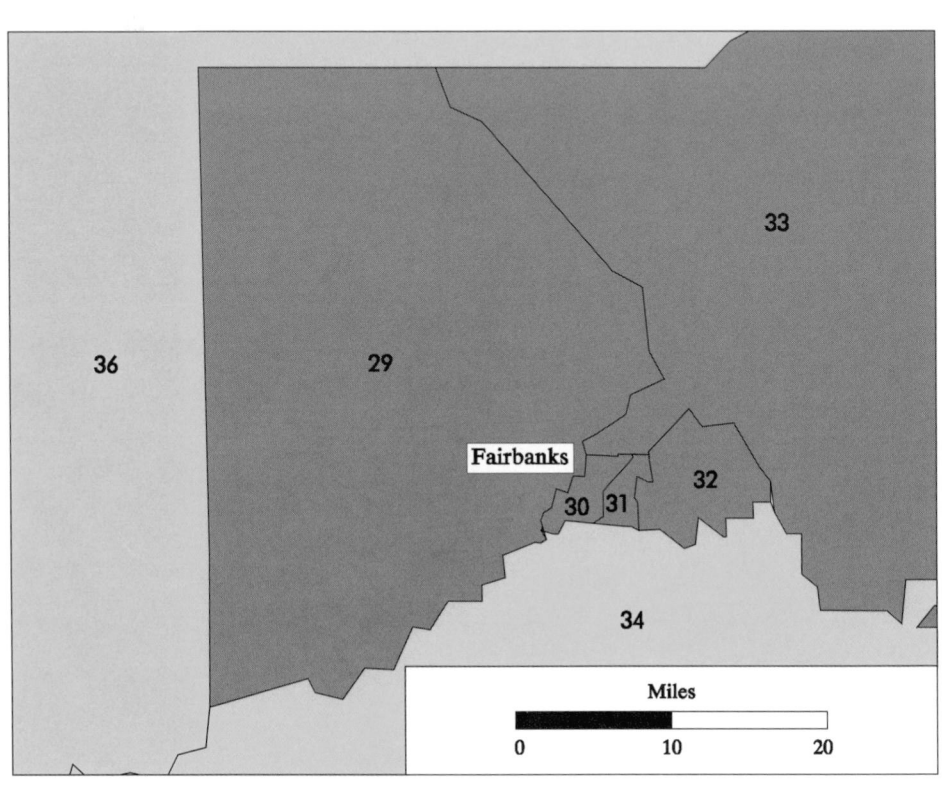

FAIRBANKS

Population Growth ☐ -35%   ☐ -7% to 6%   ☐ 7% to 21%   ☐ 25% to 43%

ANCHORAGE

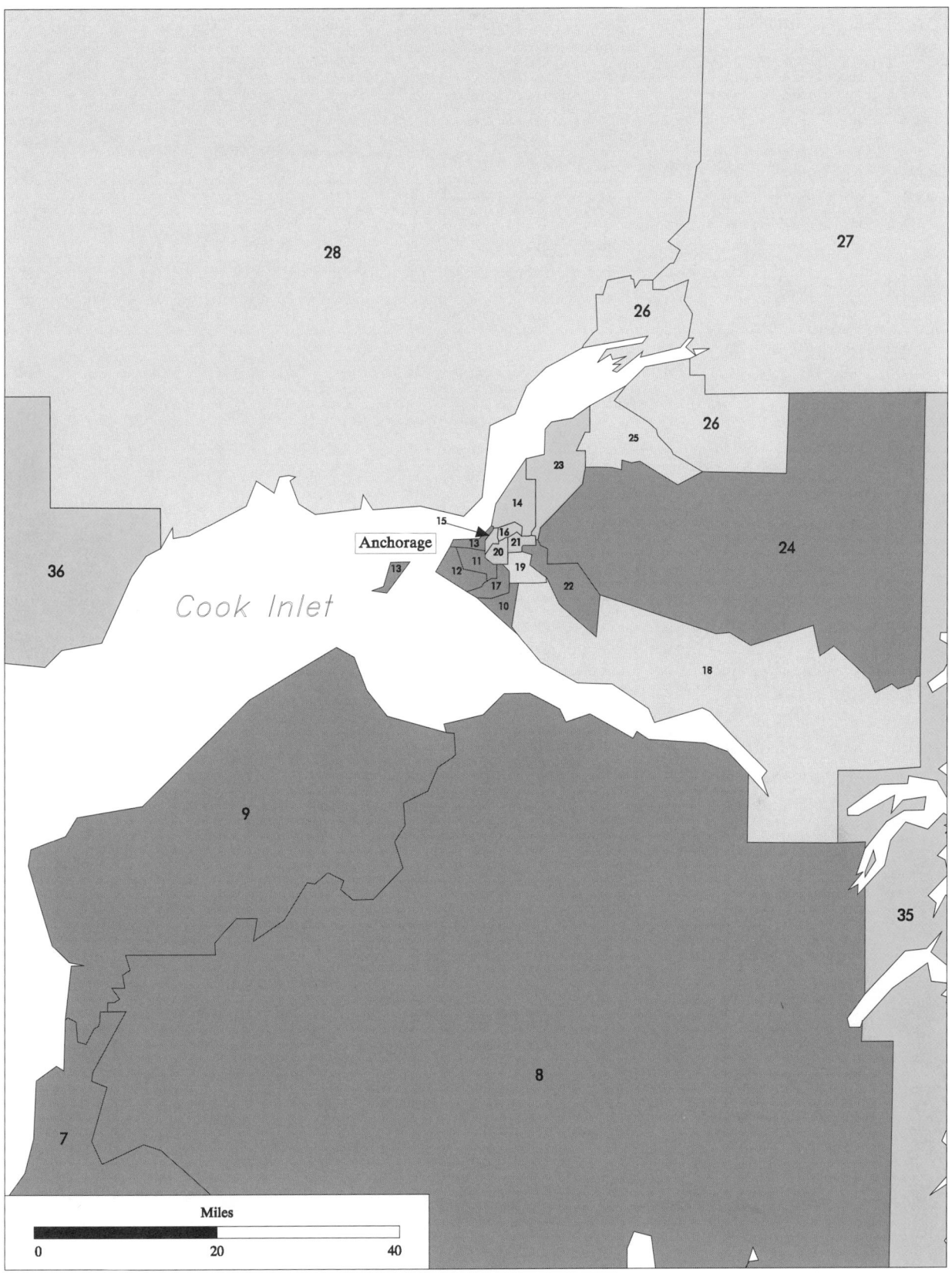

Cook Inlet

Anchorage

Population Growth

-7% to 6%   7% to 21%   25% to 43%

Alaska State House Districts: Demographic Data

House District	Population 1997	+/-	Average HH Income ($)	+/-	District Type	Unempl. Rate (%)	College Educ. (%)	White (non-Hispanic) (%)	+/-	African American (%)	+/-	Asian American (%)	+/-	Hispanic American (%)	+/-
Alaska	609,288	11	62,525	26	R	9	43	73	10	4	12	4	24	4	32
1	14,754	6	69,730	36	R	8	39	80	5	0	-2	4	26	2	18
2	14,504	0	58,492	17	R	7	40	76	-1	0	-14	3	8	3	13
3	15,132	13	63,428	27	R	6	50	75	12	1	7	5	33	4	27
4	15,004	12	75,049	30	R	4	48	83	11	1	13	5	33	3	20
5	14,970	10	48,778	13	R	12	30	62	8	0	-50	0	-21	2	7
6	14,394	15	65,632	7	R	5	41	65	11	1	10	13	39	5	24
7	16,341	17	63,905	27	R	10	41	90	16	0	0	1	23	2	43
8	15,701	21	63,262	22	R	10	39	89	20	1	5	1	46	2	52
9	16,005	15	63,193	23	R	11	36	88	13	1	20	1	32	3	60
10	16,203	19	97,074	31	U	5	57	87	17	2	34	4	41	4	60
11	16,434	14	67,473	25	U	6	47	78	10	5	32	7	37	4	33
12	15,077	16	75,658	26	U	7	48	80	12	4	31	8	38	4	45
13	14,995	7	78,517	30	U	5	55	79	3	2	28	9	36	4	43
14	13,062	-7	45,932	21	U	7	35	68	-12	14	7	6	2	7	14
15	12,466	-3	46,883	19	U	9	43	68	-8	5	10	9	17	7	24
16	15,817	0	36,000	16	U	15	28	49	-7	14	11	9	21	10	27
17	17,191	21	61,791	17	U	7	47	78	17	5	38	6	43	5	61
18	15,005	25	121,668	42	U	5	62	93	24	1	40	2	51	2	40
19	18,710	27	61,658	27	U	6	46	76	22	7	37	5	51	6	69
20	14,560	2	72,067	27	U	8	50	77	-1	6	17	7	21	4	24
21	13,010	-1	58,693	21	U	8	47	73	-5	9	12	5	14	5	23
22	16,624	13	83,389	26	U	3	53	77	9	9	25	5	32	6	49
23	10,344	-7	47,699	22	U	9	33	67	-11	16	-1	4	11	7	13
24	19,930	10	66,109	31	U	6	46	80	9	8	1	2	23	6	32
25	17,439	30	63,722	22	U	6	47	89	28	2	54	2	59	3	68
26	15,365	31	70,448	31	R	11	42	90	30	1	44	1	46	3	73
27	20,742	43	63,207	28	R	11	40	90	41	1	57	1	55	2	85
28	21,731	32	53,008	22	R	12	37	92	31	0	37	1	38	2	71
29	14,523	8	65,392	17	R	7	65	87	8	2	10	3	15	2	12
30	15,743	12	51,882	20	R	11	40	76	9	7	17	3	27	5	52
31	14,533	12	45,720	18	R	12	30	67	9	11	21	3	27	5	39
32	12,430	14	63,900	23	R	10	43	89	13	2	18	1	33	3	34
33	9,518	15	59,339	22	R	9	45	89	14	2	23	2	27	2	35
34	20,979	3	47,448	29	R	12	35	73	-1	13	2	3	9	8	34
35	12,333	1	68,144	16	R	9	38	82	0	3	-3	4	20	4	22
36	12,158	-3	38,262	34	R	23	28	34	-7	0	-35	0	-43	1	-1
37	14,721	14	59,954	24	R	17	26	17	15	0	-4	3	27	1	19
38	15,393	11	39,265	17	R	22	23	16	7	0	-32	0	-8	1	15
39	16,488	16	47,295	24	R	11	28	19	15	0	9	1	2	1	21
40	8,959	-35	60,765	33	R	5	31	47	-43	3	-52	8	-34	5	-44

Note: U=urban, S=suburban, R=rural, M=mixed, HH=households.

ARIZONA

Arizona is one of the nation's fastest-growing states, second only to another desert wonder, Nevada. Almost three-quarters of the state's population is centered around Phoenix, the country's seventh-largest city, and Tucson, which not only has more people than Atlanta but also is growing at a much faster rate.

That growth has continued during the nineties, spreading farther out across the Valley of the Sun. The Sixth State House District, just south of Tempe, has seen its population soar by 76 percent during this decade, while the neighboring Thirtieth, which includes the suburbs of Mesa, and the Twenty-eighth, which takes in most of Scottsdale, have grown by half.

The population surge is coming from two groups, the very old and the very young. Arizona exceeds the national growth rate both for persons under age fourteen and for those over age sixty-five. As it does in many places, this demographic characteristic produces political friction. Retirees, jealous of Social Security, tend to vote Democratic in national elections (though they have elected Republicans to the state legislature), while younger voters are more likely to vote for the GOP. In only three Arizona counties, in fact, do Republicans outnumber Democrats among those over age sixty.

An older citizenry is influencing Arizona, and the nation, in other ways. The University of Phoenix, for example, has grown to be the second-largest private university in the country despite having no campus (as Americans traditionally use the term), no athletic teams, and no fraternities. Instead, classes meet in sixty-five locations around the country and in Puerto Rico, often in strip malls and usually after standard business hours, although credits can also be earned over the Internet. The university markets itself toward older students and busy workers who are less interested in parsing Chaucer than they are in improving their job skills. Given its extraordinary rate of growth, the university or something much like it may become a model for the nation.

Race, at least in the old sense of black versus white, matters relatively little in Arizona. The Twenty-third House District between Phoenix and Tempe is the only area with a significant black population (18 percent). But race in the newer sense of Anglo versus Hispanic matters very much. Hispanic voters provide the Democratic Party with its political base, although their geographic distribution is surprisingly unbalanced. In only eight of the sixty state house districts do Hispanics constitute even a third of the population, five of them clustered along the Mexican border and the other three (the Twentieth, Twenty-second, and Twenty-third) forming an arc around the western and southern parts of Phoenix. Nevertheless, these areas, together with the Indian reservation in the north and east, provide the Democrats with most of their seats in the legislature.

So despite being the home state of the late Barry Goldwater, the conservative U.S. senator and 1964 presidential candidate, Arizona can be volatile politically. Republicans comfortably control both houses of the state legislature as well as the governor's mansion, but Democrats can win statewide, as former governor Bruce Babbitt and former U.S. senator Dennis DeConcini have shown. Even Bill Clinton carried Arizona in 1996, the first Democratic presidential candidate to do so since Harry Truman.

Still, as is true in many places, population trends seem to be going the Republicans' way. In a state that is experiencing phenomenal growth, eighteen of the twenty fastest-growing house districts are held by Republicans, as are seven of the ten with the fastest-growing income. This trend may be blunted as the state grows older (the number of Arizonans over age sixty-five is expected to more than double by 2020) and more Hispanic.

What else the aging of Arizona may bring carries important implications for the rest of the country. According to the Census Bureau, Arizona currently has eighty children and senior citizens for every one hundred persons of working age. By 2025, there are expected to be almost ninety-five "dependents" for each Arizona worker, the fourth-highest ratio in the country. If the country is to face an intergenerational war in the coming decades—between comfortable retirees and the strapped workers who support them—Arizona could be a battlefield, and one of the more interesting states to watch.

ARIZONA
State Legislative Districts

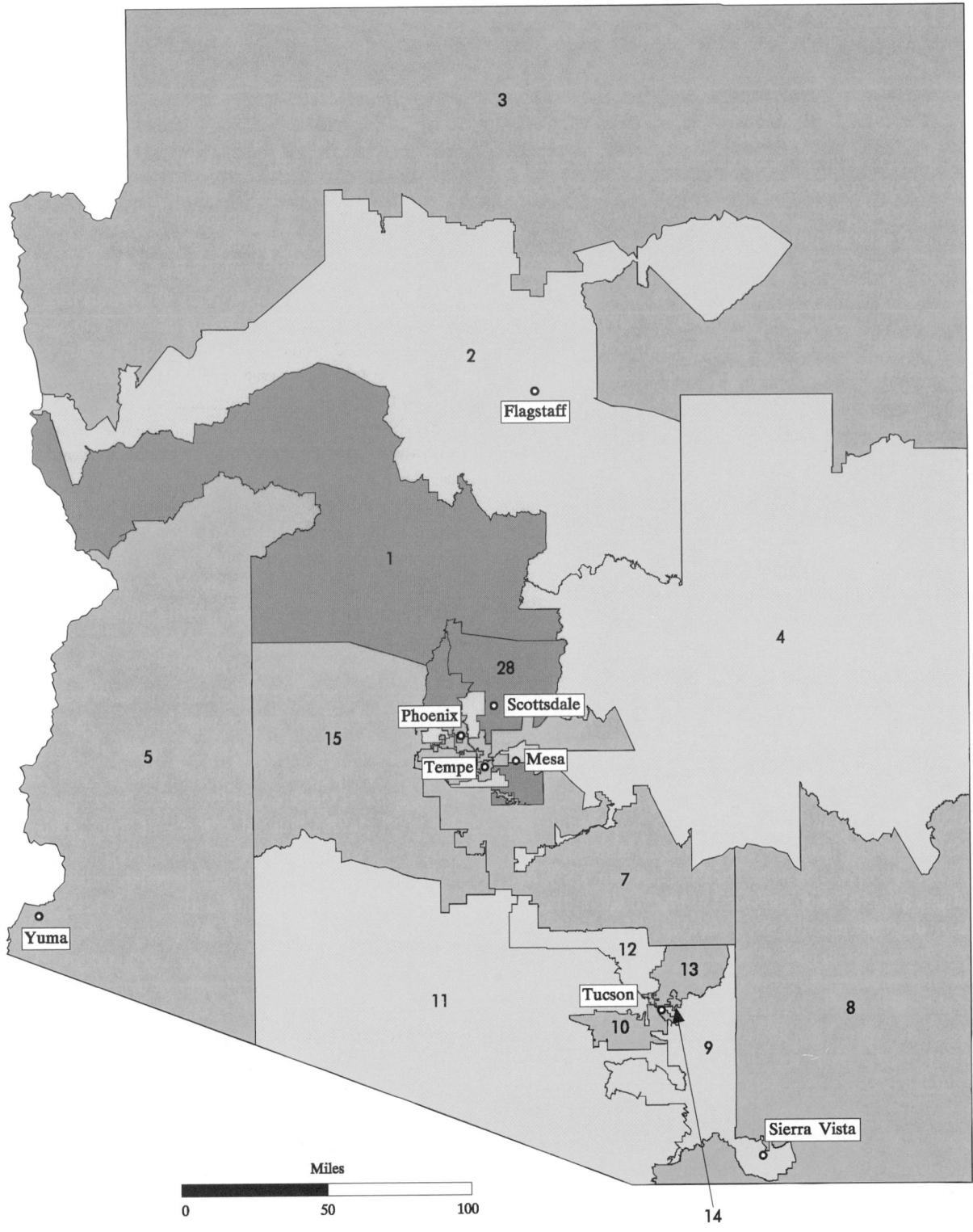

Population Growth ▨ 7% to 19% ▢ 21% to 33% ▨ 39% to 51% ▢ 76%

PHOENIX

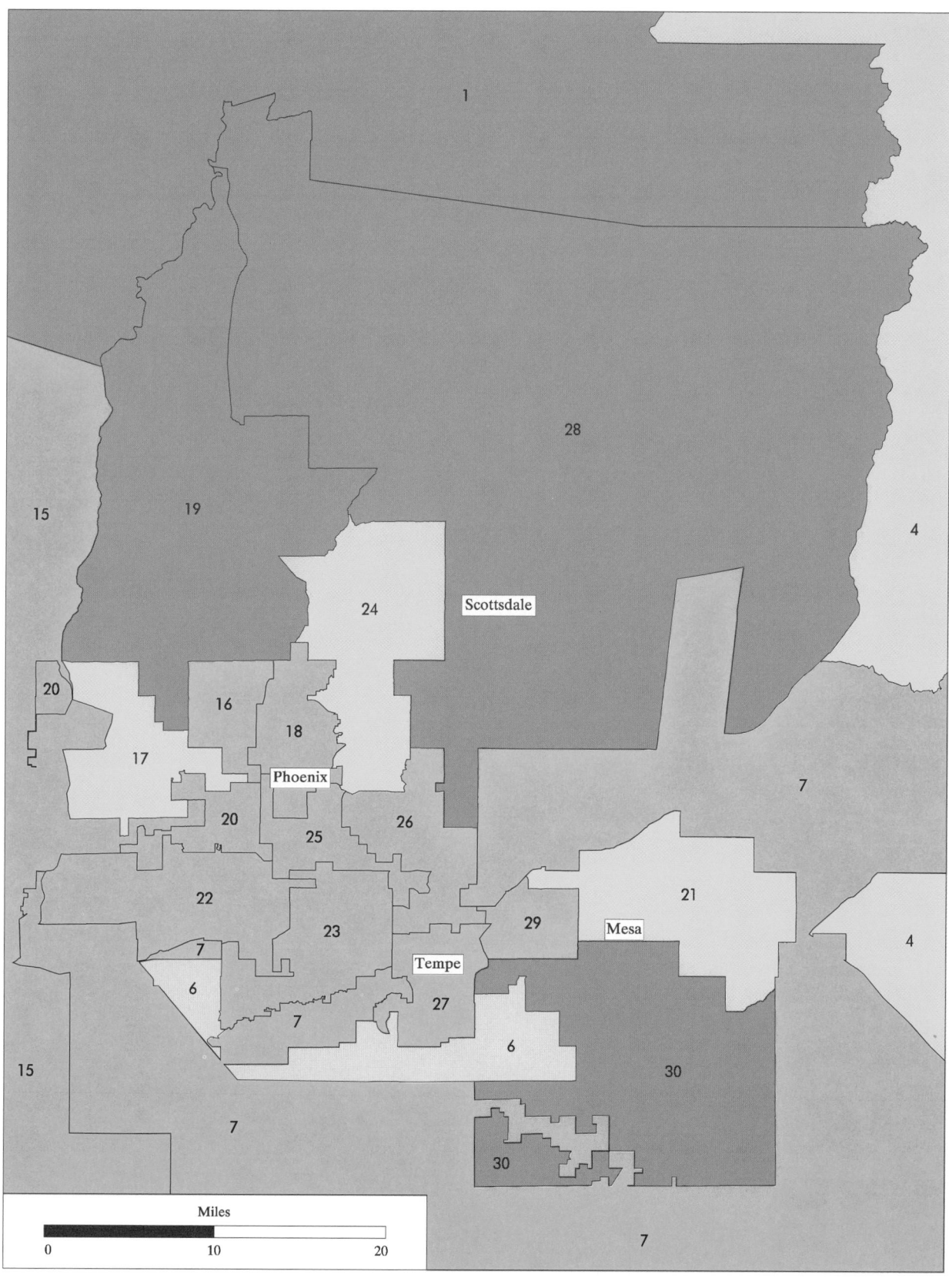

Population Growth ◻ 7% to 19%   ◻ 21% to 33%   ◼ 39% to 51%   ◻ 76%

Arizona State Legislative Districts: Demographic Data

Legis. District	Population		Average HH Income		District Type	Unempl. Rate	College Educ.	White (non-Hispanic)		African American		Asian American		Hispanic American	
	1997	+/-	($)	+/-		(%)	(%)	(%)	+/-	(%)	+/-	(%)	+/-	(%)	+/-
Arizona	4,528,581	24	47,101	33	U	7	38	69	19	3	39	2	52	21	37
1	180,363	39	40,294	37	R	6	30	91	38	0	43	1	69	7	57
2	159,615	25	45,874	43	R	7	37	78	23	1	33	1	48	11	39
3	137,788	17	27,919	39	R	22	16	20	15	0	8	0	19	2	29
4	154,198	21	36,822	28	R	11	26	61	16	1	31	0	39	19	33
5	144,465	17	35,157	20	M	11	25	52	9	3	32	1	41	42	29
6	222,890	76	67,274	45	S	4	52	79	74	3	122	3	131	14	69
7	137,402	15	32,678	27	R	10	19	46	8	4	32	0	37	37	24
8	136,315	14	35,805	32	R	10	29	53	7	4	24	2	37	41	24
9	141,757	21	48,354	36	U	7	40	76	16	5	33	2	41	16	42
10	132,805	14	29,154	24	U	11	19	30	-6	4	24	1	19	60	27
11	146,612	25	36,635	36	U	10	28	39	23	3	38	1	45	49	28
12	144,228	22	54,182	36	S	5	48	83	18	1	48	2	56	13	43
13	135,322	14	52,778	34	U	5	55	81	9	2	41	2	47	13	45
14	128,295	10	38,693	30	U	7	46	73	3	5	30	4	35	18	34
15	140,121	19	43,478	26	M	8	31	76	14	4	38	1	38	18	44
16	131,827	7	47,783	18	U	5	42	85	4	2	40	3	34	9	34
17	168,654	33	42,110	23	S	6	35	77	26	4	75	2	70	17	54
18	143,180	17	54,168	27	U	6	45	83	11	2	52	2	51	11	58
19	177,653	44	55,470	32	U	5	43	89	41	2	72	2	83	7	60
20	142,578	12	33,905	20	U	9	22	56	-2	6	43	2	32	34	38
21	158,021	32	45,072	35	U	5	33	90	29	1	64	1	71	8	62
22	133,948	15	31,941	26	U	11	15	29	-12	10	28	1	27	58	32
23	123,732	7	28,435	18	U	11	14	17	-32	18	18	1	-6	62	22
24	158,135	27	59,017	30	U	4	44	89	23	1	60	1	59	7	75
25	148,978	17	38,848	25	U	7	38	63	2	5	51	2	40	25	63
26	140,714	11	62,030	29	U	5	50	84	6	2	44	2	43	11	51
27	144,148	12	54,398	28	U	5	58	79	8	4	44	5	42	12	29
28	188,220	51	83,166	30	U	4	56	94	49	1	91	2	90	4	85
29	143,551	17	38,391	24	U	6	36	74	10	3	55	2	45	20	48
30	183,066	50	55,282	33	U	4	45	83	46	2	67	2	79	13	83

Note: U=urban, S=suburban, R=rural, M=mixed, HH=households.

ARKANSAS

Until the rise of President Bill Clinton, Arkansas was arguably the country's most obscure state. Occasionally an Arkansan would pierce the national consciousness— politicians such as Senate majority leader and Democratic vice presidential candidate Joseph Robinson and Sen. J. William Fulbright, or businessmen such as Wal-Mart founder Sam Walton—but for the most part the state remained little understood and much denigrated.

Sadly, the stereotype of Arkansas as a backward place was not without basis. Overall, the state remains poor and poorly educated. In 1997 it had the third-lowest average household income (ahead of only Mississippi and West Virginia) and the seventh-highest unemployment rate. Arkansas is also tied with West Virginia and Kentucky for the lowest college graduation rate in the country (26 percent). It also has one of the oldest populations of any state and is growing older; senior citizens may account for as much as 16 percent of its population by 2010.

Yet Arkansas is a place of great paradoxes. It is the only state with a significant frontage on the Mississippi River not to have developed a major port there. A place of wrenching poverty, it is also, like West Virginia, a place of natural beauty—home to twenty-seven species of orchids and the only state that produces diamonds and pearls. For many years it also produced almost all the country's bauxite, an essential ingredient of aluminum.

There are stark demographic and political contrasts as well. Although the state's population is growing at about the national rate, Arkansas has one of the fastest-growing house districts in the country (the Second, in the far northwest corner of the state, up 44 percent since 1990) as well as one of the fastest-shrinking (the Ninety-third, in the far northeast, which has lost 23 percent of its total population in just seven years). Despite its poverty, Arkansas has had the fourth-fastest rate of growth in average household income and boasts six of the fifty house districts in the country where income is growing fastest, more than any other state.

Most of the districts enjoying the nineties boom are located along the Mississippi River. The most peculiar of them is the above-mentioned Ninety-third, which despite its sharp population loss holds the distinction of being the house district with the fastest rate of income growth in the United States. It is centered around the town of Blytheville, just below the Missouri Bootheel. Acre Air Force Base closed there early in the decade, eliminating five thousand jobs, but at about the same time a Japanese steel manufacturer moved in, offering much higher wages than military pay. Implausible as it may seem, this area along the Mississippi muck is now one of the nation's largest producers of steel.

Blacks are a significant minority in Arkansas, but as in Alabama, they are not evenly distributed around the state. The districts along the western and northern tiers bordering Texas and Missouri are almost entirely white. On the other hand, districts in cotton and rice country along the Mississippi, as well as those around Pine Bluff, are more than 50 percent black.

In places, though, extreme differences in income and education are separated by only a few miles. For example, consider three adjoining districts just northeast of Little Rock. The Sixty-third District is the fourth-wealthiest in Arkansas, with an average household income of $56,827, and is 83 percent white. The neighboring Sixty-first District is the sixth-wealthiest and is 88 percent white. Running along the eastern boundary of these two, though, is the Fifty-ninth District, the second-poorest district in the state, where average income is just $25,787, about half the national average. It is 64 percent black.

Unlike many other southern states, Arkansas has remained strongly Democratic, helped no doubt by the presence of a native son in the White House. Republicans have made some inroads, taking the governor's mansion and a U.S. Senate seat, but they remain a distinct minority in the state legislature, outnumbered four to one in the senate and six to one in the house. And the demographic indicators in Arkansas point toward the Democrats. Six of the ten fastest-growing districts, and seven of the ten in which income is growing fastest, are currently in Democratic hands.

ARKANSAS
State Senate Districts

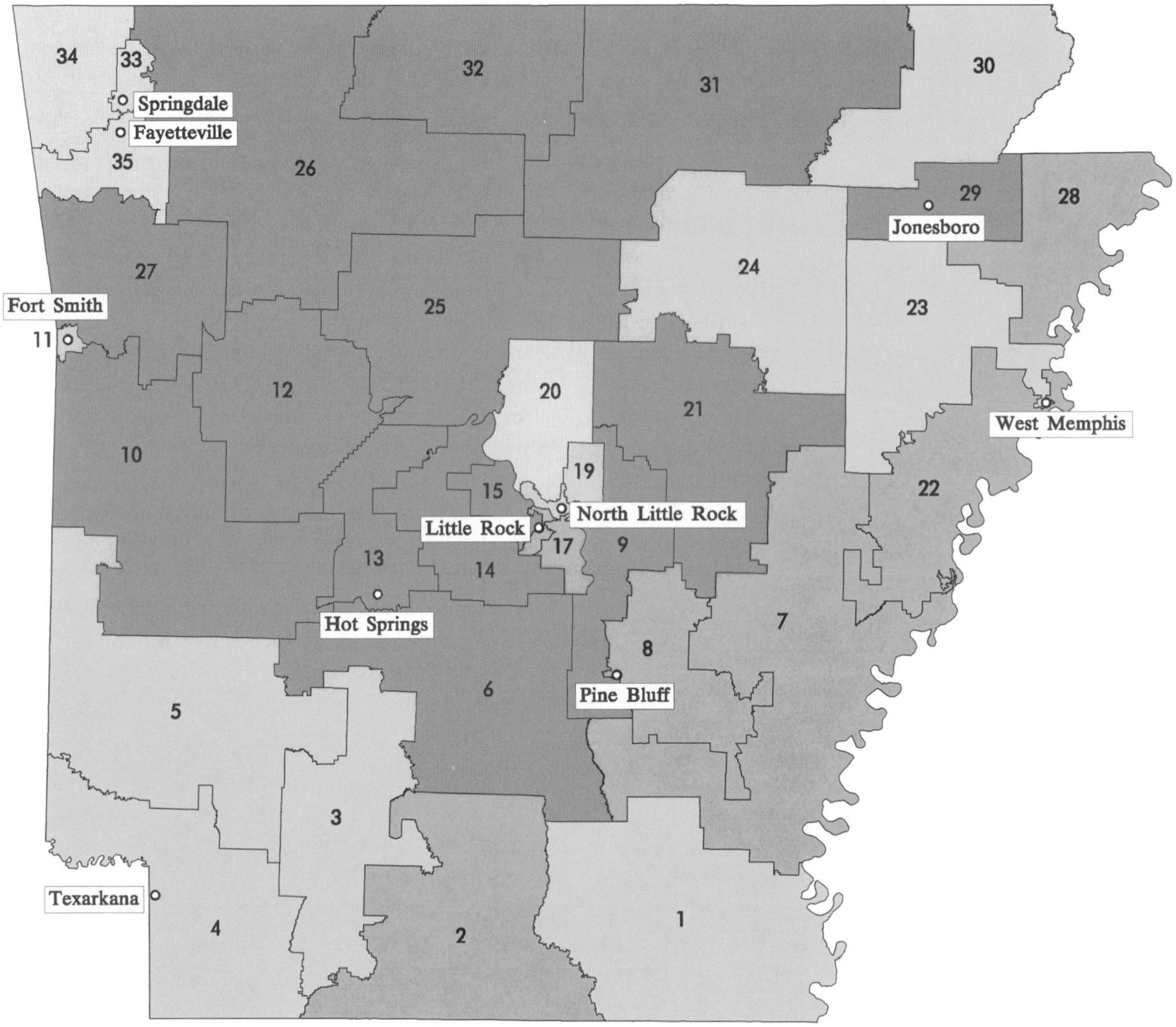

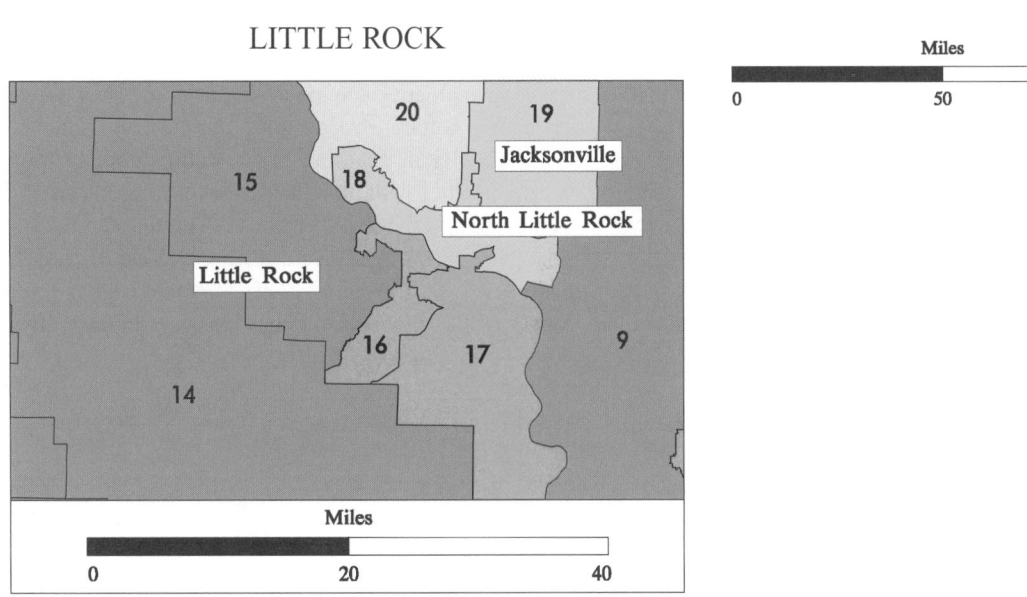

LITTLE ROCK

Miles

0	50	100

Population Growth   ▨ -10% to -2%   ▨ -1% to 6%   ▨ 8% to 19%   ▨ 21% to 35%

Arkansas State Senate Districts: Demographic Data

Senate District	Population 1997	+/-	Average HH Income ($)	+/-	District Type	Unempl. Rate (%)	College Educ. (%)	White (non-Hispanic) (%)	+/-	African American (%)	+/-	Asian American (%)	+/-	Hispanic American (%)	+/-
Arkansas	2,652,593	8	39,404	43	R	7	26	82	7	15	7	1	32	1	63
1	67,409	0	37,202	54	R	9	19	62	-3	36	4	0	-36	1	41
2	67,497	-4	37,910	40	R	8	24	68	-7	31	3	0	-9	1	40
3	65,217	0	33,582	34	R	7	27	64	-3	35	5	0	-8	1	29
4	67,345	-1	33,507	34	R	8	19	72	-4	26	5	0	6	1	43
5	69,650	6	34,704	48	R	6	19	81	4	15	10	0	-12	3	50
6	72,998	8	34,571	33	R	7	22	87	7	12	11	0	-6	1	45
7	65,924	-4	37,516	52	R	8	18	67	-6	32	1	0	-9	1	43
8	58,487	-5	29,109	39	U	13	19	30	-16	68	0	0	-10	1	42
9	77,141	12	44,820	39	M	6	29	85	10	13	24	1	36	1	71
10	71,830	11	37,210	45	R	5	21	96	10	0	-2	1	32	1	68
11	68,569	4	44,070	40	U	6	34	82	1	9	15	5	39	2	60
12	74,219	11	36,657	45	R	7	23	94	10	3	23	1	23	2	70
13	72,672	14	38,095	45	R	6	27	88	13	9	23	0	45	2	78
14	79,374	19	43,847	38	S	5	27	96	18	2	27	0	48	1	86
15	76,747	11	66,340	48	U	3	57	78	6	19	31	1	53	1	75
16	69,399	-2	54,457	39	U	4	50	74	-8	23	20	1	27	1	60
17	60,794	-10	27,757	28	U	9	21	27	-22	71	-5	0	3	1	13
18	69,091	3	46,379	46	U	5	36	76	0	21	12	1	31	1	72
19	67,934	2	47,887	41	S	6	34	82	-2	14	22	2	26	2	54
20	82,662	24	40,879	45	S	7	34	89	22	9	38	0	42	1	93
21	78,727	13	36,674	43	R	8	22	92	12	6	10	0	15	1	63
22	69,076	-3	28,529	47	R	14	15	36	-8	63	0	0	9	1	41
23	67,845	1	40,956	50	R	8	20	77	-2	22	13	0	29	1	47
24	70,606	3	35,034	42	R	8	17	91	3	8	7	0	14	1	43
25	76,395	12	33,439	39	R	7	20	94	11	4	12	0	0	1	58
26	76,910	14	33,944	41	R	6	20	98	13	0	-35	0	-10	1	66
27	76,078	14	36,389	41	M	6	18	95	13	1	18	1	40	2	73
28	62,656	-10	37,693	62	R	11	17	71	-13	27	-6	1	5	2	33
29	73,578	12	42,312	43	R	5	30	92	10	6	24	1	39	1	70
30	67,981	5	33,952	45	R	7	15	99	5	0	-9	0	-33	1	63
31	75,312	12	26,641	30	R	9	17	98	11	0	5	0	-39	1	52
32	77,795	18	31,930	30	R	6	22	98	18	0	-58	0	9	1	78
33	83,536	35	45,645	46	R	4	28	95	33	0	0	1	68	3	122
34	89,721	28	45,820	44	R	3	29	96	27	0	13	0	50	2	85
35	78,545	21	43,883	47	U	4	42	93	20	3	34	1	49	2	83

Note: U=urban, S=suburban, R=rural, M=mixed, HH=households.

ARKANSAS
State House Districts

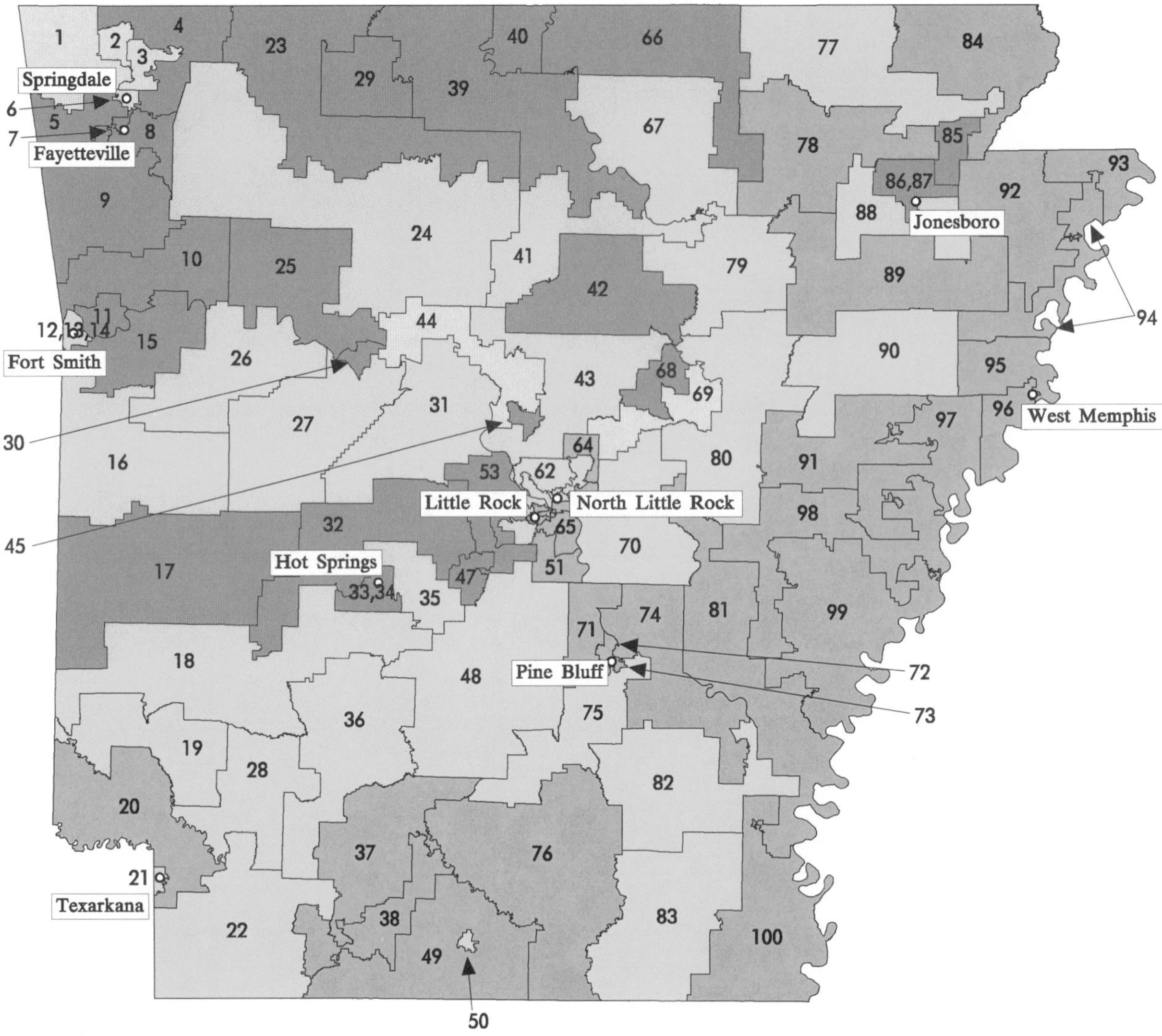

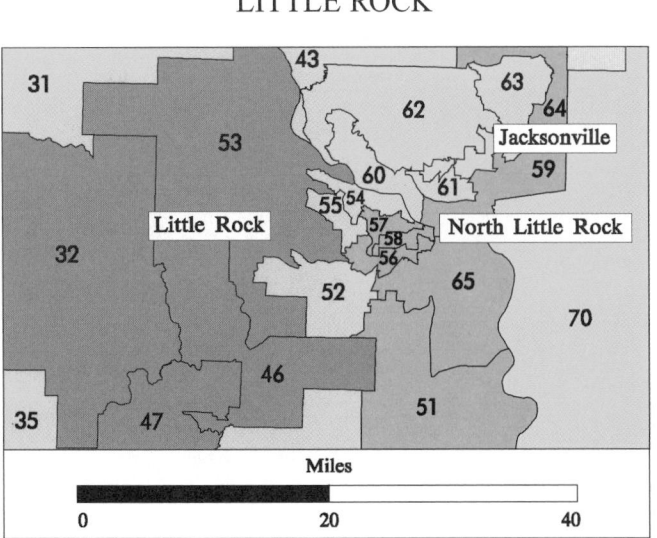

LITTLE ROCK

Miles

0   50   100

Population Growth   ■ -23% to 0%   ■ 1% to 11%   ■ 12% to 26%   ■ 30% to 44%

Arkansas State House Districts: Demographic Data

House District	Population		Average HH Income		District Type	Unempl. Rate	College Educ.	White (non-Hispanic)		African American		Asian American		Hispanic American	
	1997	+/-	($)	+/-		(%)	(%)	(%)	+/-	(%)	+/-	(%)	+/-	(%)	+/-
Arkansas	2,652,593	8	39,404	43	R	7	26	82	7	15	7	1	32	1	63
1	35,032	33	43,005	44	R	4	24	96	32	0	2	0	21	2	95
2	35,581	44	48,904	43	R	3	33	96	43	0	39	1	98	2	119
3	29,539	30	45,875	48	R	4	27	96	28	0	-20	1	55	3	118
4	30,440	25	44,662	41	R	5	32	98	25	0	-44	0	27	1	71
5	29,506	19	46,114	47	R	3	31	94	18	0	19	0	28	2	79
6	31,420	34	42,862	47	U	4	26	95	32	0	0	1	62	3	118
7	30,087	24	38,300	49	U	4	55	90	22	4	30	3	53	2	75
8	26,348	17	53,697	48	U	3	45	94	15	3	41	1	44	2	85
9	29,009	15	40,052	47	R	5	20	96	15	0	21	0	-11	2	78
10	26,599	14	38,472	42	R	6	19	97	13	0	5	0	27	1	60
11	26,877	20	33,945	36	S	7	19	93	19	2	25	2	52	2	93
12	71,845	4	43,514	41	U	6	33	82	0	9	15	6	39	2	60
13	71,845	4	43,514	41	U	6	33	82	0	9	15	6	39	2	60
14	71,845	4	43,514	41	U	6	33	82	0	9	15	6	39	2	60
15	27,902	19	44,950	45	M	4	30	95	18	0	21	2	43	2	82
16	24,596	7	37,207	49	R	6	16	97	6	0	-54	0	13	1	67
17	27,112	12	30,745	39	R	5	19	97	11	0	-50	0	-31	2	67
18	25,576	6	35,606	44	R	7	18	96	6	2	13	0	-47	1	51
19	22,220	6	36,671	48	R	6	18	76	4	19	10	0	7	4	44
20	22,156	-2	37,042	38	R	7	19	77	-5	21	6	0	-11	1	43
21	23,160	1	33,809	33	U	8	25	65	-3	33	8	1	25	1	39
22	23,510	1	29,004	31	R	9	13	73	-1	25	6	0	-37	1	48
23	28,331	13	33,200	43	R	7	17	98	12	0	-57	0	3	1	73
24	28,675	10	28,265	37	R	7	16	98	9	0	-37	0	-40	1	59
25	27,559	17	36,682	50	R	8	23	96	16	1	22	0	5	2	71
26	25,377	5	33,228	51	R	8	16	97	4	1	14	0	-32	1	54
27	24,831	9	34,546	42	R	6	14	95	9	2	19	0	2	2	68
28	23,804	2	33,497	45	R	8	21	65	-2	33	8	0	-45	2	49
29	26,897	13	33,018	30	R	5	24	98	13	0	-75	0	-10	1	79
30	25,463	13	41,997	44	R	6	33	92	12	5	26	1	49	2	78
31	27,309	10	32,861	37	R	7	20	88	9	11	12	0	-9	1	35
32	30,129	19	41,178	41	R	5	31	96	18	2	27	0	35	1	51
33	52,246	13	38,088	46	R	6	27	85	10	12	22	0	47	2	84
34	52,246	13	38,088	46	R	6	27	85	10	12	22	0	47	2	84
35	26,387	5	31,495	30	R	7	22	86	3	12	18	0	19	1	34
36	24,253	2	34,638	43	R	6	29	73	0	25	10	0	-4	1	40
37	22,780	-3	26,809	26	R	11	18	41	-8	58	1	0	-38	0	49
38	21,537	-6	39,567	32	R	5	33	80	-8	19	-1	0	-11	0	15
39	29,033	19	28,526	32	R	8	19	99	19	0	-82	0	6	1	45
40	27,217	17	32,649	31	R	7	23	98	17	0	50	0	27	1	97
41	22,858	9	35,861	39	R	8	24	96	9	2	12	0	16	1	73
42	27,013	16	30,620	30	R	8	18	99	16	0	-70	0	-13	1	48
43	28,336	7	38,189	47	R	6	20	92	5	7	24	0	-26	1	51
44	35,365	33	45,975	53	R	7	34	93	32	5	53	0	56	1	98
45	28,547	26	35,550	38	S	7	37	86	24	12	35	1	49	1	95
46	31,206	20	45,843	38	S	5	30	95	19	3	28	1	50	1	89
47	24,682	22	42,737	40	S	5	26	96	21	2	29	0	49	1	90
48	26,774	8	36,653	37	R	6	20	91	8	8	8	0	14	1	53
49	24,913	-6	43,276	47	R	7	24	77	-8	22	-1	0	-33	1	56
50	20,335	4	37,841	47	R	7	28	57	1	42	9	0	17	1	32

Note: U=urban, S=suburban, R=rural, M=mixed, HH=households.

Arkansas State House Districts: Demographic Data (cont.)

House District	Population		Average HH Income		District Type	Unempl. Rate	College Educ.	White (non-Hispanic)		African American		Asian American		Hispanic American	
	1997	+/-	($)	+/-		(%)	(%)	(%)	+/-	(%)	+/-	(%)	+/-	(%)	+/-
Arkansas	2,652,593	8	39,404	43	R	7	26	82	7	15	7	1	32	1	63
51	24,376	-5	36,788	27	U	6	23	67	-12	31	15	1	23	1	34
52	23,012	3	48,576	43	U	4	37	73	-4	25	30	1	28	1	58
53	30,580	20	64,559	49	U	3	53	89	16	8	57	1	78	1	98
54	24,706	2	80,038	42	U	3	65	91	-1	6	39	1	46	2	83
55	25,714	11	75,228	50	U	3	62	78	6	18	32	2	53	1	64
56	23,671	-3	34,392	38	U	7	31	34	-16	64	4	1	14	1	38
57	21,229	-5	50,979	38	U	5	57	80	-10	16	16	2	25	2	67
58	19,656	-10	26,995	31	U	10	25	18	-26	81	-5	0	5	0	6
59	21,402	-9	25,787	34	U	9	14	35	-20	64	-1	0	1	1	-3
60	25,042	7	49,540	48	U	4	39	82	3	15	28	0	30	2	79
61	23,636	2	52,284	44	U	4	41	88	-1	10	21	1	43	2	93
62	28,263	8	49,749	40	S	4	38	89	5	8	42	1	36	2	74
63	25,580	2	56,827	45	S	5	39	83	-2	12	22	2	20	3	59
64	24,398	-1	38,451	35	U	8	27	78	-6	17	26	2	29	2	43
65	19,807	-10	28,075	27	U	8	20	31	-22	67	-3	0	8	1	3
66	26,492	16	27,987	28	R	9	17	99	16	0	4	0	-61	0	29
67	26,204	11	29,698	34	R	7	18	97	10	1	14	0	0	1	63
68	26,473	22	41,245	39	R	6	32	94	20	4	30	0	37	2	97
69	33,250	40	39,288	41	R	8	24	95	39	3	23	0	44	1	125
70	28,020	10	41,277	45	R	6	19	81	6	18	33	0	11	1	29
71	21,949	-2	44,053	35	M	5	31	84	-4	14	13	1	30	1	66
72	21,854	-3	26,948	30	U	13	20	36	-8	64	0	0	12	0	21
73	20,977	0	28,176	31	U	12	24	30	-13	69	6	0	-10	1	52
74	19,216	-10	35,190	59	R	13	12	39	-18	59	-6	0	-11	2	46
75	23,954	1	45,629	39	R	6	31	73	-1	26	7	1	21	1	33
76	24,297	-4	30,975	30	R	9	18	67	-7	31	2	0	-16	1	31
77	24,517	5	28,622	34	R	8	15	98	5	1	10	0	-43	1	54
78	23,114	0	28,142	34	R	8	13	98	0	0	-7	0	-36	1	45
79	26,377	1	35,543	42	R	9	15	90	1	9	4	0	0	0	17
80	24,617	2	31,764	42	R	10	14	87	2	12	4	0	-9	0	11
81	20,734	-6	42,702	43	R	7	21	76	-8	23	1	0	-24	1	26
82	25,303	5	40,060	57	R	8	22	74	1	25	15	0	-15	1	48
83	24,154	2	40,857	53	R	8	20	74	-1	25	12	0	-11	1	46
84	22,438	-2	31,977	47	R	8	11	99	-2	0	-50	0	-35	1	33
85	26,292	21	38,108	48	R	7	19	99	21	0	-13	0	-24	1	108
86	49,824	13	44,166	40	R	5	35	89	12	8	23	1	39	1	75
87	49,824	13	44,166	40	R	5	35	89	12	8	23	1	39	1	75
88	25,762	10	37,657	48	R	6	19	96	9	2	30	0	29	1	52
89	22,581	-2	33,441	43	R	11	12	89	-3	10	6	0	-56	1	38
90	23,686	1	36,616	53	R	9	15	74	-2	25	11	0	2	1	44
91	23,797	-3	32,328	57	R	11	18	56	-7	42	1	0	23	1	36
92	19,588	-2	34,329	57	R	8	11	93	-3	5	-4	0	-13	2	69
93	17,971	-23	51,108	77	R	7	30	81	-26	15	-16	2	6	2	10
94	22,320	-8	30,399	54	R	15	13	40	-14	58	-5	0	-3	1	43
95	24,094	0	32,719	50	M	13	14	34	-3	65	2	0	13	1	54
96	22,838	-1	48,308	47	U	6	26	77	-5	21	12	1	41	1	44
97	16,556	-3	26,747	50	R	16	15	35	-10	63	1	0	3	2	50
98	26,572	-3	32,974	52	R	9	16	60	-7	39	3	0	6	1	40
99	20,615	-5	25,740	47	R	13	15	37	-10	62	-2	0	2	1	45
100	21,825	-6	36,035	66	R	14	15	40	-12	58	-2	0	-51	1	37

Note: U=urban, S=suburban, R=rural, M=mixed, HH=households.

CALIFORNIA

California at the end of the twentieth century dominates the country as thoroughly as New York did at the beginning. It is by far the most populous state—more than 32 million people, almost as many as New York and Florida combined. In entertainment, technology, living patterns, fashion, and a host of other fields, California sets the trends, and the rest of the United States follows.

After growing by more than 25 percent during the 1980s in the continuation of a more or less sixty-year boom, California has grown by just 8 percent in this decade. Much was written about this slump in the national press, but it is important to recognize that California continued to grow faster than the rest of the nation. The boom slowed here for many reasons, including the recession that hit the defense and aerospace industries, but also because acts of God (floods, earthquakes) and of man (the Rodney King riots, smog, and overcrowding) made the state seem a less-desirable place for working-age whites to live. They responded to these problems by moving away from the crowded cities and existing suburbs and by moving out of the state altogether.

New York may have invented the suburbs, but California perfected them. By the early 1990s, though, many older suburbs, especially those closer to Los Angeles, had become small cities themselves, with higher crime rates, more pollution, worse schools, and other problems typical of urban centers. Many who have left these areas have pushed even further out. Thus, the districts gaining population fastest today reach across the mountains—to Lake Elsinore, Lancaster, Imperial County, and the San Joaquin Valley—while the districts losing population are almost all in Los Angeles. To a lesser extent, this trend has occurred around San Francisco and San Diego as well.

Many Southern Californians also moved out of state, to places like Tucson, Las Vegas, and Boise, in search of jobs and a less hectic way of life. In the early 1990s, for the first time in memory, California experienced a net out-migration of people to other states, most of them white and middle class. This temporary exodus was one of the reasons states in the Mountain West have grown so rapidly, and its cessation (more Americans are again moving into California than are moving out) calls into question whether those boom states can sustain their growth.

California continued to expand during the recession of the early 1990s because even as whites were moving out, minority groups (chiefly Hispanics and Asians) were pouring in. This accelerated a trend that is expected to make non-Hispanic whites a minority of the state's population within the next decade.

In California, and increasingly for the nation, race and age are related. The state is growing both older and younger, and increasingly along racial lines. It is estimated that by 2010, more than two-thirds of the state's schoolchildren will be Hispanic, Asian, or African American, while the population over age fifty will remain largely non-Hispanic white. There are enormous social and political implications in these figures, as whites, with fewer children and living ever further from the cities, will be asked to provide social services to growing minority populations living in them, and urban minorities will be asked to pay more in payroll taxes to provide retirement benefits for rural whites.

California's minority groups, though, are anything but politically monolithic. The state will likely face a long period in which no ethnic or racial group predominates and in which shifting alliances between whites and Asians or blacks and Hispanics will be necessary. The state, in short, will fight more than it has in the past. The fights may be conducted along partisan divisions that are by now familiar. Whites and Asians tend to vote Republican, blacks and increasingly Hispanics, Democratic.

In this decade, Democrats have controlled both chambers of the legislature. That body is very small by national standards. A California assembly member can represent as many as a half million people; state senators, more than 900,000, making members of the legislature as distant from their constituents as TV characters. Politics here will remain wholesale rather than retail.

CALIFORNIA
State Senate Districts

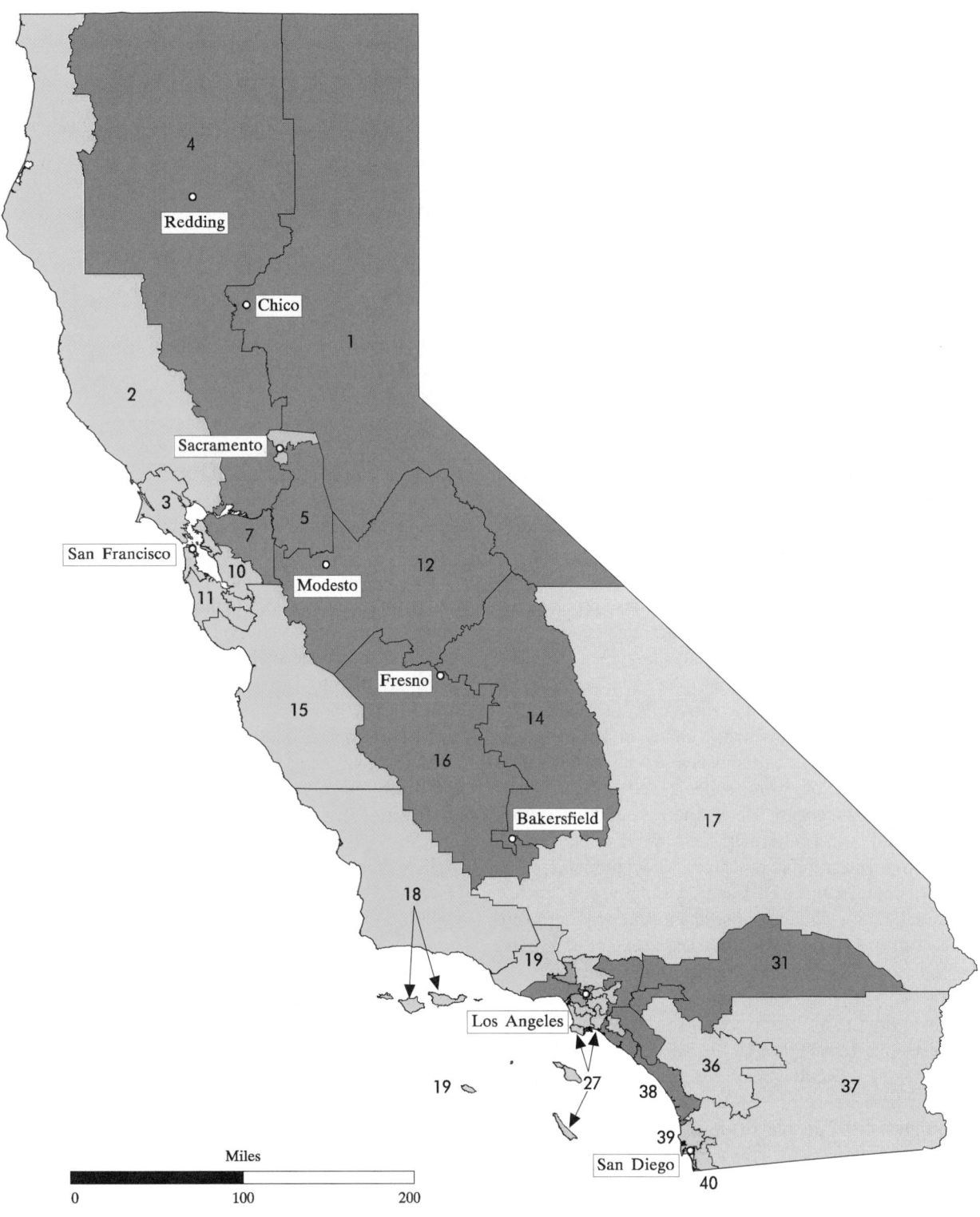

Population Growth ▨ -14% to -3% ▢ 0% to 9% ▨ 10% to 16% ▢ 18% to 24%

LOS ANGELES

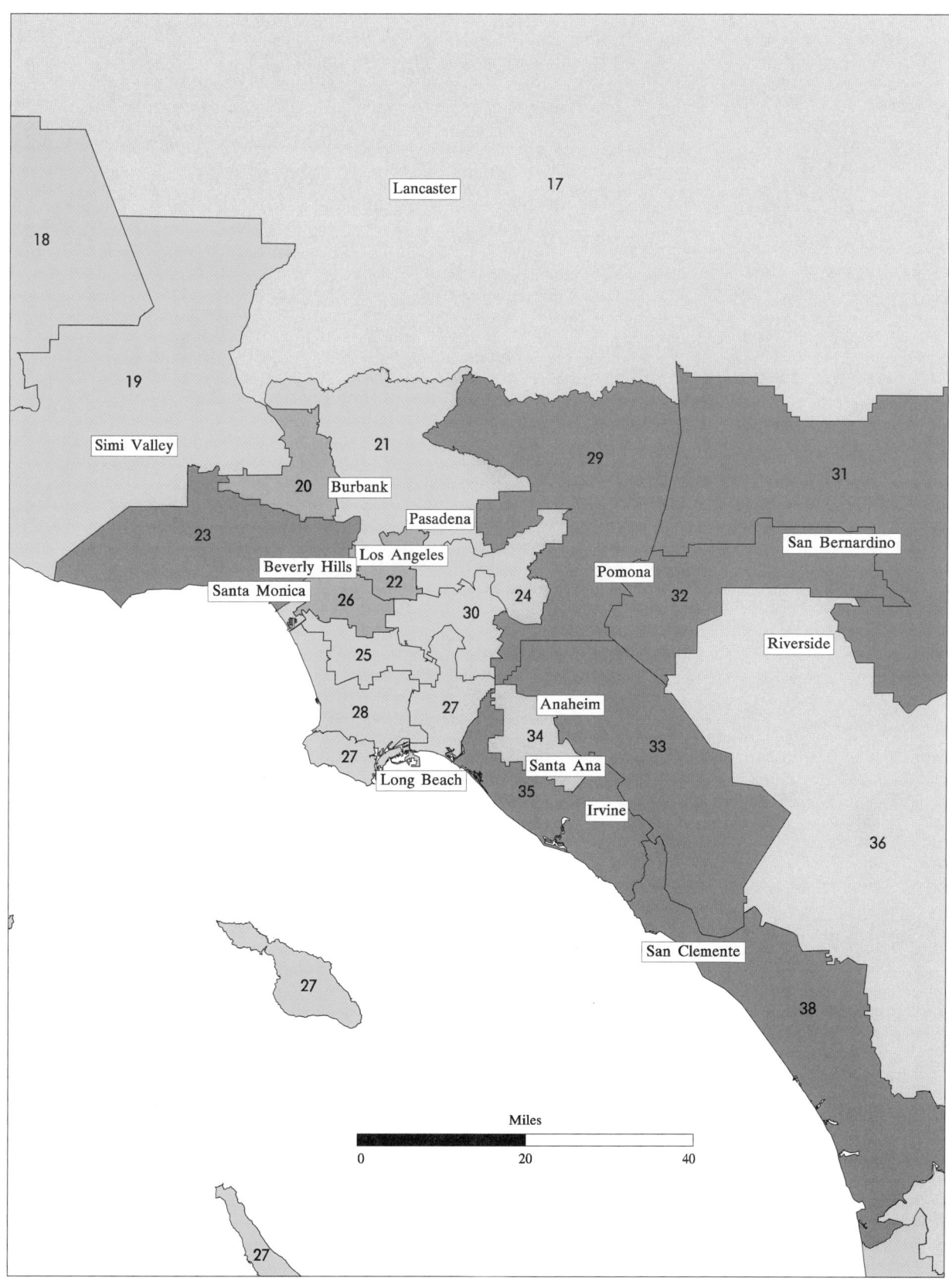

Lancaster

17

18

19

Simi Valley

21

29

31

20 Burbank

Pasadena

23

Los Angeles

San Bernardino

Beverly Hills

22

Pomona

Santa Monica

26

24

32

25

30

Riverside

28

27

Anaheim

34

33

27

Santa Ana

Long Beach

35

Irvine

36

27

San Clemente

38

Miles

0   20   40

Population Growth   ▮ -14% to -3%   ▯ 0% to 9%   ▮ 10% to 16%   ▯ 18% to 24%

SAN FRANCISCO

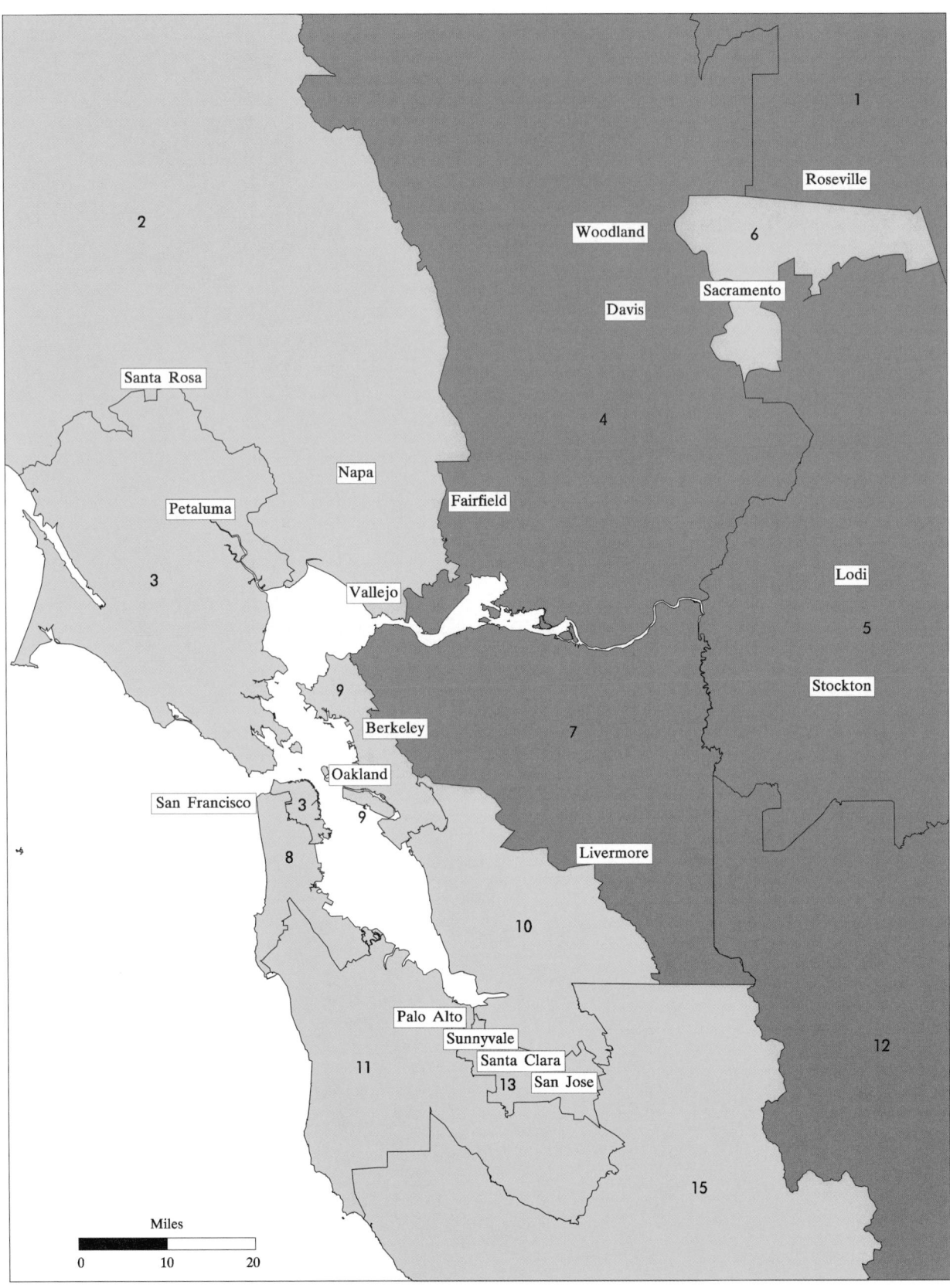

2

1

Roseville

Woodland

6

Sacramento

Davis

Santa Rosa

4

Napa

Petaluma

Fairfield

Lodi

3

Vallejo

5

Stockton

9

Berkeley

7

Oakland

San Francisco

3

9

8

Livermore

10

Palo Alto

Sunnyvale

Santa Clara

13   San Jose

11

12

15

Miles

0   10   20

Population Growth   ☐ 0% to 9%   ■ 10% to 16%

California State Senate Districts: Demographic Data

Senate District	Population		Average HH Income		District Type	Unempl. Rate	College Educ.	White non-Hispanic		African American		Asian American		Hispanic American	
	1997	+/-	($)	+/-		(%)	(%)	(%)	+/-	(%)	+/-	(%)	+/-	(%)	+/-
Calif.	32,190,255	8	57,083	23	M	7	41	52	-3	7	4	11	28	30	26
1	860,470	16	49,302	32	R	7	39	85	13	1	12	3	47	9	49
2	785,849	6	52,588	33	M	6	40	76	1	4	4	6	31	12	32
3	780,904	5	67,824	35	U	5	52	62	-3	8	4	15	25	14	26
4	819,848	10	47,532	30	M	8	37	71	3	4	17	7	37	17	35
5	846,583	13	52,387	31	S	7	37	59	2	5	14	13	40	22	37
6	801,854	7	51,167	33	S	7	40	61	-2	11	11	12	33	15	30
7	854,570	15	76,773	30	S	4	53	72	7	4	29	10	48	13	39
8	772,568	4	70,182	33	M	5	49	43	-12	5	-3	34	25	17	18
9	741,565	0	54,805	34	U	8	50	34	-18	32	3	17	19	16	26
10	809,266	9	69,340	35	S	5	44	50	-5	6	22	24	36	20	23
11	801,411	8	97,322	38	S	4	60	68	-1	4	9	13	37	15	35
12	855,077	14	45,596	22	M	10	29	61	5	3	12	6	36	29	37
13	777,273	5	61,901	30	U	6	43	40	-13	4	2	21	24	34	26
14	848,955	14	47,287	25	U	7	37	66	5	3	15	5	39	25	43
15	764,507	3	64,691	37	M	7	40	53	-7	3	-7	8	22	35	21
16	842,733	13	32,804	17	M	14	16	28	-12	6	7	7	23	59	31
17	917,105	24	48,638	12	R	7	33	67	11	5	33	4	59	22	71
18	782,527	5	56,393	25	M	5	43	66	-3	2	7	4	27	27	29
19	778,793	5	69,207	18	M	5	44	59	-5	3	-2	9	28	29	27
20	702,687	-5	45,528	11	U	7	32	30	-32	6	6	8	16	56	14
21	778,715	4	58,487	14	U	6	49	51	-11	7	17	14	30	27	27
22	637,327	-14	30,922	12	U	11	23	6	-61	5	2	18	-8	71	-8
23	844,455	14	86,797	15	U	5	61	75	7	3	26	9	47	13	45
24	754,355	2	42,630	11	S	8	27	11	-39	2	17	23	17	63	8
25	784,059	6	38,569	12	S	10	24	10	-36	31	-5	7	11	52	30
26	726,635	-3	40,687	15	U	10	33	14	-16	35	-15	5	-9	45	18
27	796,480	6	58,414	14	M	5	46	53	-8	6	8	15	31	26	34
28	766,164	3	60,845	19	S	6	46	42	-8	12	4	16	16	29	15
29	833,922	12	62,600	14	S	5	46	45	-10	6	21	16	38	33	45
30	779,513	5	38,829	11	S	9	16	10	-40	2	16	5	33	82	14
31	855,878	15	47,969	14	S	7	36	65	6	7	19	5	40	22	47
32	851,245	14	44,146	18	S	9	25	36	-8	10	14	5	33	48	36
33	835,347	13	73,386	17	S	4	51	66	3	2	10	11	44	22	39
34	785,196	6	46,656	12	U	7	27	30	-21	2	-4	16	27	52	25
35	829,903	11	75,659	21	S	4	55	71	3	2	18	13	43	15	41
36	919,323	24	50,997	16	M	6	32	61	13	5	23	4	49	29	52
37	876,018	18	55,663	20	M	7	37	59	7	2	19	5	49	33	41
38	850,350	15	64,114	22	S	5	48	68	5	3	22	6	53	23	45
39	760,463	2	54,041	23	U	5	52	66	-6	6	8	11	34	16	25
40	782,628	5	44,356	23	S	8	31	37	-12	10	0	12	20	40	26

Note: U=urban, S=suburban, R=rural, M=mixed, HH=households.

CALIFORNIA
State Assembly Districts

SAN DIEGO

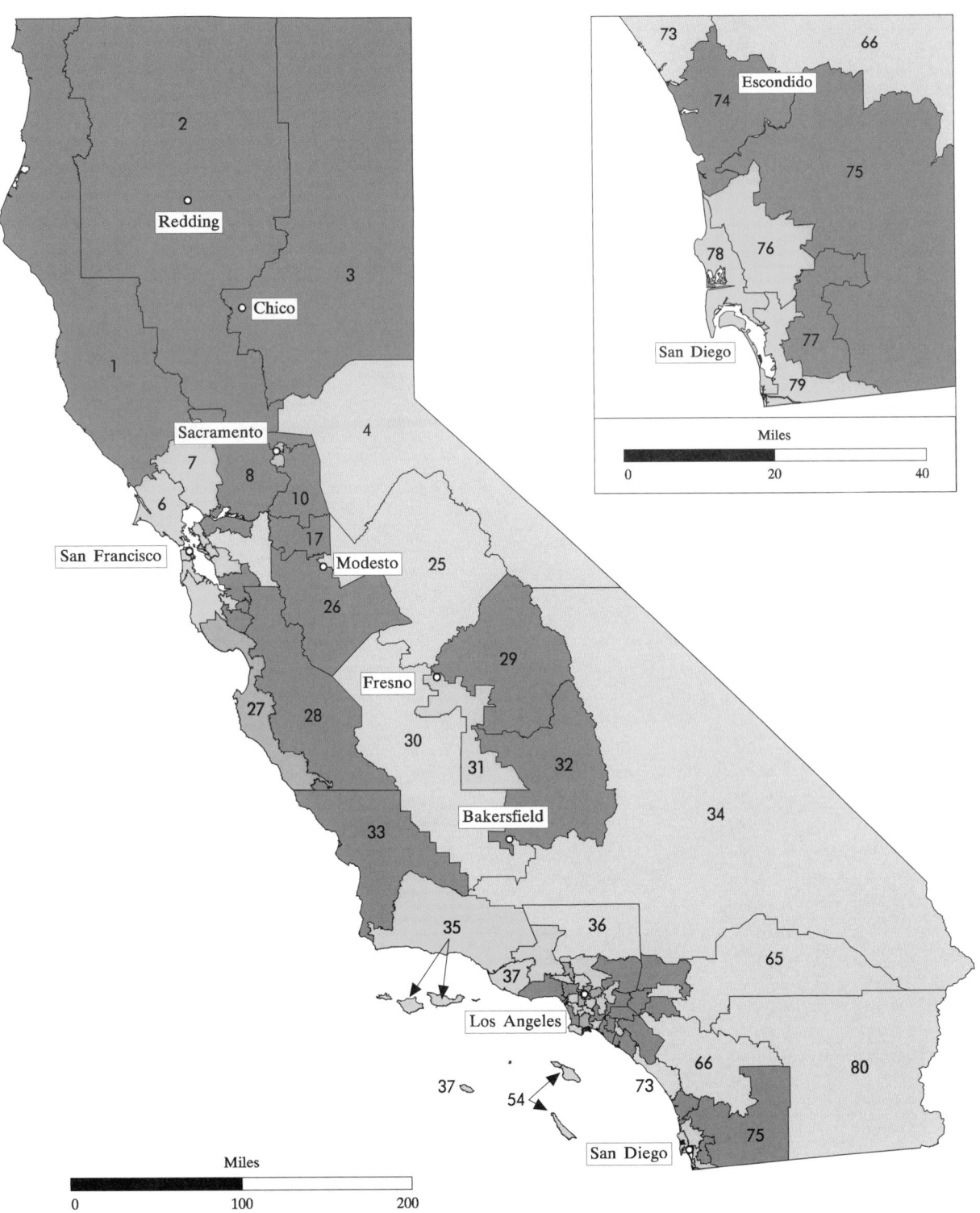

Population Growth   ▨ -16% to -3%   ▨ -1% to 7%   ▨ 8% to 16%   ▨ 17% to 35%

LOS ANGELES

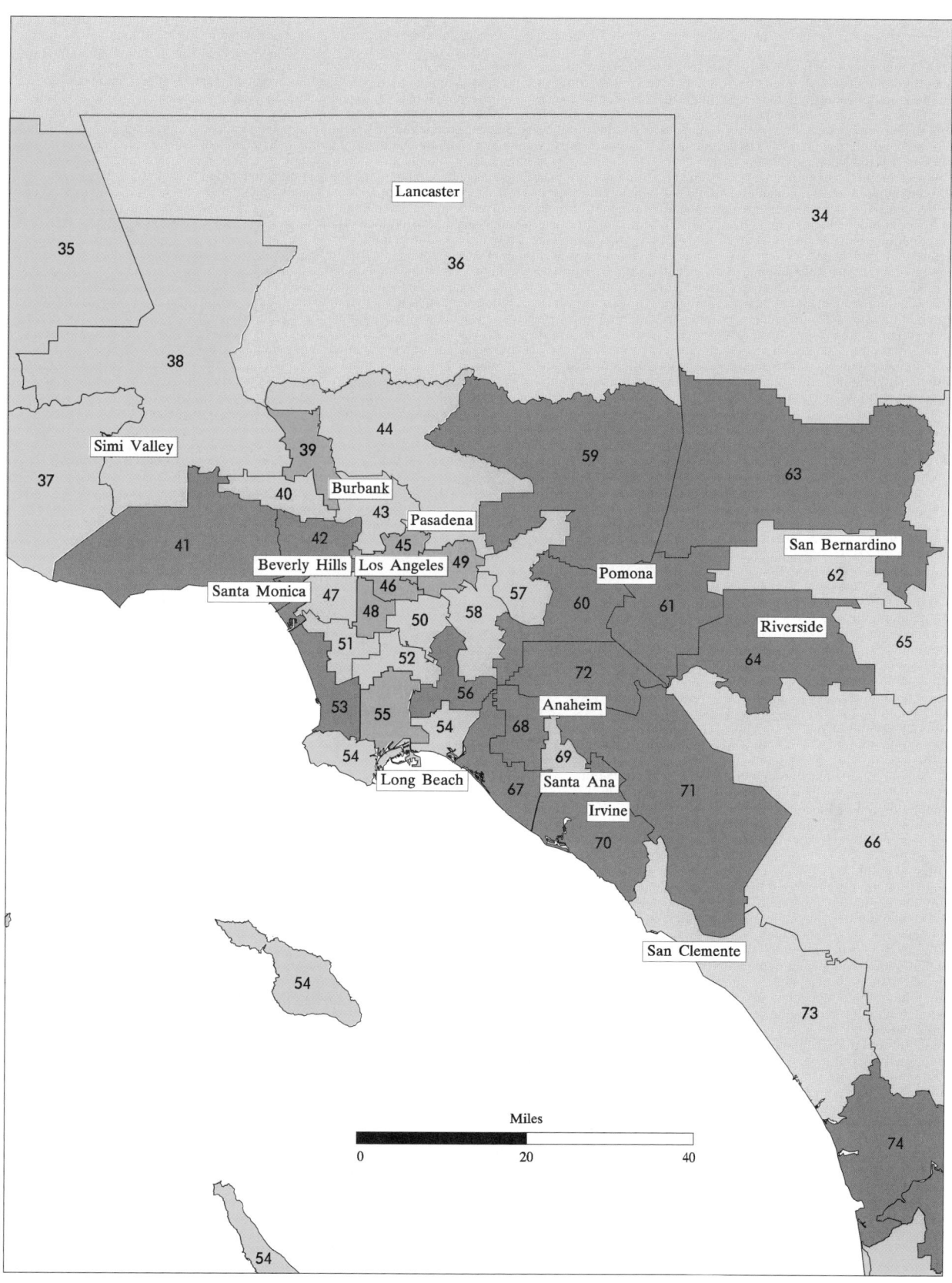

Population Growth ▨ -16% to -3%   ▨ -1% to 7%   ▨ 8% to 16%   ▨ 17% to 35%

SAN FRANCISCO

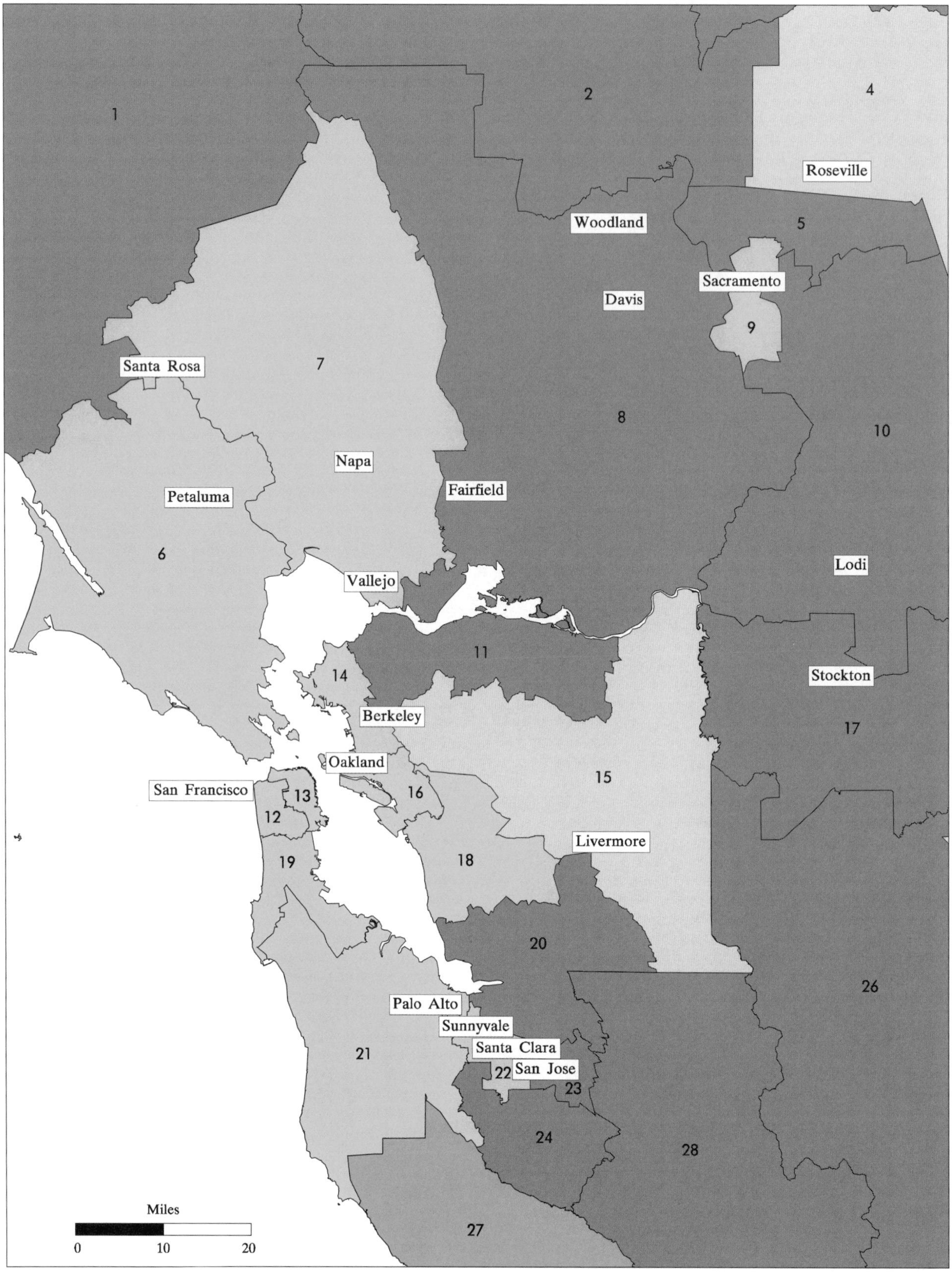

1

2

4

Roseville

Woodland

5

Davis

Sacramento

9

Santa Rosa

7

8

10

Napa

Petaluma

Fairfield

6

Lodi

Vallejo

Stockton

11

Berkeley

17

Oakland

15

San Francisco

13

16

12

Livermore

19

18

20

26

Palo Alto

Sunnyvale

Santa Clara

21

22 San Jose

23

24

28

27

Miles

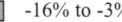

0   10   20

Population Growth   -16% to -3%   -1% to 7%   8% to 16%   17% to 35%

California State Assembly Districts: Demographic Data

Assembly District	Population		Average HH Income		District Type	Unempl. Rate	College Educ.	White non-Hispanic		African American		Asian American		Hispanic American	
	1997	+/-	($)	+/-		(%)	(%)	(%)	+/-	(%)	+/-	(%)	+/-	(%)	+/-
Calif.	32,190,255	8	57,083	23	M	7	41	52	-3	7	4	11	28	30	26
1	401,148	8	46,574	33	R	7	37	83	5	1	9	2	41	11	35
2	409,539	10	40,199	28	R	9	31	80	6	1	10	4	42	13	38
3	402,125	9	42,002	31	R	9	36	84	5	2	10	4	37	9	39
4	458,345	23	55,817	30	R	5	42	86	20	1	17	2	63	10	58
5	419,699	12	58,949	36	S	5	43	79	6	5	25	5	58	10	48
6	395,164	6	77,002	30	S	4	55	81	1	3	9	5	37	11	36
7	384,701	4	59,087	34	U	5	44	68	-3	7	3	10	29	14	29
8	410,309	10	55,634	33	M	6	43	62	0	7	18	10	35	20	34
9	382,155	2	42,799	28	U	8	37	41	-15	17	7	19	27	22	23
10	413,425	10	57,881	34	S	6	45	71	1	5	20	9	49	15	43
11	414,679	11	60,765	29	S	5	44	64	0	6	26	12	42	16	37
12	377,269	1	67,250	34	U	6	51	35	-18	7	-7	43	21	15	13
13	385,740	3	59,646	41	U	7	49	43	-10	13	2	26	23	18	20
14	370,696	-1	52,408	32	U	7	55	39	-18	31	7	15	21	14	31
15	439,891	18	91,379	30	S	3	60	80	13	2	40	8	59	9	43
16	370,869	0	57,595	37	U	8	43	28	-16	34	-1	19	16	18	23
17	433,158	15	46,203	27	U	9	29	48	2	6	10	16	35	29	34
18	390,781	6	58,609	30	S	6	38	51	-8	8	24	18	32	22	23
19	395,299	6	72,898	32	S	4	48	50	-7	4	5	26	31	19	22
20	418,485	13	80,664	37	S	5	49	49	-1	4	20	29	38	17	22
21	395,792	7	100,104	39	S	4	63	66	-1	6	8	11	35	17	34
22	372,377	1	69,698	34	S	4	55	59	-11	3	4	20	27	17	26
23	404,896	10	52,141	25	U	8	30	23	-18	5	1	21	21	50	26
24	405,619	8	94,455	38	U	3	58	71	0	2	12	15	39	12	36
25	437,895	17	49,683	24	M	8	35	70	9	2	20	4	43	22	47
26	417,182	12	40,703	19	M	11	23	52	0	3	7	8	33	36	32
27	341,976	-7	68,823	42	S	5	51	73	-10	4	-21	7	5	15	8
28	422,531	13	60,445	32	M	9	30	37	-3	3	23	9	36	50	24
29	432,441	16	48,627	27	U	6	42	65	6	2	17	7	43	25	45
30	445,831	20	34,197	16	R	14	16	32	-2	6	14	4	37	57	38
31	396,902	7	31,272	18	M	15	16	22	-24	6	0	11	18	61	24
32	416,514	12	45,857	24	U	7	31	67	3	3	13	3	30	26	42
33	403,768	8	50,515	28	R	6	38	67	0	3	10	4	29	26	32
34	440,334	18	41,860	15	R	9	29	70	11	5	18	3	38	20	50
35	374,148	3	62,513	24	M	4	46	65	-6	1	0	4	25	29	27
36	476,771	29	55,287	9	S	6	37	65	12	5	51	5	73	24	92
37	395,269	7	64,162	18	S	5	40	52	-5	3	5	7	27	37	27
38	383,524	3	74,121	17	U	4	49	66	-5	2	-9	11	29	20	26
39	333,056	-10	42,208	11	U	9	21	12	-57	7	-1	7	4	74	6
40	369,631	-1	47,618	10	U	7	40	46	-22	5	17	10	26	39	31
41	416,068	12	95,683	18	U	4	61	78	7	2	18	7	42	12	38
42	428,387	15	79,670	12	U	6	62	73	7	4	31	10	51	13	52
43	377,064	1	51,390	15	U	7	44	53	-12	2	17	15	27	30	20
44	401,651	7	65,731	14	U	5	53	50	-9	12	17	13	33	24	36
45	312,283	-16	35,290	12	U	10	26	8	-58	3	6	21	-3	68	-9
46	325,044	-13	26,835	13	U	12	20	3	-66	7	0	14	-13	75	-7
47	380,645	2	49,004	14	U	7	46	26	-11	37	-3	8	4	28	28
48	345,990	-7	27,255	13	U	15	14	1	-70	34	-27	1	-56	64	13
49	360,996	-3	40,204	10	S	8	29	11	-29	1	0	33	12	55	-4
50	381,168	3	31,624	10	S	12	9	2	-70	2	8	1	6	94	10

Note: U=urban, S=suburban, R=rural, M=mixed, HH=households.

California State Assembly Districts: Demographic Data (cont.)

Assembly District	Population 1997	+/-	Average HH Income ($)	+/-	District Type	Unempl. Rate (%)	College Educ. (%)	White non-Hispanic (%)	+/-	African American (%)	+/-	Asian American (%)	+/-	Hispanic American (%)	+/-
Calif.	32,190,255	8	57,083	23	M	7	41	52	-3	7	4	11	28	30	26
51	387,615	5	41,324	11	S	9	30	15	-29	34	1	7	15	44	28
52	396,444	7	35,242	13	S	12	17	4	-53	29	-11	7	7	60	32
53	410,626	10	70,925	17	S	4	59	68	2	3	29	14	36	14	34
54	390,701	4	63,294	14	U	5	52	60	-5	6	5	11	30	22	23
55	355,538	-4	43,133	17	U	9	27	11	-44	24	1	18	3	46	10
56	405,858	9	52,923	14	S	5	38	45	-12	7	11	18	31	29	43
57	393,359	6	45,161	11	S	8	24	11	-45	3	26	15	29	71	19
58	398,345	7	44,641	12	S	7	24	18	-31	2	25	10	37	70	20
59	413,914	11	61,145	16	S	5	47	54	-6	6	21	11	39	28	48
60	420,008	13	64,222	13	S	5	45	35	-14	6	20	21	38	38	42
61	407,345	9	49,727	20	S	7	27	37	-10	8	7	6	31	49	28
62	443,900	19	39,289	17	S	10	24	35	-5	12	18	5	34	48	45
63	413,659	11	56,018	18	S	6	43	64	3	7	14	6	38	22	36
64	417,033	13	49,465	14	U	7	32	54	-2	6	12	5	36	34	42
65	442,219	19	40,660	11	S	8	30	66	9	6	25	4	43	23	58
66	502,290	35	52,164	18	S	6	33	68	25	3	45	3	71	25	65
67	403,468	8	71,395	20	S	4	51	71	1	1	12	14	38	13	32
68	400,894	8	50,246	15	S	6	34	46	-13	2	8	21	33	31	42
69	384,302	3	41,655	8	U	8	19	14	-40	2	-16	10	16	74	18
70	426,435	15	79,354	21	S	4	59	70	5	2	21	12	50	16	49
71	420,725	14	76,557	16	S	3	54	70	6	1	7	10	46	18	41
72	414,622	12	70,135	19	S	4	49	61	0	2	13	12	42	25	37
73	433,342	17	64,025	19	R	5	48	67	7	5	21	6	54	21	47
74	417,008	13	64,205	25	S	6	47	69	3	2	28	5	51	24	43
75	418,211	13	67,492	26	S	4	49	78	6	2	21	8	53	12	42
76	390,461	5	48,714	22	U	5	49	61	-5	8	9	15	35	16	29
77	400,445	8	52,618	25	S	6	40	57	-5	6	12	12	30	24	42
78	370,002	-1	59,341	24	U	5	54	72	-7	4	5	6	31	16	22
79	382,183	3	34,119	17	U	11	21	16	-33	14	-5	12	11	58	21
80	457,807	23	44,724	13	R	9	26	43	7	2	18	2	34	52	41

Note: U=urban, S=suburban, R=rural, M=mixed, HH=households.

COLORADO

The city of Denver sits like an island in the middle of an ocean. It is the largest city between Kansas City and San Francisco and is also the most politically liberal spot in a sea of conservatism that spreads across the western plains and Rocky Mountains. Though predominantly a Republican state in a Republican region, Colorado's best-known politicians in recent decades have almost all been Democrats: Sens. Gary Hart and Tim Wirth, Rep. Patricia Schroeder, and Gov. Roy Romer, now head of the national Democratic Party. Not coincidentally, all are from Denver.

The 1990s have been a boom time for Colorado, as indeed they have been for the region as a whole. The five fastest-growing states—Arizona, Colorado, Idaho, Nevada, and Utah—are all located in the mountain time zone. Colorado is now the second-largest of the group, behind Arizona, and the fourth-fastest growing state in the country. This population growth will bring it at least one new congressional seat in 2002 and perhaps more to come. Given Colorado's reputation as the most competitive state for Democrats in the region, it may also bring increased attention and even more political competition.

Colorado's growth, however, has not been so much in Denver as in its less-crowded, less-polluted southern suburbs and in the area just behind them stretching down toward Colorado Springs. The Sixty-fourth State House District, which includes Douglas County (the nation's fastest-growing county), has doubled in population in the last seven years and is the eighth-fastest growing district in the United States. Just below it, the Twentieth House District has grown by 47 percent.

The southern suburbs are home to Colorado's youngest, wealthiest, and most Republican voters. Average household income in the Thirty-seventh and Thirty-ninth House Districts, which take in Denver's southwestern suburbs, is $99,000 and $104,000, respectively; in the Sixty-fourth District, it is more than $86,000, and in the Twentieth, $72,000. Household income levels off in Colorado Springs, which is filling with couples with young children and is dominated by the military (the Air Force Academy and the U.S. Army's Fort Carson) and the conservative Christian organization Focus on the Family.

This area has proved fertile ground for Republicans, who hold all the state house and senate seats between downtown Denver and downtown Colorado Springs. Often, Democrats do not even try to contest this region; the party has fielded a candidate in the Sixty-fourth District only once in three elections between 1992 and 1996, and not at all in the Twentieth District.

Democratic strength centers on the corridor north of Denver to Boulder, which includes the University of Colorado and some of the trendy ski resorts. The corridor also includes the only two state house districts that have any significant concentration of African Americans (the Seventh and Eighth, in northeast Denver), as well as three of the state's four Hispanic-majority districts (the Second, Fourth, and Fifth, in northwest Denver). Colorado does have a significant Hispanic population (14 percent, eighth-highest in the country), and it is growing. The Hispanic community in Denver has already flexed its political muscle, helping to elect Federico Peña, now secretary of energy, as mayor during the 1980s.

Republicans control both houses of the legislature rather comfortably, though things were close earlier in the decade. Boosted by President Bill Clinton in 1992, Democrats came within three seats of gaining control in both the state house and senate. In 1996 the GOP moved back to a 41–24 advantage in the lower house and a 20–15 advantage in the upper house, and having voted for Bill Clinton in 1992, the state switched its presidential vote to Bob Dole in 1996. It seems risky to make any political predictions based on demographics, though. Republicans control seven of the ten fastest-growing house districts—but two of the four fastest-shrinking ones as well.

One factor that does bear watching is age. Colorado is a young state; only 19 percent of the population is older than fifty-five, and only 10 percent is over sixty-five. The Census Bureau expects the number of senior citizens to more than double over the next quarter century.

COLORADO
State Senate Districts

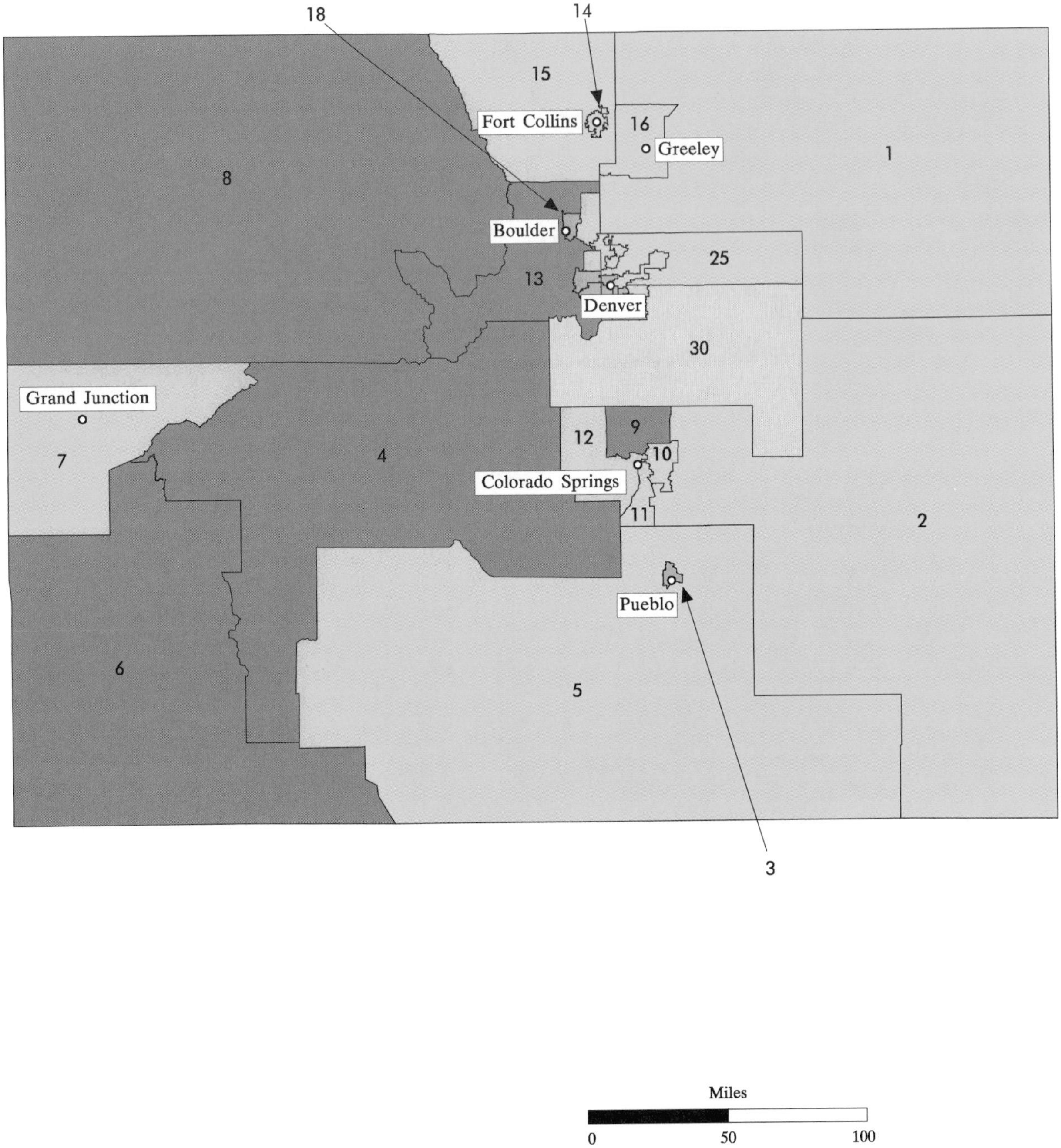

18

14

15

Fort Collins

16 Greeley

8

1

Boulder

13

25

Denver

30

Grand Junction

7

4

12

9

10

Colorado Springs

11

2

Pueblo

5

6

3

Miles

0   50   100

Population Growth   ☐ -3% to 9%   ☐ 12% to 22%   ☐ 25% to 39%   ☐ 86%

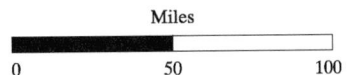

DENVER

13

18

17

1

23

25

13

19

24

33

25

20

34

33

Denver

21

31

32

35

29

25

22

28

30

26

27

Miles

0   5   10

Population Growth   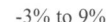 -3% to 9%   12% to 22%    25% to 39%   86%

Colorado State Senate Districts: Demographic Data

Senate District	Population		Average HH Income		District Type	Unempl. Rate	College Educ.	White (non-Hispanic)		African American		Asian American		Hispanic American	
	1997	+/-	($)	+/-		(%)	(%)	(%)	+/-	(%)	+/-	(%)	+/-	(%)	+/-
Colorado	3,885,429	18	51,964	38	M	6	47	79	16	4	22	2	38	14	26
1	107,996	12	40,966	39	R	5	29	83	10	0	11	0	14	16	24
2	102,865	13	35,774	31	R	7	30	76	10	3	31	1	36	18	18
3	92,691	3	32,395	31	U	9	28	52	-6	2	17	0	9	45	15
4	119,660	26	44,929	40	R	7	40	90	26	1	19	0	5	8	36
5	108,302	14	35,889	34	R	8	33	60	13	1	20	0	18	38	17
6	121,658	26	43,503	47	R	7	39	83	24	0	-2	0	5	12	40
7	110,168	18	41,794	39	R	7	36	89	17	0	21	1	33	9	32
8	115,941	25	57,057	52	R	5	48	91	23	0	4	0	18	8	45
9	128,550	36	63,141	30	U	5	62	89	33	3	40	2	65	6	66
10	110,709	17	44,137	27	U	7	45	80	13	7	28	3	44	10	41
11	109,559	15	32,017	26	U	11	32	61	8	17	24	4	38	17	33
12	115,585	20	47,805	30	U	6	50	89	18	2	27	1	46	8	33
13	139,862	39	77,866	41	S	4	63	94	39	0	39	1	65	4	56
14	110,992	20	50,220	45	U	6	60	88	19	1	28	3	41	8	34
15	114,855	22	54,537	43	M	5	45	92	21	0	15	1	36	7	39
16	111,208	17	42,493	39	U	5	39	75	13	0	20	1	40	23	28
17	114,642	22	60,539	41	U	5	51	87	20	1	33	2	53	10	32
18	94,586	3	60,396	46	U	5	70	88	1	1	19	4	25	5	16
19	108,482	13	62,581	35	S	4	50	88	11	1	29	2	41	9	28
20	99,491	9	47,652	29	S	5	43	89	7	1	16	2	29	8	29
21	91,270	-3	47,203	25	S	5	47	84	-6	1	16	2	19	12	22
22	106,610	15	68,371	36	S	3	58	89	14	1	30	2	49	7	23
23	116,087	20	54,985	37	S	5	42	81	17	1	29	4	50	14	31
24	103,176	16	44,851	32	S	6	31	74	12	1	23	2	34	22	29
25	113,708	20	41,189	37	S	8	26	65	14	7	28	2	35	25	35
26	109,699	16	65,530	34	S	5	52	89	14	1	22	2	43	7	31
27	112,991	19	93,564	39	S	3	69	91	18	2	31	3	48	3	23
28	108,457	17	55,805	29	S	3	54	82	14	7	26	4	43	6	38
29	107,446	15	41,493	25	S	5	42	71	11	14	24	5	39	9	34
30	172,314	86	76,728	36	S	3	57	94	85	1	93	1	120	3	104
31	97,550	4	34,834	34	U	9	30	45	-7	2	0	3	15	49	17
32	98,727	4	58,232	40	U	5	56	80	0	2	4	3	24	14	27
33	113,350	19	43,838	38	U	9	40	37	10	47	23	2	42	13	36
34	92,066	-1	33,082	36	U	9	32	43	-12	5	-4	2	9	49	11
35	104,361	8	58,055	33	U	4	59	83	6	7	6	3	28	7	42

Note: U=urban, S=suburban, R=rural, M=mixed, HH=households.

COLORADO
State House Districts

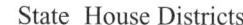

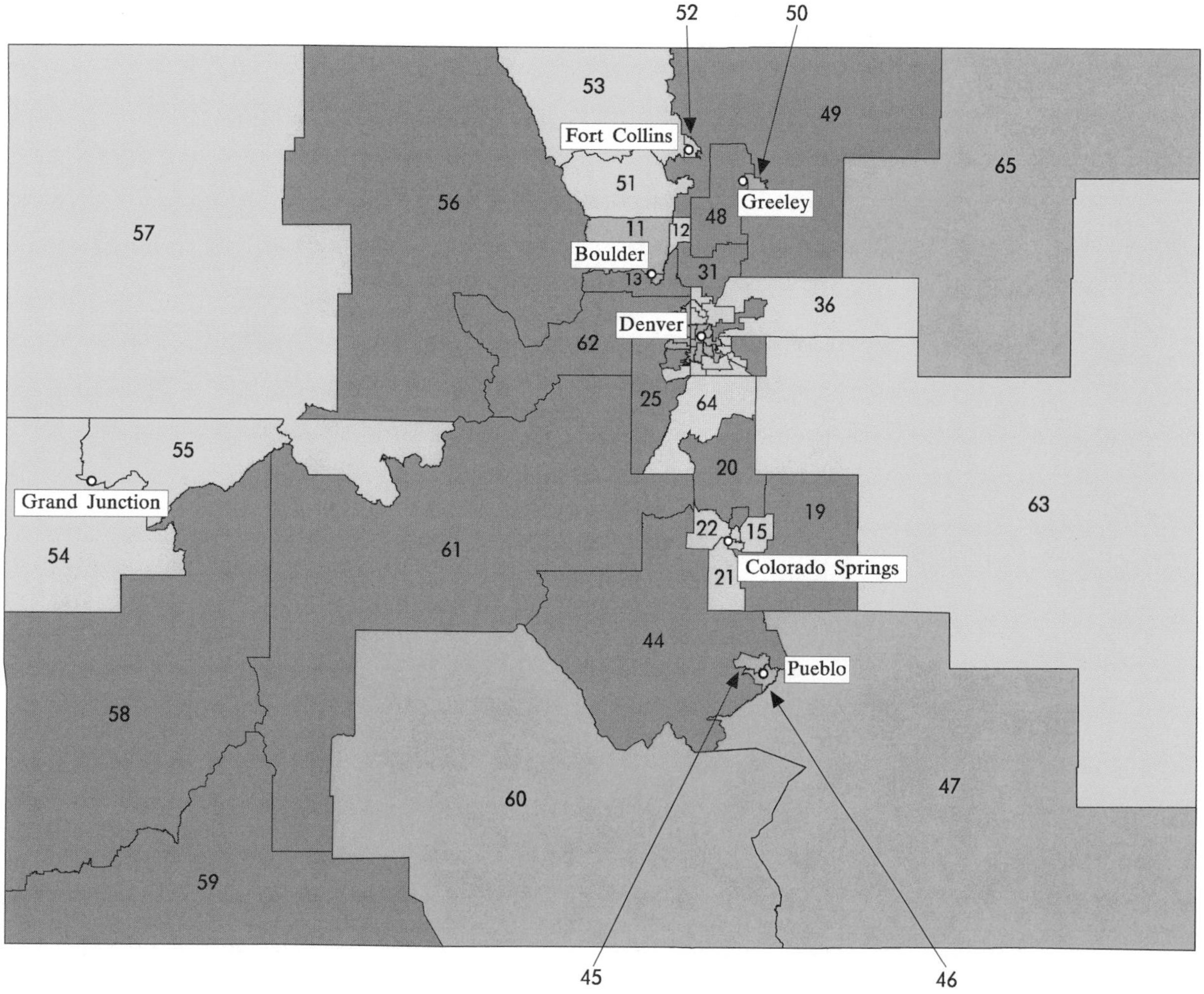

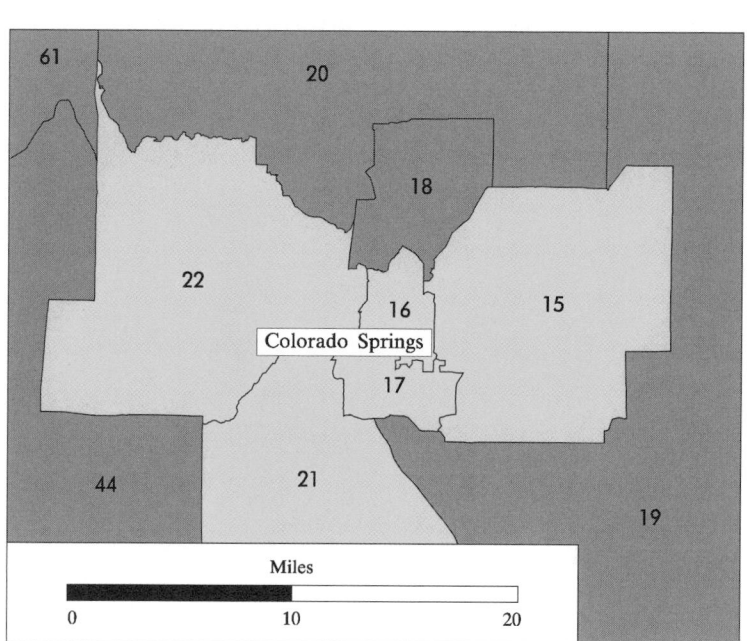

COLORADO SPRINGS

Miles
0 50 100

Population Growth -5% to 10% 11% to 23% 25% to 47% 100%

DENVER

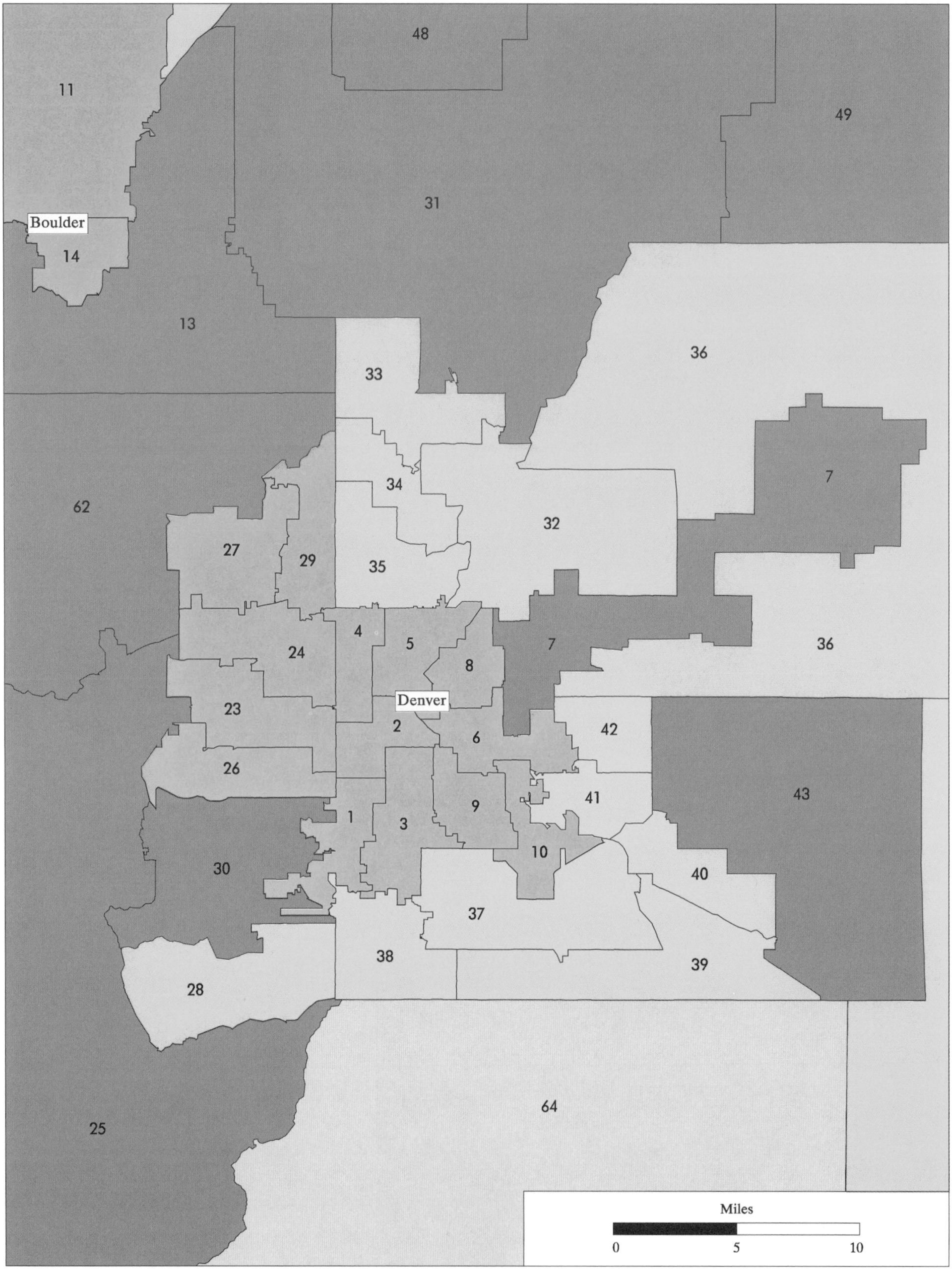

11

48

49

Boulder

14

31

13

36

33

62

34

32

7

35

27

29

4   5

8   7

24   Denver

23   2   6   42   36

26   1   3   9   41   43

30   10   40

37

38   39

28   64

25

Population Growth   ▢ -5% to 10%   ▢ 11% to 23%   ▢ 25% to 47%   ▢ 100%

Colorado State House Districts: Demographic Data

House District	Population		Average HH Income		District Type	Unempl. Rate	College Educ.	White (non-Hispanic)		African American		Asian American		Hispanic American	
	1997	+/-	($)	+/-		(%)	(%)	(%)	+/-	(%)	+/-	(%)	+/-	(%)	+/-
Colorado	3,885,429	18	51,964	38	M	6	47	79	16	4	22	2	38	14	26
1	51,794	4	47,732	32	U	5	41	70	-1	1	-13	3	14	25	24
2	53,776	10	32,142	36	U	10	27	40	0	3	6	3	27	52	18
3	55,031	7	38,679	33	S	6	36	74	4	1	2	2	19	21	16
4	50,152	0	33,394	27	U	7	29	44	-14	1	-11	2	9	51	18
5	49,138	-3	31,016	40	U	11	30	36	-14	7	-3	2	10	53	7
6	53,642	7	64,812	37	U	4	61	83	4	7	8	3	22	7	38
7	65,760	33	50,236	32	U	8	40	39	23	47	38	3	63	11	52
8	51,276	3	37,882	41	U	10	38	35	-8	44	7	1	4	19	19
9	53,894	7	55,109	37	U	4	61	88	4	2	19	3	33	6	43
10	53,004	7	59,611	37	U	4	61	83	4	7	3	3	29	7	36
11	55,220	6	63,842	44	U	4	67	90	5	1	18	2	24	6	24
12	56,369	13	53,320	41	U	5	44	86	11	0	6	2	42	12	27
13	74,950	36	73,722	39	S	4	64	92	35	1	45	2	61	4	44
14	47,415	3	57,899	46	U	5	73	87	1	2	18	6	25	5	10
15	60,344	16	46,915	28	U	7	47	80	12	7	28	3	42	9	40
16	58,076	11	40,057	26	U	7	43	79	7	7	25	2	38	11	40
17	58,425	14	29,707	25	U	11	28	57	6	18	23	5	34	19	31
18	66,468	33	55,045	29	U	5	58	86	29	4	44	3	65	8	72
19	64,218	27	39,334	24	S	8	32	75	23	9	36	4	49	12	45
20	74,100	47	72,058	31	M	4	62	92	46	2	35	2	67	4	68
21	60,561	18	52,962	32	U	7	52	78	15	9	24	3	46	9	30
22	58,432	18	42,940	26	U	7	51	87	16	2	29	2	51	9	34
23	48,512	-5	48,723	23	S	5	50	85	-8	1	11	2	16	11	20
24	55,024	6	42,177	27	S	6	39	85	2	1	14	2	31	12	34
25	68,541	37	77,219	43	S	4	60	94	36	1	35	1	39	3	46
26	48,585	-5	56,962	31	S	4	52	87	-7	1	20	2	20	9	11
27	56,598	10	64,041	35	S	5	50	91	8	0	14	2	34	7	26
28	59,033	18	78,805	36	S	4	60	92	17	1	33	2	50	5	21
29	52,758	4	49,244	31	S	5	41	85	1	1	17	3	28	11	22
30	67,971	31	69,253	36	S	3	58	89	30	1	39	2	67	8	39
31	68,540	36	57,249	42	S	5	41	79	33	1	55	2	61	18	47
32	56,980	12	37,302	26	S	8	20	66	6	2	19	1	25	30	28
33	59,282	17	54,238	36	S	4	41	82	15	1	28	2	38	13	27
34	57,570	13	48,866	37	S	6	36	75	10	1	21	3	42	20	22
35	57,350	16	40,474	29	S	6	27	68	9	1	19	6	45	25	33
36	60,795	22	41,616	36	S	8	29	66	17	12	29	3	36	18	41
37	61,339	22	98,804	33	S	4	63	92	21	2	35	3	50	4	33
38	55,845	13	66,228	38	S	4	59	91	11	1	20	2	43	5	33
39	61,897	20	104,277	43	S	3	71	92	19	2	32	3	49	3	16
40	60,923	18	55,925	26	S	3	53	84	16	6	28	3	44	6	37
41	56,104	12	51,095	25	S	4	56	78	8	10	20	5	37	7	37
42	57,746	13	38,002	22	S	6	40	70	8	16	23	5	39	9	35
43	64,172	27	53,116	34	S	4	47	78	24	10	33	4	49	7	38
44	72,739	33	39,322	38	R	8	33	84	33	2	30	0	26	13	31
45	55,186	9	37,178	36	U	9	34	64	2	2	27	1	21	33	24
46	51,540	3	30,416	28	U	10	23	46	-6	2	15	0	-2	51	12
47	52,230	5	32,616	33	R	7	29	64	1	1	-1	0	-1	34	12
48	63,092	25	53,533	41	M	4	43	83	24	0	36	1	50	15	31
49	68,336	27	58,685	44	S	5	43	89	26	0	12	1	42	9	29
50	52,688	9	31,767	32	U	7	32	66	1	1	17	1	30	32	28

Note: U=urban, S=suburban, R=rural, M=mixed, HH=households.

Colorado State House Districts: Demographic Data (cont.)

House District	Population		Average HH Income		District Type	Unempl. Rate	College Educ.	White (non-Hispanic)		African American		Asian American		Hispanic American	
	1997	+/-	($)	+/-		(%)	(%)	(%)	+/-	(%)	+/-	(%)	+/-	(%)	+/-
Colorado	3,885,429	18	51,964	38	M	6	47	79	16	4	22	2	38	14	26
51	61,262	22	52,156	42	U	5	44	92	21	0	14	1	35	6	44
52	60,016	18	53,869	48	U	5	60	88	17	1	26	2	43	9	32
53	58,248	17	41,103	37	U	6	57	88	15	1	27	3	38	7	31
54	59,861	20	41,618	42	R	7	34	88	19	0	18	1	28	11	29
55	59,660	17	40,744	37	R	7	36	89	16	1	20	1	34	9	36
56	66,294	32	64,114	54	R	4	53	90	30	0	16	0	23	10	57
57	58,439	15	54,986	48	R	5	45	94	14	0	-10	0	12	5	22
58	67,989	26	40,315	42	R	6	36	90	26	0	-18	0	1	8	35
59	61,028	26	46,050	51	R	7	43	79	24	0	8	0	7	14	45
60	55,657	9	29,677	26	R	8	30	51	4	0	-12	0	0	48	16
61	62,617	30	48,142	39	R	6	48	91	30	1	-5	0	0	7	29
62	72,395	35	63,250	41	S	4	54	92	34	0	35	2	63	5	45
63	63,293	23	40,277	35	R	4	34	91	23	0	32	0	15	8	15
64	100,080	100	86,368	36	S	3	62	94	99	1	123	1	143	3	118
65	54,984	7	38,255	39	R	5	31	86	6	0	-9	0	-7	13	20

Note: U=urban, S=suburban, R=rural, M=mixed, HH=households.

CONNECTICUT

When Connecticut was founded in 1682, its western boundary stretched all the way to the Pacific Ocean. Now it is the third-smallest state by land area, although one of the most densely populated. Connecticut's southwestern border on its nubby Panhandle is only twelve miles from New York City, which accounts for its popularity as a place to live for the many wealthy professionals who crowd the morning and evening commuter trains.

Like most of New England, Connecticut has fared badly during the 1990s. Long known for its manufacturing, the state has suffered as manufacturing jobs have disappeared. The end of the cold war forced cutbacks in the state's ship-building and helicopter-making industries, while the prominent insurance firms in Hartford also struggled. Areas like downtown Bridgeport were hit especially hard; the unemployment rate there in 1997 was 19 percent. In all, Connecticut had the nation's eighth-slowest rate of income growth during the 1990s, though perhaps buoyed by the earnings of those Wall Street bond traders who live in Greenwich and Stamford, it was the fastest in New England.

The state's population, once swelled by immigrants, has grown not at all during the decade; in fact, Connecticut has lost several thousand people. Four of the fastest-shrinking state house districts in the United States are here, three of them in New Haven (the other in New London). In all, fifty-nine Connecticut house districts have lost population during the 1990s, more than a third of the total. Twenty-two districts have lost more than 10 percent of their population; four have lost more than 20 percent.

The only areas of the state that are growing, in fact, are suburban areas far from the major cities. Connecticut is the second-most-suburban state in the country (behind Maryland, tied with Utah), and 80 percent of its house districts that have gained any population at all have been suburban. In contrast, forty-four of the fifty-two house districts classified as urban either lost population or recorded no gain.

Connecticut is a state of deep divisions; perhaps nowhere else in the country can the split between rich and poor be so clearly seen as here. It is the wealthiest state, with an average household income of almost $67,000. It is also home to seven of the ten wealthiest house districts in the country, all clustered on the New York border. The One Hundred Forty-ninth District is the single richest house district in the United States; the *average* household income there is $201,778. But Connecticut also has pockets of great poverty. In Hartford's Fifth District, household income is less than $25,000.

Given that income distribution is so uneven, it is not surprising that racial distribution is uneven too. Three house districts in downtown Hartford (the First, Second, and Seventh) are more than 56 percent African American, while four other districts scattered in more rural areas of the state are less than 1 percent black.

Hispanics have also joined the Connecticut melting pot. Four state house districts have Hispanic majorities (two in Hartford, two in Bridgeport). One of those Hartford districts has the second-largest percentage of Puerto Ricans of any district in the country. The presence of so many prominent colleges and universities—Yale, Wesleyan, and Trinity, among others—accounts for the high number of college graduates here. Almost half of all Connecticut residents have finished at least two years of college. In twelve districts, 70 percent or more have done so. On the other hand, in two districts, both in Bridgeport, the figure is only 11 percent, among the worst in the country.

Democrats control the state house of representatives by a large and growing margin, as Connecticut has been one of the party's best states nationally, voting for Democratic presidential candidates Michael Dukakis and Bill Clinton (twice, by large margins) and electing two Democratic U.S. senators.

In the state senate, though, control has swung every two years between the Democrats and Republicans. Democrats regained the edge in 1996, and much may be determined by which party holds the governor's chair when the next round of reapportionment is done. The demographic evidence suggests that contests between the parties will continue to be close.

CONNECTICUT
State Senate Districts

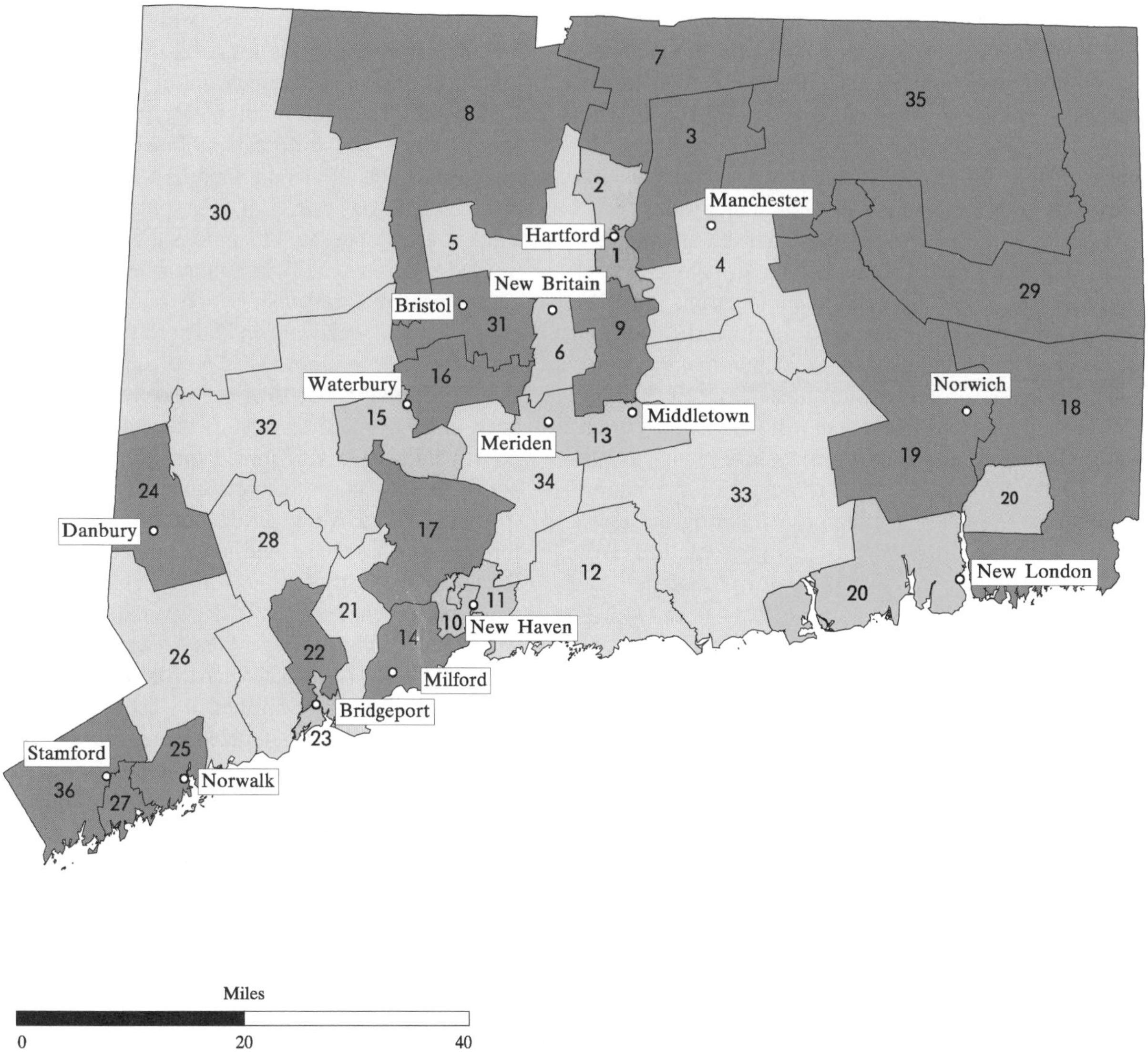

7

8

35

30

2

3

5

Manchester

Hartford

1

4

New Britain

Bristol

31

9

29

6

Waterbury

16

Norwich

18

32

15

Middletown

19

Meriden

13

34

24

33

20

28

17

Danbury

12

New London

11

21

10

14

New Haven

20

26

22

Milford

23

Bridgeport

Stamford

25

36

Norwalk

27

Miles

0   20   40

Population Growth   ■ -19%   ☐ -12% to -4%   ■ -2% to 3%   ☐ 4% to 10%

Connecticut State Senate Districts: Demographic Data

Senate District	Population		Average HH Income		District Type	Unempl. Rate	College Educ.	White (non-Hispanic)		African American		Asian American		Hispanic American	
	1997	+/-	($)	+/-		(%)	(%)	(%)	+/-	(%)	+/-	(%)	+/-	(%)	+/-
Conn.	3,275,194	0	66,982	26	S	5	49	81	-3	8	6	2	33	8	21
1	71,872	-19	37,978	19	U	9	31	37	-38	14	-5	2	-16	46	1
2	79,247	-12	39,291	15	U	10	33	22	-31	58	-9	1	-6	18	15
3	91,857	0	56,250	19	S	4	42	83	-5	8	37	3	37	6	56
4	95,038	4	64,609	19	S	3	59	90	1	4	50	2	45	3	66
5	97,410	4	82,569	20	S	4	66	89	1	4	46	3	44	4	59
6	84,367	-9	46,694	18	U	7	34	71	-18	8	29	2	20	19	25
7	92,552	1	62,798	20	S	4	45	90	-2	5	32	2	44	3	48
8	95,876	3	78,791	20	S	3	62	96	2	1	39	1	44	1	44
9	91,182	2	61,568	20	S	3	52	91	0	4	27	2	44	3	51
10	84,871	-10	38,066	19	U	9	36	35	-26	46	-4	3	11	16	17
11	80,187	-9	47,313	23	U	6	49	68	-17	18	9	2	22	11	12
12	100,610	7	72,892	24	S	4	57	96	6	1	47	1	51	2	45
13	85,335	-5	48,723	19	U	5	39	78	-10	8	17	1	28	12	16
14	91,711	1	61,348	20	U	5	46	93	-1	3	32	2	40	3	35
15	90,710	-4	50,743	22	U	6	37	80	-7	6	22	1	26	12	12
16	90,475	-2	51,640	21	U	6	36	79	-6	11	5	1	28	9	32
17	95,883	2	60,399	20	S	5	49	89	-1	6	36	2	42	3	39
18	88,731	2	56,000	30	S	5	42	91	0	4	21	2	41	3	33
19	86,614	0	54,786	31	M	6	42	90	-2	4	16	2	31	3	36
20	87,707	-6	64,532	34	S	5	51	85	-7	6	-7	2	27	6	15
21	99,093	5	64,883	27	S	5	45	89	3	5	17	1	51	4	41
22	87,829	-2	69,548	31	U	5	45	81	-7	6	12	2	38	10	32
23	83,609	-10	38,871	25	U	13	18	20	-39	36	-4	3	3	41	8
24	97,492	1	71,715	31	U	5	50	82	-3	5	17	4	35	8	34
25	91,658	2	92,313	30	U	5	54	72	-4	15	16	2	41	11	32
26	95,540	8	152,974	32	S	3	76	94	6	1	32	2	56	2	40
27	90,276	-1	75,780	28	U	5	52	60	-11	22	12	3	35	15	30
28	93,344	5	95,667	30	S	4	63	95	4	1	32	2	51	2	33
29	91,485	0	48,187	24	R	7	35	90	-2	1	7	2	43	6	23
30	92,225	4	62,382	18	R	5	49	96	3	1	13	1	42	1	26
31	95,063	0	52,119	18	U	5	36	92	-3	3	50	1	40	4	50
32	97,809	10	68,933	20	S	5	54	96	9	1	21	1	54	2	45
33	101,748	9	66,092	23	S	4	53	96	8	1	22	1	43	2	40
34	92,396	4	68,745	21	S	4	52	92	2	3	38	2	47	3	40
35	93,329	3	58,215	21	S	4	48	95	3	1	9	2	31	2	33
36	89,124	0	167,770	33	S	3	70	88	-4	3	23	4	40	5	41

Note: U=urban, S=suburban, R=rural, M=mixed, HH=households.

CONNECTICUT
State Assembly Districts

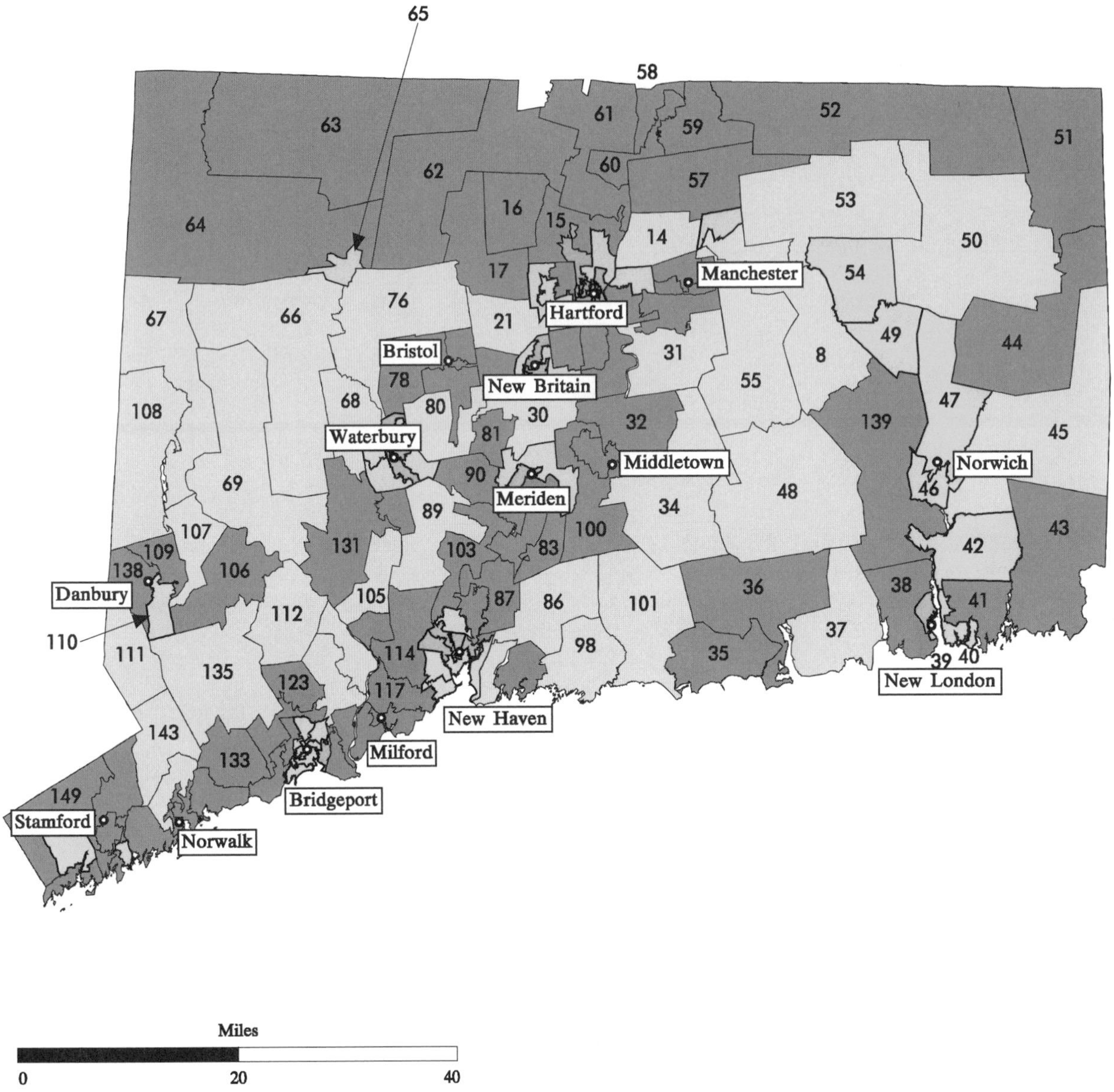

65

58

63

61

52

51

62

59

60

57

53

50

16

15

64

14

54

17

Manchester

76

67

66

21

Hartford

31

44

Bristol

78

New Britain

55

8

49

47

68

80

30

32

139

45

108

Waterbury

81

Middletown

Norwich

69

90

34

48

46

Meriden

89

43

107

131

100

42

109

103

83

138

106

36

38

Danbury

87

86

101

41

110

105

35

37

39 40

111

112

114

98

New London

135

123

117

143

New Haven

149

133

Milford

Stamford

Bridgeport

Norwalk

Miles

0   20   40

Population Growth   ▨ -26% to -12%   ☐ -11% to -3%   ▨ -2% to 5%   ☐ 6% to 19%

HARTFORD

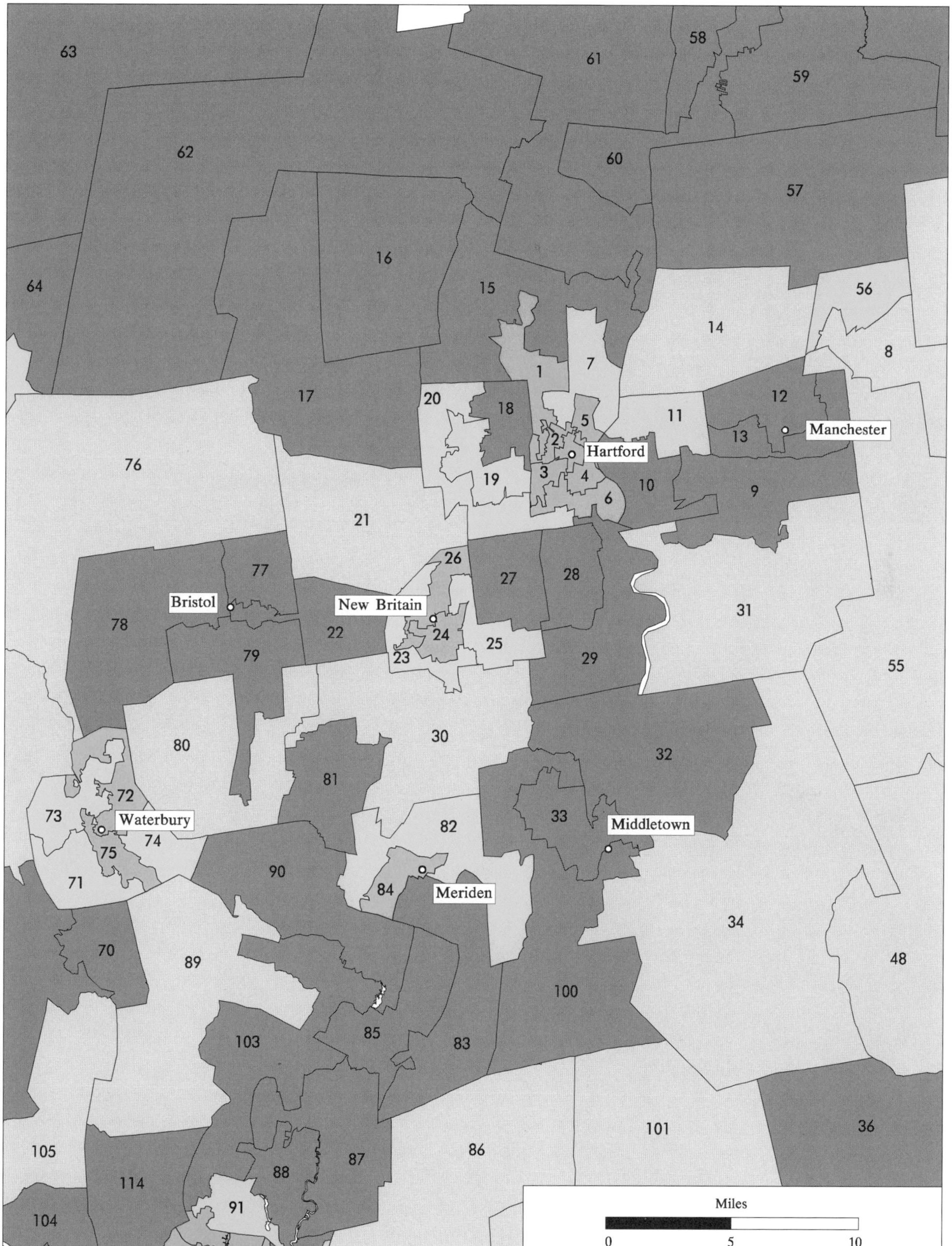

63

58

61

59

62

60

57

64

56

16

8

15

14

17

7

1

20

18

11

12

Manchester

5

13

76

2   Hartford

19   3   4

10

6

9

21

26

27   28

77

Bristol

New Britain

31

78

22

24

25

55

79

23

29

30

32

80

81

82

33   Middletown

72

73   Waterbury

90

84   Meriden

34

48

75   74

71

100

70

89

85

83

103

101

36

105

87

86

114

88

104

91

  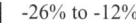 -26% to -12%   -11% to -3%   -2% to 5%   6% to 19%

Miles

0   5   10

BRIDGEPORT/NEW HAVEN

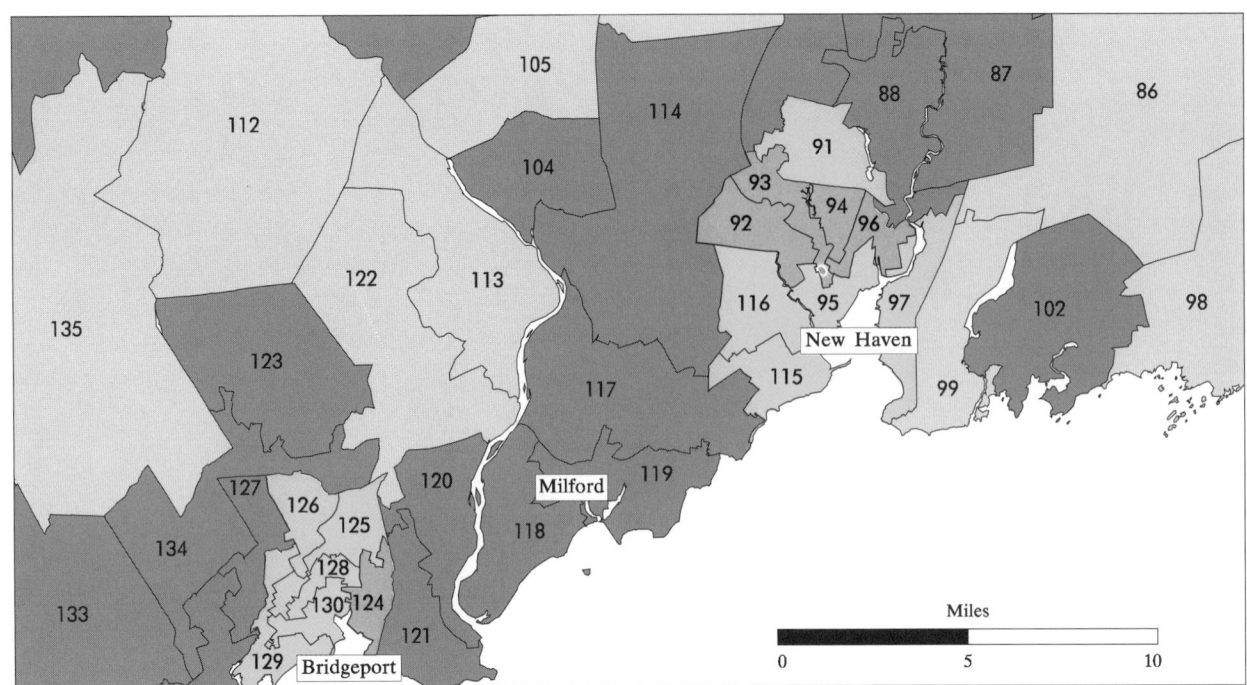

STAMFORD/WESTPORT

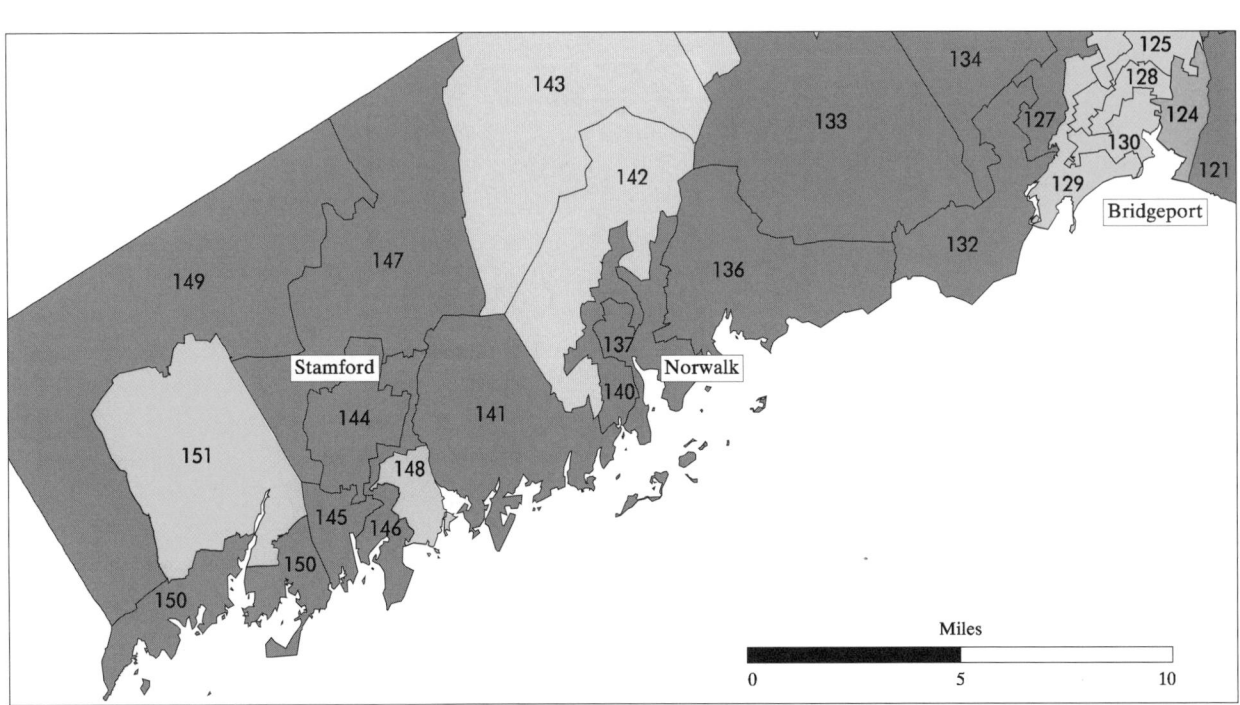

Population Growth ⬛ -26% to -12%　⬛ -11% to -3%　⬛ -2% to 5%　⬜ 6% to 19%

Connecticut State Assembly Districts: Demographic Data

Assembly District	Population		Average HH Income		District Type	Unempl. Rate	College Educ.	White (non-Hispanic)		African American		Asian American		Hispanic American	
	1997	+/-	($)	+/-		(%)	(%)	(%)	+/-	(%)	+/-	(%)	+/-	(%)	+/-
Conn.	3,275,194	0	66,982	26	S	5	49	81	-3	8	6	2	33	8	21
1	17,732	-12	49,145	18	U	8	38	27	-29	63	-6	1	-3	7	16
2	16,599	-18	31,729	13	U	11	38	16	-50	56	-12	2	-18	25	7
3	14,283	-24	27,758	10	U	13	21	11	-70	17	-11	2	-31	69	-5
4	14,658	-22	27,679	18	U	12	22	11	-66	20	-7	1	-25	66	-6
5	18,657	-14	24,930	11	U	15	18	5	-60	45	-21	1	-33	49	7
6	20,125	-23	36,680	16	U	9	26	36	-48	15	-4	1	-11	47	10
7	19,380	-10	43,683	17	U	10	26	19	-31	68	-7	1	11	12	33
8	23,560	7	64,092	18	S	4	53	97	7	1	11	1	21	1	39
9	21,668	0	76,505	20	S	3	58	90	-4	3	48	2	42	4	64
10	22,221	0	44,308	15	S	4	31	76	-10	12	45	3	39	9	58
11	19,769	-6	45,027	16	S	6	32	70	-17	14	28	4	22	11	53
12	21,155	3	50,578	17	S	4	47	89	-2	5	60	2	47	4	66
13	22,266	0	48,746	18	S	4	47	86	-6	7	46	2	35	5	71
14	24,093	9	77,587	21	S	2	57	91	6	3	53	3	52	3	70
15	22,241	1	67,706	19	S	4	55	62	-10	31	22	2	22	4	52
16	22,819	4	95,374	21	S	3	75	95	2	1	51	2	48	2	50
17	23,073	4	95,257	22	S	3	69	96	3	1	47	2	45	1	50
18	21,593	0	83,277	19	S	5	70	90	-3	2	43	3	42	4	65
19	21,567	-3	78,406	18	S	3	68	89	-7	3	39	4	39	5	62
20	21,404	-7	71,017	19	S	4	54	83	-13	4	29	4	36	9	46
21	23,436	14	84,102	19	S	3	65	93	11	2	67	3	62	2	76
22	22,381	-1	49,288	16	S	5	36	93	-3	3	46	1	40	3	42
23	19,487	-8	47,158	13	U	6	33	61	-23	13	32	4	16	22	30
24	16,746	-17	33,190	14	U	10	25	54	-34	9	20	1	-2	35	16
25	20,921	-5	56,149	22	U	5	39	79	-12	7	32	2	35	11	35
26	18,302	-13	41,643	15	U	8	33	74	-22	7	31	2	15	17	29
27	21,400	1	57,241	16	S	3	45	93	-1	2	49	2	45	3	63
28	21,792	1	67,846	20	S	4	52	94	-2	1	47	1	41	3	78
29	22,352	3	60,889	20	S	2	54	91	0	3	47	2	48	4	60
30	24,331	7	69,972	20	S	4	48	95	5	1	52	1	52	2	70
31	24,203	10	82,204	19	S	3	70	94	8	1	54	3	56	2	73
32	22,677	2	61,083	20	S	3	53	94	1	3	13	1	35	2	32
33	21,503	-1	47,539	23	U	6	40	77	-6	14	10	3	36	5	23
34	24,707	6	66,031	23	S	4	51	93	5	4	18	1	40	2	28
35	21,329	0	65,392	24	R	5	50	95	-1	1	14	1	37	3	35
36	22,174	5	69,682	23	R	3	56	96	5	1	15	1	43	1	35
37	23,419	7	75,997	31	S	4	60	93	6	2	0	2	57	3	56
38	20,815	-1	65,460	32	S	4	48	92	-3	3	20	2	45	3	41
39	15,375	-26	35,392	24	U	10	28	54	-37	21	-14	3	-9	21	6
40	21,156	-4	43,102	24	M	8	36	79	-8	11	13	3	31	6	24
41	21,883	0	58,703	31	S	4	50	88	-3	5	26	3	35	4	30
42	18,483	-4	68,361	29	S	5	52	90	-6	4	9	2	36	3	24
43	21,925	1	66,247	33	R	5	50	96	0	1	28	1	50	2	38
44	23,331	3	48,519	26	R	7	27	97	2	0	14	1	34	1	24
45	23,917	8	53,038	31	S	6	31	96	7	1	17	1	74	2	44
46	19,597	-6	46,690	30	U	7	34	83	-10	8	13	2	23	5	37
47	21,366	-4	50,911	31	U	7	34	92	-5	3	21	1	27	3	37
48	24,991	19	63,503	28	S	5	51	96	18	1	40	1	62	1	46
49	20,492	-7	42,676	23	R	7	33	76	-13	3	4	1	23	20	22
50	23,442	6	54,560	28	R	7	39	95	5	1	17	1	41	2	42

Note: U=urban, S=suburban, R=rural, M=mixed, HH=households.

Connecticut State Assembly Districts: Demographic Data (cont.)

Assembly District	Population 1997	+/-	Average HH Income ($)	+/-	District Type	Unempl. Rate (%)	College Educ. (%)	White (non-Hispanic) (%)	+/-	African American (%)	+/-	Asian American (%)	+/-	Hispanic American (%)	+/-
Conn.	3,275,194	0	66,982	26	S	5	49	81	-3	8	6	2	33	8	21
51	22,269	0	46,692	24	R	7	30	97	0	1	5	1	34	1	25
52	21,687	3	56,996	22	R	5	44	97	3	0	7	1	34	1	24
53	24,165	12	62,216	17	S	3	56	96	11	1	23	1	45	1	43
54	20,232	-4	64,113	28	R	4	70	84	-8	3	5	9	41	3	18
55	23,767	8	69,610	17	S	3	62	97	7	1	27	1	32	1	41
56	20,273	-6	48,835	18	S	4	44	91	-8	3	3	3	23	3	25
57	21,323	0	56,818	19	S	4	45	94	-2	3	34	1	42	2	36
58	21,131	-1	49,230	17	R	4	37	94	-4	2	48	1	39	3	47
59	19,687	0	65,547	19	R	4	39	85	-3	8	12	1	38	6	38
60	22,465	-1	57,275	20	S	4	43	94	-3	2	48	2	43	2	59
61	23,561	5	78,239	21	S	3	57	87	0	7	47	3	50	3	62
62	23,649	5	72,082	18	S	3	62	97	4	1	43	1	41	1	54
63	21,493	2	52,484	17	R	5	41	98	1	1	5	0	31	1	31
64	24,543	5	68,470	18	R	4	54	96	5	1	16	1	48	1	20
65	20,111	-5	39,155	11	R	6	29	95	-6	2	6	2	29	2	16
66	22,641	6	69,479	16	S	5	59	97	6	1	6	1	46	1	34
67	23,222	9	65,537	16	S	5	54	93	8	2	17	2	50	3	41
68	24,269	6	59,156	15	S	5	43	97	6	1	16	1	51	1	34
69	24,924	16	72,588	18	S	4	56	97	15	1	42	1	63	1	61
70	20,905	2	53,433	20	S	4	38	92	0	2	39	1	37	5	34
71	21,118	-6	49,222	22	U	5	34	86	-10	5	28	1	22	8	20
72	18,328	-13	32,539	15	U	12	20	39	-32	37	-3	1	-11	22	25
73	20,367	-5	50,660	19	U	6	43	81	-10	8	27	1	23	9	38
74	21,577	-3	42,868	17	U	6	33	81	-9	9	26	1	35	8	51
75	18,478	-16	33,178	17	U	10	19	42	-34	15	8	1	-4	42	5
76	23,092	11	70,903	20	S	5	51	98	11	0	37	0	54	1	30
77	22,586	-1	52,744	18	U	4	36	90	-4	3	56	1	42	5	56
78	22,468	0	51,076	16	S	4	35	96	-1	1	39	1	35	2	31
79	24,566	1	49,492	17	U	7	33	91	-2	3	52	1	‹36	4	53
80	24,223	7	65,064	21	S	5	39	96	6	2	53	1	47	2	57
81	20,612	3	61,410	19	S	4	44	96	1	1	50	1	39	2	55
82	21,835	-4	51,950	17	U	4	43	84	-9	4	30	1	21	11	33
83	22,093	1	57,591	20	U	3	44	91	-1	3	35	1	43	6	26
84	19,540	-12	36,748	17	U	8	24	60	-22	8	22	1	1	31	9
85	21,696	1	55,849	20	S	4	44	93	-1	1	41	1	42	5	23
86	23,065	9	67,016	21	S	4	50	96	8	2	52	1	45	2	55
87	23,736	4	63,876	17	S	3	46	92	2	4	41	2	47	2	45
88	21,412	0	64,128	24	S	5	61	86	-4	7	29	3	40	3	43
89	22,718	9	78,271	22	S	4	58	94	7	2	51	2	50	2	52
90	22,624	4	70,244	18	S	4	52	86	-1	6	33	2	41	6	57
91	20,366	-4	52,141	21	S	5	48	76	-10	18	19	2	29	4	46
92	18,422	-16	48,451	19	U	7	54	51	-28	37	-1	2	2	9	18
93	18,703	-14	35,742	17	U	11	42	30	-34	56	-4	2	1	11	23
94	17,487	-13	35,941	20	U	8	42	24	-25	61	-12	8	14	6	13
95	18,893	-10	30,589	20	U	15	24	12	-48	47	-7	0	-33	40	10
96	18,418	-13	39,206	21	U	8	60	50	-26	20	8	6	25	23	-2
97	18,949	-11	40,255	19	U	7	34	74	-19	13	20	1	14	11	28
98	22,767	7	85,899	25	S	4	66	96	6	1	40	1	49	2	28
99	23,211	7	51,863	23	S	5	32	96	5	1	41	1	54	3	54
100	21,465	2	63,194	23	U	3	58	90	1	6	11	2	38	2	19

Note: U=urban, S=suburban, R=rural, M=mixed, HH=households.

Connecticut State Assembly Districts: Demographic Data (cont.)

Assembly District	Population		Average HH Income		District Type	Unempl. Rate	College Educ.	White (non-Hispanic)		African American		Asian American		Hispanic American	
	1997	+/-	($)	+/-		(%)	(%)	(%)	+/-	(%)	+/-	(%)	+/-	(%)	+/-
Conn.	3,275,194	0	66,982	26	S	5	49	81	-3	8	6	2	33	8	21
101	23,921	12	93,653	25	S	5	67	97	11	1	40	1	65	2	46
102	23,713	5	60,095	20	S	4	57	94	3	2	44	2	48	2	51
103	22,975	5	70,042	21	S	4	62	92	3	4	40	2	52	2	44
104	24,038	-2	44,566	18	S	8	32	84	-7	9	32	1	26	5	35
105	21,091	9	56,236	21	S	5	42	96	8	1	54	1	54	2	47
106	23,489	4	81,181	29	S	5	59	94	2	1	24	2	44	2	27
107	24,271	8	85,745	31	S	4	63	93	6	1	30	3	55	3	40
108	23,973	14	88,443	29	S	4	60	96	13	0	30	1	60	2	32
109	22,573	2	71,269	30	U	5	48	80	-4	7	22	4	37	8	35
110	20,433	-6	49,145	30	U	6	33	66	-16	9	11	6	24	18	33
111	22,823	9	124,773	32	S	3	73	95	8	1	30	2	55	2	47
112	25,039	13	86,921	29	S	4	60	94	11	2	42	2	60	3	55
113	23,364	6	65,743	30	S	4	44	93	4	1	34	2	58	4	33
114	21,929	2	94,149	21	S	4	63	94	0	1	40	3	45	2	29
115	21,916	-3	45,121	18	S	6	35	84	-7	10	21	2	27	4	36
116	21,031	-5	45,052	20	S	5	34	61	-18	27	19	4	20	8	40
117	22,441	0	67,523	20	S	4	48	94	-2	2	38	2	37	2	30
118	21,766	3	57,979	20	U	5	41	92	1	2	44	1	44	4	45
119	21,736	4	62,649	21	U	6	49	94	3	2	43	1	47	3	37
120	23,592	4	64,054	26	S	4	45	93	2	2	29	1	45	4	48
121	20,382	0	49,344	26	S	6	34	72	-6	18	13	1	35	7	38
122	24,984	9	86,387	26	S	4	57	95	8	1	38	1	57	2	47
123	22,175	5	102,587	33	S	4	58	94	3	1	37	2	52	2	41
124	17,564	-17	36,811	25	U	15	13	18	-44	50	-13	1	-3	30	5
125	20,804	-10	46,637	21	U	8	27	50	-27	20	8	3	17	27	23
126	19,549	-6	50,887	25	U	8	27	37	-28	39	7	2	21	21	31
127	22,213	-2	61,687	29	U	5	43	88	-5	3	17	2	44	7	33
128	18,646	-9	33,675	22	U	14	11	11	-54	25	-1	5	1	58	6
129	20,423	-10	47,346	27	U	8	34	61	-18	15	-4	3	20	21	15
130	18,872	-8	30,943	26	U	19	11	8	-56	32	-4	3	-4	56	4
131	25,469	5	68,574	22	S	5	52	95	4	1	43	1	45	2	36
132	22,901	3	84,016	32	S	5	59	95	1	1	34	2	49	2	26
133	23,395	4	158,947	31	S	4	76	95	3	1	30	2	51	2	43
134	23,135	2	90,900	25	S	4	61	94	1	1	24	2	50	2	30
135	24,461	11	146,135	34	S	4	73	95	10	1	39	2	64	2	51
136	22,985	2	128,681	35	S	4	66	89	-1	3	22	3	47	4	34
137	23,285	0	61,766	26	U	4	45	65	-11	18	22	3	33	14	32
138	21,314	-2	79,737	27	U	4	56	83	-7	6	20	5	35	6	37
139	23,078	4	61,182	35	S	6	41	93	2	2	28	1	45	3	44
140	19,852	0	57,418	30	U	7	33	39	-18	36	11	1	26	23	25
141	23,850	5	177,502	32	S	3	77	94	4	1	23	3	53	2	44
142	24,412	7	98,554	28	U	3	62	87	3	6	28	3	53	5	52
143	24,018	8	165,823	31	S	4	78	94	6	2	33	3	54	2	36
144	22,718	0	83,449	27	U	4	59	78	-5	10	18	4	40	8	35
145	20,036	-2	50,417	25	U	9	25	19	-37	52	7	1	14	27	26
146	22,180	0	77,427	29	U	5	57	68	-9	14	20	4	39	14	33
147	22,342	3	184,036	36	U	3	73	92	1	2	26	3	47	2	32
148	19,921	-3	63,255	24	U	6	49	62	-15	19	18	4	28	15	33
149	23,118	0	201,778	32	S	4	72	90	-3	2	23	3	41	4	37
150	22,719	-1	128,983	34	S	4	65	82	-6	4	24	5	39	9	47

Note: U=urban, S=suburban, R=rural, M=mixed, HH=households.

Connecticut State Assembly Districts: Demographic Data (cont.)

Assembly District	Population		Average HH Income		District Type	Unempl. Rate	College Educ.	White (non-Hispanic)		African American		Asian American		Hispanic American	
	1997	+/-	($)	+/-		(%)	(%)	(%)	+/-	(%)	+/-	(%)	+/-	(%)	+/-
Conn.	3,275,194	0	66,982	26	S	5	49	81	-3	8	6	2	33	8	21
151	21,289	-4	167,330	33	S	3	72	87	-8	2	18	6	36	5	37

Note: U=urban, S=suburban, R=rural, M=mixed, HH=households.

DELAWARE

The only part of Delaware most Americans ever see is the busy part of Interstate 95 that cuts through downtown Wilmington (and even that may be bypassed) on the route between New York and Washington. Indeed, if one goes by population, Wilmington more or less *is* Delaware; nearly two-thirds of its citizens live in the city or its suburbs. Yet the city has no network television stations and no significant airport; it relies on Philadelphia, about twenty miles away, for both.

Look at Delaware on a map and you will see two geographic curiosities. For one, it has only three counties, the fewest of any state. Second, Delaware has the only state boundary, perhaps the only boundary in the world, to be defined by the arc of a circle. Stick a compass point on Fenwick Island in Delaware Bay, set the radius at twenty-five miles, and you can draw the state's border with Pennsylvania. The Mason-Dixon line, which separates Pennsylvania from Maryland (and in national mythology, North from South), originates at the point where Delaware's western boundary intersects with that arc.

South of Wilmington, along Route 13, which leads to Maryland's Eastern Shore, one finds low, rural country filled with crossroads towns, small farms, and poultry processing plants. Southern Delaware also has Rehoboth, Dewey, and Bethany Beaches, increasingly popular weekend destinations for people from Baltimore and Washington.

Delaware was slave-holding territory until the Civil War. Even today, the state is 19 percent African American, the ninth-highest percentage in the country, almost the same as Virginia and ranked squarely in the middle of the southern states. It also has one of the ten fastest rates of black population growth.

Racially, Wilmington is rather like an onion, with a core of heavily black districts downtown (the First, Second, Third, and Fifth) surrounded by a layer of almost entirely white suburban districts (the Tenth, Eleventh, Thirteenth, and Twentieth). The Fifth House District, which includes the heart of Wilmington, is 24 percent Hispanic, the only large concentration of Hispanics in the state.

This racial split accounts for most of the population growth and income divisions in the state. That outer crescent, the predominantly white suburbs, is the wealthiest part of Delaware. In the Twelfth District, home to many DuPonts, average household income is more than $111,000.

Indeed, though, the outer crescent is also the part of the state that has been losing population during the decade. The Sixteenth District has lost 12 percent of its population in seven years, and the Sixth, Eighth, Eleventh, Thirteenth, and Nineteenth Districts have also had significant losses. Population has grown by 55 percent in the Twenty-seventh District, between Wilmington and Newark (pronounced "newARK"), where the state university is located. It has also grown at the beach, which is the poorest part of Delaware and one of its oldest. More than a third of the residents of the Thirty-seventh and Thirty-eighth Districts are over age fifty-five.

Politically, Delaware is mixed. It has one Democratic U.S. senator and one Republican U.S. senator; the governor is a Democrat, the lone U.S. representative a Republican (they switched jobs in 1992). Democrats control the state senate, Republicans the house.

One political curiosity is the Second Senate District, which encompasses downtown Wilmington. It is 71 percent African American, household income is 25 percent below the state average, and the unemployment rate is 10 percent. Yet in 1994, it elected a Republican state senator with 58 percent of the vote, replacing a Democrat who had run unopposed two years earlier. However, soon after the election the senator switched to the Democratic Party and successfully ran for re-election under that banner.

DELAWARE
State Senate Districts

Population Growth　　　▮ -5% to -2%　　　▯ 3% to 8%　　　▮ 12% to 24%　　　□ 42%

Delaware State Senate Districts: Demographic Data

Senate District	Population		Average HH Income		District Type	Unempl. Rate	College Educ.	White (non-Hispanic)		African American		Asian American		Hispanic American	
	1997	+/-	($)	+/-		(%)	(%)	(%)	+/-	(%)	+/-	(%)	+/-	(%)	+/-
Delaware	731,349	10	53,259	27	M	4	42	76	6	19	22	2	50	3	37
1	31,896	-2	58,190	30	U	3	51	63	-9	32	14	1	22	3	22
2	29,455	-3	39,381	29	U	10	21	25	-19	71	2	1	6	3	18
3	32,741	3	36,182	24	U	8	23	36	-14	47	14	0	2	16	26
4	28,979	-5	67,438	24	S	2	57	90	-8	6	23	2	29	2	21
5	32,219	-5	66,680	23	S	4	58	86	-9	9	24	3	28	2	27
6	38,495	16	109,196	33	S	3	71	90	13	4	45	5	67	1	30
7	29,152	-4	63,398	34	S	3	43	91	-6	5	19	2	42	2	24
8	32,408	12	69,629	34	S	2	64	90	9	3	46	4	67	2	44
9	34,098	3	52,252	26	S	2	46	84	-1	10	30	2	39	3	44
10	37,230	8	59,274	31	R	3	60	86	4	8	37	4	40	2	32
11	39,023	18	51,438	24	S	3	42	78	11	16	49	3	53	4	65
12	41,431	42	54,884	28	S	3	43	80	34	16	81	2	99	3	106
13	34,686	4	49,737	31	S	4	30	75	0	21	12	1	51	3	33
14	35,588	21	56,325	32	R	4	30	83	18	14	39	1	78	2	50
15	38,705	16	44,204	30	R	4	20	84	13	12	30	1	57	2	36
16	33,749	8	47,663	29	R	4	38	74	3	20	23	2	48	4	34
17	32,991	7	46,870	32	R	5	41	62	1	31	17	3	51	4	46
18	38,388	21	40,315	22	R	4	31	81	17	15	37	1	59	2	51
19	38,291	13	38,400	17	R	4	28	72	8	25	27	1	62	3	55
20	37,264	24	36,470	15	R	4	29	81	22	16	32	1	45	1	30
21	34,795	13	36,374	14	R	5	28	81	9	17	29	1	62	1	38

Note: U=urban, S=suburban, R=rural, M=mixed, HH=households.

DELAWARE
State House Districts

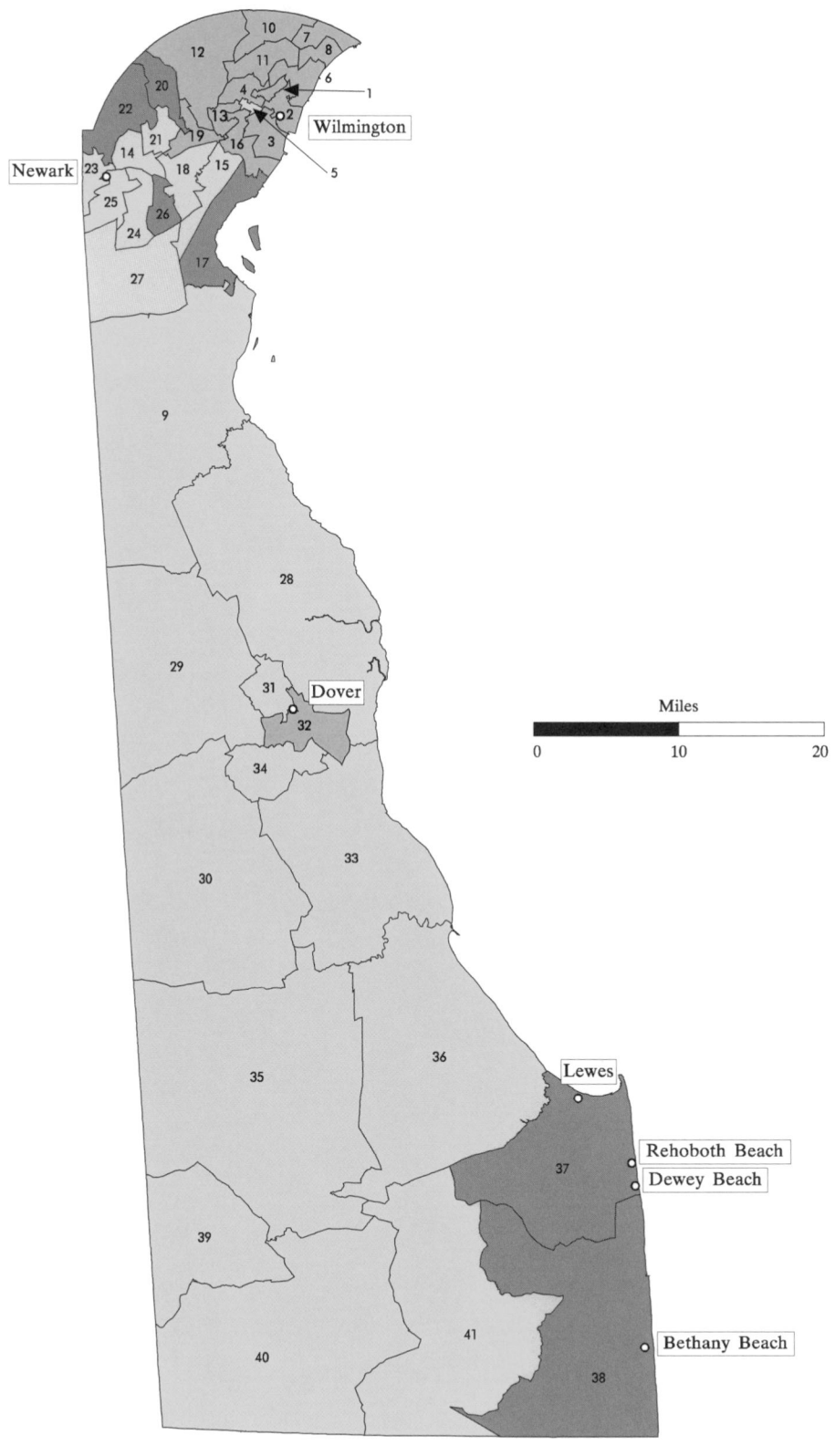

Population Growth   ▢ -12% to 1%   ▢ 5% to 19%   ▢ 22% to 33%   ▢ 55%

Delaware State House Districts: Demographic Data

House District	Population		Average HH Income		District Type	Unempl. Rate	College Educ.	White (non-Hispanic)		African American		Asian American		Hispanic American	
	1997	+/-	($)	+/-		(%)	(%)	(%)	+/-	(%)	+/-	(%)	+/-	(%)	+/-
Delaware	731,349	10	53,259	27	M	4	42	76	6	19	22	2	50	3	37
1	16,098	0	51,902	36	U	5	46	45	-10	51	10	1	21	2	18
2	16,281	-1	35,486	27	U	11	21	14	-19	83	2	1	6	3	11
3	15,335	-5	32,132	21	U	11	14	21	-22	73	-1	0	-5	6	37
4	17,034	1	73,019	30	U	3	54	62	-8	32	23	1	21	5	14
5	17,106	5	37,878	25	U	8	22	30	-17	46	14	0	4	24	27
6	16,016	-7	63,551	25	S	3	57	84	-10	13	12	2	26	1	3
7	15,732	-4	56,498	22	S	5	54	82	-9	13	25	3	27	2	35
8	14,580	-7	53,066	20	S	3	44	89	-9	8	22	2	23	2	24
9	18,031	15	54,586	30	R	4	30	86	13	12	35	0	56	1	30
10	15,116	-5	84,462	25	S	2	64	91	-7	4	20	4	31	1	3
11	14,332	-7	89,295	29	S	2	68	94	-9	2	23	3	29	2	22
12	16,382	-3	111,233	38	S	2	59	90	-5	6	15	3	38	1	8
13	15,488	-7	46,914	26	S	4	27	92	-10	4	28	1	20	3	34
14	16,226	12	49,834	26	R	3	50	77	5	13	40	4	44	6	65
15	20,742	19	49,064	28	S	4	33	78	12	17	51	1	69	3	50
16	15,672	-12	42,866	24	S	4	19	81	-16	14	8	1	4	4	10
17	20,127	22	50,976	25	S	4	35	79	14	18	62	1	87	2	82
18	18,303	18	56,387	28	S	2	48	81	12	13	52	3	50	3	69
19	16,116	-9	46,476	23	S	3	36	89	-12	7	19	2	31	2	18
20	19,914	27	86,262	33	S	2	69	90	24	3	64	5	81	2	56
21	16,420	11	62,538	26	S	2	61	89	8	4	42	3	53	3	40
22	23,414	30	91,363	39	S	2	74	88	27	4	48	6	83	2	52
23	14,660	6	63,695	35	R	3	69	87	3	7	34	4	41	2	30
24	17,037	11	52,012	25	S	2	42	85	7	11	37	1	48	2	34
25	19,344	5	52,994	28	R	4	51	85	2	9	36	4	37	2	17
26	21,926	31	52,010	24	S	4	42	75	23	19	59	2	72	4	87
27	23,166	55	64,318	30	S	3	46	86	49	10	96	2	107	2	125
28	17,917	8	45,751	31	R	6	26	68	2	26	21	1	40	3	39
29	22,704	17	46,001	29	R	4	23	86	15	10	34	1	57	2	33
30	18,746	15	40,766	32	R	4	20	84	12	14	33	1	52	1	43
31	15,033	9	53,074	35	R	5	50	61	3	32	16	3	60	4	50
32	17,056	0	44,874	28	R	5	41	63	-7	30	15	3	40	4	25
33	18,772	9	42,018	33	R	5	27	76	5	18	24	1	43	3	40
34	13,421	19	49,155	24	R	4	39	72	12	21	37	2	64	4	62
35	20,421	14	39,712	16	R	4	27	75	9	21	27	1	62	3	61
36	20,840	16	36,864	19	R	4	29	71	11	24	29	1	58	4	48
37	20,246	27	42,328	17	R	4	35	85	24	13	49	1	64	1	46
38	22,594	33	35,560	14	R	3	30	85	32	12	43	0	40	1	40
39	15,527	11	38,012	15	R	5	38	77	6	21	27	1	65	1	45
40	20,304	15	35,752	15	R	5	22	82	12	16	31	1	60	1	33
41	16,934	8	35,845	17	R	3	25	75	4	23	20	1	61	1	26

Note: U=urban, S=suburban, R=rural, M=mixed, HH=households.

FLORIDA

Sometime earlier in this decade, Hispanics supplanted African Americans as Florida's largest minority group. Forty years ago, before the Castro revolution in Cuba, Florida had very few Hispanics and proportionately many more blacks. It also had just begun to welcome retirees. Miami Beach was the ritzy vacation spot, while Orlando was a sleepy town amid the orange groves. No state has changed more in the last two generations, and few have a better claim to national importance in the next two.

Florida is now a mega-state, the fourth largest behind California, New York, and Texas. During the 1990s its population has grown at a pace almost twice the national average. The fastest-growing districts neatly reflect three of the state's most demographically significant groups. They include the heavily Hispanic districts around Homestead and Kendall, in southern Dade County; the district around Plantation, popular with retirees; and districts south of Orlando and Jacksonville, which are filling with young white families. Only seven districts in the state are shrinking—the area south of Coral Gables, downtown St. Petersburg, and downtown Jacksonville.

Florida has the smallest percentage of African Americans of any southern state, although it is growing at a faster rate. They are concentrated in a relatively small geographic area. Only 13 of the 120 Florida house districts have a black majority, including districts in Hillsborough County (Tampa), Jacksonville, and outside Orlando. Most, though, are found in a strip of districts in Dade and Broward Counties just off the ocean, running with a few interruptions from Pompano Beach to Hialeah.

The Hispanic population has been growing almost half again as quickly as the black population, largely due to immigration. The influx of immigrants has also made the Hispanic population more diverse, as second- or third-generation Cubans have moved over to make room for new arrivals from the Caribbean and South America.

Ten house districts have a Hispanic majority. All are located in south Florida, starting at Miami Beach and Hialeah (forming a Y around a black-majority One Hundred Ninth District in between), then running south and southwest to Homestead. In only two house districts are the black and Hispanic populations fairly equal, which probably proves that the reapportioners have succeeded in separating the groups in order to maximize their political strength.

Hispanics here are, as a whole, wealthier than blacks, and almost all the Hispanic-majority house districts are represented by Republicans. Every black-majority district in the state is represented by a Democrat. There is considerable friction between the two groups, which has bubbled over more than once into riots.

Florida also has a higher percentage of senior citizens than any other state. Twenty-eight percent of its population is over age fifty-five, although in only two house districts do senior citizens constitute a majority: one north of Tampa (the Forty-sixth) and one south of there (the Seventieth). The newer Florida retirees are wealthier and more mobile than the generation that arrived in the 1960s and 1970s; they are more likely, for example, to settle in Broward County, where one needs a car, than in Miami Beach, where many of the previous generation of retirees from the northeast rode the busses. Florida's senior citizens are also overwhelmingly white, a characteristic that is not often mentioned. Twenty-one Florida house districts are more than 90 percent white, most of them in the retirement areas on the Gulf Coast.

Given its percolating racial and ethnic makeup, political change in Florida has been sweeping. In 1990 Democrats controlled both houses of the legislature; by 1996 they controlled neither. As it did elsewhere, racial gerrymandering in Florida shook loose several congressional and state seats for the GOP. Democrats, in fact, have not added to their number of seats in the state house since 1982. In recent elections, though, as many as half the seats in both chambers of the legislature go uncontested.

Florida seems still to be adjusting to its prominence. It has not yet produced a national political figure of any note, nor has a Floridian ever served on a major party presidential ticket. Given its rich pot of electoral votes (likely to grow richer as the state gains congressional seats after the next census) and the key constituencies that both parties find here, someone in the current generation of Florida politicians will surely change that.

FLORIDA
State Senate Districts

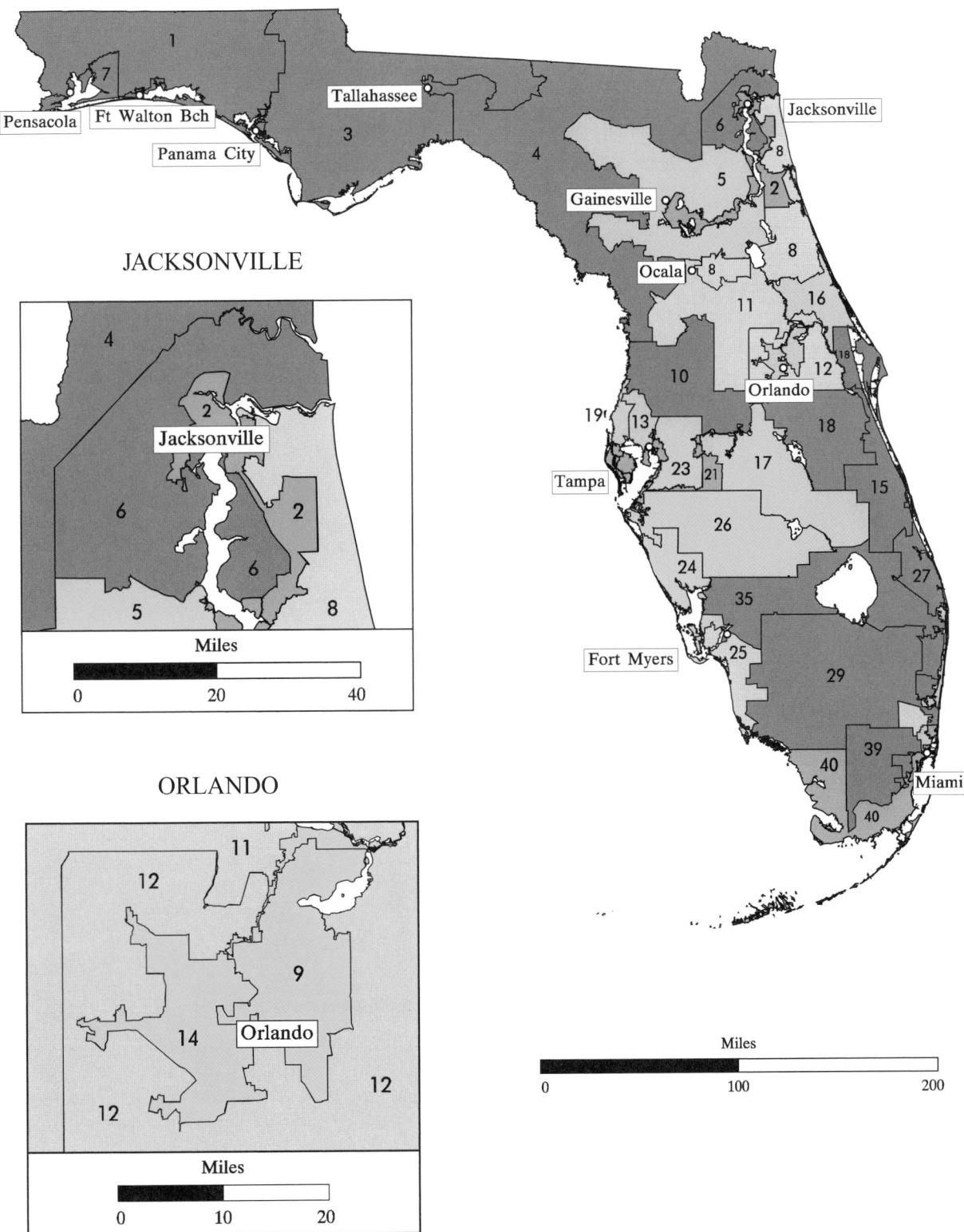

JACKSONVILLE

ORLANDO

Population Growth | -3% to 5% | 6% to 13% | 14% to 19% | 21% to 29%

MIAMI

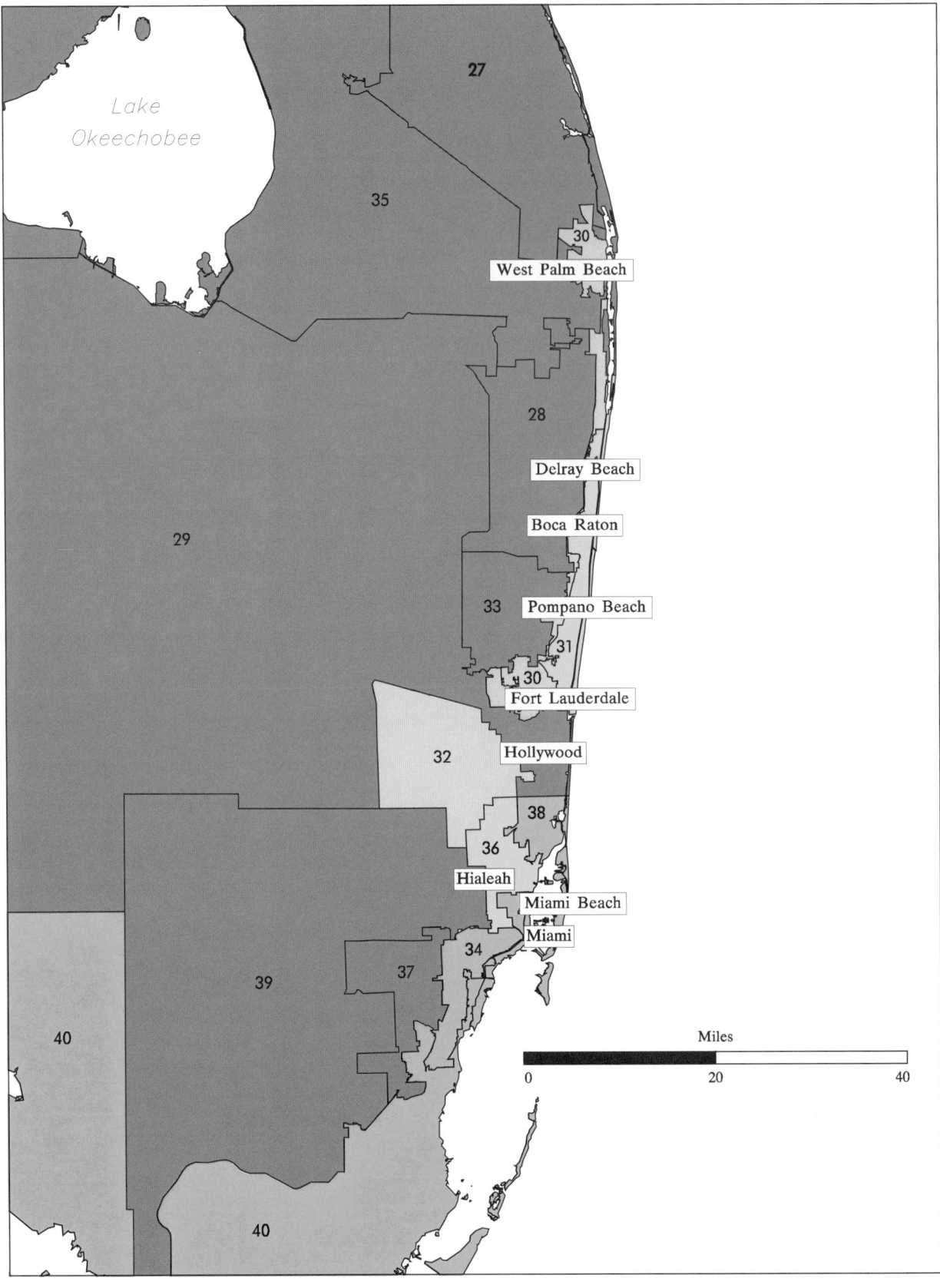

Lake Okeechobee

27

35

30

West Palm Beach

28

Delray Beach

Boca Raton

29

33   Pompano Beach

31

30

Fort Lauderdale

32   Hollywood

38

36

Hialeah

Miami Beach

Miami

34

39

37

40

40

Miles

0   20   40

Population Growth   ▢ -3% to 5%   ▢ 6% to 13%   ▢ 14% to 19%   ▢ 21% to 29%

TAMPA

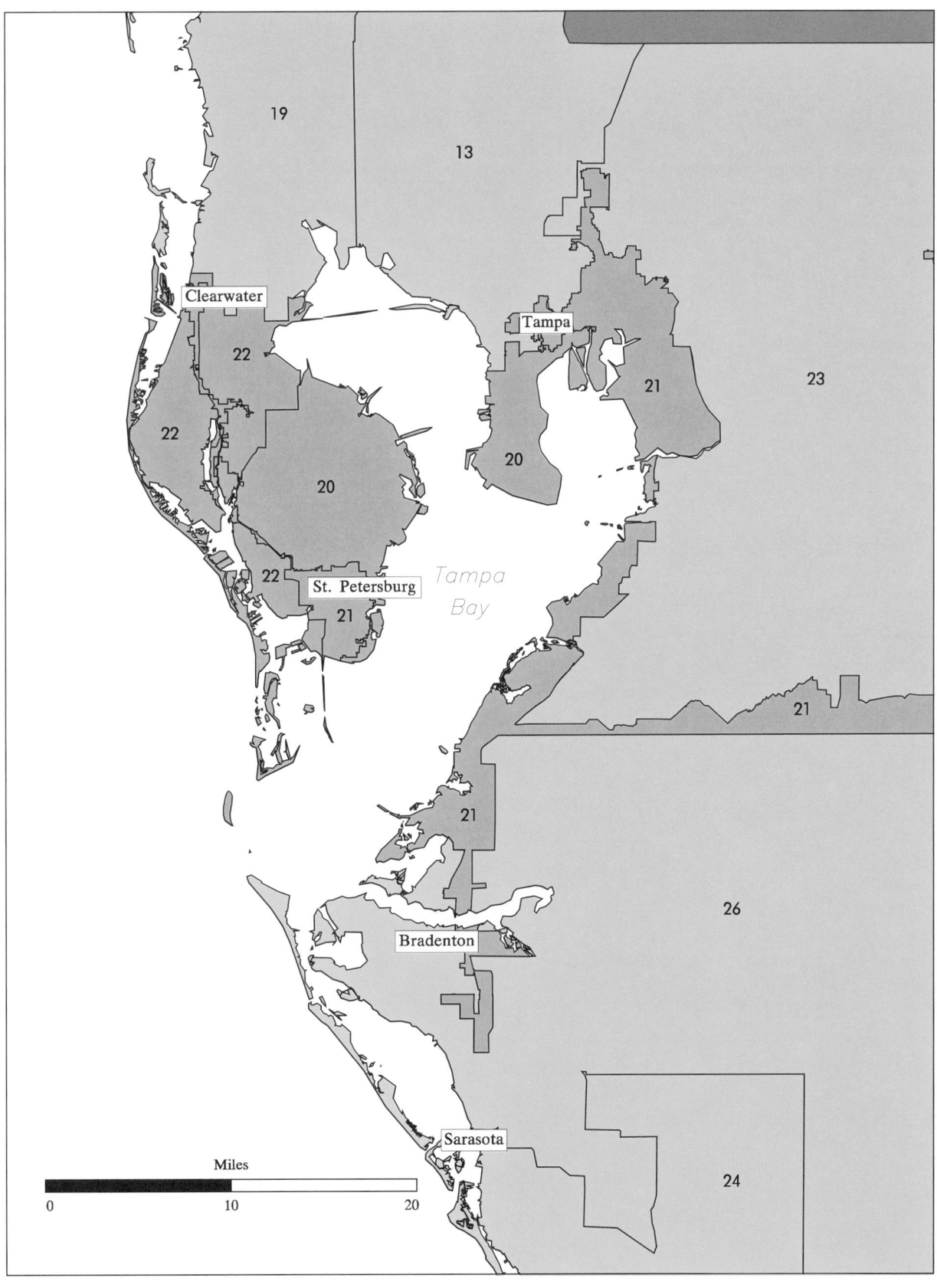

Population Growth   -3% to 5%   6% to 13%   14% to 19%

Florida State Senate Districts: Demographic Data

Senate District	Population 1997	+/-	Average HH Income ($)	+/-	District Type	Unempl. Rate (%)	College Educ. (%)	White (non-Hispanic) (%)	+/-	African American (%)	+/-	Asian American (%)	+/-	Hispanic American (%)	+/-
Florida	14,556,962	13	46,784	28	S	6	36	70	7	14	22	2	53	14	32
1	371,308	15	36,502	31	M	7	28	75	11	20	24	2	58	2	56
2	327,950	1	34,321	27	U	8	26	43	-12	53	13	1	27	2	32
3	366,056	14	39,829	36	M	6	37	65	9	30	23	1	49	3	46
4	372,468	16	41,691	30	R	6	32	80	12	16	31	1	51	2	50
5	356,704	11	39,006	33	M	6	42	78	6	16	31	2	48	4	43
6	378,364	17	54,098	28	U	4	42	85	12	8	53	3	64	4	61
7	372,246	16	48,069	35	S	6	42	84	12	9	29	3	63	3	57
8	398,744	25	51,555	30	M	5	43	82	19	10	61	2	72	6	68
9	359,975	13	52,596	28	S	4	47	78	6	5	39	3	55	13	48
10	385,951	18	35,509	25	R	7	23	88	15	6	36	1	69	4	52
11	406,751	24	37,980	25	R	6	28	84	20	11	42	1	77	4	70
12	388,449	21	57,896	30	S	5	46	80	14	6	58	3	71	11	58
13	352,987	9	49,915	31	S	4	41	75	2	5	37	2	50	18	34
14	356,495	10	41,592	28	S	5	33	55	-1	33	22	2	48	10	42
15	371,138	15	39,783	22	M	7	32	76	9	16	28	2	62	5	58
16	361,834	12	37,216	21	S	6	32	84	9	11	27	1	58	4	43
17	353,583	9	40,273	25	M	7	28	79	3	13	32	1	53	7	45
18	374,971	16	45,485	20	M	5	40	84	11	6	33	2	66	8	58
19	356,428	11	43,991	31	S	5	34	93	8	2	53	1	60	3	57
20	320,944	1	46,210	35	U	4	39	87	-3	4	38	3	42	5	30
21	325,398	1	29,679	27	U	9	21	36	-15	51	10	1	22	12	28
22	322,265	0	49,711	34	S	4	39	92	-2	3	41	1	46	3	35
23	366,468	12	49,447	36	S	5	38	77	5	7	38	2	59	13	59
24	358,683	11	45,556	24	R	4	37	94	9	2	43	1	63	3	54
25	392,730	21	59,128	27	S	4	41	90	17	2	82	1	75	7	70
26	355,018	10	47,555	33	S	5	35	86	7	7	23	1	52	6	35
27	381,178	19	68,594	29	M	4	45	90	15	4	76	1	74	5	59
28	382,877	19	67,830	45	S	4	44	85	14	5	76	2	73	9	54
29	379,060	16	46,325	26	S	6	34	66	8	15	23	1	63	17	44
30	352,038	11	36,741	26	S	8	25	31	-10	58	20	1	22	11	44
31	346,281	6	60,489	21	U	4	44	83	1	7	40	1	43	9	40
32	415,123	29	52,789	22	S	5	41	62	19	12	37	2	74	24	53
33	385,785	17	49,701	24	S	5	41	81	11	7	45	2	60	9	52
34	333,603	3	49,528	20	S	7	36	26	-14	2	2	1	26	70	12
35	377,702	16	43,243	32	S	5	30	72	7	15	37	1	51	11	53
36	342,101	7	31,914	15	S	11	21	11	-13	55	7	1	25	32	14
37	367,986	14	52,520	18	S	5	45	22	-20	3	7	2	34	72	30
38	341,538	5	52,226	23	S	7	42	49	-8	11	12	2	32	37	25
39	386,367	19	41,334	21	U	7	27	17	-7	3	22	1	56	79	26
40	311,399	-3	44,108	26	M	9	28	35	-13	37	0	1	11	27	8

Note: U=urban, S=suburban, R=rural, M=mixed, HH=households.

FLORIDA
State House Districts

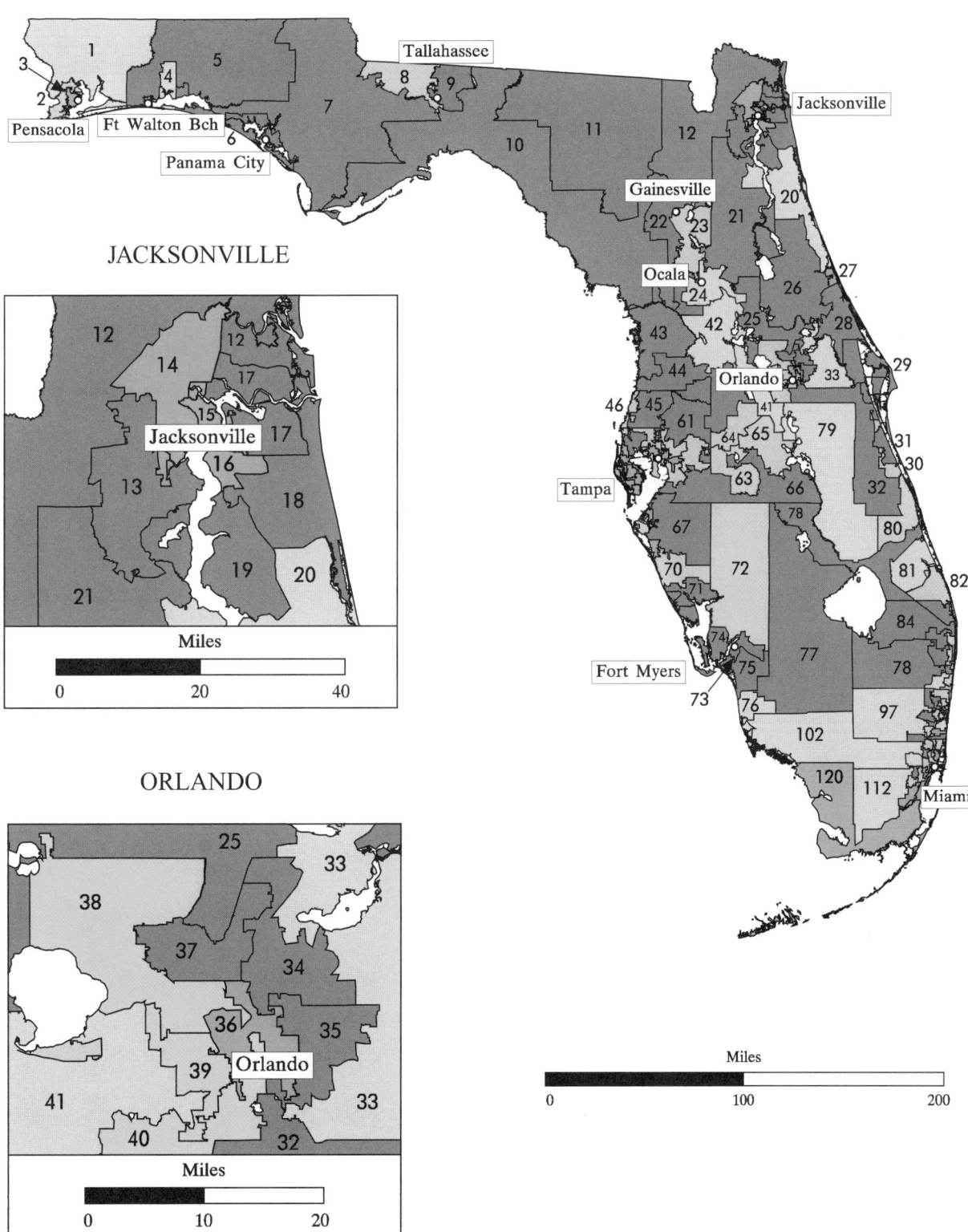

JACKSONVILLE

ORLANDO

Population Growth — -12% to 4% — 5% to 12% — 13% to 22% — 23% to 37%

MIAMI

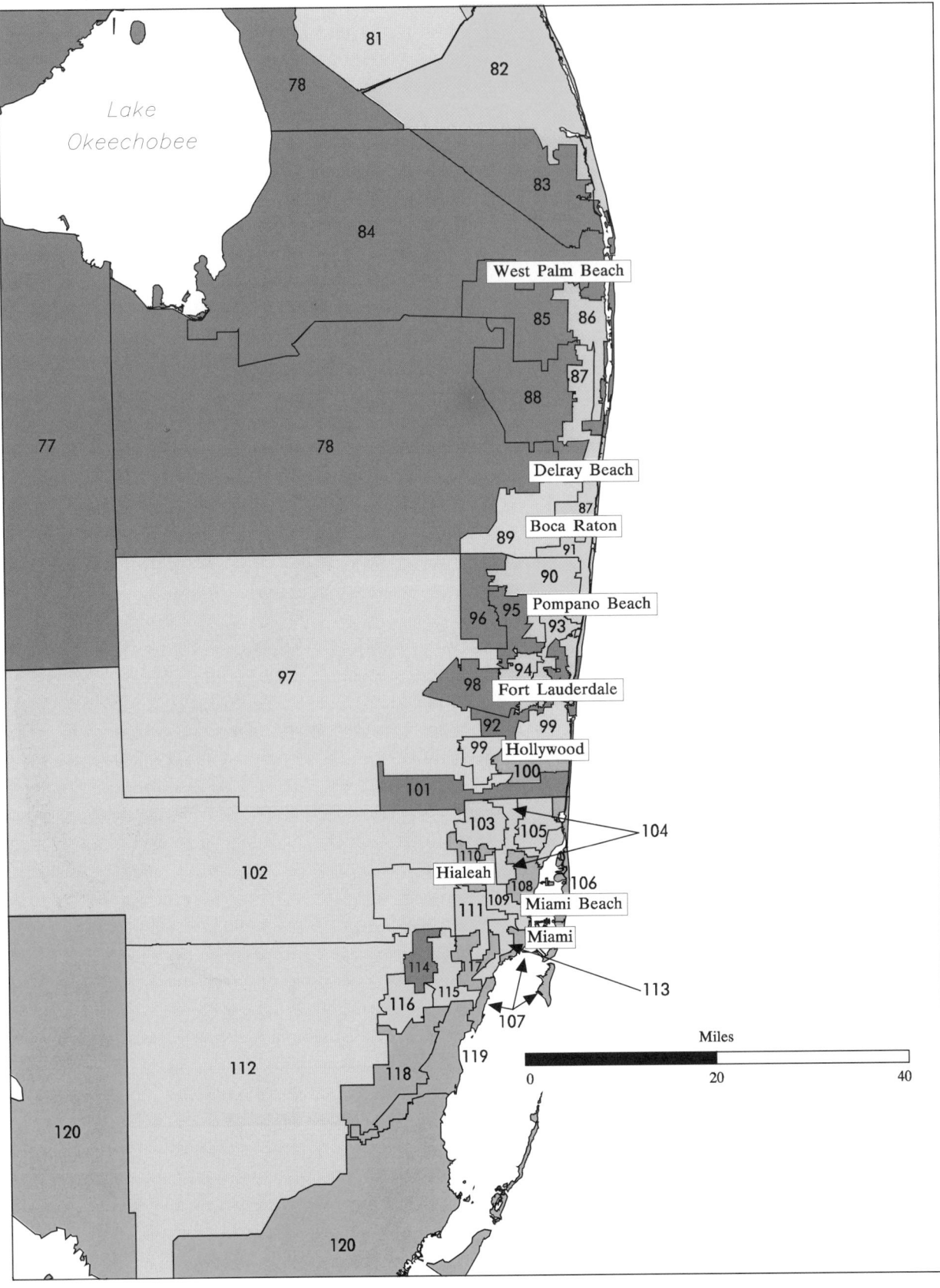

Lake Okeechobee

81

78

82

83

84

West Palm Beach

85 86

87

88

77

78

Delray Beach

87

Boca Raton

89

91

90

95

Pompano Beach

96

93

94

98

Fort Lauderdale

92 99

99 Hollywood

100

101

103 105

104

110

Hialeah

108 106

111 109

Miami Beach

102

Miami

114 117

113

115

116

107

112

119

118

Miles

0 20 40

120

120

Population Growth   -12% to 4%   5% to 12%   13% to 22%   23% to 37%

TAMPA

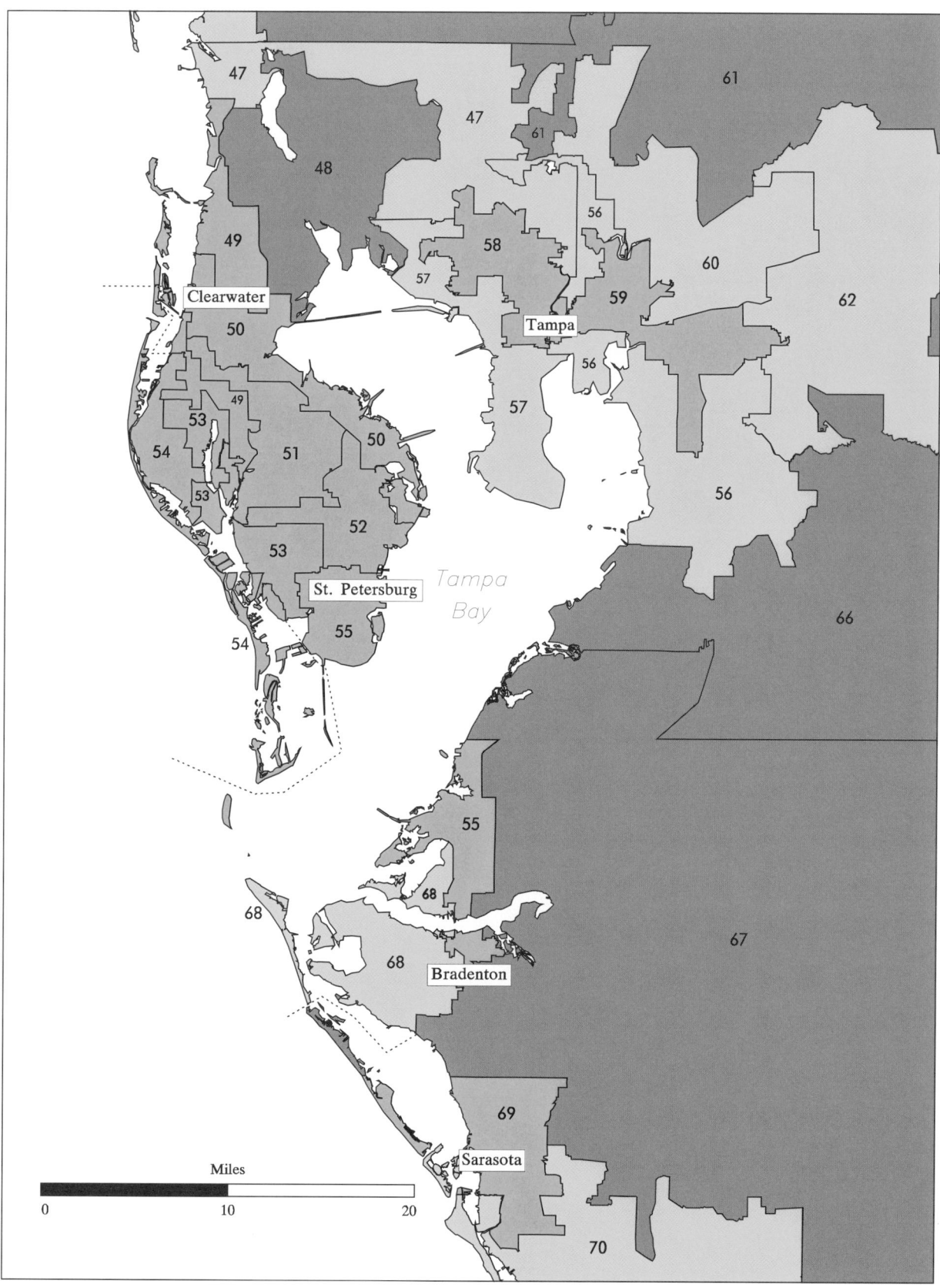

47

47

61

61

48

56

49

58

60

57

59

62

Clearwater

Tampa

50

56

49

53

57

56

54

51

50

53

52

66

53

55

St. Petersburg

Tampa Bay

54

55

68

68

68

67

Bradenton

69

Sarasota

70

Miles

0   10   20

Population Growth   ▢ -12% to 4%   ▢ 5% to 12%   ▢ 13% to 22%

Florida State House Districts: Demographic Data

House District	Population 1997	+/-	Average HH Income ($)	+/-	District Type	Unempl. Rate (%)	College Educ. (%)	White (non-Hispanic) (%)	+/-	African American (%)	+/-	Asian American (%)	+/-	Hispanic American (%)	+/-
Florida	14,556,962	13	46,784	28	S	6	36	70	7	14	22	2	53	14	32
1	138,806	25	40,643	33	R	7	32	86	21	10	45	1	80	2	62
2	118,107	8	46,744	32	S	6	41	83	3	9	34	3	56	3	57
3	104,535	1	33,507	28	S	9	30	52	-9	42	14	3	41	3	36
4	134,049	23	53,564	34	S	5	48	88	20	5	29	3	76	4	75
5	127,232	18	33,788	30	R	7	24	81	14	13	35	2	59	3	51
6	124,144	16	43,269	38	S	7	34	80	11	14	31	3	63	3	59
7	126,477	14	37,961	37	R	5	25	79	11	18	26	0	43	2	47
8	115,478	10	29,197	31	U	8	36	41	-1	54	17	2	39	3	37
9	123,000	14	63,836	41	U	3	66	79	8	15	40	2	64	3	52
10	127,566	19	34,340	31	R	6	23	79	15	19	35	0	26	2	50
11	126,093	16	32,868	24	R	7	22	73	12	24	26	0	47	2	47
12	126,202	16	43,836	35	R	6	23	82	13	15	32	0	39	2	51
13	124,094	17	48,379	26	U	5	37	79	9	12	57	4	59	5	61
14	110,763	3	35,188	28	U	8	22	37	-10	60	12	1	25	2	32
15	99,018	-6	31,102	25	U	9	24	35	-21	62	5	1	14	2	20
16	110,850	2	44,437	27	U	4	38	76	-6	18	43	2	42	4	42
17	128,001	18	51,196	30	U	5	44	77	9	13	59	4	68	5	72
18	121,342	17	64,321	39	U	4	54	82	11	11	57	3	57	4	53
19	130,820	22	63,681	28	S	3	52	88	18	5	56	3	78	4	69
20	140,166	31	43,051	23	R	5	36	84	26	11	52	1	95	4	82
21	122,894	14	35,882	30	R	7	22	83	11	14	24	0	54	3	48
22	128,539	14	50,107	35	S	5	54	78	8	14	38	2	60	5	50
23	113,047	7	29,019	30	U	8	45	56	-3	36	19	4	39	5	30
24	130,955	26	39,152	24	S	6	33	85	21	10	52	1	78	4	70
25	128,203	18	48,014	28	R	6	34	86	14	7	47	1	75	6	63
26	125,590	14	38,368	25	R	6	29	79	8	11	40	1	60	9	55
27	111,826	4	36,175	22	S	7	34	75	0	21	18	1	49	3	26
28	127,033	17	38,273	21	S	5	33	93	15	4	55	1	68	2	43
29	119,716	13	40,689	20	M	6	37	78	9	17	23	1	62	3	46
30	123,519	12	52,262	20	S	5	50	91	10	3	34	2	59	4	46
31	125,456	17	36,904	19	U	6	36	83	12	9	43	2	65	5	60
32	134,591	20	48,911	22	M	5	39	81	13	7	53	2	65	10	72
33	133,838	25	49,209	36	S	5	34	76	20	15	30	1	81	8	68
34	127,861	19	58,229	28	S	4	49	83	13	5	50	2	64	9	59
35	127,479	18	47,216	28	S	4	49	74	8	4	52	4	61	18	56
36	109,070	0	48,907	27	U	4	47	79	-5	5	16	2	36	13	33
37	124,010	14	59,454	30	S	5	51	82	8	6	43	3	64	9	45
38	114,863	10	42,549	29	S	6	31	64	2	24	24	2	45	9	41
39	113,425	9	33,857	23	S	7	23	32	-12	57	21	1	26	9	35
40	119,030	10	56,212	29	S	4	46	74	2	7	28	4	59	15	41
41	141,148	33	51,952	28	S	4	41	77	26	11	64	3	85	9	65
42	136,950	27	32,942	23	R	7	22	85	24	11	42	0	67	3	80
43	129,387	19	32,974	21	R	7	24	94	18	3	38	1	73	2	57
44	132,489	21	34,836	21	R	7	24	89	18	5	36	1	75	5	67
45	126,330	17	34,418	26	R	6	22	91	15	3	22	1	74	5	47
46	114,407	6	31,316	25	R	6	20	96	5	0	31	1	59	3	54
47	121,113	11	53,807	30	S	5	47	80	5	6	45	2	53	12	42
48	126,716	18	59,085	33	S	4	46	93	15	2	61	1	71	4	64
49	115,291	3	49,195	33	S	4	38	95	1	1	50	1	50	3	41
50	110,888	1	42,301	28	U	4	40	84	-3	10	26	2	49	4	39

Note: U=urban, S=suburban, R=rural, M=mixed, HH=households.

Florida State House Districts: Demographic Data (cont.)

House District	Population 1997	+/-	Average HH Income ($)	+/-	District Type	Unempl. Rate (%)	College Educ. (%)	White (non-Hispanic) (%)	+/-	African American (%)	+/-	Asian American (%)	+/-	Hispanic American (%)	+/-
Florida	14,556,962	13	46,784	28	S	6	36	70	7	14	22	2	53	14	32
51	108,364	3	40,214	34	S	4	28	90	0	4	37	2	47	4	43
52	105,052	-3	39,423	33	U	4	33	90	-6	3	40	3	36	4	32
53	104,702	-2	39,009	32	U	4	32	90	-5	5	35	2	42	3	30
54	106,916	-1	60,796	36	S	3	46	96	-2	0	43	1	46	2	29
55	106,298	0	33,434	29	U	7	27	36	-17	56	10	1	15	7	41
56	116,843	7	44,826	32	S	5	36	72	-1	12	28	2	44	14	37
57	111,845	6	60,961	39	U	5	49	78	0	6	34	3	45	13	37
58	108,865	4	41,347	28	S	5	34	52	-10	9	25	2	43	37	22
59	108,502	4	29,756	27	U	10	21	28	-13	58	10	1	30	13	25
60	116,441	8	44,010	36	S	5	46	73	-1	13	32	2	54	11	45
61	125,820	17	45,729	38	S	5	33	83	12	8	32	1	72	7	61
62	121,819	10	56,095	38	S	5	37	81	3	4	37	1	53	13	64
63	119,172	8	45,235	27	S	5	31	84	4	10	32	1	55	5	37
64	117,928	10	35,578	25	S	7	26	78	7	17	14	1	56	4	54
65	117,680	10	37,235	27	S	9	23	72	5	22	24	0	42	5	42
66	121,214	13	44,203	25	S	6	29	75	4	9	45	1	55	14	64
67	128,512	18	49,578	35	S	4	36	90	16	3	36	1	63	5	44
68	115,079	5	46,104	36	S	4	36	93	3	2	42	1	51	4	41
69	110,274	3	46,405	24	S	4	39	82	-1	12	21	1	45	5	43
70	116,006	7	58,453	30	S	4	45	97	6	1	37	1	55	2	33
71	127,180	19	36,582	20	R	5	30	92	16	3	51	1	79	3	70
72	117,813	9	37,747	21	R	5	23	82	5	7	22	0	44	10	33
73	123,289	14	38,064	23	S	5	29	69	5	20	29	1	58	10	55
74	129,551	18	49,668	22	U	4	37	94	16	1	70	1	72	4	71
75	127,640	19	53,022	28	S	4	40	94	17	1	79	1	72	4	46
76	136,477	27	74,498	28	S	3	47	88	22	3	82	1	89	8	82
77	122,150	14	32,999	21	R	7	20	62	4	13	22	1	55	24	44
78	124,580	14	47,832	41	M	7	30	67	11	25	17	1	59	8	33
79	139,158	25	38,996	21	R	5	28	74	16	7	39	2	79	17	62
80	121,603	9	52,618	28	R	6	36	88	6	9	33	1	50	2	32
81	136,517	27	48,611	17	R	5	36	87	21	6	133	1	85	5	72
82	116,333	12	70,699	35	R	4	45	90	10	5	36	1	54	4	53
83	123,029	14	78,204	34	S	3	48	91	11	3	79	1	75	4	56
84	126,149	15	46,469	45	M	9	27	30	2	56	17	1	31	13	41
85	127,972	20	52,812	37	S	4	37	78	11	8	73	1	50	13	67
86	119,902	9	42,256	34	S	6	30	58	-8	18	47	1	34	23	53
87	120,936	10	71,139	34	S	4	46	84	4	5	73	2	52	9	50
88	130,845	21	55,914	37	S	5	38	76	15	12	34	1	79	10	54
89	130,197	25	83,779	55	S	4	49	91	22	1	109	2	86	5	56
90	118,711	10	47,723	28	S	5	37	73	3	16	28	1	47	9	41
91	116,173	7	73,756	21	U	4	51	92	5	1	59	1	54	5	41
92	120,153	14	47,958	19	S	5	39	81	8	6	50	2	53	11	45
93	118,196	12	33,373	16	U	9	22	33	-4	57	20	1	33	8	40
94	113,235	9	32,853	16	S	8	26	28	-17	61	22	1	19	9	33
95	123,312	16	42,334	18	S	5	36	82	10	6	55	2	60	10	55
96	131,128	17	59,490	29	S	4	47	83	13	6	43	2	58	9	47
97	162,615	37	60,243	23	S	4	47	78	28	5	79	2	89	14	82
98	127,390	21	55,799	21	S	4	47	81	15	6	56	2	68	10	58
99	128,163	26	50,259	24	S	5	39	71	17	12	41	3	84	13	63
100	110,798	2	45,173	20	U	6	33	77	-4	5	38	2	39	15	32

Note: U=urban, S=suburban, R=rural, M=mixed, HH=households.

Florida State House Districts: Demographic Data (cont.)

House District	Population 1997	+/-	Average HH Income ($)	+/-	District Type	Unempl. Rate (%)	College Educ. (%)	White (non-Hispanic) (%)	+/-	African American (%)	+/-	Asian American (%)	+/-	Hispanic American (%)	+/-
Florida	14,556,962	13	46,784	28	S	6	36	70	7	14	22	2	53	14	32
101	131,126	20	39,442	20	S	6	30	61	9	19	37	2	55	17	53
102	150,504	32	43,627	17	U	6	28	20	-10	4	43	1	54	74	49
103	118,716	12	38,952	17	S	9	27	9	-18	59	12	1	32	31	25
104	111,938	6	39,599	18	S	9	29	22	-8	58	9	1	27	18	20
105	114,046	6	45,688	20	S	7	38	51	-8	20	15	3	33	25	35
106	113,850	3	54,461	25	U	7	42	57	-7	4	5	1	26	38	21
107	109,942	4	45,071	24	U	8	36	26	-14	2	0	1	32	71	13
108	112,951	4	32,700	17	S	13	25	19	-3	64	6	1	31	16	4
109	115,066	7	24,298	16	U	14	12	3	-34	58	4	0	13	38	19
110	101,628	1	37,268	17	U	8	19	10	-31	2	-3	1	16	87	7
111	111,317	7	36,155	15	U	8	27	16	-17	2	1	1	31	81	13
112	155,793	33	51,036	18	S	5	43	21	0	4	33	2	65	72	46
113	114,544	7	38,261	17	U	9	25	14	-10	9	12	1	33	76	10
114	120,490	14	45,745	20	S	7	37	13	-28	1	-4	1	31	85	25
115	113,978	10	59,874	22	S	6	45	24	-17	1	11	2	36	72	22
116	116,186	12	54,812	15	S	5	57	35	-16	5	15	4	38	57	39
117	113,583	4	46,615	19	S	7	34	22	-14	4	7	1	27	73	11
118	97,843	-5	51,213	26	S	7	37	33	-15	32	-8	2	16	32	12
119	89,245	-12	71,410	32	S	4	48	57	-19	11	-10	2	10	29	4
120	113,297	-1	52,885	32	R	5	35	65	-5	11	-2	1	22	22	13

Note: U=urban, S=suburban, R=rural, M=mixed, HH=households.

GEORGIA

Atlanta, home of Coca-Cola, CNN, and the 1996 Summer Olympics, is one of the preeminent places in the United States at the end of the twentieth century, though it is not an especially large one. It is still only the country's thirty-seventh largest city and has fewer people than Albuquerque, Fort Worth, or Oklahoma City.

It owes its position to its geographical location as a shipping point for both east-west and north-south traffic, to a large airport, good universities, and a comparatively tolerant racial attitude. Some credit should also be given to an impressive list of political figures. In the last fifty years Georgia has produced civil rights leader Martin Luther King Jr., President Jimmy Carter, Sen. Richard Russell, Sen. Sam Nunn, and House Speaker Newt Gingrich.

While Atlanta may get all the attention, the surrounding metropolitan area has made it a boomtown, much like Los Angeles in the twenties or Chicago in the late nineteenth century. That surge has made Georgia the tenth-most-populous state and may lift it to ninth, past New Jersey, early in the next century.

More than half of those new arrivals are moving to Georgia from other states, and almost all of them, it seems, are moving to Atlanta's outer suburbs—Henry, Gwinnett, and Dawson Counties, in particular. Georgia has eleven of the fifty fastest-growing state house districts in the United States, more than any other state. The Forty-first House District, at the extreme northeast edge of the Atlanta suburbs, has more than doubled in population in the last seven years. The Eighty-fifth District, slightly further out, has grown by 75 percent; the Eightieth District, just to the south, by 72 percent. Two other districts, the Twenty-eighth and Eighty-second, have grown by two-thirds.

The only parts of the state that are losing people are the cities—downtown Atlanta, Augusta, Columbus, and Albany. Georgia is yet another state in which population shifts have created what might be called the metropolitan doughnut, an increasingly hollow urban core surrounded by growing suburbs that are pushing into previously rural areas. Of the state's fifty fastest-growing districts, thirty are classified as rural, nineteen as suburban, and only one as urban.

Although the booming Atlanta suburbs include the wealthiest parts of the state (average income in the Forty-fifth House District is $130,000), income growth in Georgia as a whole is only a shade above the national average. The new arrivals tend to be young, well educated families with children. Metro Atlanta, which is home to several black universities and has long had a large black middle class, also has some of the wealthiest black-majority districts. However, the Forty-eighth District in Atlanta, 88 percent black, is the fourth-poorest district in the country.

Georgia has more counties (159) than any other state except Texas, and as a consequence its house of representatives is unusually large, at 180 members. The most recent round of reapportionment was a mess, pitting black legislators against white, and liberal and moderate blacks against each other. The state's congressional districts went up to the U.S. Supreme Court three times, though its legislative districts were also redrawn. The dispute over the congressional districts turned on attempts to create a third black-majority congressional district by linking black neighborhoods in Atlanta with black neighborhoods in Savannah, 250 miles away. Although the black incumbents won reelection in their redrawn districts, the state's congressional delegation has changed from 9–1 Democratic in 1990 to 8–3 Republican in 1996. The Democrats have, however, maintained control of the legislature, though by small margins.

One other note about race should be made. Although almost all the boom districts are heavily white, the percentage of minorities, while still small in overall numbers, is increasing rapidly. Georgia has twelve of the fastest-growing African-American districts in the country, fourteen of the fastest-growing Hispanic districts, and ten of the fastest-growing Asian districts. (As much as 10 percent of Georgia's growth has come by immigration from other countries.) It should be a question of some concern to Republicans whether their opposition to bilingual education and illegal immigration in places like California might backfire on them in what ought to be receptive parts of the new South.

GEORGIA
State Senate Districts

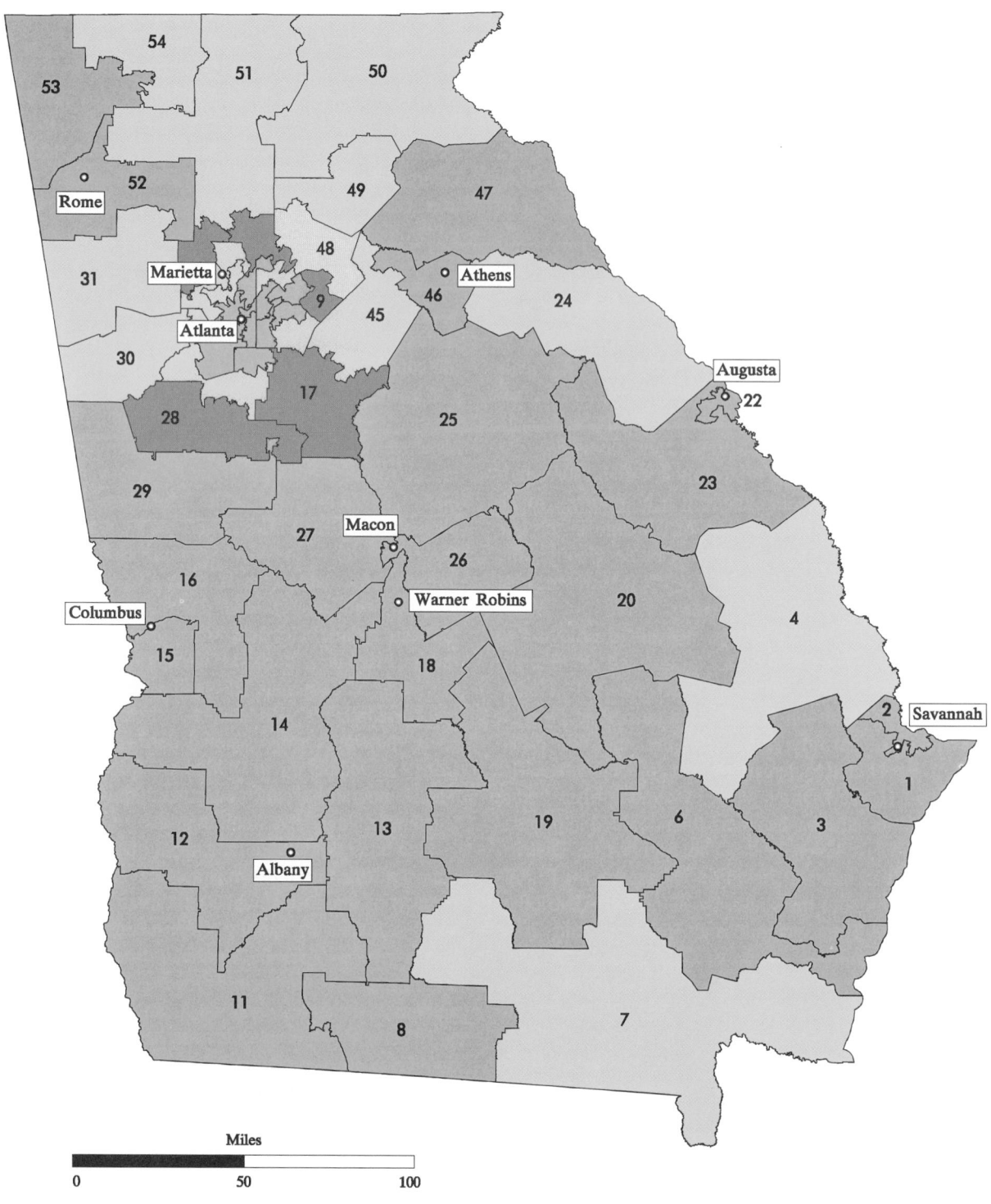

Miles

0   50   100

Population Growth   -3% to 13%   15% to 29%   33% to 47%   80%

ATLANTA

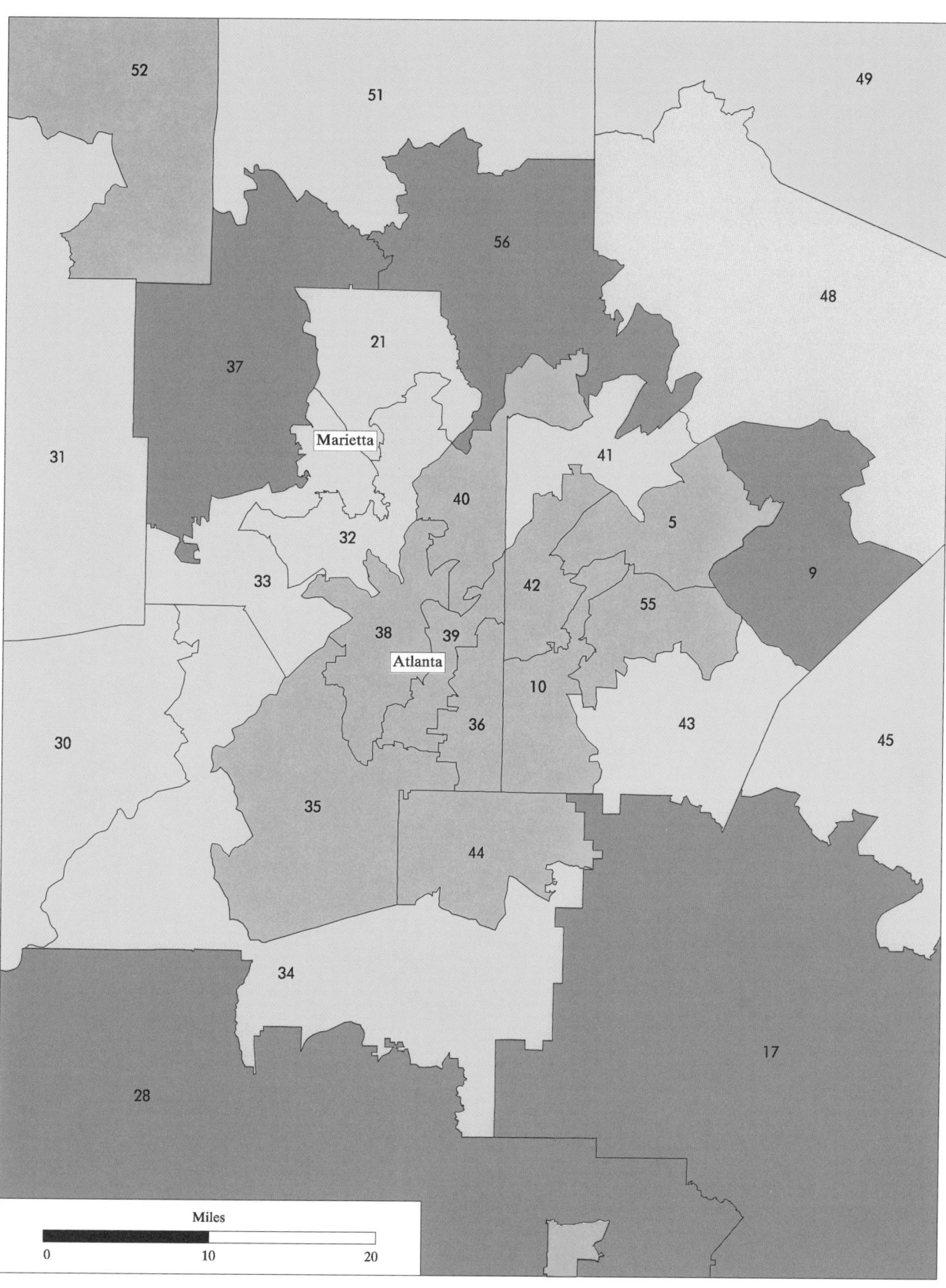

Population Growth   ▢ -3% to 13%   ▢ 15% to 29%   ▢ 33% to 47%   ▢ 80%

Georgia State Senate Districts: Demographic Data

Senate District	Population 1997	+/-	Average HH Income ($)	+/-	District Type	Unempl. Rate (%)	College Educ. (%)	White (non-Hispanic) (%)	+/-	African American (%)	+/-	Asian American (%)	+/-	Hispanic American (%)	+/-
Georgia	7,460,487	15	48,918	33	M	6	35	68	12	28	20	2	63	2	51
1	127,220	11	53,753	27	M	4	45	80	5	16	41	2	56	2	57
2	113,354	3	33,633	32	U	10	23	31	-9	66	10	1	42	1	19
3	126,531	13	36,064	31	R	8	25	58	5	35	23	2	49	4	42
4	135,811	16	35,821	31	R	6	24	68	12	30	25	0	38	1	37
5	130,279	10	69,648	26	S	3	58	81	4	7	30	8	71	4	62
6	131,118	10	40,831	33	R	6	27	76	6	22	22	0	23	2	41
7	135,170	17	34,429	29	R	6	22	72	12	25	29	1	71	2	57
8	130,657	10	41,262	40	R	6	29	63	3	35	21	1	43	2	41
9	159,421	34	65,373	25	R	3	50	92	30	3	72	3	126	3	99
10	118,241	7	39,094	23	S	10	31	21	-3	76	9	1	54	1	20
11	126,509	5	34,345	36	R	6	20	53	-2	44	14	0	-13	2	25
12	118,684	0	39,797	38	U	10	30	43	-8	55	7	1	32	1	21
13	129,039	7	38,151	44	R	7	20	63	1	34	17	0	13	3	31
14	119,893	8	37,706	36	N.A.	8	24	51	3	48	14	0	22	1	26
15	106,985	-3	32,504	31	U	11	25	29	-24	62	7	2	21	6	22
16	127,280	10	48,983	33	U	6	36	75	5	21	28	1	74	2	56
17	161,033	46	50,862	23	R	5	27	84	43	14	58	1	110	1	95
18	130,647	12	41,125	22	M	6	32	71	7	25	27	1	59	2	54
19	119,974	8	34,685	36	R	6	19	70	4	29	20	0	4	1	28
20	116,978	6	33,546	29	R	6	20	58	-1	41	16	0	32	1	19
21	141,423	16	77,870	25	S	3	61	90	13	4	33	3	78	2	56
22	106,401	0	34,542	33	S	8	26	34	-14	62	7	2	46	2	33
23	130,396	4	45,679	35	N.A.	6	34	61	-3	35	15	2	44	2	26
24	139,823	23	47,631	25	R	4	36	74	19	23	28	2	96	2	74
25	129,317	10	41,632	34	R	7	24	55	3	44	18	0	31	1	29
26	110,646	0	31,618	23	U	9	18	35	-14	64	10	0	10	1	21
27	129,619	11	50,514	30	R	5	35	73	6	25	28	1	44	1	37
28	164,229	33	53,295	28	R	5	34	79	28	18	52	1	98	1	95
29	120,669	7	36,557	27	R	7	20	61	1	38	17	0	40	1	26
30	142,154	16	45,276	30	R	5	25	84	13	14	31	1	64	1	59
31	154,745	28	40,113	28	R	6	18	89	27	10	38	0	48	1	72
32	129,903	15	66,691	24	S	4	60	82	10	11	36	4	74	3	66
33	145,010	21	43,392	27	S	6	34	72	14	22	35	2	74	4	78
34	151,083	24	58,425	27	S	4	36	83	19	13	51	2	80	2	71
35	122,735	10	43,071	27	S	8	36	15	-41	82	31	1	-2	2	21
36	114,587	3	34,752	42	U	11	30	17	-34	78	16	1	-26	4	35
37	178,073	46	66,277	33	S	4	48	92	44	4	60	1	114	2	97
38	109,657	2	56,102	44	N.A.	9	38	16	-9	83	4	0	28	1	8
39	108,191	-2	46,203	41	U	10	42	24	-27	71	8	2	19	3	26
40	124,564	11	99,682	30	S	3	70	80	-1	14	148	2	68	3	41
41	130,158	15	75,280	30	S	3	61	75	7	12	33	7	78	5	71
42	120,864	7	54,220	27	S	4	60	69	-2	15	21	6	50	9	45
43	132,967	19	51,979	21	S	6	47	26	5	70	25	2	54	2	42
44	126,164	6	42,289	24	S	6	30	59	-4	33	20	4	53	3	46
45	141,964	25	46,410	30	R	5	23	78	20	20	44	1	76	1	75
46	133,075	11	43,998	39	M	6	48	71	6	24	22	2	47	2	41
47	131,533	13	36,995	31	R	5	19	83	11	16	25	0	11	1	50
48	213,577	80	64,140	39	R	4	42	92	76	4	104	2	196	3	158
49	152,684	29	52,673	39	R	4	29	87	27	7	36	1	63	5	61
50	141,049	19	39,807	38	R	4	23	93	18	4	26	1	53	1	51

Note: U=urban, S=suburban, R=rural, M=mixed, HH=households.

Georgia State Senate Districts: Demographic Data (cont.)

Senate District	Population		Average HH Income		District Type	Unempl. Rate	College Educ.	White (non-Hispanic)		African American		Asian American		Hispanic American	
	1997	+/-	($)	+/-		(%)	(%)	(%)	+/-	(%)	+/-	(%)	+/-	(%)	+/-
Georgia	7,460,487	15	48,918	33	M	6	35	68	12	28	20	2	63	2	51
51	146,966	24	42,551	36	R	5	21	96	23	3	48	0	45	1	83
52	124,507	9	44,041	40	R	6	24	85	7	13	22	1	56	1	47
53	126,674	7	37,910	31	R	5	19	94	6	5	24	0	31	1	56
54	134,541	15	42,370	32	R	5	21	94	14	3	26	1	65	2	55
55	120,513	5	48,277	21	S	6	48	45	-6	46	14	5	42	3	33
56	165,206	47	86,050	39	S	3	61	87	39	7	193	3	147	3	94

Note: U=urban, S=suburban, R=rural, M=mixed, HH=households.

GEORGIA
State House Districts

SAVANNAH

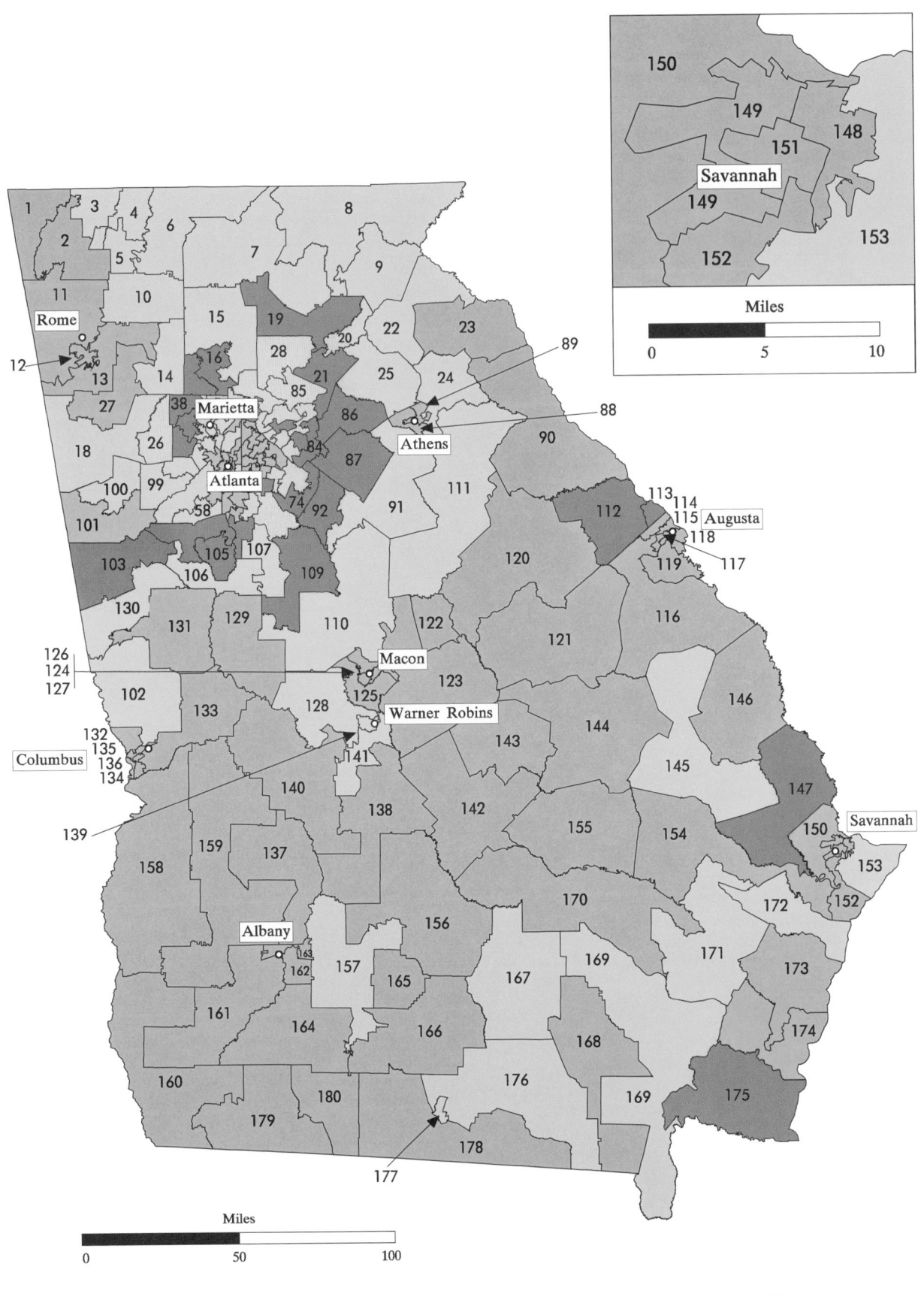

Population Growth   ▢ -10% to 10%   ▢ 11% to 26%   ▢ 27% to 52%   ▢ 59% to 108%

ATLANTA

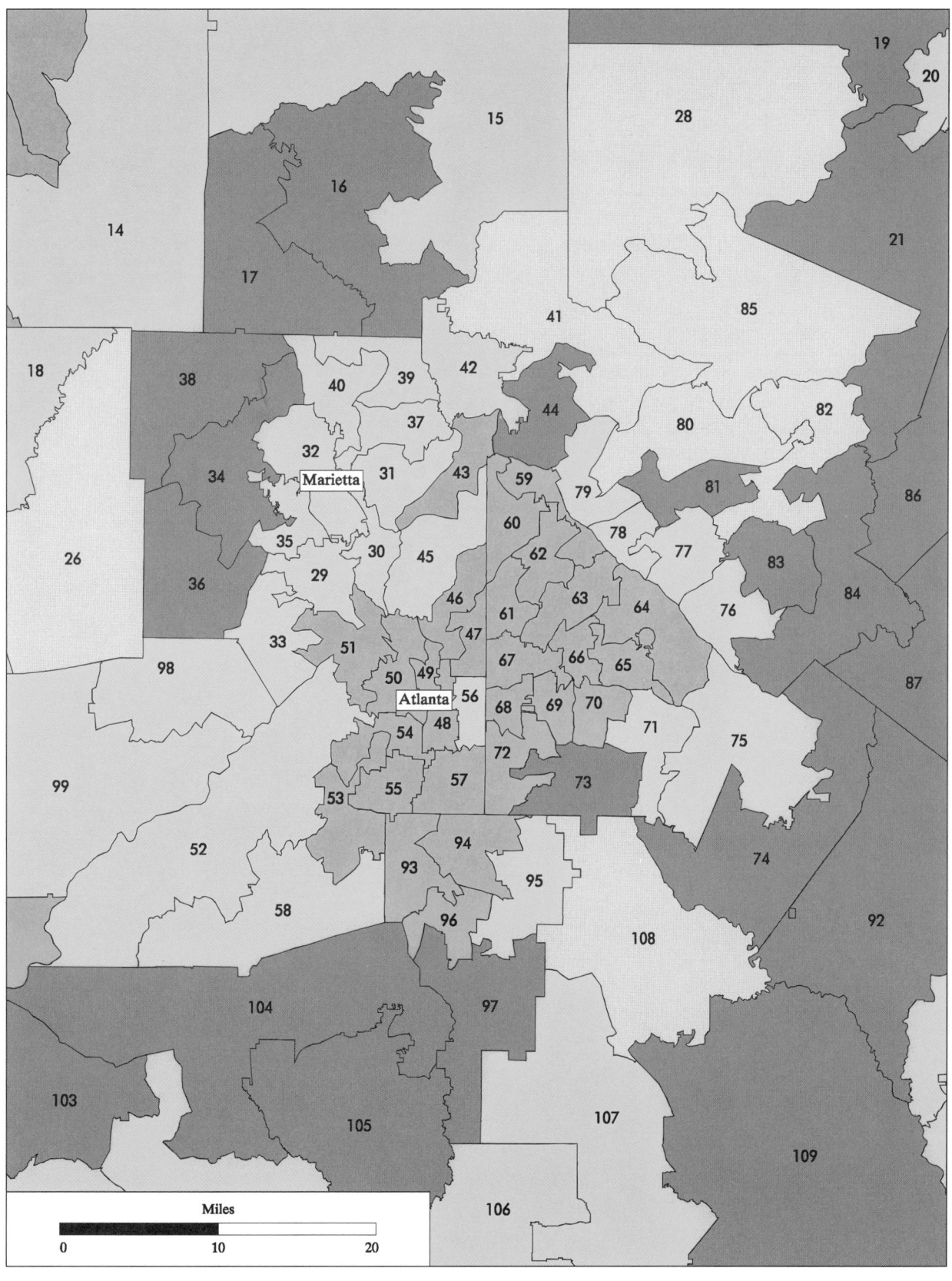

Population Growth · -10% to 10% · 11% to 26% · 27% to 52% · 59% to 108%

Georgia State House Districts: Demographic Data

House District	Population 1997	+/-	Average HH Income ($)	+/-	District Type	Unempl. Rate (%)	College Educ. (%)	White (non-Hispanic) (%)	+/-	African American (%)	+/-	Asian American (%)	+/-	Hispanic American (%)	+/-
Georgia	7,460,487	15	48,918	33	M	6	35	68	12	28	20	2	63	2	51
1	39,775	5	36,391	31	S	6	22	97	5	2	13	0	20	1	48
2	40,189	8	34,507	24	R	5	18	93	6	5	27	0	30	1	63
3	44,556	18	37,936	27	S	6	21	97	17	1	33	1	79	1	65
4	40,837	14	42,712	32	R	4	18	89	12	6	22	0	48	5	52
5	40,495	11	53,907	38	R	5	28	91	8	3	37	1	64	4	56
6	41,431	17	37,515	35	R	4	13	99	16	0	-12	0	46	1	72
7	42,867	24	35,987	31	R	5	19	97	23	1	32	0	24	1	66
8	43,344	22	38,875	42	R	5	24	98	21	1	36	0	-6	1	39
9	41,090	16	41,569	40	R	4	23	91	15	5	25	2	65	1	46
10	39,915	14	43,109	37	R	5	18	94	13	4	33	0	54	1	61
11	41,690	6	40,308	38	R	5	19	92	4	7	24	0	40	1	25
12	34,466	2	42,783	49	R	7	26	67	-4	30	15	1	45	2	47
13	42,789	7	42,343	34	R	6	23	90	5	8	34	1	61	1	31
14	46,425	22	45,452	36	R	6	20	87	19	11	42	0	68	2	80
15	44,524	25	50,102	35	R	4	24	98	25	1	38	0	43	0	40
16	46,791	39	53,511	32	S	3	35	93	36	4	70	0	70	2	123
17	51,969	47	61,646	39	S	4	42	95	46	2	56	1	113	2	100
18	48,222	22	37,012	29	R	5	15	92	20	7	38	0	23	1	66
19	44,221	27	53,705	39	R	4	30	97	26	1	49	0	69	2	63
20	41,152	16	45,601	36	R	5	27	65	5	20	34	1	47	13	59
21	48,076	38	54,100	39	R	4	30	93	37	4	59	1	95	2	70
22	39,086	12	37,691	33	R	5	23	88	10	10	27	0	32	1	44
23	38,069	9	34,581	25	R	4	19	81	6	18	23	0	-15	0	26
24	41,555	11	45,968	38	S	5	39	82	8	15	29	1	45	2	50
25	41,339	19	39,779	34	R	6	18	86	17	13	40	0	28	1	62
26	50,098	63	42,229	18	S	5	20	94	61	5	94	0	106	1	140
27	39,587	9	38,054	34	R	8	16	83	7	15	21	0	34	2	40
28	62,118	66	57,988	34	R	4	29	97	65	0	-14	0	132	2	135
29	41,809	11	52,822	27	S	5	45	77	5	16	29	3	67	4	65
30	41,366	14	54,775	22	S	3	66	75	7	17	34	4	72	4	65
31	41,920	15	94,300	27	S	3	69	91	12	4	32	3	77	2	50
32	47,203	20	40,743	26	U	6	42	66	10	25	33	3	77	6	79
33	39,999	15	46,098	21	N.A.	5	30	74	11	22	26	1	71	2	62
34	48,479	37	74,159	32	S	4	54	89	35	7	51	1	102	2	78
35	44,659	19	46,475	26	S	6	37	77	12	14	41	3	78	4	85
36	51,897	45	55,414	29	S	4	35	85	40	11	78	1	114	2	105
37	42,369	15	94,963	27	S	3	68	90	12	3	30	5	74	2	52
38	57,164	52	64,111	31	S	3	46	92	49	4	71	1	120	2	109
39	43,670	15	82,786	25	S	4	63	92	13	4	32	2	76	2	52
40	42,271	15	69,813	23	S	3	56	90	12	5	32	3	78	2	60
41	71,741	108	101,244	48	S	3	63	89	97	5	358	4	254	3	185
42	44,062	23	91,897	41	S	3	61	86	15	9	181	2	80	3	50
43	36,634	4	78,361	19	S	3	67	75	-10	19	129	2	48	3	31
44	50,429	31	97,908	30	S	2	70	85	21	8	189	4	103	3	51
45	42,848	14	130,422	30	S	3	71	81	3	12	179	2	71	4	54
46	35,794	1	98,955	40	U	3	71	83	-8	13	131	2	53	3	26
47	41,157	10	63,639	42	U	5	66	63	-12	27	125	3	58	6	40
48	33,073	-10	20,216	33	U	14	15	9	-48	88	-2	2	-35	1	-26
49	36,048	-3	26,426	29	U	15	25	11	-26	87	1	1	25	1	-9
50	36,919	-1	38,984	35	U	8	33	13	-29	86	5	0	2	1	6

Note: U=urban, S=suburban, R=rural, M=mixed, HH=households.

Georgia State House Districts: Demographic Data (cont.)

House District	Population 1997	+/-	Average HH Income ($)	+/-	District Type	Unempl. Rate (%)	College Educ. (%)	White (non-Hispanic) (%)	+/-	African American (%)	+/-	Asian American (%)	+/-	Hispanic American (%)	+/-
Georgia	7,460,487	15	48,918	33	M	6	35	68	12	28	20	2	63	2	51
51	35,765	2	33,244	33	N.A.	11	27	17	2	82	1	0	53	1	28
52	41,330	13	50,731	28	N.A.	8	38	14	-25	85	24	0	-9	1	17
53	39,428	6	38,747	28	N.A.	9	37	3	-60	94	14	1	-26	1	22
54	35,707	-1	38,688	30	U	9	31	3	-59	96	4	0	-41	1	3
55	33,053	-3	40,756	36	S	9	28	20	-49	77	25	1	-19	3	15
56	40,545	11	32,077	44	U	11	27	15	-42	76	33	0	-34	8	47
57	36,872	0	30,949	29	U	13	14	12	-41	83	10	2	13	2	29
58	43,029	16	44,032	23	N.A.	6	37	20	-37	78	47	0	-1	2	25
59	37,299	4	75,484	30	S	3	65	74	-3	11	20	9	53	5	45
60	36,529	10	86,661	33	S	4	66	81	5	10	29	4	65	4	48
61	38,647	10	49,753	22	S	4	57	65	0	17	23	7	55	10	44
62	37,063	3	53,362	23	S	5	52	55	-11	21	14	9	42	14	47
63	37,955	4	67,819	25	S	3	61	88	0	4	27	5	60	3	37
64	42,570	8	70,567	28	S	4	54	69	0	23	27	4	51	3	39
65	38,333	6	54,288	20	S	5	56	56	-5	34	19	6	45	3	36
66	34,864	4	37,822	19	S	7	43	35	-10	55	11	6	39	3	31
67	40,363	8	62,480	34	S	4	69	83	3	11	29	3	65	2	30
68	36,470	6	27,785	22	U	13	17	7	-13	93	8	0	31	1	-3
69	35,115	4	39,857	26	S	10	33	19	-9	79	7	1	39	1	-9
70	35,755	6	46,535	16	S	7	42	24	-13	70	12	3	41	2	24
71	41,862	18	50,532	18	S	5	51	27	-1	67	26	2	54	3	58
72	34,535	2	38,385	18	S	10	25	7	-16	92	4	0	16	1	3
73	46,927	32	52,345	17	S	6	44	11	5	88	37	0	54	0	-9
74	44,172	29	65,298	27	N.A.	4	42	92	27	5	52	1	90	1	59
75	42,743	19	51,185	31	N.A.	5	33	67	12	29	32	1	78	2	77
76	42,233	21	70,131	23	R	2	55	94	18	1	48	2	103	2	68
77	40,508	13	74,441	27	S	3	55	90	9	2	42	5	92	3	68
78	39,457	13	50,412	22	S	3	51	65	-1	14	29	13	73	8	79
79	44,054	22	68,824	34	S	4	59	74	13	13	37	7	93	5	83
80	66,137	72	65,292	32	R	3	54	86	65	6	98	4	172	4	156
81	49,441	37	59,775	26	R	3	52	79	27	7	62	7	115	6	120
82	55,180	66	63,034	31	R	3	47	93	63	3	84	2	175	2	131
83	43,840	27	70,508	25	R	2	52	96	25	1	54	2	112	1	49
84	48,313	48	60,229	30	R	4	40	91	45	5	72	2	123	2	116
85	59,438	75	58,917	39	R	4	32	92	73	5	82	1	197	2	143
86	48,586	34	42,876	28	R	5	22	87	32	11	51	1	101	1	84
87	46,660	30	44,909	33	R	5	19	76	24	22	49	0	82	1	83
88	40,182	4	47,928	40	S	5	64	74	-2	19	24	4	48	3	42
89	33,784	3	27,994	36	U	9	37	49	-7	46	13	3	37	2	25
90	37,994	3	34,150	32	R	6	18	59	-3	40	13	0	-5	1	18
91	46,010	25	52,360	36	R	4	35	80	23	19	33	0	52	1	61
92	45,619	28	39,908	23	R	7	18	71	22	27	46	0	43	1	68
93	39,109	8	39,995	19	S	6	40	35	-8	58	18	5	46	2	35
94	34,934	-1	39,590	26	S	8	21	65	-9	26	17	5	48	3	37
95	42,641	14	51,348	29	S	5	34	79	8	15	35	3	68	3	58
96	40,028	10	44,232	23	S	5	29	70	1	21	30	5	67	3	55
97	48,315	31	59,343	27	S	4	38	80	27	14	44	3	90	3	76
98	43,793	22	49,214	27	S	5	25	85	19	12	41	1	75	2	84
99	42,352	20	55,869	28	S	4	30	92	19	6	36	1	63	1	59
100	41,494	18	38,564	28	R	5	22	82	14	16	35	0	54	1	64

Note: U=urban, S=suburban, R=rural, M=mixed, HH=households.

Georgia State House Districts: Demographic Data (cont.)

House District	Population 1997	+/-	Average HH Income ($)	+/-	District Type	Unempl. Rate (%)	College Educ. (%)	White (non-Hispanic) (%)	+/-	African American (%)	+/-	Asian American (%)	+/-	Hispanic American (%)	+/-
Georgia	7,460,487	15	48,918	33	M	6	35	68	12	28	20	2	63	2	51
101	38,750	7	40,444	28	R	6	24	78	4	20	22	0	47	1	42
102	42,996	21	46,352	29	R	5	29	73	16	25	37	1	84	1	59
103	48,366	37	41,489	23	R	6	23	68	29	30	55	0	68	1	85
104	54,347	36	65,483	25	R	3	38	87	32	10	64	1	82	2	80
105	48,538	40	73,482	29	S	4	52	90	35	4	71	3	109	3	110
106	43,841	18	45,140	32	R	6	25	74	12	24	37	1	53	1	66
107	46,023	25	42,244	29	R	5	20	70	25	28	22	1	92	1	80
108	57,232	59	48,965	16	S	4	28	91	55	7	94	1	138	1	141
109	46,395	30	44,781	37	R	5	19	63	26	36	39	0	44	1	50
110	40,772	12	43,991	33	R	6	27	66	7	33	25	0	-8	1	31
111	40,990	15	38,618	32	R	6	22	59	9	40	25	0	6	1	12
112	53,761	31	45,387	24	R	4	32	77	28	20	38	1	103	2	88
113	44,021	29	62,268	18	S	3	55	85	24	7	50	5	98	2	89
114	33,633	5	62,039	35	S	3	57	75	-1	18	26	4	58	2	46
115	33,152	-5	41,034	36	U	6	38	56	-15	40	13	1	34	1	19
116	43,784	10	35,863	38	R	7	25	41	-2	53	18	2	46	3	29
117	32,352	3	37,339	35	S	8	25	26	-14	68	10	3	50	3	39
118	33,052	-8	23,894	21	S	11	16	24	-22	74	-3	1	24	1	-7
119	38,713	7	44,196	29	S	6	25	69	0	27	23	2	44	2	35
120	35,353	6	34,473	38	R	6	17	43	-1	57	12	0	-50	0	-9
121	37,917	4	36,182	40	R	8	16	42	-5	57	11	0	-10	0	-1
122	38,587	6	41,770	33	R	7	28	51	-3	47	15	1	44	1	44
123	36,803	5	38,825	24	R	7	18	58	-1	41	16	0	-9	0	3
124	34,842	0	29,759	25	U	11	21	26	-18	72	8	0	19	1	20
125	41,193	7	47,880	23	S	4	29	74	0	24	32	1	40	1	33
126	39,119	8	62,084	32	U	4	54	75	2	22	27	2	59	1	45
127	35,271	0	28,676	21	U	10	16	25	-21	74	9	0	-4	1	24
128	45,286	19	41,137	19	S	5	28	67	10	30	38	1	56	2	55
129	38,931	7	39,003	33	R	7	19	71	2	28	19	0	-18	0	17
130	41,698	12	46,688	28	R	5	32	80	8	18	31	1	52	1	44
131	38,498	2	29,448	23	R	10	13	45	-7	54	11	0	-16	1	12
132	38,706	7	58,930	37	U	5	40	87	3	9	26	2	80	2	64
133	40,696	-1	40,113	36	N.A.	8	26	36	-19	56	13	2	23	6	17
134	27,750	-2	28,203	23	U	13	24	20	-31	72	9	2	15	5	30
135	36,683	4	43,446	30	U	7	40	72	-3	24	27	1	64	2	52
136	34,620	-4	29,058	25	U	11	20	26	-22	68	3	2	25	3	20
137	42,127	8	40,270	40	R	7	30	58	5	40	13	0	23	1	31
138	36,675	3	37,060	39	R	7	20	57	-4	42	13	0	-18	1	10
139	39,493	14	39,859	17	U	5	35	78	9	17	33	2	68	3	68
140	36,513	3	33,388	35	R	10	19	36	-5	63	9	0	-4	1	8
141	46,061	18	44,289	22	N.A.	6	38	69	12	27	31	2	63	2	46
142	37,127	5	33,868	34	R	5	20	70	1	29	16	0	9	1	14
143	40,438	10	35,571	24	R	7	26	61	4	38	21	1	54	1	27
144	35,205	1	29,421	26	R	6	17	63	-4	36	12	0	6	0	-1
145	45,667	13	33,667	30	R	7	27	68	8	31	25	0	43	1	46
146	36,008	10	34,954	34	R	6	30	58	3	40	21	0	53	1	6
147	48,629	36	38,167	25	R	5	18	81	32	18	58	0	48	1	80
148	36,167	-2	29,226	25	U	11	19	28	-21	70	7	1	32	1	2
149	35,714	6	28,127	28	U	12	23	23	-11	74	11	1	33	2	19
150	39,872	9	44,859	36	S	6	27	74	2	23	34	1	63	1	59

Note: U=urban, S=suburban, R=rural, M=mixed, HH=households.

Georgia State House Districts: Demographic Data (cont.)

House District	Population		Average HH Income		District Type	Unempl. Rate	College Educ.	White (non-Hispanic)		African American		Asian American		Hispanic American	
	1997	+/-	($)	+/-		(%)	(%)	(%)	+/-	(%)	+/-	(%)	+/-	(%)	+/-
Georgia	7,460,487	15	48,918	33	M	6	35	68	12	28	20	2	63	2	51
151	35,587	-1	41,687	32	U	7	33	42	-11	56	7	1	35	1	22
152	38,104	5	45,052	23	U	5	44	67	-7	26	38	3	49	4	53
153	42,377	13	71,161	28	S	4	54	89	9	7	48	2	75	1	43
154	48,913	8	36,492	31	R	6	23	63	6	31	11	1	7	5	25
155	38,329	6	34,566	32	R	6	22	68	1	28	17	0	21	4	32
156	37,551	6	36,279	44	R	7	17	65	0	34	17	0	-25	1	7
157	38,965	11	37,487	39	N.A.	8	18	64	5	33	22	0	-5	2	34
158	35,541	-2	33,372	44	R	10	24	43	-11	49	5	2	20	6	23
159	38,247	10	37,134	40	R	8	19	51	5	48	16	0	14	1	24
160	35,804	3	32,183	36	R	6	18	54	-4	42	13	0	-14	3	25
161	38,723	1	38,782	38	N.A.	11	28	33	-5	66	5	0	42	0	10
162	33,795	-4	30,773	30	U	13	18	32	-21	66	6	0	8	1	8
163	33,642	3	53,719	41	U	5	45	74	-3	23	21	1	50	1	48
164	37,615	6	34,875	41	R	6	17	52	-1	45	13	0	-19	3	26
165	37,069	6	44,586	51	R	6	27	65	0	29	17	1	39	4	34
166	41,806	9	33,989	35	R	5	16	76	5	20	22	0	-15	4	32
167	40,765	14	38,402	43	R	7	21	69	8	28	27	0	33	2	40
168	35,515	0	34,565	34	R	6	22	70	-4	29	12	0	29	1	24
169	45,437	15	34,254	31	R	6	16	85	13	14	30	0	-31	1	31
170	40,015	4	33,602	29	R	5	17	76	0	22	17	0	-10	1	21
171	31,852	15	31,934	22	R	7	22	70	10	27	25	0	5	3	50
172	45,598	26	37,143	38	R	11	32	49	14	41	35	3	73	7	60
173	36,749	6	34,561	28	R	6	23	51	-3	47	15	1	50	1	31
174	38,900	7	56,644	35	R	3	42	83	3	15	28	1	53	1	47
175	47,317	43	36,549	18	R	7	32	71	36	24	58	2	101	3	95
176	38,277	13	36,355	33	R	7	22	66	6	31	30	1	30	2	46
177	41,291	15	43,831	38	R	8	37	54	9	43	21	1	66	1	41
178	36,953	4	36,246	37	R	6	21	66	-2	32	16	0	18	2	25
179	37,241	6	36,441	35	R	5	23	60	0	38	16	0	-13	2	30
180	38,917	9	39,679	47	R	5	26	57	2	41	18	0	-9	1	40

Note: U=urban, S=suburban, R=rural, M=mixed, HH=households.

HAWAII

Nowhere else in the United States do Asians and Pacific Islanders exert as much influence as they do in Hawaii. They comprise 59 percent of the state's population, more than five times the percentage in any other state. Looked at another way, the percentage of Asians in Hawaii is roughly the same as the percentage of whites in Texas. The top forty-one state house districts in the United States by Asian percentage, and forty-seven of the top fifty, are in Hawaii. Of course, given that Hawaii *is* a Pacific island and is the state geographically closest to Asia, it is not surprising that people from these areas should predominate.

The Asian population is ethnically diverse and includes a mixture of native Hawaiians (who account for about 20 percent of the state's population), Japanese (Hawaii is a popular tourist destination on both sides of the Pacific), Chinese, and Filipinos. The current governor, Ben Cayetano, is the only governor of predominantly Filipino extraction in American history, and both of Hawaii's U.S. senators are of Japanese ancestry.

The flip side is that Hawaii has the smallest percentage of whites and one of the smallest percentages of African Americans. Only 30 percent of Hawaii's residents are white, and in only three of its fifty-one house districts do they constitute a majority—two on Oahu, one on Maui. The Twenty-eighth House District in Honolulu, which is 85 percent Asian (the highest Asian percentage of any district in the country), is only 8 percent white. The only significant concentration of African Americans on the islands is in the Forty-fifth House District, which takes in the large western end of Oahu and is 13 percent black.

Population has been growing rapidly on the Big Island of Hawaii and on Maui. It has been falling on Oahu, the state's most populous island, a development that may parallel the suburbanization that is taking place elsewhere in the country. Hawaii is the third-wealthiest state after Connecticut and New Jersey, has one of the highest percentages of college graduates, and has the third-lowest rate of unemployment. The wealthiest districts are located on the eastern end of Honolulu (the Fifteenth, Sixteenth, and Seventeenth House Districts) and in Pacific Palisades (the Thirty-fifth District). Not far away, in downtown Honolulu, are two of Hawaii's poorest districts, the Twenty-fifth and the Thirtieth.

Hawaii is perhaps the country's most Democratic, and liberal, state; the party holds the governorship and all four seats in Congress and has carried Hawaii in every presidential election since statehood, with the exception of the Reagan landslide in 1984. Republicans have made some gains in the state house of representatives, picking up five seats in 1996, but still trail, 39–14. Republican state senators can caucus in a phone booth; Democrats hold a 23–2 edge in that body. The situation seems unlikely to change in Hawaii anytime soon.

Hawaii is also one of only two states that does not have a lottery and that prohibits all forms of gambling—perhaps from a belief that those who live there have already won.

HAWAII
State Senate Districts

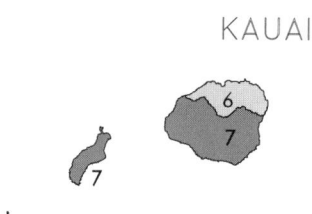

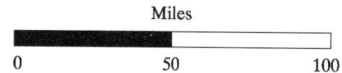

Population Growth ▢ -7% to -2%   ▢ 0% to 4%   ▢ 5% to 11%   ▢ 18% to 27%

OAHU

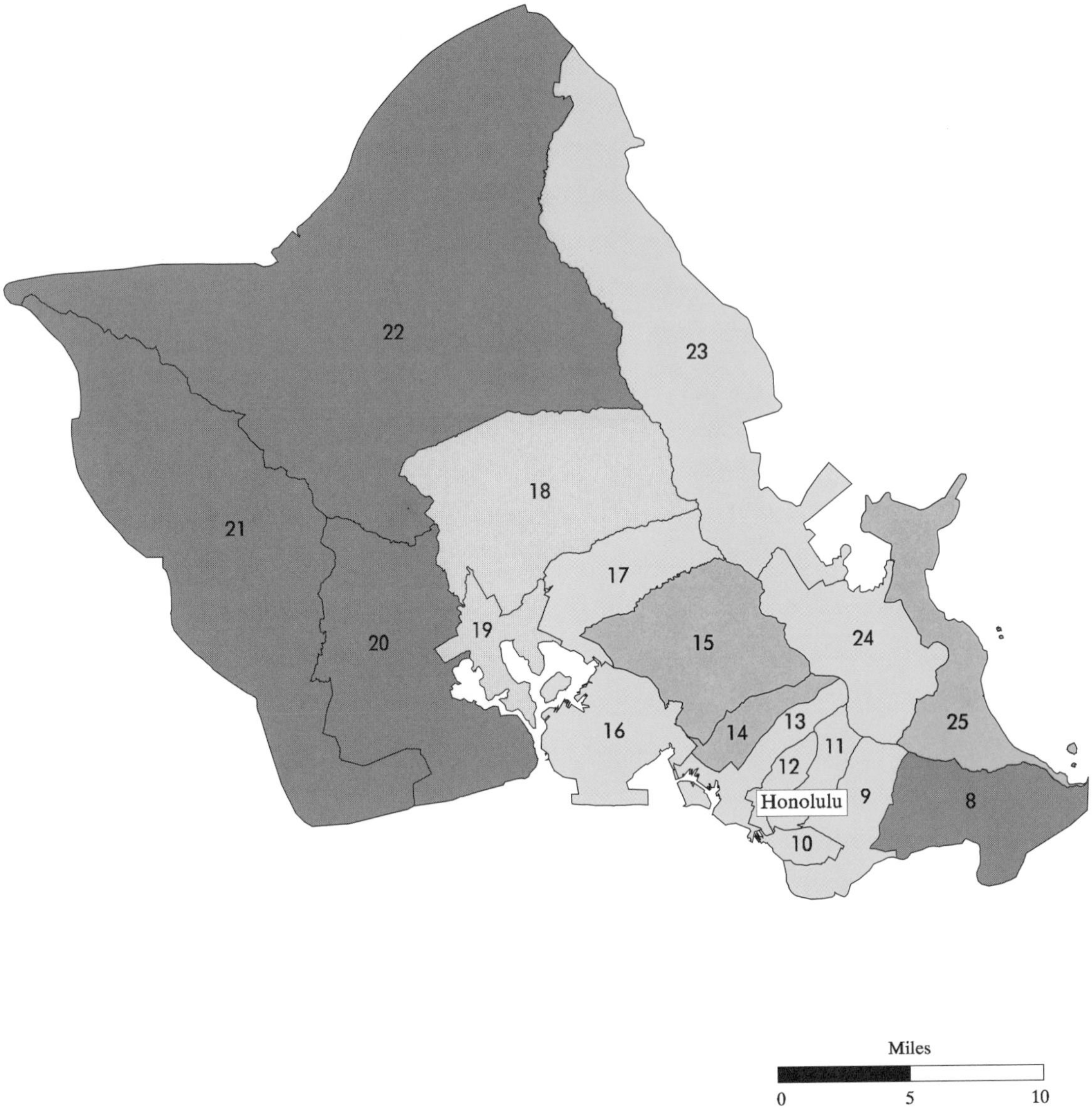

22

23

21

18

17

20

19

15

24

16

14

13

25

12

11

Honolulu

9

8

10

Miles

0   5   10

Population Growth   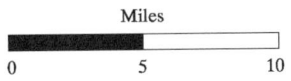 -7% to -2%   0% to 4%   5% to 11%   18% to 27%

Hawaii State Senate Districts: Demographic Data

Senate District	Population 1997	+/-	Average HH Income ($)	+/-	District Type	Unempl. Rate (%)	College Educ. (%)	White (non-Hispanic) (%)	+/-	African American (%)	+/-	Asian American (%)	+/-	Hispanic American (%)	+/-
Hawaii	1,185,546	7	64,104	33	M	4	44	30	2	2	0	59	7	9	31
1	48,842	24	54,791	33	R	4	40	39	21	0	27	47	22	12	50
2	42,996	2	44,589	21	R	5	45	23	-6	1	3	64	2	11	27
3	48,099	24	42,846	22	R	6	37	43	15	1	30	45	28	10	43
4	45,293	19	64,748	42	R	3	33	26	9	0	31	65	21	8	43
5	38,485	6	63,747	37	R	3	38	27	-1	0	8	60	5	12	35
6	50,210	19	59,691	39	R	5	34	52	14	1	24	36	20	10	36
7	41,759	8	60,155	35	R	3	35	27	4	0	0	59	7	13	27
8	43,919	5	106,710	30	U	2	63	35	0	0	-11	61	7	3	25
9	42,526	1	87,219	32	U	3	54	26	-4	0	-15	69	2	4	27
10	43,088	2	51,312	26	U	3	46	32	-3	1	1	62	3	5	17
11	40,927	0	58,590	29	U	2	55	20	-6	1	-10	75	1	4	29
12	41,452	1	53,464	29	U	3	53	32	-4	1	-1	62	3	4	17
13	44,152	1	57,390	33	U	3	43	20	-5	1	-5	72	1	6	25
14	40,686	-2	60,260	29	U	4	32	9	-8	0	-16	84	-3	6	9
15	47,908	-3	68,197	31	U	3	38	17	-7	2	-9	73	-2	7	8
16	75,037	4	59,392	38	U	4	41	37	-1	7	-1	45	5	10	31
17	46,724	2	81,916	38	S	2	50	20	-2	1	-3	72	2	6	19
18	57,425	27	74,138	36	S	3	57	33	22	4	23	56	30	6	30
19	54,136	18	61,487	31	S	5	30	14	6	2	4	72	17	12	45
20	51,490	9	63,556	34	S	4	39	29	3	2	4	56	10	12	25
21	48,048	11	51,098	36	S	8	26	23	0	2	-4	57	10	17	35
22	62,467	7	52,592	33	S	6	33	36	1	10	4	41	6	12	34
23	37,940	2	73,100	37	S	3	48	29	-4	1	-11	59	2	10	37
24	44,165	4	80,777	34	S	2	52	31	-2	1	-4	60	5	7	26
25	48,034	-7	77,615	41	S	3	49	49	-13	4	-27	37	-1	10	11

Note: U=urban, S=suburban, R=rural, M=mixed, HH=households.

HAWAII
State House Districts

KAUAI

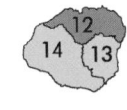

12
14 13

14

OAHU

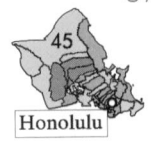

45

Honolulu

9 10

MAUI

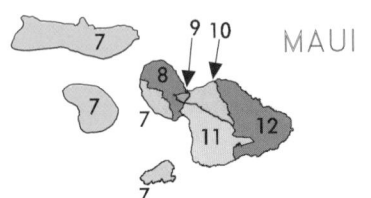

7

8

7

7

11

12

7

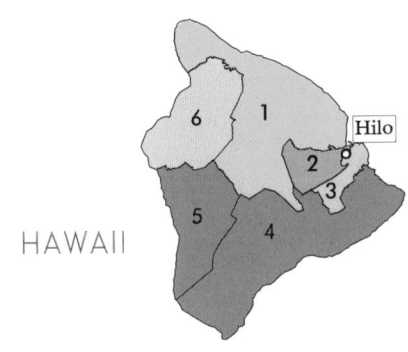

6

1

Hilo

2

3

5

4

HAWAII

Miles

0   50   100

Population Growth   ☐ -11% to 3%   ☐ 4% to 13%   ☐ 18% to 28%   ☐ 41% to 42%

OAHU

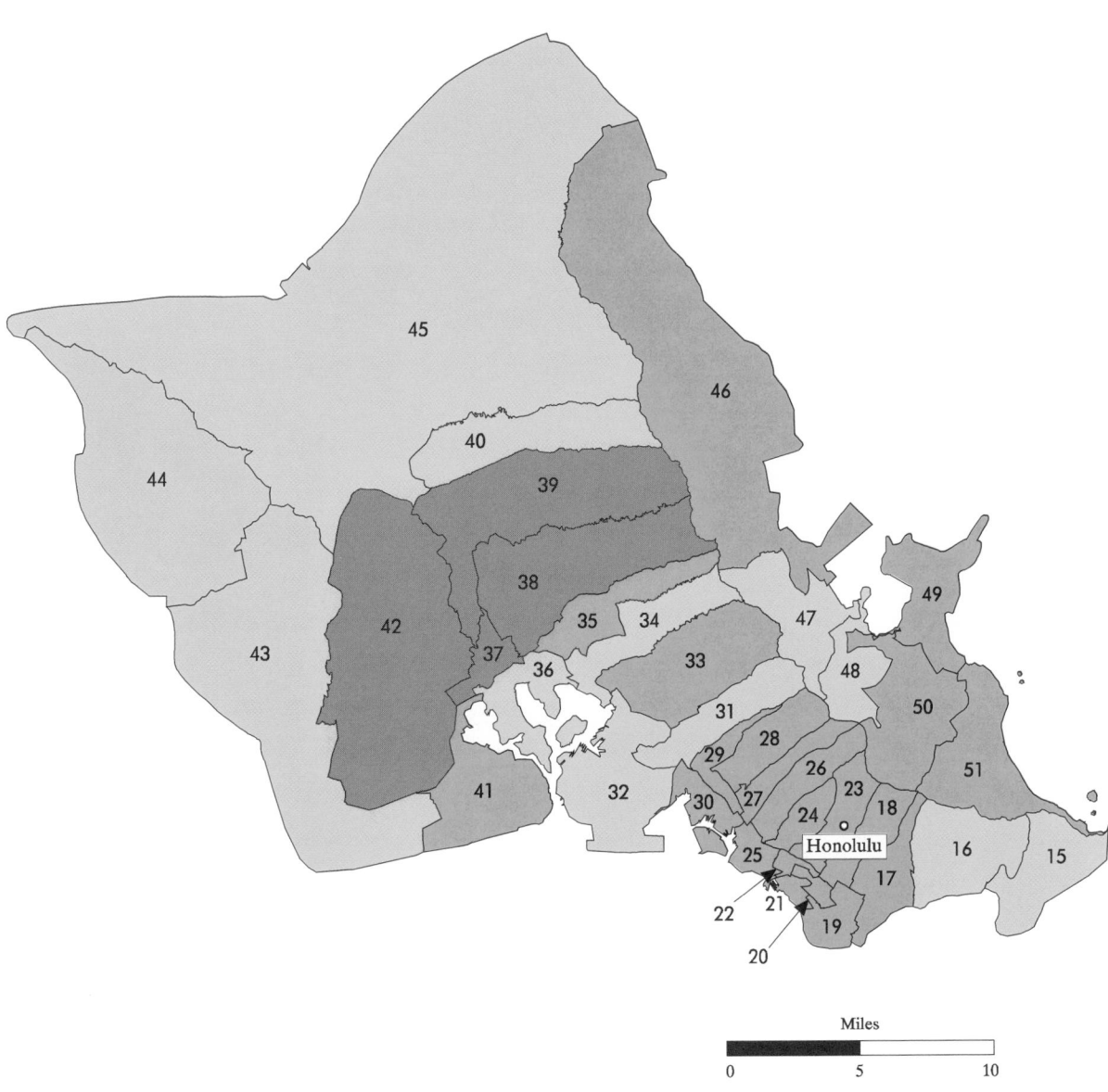

Population Growth   ⬜ -11% to 3%   ⬜ 4% to 13%   ⬛ 18% to 28%

Hawaii State House Districts: Demographic Data

House District	Population 1997	+/-	Average HH Income ($)	+/-	District Type	Unempl. Rate (%)	College Educ. (%)	White (non-Hispanic) (%)	+/-	African American (%)	+/-	Asian American (%)	+/-	Hispanic American (%)	+/-
Hawaii	1,185,546	7	64,104	33	M	4	44	30	2	2	0	59	7	9	31
1	21,110	7	41,695	26	R	5	30	27	-1	0	0	58	7	13	29
2	21,208	-1	43,691	25	R	4	44	25	-10	1	-4	62	0	12	20
3	21,781	5	45,537	17	R	5	47	22	-1	0	17	66	3	10	36
4	24,128	25	31,330	16	R	7	31	38	14	1	34	48	28	12	53
5	23,971	23	53,769	25	R	4	43	48	17	0	24	43	28	8	31
6	27,732	42	64,556	31	R	3	48	48	33	0	49	39	45	11	75
7	20,818	13	57,290	38	R	3	26	20	-2	0	21	72	16	7	35
8	24,165	25	70,352	44	R	3	38	31	16	1	36	59	27	9	49
9	18,296	-1	60,559	34	R	2	34	13	-16	0	0	76	-2	11	33
10	19,638	13	67,281	38	R	3	41	40	4	0	16	47	16	12	36
11	26,251	41	83,793	59	R	3	45	60	33	1	75	31	55	8	63
12	24,387	18	57,923	39	R	4	37	44	11	0	25	42	20	13	43
13	20,684	11	63,196	35	R	4	37	28	4	0	-4	60	11	11	31
14	21,504	6	57,182	34	R	3	34	27	4	0	4	58	4	14	24
15	21,564	5	98,601	30	U	3	61	37	0	1	-18	58	7	4	27
16	19,304	5	93,205	27	U	2	62	33	0	0	1	63	7	3	24
17	19,942	2	130,098	39	U	2	63	34	-4	0	-11	63	4	2	19
18	21,244	2	62,998	30	U	3	47	16	-4	0	-22	77	2	6	28
19	21,793	2	65,715	27	U	3	47	31	-2	1	2	63	2	4	25
20	19,902	1	46,425	27	U	3	44	17	-5	1	-7	77	2	5	21
21	21,609	2	48,096	24	U	4	52	50	-3	2	3	43	7	4	12
22	18,290	1	38,523	24	U	2	42	19	-4	1	-4	76	2	4	19
23	19,529	0	87,999	34	U	2	66	23	-6	0	-16	72	0	4	33
24	20,342	1	63,864	33	U	2	59	30	-6	1	0	64	3	4	19
25	21,910	3	46,092	28	U	3	46	26	-4	1	-4	65	4	7	32
26	19,562	0	76,543	38	U	2	52	22	-6	1	-7	72	1	5	17
27	21,415	-1	67,534	31	U	2	38	12	-7	0	-14	82	-1	5	16
28	20,287	-3	60,911	24	U	3	25	8	-9	0	-18	85	-3	7	4
29	21,275	-3	44,012	24	U	5	26	11	-12	3	-12	79	-3	7	8
30	18,381	-6	40,808	23	U	6	22	9	-11	1	-16	79	-7	10	15
31	27,988	6	74,411	40	U	2	46	19	3	3	3	71	6	7	12
32	47,368	4	51,966	34	S	5	41	48	-1	10	-1	30	5	11	38
33	25,340	0	72,310	34	S	3	50	29	-4	2	-6	60	0	9	18
34	20,326	5	86,775	38	S	2	53	18	-1	2	0	74	5	5	16
35	21,399	0	94,147	41	S	2	48	14	-3	1	-5	80	0	5	12
36	25,948	13	55,191	32	S	5	26	16	1	3	1	69	14	11	33
37	25,299	25	64,623	31	S	5	32	12	14	2	9	72	22	14	57
38	26,901	28	76,287	38	S	2	60	30	24	3	27	61	32	5	17
39	30,519	25	72,108	35	S	4	54	36	20	5	21	51	27	7	40
40	23,736	11	55,870	35	S	6	29	19	3	4	3	64	10	12	39
41	26,037	2	54,444	33	S	5	32	31	-3	3	0	53	2	12	15
42	26,263	18	71,711	33	S	4	44	26	11	2	11	60	18	11	37
43	25,612	9	55,744	42	S	9	22	24	-2	3	-2	57	10	16	32
44	22,436	13	46,588	29	S	7	30	23	4	1	-8	56	11	19	38
45	39,989	4	49,394	31	S	5	36	45	0	13	4	28	0	13	31
46	18,251	-2	66,803	37	S	4	42	29	-9	1	-20	58	-3	11	40
47	21,279	8	84,591	38	S	3	56	32	1	1	-3	57	8	9	37
48	22,150	6	71,781	30	S	2	47	23	0	1	-6	68	6	8	29
49	27,717	-11	73,458	39	S	3	48	56	-16	6	-28	27	-1	10	8
50	19,755	1	86,560	36	S	3	56	42	-3	1	-3	50	3	6	15

Note: U=urban, S=suburban, R=rural, M=mixed, HH=households.

House District	Population		Average HH Income		District Type	Unempl. Rate	College Educ.	White (non-Hispanic)		African American		Asian American		Hispanic American	
	1997	+/-	($)	+/-		(%)	(%)	(%)	+/-	(%)	+/-	(%)	+/-	(%)	+/-
Hawaii	1,185,546	7	64,104	33	M	4	44	30	2	2	0	59	7	9	31
51	18,949	-1	84,115	43	S	4	49	36	-6	1	-13	54	-1	9	19

Hawaii State House Districts: Demographic Data (cont.)

Note: U=urban, S=suburban, R=rural, M=mixed, HH=households.

IDAHO

There is irony in the fact that Idaho, now regarded as one of the most Republican and conservative states in the country, has produced three notable U.S. senators from three different political parties. Republican William E. Borah was a national figure in the 1910s and 1920s, a brilliant orator and staunch opponent of the League of Nations. More recently, Democratic senator Frank Church chaired hearings on misconduct by the CIA in the seventies and made a respectable though too-late run for the presidential nomination in 1976. In between was Sen. Glen Taylor, who became an early critic of nuclear proliferation and who served as Henry Wallace's running mate on the Progressive Party ticket in 1948 (and gained some notoriety at the time for singing his acceptance speech to the convention). Clearly, Idaho appreciates mavericks.

Indeed, there are many un-ironed corners here. The state, which made its reputation by pulling gold and silver from the ground, now has a reputation for pulling something decidedly less glamorous—potatoes. One of its largest ethnic groups is the Basques. And on a more ominous note, Idaho is home to the ultra-right-wing Aryan Nations (its national headquarters are in Hayden Lake) and earlier this decade was the site of the infamous FBI shoot-out at Ruby Ridge.

Idaho has been very much a part of the Rocky Mountain surge of the 1990s; it is the third-fastest-growing state in the country. The population here has grown 20 percent in seven years, perhaps enough to earn it another U.S. House seat after the next round of reapportionment. Two state house districts have grown by 50 percent or more during that time and are among the fastest-growing districts in the country: the Fourteenth, near Boise, and the Second, near Coeur d'Alene. The city of Boise,

in fact, grew by 16.4 percent from 1990 to 1994. Only twelve cities in the country with at least one hundred thousand people grew faster.

Household income in Idaho is also growing at a rate faster than the national average, fastest in the districts around Boise. However, the state has no great extremes of wealth and poverty as do Missouri and many other states in the East and Midwest. The wealthiest sections include all the districts in and around Boise in the west and Idaho Falls in the east. The poorest sections include the Twentieth House District, which takes in much of the sheep-grazing and fruit-growing region in the far southwest, and the logging areas in the mid-panhandle, where the unemployment rate is 13 percent.

Race is not an issue in Idaho politics. Twenty-six of its thirty-five senate districts and twenty-seven of its seventy house districts are at least 90 percent white. Although Idaho has one of the fastest-growing black populations, this trend merely shows the mirage of small numbers; according to the Census Bureau, there are still fewer than ten thousand African Americans in the entire state. The only district with any Hispanic concentration is the Tenth, northwest of Boise, where migrant farm workers account for most of the 24-percent-Hispanic population.

Idaho has thirty-five legislative districts and elects one senator and two representatives from each, a practice used in many other states. Although Democrats have been able to win elections here (the state had Democratic governors continuously from 1970 to 1994), the many new arrivals have, if anything, made the state more conservative, as the governor, all the congressional representatives, and almost all statewide elected officials are now Republicans. In the legislature, Democrats have lost seven seats in the senate and nine in the house since 1992.

IDAHO
State Legislative Districts

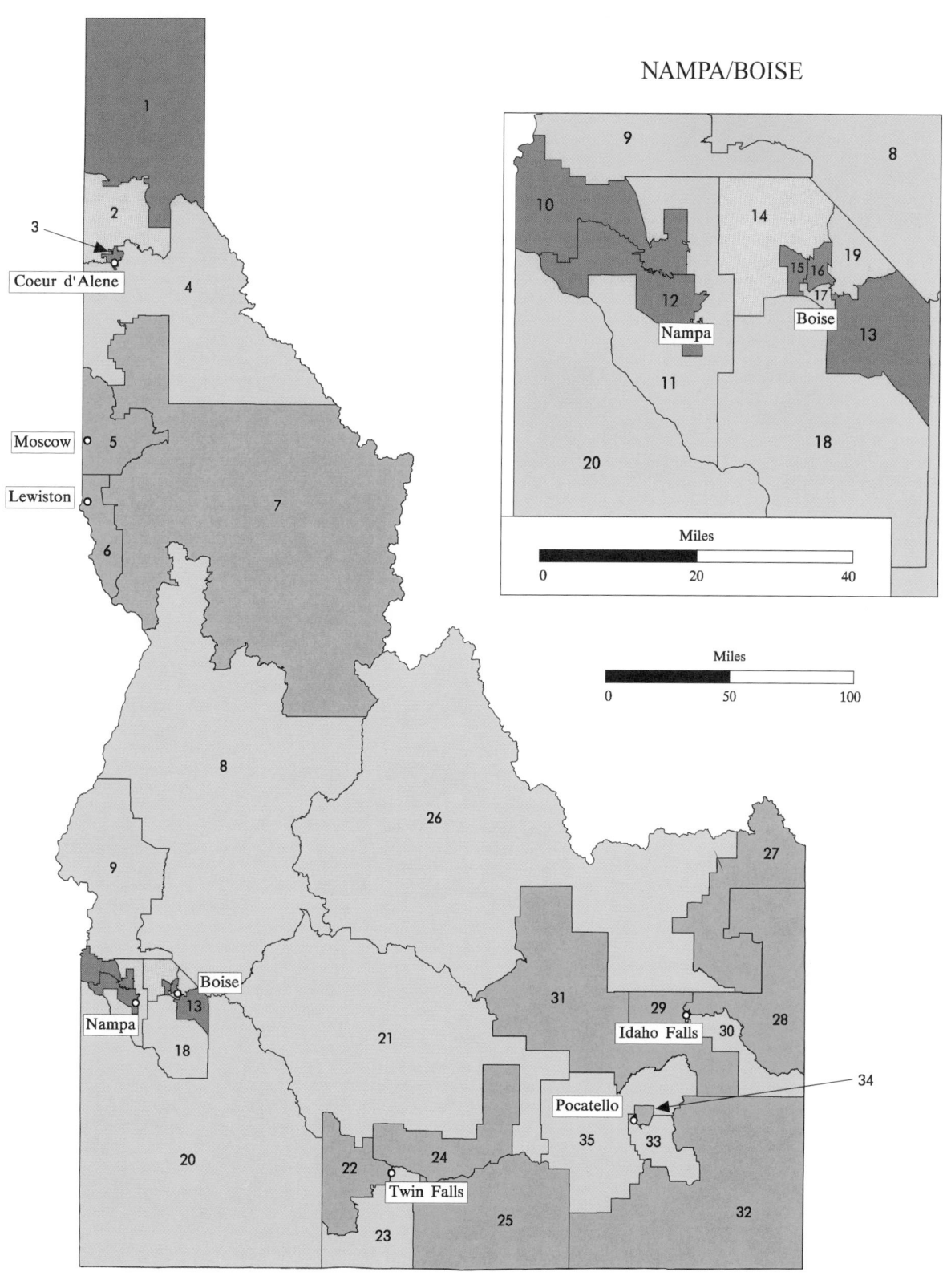

NAMPA/BOISE

Population Growth ▢ -1% to 13%   ▢ 15% to 24%   ▢ 27% to 38%   ▢ 50% to 56%

Idaho State Legislative Districts: Demographic Data

Legis. District	Population		Average HH Income		District Type	Unempl. Rate	College Educ.	White (non-Hispanic)		African American		Asian American		Hispanic American	
	1997	+/-	($)	+/-		(%)	(%)	(%)	+/-	(%)	+/-	(%)	+/-	(%)	+/-
Idaho	1,210,930	20	44,254	40	R	6	36	91	19	0	54	1	30	6	42
1	39,061	27	39,794	46	R	10	32	96	27	0	57	0	4	2	53
2	45,643	50	40,310	41	R	11	31	97	50	0	92	0	55	2	79
3	38,794	37	44,473	43	R	6	36	97	37	0	73	1	50	2	76
4	36,206	16	44,457	45	R	9	34	95	15	0	4	0	11	2	44
5	32,099	9	40,802	43	R	6	57	94	9	1	31	3	18	2	33
6	33,237	9	42,006	36	R	7	37	95	9	0	46	1	16	1	32
7	34,062	13	35,121	29	R	13	28	93	13	0	48	0	-25	1	20
8	33,479	24	38,206	30	R	10	30	96	24	0	-29	0	2	3	41
9	35,288	21	33,343	27	R	8	23	89	20	0	132	1	27	9	42
10	38,799	37	36,439	37	R	6	22	74	30	0	113	1	46	24	60
11	36,833	19	39,708	40	R	6	27	86	16	0	105	1	35	12	38
12	39,698	29	40,887	40	R	5	29	88	27	0	102	1	55	10	46
13	37,065	30	64,423	62	U	4	52	94	29	1	71	2	48	3	62
14	43,652	56	56,642	53	S	3	42	95	55	0	98	1	76	3	97
15	41,922	38	65,190	50	S	3	45	94	36	1	79	2	55	3	69
16	39,299	31	49,312	52	U	5	42	94	30	0	69	1	53	4	66
17	35,271	19	46,789	44	U	4	37	93	18	1	44	2	39	4	46
18	34,614	16	61,206	51	S	5	40	94	15	0	39	1	22	4	51
19	34,722	17	58,220	51	U	4	51	93	16	1	66	2	35	4	47
20	33,811	17	32,270	17	R	6	30	82	14	3	29	2	29	12	43
21	34,307	23	55,184	48	R	4	42	93	22	0	-52	0	18	6	42
22	28,804	11	35,867	26	R	4	27	91	9	0	29	1	22	7	34
23	33,741	17	40,235	30	R	4	33	91	16	0	18	1	28	7	41
24	30,938	12	36,697	25	R	6	24	85	10	0	214	0	-3	13	29
25	30,005	10	36,604	26	R	9	27	80	6	0	131	0	1	19	32
26	32,598	15	38,504	31	R	5	32	93	14	0	180	0	-14	6	39
27	28,363	-1	37,304	28	R	7	41	94	-2	0	92	1	-2	4	19
28	28,960	7	38,466	25	R	5	32	92	6	0	9	0	2	7	33
29	30,369	12	45,054	32	R	5	46	91	10	1	43	1	24	7	41
30	32,920	19	53,370	36	R	5	51	95	19	1	48	1	34	3	28
31	32,192	10	39,889	24	R	5	34	89	8	0	124	1	14	9	29
32	30,505	11	38,509	35	R	8	32	97	10	0	42	0	-24	3	37
33	31,771	15	42,286	41	R	6	36	92	14	1	62	1	29	5	46
34	29,968	10	44,996	41	R	6	46	91	8	2	61	2	27	5	31
35	31,934	16	36,596	26	R	8	30	78	16	0	88	1	24	12	32

Note: U=urban, S=suburban, R=rural, M=mixed, HH=households.

ILLINOIS

Illinois claims to be a bellwether, the representative American state, and in many ways it is. In an uncanny number of demographic categories, Illinois is almost exactly at the national average. When such a state changes, then, it should be of more than passing interest to the rest of the country.

Illinois has recuperated, or at least stabilized, after a rough twenty years. The state's population grew just 3 percent during the 1970s, and not at all during the 1980s. But in the first seven years of the 1990s, it has grown by 4 percent—a small increase, but still better than the growth rate in other Rust Belt behemoths such as New York, Pennsylvania, Ohio, and Michigan. As Pennsylvania's population continues to decline, the Census Bureau projects that Illinois will become the fifth-largest state by early in the next century.

The state's population gains have occurred almost entirely in Chicago's outer suburbs. Eleven Illinois state house districts have grown by at least 20 percent, ten of them in Kane, Will, DuPage, Lake, Kendall, or McHenry Counties (the other district, the Forty-ninth, includes Schaumburg, at the outer edge of Cook County). The original ring suburbs—Cicero, Des Plaines, Skokie, Evanston—are full, and many are developing urban-type problems of their own. So residents, predominantly white, have moved still farther out to places like Aurora and Elgin, as many as forty miles from the Loop. Increasingly, they commute not to jobs downtown but to other suburbs.

Population loss, on the other hand, has been concentrated in Cook County and East St. Louis. Downstate farming counties have either grown not at all or by small amounts. What Chicago has seen, and what many other states are seeing, is a hollowing out of the urban core and a widening of the suburban doughnuts around them.

The racial composition of Chicago is also changing. Illinois is 15 percent black, slightly above the national average but second only to New York among nonsouthern states. Its African-American population is overwhelmingly centered in Chicago, the legacy of the great migration of southern blacks in search of industrial jobs after World War II. Today, eight state house dis[tricts in] the city are more than 70 percent African Am[erican,] many of them appallingly poor. To the extent bla[cks are] migrating, it is to some of the older, closer-in s[uburbs] that whites are leaving.

What is changing the face of Chicago is its H[ispanic] population. Illinois is 10 percent Hispanic, but as [much] as 92 percent of that Hispanic population lives in [Chica]go and the surrounding suburban counties. An[d the] group's rapid rate of increase—27 percent durin[g the] decade—accounts for more than half the state's [total] population gain. The implications of these developm[ents] could be substantial. Although the state as a whole is [also] expected to age significantly in the coming decades, r[ural] counties without an influx of young families will g[row] older, while an increasingly black and Hispanic Chica[go] grows younger. As Cook County comes to cast a smal[ler] share of the state's vote, the current mayor, Richard M[.] Daley, will not have the same ability his father once ha[d] to influence state or even national elections by deliverin[g] the county to offset votes downstate. The days whe[n a] Daley could hope to control the city without Hispanic support have already ended.

Chicago's Hispanic population is not monolithic, though; it is roughly two-thirds Mexican and one-third Puerto Rican, and there has been some friction between the groups. There has also been friction between Hispanics and blacks in Chicago, most notably over the effect that creation of a Hispanic-majority congressional district would have on black political influence in surrounding districts. Certainly, this is not the last struggle between the groups.

The Illinois legislature has been one of the nation's battlegrounds. The Democrats controlled both chambers in 1990 but lost both in the Republican sweep of 1994. Two years later Democrats retook the house by the slimmest of margins, 60–58, while the GOP held on to the senate, 31–28. Both chambers were fiercely contested in 1998. Control of the governor's mansion may determine which party controls the legislature after the next round of reapportionment.

ILLINOIS
State Senate Districts

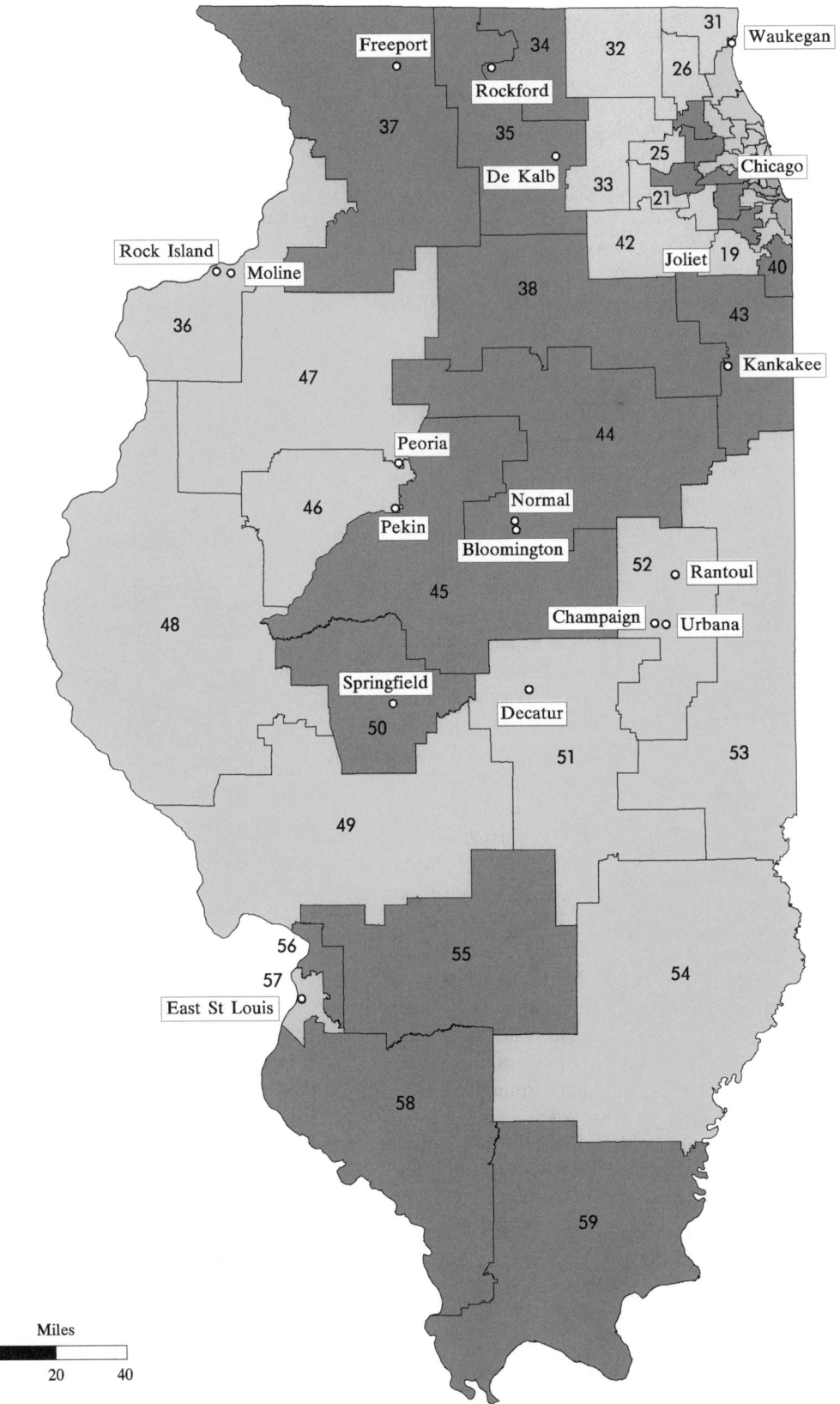

Freeport

34

32

31

Waukegan

Rockford

26

37

35

25

Chicago

De Kalb

33

21

Rock Island

42

Joliet

19

Moline

38

40

36

43

47

Kankakee

44

Peoria

52

Rantoul

Normal

46

Pekin

Bloomington

Champaign

Urbana

45

48

Springfield

Decatur

50

51

53

49

56

55

54

57

East St Louis

58

59

Miles

0   20   40

Population Growth   ■ -11% to -7%   ☐ -4% to 2%   ■ 3% to 9%   ☐ 15% to 28%

CHICAGO

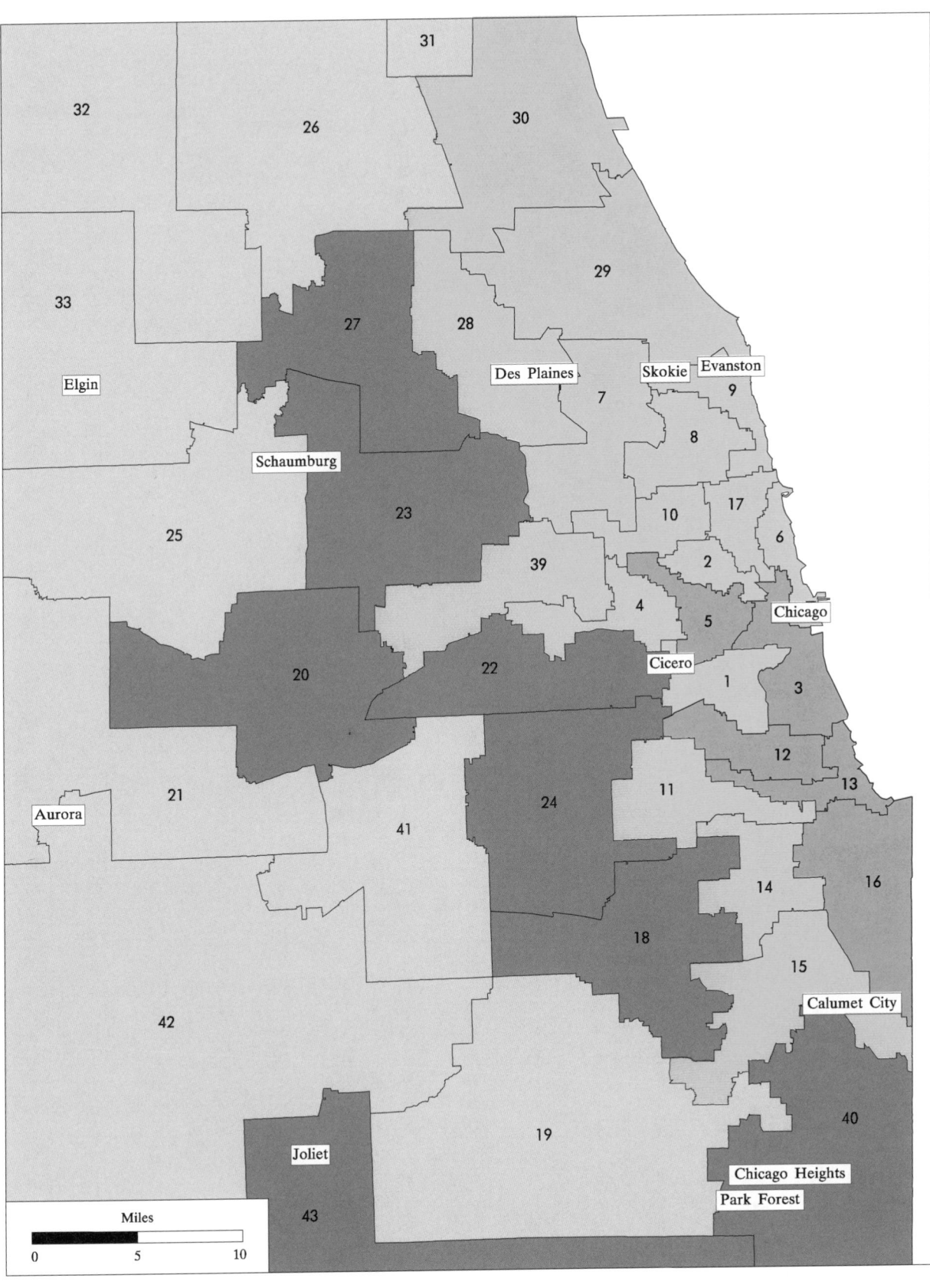

Population Growth   ■ -11% to -7%   ■ -4% to 2%   ■ 3% to 9%   □ 15% to 28%

Illinois State Senate Districts: Demographic Data

Senate District	Population 1997	+/-	Average HH Income ($)	+/-	District Type	Unempl. Rate (%)	College Educ. (%)	White (non-Hispanic) (%)	+/-	African American (%)	+/-	Asian American (%)	+/-	Hispanic American (%)	+/-
Illinois	11,893,640	4	54,426	33	M	6	39	72	0	15	7	3	26	10	27
1	187,023	-3	30,963	19	U	12	9	10	-46	5	12	1	0	84	6
2	184,934	-3	30,361	21	U	13	16	9	-57	12	31	1	-29	78	9
3	176,091	-9	34,540	46	U	17	29	19	-19	64	-10	8	3	9	10
4	188,733	-3	48,585	31	S	11	35	22	-22	71	3	1	5	6	28
5	173,229	-11	27,573	22	U	21	15	6	-39	79	-10	1	-12	14	1
6	197,660	2	87,313	41	U	4	73	74	-5	14	64	5	27	7	-2
7	191,412	-2	64,075	30	S	3	39	88	-6	1	70	6	32	5	51
8	194,823	1	50,655	23	U	6	44	64	-11	4	58	19	23	13	41
9	188,676	-2	47,147	25	U	6	54	41	-27	31	37	10	10	17	27
10	192,970	-1	43,092	23	U	7	27	66	-14	1	80	6	21	27	50
11	191,761	-1	43,659	23	U	9	22	57	-6	33	-1	1	20	9	54
12	176,728	-9	29,709	24	U	19	14	17	-26	65	-11	0	-6	17	32
13	175,785	-9	36,367	25	U	14	35	12	-38	76	-7	2	-7	10	36
14	185,330	-3	50,595	27	U	11	32	27	-15	69	1	0	-14	4	31
15	196,912	2	40,649	23	S	13	24	22	-25	71	13	0	-9	6	30
16	180,959	-7	38,932	22	U	13	25	14	-29	67	-5	0	-21	19	8
17	196,438	0	43,044	33	U	8	38	38	-24	12	58	10	11	39	20
18	201,964	4	58,529	29	S	4	37	90	0	3	71	2	37	5	51
19	238,503	25	69,301	33	S	4	46	85	21	9	53	2	56	3	68
20	207,850	8	76,098	30	S	3	62	88	5	2	16	5	38	4	42
21	240,707	24	72,143	30	S	3	58	84	21	5	33	4	60	7	61
22	202,161	5	59,911	28	S	5	39	76	-6	2	62	4	30	17	68
23	200,662	4	65,238	29	S	4	43	81	-2	2	39	7	33	10	38
24	203,072	4	64,138	32	S	5	39	87	0	4	59	2	36	7	45
25	237,742	22	73,622	33	R	3	49	83	17	2	60	6	49	8	51
26	235,113	21	93,484	42	S	3	55	87	16	1	78	3	51	8	68
27	198,729	3	69,646	33	S	3	53	82	-4	3	80	6	33	8	48
28	193,885	0	72,039	34	S	3	52	84	-5	2	75	7	29	7	46
29	198,015	2	138,706	39	S	3	70	85	-3	3	69	8	31	4	42
30	196,703	2	99,446	42	S	4	54	69	-4	13	14	4	29	14	25
31	229,168	19	67,842	40	S	4	45	82	14	7	42	3	45	8	58
32	248,407	28	67,471	26	R	3	44	94	27	0	32	1	55	4	63
33	228,194	17	63,222	31	M	4	39	78	11	4	35	3	44	15	53
34	213,868	9	46,243	25	U	6	35	81	7	11	15	1	30	6	40
35	202,295	5	48,148	28	R	4	39	92	4	2	17	2	29	3	40
36	193,970	0	42,920	31	M	7	32	87	-2	6	9	1	17	6	30
37	197,761	3	41,442	27	R	5	31	93	1	3	11	0	8	4	30
38	211,602	9	47,325	36	R	7	30	95	8	1	18	1	26	4	40
39	192,289	-1	61,011	30	S	4	41	80	-7	3	48	3	27	14	32
40	205,799	5	56,986	29	S	6	35	66	-8	26	44	1	20	7	34
41	223,568	15	76,013	30	S	3	55	83	10	6	45	7	43	4	50
42	238,239	23	60,581	30	S	5	37	78	18	5	34	1	55	15	46
43	209,580	8	43,113	29	M	8	27	67	1	23	21	1	18	9	44
44	203,763	6	50,427	40	M	4	44	92	5	4	16	1	32	2	34
45	205,098	4	47,129	32	R	5	33	98	4	1	5	0	9	1	35
46	192,928	0	38,381	33	U	8	28	84	-2	13	8	1	14	2	29
47	194,791	1	47,458	34	R	5	40	93	0	4	17	1	21	2	34
48	195,134	1	37,810	36	R	6	31	96	0	3	10	1	13	1	18
49	196,402	2	40,437	32	R	6	27	98	1	1	9	0	-5	1	23
50	209,808	8	48,894	35	U	4	43	90	7	8	20	1	34	1	41

Note: U=urban, S=suburban, R=rural, M=mixed, HH=households.

Illinois State Senate Districts: Demographic Data (cont.)

Senate District	Population		Average HH Income		District Type	Unempl. Rate	College Educ.	White (non-Hispanic)		African American		Asian American		Hispanic American	
	1997	+/-	($)	+/-		(%)	(%)	(%)	+/-	(%)	+/-	(%)	+/-	(%)	+/-
Illinois	11,893,640	4	54,426	33	M	6	39	72	0	15	7	3	26	10	27
51	194,356	0	43,547	30	M	6	32	91	-1	8	8	0	7	0	22
52	188,930	-3	46,197	38	U	4	55	83	-5	9	7	5	19	2	19
53	193,061	-1	39,629	35	R	7	30	93	-1	5	5	1	15	1	25
54	196,584	2	37,793	35	R	8	28	98	2	1	14	0	-11	0	11
55	204,680	6	44,841	33	R	6	31	92	3	5	48	1	15	1	32
56	204,711	5	45,195	28	S	7	35	88	2	9	33	1	32	2	43
57	183,952	-4	35,458	27	U	12	23	59	-9	38	2	0	9	2	24
58	199,017	3	36,308	24	R	8	33	91	2	5	11	1	18	1	27
59	200,146	3	33,294	31	R	11	25	93	3	6	9	0	-6	1	25

Note: U=urban, S=suburban, R=rural, M=mixed, HH=households.

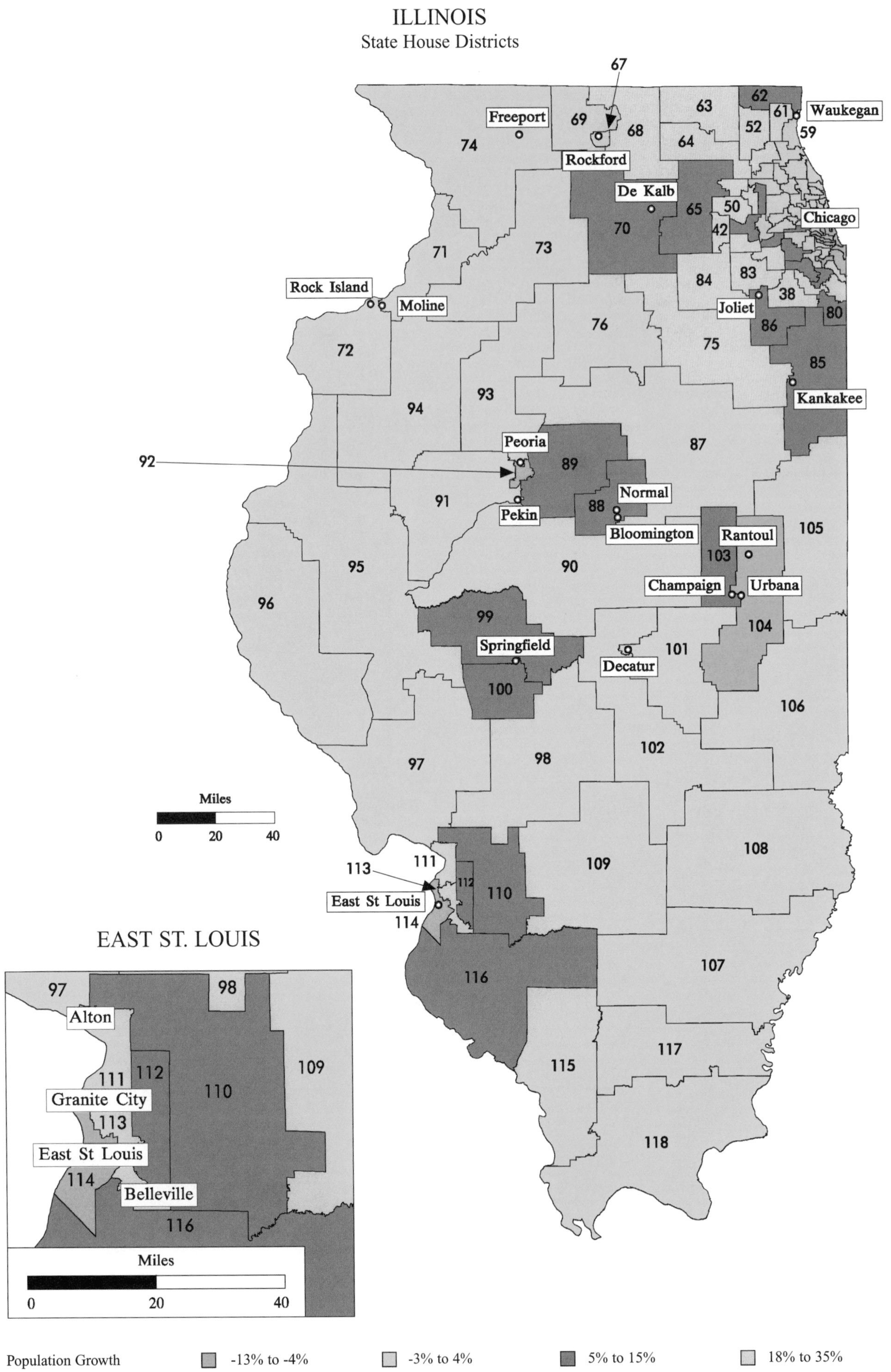

ILLINOIS
State House Districts

67

Freeport
69
68
74
Rockford
63
62
52
61
Waukegan
59

De Kalb
65
50
Chicago
70
42
84
83

Rock Island
Moline
72
73
71
76
38
Joliet
86
80
75
85
Kankakee

94
93
87
105

92
Peoria
89
91
Pekin
88
Normal
Bloomington
Rantoul
103
Champaign
Urbana
104

95
90
99
Springfield
101
Decatur
106

96
100
102

97
98
109
108

113
111
112
110
East St Louis
114
107

116
115
117

118

Miles
0   20   40

EAST ST. LOUIS

97
98
Alton
111
112
109
Granite City
110
113
East St Louis
114
Belleville
116

Miles
0   20   40

Population Growth ▢ -13% to -4%   ▢ -3% to 4%   ▢ 5% to 15%   ▢ 18% to 35%

CHICAGO

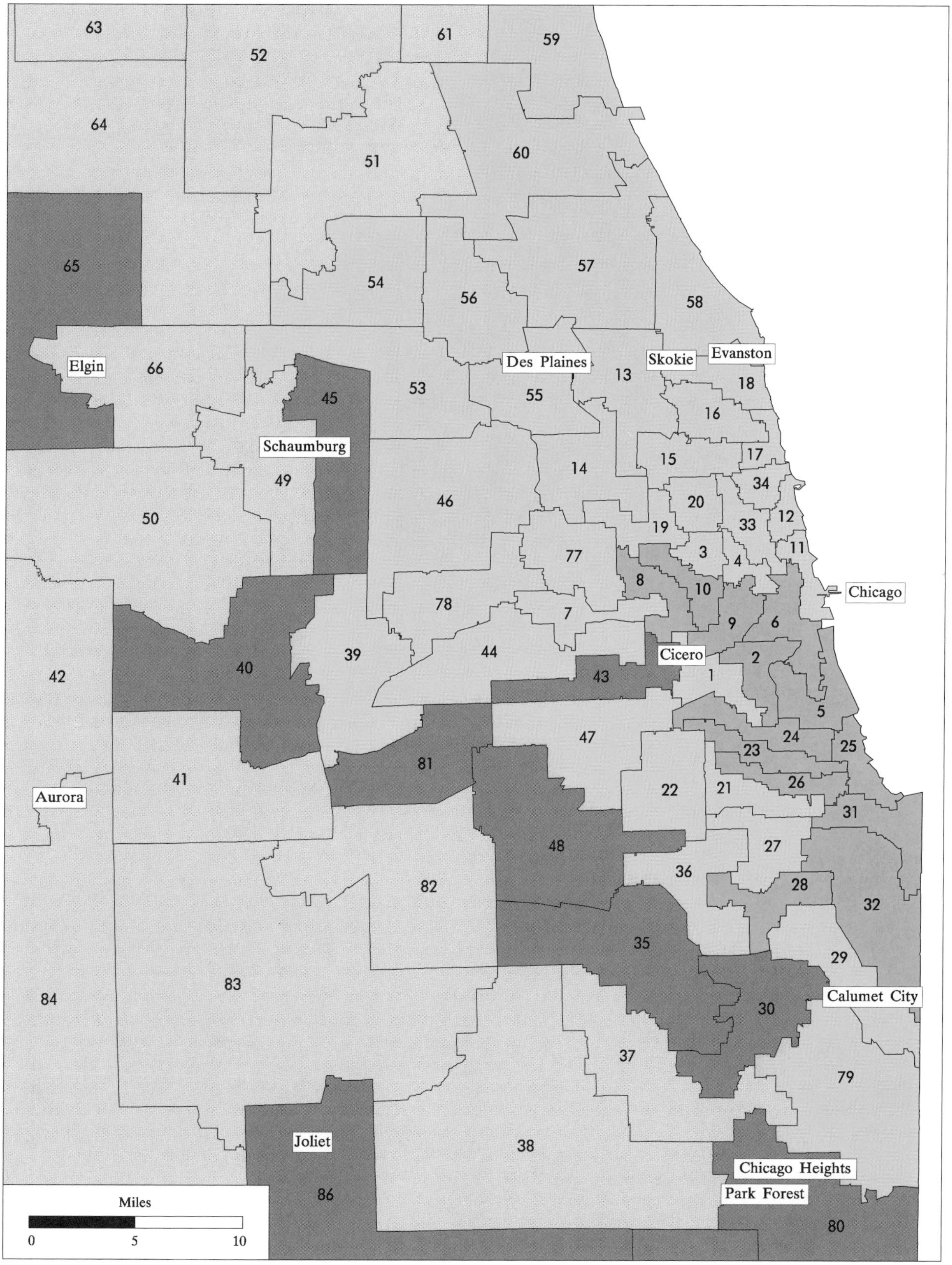

63

52

64

61

59

65

51

60

Elgin
66

54

56

57

58

45

53

Des Plaines
13

Skokie
18

Evanston

Schaumburg

55

16

49

46

14

15

17

34

50

19

20

33

12

77

3

4

11

78

8
10

Chicago

42

39

7

9

6

40

44

Cicero
2

1

5

43

47

23

24

25

81

22

21

26

31

41

Aurora

48

27

82

36

28

32

83

35

29

84

30

Calumet City

37

79

86

Joliet

38

Chicago Heights

Park Forest

80

Miles

0   5   10

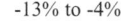

Illinois State House Districts: Demographic Data

House District	Population 1997	+/-	Average HH Income ($)	+/-	District Type	Unempl. Rate (%)	College Educ. (%)	White (non-Hispanic) (%)	+/-	African American (%)	+/-	Asian American (%)	+/-	Hispanic American (%)	+/-
Illinois	11,893,640	4	54,426	33	M	6	39	72	0	15	7	3	26	10	27
1	91,077	-3	32,847	16	U	12	9	12	-45	6	7	1	6	81	9
2	96,127	-4	29,315	20	U	13	9	9	-46	4	19	0	-7	86	4
3	94,820	-2	30,458	16	U	13	14	6	-66	12	17	1	-36	81	12
4	90,114	-3	30,267	26	U	12	18	11	-49	12	47	1	-20	75	5
5	85,114	-13	27,554	28	U	19	21	19	-24	64	-15	5	12	12	18
6	91,339	-5	40,756	59	U	15	36	19	-14	64	-4	11	0	6	-2
7	96,978	0	47,816	29	S	10	36	21	-27	71	11	2	2	5	21
8	92,012	-6	49,429	32	U	13	33	22	-18	70	-4	1	9	6	37
9	86,610	-13	24,207	25	U	24	14	8	-28	78	-13	1	-1	13	2
10	86,960	-10	31,160	20	U	19	15	5	-52	80	-7	1	-18	14	0
11	97,559	2	111,180	42	U	4	78	81	-4	11	75	4	34	4	7
12	100,389	2	62,958	39	U	4	68	67	-6	16	58	6	23	10	-5
13	96,331	-1	71,644	33	S	3	44	86	-5	0	88	9	32	4	50
14	95,081	-2	57,007	28	U	4	33	89	-6	1	64	3	32	7	51
15	97,201	0	49,308	24	U	6	39	67	-10	2	66	17	21	14	40
16	97,622	1	52,029	22	U	6	49	61	-12	5	56	20	24	13	43
17	93,457	-3	38,354	22	U	7	50	34	-34	29	47	12	6	24	25
18	95,219	-2	57,233	27	U	5	58	48	-21	33	30	9	15	11	30
19	97,322	0	44,656	22	U	6	25	75	-10	1	83	3	29	21	59
20	95,495	-1	41,507	24	U	7	30	57	-19	1	79	9	18	32	44
21	94,399	-2	39,058	21	U	13	23	23	-18	67	-1	1	4	9	55
22	97,362	1	47,773	24	U	5	21	89	-3	0	70	1	33	9	52
23	88,683	-8	31,275	23	U	18	14	18	-28	64	-11	0	-16	18	43
24	88,292	-9	28,082	24	U	20	13	16	-24	67	-11	0	5	16	23
25	86,731	-11	40,503	28	U	12	49	15	-32	79	-5	3	-5	2	5
26	88,989	-8	30,843	20	U	18	17	9	-45	73	-8	0	-15	17	42
27	95,054	-3	54,538	27	U	10	36	28	-17	69	4	0	-13	2	37
28	90,015	-4	46,396	27	U	12	28	27	-12	68	-2	0	-17	5	28
29	97,049	-1	40,160	21	S	13	24	24	-22	70	8	0	-7	5	16
30	99,878	5	41,141	24	S	13	24	21	-28	71	18	0	-11	8	41
31	88,223	-9	35,570	21	U	14	24	8	-42	67	-7	0	-47	25	3
32	92,961	-6	42,233	22	U	13	25	20	-23	67	-3	0	-10	13	17
33	98,933	0	47,842	35	U	8	34	37	-25	6	80	7	15	49	21
34	97,698	0	38,740	30	U	8	41	39	-23	17	51	13	9	30	18
35	102,300	6	65,161	29	S	4	38	90	2	4	66	2	39	4	51
36	99,762	2	52,471	28	S	4	36	90	-2	2	81	1	34	6	51
37	111,403	18	70,425	35	S	3	48	84	13	10	52	3	61	3	59
38	127,100	32	68,248	31	S	4	45	86	28	9	55	1	49	3	77
39	100,172	4	69,747	27	S	3	60	89	1	2	12	5	32	3	34
40	107,619	12	82,724	32	S	3	63	87	9	3	19	5	44	5	48
41	120,588	24	86,233	31	S	2	70	89	21	3	32	6	62	3	69
42	120,119	24	57,470	28	M	4	44	80	20	8	34	1	54	11	59
43	103,587	8	47,412	24	S	6	33	71	-6	0	94	2	38	27	72
44	98,309	1	72,376	31	S	4	45	82	-6	5	60	6	28	7	55
45	103,881	8	68,405	30	R	3	48	82	3	3	49	9	38	6	44
46	96,781	0	61,724	27	S	4	36	80	-6	1	8	5	26	14	36
47	102,575	3	60,698	31	S	5	39	84	-2	4	46	1	32	10	46
48	100,523	5	67,724	33	S	5	39	89	1	4	74	3	38	4	44
49	120,032	21	69,497	34	S	4	46	79	15	4	75	9	44	8	56
50	117,804	23	77,923	33	R	3	51	86	20	1	29	4	61	8	47

Note: U=urban, S=suburban, R=rural, M=mixed, HH=households.

Illinois State House Districts: Demographic Data (cont.)

House District	Population 1997	+/-	Average HH Income ($)	+/-	District Type	Unempl. Rate (%)	College Educ. (%)	White (non-Hispanic) (%)	+/-	African American (%)	+/-	Asian American (%)	+/-	Hispanic American (%)	+/-
Illinois	11,893,640	4	54,426	33	M	6	39	72	0	15	7	3	26	10	27
51	117,224	20	105,464	43	S	3	64	85	14	2	84	5	50	7	63
52	117,889	22	81,488	41	R	4	43	89	18	1	62	1	52	9	73
53	99,958	3	61,941	30	S	3	50	76	-6	4	80	9	33	11	49
54	98,771	3	77,781	35	S	3	56	88	-1	2	80	4	34	5	48
55	95,096	-1	63,457	31	S	3	48	79	-8	2	70	9	27	10	43
56	98,886	2	80,840	36	S	3	57	89	-2	1	84	5	35	5	50
57	99,489	2	129,745	38	S	3	64	84	-3	1	75	8	33	7	49
58	98,529	2	148,011	41	S	3	77	85	-2	4	67	9	30	2	25
59	100,187	2	91,840	47	U	5	46	54	-8	23	11	3	21	19	23
60	96,504	2	105,674	40	S	3	61	86	-2	2	51	5	34	8	32
61	116,839	22	74,035	41	S	3	52	81	16	5	50	4	50	9	61
62	112,413	15	60,972	38	S	5	36	83	11	8	37	1	32	7	54
63	118,029	22	57,861	24	R	4	35	94	20	0	1	1	44	5	64
64	130,402	35	76,268	26	R	3	51	95	34	0	53	2	60	3	62
65	111,790	14	71,009	32	S	4	42	88	11	2	18	1	39	8	48
66	116,404	21	56,331	32	U	5	36	69	12	6	42	4	46	21	55
67	94,654	-1	35,517	18	U	8	28	67	-8	24	14	2	17	7	30
68	119,194	19	55,681	26	S	4	40	92	17	2	32	1	46	4	56
69	97,594	3	51,878	29	S	4	34	94	1	3	20	1	32	2	39
70	104,701	8	44,330	27	R	4	44	91	6	2	13	2	28	4	40
71	97,145	1	43,982	31	M	6	33	89	-2	3	16	1	20	6	32
72	96,810	0	41,843	31	U	7	31	86	-2	8	6	1	14	5	27
73	98,965	4	39,203	23	R	6	31	91	2	2	10	0	4	6	31
74	98,798	2	43,629	31	R	5	31	94	1	4	12	0	12	1	24
75	114,411	19	53,139	34	R	6	32	96	18	1	27	1	35	2	60
76	97,191	-1	41,370	35	R	7	28	93	-2	1	1	1	17	5	32
77	97,054	-1	58,368	31	S	5	38	76	-8	4	53	2	25	17	32
78	95,351	-1	63,868	30	S	4	44	84	-5	1	36	4	28	10	31
79	101,956	4	53,868	27	S	5	34	70	-7	24	46	1	19	5	43
80	103,888	6	60,114	31	S	6	37	61	-8	28	42	1	21	10	30
81	104,531	7	79,076	29	S	3	60	87	4	2	14	7	35	4	39
82	119,038	23	72,994	32	S	3	49	79	17	10	53	7	53	5	57
83	119,565	23	67,353	31	S	4	43	88	20	4	44	2	60	5	63
84	118,674	22	53,820	28	M	5	31	69	16	6	27	1	44	24	43
85	106,502	9	43,270	34	M	7	27	74	5	22	23	0	16	3	44
86	103,077	7	42,942	24	U	8	27	59	-4	24	19	1	20	15	44
87	99,260	4	48,277	40	R	4	34	94	3	3	11	1	23	2	29
88	104,537	8	52,542	40	U	4	53	91	7	6	19	2	36	2	40
89	104,657	6	51,182	33	S	4	36	98	6	0	-19	0	20	1	44
90	100,425	3	42,892	32	R	6	30	97	2	1	8	0	-4	1	24
91	102,818	3	39,992	32	M	7	27	96	2	3	24	0	18	1	35
92	90,095	-4	36,564	34	U	9	30	71	-8	25	6	1	12	2	27
93	98,082	3	55,851	35	M	4	47	93	2	3	31	1	27	2	38
94	96,752	-1	38,722	31	R	7	32	93	-2	4	7	0	6	3	32
95	96,822	0	36,440	36	R	6	32	95	-1	3	7	1	15	1	15
96	98,312	1	39,094	37	R	6	30	97	1	2	14	0	9	0	25
97	97,545	2	42,968	30	R	6	31	98	1	1	13	0	-1	1	23
98	98,858	2	38,001	34	R	7	23	98	2	1	5	0	-11	1	24
99	104,825	8	49,202	35	M	4	42	95	7	3	33	1	23	1	27
100	104,952	9	48,597	34	U	5	45	84	7	13	17	1	41	1	52

Note: U=urban, S=suburban, R=rural, M=mixed, HH=households.

Illinois State House Districts: Demographic Data (cont.)

House District	Population		Average HH Income		District Type	Unempl. Rate	College Educ.	White (non-Hispanic)		African American		Asian American		Hispanic American	
	1997	+/-	($)	+/-		(%)	(%)	(%)	+/-	(%)	+/-	(%)	+/-	(%)	+/-
Illinois	11,893,640	4	54,426	33	M	6	39	72	0	15	7	3	26	10	27
101	95,329	0	40,517	32	U	7	27	86	-1	14	6	0	2	0	11
102	99,145	1	46,546	29	R	5	36	96	0	2	17	0	9	1	34
103	101,980	6	49,321	38	U	4	67	83	2	6	24	8	23	3	47
104	86,951	-11	42,882	36	M	5	41	83	-13	13	1	2	5	2	-13
105	94,750	-3	40,268	33	R	7	28	88	-4	9	5	1	14	2	26
106	98,310	1	39,000	36	R	7	33	97	1	1	5	0	16	1	22
107	97,110	0	36,801	34	R	9	27	97	0	2	16	0	-5	0	10
108	99,475	3	38,768	36	R	7	28	99	3	0	-7	0	-20	0	11
109	100,864	4	38,137	34	R	8	24	95	3	4	14	0	8	1	32
110	103,816	7	51,668	32	S	5	38	90	4	7	77	1	18	2	33
111	95,202	-2	39,674	26	S	8	26	89	-3	9	10	0	11	1	22
112	109,506	12	50,030	29	S	5	43	88	7	8	65	1	39	2	57
113	93,683	-2	40,255	25	U	7	30	87	-7	10	64	1	14	2	33
114	90,272	-7	29,422	29	S	19	15	30	-13	68	-4	0	-3	1	11
115	97,278	1	32,244	27	R	10	39	87	-1	8	11	3	20	2	25
116	101,739	5	40,487	21	R	6	26	95	5	3	10	0	-4	1	30
117	99,665	3	32,479	29	R	12	25	98	3	1	12	0	3	1	31
118	100,436	3	34,147	34	R	10	24	88	2	11	9	0	-15	1	21

Note: U=urban, S=suburban, R=rural, M=mixed, HH=households.

INDIANA

Demographically, Indiana is two states in one—the North and the South—and takes on the flavor of both. Gary, which is heavily African American, abuts Chicago. New Albany, which lies across from Louisville, has very few blacks. Southern Indiana is rural and agricultural, while in the cities of Gary, Hammond, and Fort Wayne, northern Indiana has (or in many cases, had) some of the heaviest industry in the United States.

In between these states within a state sits Indianapolis, a city planned for the center of the state and in many ways still the pin on which it revolves. It is the twelfth-largest city in the country and second-largest capital city, after Phoenix. It is also one of the largest cities in the United States that is not on a navigable body of water. Despite being situated between two important waterways, Lake Michigan and the Ohio River, Indiana seems to have emphasized overland travel, a tradition nicely reflected in the state's most important annual sporting event, the Indianapolis 500.

Indiana has grown at a rate of about 6 percent since 1990, slightly below the national average but much faster than in the 1980s, when it grew by just 1 percent. It has also grown faster than any other midwestern or Great Lakes state except Minnesota. However, the Census Bureau, at least, does not believe that Indiana can keep up its current pace; it projects that only seven states will grow more slowly than Indiana over the next quarter century.

The fastest-growing areas of the state almost perfectly surround the city of Indianapolis. The suburban Twenty-ninth House District, which includes Tipton and Hamilton Counties northeast of the city, has grown by 45 percent during the 1990s. The Thirty-ninth, Fortieth, and Fifty-eighth Districts have also grown by more than 20 percent.

Population loss has occurred in several places—in the black neighborhoods of Gary, as well as in some white districts northwest of Indianapolis and in Fort Wayne. Miami County, in the Twenty-third House District, is one of the fastest-shrinking counties in the country, having lost almost 12 percent of its population during the decade. Far northwest Indianapolis and the city's northern suburbs are also the wealthiest areas, with more pockets of affluence scattered in the Eighth (South Bend), Fifteenth (south of Hammond), and Seventy-eighth (Evansville) Districts.

Although Indiana has a significant black population, it is almost entirely concentrated in Gary and downtown Indianapolis, the result of the great migration of African Americans to northern factories around the middle of the century. Seven of the one hundred state house districts are more than 60 percent black, but forty-eight of them are less than 2 percent black. Hard times in the state's most industrial areas have disproportionately meant hard times for blacks; unemployment, for example, is 15 percent in the Second and Fourteenth Districts, both in Gary. In the northeast suburbs of Indianapolis, heavily white areas, it is only 2 percent.

Northwest Indiana is home to the state's only significant Hispanic neighborhoods. The Second District and another Gary district, the Twelfth, are both more than 20 percent Hispanic. The only concentration of Asians is in West Lafayette, home of Purdue University; the Twenty-sixth District is 9 percent Asian. It also has the highest percentage of college graduates—71 percent.

Indiana has a reputation for being a staunchly Republican state, and it is in presidential elections. But in statewide contests, it fluctuates. Though its two most famous U.S. senators recently have been Richard Lugar and Dan Quayle, they won their seats by defeating liberal Democrats Vance Hartke and Birch Bayh, respectively. A Democrat currently sits in the governor's mansion, and Bayh's son, Evan, is expected to reclaim the family Senate seat in 1998.

In the state legislature Democrats were close to a majority in the senate as recently as 1990 but now trail, 31–19. The house of representatives has been much more closely contested throughout the decade, and after the 1996 elections stood deadlocked, with 50 Democrats and 50 Republicans. Indiana may be feeling the tide that is pulling much of the rest of the industrial Midwest toward the Democrats.

INDIANA
State Senate Districts

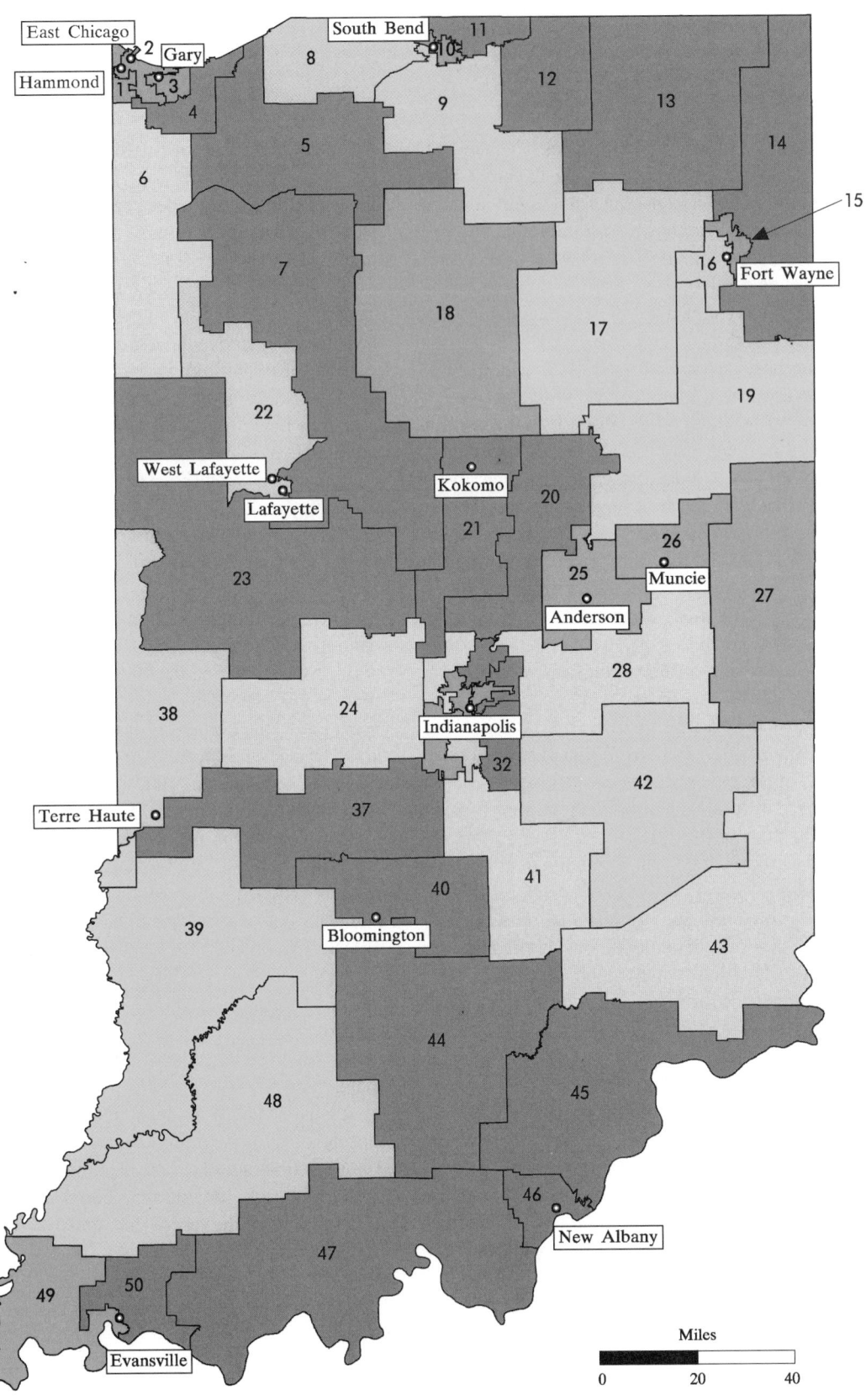

Population Growth
-6% to 1%   2% to 6%   7% to 11%   14% to 20%

INDIANAPOLIS

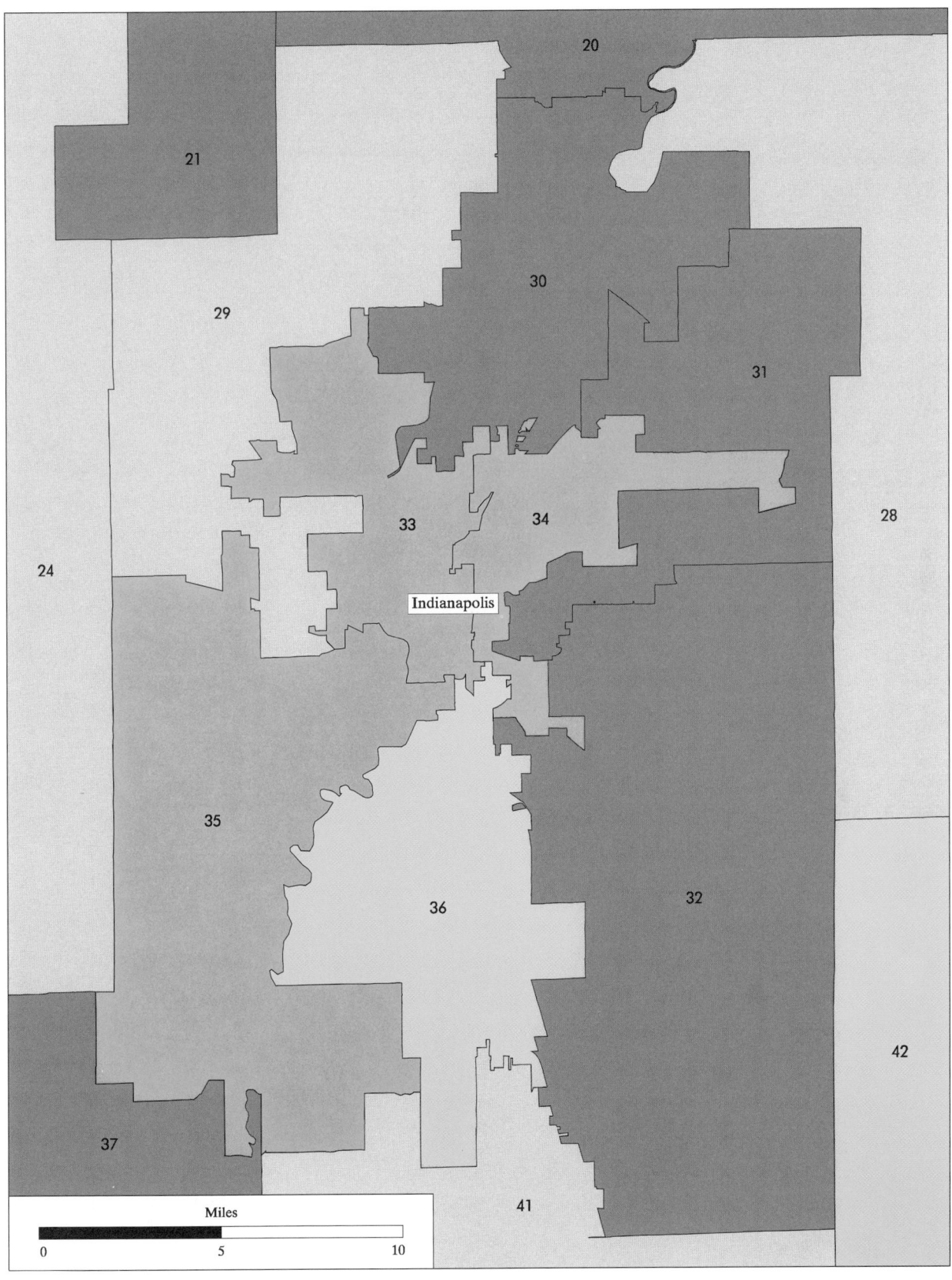

Indianapolis

Miles
0   5   10

Population Growth   ☐ -6% to 1%   ☐ 2% to 6%   ☐ 7% to 11%   ☐ 14% to 20%

Indiana State Senate Districts: Demographic Data

Senate District	Population		Average HH Income		District Type	Unempl. Rate	College Educ.	White (non-Hispanic)		African American		Asian American		Hispanic American	
	1997	+/-	($)	+/-		(%)	(%)	(%)	+/-	(%)	+/-	(%)	+/-	(%)	+/-
Indiana	5,874,429	6	47,795	37	M	6	35	89	5	8	10	1	28	2	29
1	106,651	-3	49,667	29	U	6	34	83	-10	4	87	1	29	12	40
2	103,302	-6	34,001	22	U	12	19	30	-30	44	10	0	-12	26	11
3	105,788	-4	33,928	26	U	14	21	26	-15	66	0	0	-24	7	17
4	118,562	7	55,186	33	S	5	33	90	4	2	62	1	37	7	46
5	124,104	11	53,037	38	R	5	39	97	11	0	13	1	44	2	36
6	129,231	16	58,753	35	S	5	39	94	14	1	99	1	52	4	71
7	123,422	10	46,823	38	R	5	34	97	9	0	17	1	23	1	40
8	113,764	2	45,577	31	R	6	30	88	1	10	12	0	22	2	29
9	121,910	6	48,632	35	R	4	32	91	5	5	13	1	32	3	35
10	110,481	0	38,578	33	U	7	34	78	-4	17	12	1	16	3	28
11	121,162	11	62,743	40	S	3	46	94	10	2	32	2	37	1	42
12	120,796	10	48,651	37	M	4	28	90	9	6	18	1	31	3	38
13	119,336	9	46,497	40	R	5	25	98	8	0	-6	0	9	2	35
14	130,280	8	53,772	30	S	4	42	96	7	2	36	1	32	1	42
15	104,814	0	45,432	28	U	6	40	71	-3	24	6	2	24	3	26
16	113,733	4	50,043	33	U	5	43	90	2	5	37	1	33	3	37
17	116,051	4	45,398	35	R	5	30	98	4	0	-17	0	6	1	27
18	109,721	-1	38,878	31	R	7	26	96	-1	1	-2	0	7	1	18
19	115,063	4	44,693	33	R	5	29	97	3	0	6	0	12	2	26
20	120,102	11	55,549	43	R	5	39	93	10	4	7	1	52	2	31
21	118,049	7	55,411	41	M	6	37	94	6	4	13	1	28	1	28
22	115,598	4	47,884	44	U	5	54	91	3	2	16	5	23	2	32
23	119,155	7	44,140	41	R	5	29	98	7	0	-5	0	4	1	30
24	129,013	17	57,997	41	S	3	38	97	16	1	24	0	40	1	48
25	114,660	1	43,628	29	U	6	30	89	0	10	11	0	18	1	31
26	109,905	-1	42,608	38	U	8	34	91	-2	7	9	1	17	1	24
27	111,617	0	38,714	32	R	7	25	95	0	4	9	0	18	1	22
28	132,485	20	56,185	44	S	5	39	98	19	1	29	0	75	1	65
29	126,280	14	66,282	43	U	3	56	83	10	13	38	2	45	1	49
30	123,283	11	71,339	37	U	2	67	90	9	7	25	2	50	1	46
31	122,405	7	52,683	39	U	5	41	85	3	11	34	2	37	2	35
32	120,606	8	52,471	38	U	4	34	95	7	3	34	1	46	1	38
33	108,442	-2	39,237	36	U	9	32	33	-12	64	4	1	21	1	28
34	106,212	0	34,900	30	U	11	22	32	-12	66	7	1	10	1	24
35	107,205	-2	43,853	34	U	5	28	94	-4	3	31	1	24	1	32
36	117,180	6	49,277	34	U	4	35	96	5	2	33	1	39	1	37
37	120,650	9	49,542	38	S	5	31	97	9	1	-2	1	11	1	38
38	115,301	3	37,887	41	M	8	29	93	2	5	13	1	15	1	26
39	114,641	4	39,071	38	R	7	30	98	4	1	6	0	-9	1	23
40	120,025	8	45,517	43	U	6	51	93	7	3	18	3	24	2	38
41	126,611	14	51,400	40	R	5	34	96	13	2	23	1	39	1	43
42	117,469	6	46,165	41	R	6	24	98	6	1	8	0	19	0	9
43	125,650	14	44,013	36	R	6	24	99	14	1	17	0	1	0	29
44	120,803	9	41,504	41	R	7	24	99	8	0	-3	0	26	0	27
45	120,865	8	43,587	39	R	7	24	98	7	1	17	0	16	1	28
46	119,899	8	45,553	40	S	6	30	92	7	6	18	0	30	1	38
47	118,889	7	41,067	35	R	6	23	99	7	0	8	0	-7	1	25
48	114,293	3	39,193	31	R	5	26	98	3	1	3	0	-20	0	16
49	111,135	1	37,198	35	U	8	24	89	0	10	10	0	11	1	19
50	117,934	7	56,473	36	S	4	45	96	6	3	18	1	31	1	43

Note: U=urban, S=suburban, R=rural, M=mixed, HH=households.

INDIANA
State House Districts

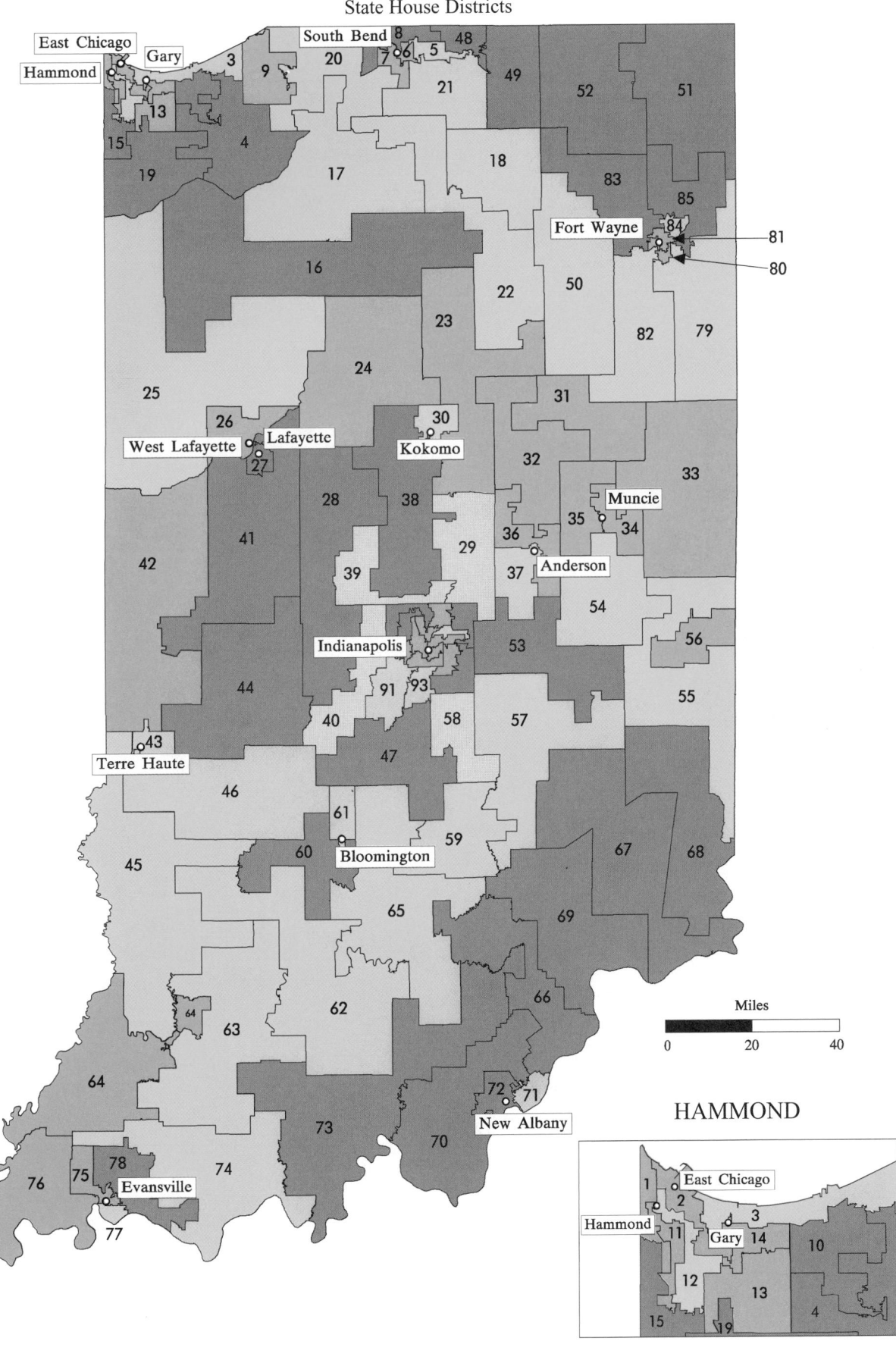

HAMMOND

Population Growth · -6% to 1% · 2% to 8% · 9% to 16% · 23% to 45%

INDIANAPOLIS

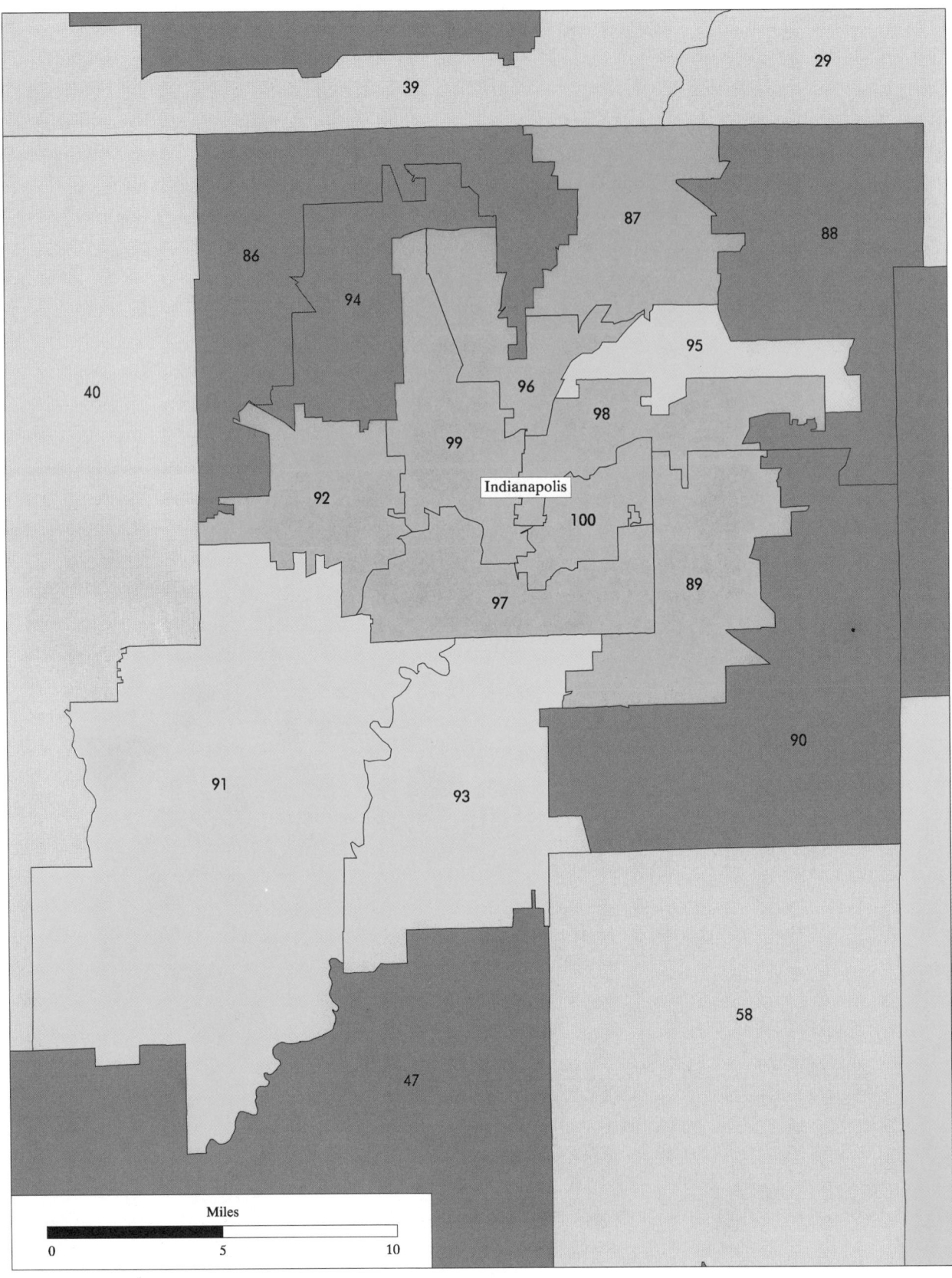

Population Growth ▦ -6% to 1%   ▦ 2% to 8%   ▦ 9% to 16%   ▦ 23% to 45%

Indiana State House Districts: Demographic Data

House District	Population		Average HH Income		District Type	Unempl. Rate	College Educ.	White (non-Hispanic)		African American		Asian American		Hispanic American	
	1997	+/-	($)	+/-		(%)	(%)	(%)	+/-	(%)	+/-	(%)	+/-	(%)	+/-
Indiana	5,874,429	6	47,795	37	M	6	35	89	5	8	10	1	28	2	29
1	52,571	-5	39,603	26	U	9	26	76	-14	8	68	1	5	15	37
2	51,075	-6	31,660	24	U	15	18	15	-31	61	0	0	-32	23	3
3	58,349	2	42,569	32	U	12	32	31	-4	64	4	0	-2	5	4
4	56,480	12	64,308	38	R	4	47	96	11	0	15	1	46	2	43
5	56,007	5	41,438	35	U	6	29	88	3	9	18	1	25	2	41
6	51,162	-1	41,376	34	U	6	36	81	-4	14	11	1	16	3	27
7	55,326	-2	37,274	29	U	9	29	67	-7	27	10	1	11	5	27
8	66,044	11	65,019	43	S	4	52	90	9	6	28	2	33	2	45
9	58,909	0	44,773	32	R	6	28	80	-3	17	11	1	25	2	23
10	63,819	10	50,960	34	S	6	33	93	9	0	17	1	39	6	41
11	53,006	-2	47,735	29	U	6	33	75	-10	13	29	1	32	12	39
12	57,377	3	45,652	31	S	7	25	68	-5	9	32	1	27	22	24
13	58,038	0	50,905	28	S	5	32	82	-6	8	46	1	29	9	44
14	51,552	-5	28,831	21	U	15	15	27	-18	63	-2	0	-39	9	18
15	65,171	16	68,511	33	S	3	45	93	13	1	104	2	46	4	68
16	61,959	11	38,609	27	R	5	27	98	10	0	2	0	-32	1	43
17	57,924	6	42,747	40	R	6	25	96	5	1	8	0	25	2	33
18	59,940	8	51,624	37	R	3	35	96	7	1	11	1	36	3	37
19	61,978	10	57,855	33	S	5	40	96	9	0	79	1	34	3	52
20	55,843	8	45,400	30	R	5	31	97	7	1	24	0	16	2	34
21	61,247	6	48,337	33	M	4	31	94	5	4	24	1	26	2	39
22	56,127	3	43,567	36	R	4	27	98	2	0	-6	0	13	1	30
23	52,108	-6	45,049	38	R	6	28	95	-6	2	0	1	9	1	13
24	56,084	0	39,816	28	R	6	27	98	0	1	-7	0	13	1	15
25	59,938	7	43,616	37	R	4	28	99	7	0	-42	0	-4	1	25
26	54,805	0	48,872	42	M	5	71	86	-3	3	7	9	22	2	25
27	60,547	11	48,580	50	U	4	42	93	9	3	29	2	33	2	47
28	60,845	9	49,825	42	R	5	31	98	9	0	-18	0	-18	1	36
29	81,576	45	68,278	42	S	2	56	97	45	1	67	1	119	1	104
30	57,177	3	43,927	35	U	8	29	89	2	8	12	1	30	2	27
31	53,482	-1	39,067	32	R	9	24	87	-3	9	7	0	15	3	21
32	58,280	1	44,275	29	R	5	29	97	0	1	7	0	21	1	33
33	55,419	1	37,152	30	R	7	24	99	1	0	-13	0	-9	1	23
34	53,924	-2	39,337	41	U	9	27	87	-3	12	7	0	14	1	11
35	55,129	0	48,311	35	M	6	42	95	-1	2	15	1	18	1	35
36	55,748	1	47,556	30	S	6	32	96	0	2	18	0	21	1	33
37	56,243	2	37,545	25	U	8	24	82	0	17	10	0	19	1	28
38	64,755	14	71,152	42	S	4	52	97	13	1	26	1	49	1	48
39	70,667	27	87,066	44	S	3	60	97	27	0	20	2	73	1	55
40	68,418	23	63,221	42	S	3	39	98	22	1	26	0	57	1	56
41	61,726	9	50,794	46	R	4	38	98	9	1	9	0	20	1	31
42	56,231	1	41,306	39	R	7	24	99	1	0	1	0	-15	0	4
43	55,727	3	41,030	43	U	7	36	91	2	7	13	1	17	1	35
44	60,359	10	43,592	41	R	5	28	97	10	2	17	0	12	1	24
45	60,429	4	36,807	35	R	7	27	99	4	0	-17	0	-24	1	24
46	58,069	5	42,816	39	R	6	32	93	5	4	9	1	15	1	37
47	64,431	14	57,461	40	S	4	34	98	14	1	27	0	42	1	39
48	59,845	9	57,994	37	S	4	38	94	8	3	25	1	39	1	31
49	64,950	15	51,868	37	S	3	30	95	14	1	21	1	49	3	40
50	58,657	7	46,509	36	R	5	30	98	7	0	-29	0	1	1	30

Note: U=urban, S=suburban, R=rural, M=mixed, HH=households.

Indiana State House Districts: Demographic Data (cont.)

House District	Population 1997	+/-	Average HH Income ($)	+/-	District Type	Unempl. Rate (%)	College Educ. (%)	White (non-Hispanic) (%)	+/-	African American (%)	+/-	Asian American (%)	+/-	Hispanic American (%)	+/-
Indiana	5,874,429	6	47,795	37	M	6	35	89	5	8	10	1	28	2	29
51	62,289	12	46,005	35	R	5	32	98	12	0	-21	0	5	1	48
52	62,435	13	45,404	42	R	5	20	98	13	0	-19	0	15	2	42
53	61,105	14	55,492	40	S	4	33	98	14	0	-30	0	35	1	45
54	56,018	2	42,452	37	R	8	25	98	2	1	8	0	-24	1	29
55	57,812	4	43,806	35	R	7	23	98	4	1	8	0	-12	0	1
56	54,921	-1	38,453	34	R	8	26	91	-2	7	10	1	29	1	24
57	62,252	7	49,104	42	R	5	27	98	7	1	9	0	24	0	32
58	68,786	23	48,184	33	S	4	33	97	22	1	33	1	63	1	63
59	59,455	8	54,364	46	R	5	38	96	7	2	19	1	37	1	27
60	61,230	10	48,908	42	S	5	41	96	10	1	22	1	22	1	54
61	57,082	5	39,095	41	U	7	64	88	3	4	17	5	25	2	30
62	60,045	7	35,936	37	R	9	21	99	7	0	-3	0	-8	0	21
63	55,021	3	37,177	29	R	5	24	99	3	0	-15	0	-24	0	7
64	56,844	0	38,605	33	R	6	30	97	0	2	7	0	-8	1	18
65	58,052	7	44,094	42	R	6	28	99	7	0	-7	0	14	1	38
66	60,056	11	43,011	42	R	8	22	98	11	1	17	1	37	0	34
67	60,196	9	46,483	46	R	5	24	99	9	0	-14	0	27	0	6
68	63,331	14	42,832	31	R	6	24	99	14	1	22	0	0	0	34
69	60,781	9	42,205	40	R	6	25	98	9	1	11	0	6	0	23
70	64,722	13	47,919	40	S	5	26	98	13	1	21	0	35	0	37
71	57,689	5	43,420	40	S	6	29	89	3	9	16	1	32	1	29
72	60,148	9	47,189	40	U	6	32	94	8	5	21	0	22	1	40
73	61,419	9	42,816	39	R	7	22	99	9	0	6	0	-47	1	33
74	57,440	5	40,534	30	R	6	25	99	5	0	6	0	-6	0	25
75	53,831	0	38,733	33	U	6	27	96	-1	3	12	1	22	1	32
76	53,576	-2	43,183	36	M	6	27	97	-3	2	9	0	-2	1	16
77	57,861	5	40,233	35	U	8	33	79	3	19	11	1	23	1	31
78	62,255	12	65,333	35	S	4	49	97	12	1	21	1	38	1	42
79	61,488	4	45,318	30	R	5	32	94	3	3	31	0	9	3	39
80	49,763	-5	35,275	24	U	7	30	71	-12	22	20	1	3	5	27
81	52,172	-5	35,092	26	U	8	28	64	-8	32	0	1	5	3	19
82	56,356	6	55,224	36	R	4	42	96	5	1	46	0	34	2	35
83	61,579	10	58,374	36	S	4	44	96	9	2	59	1	52	1	45
84	52,685	4	58,403	28	U	3	54	91	1	5	47	2	39	2	45
85	65,682	10	58,264	29	S	4	45	97	9	1	52	1	40	1	38
86	63,996	13	85,564	42	U	2	67	90	10	7	46	2	49	1	61
87	54,270	1	64,749	36	U	2	67	90	-1	7	31	2	35	1	42
88	72,309	14	63,464	40	U	3	54	86	11	10	38	2	45	2	41
89	55,096	0	46,521	35	U	4	32	96	-1	2	29	1	33	1	28
90	61,377	11	55,361	37	U	3	39	97	10	1	40	1	45	1	48
91	56,816	5	51,435	36	U	4	29	97	5	1	18	0	26	1	30
92	55,840	-3	40,829	30	U	4	32	91	-5	7	29	1	23	1	28
93	58,624	6	57,020	35	U	3	40	96	5	1	35	1	38	1	28
94	61,465	12	46,198	32	U	4	50	67	3	28	36	2	33	2	43
95	52,213	2	40,809	28	U	8	30	32	-11	65	10	1	16	1	31
96	52,941	-5	45,651	34	U	7	41	33	-17	65	3	1	4	1	25
97	55,843	-2	32,340	31	U	9	13	86	-5	12	26	0	12	2	29
98	54,850	-1	35,278	37	U	11	22	35	-9	63	4	1	21	1	25
99	50,741	-4	35,428	33	U	10	27	32	-15	66	1	1	21	1	18
100	56,093	-1	30,595	32	U	10	15	87	-4	10	29	0	6	2	28

Note: U=urban, S=suburban, R=rural, M=mixed, HH=households.

IOWA

Iowa, land of hogs, corn, and insurance companies, is the slowest-growing state in the Farm Belt and the ninth-slowest in the nation. Between 1990 and 1997, Iowa's population grew by just 3 percent, a figure that nevertheless represented a dramatic improvement over the growth rate of the 1980s, when in the midst of a deep agricultural recession it fell fully 7 percent. Furthermore, more people are moving into Iowa than are leaving it, for the first time since the 1910s. But the Census Bureau thinks the growth rate will slow here. It projects Iowa as the fifth-slowest-growing state over the next generation.

Two important reasons for Iowa's sluggishness are its economy, which is based on agriculture, and its population, which is old. Four-fifths of the state house districts that lost population in the 1990s were rural, in sharp contrast to the situation in many other states, where urban areas are the ones losing people. Nowhere in the state was the loss severe, just steady and widespread. The Sixty-first House District, which includes the town of Ames and Iowa State University, shrank by 6 percent from 1990 to 1997, the fastest rate in the state. The Twenty-fifth District (Waterloo) shrank by 4 percent, part of a broad band of districts and counties along Iowa's northern tier that lost population. Mitchell County was the only county in northern Iowa to have grown during the nineties, and it has gained just 135 residents.

To the extent that Iowa has gained population, it has done so almost entirely in the northern and northwestern suburbs of Des Moines. The Sixty-fifth, Seventy-fifth, and Seventy-sixth House Districts all grew by at least 20 percent. Growth in those districts, which include Polk, Dallas, Madison, and Warren Counties, accounted for half the state's population gain.

The state's wealth is also centered around Des Moines, which is home to several large insurance companies. In the Seventy-third District, in the city's southwestern suburbs, average household income is $89,000, by far the highest in the state. With the exception of two districts in downtown Des Moines and another on the Mississippi River north of Dubuque, the poorest sections of the state are along the southern tier of counties on the Missouri border. (Iowa's counties are stacked neatly, like blocks, and are named after presidents and statesmen from the time when the state was settled—hence, Polk, Dallas, Madison, DeWitt, Clinton, and Marshall Counties, among others.)

Less than 2 percent of the state's residents are black, and it has the highest percentage of white residents of any state outside New England. The only districts with a significant share of African Americans are the Twenty-fifth, which is 26 percent black, and the Seventy-first (central Des Moines), which is 21 percent black. Only one district is at least 10 percent Hispanic (the Forty-eighth, comprising the packing houses of Davenport). Similarly, Iowa took in many Vietnamese refugees during the mid-seventies, and today the Sixty-first District is 10 percent Asian.

Iowa has the third-highest percentage of citizens age fifty-five or older, trailing only Florida and West Virginia. A quarter of the state is at least fifty-five years old, and in three rural farm districts—the Seventy-eighth, Eighty-seventh, and Ninety-first—the fraction is almost one-third.

The state legislature is organized around legislative districts, with one senator and two representatives elected from each. Although it has become a firmly Democratic state in presidential elections, the partisan fortunes in the legislature have almost perfectly flipped during the decade. In 1990 the state house had fifty-five Democrats and forty-five Republicans; in 1996 it had forty-six Democrats and fifty-four Republicans. The state senate in 1990 had twenty-nine Democrats and twenty-one Republicans; in 1996 it had twenty-one Democrats and twenty-nine Republicans. This pattern of partisan fluctuation in the legislature is not new to Iowa politics. As early as the 1940s political commentator John Gunther noted a connection between the fortunes of the parties and those of the Iowa farmer. "When the farmer is rich," he wrote in *Inside USA,* "he placidly votes Republican by and large. When poor, his vote will be a protest vote." If not rich, perhaps, most Iowans must be thankful that things have at least quieted down in the state after the dismal eighties.

IOWA
State Senate Districts

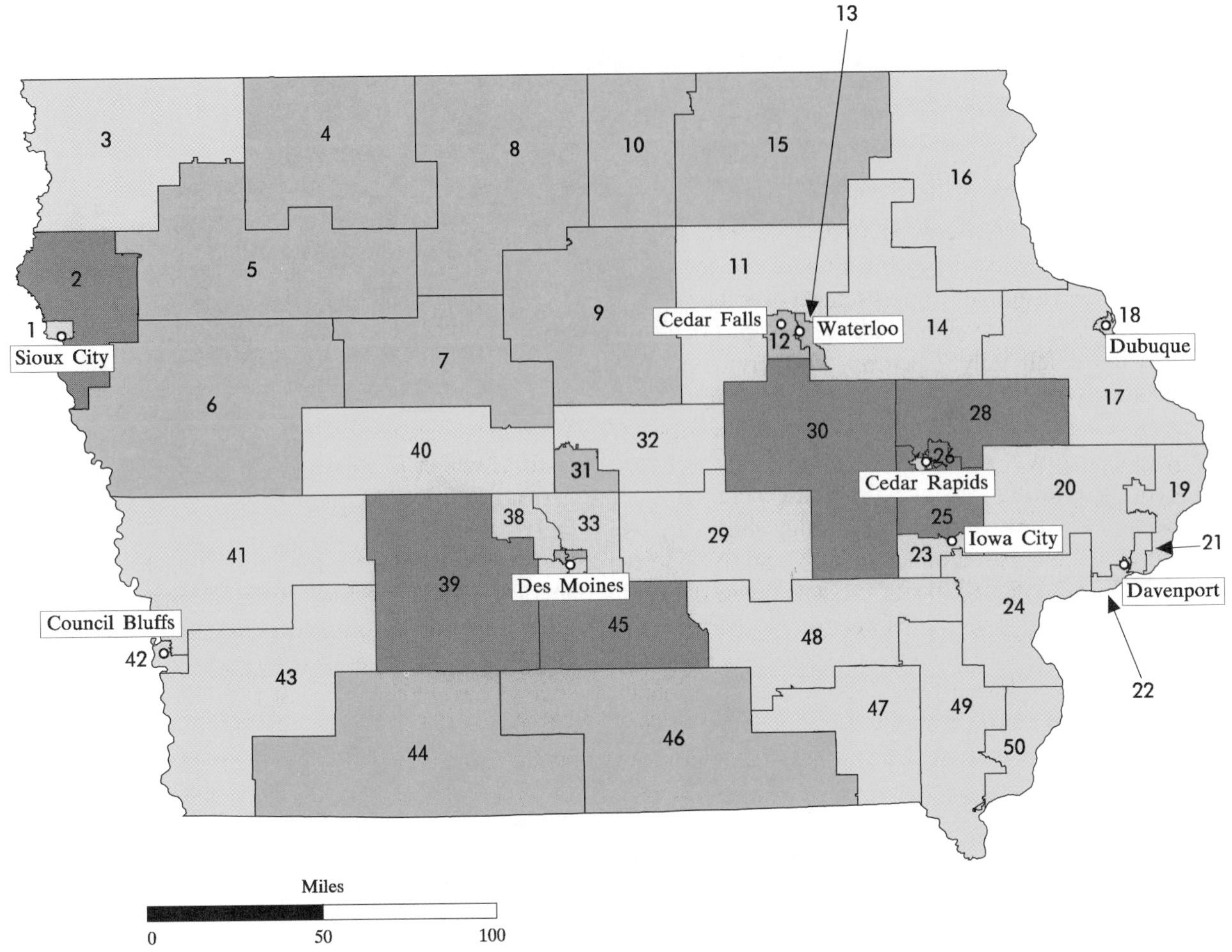

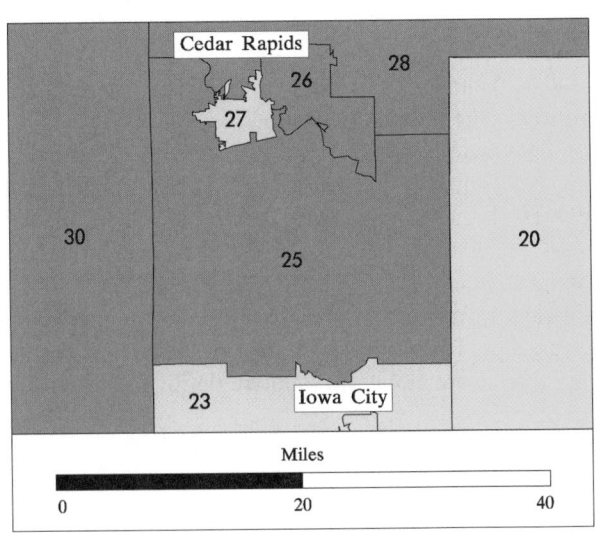

DES MOINES

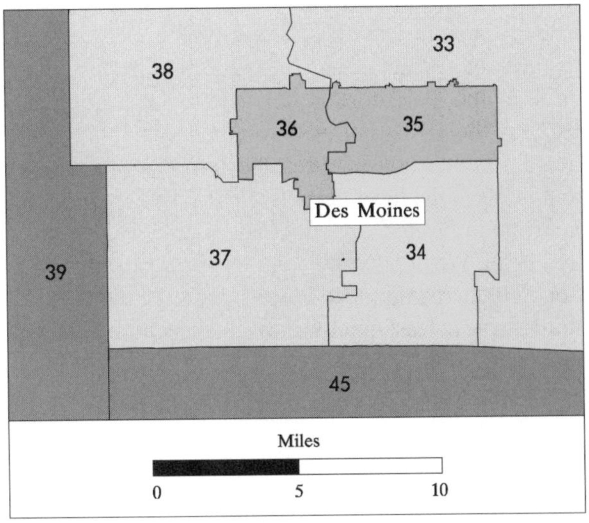

CEDAR RAPIDS/IOWA CITY

Population Growth ▨ -3% to 0% ☐ 1% to 5% ▨ 6% to 11% ☐ 15% to 23%

Iowa State Senate Districts: Demographic Data

Senate District	Population 1997	+/-	Average HH Income ($)	+/-	District Type	Unempl. Rate (%)	College Educ. (%)	White (non-Hispanic) (%)	+/-	African American (%)	+/-	Asian American (%)	+/-	Hispanic American (%)	+/-
Iowa	2,859,077	3	45,070	41	R	5	41	95	2	2	17	1	29	2	55
1	57,242	4	49,049	53	U	6	37	86	1	3	18	2	35	6	53
2	59,125	7	46,854	45	M	3	40	97	6	0	16	1	36	1	45
3	57,960	2	40,501	38	R	2	32	99	1	0	-25	1	19	0	20
4	55,266	0	42,510	45	R	3	40	99	-1	0	-34	0	-5	0	24
5	53,174	-3	40,083	41	R	3	37	98	-4	0	-14	1	24	1	36
6	54,555	-2	38,118	44	R	4	31	99	-2	0	-20	0	-24	0	22
7	53,910	-3	40,748	46	R	5	36	96	-4	2	7	0	-9	1	40
8	53,112	-3	40,121	40	R	5	37	99	-3	0	-32	0	-14	1	35
9	55,642	-1	39,232	36	R	5	35	98	-2	0	-20	0	-3	1	41
10	55,170	-1	42,853	45	R	5	42	96	-2	1	0	1	16	3	47
11	57,808	2	45,621	47	R	4	35	99	1	0	5	0	-12	0	32
12	54,230	-1	50,354	42	U	5	53	95	-2	2	29	2	36	1	48
13	53,493	-2	39,378	39	U	8	32	83	-4	15	9	1	24	1	51
14	56,199	1	39,977	34	R	6	35	99	1	0	-16	0	-13	1	50
15	54,980	-1	37,695	37	R	5	32	99	-1	0	-80	0	-28	0	19
16	56,311	2	35,941	34	R	4	34	99	1	0	7	0	3	0	33
17	58,373	1	44,918	37	R	5	31	99	1	0	-31	0	4	0	43
18	55,157	2	44,416	37	U	5	41	97	2	1	5	1	22	1	51
19	57,278	2	46,618	39	R	6	40	96	1	1	10	1	31	1	68
20	58,258	4	42,797	34	R	4	36	94	3	3	35	1	24	2	66
21	60,255	5	55,896	41	U	5	55	87	3	8	12	1	41	4	59
22	52,992	1	39,406	32	U	7	33	87	-3	6	23	1	33	6	54
23	52,599	3	54,729	55	U	3	70	88	-1	3	19	6	36	2	61
24	62,043	3	47,938	46	R	5	35	90	0	1	14	1	16	8	52
25	64,816	11	55,562	44	S	4	58	93	9	2	27	3	30	2	75
26	58,600	9	58,839	34	U	4	55	96	8	2	22	1	38	1	65
27	53,286	2	40,227	34	U	7	36	92	1	5	19	1	30	2	66
28	62,664	8	52,479	39	M	5	47	97	8	1	27	1	40	1	61
29	57,096	1	44,264	37	R	4	36	98	1	0	-3	1	13	1	44
30	59,605	6	42,615	42	R	5	32	98	6	0	-29	0	-1	1	41
31	55,986	-1	47,745	49	R	4	67	88	-4	2	12	7	21	2	54
32	56,142	3	47,410	41	R	4	43	97	3	1	2	1	43	1	51
33	64,438	15	54,012	39	S	3	46	97	14	1	40	1	51	2	89
34	56,623	3	36,397	33	U	6	27	85	-2	5	34	3	47	6	61
35	54,257	-2	35,872	29	U	6	24	80	-6	12	14	4	30	4	59
36	54,520	0	44,410	35	U	4	53	82	-5	12	23	3	34	3	71
37	64,586	16	79,497	46	S	3	64	94	13	2	46	2	75	2	68
38	68,494	23	66,932	39	S	2	61	96	21	1	57	2	76	1	105
39	62,070	10	44,623	43	R	4	37	99	10	0	-26	0	-31	1	53
40	56,394	2	40,750	39	R	4	36	99	2	0	-9	0	0	0	33
41	57,363	2	43,369	41	R	4	34	99	2	0	-41	0	11	1	49
42	56,357	2	40,321	41	U	5	26	95	1	1	13	0	37	4	53
43	55,560	1	39,022	38	R	4	33	99	1	0	-17	0	-51	1	25
44	54,634	-1	33,799	36	R	5	33	98	-2	0	-7	0	-15	1	36
45	59,667	8	48,535	45	R	3	38	98	8	0	6	0	21	1	59
46	55,047	-1	34,382	38	R	7	28	99	-1	0	-13	0	-24	0	13
47	55,588	1	36,811	38	R	6	36	97	1	1	2	1	17	1	48
48	58,319	4	41,406	40	R	4	33	98	4	0	-7	1	30	1	42
49	56,797	1	41,376	41	R	5	33	96	0	2	13	1	19	1	54
50	55,172	1	41,775	38	R	6	34	93	-1	4	14	1	23	3	57

Note: U=urban, S=suburban, R=rural, M=mixed, HH=households.

IOWA
State House Districts

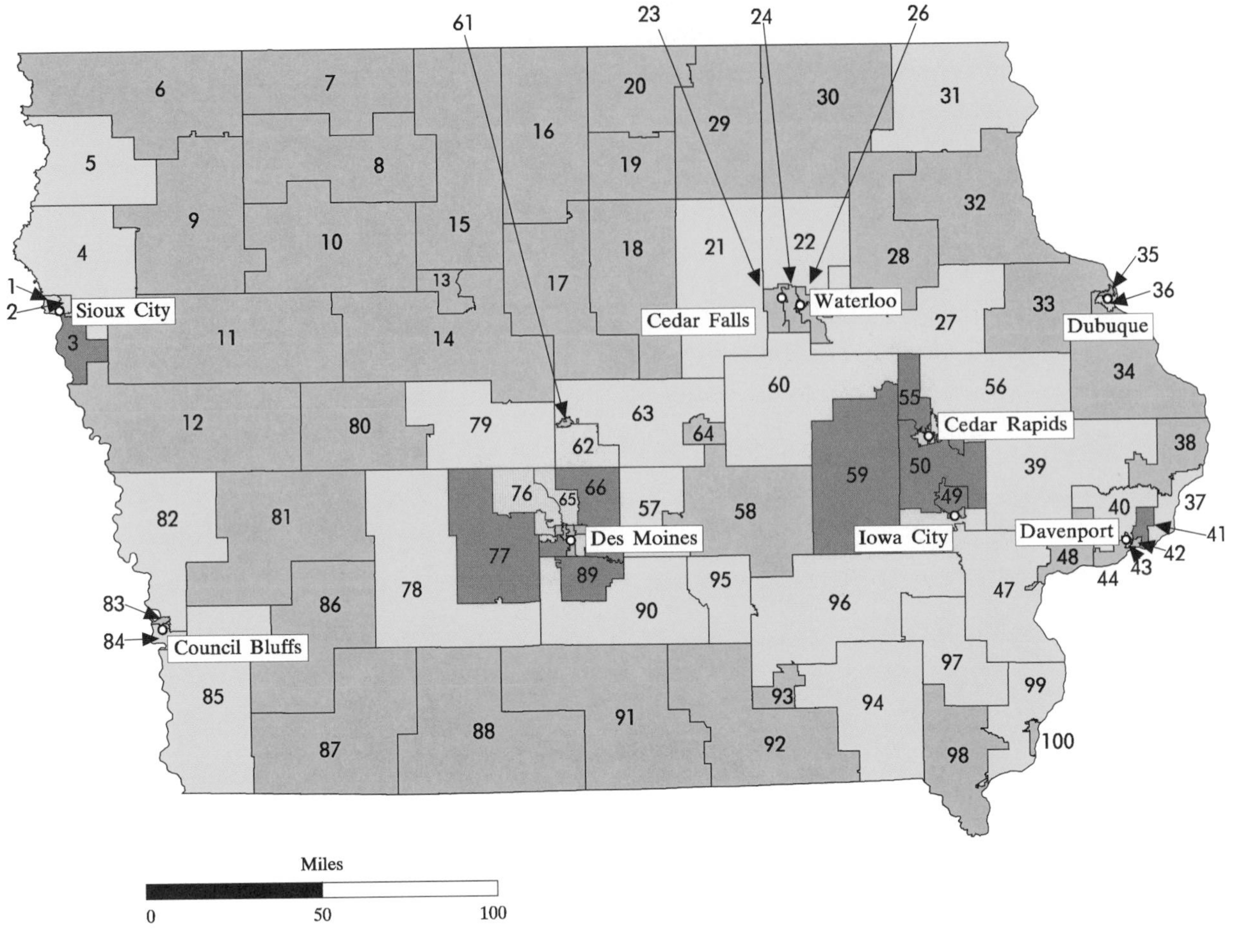

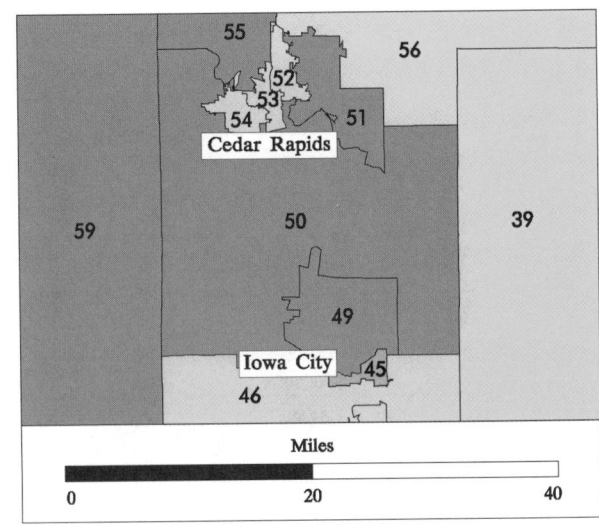

Miles

0　50　100

DES MOINES

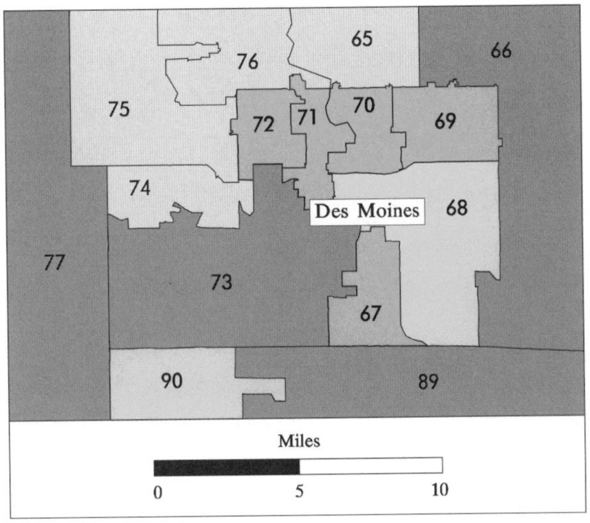

CEDAR RAPIDS/IOWA CITY

Miles

0　5　10

Miles

0　20　40

Population Growth　■ -6% to 1%　□ 2% to 7%　■ 8% to 15%　□ 18% to 24%

Iowa State House Districts: Demographic Data

House District	Population		Average HH Income		District Type	Unempl. Rate	College Educ.	White (non-Hispanic)		African American		Asian American		Hispanic American	
	1997	+/-	($)	+/-		(%)	(%)	(%)	+/-	(%)	+/-	(%)	+/-	(%)	+/-
Iowa	2,859,077	3	45,070	41	R	5	41	95	2	2	17	1	29	2	55
1	28,754	2	57,821	57	U	6	38	88	0	4	16	1	27	5	44
2	28,361	6	40,699	48	U	7	36	84	2	3	20	4	38	7	61
3	29,440	8	50,044	49	U	3	43	96	7	1	17	1	47	2	44
4	29,684	6	43,778	40	R	3	38	98	6	0	16	0	11	1	48
5	29,197	5	42,097	37	R	2	35	99	5	0	-8	1	30	0	36
6	28,767	-2	39,072	39	R	2	30	99	-2	0	-58	0	-3	0	0
7	28,244	1	43,006	46	R	4	41	99	1	0	-31	0	-25	1	30
8	27,022	-2	41,980	44	R	2	39	99	-2	0	-42	0	6	0	14
9	26,024	-4	39,903	45	R	4	34	99	-4	0	-17	0	-4	1	42
10	27,183	-3	40,244	37	R	3	40	97	-3	0	-12	2	31	1	31
11	26,849	-2	38,089	40	R	4	32	99	-2	0	-83	0	-65	0	7
12	27,709	-1	38,149	47	R	5	29	98	-1	0	-8	0	-3	1	30
13	22,732	-5	39,418	47	R	5	38	93	-6	4	5	1	1	2	44
14	31,156	-2	41,755	46	R	4	35	98	-2	0	19	0	-29	1	34
15	26,930	-3	39,523	36	R	4	37	99	-4	0	-63	0	-27	1	25
16	26,184	-2	40,751	45	R	5	38	98	-3	0	-18	0	-4	1	40
17	28,734	0	38,137	31	R	5	35	98	0	0	-61	0	10	1	43
18	26,911	-3	40,418	42	R	5	35	98	-3	0	-14	0	-29	1	38
19	28,599	1	43,129	46	R	5	43	96	0	0	4	1	25	2	46
20	26,529	-2	42,512	45	R	4	40	95	-3	1	-4	0	3	3	49
21	28,180	2	44,198	48	R	4	32	99	1	0	-36	0	-41	0	23
22	29,631	2	47,051	46	R	4	39	98	1	1	8	0	-3	1	38
23	25,563	-2	47,541	41	U	5	59	95	-3	2	26	2	35	1	54
24	28,704	0	52,460	43	U	5	48	95	-1	3	31	2	36	1	39
25	26,671	-4	37,019	39	U	10	32	71	-8	26	6	1	22	1	47
26	26,850	0	41,702	39	U	6	32	94	-2	4	29	1	26	1	55
27	30,727	2	43,343	34	R	5	36	99	2	0	-16	0	-9	1	51
28	25,473	0	36,156	34	R	6	33	98	0	0	-15	0	-18	1	52
29	26,875	-1	37,898	36	R	5	34	99	-2	0	-78	0	-12	1	25
30	28,104	-1	37,497	39	R	4	29	99	-1	0	-82	0	-48	0	10
31	29,498	2	38,315	36	R	4	38	99	2	0	0	1	11	0	27
32	26,815	1	33,445	30	R	4	31	99	1	0	15	0	-31	1	39
33	28,501	1	46,914	36	R	4	30	99	1	0	-29	0	16	0	47
34	29,874	1	43,145	38	R	6	33	99	1	0	-32	0	-12	1	41
35	27,546	1	40,113	34	U	5	35	98	1	0	3	1	19	1	52
36	27,627	4	48,448	39	U	5	47	97	3	1	6	1	24	1	50
37	28,123	4	48,536	41	R	7	38	95	2	2	8	1	40	2	74
38	29,306	1	44,724	37	R	6	42	97	0	1	13	1	23	1	54
39	28,633	2	41,440	37	R	4	34	99	2	0	-58	0	-38	1	39
40	29,606	7	44,206	32	M	5	38	89	4	6	36	1	37	3	74
41	34,340	12	62,916	40	S	4	58	92	9	3	39	1	52	3	77
42	25,859	-2	47,078	40	U	7	50	80	-6	14	6	1	26	5	46
43	27,479	2	40,642	32	U	5	38	86	-2	7	27	1	36	6	52
44	25,478	0	38,049	31	U	8	27	88	-4	4	17	1	30	6	55
45	26,747	1	55,705	55	U	4	71	90	-1	3	13	5	19	2	44
46	26,020	5	53,813	55	U	3	69	86	0	3	25	8	48	3	74
47	34,432	5	48,116	44	R	4	36	91	2	1	1	1	21	7	57
48	27,627	1	47,732	49	R	6	32	88	-2	1	35	1	5	10	48
49	26,636	9	58,542	45	S	4	70	90	6	3	27	5	26	3	74
50	38,067	12	53,376	42	M	5	46	96	11	1	28	1	43	1	75

Note: U=urban, S=suburban, R=rural, M=mixed, HH=households.

Iowa State House Districts: Demographic Data (cont.)

House District	Population 1997	+/-	Average HH Income ($)	+/-	District Type	Unempl. Rate (%)	College Educ. (%)	White (non-Hispanic) (%)	+/-	African American (%)	+/-	Asian American (%)	+/-	Hispanic American (%)	+/-
Iowa	2,859,077	3	45,070	41	R	5	41	95	2	2	17	1	29	2	55
51	30,125	13	59,065	32	S	4	54	97	12	1	13	1	47	1	80
52	28,463	6	58,496	36	U	5	56	95	4	2	25	1	31	2	55
53	27,392	2	36,174	34	U	8	32	88	0	7	18	1	26	2	61
54	25,816	3	44,655	33	U	7	40	95	1	2	24	1	34	2	71
55	31,733	13	60,107	41	U	5	56	97	12	1	33	1	46	1	61
56	30,958	4	43,985	34	R	5	37	97	3	1	23	0	20	1	60
57	28,353	3	44,450	38	R	4	35	98	2	0	-2	1	24	1	46
58	28,754	0	44,063	37	R	4	37	98	0	0	-4	1	5	1	45
59	30,031	8	45,668	48	R	4	32	99	8	0	-100	0	-8	0	32
60	29,574	5	39,507	36	R	5	31	96	5	0	-11	0	2	1	45
61	24,368	-6	56,524	59	R	4	74	85	-9	3	0	10	12	3	40
62	31,613	3	41,751	43	R	4	61	91	0	2	26	5	39	2	72
63	30,706	5	50,048	46	R	4	45	98	5	0	-22	1	46	1	58
64	25,462	1	44,385	35	R	5	41	96	0	1	8	1	39	1	47
65	32,688	20	54,911	37	S	3	53	98	19	1	50	1	56	1	77
66	31,756	11	53,067	41	S	3	38	97	10	0	29	1	47	2	96
67	27,746	1	41,288	34	U	4	30	90	-3	2	35	2	45	5	64
68	28,963	6	32,051	33	U	8	24	80	0	8	33	4	49	6	58
69	27,287	-1	39,034	30	U	6	24	88	-4	7	16	2	35	3	67
70	26,868	-3	32,793	28	U	7	25	72	-10	17	14	6	29	4	53
71	26,624	0	38,899	33	U	5	48	69	-9	21	22	5	31	4	71
72	27,733	0	49,586	36	U	3	58	94	-2	2	34	2	44	2	73
73	34,027	13	89,022	53	U	2	65	94	12	2	38	1	71	2	69
74	30,491	18	69,138	37	S	3	64	93	16	2	57	2	78	3	67
75	31,499	21	70,684	37	S	2	64	95	19	1	65	2	73	1	108
76	36,961	24	63,442	41	S	3	58	96	23	1	49	1	80	1	103
77	33,894	15	50,872	46	R	3	40	98	15	0	-25	0	-8	1	77
78	28,168	4	37,559	36	R	4	32	99	4	0	-36	0	-69	0	16
79	30,369	4	41,930	42	R	4	38	99	3	0	-2	0	0	0	44
80	26,008	1	39,334	34	R	4	34	99	1	0	-44	0	1	0	17
81	27,536	-2	38,036	36	R	4	33	99	-2	0	-60	0	-15	0	21
82	29,810	6	48,585	44	R	4	34	98	5	0	-38	0	21	1	66
83	28,119	1	37,331	36	U	5	24	95	0	1	13	0	35	4	53
84	28,299	4	43,235	46	U	5	28	95	2	1	13	0	39	4	53
85	27,589	3	42,827	44	R	4	33	99	3	0	6	0	-57	1	36
86	27,971	-2	35,663	31	R	5	34	99	-2	0	-63	0	-41	0	11
87	27,576	-1	35,878	40	R	4	34	98	-2	0	-6	0	-6	1	43
88	27,059	-1	31,688	32	R	6	33	99	-1	0	-9	0	-21	0	18
89	27,356	12	51,872	45	S	3	46	98	11	0	8	0	35	1	73
90	32,310	5	45,732	44	R	4	32	98	4	0	5	0	10	1	46
91	27,403	-1	33,514	31	R	7	27	99	-1	0	-45	0	-27	0	5
92	27,647	0	35,277	46	R	7	29	99	0	0	-9	0	-23	1	20
93	25,887	0	35,858	38	R	8	29	97	-1	1	8	1	15	1	49
94	29,707	2	37,686	38	R	5	42	98	2	0	-9	1	19	1	47
95	27,499	5	43,577	42	R	4	34	97	4	0	7	2	39	1	57
96	30,817	4	39,526	38	R	4	31	99	4	0	-21	0	-11	0	24
97	28,829	4	41,610	41	R	4	38	96	3	1	8	1	18	1	61
98	27,950	-2	41,135	41	R	6	29	95	-3	3	16	0	26	2	49
99	27,741	2	43,297	37	R	6	35	93	0	2	16	0	24	3	65
100	27,405	0	40,288	38	R	7	34	92	-1	5	12	1	22	2	43

Note: U=urban, S=suburban, R=rural, M=mixed, HH=households.

KANSAS

In the 1930s, Professor Walter Prescott Webb popularized the theory that the Great Plains begin at the hundredth meridian, for it is west of there that the annual rainfall drops below twenty inches. To the east of that line, there is enough rain to grow crops without irrigation. To the west, the land is drier and better suited to grazing. Kansas sits astride the hundredth meridian, which passes almost exactly through Dodge City, perhaps the most notorious of the frontier towns a century ago. It is the gateway to the Plains and to the West.

The hundredth meridian is not a bad dividing line for Kansas. The eastern part of the state is hilly and green. As the Plains roll west past the two university towns of Lawrence and Manhattan on I-70, the landscape turns yellow, and the trees give way to wheat fields, oil wells, and cattle. The table-flat Plains roll out interminably until they meet the foothills of the Rockies in Colorado. (The land is flat, but not exactly level. Kansas, like the continent, slopes upward; its highest point, Mt. Sunflower, is at a higher elevation than any point in Pennsylvania.)

Eastern Kansas is wealthy and gaining population. Although the state as a whole is growing at a rate less than the national average, the Twenty-seventh House District, which includes the fancy Kansas City suburb of Overland Park, has grown by 76 percent since 1990, making it the eleventh fastest-growing district in the United States. Neighboring districts are also growing rapidly: the Twenty-eighth District by 37 percent, and the Fourteenth District (Olathe) by 35 percent.

Those Kansas City suburbs are also the wealthiest part of the state. In four districts, three of them surrounding Kansas City, average household income exceeds $100,000. Average income in the Twenty-eighth District around Overland Park is $126,000—as high as in Greenwich, Connecticut. But only a few miles from the Eighty-third District, just northeast of Wichita (average income $108,000), is the One Hundred Third District,

one of the state's poorest, where average income is less than $26,000 and where the unemployment rate is 13 percent. Kansas may be a predominantly rural state, but its worst poverty remains in urban areas.

Only 87 percent of Kansans are white, one of the lowest percentages in the Farm Belt. The state is 6 percent African American, almost the same percentage as in California and greater than in Massachusetts. That is not surprising, if one thinks about it; the state was home to John Brown and was born amid a bloody feud over whether it would permit slavery. After the Civil War, a few groups of ex-slaves homesteaded in the northwest part of the state. Sadly, there are no large pockets of black farmers in the state today. The districts with the largest percentage of African-American residents, the Thirty-fourth and Thirty-fifth in downtown Kansas City, are urban and among the poorest in the state.

In western Kansas, which is geographically and culturally similar to West Texas and Oklahoma, there are sizable Hispanic communities, composed in large measure of oil field workers who have traveled up Highway 83, which runs from Canada to Mexico. Five districts in this area are more than one-fifth Hispanic: the One Hundred Fourth (Wichita), One Hundred Twenty-third (Garden City), One Hundred Sixteenth and One Hundred Seventeenth (Dodge City), and One Hundred Twenty-fifth (Liberal). One district in downtown Wichita, the Eighty-eighth, is 9 percent Asian.

Unlike most other states in the region, Kansas has a large state house of representatives, with 125 members. Hard as it may be to remember in a place known as a bastion of the Republican Party, Kansas has had competitive gubernatorial races, and as recently as 1990 Democrats controlled the state house of representatives, 63–62. As the rural economy has improved in this decade, Kansas seems to have reverted more to form, and the GOP now controls the house, 77–48, a gain of fifteen seats in six years.

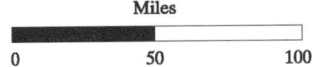

KANSAS
State Senate Districts

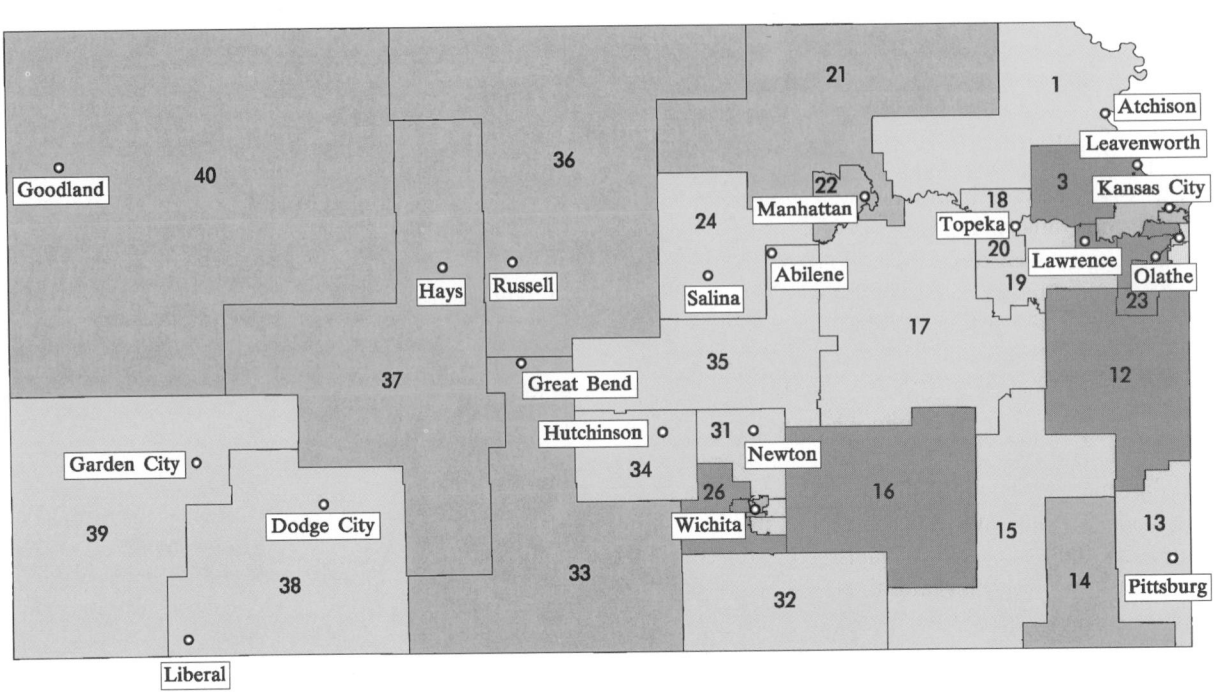

WICHITA

KANSAS CITY

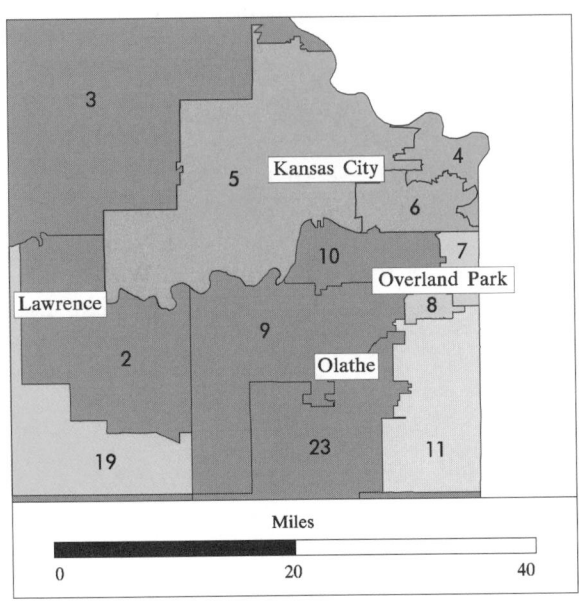

Population Growth   -9% to -2%   0% to 8%   10% to 20%   43%

Kansas State Senate Districts: Demographic Data

Senate District	Population		Average HH Income		District Type	Unempl. Rate	College Educ.	White (non-Hispanic)		African American		Asian American		Hispanic American	
	1997	+/-	($)	+/-		(%)	(%)	(%)	+/-	(%)	+/-	(%)	+/-	(%)	+/-
Kansas	2,583,015	4	47,174	38	R	5	41	87	3	6	8	2	28	5	27
1	62,849	2	38,487	41	R	5	31	93	2	2	3	0	-19	2	20
2	81,429	12	41,768	35	U	5	60	86	11	5	20	4	30	3	32
3	70,879	11	44,959	33	U	6	43	83	9	10	19	2	34	4	43
4	57,917	-5	30,727	33	U	11	23	36	-14	55	0	2	18	6	19
5	57,778	-3	50,270	35	U	5	34	82	-4	14	4	0	13	3	8
6	54,230	-7	36,328	35	U	9	20	73	-13	10	6	2	14	14	15
7	57,997	0	81,600	32	S	3	65	94	-1	1	6	1	36	3	27
8	64,048	8	58,847	26	S	3	59	92	6	2	24	3	47	3	43
9	74,432	18	62,666	32	S	3	57	92	16	3	28	2	52	2	47
10	65,575	10	57,234	29	S	4	53	91	8	3	22	2	39	4	44
11	84,290	43	102,693	37	S	3	71	94	41	2	58	2	85	2	87
12	67,647	10	37,883	28	R	6	29	96	9	2	16	0	-19	2	36
13	64,624	3	33,507	35	R	7	32	95	3	2	10	1	9	1	25
14	58,270	-4	33,109	27	R	7	29	90	-5	5	2	0	1	2	19
15	62,954	0	34,315	31	R	5	29	95	-1	2	7	0	-20	2	17
16	71,810	16	45,490	37	R	4	33	96	16	1	16	0	36	2	40
17	63,273	0	38,912	36	R	5	34	91	-1	2	-5	1	16	5	20
18	64,505	5	43,760	33	U	4	39	86	3	7	12	1	31	5	37
19	63,434	0	39,251	28	U	5	27	78	-3	12	9	0	-2	8	23
20	59,682	5	52,430	27	U	3	51	90	3	4	25	1	41	4	42
21	59,371	-3	39,488	49	R	3	33	98	-3	1	-6	0	-3	1	4
22	76,778	-9	38,301	39	R	8	50	73	-11	15	-9	5	14	6	11
23	71,261	20	59,202	32	U	4	53	93	19	2	34	2	59	2	67
24	63,745	5	43,377	38	R	5	37	93	4	3	14	1	33	3	32
25	60,003	-4	34,964	23	U	6	32	85	-8	5	37	2	29	7	28
26	78,299	17	58,880	33	S	4	41	95	16	1	55	1	52	3	54
27	59,843	10	53,824	32	U	4	47	90	7	3	57	2	56	4	42
28	66,878	3	39,882	27	U	6	25	81	-2	8	38	5	27	5	30
29	60,242	-5	31,947	27	U	9	32	43	-16	41	1	4	9	12	21
30	64,428	5	72,006	35	U	4	59	86	1	7	45	3	45	3	37
31	66,375	7	50,216	37	M	3	40	90	5	3	40	1	37	6	33
32	63,794	2	38,404	26	R	5	30	92	1	2	7	1	13	4	27
33	58,961	-4	39,616	43	R	3	32	96	-5	1	-6	0	-15	2	14
34	62,966	1	41,022	38	R	4	33	91	0	3	4	0	4	5	26
35	63,555	1	41,111	44	R	3	33	97	1	1	-4	0	-5	2	22
36	56,423	-5	37,537	52	R	3	29	98	-5	0	-8	0	-34	1	4
37	58,008	-2	41,614	48	R	4	36	97	-3	1	-5	0	-6	2	13
38	64,436	6	46,289	50	R	4	32	78	3	3	11	2	27	16	24
39	62,647	6	48,666	48	R	3	30	71	0	1	2	3	24	25	25
40	57,528	-4	39,226	46	R	3	32	96	-5	0	-12	0	-27	3	14

Note: U=urban, S=suburban, R=rural, M=mixed, HH=households.

KANSAS
State House Districts

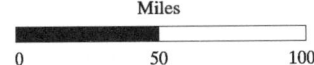

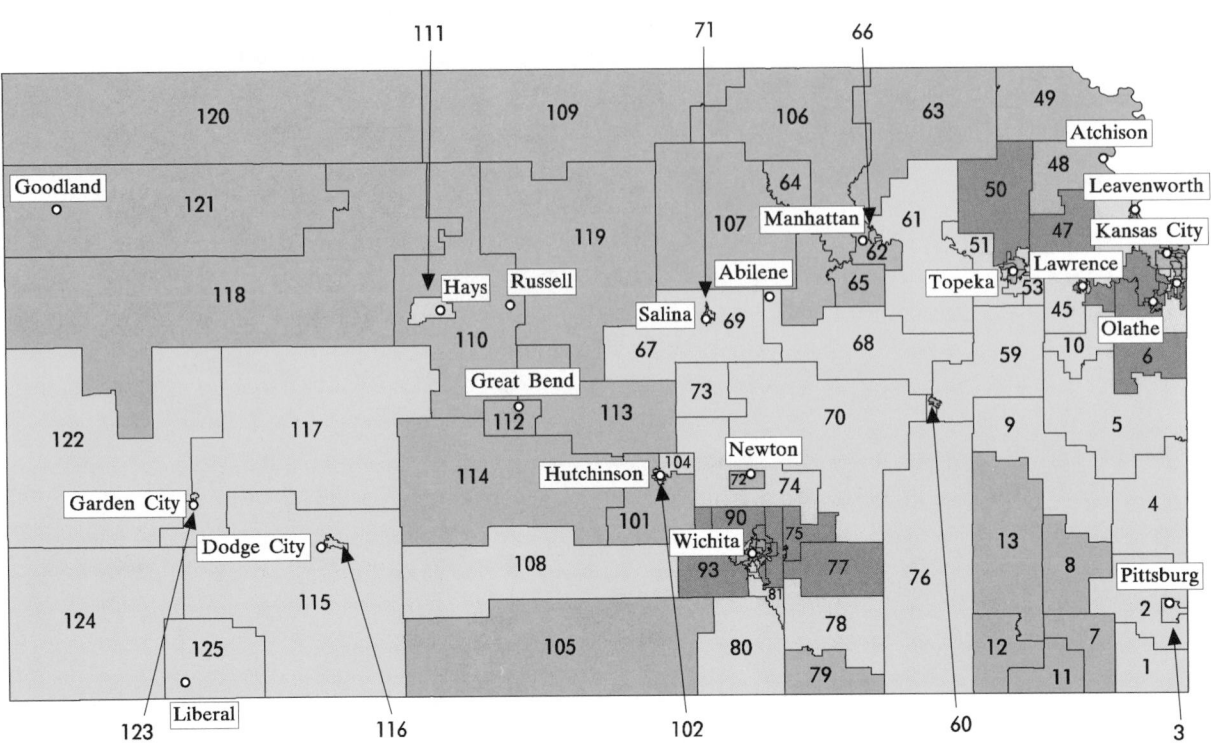

TOPEKA

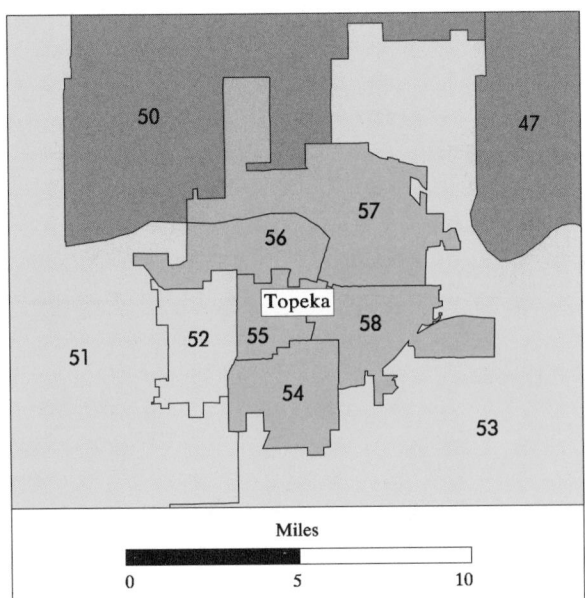

Population Growth   ▨ -20% to 0%   ▨ 1% to 11%   ▨ 12% to 37%   ▨ 76%

WICHITA

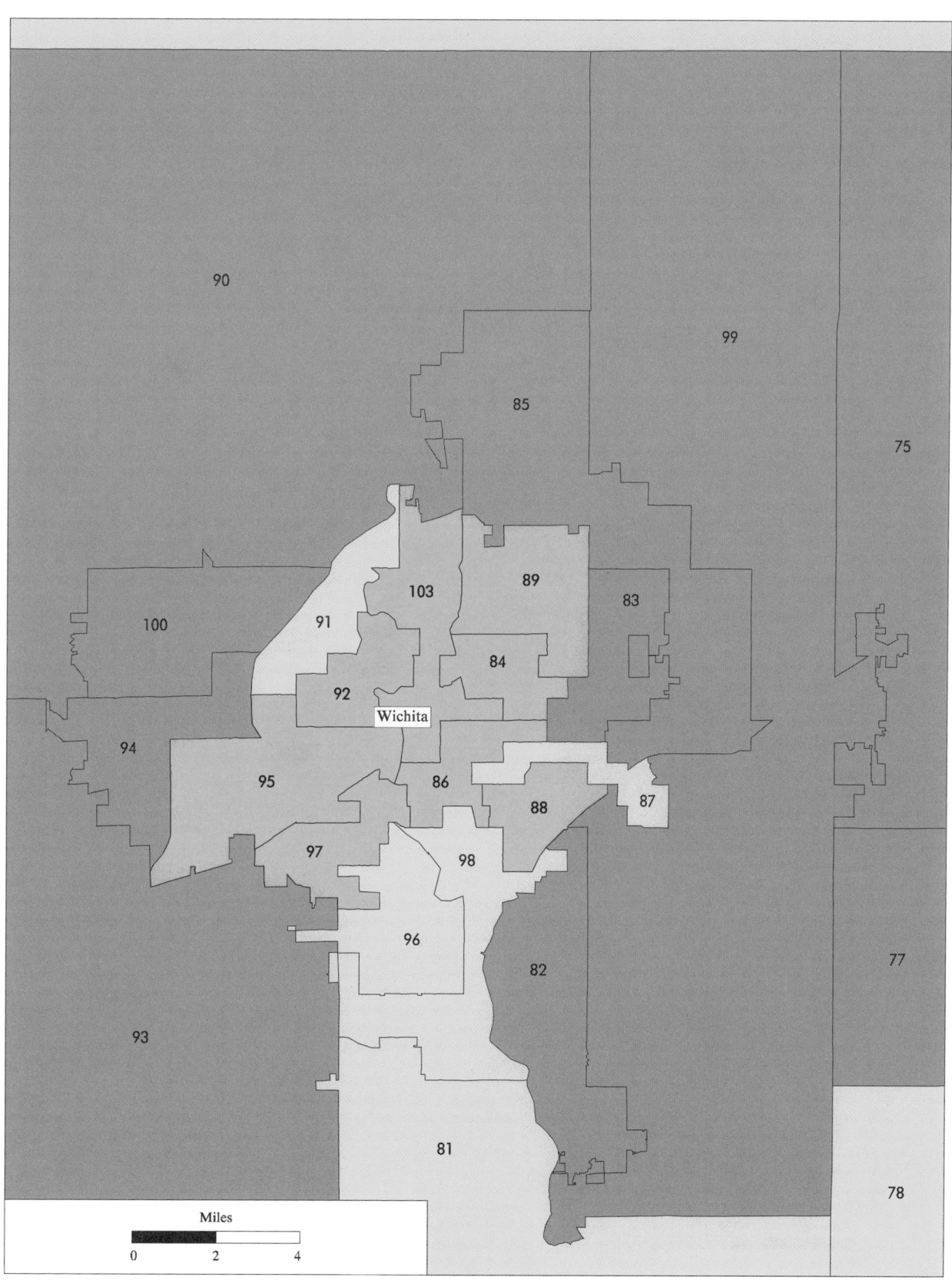

Population Growth   ☐ -20% to 0%   ☐ 1% to 11%   ☐ 12% to 37%

KANSAS CITY

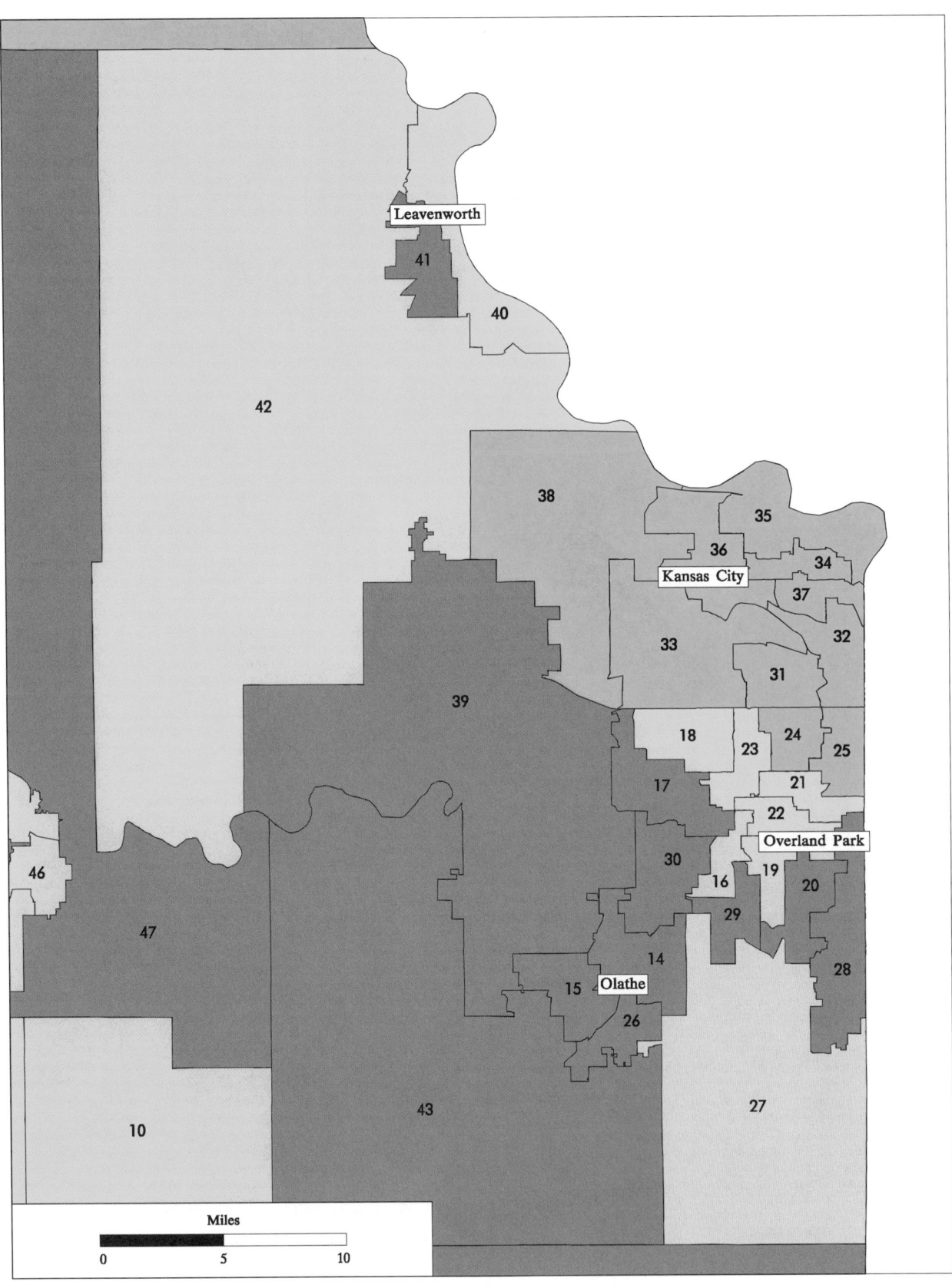

Leavenworth

41

40

42

38

35

36

Kansas City

34

37

33

32

31

39

18

24

23

25

17

21

22

Overland Park

30

19

16

20

29

14

28

15

Olathe

26

27

10

47

46

43

Miles

0   5   10

Population Growth   -20% to 0%   1% to 11%   12% to 37%   76%

Kansas State House Districts: Demographic Data

House District	Population 1997	+/-	Average HH Income ($)	+/-	District Type	Unempl. Rate (%)	College Educ. (%)	White (non-Hispanic) (%)	+/-	African American (%)	+/-	Asian American (%)	+/-	Hispanic American (%)	+/-
Kansas	2,583,015	4	47,174	38	R	5	41	87	3	6	8	2	28	5	27
1	19,793	6	33,128	35	R	7	24	94	5	1	-4	0	-8	1	35
2	20,698	3	37,391	41	R	6	28	98	3	0	-7	0	-38	1	20
3	19,752	3	33,227	37	R	8	41	93	2	2	11	2	15	1	25
4	19,256	3	29,051	18	R	6	30	96	3	2	11	0	-27	0	7
5	23,436	7	37,624	26	R	6	29	98	7	1	1	0	-23	1	21
6	22,176	13	44,758	30	R	5	32	95	13	3	25	0	-60	2	42
7	19,412	-5	31,922	18	R	6	28	89	-6	6	5	0	12	3	18
8	18,491	0	35,769	37	R	6	30	94	-1	1	0	0	-31	3	26
9	20,561	2	36,070	37	R	5	30	97	2	1	2	0	-26	1	10
10	21,456	8	38,472	31	R	5	33	94	8	2	16	0	-1	3	39
11	18,230	-7	33,022	29	R	7	29	86	-8	9	2	0	1	2	11
12	19,582	-1	37,357	31	R	5	32	91	-2	4	10	0	-3	3	24
13	18,448	-1	31,465	30	R	5	25	98	-1	0	-23	0	-52	1	2
14	27,542	35	63,436	37	U	3	61	91	33	3	43	2	69	3	88
15	17,732	12	38,391	21	U	5	38	91	10	4	26	2	48	2	49
16	20,001	9	61,767	25	S	3	66	91	7	3	23	3	47	3	39
17	23,940	12	76,742	34	S	3	66	91	11	3	22	3	42	3	51
18	20,361	5	58,930	27	S	4	49	92	4	2	15	2	28	4	44
19	22,146	9	62,452	29	S	3	62	92	7	2	25	3	51	3	52
20	21,352	16	84,755	25	S	2	68	95	14	1	40	2	61	2	55
21	19,154	2	66,229	31	S	3	61	95	2	1	16	1	38	3	28
22	20,007	6	60,883	24	S	4	51	92	4	2	21	3	44	3	45
23	19,998	9	48,184	25	S	4	53	89	6	4	25	2	51	4	44
24	19,250	-2	49,408	28	S	3	56	90	-4	3	9	1	30	5	32
25	19,674	-1	106,717	39	S	3	69	95	-2	1	7	1	29	3	24
26	22,231	17	64,017	27	U	3	58	93	16	3	30	2	55	2	53
27	33,627	76	105,695	36	S	3	67	95	74	1	105	2	134	1	133
28	26,011	37	126,032	36	S	2	72	95	35	1	61	3	88	1	69
29	20,319	17	75,739	33	S	2	70	92	15	3	34	3	51	2	59
30	22,990	13	61,758	32	S	3	63	92	11	3	25	3	52	2	42
31	18,274	-9	39,483	37	U	8	19	72	-14	8	4	2	15	18	12
32	18,602	-6	30,094	37	U	8	26	62	-14	13	5	4	18	21	18
33	18,017	-8	44,207	35	U	7	24	78	-12	15	3	1	3	5	14
34	18,003	-4	28,732	27	U	12	19	23	-17	73	0	1	7	2	9
35	18,033	-5	31,597	36	U	12	20	28	-14	69	-1	0	3	2	13
36	17,846	-5	38,905	32	U	9	25	61	-10	35	2	0	9	3	17
37	17,860	-6	30,170	33	U	11	21	64	-14	18	5	3	21	14	21
38	17,782	-12	54,980	40	U	4	37	83	-14	13	0	0	-5	3	-2
39	26,391	26	63,117	35	S	4	43	94	26	3	35	1	66	2	29
40	23,805	11	41,548	38	U	11	49	70	7	21	15	2	34	7	43
41	20,427	15	44,407	29	U	6	43	80	11	12	26	2	41	5	46
42	22,281	5	52,536	30	M	5	41	93	4	4	16	1	21	2	32
43	23,878	17	52,869	31	S	4	37	96	16	1	29	1	46	2	53
44	29,521	19	54,573	38	U	5	73	88	18	3	27	6	35	3	28
45	24,853	8	41,221	30	U	5	53	87	6	5	21	2	25	3	37
46	23,053	4	28,634	25	U	8	56	81	2	6	14	5	25	4	27
47	24,300	15	45,032	35	R	4	30	96	14	1	17	0	0	2	49
48	18,178	-4	37,246	39	R	6	32	91	-5	6	6	1	-8	3	18
49	18,650	-3	37,831	49	R	5	30	93	-3	1	-5	0	-33	1	5
50	22,582	15	48,722	39	R	3	33	94	15	1	29	0	38	2	42

Note: U=urban, S=suburban, R=rural, M=mixed, HH=households.

Kansas State House Districts: Demographic Data (cont.)

House District	Population		Average HH Income		District Type	Unempl. Rate	College Educ.	White (non-Hispanic)		African American		Asian American		Hispanic American	
	1997	+/-	($)	+/-		(%)	(%)	(%)	+/-	(%)	+/-	(%)	+/-	(%)	+/-
Kansas	2,583,015	4	47,174	38	R	5	41	87	3	6	8	2	28	5	27
51	21,680	8	60,152	26	M	2	51	95	7	1	28	1	41	2	38
52	22,036	6	49,652	27	U	3	53	91	4	3	33	1	50	3	45
53	24,611	10	53,151	32	S	3	39	88	7	5	25	0	25	5	50
54	19,061	0	46,419	28	U	5	46	80	-4	12	19	1	24	5	36
55	18,151	-5	43,111	28	U	6	47	80	-9	12	9	1	24	6	35
56	18,601	-1	38,667	32	U	5	41	83	-4	10	11	1	33	5	41
57	18,002	-7	30,531	27	U	7	14	72	-11	9	6	0	-4	16	15
58	15,171	-5	33,663	27	U	7	23	61	-12	28	6	1	1	10	23
59	24,007	7	36,788	28	R	5	25	95	6	1	-1	0	-8	3	31
60	18,014	-1	39,383	40	R	5	46	86	-3	3	4	3	22	8	13
61	21,256	10	39,312	34	R	4	32	97	9	1	-2	0	-13	2	30
62	21,379	-6	53,240	48	R	5	61	89	-7	4	-1	3	30	3	13
63	19,465	-2	40,671	52	R	3	28	99	-2	0	-36	0	-81	0	-2
64	19,618	-3	40,644	39	R	6	34	85	-3	9	-6	2	14	3	3
65	16,555	-20	31,513	28	R	12	31	61	-25	25	-18	5	7	8	5
66	27,117	-4	29,095	35	R	7	57	85	-6	5	-6	5	11	4	24
67	24,202	6	49,900	39	R	4	41	94	5	2	8	1	36	2	26
68	20,998	5	38,724	40	R	4	28	97	4	1	1	0	-8	2	22
69	17,683	2	34,637	34	R	5	28	89	0	4	14	2	33	4	29
70	21,283	4	40,011	41	R	4	29	97	4	1	14	0	-28	1	20
71	17,242	7	44,426	36	R	5	40	92	6	4	14	1	40	3	39
72	19,221	0	45,642	42	R	3	38	87	-2	2	7	1	14	9	26
73	19,937	2	46,058	48	R	3	38	96	2	1	-3	1	8	2	30
74	20,604	4	48,222	43	R	3	36	97	3	1	-5	0	-8	2	38
75	24,817	16	46,526	35	R	4	37	95	15	1	19	0	42	2	42
76	21,470	1	32,437	26	R	4	26	94	1	0	-20	1	12	4	22
77	22,921	18	49,383	40	S	4	33	97	18	0	10	0	40	2	44
78	19,955	5	37,600	25	R	5	32	92	4	2	7	2	22	3	21
79	19,331	-1	36,718	20	R	5	32	90	-2	4	9	0	5	4	27
80	20,997	3	41,154	30	R	5	27	93	2	1	-1	0	-8	5	32
81	19,439	11	49,500	32	S	6	34	95	10	0	43	1	43	3	43
82	20,263	15	56,609	37	S	5	40	87	13	6	41	3	40	3	28
83	20,395	14	108,001	41	U	3	69	91	11	4	75	3	65	3	52
84	15,888	-10	38,044	27	U	9	36	39	-16	54	-7	2	-3	3	21
85	22,171	15	59,986	30	S	3	53	87	11	6	62	2	55	4	46
86	18,158	-5	35,099	24	U	5	33	85	-9	6	34	2	28	6	23
87	19,000	1	42,533	25	U	4	48	81	-4	10	42	3	36	4	33
88	19,436	-3	32,373	22	U	8	30	70	-11	13	28	9	18	6	28
89	20,469	-2	42,587	30	U	7	42	39	-9	52	2	5	10	3	33
90	29,097	13	60,856	33	M	3	40	95	11	1	53	1	53	3	56
91	19,408	1	47,779	27	U	4	42	89	-1	3	47	1	42	5	31
92	19,836	-2	36,859	26	U	5	36	81	-7	5	34	1	27	11	26
93	25,096	25	56,386	31	S	4	37	96	23	0	39	1	71	2	84
94	19,350	14	54,117	29	U	3	53	89	11	4	62	2	60	4	55
95	20,836	0	32,100	21	U	7	26	86	-4	4	45	2	39	7	29
96	20,135	3	39,770	27	U	6	25	88	0	4	50	2	45	5	45
97	19,450	-1	37,170	22	U	6	26	84	-5	6	43	3	34	6	26
98	19,564	2	37,458	23	U	6	19	82	-3	8	42	3	36	5	34
99	26,519	15	63,842	30	S	4	54	89	13	5	41	3	45	3	29
100	16,991	14	74,179	36	U	3	56	93	12	2	59	2	60	3	53

Note: U=urban, S=suburban, R=rural, M=mixed, HH=households.

Kansas State House Districts: Demographic Data (cont.)

House District	Population		Average HH Income		District Type	Unempl. Rate	College Educ.	White (non-Hispanic)		African American		Asian American		Hispanic American	
	1997	+/-	($)	+/-		(%)	(%)	(%)	+/-	(%)	+/-	(%)	+/-	(%)	+/-
Kansas	2,583,015	4	47,174	38	R	5	41	87	3	6	8	2	28	5	27
101	20,440	-3	43,902	43	R	4	32	96	-3	1	0	0	-13	2	12
102	19,650	2	24,217	20	R	6	18	81	-1	7	5	1	1	11	40
103	19,066	-6	25,916	23	U	13	21	49	-20	19	8	4	14	26	20
104	20,338	3	56,082	45	R	2	45	96	3	1	8	0	27	2	-13
105	19,001	-5	36,499	38	R	3	30	98	-5	0	-46	0	-55	1	8
106	29,263	-3	36,958	53	R	6	29	77	-5	15	-1	2	15	5	12
107	19,201	-4	37,071	46	R	4	34	99	-4	0	-30	0	-55	1	3
108	20,660	1	42,633	49	R	3	34	97	1	1	-6	0	-32	2	15
109	17,906	-6	37,045	58	R	2	29	99	-6	0	-56	0	-27	0	-5
110	19,254	-5	38,540	45	R	3	29	98	-5	0	-12	0	-15	1	11
111	19,358	3	43,782	50	R	4	44	98	3	0	-10	1	0	1	22
112	18,659	-5	39,950	36	R	4	32	93	-6	2	-1	0	-1	4	18
113	18,893	-5	37,229	43	R	4	33	96	-5	1	-15	0	-32	2	12
114	18,520	-3	40,670	45	R	5	34	94	-4	1	6	0	-4	4	17
115	27,491	4	46,072	49	R	3	34	89	2	1	4	2	21	9	26
116	15,502	8	43,776	47	R	5	36	72	4	2	12	3	30	22	22
117	25,660	4	42,637	46	R	3	30	72	-3	1	-1	4	32	22	30
118	18,798	-4	36,667	38	R	2	31	96	-5	1	-9	0	-17	2	12
119	17,544	-4	39,258	58	R	3	34	99	-5	0	0	0	-80	0	3
120	17,224	-6	38,136	48	R	3	30	98	-6	1	-14	0	-49	1	3
121	18,380	-3	40,638	53	R	3	35	95	-3	0	-18	0	-14	4	18
122	19,699	2	46,105	52	R	2	28	82	-1	0	-27	1	-3	16	26
123	13,717	3	57,248	49	R	2	34	73	-1	1	11	2	25	23	14
124	20,335	4	46,751	48	R	4	31	79	0	0	-24	0	-2	19	25
125	21,459	7	48,502	52	R	4	28	69	2	6	12	3	30	22	24

Note: U=urban, S=suburban, R=rural, M=mixed, HH=households.

KENTUCKY

Kentucky is a state that defies easy classification. Although it sits along some of the most important transportation routes in America, both water (the Mississippi, Ohio, Cumberland, and Tennessee Rivers) and land, it is not a popular destination, except for passengers changing planes at Cincinnati's airport, which is located in Covington. Politically, the home of Henry Clay has produced few leaders of note since 1860, when it was the birthplace of all three major presidential candidates: Abraham Lincoln, Stephen Douglas, and John Breckinridge. It is also, as author John Gunther pointed out, the only state in which one part, a little peninsula sticking out from Tennessee into the Mississippi, cannot be reached by land without passing through another state.

The Kentucky that most Americans see on television each May, and the part that is foremost in national mythology, is bluegrass horse country, home to the Kentucky Derby and mint juleps. It is a land of surpassing beauty, one not exceeded even by an area most of the country does not see: the mountains, where wrenching poverty prevails. Kentucky is the sixth-poorest state in terms of average household income and is tied with Arkansas and West Virginia for the lowest percentage of college graduates, 26 percent. The unemployment rate in some parts of the mountains, mining country, is more than 14 percent.

An economy so reliant on coal and tobacco would be precarious at any time but is particularly so today. The state's overall rate of income growth is right at the national average. But growth is falling sharply in downtown Louisville and Covington, in the Ninth House District outside Hopkinsville in the southwest, and to a lesser extent in the eastern coal counties. On the other hand, the Louisville suburbs and the Cincinnati suburbs around Covington are growing economically, and, in a process seen around the nation, they are spreading into outlying rural areas.

The wealthiest Kentucky districts are not so wealthy by the standards of other states. There are no $100,000 income districts here. Suburban Louisville, particularly the Forty-seventh and Forty-eighth House Districts, has the highest average household income. Not surprisingly, the poorest districts are in the mountains: the Ninety-first, Ninety-second, and Eighty-seventh Districts in particular, where only about 12 percent of the residents have gone to college.

Kentucky is one of the least racially diverse states, though slavery was once permitted here. Fifty-four of the one hundred districts in the state house of representatives are more than 95 percent white. African Americans are found in significant numbers in only three urban house districts: the Forty-second and Forty-third in downtown Louisville (73 and 69 percent black, respectively) and the Seventy-seventh, in Lexington (54 percent black). There are no large pockets of Asians or Hispanics.

The Republican tide in the South has not lapped as far north as Kentucky, which of course was always a border state. GOP strength is scattered through some of the rural bluegrass districts and in the mountains, which were strongly Unionist during the Civil War. Democrats control both houses of the legislature, although their control in the senate has gotten thin. Kentucky remains one of four states (Mississippi, New Jersey, and Virginia are the others) that hold their gubernatorial elections in odd-numbered years.

KENTUCKY
State Senate Districts

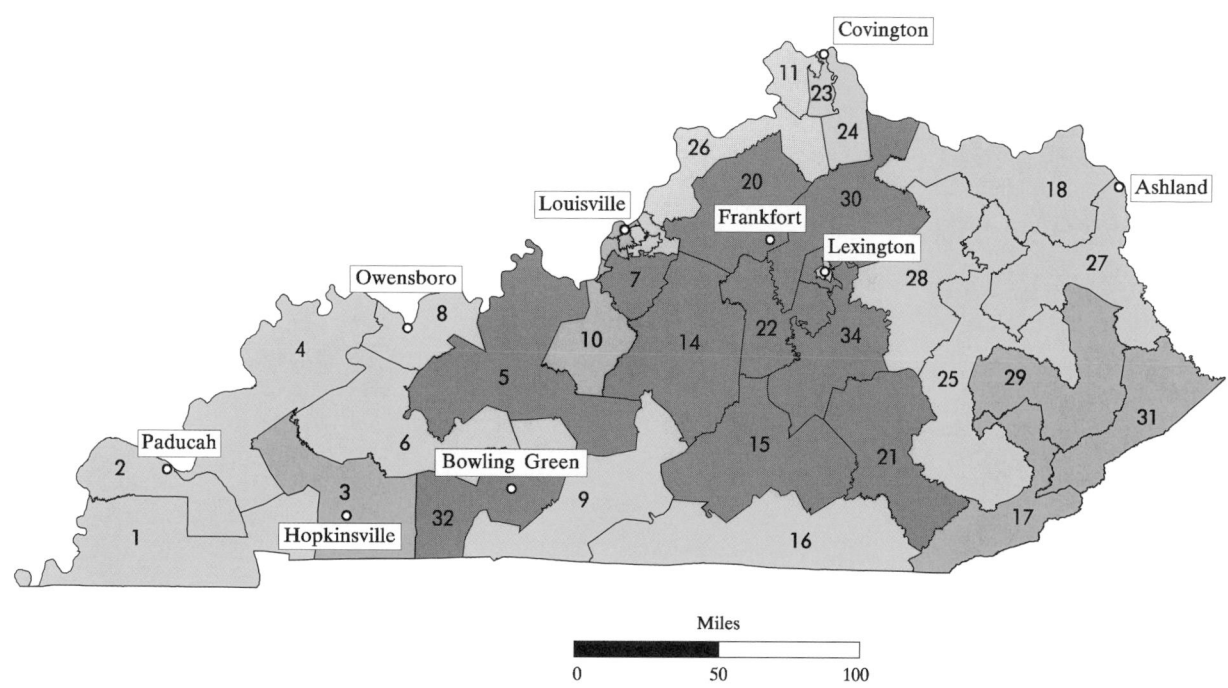

Covington

Louisville

Owensboro

Frankfort

Lexington

Ashland

Paducah

Bowling Green

Hopkinsville

Miles

0   50   100

LOUISVILLE

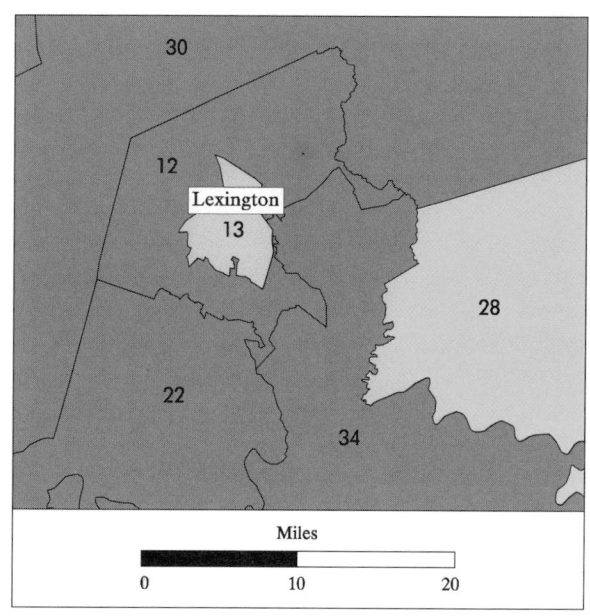

Louisville

Miles

0   10   20

LEXINGTON

Lexington

Miles

0   10   20

Population Growth   -4% to 1%   2% to 7%   9% to 14%   18% to 21%

Kentucky State Senate Districts: Demographic Data

Senate District	Population		Average HH Income		District Type	Unempl. Rate	College Educ.	White (non-Hispanic)		African American		Asian American		Hispanic American	
	1997	+/-	($)	+/-		(%)	(%)	(%)	+/-	(%)	+/-	(%)	+/-	(%)	+/-
Kentucky	3,906,528	6	40,913	39	R	7	26	92	6	7	4	1	30	1	33
1	99,066	6	36,638	41	R	8	23	93	6	6	5	0	7	0	22
2	103,465	6	42,288	45	R	7	28	92	5	7	4	0	24	1	43
3	89,775	-4	37,040	47	R	9	24	76	-4	20	-5	1	18	3	12
4	101,223	3	39,864	37	R	8	21	92	3	7	1	0	4	0	12
5	106,719	9	31,500	33	R	10	16	94	9	4	11	0	30	1	44
6	100,103	2	33,654	29	R	9	17	95	2	5	2	0	2	0	23
7	114,387	12	47,088	40	N.A.	6	21	98	11	1	11	0	34	1	48
8	100,117	5	41,083	37	U	7	29	95	5	4	5	0	21	0	38
9	100,132	7	34,516	46	R	8	14	95	7	5	7	0	1	0	27
10	96,135	0	41,194	38	R	9	28	84	-1	10	-2	2	35	3	20
11	121,331	18	60,553	40	S	3	39	98	18	1	19	1	57	1	60
12	107,711	10	55,514	35	N.A.	3	53	89	8	7	9	2	44	2	49
13	103,528	3	39,853	29	U	6	41	74	1	22	7	2	29	1	36
14	107,522	12	36,944	37	R	6	20	93	12	6	11	0	5	0	22
15	103,517	10	31,785	39	R	7	17	98	10	1	9	0	20	1	49
16	99,872	6	26,634	41	R	12	14	98	6	1	3	0	-18	0	20
17	95,732	-2	28,039	36	R	14	14	97	-2	3	0	0	8	0	25
18	96,772	4	34,406	34	R	9	19	98	4	2	1	0	4	0	22
19	100,123	4	49,602	42	S	5	33	84	3	14	5	1	33	1	47
20	106,233	12	50,327	49	R	4	31	92	12	7	11	1	39	0	29
21	109,879	10	30,249	35	R	11	14	99	10	1	7	0	16	0	48
22	113,992	14	45,691	39	R	5	32	94	14	5	12	1	35	1	45
23	99,519	3	44,195	43	S	5	25	95	2	4	2	0	20	1	47
24	101,487	6	44,046	34	N.A.	5	29	98	6	1	2	0	24	0	37
25	99,033	6	27,148	43	R	14	14	99	6	1	6	0	11	0	19
26	110,661	21	54,152	30	N.A.	5	37	94	21	4	18	0	37	1	49
27	97,812	3	35,043	32	R	11	19	98	3	1	-1	0	20	1	33
28	103,828	7	34,312	35	R	9	18	96	7	3	10	0	-23	0	19
29	102,431	1	29,965	39	R	13	16	99	1	0	-4	0	20	0	30
30	103,350	10	43,869	41	R	5	26	94	10	6	12	0	14	0	28
31	99,400	0	31,886	39	R	13	14	99	0	0	1	0	19	0	32
32	112,585	11	43,830	48	R	6	30	90	11	8	13	1	45	1	43
33	96,850	-2	30,216	43	U	13	18	31	-4	68	-1	0	18	1	17
34	118,550	13	40,988	43	R	7	28	94	12	5	12	1	43	0	37
35	97,122	2	55,552	46	U	4	51	89	1	9	7	1	33	1	37
36	97,984	3	77,794	35	N.A.	3	59	94	2	3	11	2	33	1	46
37	93,975	1	43,274	42	S	6	20	92	0	7	8	0	26	1	31
38	94,576	-4	32,585	38	U	8	22	84	-6	13	4	1	27	1	39

Note: U=urban, S=suburban, R=rural, M=mixed, HH=households.

KENTUCKY
State House Districts

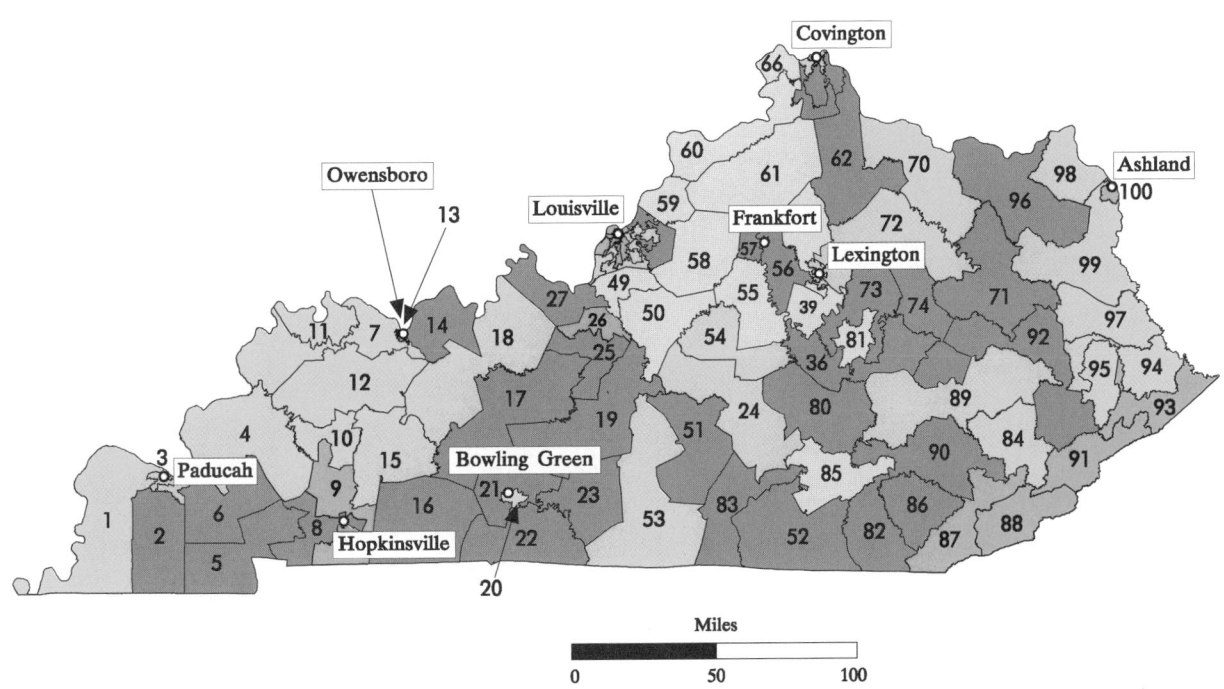

COVINGTON

LEXINGTON

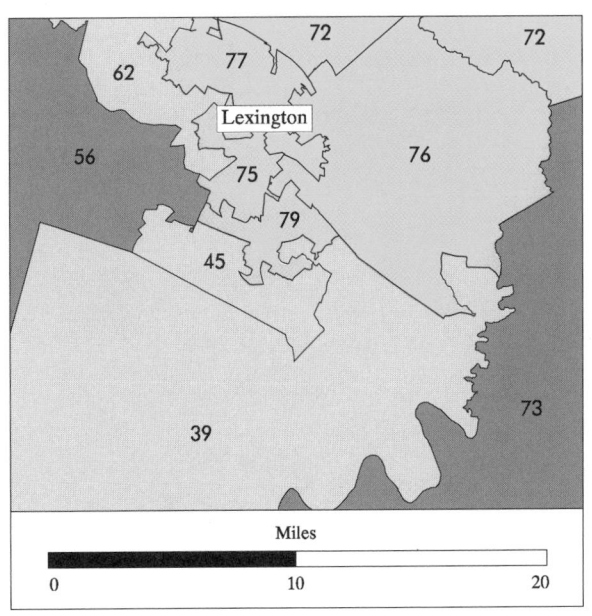

Population Growth   ☐ -17% to -1%   ☐ 0% to 5%   ☐ 6% to 13%   ☐ 14% to 29%

LOUISVILLE

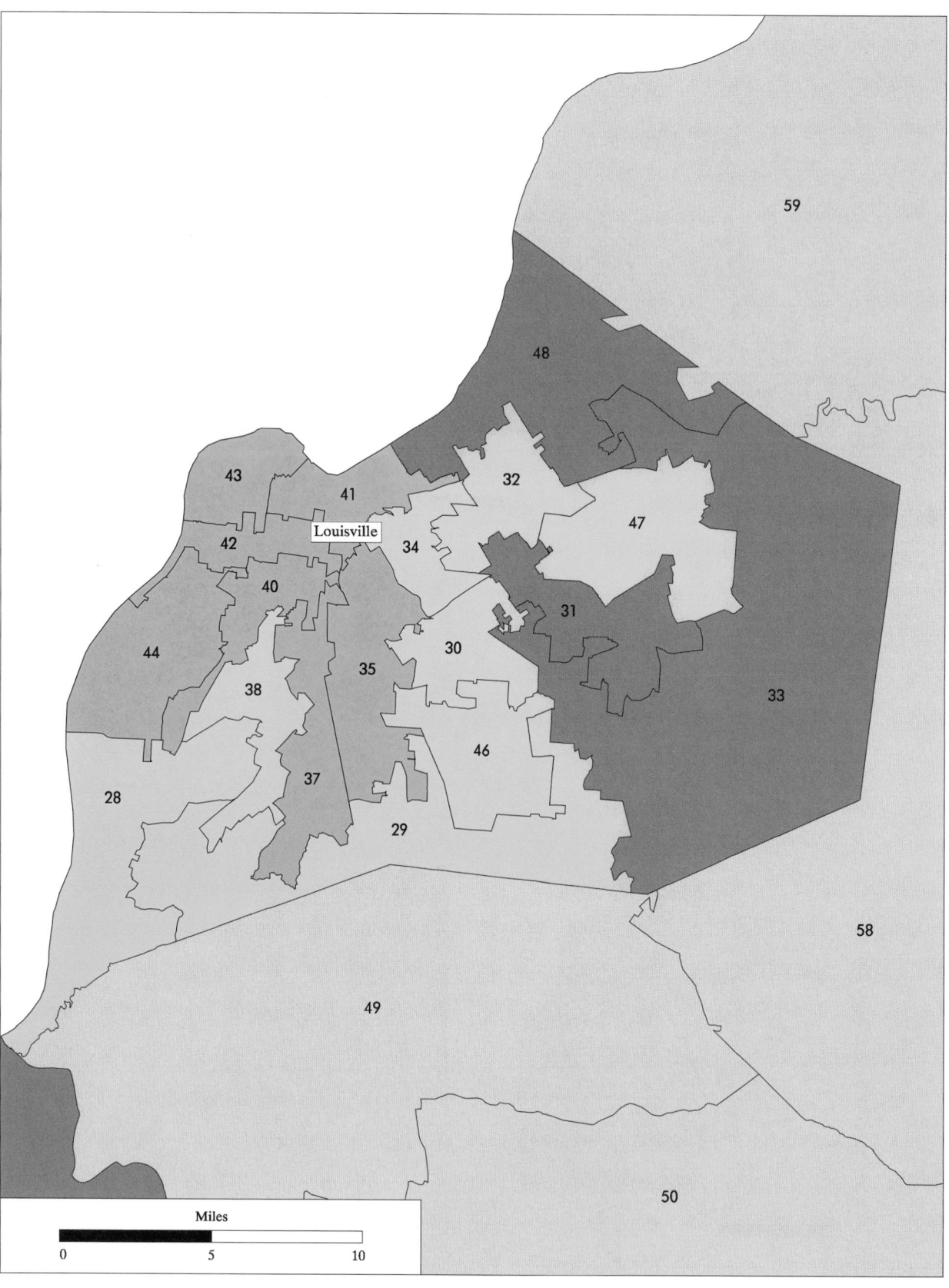

Population Growth   -17% to -1%   0% to 5%   6% to 13%   14% to 29%

Kentucky State House Districts: Demographic Data

House District	Population 1997	+/-	Average HH Income ($)	+/-	District Type	Unempl. Rate (%)	College Educ. (%)	White (non-Hispanic) (%)	+/-	African American (%)	+/-	Asian American (%)	+/-	Hispanic American (%)	+/-
Kentucky	3,906,528	6	40,913	39	R	7	26	92	6	7	4	1	30	1	33
1	38,403	2	40,146	50	R	8	23	92	2	7	-1	0	-16	0	25
2	42,098	8	37,991	35	R	8	21	95	8	4	8	0	7	0	31
3	36,615	0	39,062	45	R	7	30	83	-1	16	3	0	33	1	36
4	40,317	3	38,238	45	R	8	19	97	3	3	2	0	0	0	20
5	40,859	9	38,232	45	R	7	29	94	8	5	12	0	15	1	27
6	40,229	12	39,613	38	R	8	23	98	12	1	18	0	-2	1	44
7	43,759	5	43,768	35	R	6	29	92	5	7	0	0	12	0	3
8	37,046	12	36,572	42	U	9	27	69	11	29	10	1	82	1	59
9	31,761	-17	38,087	49	R	10	25	73	-17	17	-26	2	4	7	5
10	35,791	1	33,402	26	R	10	20	91	0	8	2	0	13	1	38
11	37,262	4	42,107	38	U	7	27	91	3	8	4	0	21	0	37
12	36,324	2	37,845	32	R	7	18	97	2	3	-1	0	12	0	8
13	32,391	-2	38,284	35	U	8	33	91	-3	8	2	0	13	1	36
14	41,635	9	42,428	41	N.A.	8	25	97	8	2	5	0	25	0	46
15	36,200	0	33,888	30	R	10	14	95	0	4	1	0	-19	0	13
16	37,336	6	37,022	46	R	6	15	90	5	9	7	0	-9	0	25
17	38,978	7	30,127	32	R	8	12	99	7	0	-4	0	-11	0	23
18	38,899	4	30,949	36	R	11	14	97	4	2	5	0	-24	0	26
19	40,578	10	30,945	39	R	9	14	95	10	5	11	0	-17	0	15
20	40,784	17	50,783	56	R	5	43	88	17	9	16	2	53	1	61
21	37,665	7	39,867	39	R	8	25	90	7	9	12	1	26	1	26
22	38,925	10	36,731	40	R	8	18	94	10	5	9	0	23	0	21
23	37,868	7	38,675	52	R	7	16	94	7	5	7	0	5	0	44
24	36,472	3	31,990	40	R	7	13	95	3	4	5	0	10	0	32
25	40,185	7	43,244	40	R	7	31	92	5	5	17	2	59	1	32
26	37,559	-3	41,149	35	R	12	29	75	-5	16	-3	4	29	5	21
27	35,666	9	34,116	27	R	12	26	82	9	12	-1	1	29	4	32
28	39,732	0	45,718	40	S	7	20	96	0	3	9	0	19	1	30
29	37,845	3	49,574	47	S	6	25	97	3	2	11	1	31	1	26
30	35,943	1	37,403	38	S	7	29	64	-1	34	5	1	31	1	34
31	41,256	8	53,803	43	S	3	43	92	7	6	15	1	41	1	62
32	36,028	0	74,272	39	S	3	61	96	0	2	5	1	34	1	55
33	44,255	10	71,214	52	S	4	44	91	9	7	14	1	47	1	66
34	37,468	2	60,880	51	U	3	60	96	1	2	9	1	34	1	38
35	34,341	-4	45,168	46	U	6	27	96	-5	3	6	1	18	0	11
36	43,695	12	32,475	34	R	9	18	97	12	2	14	0	31	0	18
37	36,323	-4	35,415	42	U	7	22	89	-5	7	-1	3	29	1	48
38	36,414	2	39,020	39	U	7	22	90	1	8	9	1	33	1	37
39	51,293	18	50,557	39	N.A.	4	42	93	18	4	17	1	45	1	48
40	36,126	-2	30,248	36	U	10	17	68	-5	29	2	1	32	1	42
41	33,153	-3	27,587	49	U	11	23	59	-3	39	-4	1	27	1	29
42	34,341	-1	26,745	43	U	13	20	26	-4	73	0	0	23	1	24
43	34,466	-2	30,662	39	U	12	15	30	-5	69	-1	0	-20	0	-1
44	37,093	-1	42,636	43	S	8	17	83	-2	16	2	0	11	1	17
45	38,332	15	63,452	36	U	3	60	92	15	4	13	3	48	1	49
46	37,860	1	49,144	44	S	4	25	86	1	13	2	1	28	1	30
47	38,850	2	78,692	35	S	3	60	93	1	4	14	1	30	2	50
48	39,539	6	89,554	33	S	3	61	90	5	7	11	2	36	1	25
49	46,373	21	44,378	36	N.A.	7	19	99	21	0	11	0	39	1	84
50	42,633	19	40,272	39	N.A.	7	22	94	19	5	19	0	24	1	42

Note: U=urban, S=suburban, R=rural, M=mixed, HH=households.

Kentucky State House Districts: Demographic Data (cont.)

House District	Population		Average HH Income		District Type	Unempl. Rate	College Educ.	White (non-Hispanic)		African American		Asian American		Hispanic American	
	1997	+/-	($)	+/-		(%)	(%)	(%)	+/-	(%)	+/-	(%)	+/-	(%)	+/-
Kentucky	3,906,528	6	40,913	39	R	7	26	92	6	7	4	1	30	1	33
51	39,486	8	32,138	33	R	5	18	95	8	4	10	0	-2	0	22
52	40,606	8	26,597	49	R	13	12	98	8	1	6	0	0	0	18
53	38,348	2	29,670	45	R	6	12	96	2	3	3	0	-33	1	14
54	37,989	5	41,248	46	R	7	25	90	5	9	6	0	17	1	20
55	39,760	15	42,209	40	R	5	20	95	14	4	15	0	13	1	48
56	46,448	13	59,661	44	N.A.	3	42	92	12	6	17	1	90	1	44
57	36,653	9	44,325	42	R	5	37	91	9	8	3	1	36	0	22
58	41,836	20	47,924	41	R	3	24	92	21	7	15	0	34	0	31
59	45,858	29	55,617	20	S	4	41	93	29	5	26	0	55	1	74
60	47,761	22	45,391	41	N.A.	6	22	98	22	1	8	0	36	0	25
61	44,507	18	38,643	42	R	6	17	98	19	2	12	0	-53	0	25
62	44,919	14	46,208	39	N.A.	4	33	90	13	8	13	0	21	2	54
63	37,583	2	73,399	48	S	2	51	98	2	1	10	1	38	1	24
64	42,091	12	51,242	41	S	4	27	98	12	0	16	0	25	1	59
65	34,320	-8	36,044	44	S	8	22	89	-9	9	-1	0	6	1	41
66	47,985	29	52,924	39	N.A.	3	34	97	29	1	32	1	73	1	88
67	39,046	1	37,708	37	S	7	23	97	0	2	2	0	22	1	41
68	38,760	7	51,521	30	S	3	40	99	7	0	14	0	27	0	31
69	38,771	7	51,693	42	N.A.	3	28	97	6	2	14	0	44	1	55
70	38,386	5	33,787	38	R	6	19	95	5	4	2	0	-50	0	17
71	40,924	10	28,757	39	R	11	19	98	10	1	5	0	25	0	24
72	41,301	5	36,707	36	N.A.	7	21	93	5	6	8	0	10	1	42
73	41,081	7	42,693	38	N.A.	6	24	95	7	5	11	0	-18	0	34
74	41,018	6	30,193	32	N.A.	11	14	97	6	2	9	0	-19	0	17
75	38,971	3	40,864	30	U	6	54	86	1	7	10	4	30	2	38
76	37,783	0	43,558	27	N.A.	5	39	89	-1	9	5	1	24	1	23
77	33,938	4	29,236	30	U	10	19	44	0	54	7	0	13	1	47
78	38,979	10	39,222	39	N.A.	6	18	98	10	1	8	0	-4	0	13
79	41,169	3	59,350	33	U	3	60	91	2	5	6	3	33	1	30
80	41,274	8	31,255	46	R	10	12	98	8	2	14	0	-23	0	13
81	41,252	16	40,302	45	N.A.	8	34	91	15	7	14	1	40	1	45
82	41,113	8	28,621	30	R	13	19	99	8	1	2	0	8	0	40
83	40,913	11	29,444	35	R	7	17	98	11	1	9	0	5	0	37
84	36,502	2	32,036	40	R	13	13	98	2	2	5	0	7	0	27
85	46,213	18	35,842	39	R	7	19	98	18	1	12	0	32	1	73
86	40,922	7	27,572	32	R	12	14	98	7	1	2	0	-11	0	64
87	34,473	-4	26,303	40	R	14	14	97	-4	2	-1	0	18	0	19
88	35,270	-4	27,202	32	R	14	13	96	-4	3	-2	0	-8	0	24
89	37,979	5	26,720	42	R	14	12	99	5	0	3	0	-8	0	6
90	39,307	7	27,413	36	R	13	13	98	7	1	10	0	-6	0	43
91	35,104	-2	26,203	28	R	14	12	99	-2	1	-2	0	-12	0	13
92	39,591	6	25,580	38	R	16	12	99	6	0	-4	0	-27	0	11
93	35,570	-1	30,881	39	R	14	13	99	-1	0	-2	0	12	0	26
94	39,027	4	38,451	45	R	11	19	99	4	1	4	0	30	0	51
95	34,192	0	29,002	37	R	13	16	98	0	1	-5	0	18	0	50
96	40,162	7	30,339	40	R	11	14	99	7	0	-11	0	5	0	21
97	36,883	3	31,965	37	R	12	16	99	3	0	2	0	35	0	15
98	37,222	1	38,972	28	S	8	23	99	1	0	-1	0	15	0	25
99	37,008	3	34,689	34	R	13	14	99	3	0	-46	0	14	0	-6
100	35,340	-1	39,777	33	U	7	28	95	-2	3	0	0	26	2	43

Note: U=urban, S=suburban, R=rural, M=mixed, HH=households.

LOUISIANA

Traditionally, there are two Louisianas: the northern half, which is Protestant and grows cotton, and the southern half, which is Catholic and grows rice and sugar. Both depend on the petroleum industry, though, which is why Louisiana in the 1990s remains one of the poorest states in the country and one that has been mostly a bystander to the boom sweeping the rest of the region.

From 1980 to 1990, Louisiana's population grew by just three-tenths of a percent. It has fared somewhat better in the 1990s, but its 3 percent growth rate is still half that of the next-most-sluggish southern state, Alabama. Districts in Alexandria, Shreveport, and the French Quarter of New Orleans have lost significant parts of their population.

Many of the people leaving New Orleans had fled across Lake Pontchartrain. Two house districts across the causeway or in Slidell, east on Interstate 10, have gained population during the 1990s, as have two suburban districts southeast of Baton Rouge. The state is almost evenly divided between urban, suburban, and rural areas, yet eight of the ten Louisiana districts that are losing population fastest are classified as urban, while seven of the ten that are gaining population fastest are suburban (and two more of the ten, though classified as rural, are across the lake from New Orleans).

Poverty, however, remains predominantly urban. The eleven poorest districts are all located in cities, led by the Sixty-seventh District in Baton Rouge, where average household income is just $19,000 a year. In central New Orleans (as well as Shreveport), more than 20 percent of the people are unemployed. That has helped give New Orleans by far the highest per capita murder rate of any large city in the country.

Even Louisiana's wealthy districts are modest by national standards. The wealthiest is the Eighty-ninth District, which takes in the Garden District of New Orleans, where the average income is a comfortable but not ostentatious $81,000.

Almost one-third of Louisiana residents are African American, the second-highest percentage in the country. The state has more black residents than Michigan or Ohio and five of the state house districts in the country with the highest percentage of African Americans. Yet with the exception of the Cajun areas, which are overwhelmingly white, racial distribution in Louisiana is not so much geographic as residential. In other words, blacks are concentrated not in certain parts of the state but in certain areas of each major city, a stark and startling reminder of residential segregation.

Consider, as an example, three adjoining house districts in New Orleans and Metairie, its closest suburb. The distance across them could easily be walked, yet the social and political gaps they span are perhaps infinite:

District	% White	% Black	Ave. HH Income
81	91	1	$52,330
94	77	14	63,134
96	9	89	20,558

Or consider the following contiguous districts in Shreveport:

District	% White	% Black	Ave. HH Income
6	81	16	$60,777
2	18	80	21,234

The same demonstration could be repeated in Alexandria, Baton Rouge, Lake Charles, or Monroe, each in a different corner of the state.

After the Vietnam War, the Gulf area attracted Vietnamese refugees, many of them fishermen who found the steamy climate amenable. As a consequence, the One Hundred Third District (St. Bernard Parish) is 12 percent Asian. Curiously, given that Louisiana was once a Spanish possession and sits on the Latin American rim, the state is only 2 percent Hispanic.

Like several other southern states, Louisiana attempted to play racial politics in reapportionment but experienced a nightmare. Since 1989, the state has held congressional elections under four different maps. Racial gerrymandering has not cost the Democratic Party here as dearly as it has elsewhere, due in large part to the state's unique unified primary system; all candidates run together, and if any wins an absolute majority in the primary, he or she is elected. Louisiana may remain a Democratic holdout in the South, but the next round of reapportionment should be no less ugly.

LOUISIANA
State Senate Districts

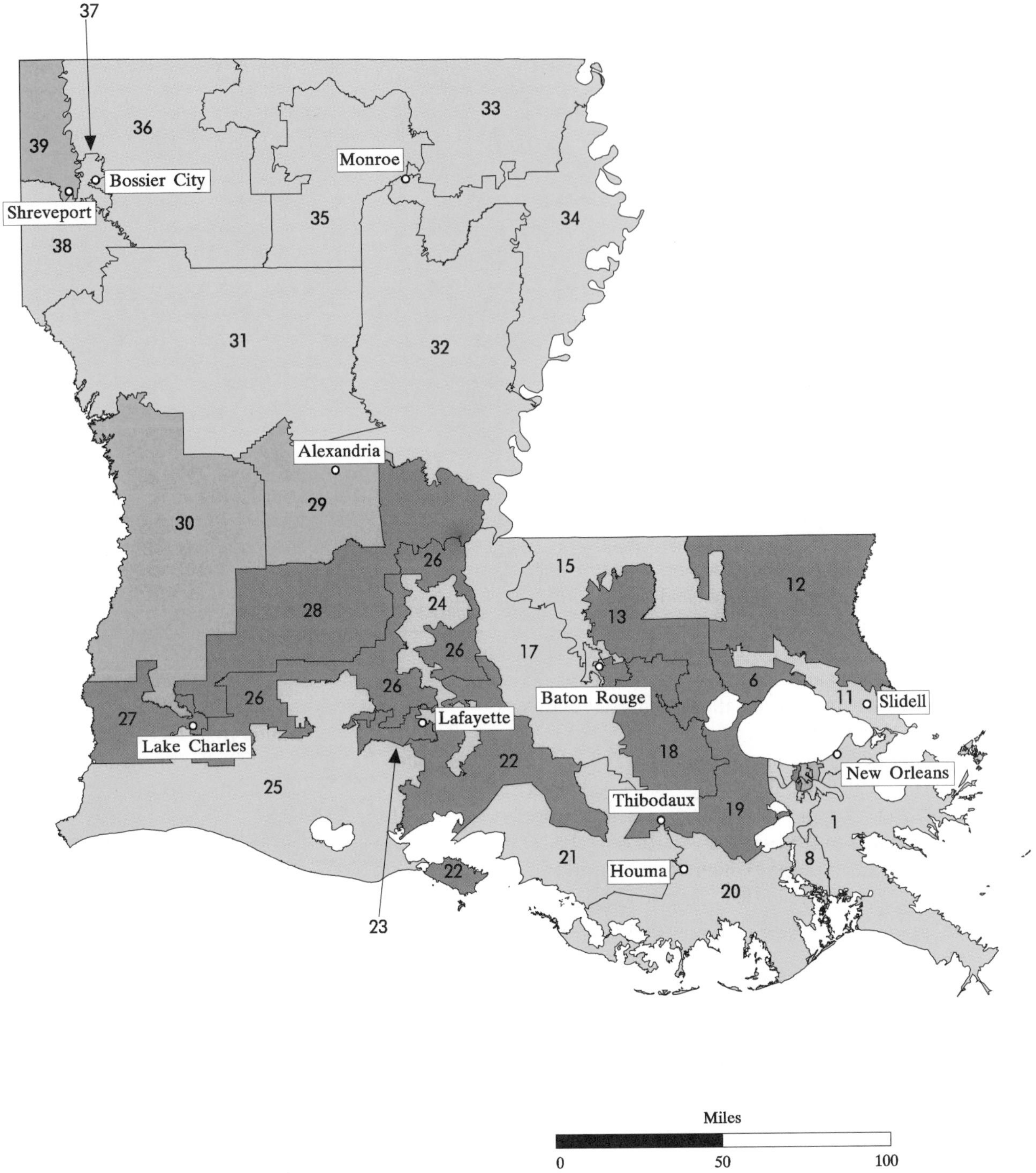

37

39

36

Bossier City

Monroe

Shreveport

38

35

34

31

32

Alexandria

29

30

26

15

12

24

28

13

26

17

26

Baton Rouge

6

26

11 Slidell

27

Lafayette

22

18

New Orleans

Lake Charles

25

Thibodaux

19

1

21

Houma

8

22

20

23

Miles

0   50   100

Population Growth   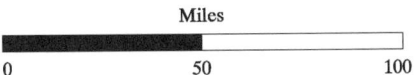 -7% to -5%   -1% to 5%   6% to 16%   27%

BATON ROUGE/NEW ORLEANS

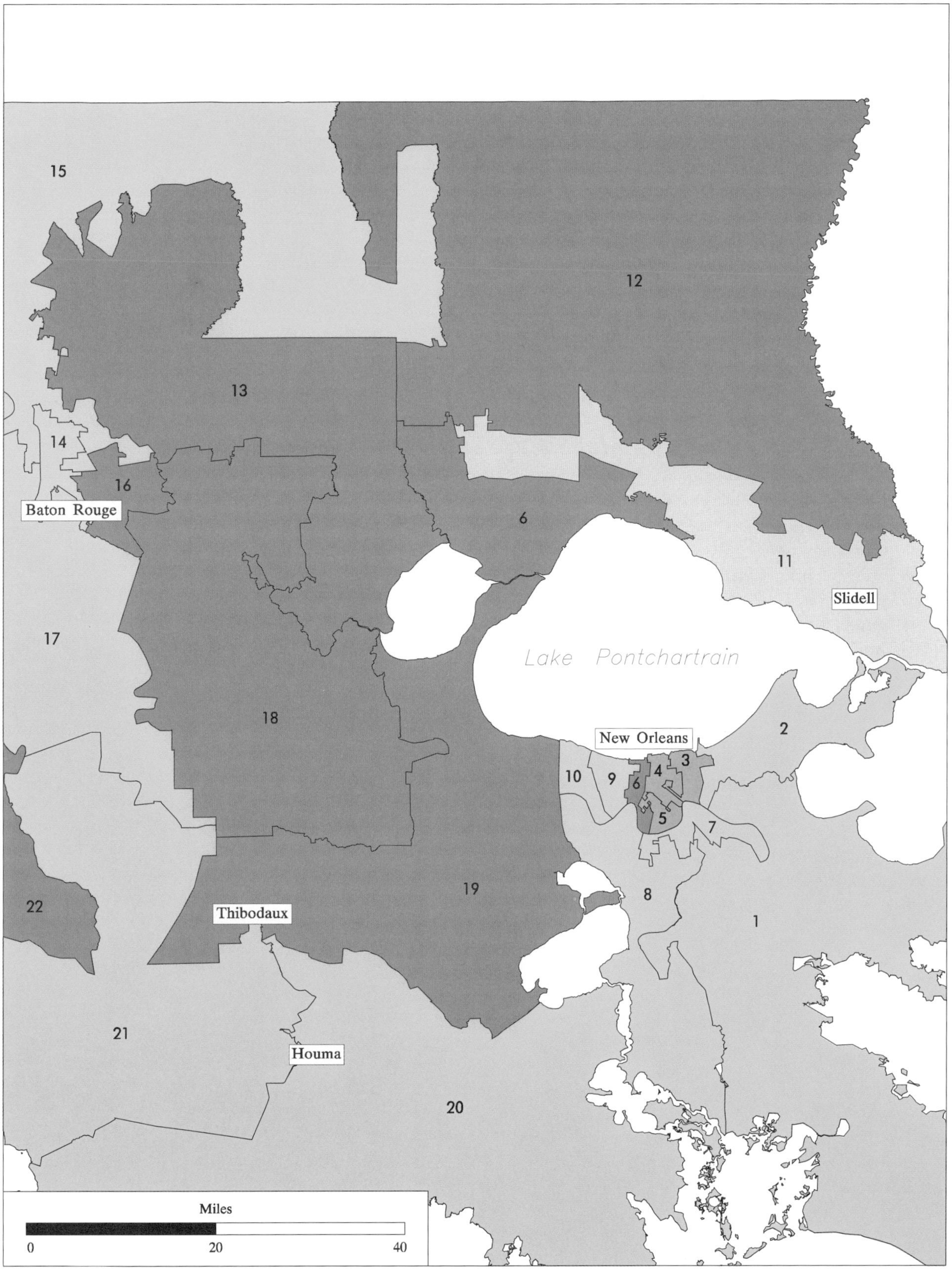

15

12

13

14

16

Baton Rouge

6

11

Slidell

17

Lake   Pontchartrain

18

New Orleans

2

10   9

3
4
6
5
7

1

8

22

Thibodaux

19

21

Houma

20

Miles

0   20   40

Population Growth   -7% to -5%   -1% to 5%   6% to 16%   27%

Louisiana State Senate Districts: Demographic Data

Senate District	Population 1997	+/-	Average HH Income ($)	+/-	District Type	Unempl. Rate (%)	College Educ. (%)	White (non-Hispanic) (%)	+/-	African American (%)	+/-	Asian American (%)	+/-	Hispanic American (%)	+/-
Louisiana	4,364,600	3	41,211	40	M	9	29	64	1	32	8	1	28	2	13
1	113,148	0	40,281	31	S	9	20	79	-3	12	10	2	27	6	12
2	102,808	-1	37,102	30	U	11	33	21	-17	70	2	6	21	3	14
3	96,783	-6	32,648	33	U	13	30	25	-15	70	-2	1	23	4	-5
4	96,988	-6	38,909	44	U	13	32	31	-9	63	-6	1	17	5	2
5	96,035	-7	39,987	51	U	14	37	26	-14	70	-5	1	17	3	4
6	117,472	8	61,003	43	M	7	47	81	5	14	21	1	39	3	9
7	111,315	-1	34,464	26	U	12	28	41	-8	50	4	3	23	5	18
8	114,521	3	42,261	30	S	8	27	66	-2	23	11	5	33	5	13
9	114,131	4	48,561	31	S	5	43	85	0	4	29	3	40	8	22
10	112,600	-1	49,225	33	S	6	37	73	-4	17	4	2	31	9	13
11	139,628	27	50,211	33	S	7	38	82	24	14	35	1	65	3	44
12	114,435	9	34,598	38	R	10	21	76	7	22	15	0	4	1	19
13	120,984	11	46,725	42	S	8	24	84	8	15	28	0	20	1	17
14	106,411	1	29,990	29	U	13	33	27	-11	70	6	2	28	1	4
15	114,733	2	33,172	32	M	13	23	35	-8	63	9	1	17	1	14
16	122,925	7	67,252	45	U	4	57	86	4	9	41	2	40	2	23
17	119,921	4	47,285	44	R	9	34	59	-1	37	11	2	31	2	8
18	132,364	16	45,876	43	S	8	22	72	14	26	19	0	37	1	38
19	120,953	7	44,176	35	R	8	29	70	4	26	18	1	33	2	19
20	112,670	4	33,250	33	M	8	14	79	1	13	16	1	35	2	20
21	112,930	2	41,005	41	R	10	19	68	-1	27	8	1	23	2	17
22	111,839	7	40,794	38	R	8	22	75	4	21	17	1	34	2	21
23	117,116	12	50,462	42	U	6	43	83	8	13	32	2	41	2	28
24	107,210	4	28,138	30	R	15	16	40	-5	57	10	1	17	1	8
25	116,772	5	42,087	46	R	7	25	88	3	10	16	1	31	1	20
26	115,739	7	33,603	39	R	10	18	69	3	29	17	0	-11	1	13
27	119,479	6	40,164	43	M	10	24	65	2	33	13	0	23	1	17
28	116,244	6	29,289	41	R	13	16	72	3	26	14	0	-18	2	18
29	102,539	-5	38,980	40	M	9	29	62	-10	35	2	1	27	1	5
30	107,743	-5	37,395	46	R	12	24	75	-7	19	2	2	19	4	-3
31	105,546	3	32,300	43	R	12	20	64	0	33	8	0	-15	2	9
32	104,003	0	35,590	45	R	9	18	81	-1	18	8	0	-4	1	9
33	107,971	1	35,477	44	R	11	24	59	-3	39	6	0	20	1	3
34	106,111	3	26,923	41	R	16	18	34	-7	65	8	0	3	1	-6
35	113,684	3	47,681	42	R	7	38	82	1	16	13	1	32	1	20
36	106,248	4	35,301	37	R	11	22	64	1	34	11	0	15	1	4
37	106,509	2	49,243	46	U	8	40	72	0	25	8	1	43	2	22
38	108,702	3	51,416	45	U	8	36	74	-2	24	22	1	32	2	14
39	96,960	-6	28,668	33	U	16	19	31	-15	68	-1	0	-9	1	-19

Note: U=urban, S=suburban, R=rural, M=mixed, HH=households.

LOUISIANA
State House Districts

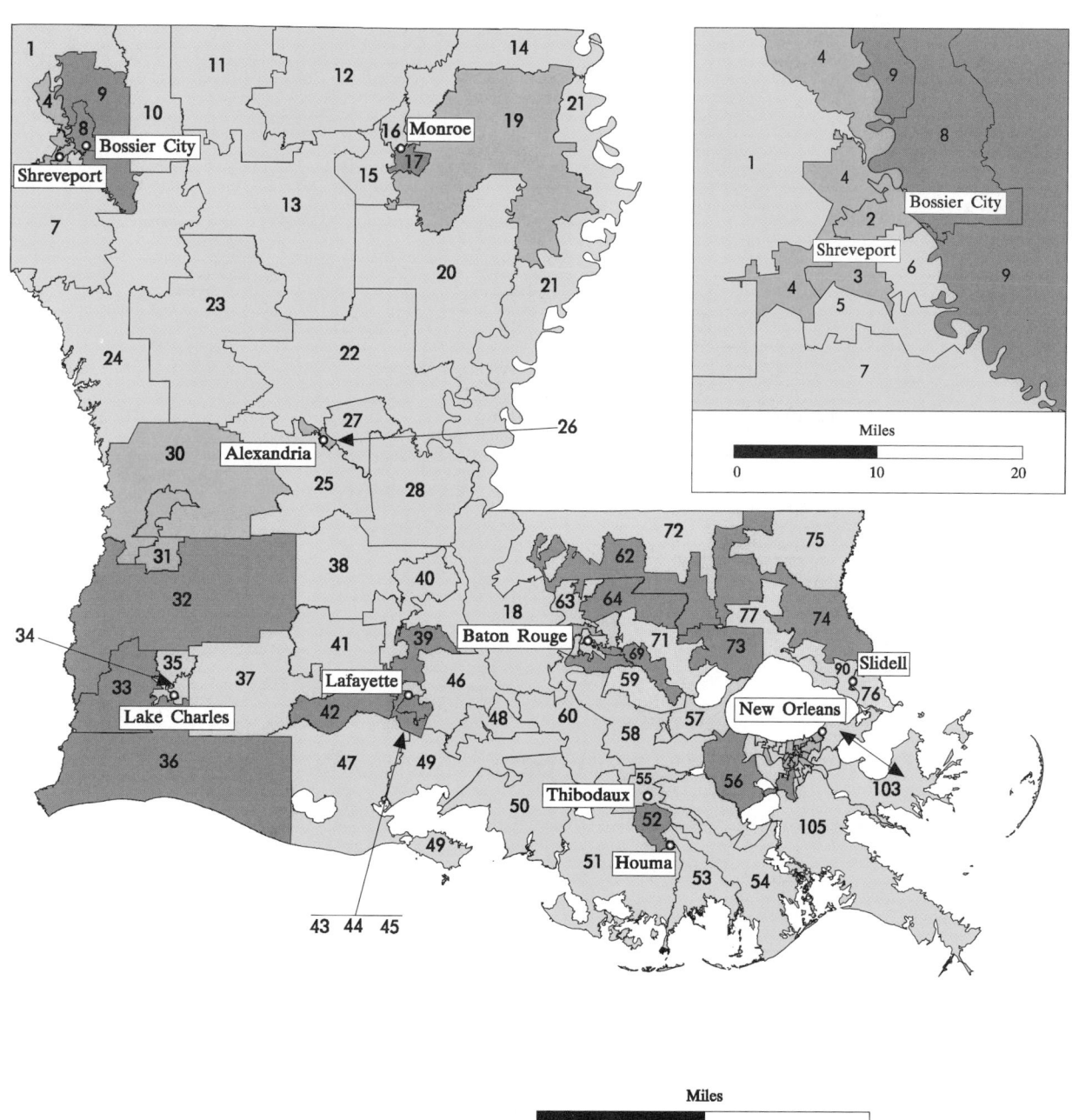

SHREVEPORT

Population Growth   ▨ -16% to -2%   ▢ -1% to 6%   ▨ 7% to 15%   ▢ 20% to 29%

BATON ROUGE

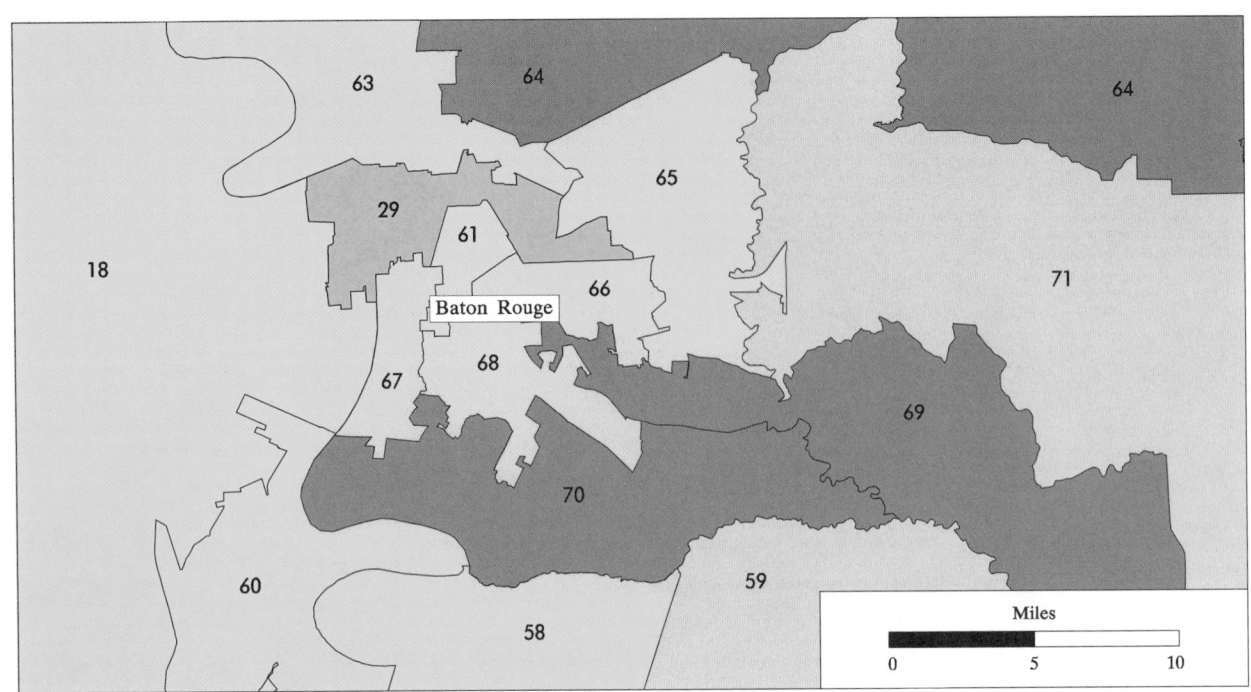

NEW ORLEANS

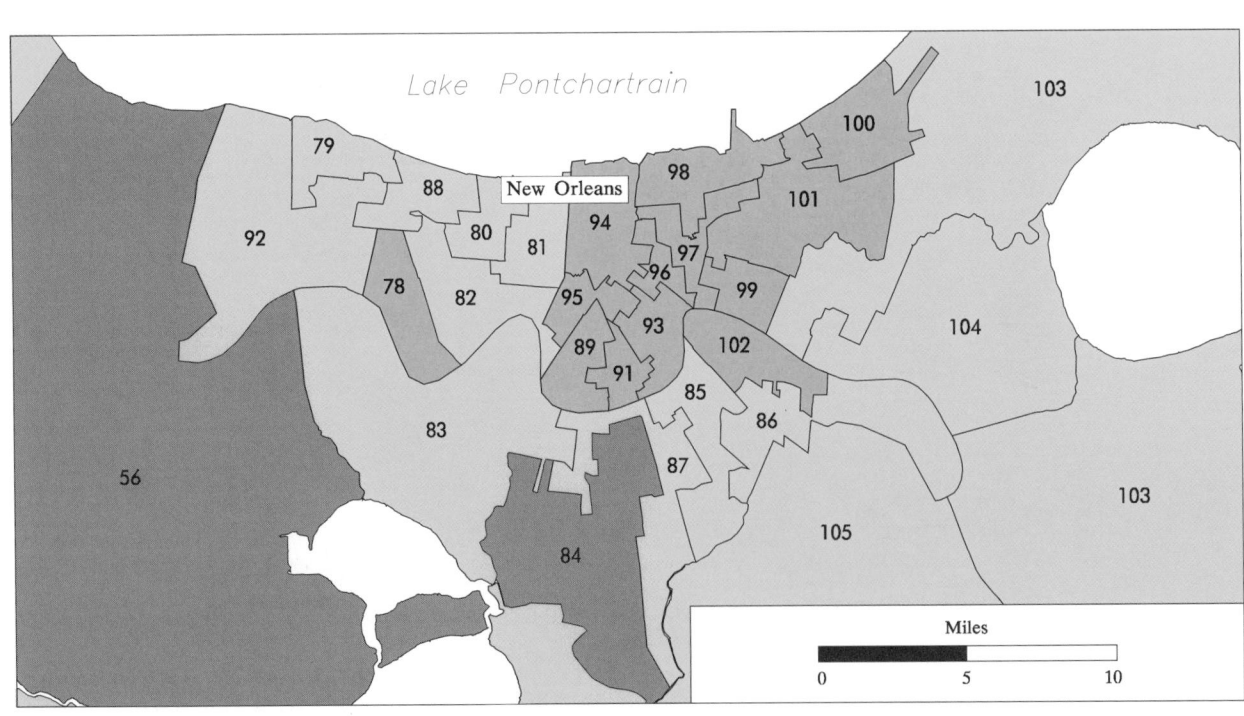

Population Growth   ▨ -16% to -2%   ▨ -1% to 6%   ■ 7% to 15%   ▨ 20% to 29%

Louisiana State House Districts: Demographic Data

House District	Population		Average HH Income		District Type	Unempl. Rate	College Educ.	White (non-Hispanic)		African American		Asian American		Hispanic American	
	1997	+/-	($)	+/-		(%)	(%)	(%)	+/-	(%)	+/-	(%)	+/-	(%)	+/-
Louisiana	4,364,600	3	41,211	40	M	9	29	64	1	32	8	1	28	2	13
1	43,957	-1	43,721	41	S	10	27	67	-8	32	17	0	11	1	-8
2	34,590	-9	21,234	27	U	22	18	18	-17	80	-7	0	9	1	-2
3	37,289	-8	24,376	26	U	17	11	26	-24	73	0	0	-11	1	-24
4	34,107	-3	35,129	38	U	13	27	33	-15	65	3	0	5	1	1
5	36,090	4	58,004	45	U	7	43	86	0	11	37	1	37	2	23
6	41,963	0	60,777	44	U	5	53	81	-4	16	23	1	31	2	27
7	44,113	3	43,680	48	R	10	29	66	0	32	8	0	38	1	2
8	39,430	9	47,312	54	U	8	35	77	6	18	20	2	49	3	20
9	45,887	9	48,128	43	M	8	31	76	5	20	21	1	44	2	18
10	42,856	2	31,021	29	R	12	19	65	-1	34	9	0	-12	1	-1
11	40,824	0	29,297	37	R	13	26	39	-7	60	5	0	10	0	-5
12	41,627	2	43,954	56	R	8	32	75	-1	24	14	1	24	1	4
13	41,566	1	34,663	31	R	10	20	70	-1	29	7	0	-67	1	5
14	41,786	4	38,717	49	R	11	20	66	2	33	8	0	-9	1	9
15	42,764	3	37,719	31	S	7	26	89	2	10	7	0	21	1	36
16	42,749	1	54,702	42	U	5	51	85	-1	12	7	2	38	1	9
17	44,727	8	21,785	29	U	18	16	15	-11	84	12	0	12	0	-18
18	43,420	4	38,732	41	R	10	16	59	0	40	10	0	-42	1	8
19	42,568	-2	35,266	50	R	10	18	65	-5	34	5	0	-50	1	3
20	40,531	-1	34,258	56	R	11	17	71	-3	27	5	0	-44	1	4
21	41,105	0	30,946	54	R	17	17	43	-4	56	4	0	-32	1	0
22	44,297	4	33,525	39	R	8	19	82	3	17	14	0	-10	1	8
23	44,428	6	33,361	45	R	14	25	58	1	39	12	0	1	1	8
24	43,386	4	30,864	41	R	12	16	68	1	27	10	0	-17	3	19
25	42,952	0	48,162	42	M	7	34	71	-7	25	22	1	42	2	21
26	31,224	-16	27,805	31	U	14	22	35	-25	63	-10	1	-8	1	-22
27	40,472	1	38,504	36	S	7	27	83	-3	15	27	1	38	1	10
28	40,554	4	30,335	55	R	15	14	69	1	29	11	0	-39	2	14
29	37,490	-3	32,696	30	U	13	22	29	-16	70	4	0	3	1	-9
30	50,884	-12	36,228	48	R	13	24	72	-14	19	-6	3	19	5	-4
31	22,851	-6	39,018	49	R	14	32	68	-9	26	1	2	18	4	-11
32	45,922	10	30,299	31	R	11	15	80	8	17	23	0	-7	2	24
33	45,821	10	45,520	44	S	7	26	88	7	11	34	0	22	1	34
34	41,130	2	30,332	37	U	14	20	27	-9	71	7	0	13	1	-7
35	40,416	6	50,025	46	M	8	30	85	2	13	41	0	32	1	13
36	45,407	9	57,695	53	M	5	37	90	7	7	39	1	48	2	26
37	44,975	4	31,820	30	R	10	16	81	2	18	16	0	-13	1	3
38	44,688	5	29,614	45	R	11	16	70	1	29	13	0	-45	1	19
39	49,028	15	39,841	43	S	7	25	74	10	24	32	0	30	1	4
40	40,162	1	29,631	33	R	16	20	41	-8	58	7	0	-24	1	-1
41	41,361	2	29,922	37	R	11	15	76	-1	22	11	0	-6	1	14
42	45,055	10	30,257	29	R	10	18	75	7	23	19	0	10	1	34
43	45,692	12	71,407	52	U	5	54	89	10	8	40	1	39	2	31
44	40,458	5	24,086	22	U	14	20	36	-6	61	11	1	38	2	19
45	48,916	11	44,120	35	U	6	43	85	8	10	34	2	40	2	24
46	44,333	6	31,396	31	S	10	14	61	2	37	13	1	22	1	15
47	41,676	2	33,620	38	R	9	17	80	0	16	11	2	26	1	22
48	41,222	5	36,959	37	R	12	19	63	1	32	14	2	30	2	21
49	42,081	5	38,567	36	R	9	16	73	2	24	12	1	37	2	15
50	42,003	2	34,988	39	R	11	15	60	-2	36	8	1	53	1	0

Note: U=urban, S=suburban, R=rural, M=mixed, HH=households.

Louisiana State House Districts: Demographic Data (cont.)

House District	Population 1997	+/-	Average HH Income ($)	+/-	District Type	Unempl. Rate (%)	College Educ. (%)	White (non-Hispanic) (%)	+/-	African American (%)	+/-	Asian American (%)	+/-	Hispanic American (%)	+/-
Louisiana	4,364,600	3	41,211	40	M	9	29	64	1	32	8	1	28	2	13
51	41,143	-1	36,627	36	R	10	15	65	-5	22	6	3	18	3	26
52	43,652	7	44,397	40	S	8	24	78	4	18	20	0	32	2	19
53	43,297	5	37,620	43	S	7	16	78	3	16	14	1	37	1	15
54	39,386	2	32,674	28	R	8	14	90	2	4	16	1	34	2	29
55	37,835	3	40,577	40	M	8	27	74	0	23	14	1	34	1	5
56	44,243	10	45,730	32	R	8	30	71	7	26	19	0	48	2	17
57	43,833	5	44,899	32	R	7	26	63	0	33	14	0	11	3	18
58	42,051	2	37,640	43	R	14	17	31	-9	67	9	0	2	1	9
59	51,008	24	48,077	42	S	6	21	86	20	12	51	0	39	2	48
60	37,626	1	37,004	37	R	10	17	61	-3	37	10	0	-23	2	5
61	38,759	-1	26,662	26	U	12	23	25	-17	73	7	1	5	1	-8
62	43,019	10	40,038	48	R	10	24	68	6	30	18	0	22	1	27
63	39,158	0	36,717	31	S	14	29	22	-11	77	4	0	-9	0	-17
64	47,546	8	46,699	39	S	8	25	80	3	18	32	0	14	1	15
65	40,061	6	55,411	31	S	5	42	88	3	8	32	1	34	2	21
66	44,278	5	49,578	36	U	7	46	70	-2	26	26	2	31	2	24
67	34,280	4	19,458	24	U	15	34	30	-5	62	6	5	29	2	12
68	41,802	5	69,685	45	U	5	61	78	0	19	23	1	40	2	21
69	46,068	13	67,154	48	S	4	52	91	11	5	43	2	43	2	26
70	50,006	12	69,587	46	S	5	63	76	7	18	35	4	42	3	20
71	49,043	20	43,861	46	S	8	20	92	19	6	33	0	38	1	21
72	40,696	5	30,681	45	R	13	17	40	-1	59	10	0	-43	1	19
73	47,290	14	36,465	44	R	10	23	72	10	26	25	0	34	1	12
74	49,655	15	35,556	31	R	9	22	84	13	14	25	0	29	2	31
75	42,034	1	32,717	45	R	12	19	66	-2	34	8	0	-36	1	8
76	51,253	28	55,749	33	S	6	44	85	25	10	44	1	66	3	51
77	50,288	24	52,158	35	S	7	40	81	22	16	30	1	68	2	34
78	37,443	-4	49,497	32	S	6	35	81	-5	14	1	1	28	4	4
79	40,391	4	60,598	35	S	5	49	77	0	9	19	3	37	11	18
80	39,164	6	46,355	27	S	5	46	82	1	5	29	3	40	10	29
81	38,513	0	52,330	37	S	5	45	91	-1	1	10	2	35	5	9
82	39,231	3	42,180	35	S	6	36	82	0	12	14	1	36	5	8
83	40,068	-1	31,881	28	S	10	13	58	-7	34	8	3	30	4	3
84	41,274	7	39,469	22	S	6	24	75	3	14	22	5	40	5	19
85	39,636	5	43,024	32	S	8	31	62	-1	28	15	3	40	5	14
86	42,255	0	48,387	27	S	8	42	60	-7	27	11	6	22	7	12
87	39,217	-1	30,745	20	S	13	19	32	-10	59	4	4	22	5	5
88	41,121	2	56,048	32	S	5	46	84	-1	4	21	3	39	8	20
89	36,908	-4	80,888	57	U	8	57	59	-8	35	2	2	30	3	-6
90	56,601	29	52,498	29	S	6	39	82	27	14	40	1	65	3	43
91	36,495	-6	43,512	47	U	13	41	31	-12	66	-4	1	21	3	1
92	37,594	0	39,602	34	S	8	26	57	-4	30	5	1	24	11	13
93	34,764	-9	28,408	59	U	20	30	22	-8	74	-11	1	9	3	17
94	37,441	-3	63,134	49	U	5	49	77	-6	14	7	1	28	8	6
95	37,353	-5	31,385	38	U	14	27	19	-19	76	-2	1	13	4	1
96	34,724	-9	20,558	30	U	22	18	9	-15	89	-8	0	31	2	-13
97	36,218	-4	30,358	30	U	13	28	16	-18	79	0	1	11	4	-5
98	36,791	-5	47,294	34	U	8	43	45	-15	49	5	2	34	5	-1
99	37,300	-6	22,498	31	U	20	12	6	-25	92	-4	0	0	2	-10
100	38,280	-2	45,423	31	U	9	39	25	-17	68	5	4	26	2	0

Note: U=urban, S=suburban, R=rural, M=mixed, HH=households.

Louisiana State House Districts: Demographic Data (cont.)

House District	Population		Average HH Income		District Type	Unempl. Rate	College Educ.	White (non-Hispanic)		African American		Asian American		Hispanic American	
	1997	+/-	($)	+/-		(%)	(%)	(%)	+/-	(%)	+/-	(%)	+/-	(%)	+/-
Louisiana	4,364,600	3	41,211	40	M	9	29	64	1	32	8	1	28	2	13
101	36,602	-5	27,906	25	U	13	28	14	-18	84	-3	1	14	2	-9
102	37,760	-5	37,774	34	U	13	34	37	-12	55	-2	1	19	6	30
103	40,850	1	33,963	28	S	11	21	62	-5	17	7	12	20	9	22
104	39,208	2	43,839	38	S	8	17	88	0	5	13	1	34	6	21
105	39,684	1	37,735	36	R	10	14	72	-2	22	8	2	29	2	7

Note: U=urban, S=suburban, R=rural, M=mixed, HH=households.

MAINE

The 1990s have been a difficult decade for New England, and for few states more than Maine. Perhaps because it was settled later than the others (the only state, as has been pointed out, to be settled from southwest to northeast), it never developed the manufacturing base that helped Connecticut and Massachusetts thrive; did not receive as many immigrants as, say, Rhode Island; and, more recently, has been too far from the Boston sprawl to lure as many transplants as tax-free New Hampshire.

Maine's population has grown barely 1 percent since 1990, forty-sixth among the states but in line with the rest of New England. This is a far cry from the 1980s, when Maine grew by more than 9 percent. In some areas, population losses have been staggering. It is a cruel irony that dovish Maine has been so badly hurt by military cutbacks. The closing of Loring Air Force Base in Aroostoock County cut population in the One Hundred Forty-eighth House District by 35 percent, and in the neighboring One Hundred Forty-ninth District by 28 percent. In all, fifteen house districts have lost 10 percent or more of their population.

But there have been pockets of growth here. Twenty-eight house districts have enjoyed double-digit growth since 1990. The Twenty-third District in suburban Portland has grown by 26 percent, while the Eightieth District outside Augusta has grown by 24 percent.

Income growth, however, has been the slowest in the nation, leaving Maine's average household income just two-thirds of that in Massachusetts. The wealthiest areas are four suburban house districts along the waterfront outside Portland; the poorest are scattered among downtown Portland, Lewiston, and the frontier. Bar Harbor, long a resort for wealthy easterners (who never lived there year-round), is one of the poorest districts in the state.

As might be expected in a state that is experiencing little growth and a lot of emigration, Maine is one of the older states; 23 percent of its population is over age fifty-five. Maine has one of the highest rates of unemployment in the country; it is worst in downtown Portland and in the districts along the Canadian border.

Maine has ethnic minorities, but they are Indians and French Canadians, groups found in few other states. It is 98 percent white; statistically, it is the whitest state in the Union. Its African American population is listed as less than 1 percent and is falling rapidly. Here, as in West Virginia and Kentucky, poverty is largely a white (and Indian) phenomenon.

Politically, Maine is unpredictable. Its reputation as one of the most Republican states notwithstanding, it actually has been more competitive than people have recognized. Franklin Roosevelt came close to carrying it twice, in 1940 and 1944. In more recent presidential races, Maine has been the country's worst bellwether (the opposite of Illinois). As political commentator Michael Barone points out, it voted for the losing candidate in 1948, 1960, 1968, and 1976 and almost did so in 1980.

In 1946, John Gunther wrote in *Inside USA,* "The trend—in Maine as elsewhere in New England—is all toward urbanization, industrialization, which, as we know, usually means more Democrats." Gunther was right about the trend, if not the cause; he did not foresee environmentalists or the cultural liberalism that have made Maine more Democratic. The state did vote twice for Bill Clinton by large margins, yet it has two Republican U.S. senators and an independent as governor (its second independent governor in a generation). Twice it was Ross Perot's best state; in 1992, he actually finished ahead of George Bush, who more or less lived there.

Maine's legislature has been in turmoil. Like other New England states, it has a huge house of representatives: 151 members. The effect has been to give rural interests greater influence. Democrats still control the senate, as they have throughout the decade, but they have lost 16 seats. They lost control of the senate in 1994 but won it back in 1996. In those two elections, almost half the seats (17 of 35 in the senate, 75 of 151 in the house) changed hands.

MAINE
State Senate Districts

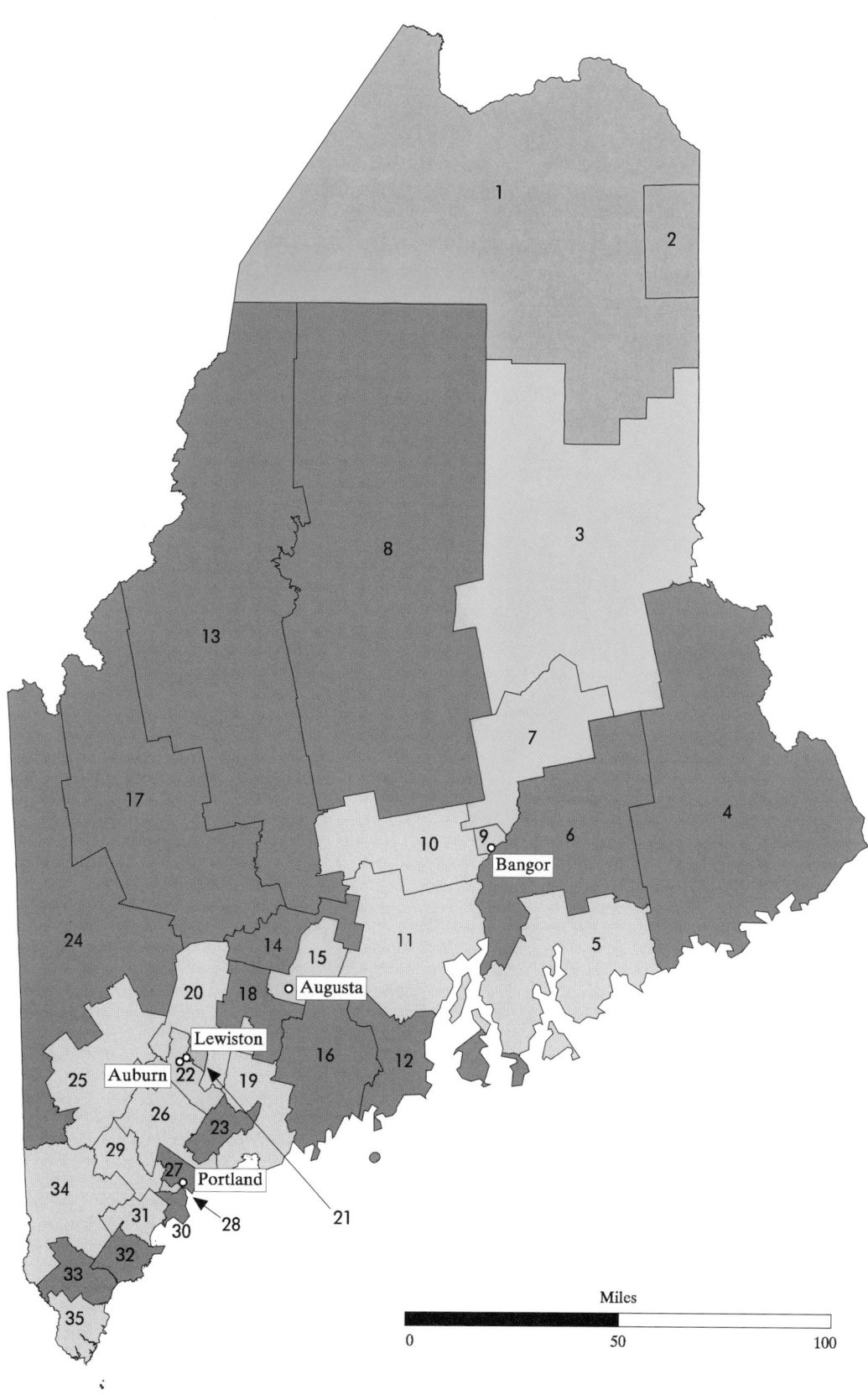

Population Growth   ▨ -16% to -11%   ▨ -7% to -4%   ▨ 1% to 4%   ▨ 6% to 10%

Maine State Senate Districts: Demographic Data

Senate District	Population		Average HH Income		District Type	Unempl. Rate	College Educ.	White non-Hispanic		African American		Asian American		Hispanic American	
	1997	+/-	($)	+/-		(%)	(%)	(%)	+/-	(%)	+/-	(%)	+/-	(%)	+/-
Maine	1,244,503	1	40,726	21	R	7	41	98	1	0	-23	1	23	1	7
1	33,484	-12	32,053	19	R	9	26	98	-12	1	-40	0	-18	0	-24
2	26,602	-16	30,996	14	R	7	33	96	-16	1	-30	1	10	1	-13
3	33,114	-4	34,110	17	R	10	29	98	-4	0	-24	0	21	0	28
4	36,260	3	29,404	19	R	11	30	95	3	0	-34	0	11	0	5
5	36,410	6	38,035	25	R	6	47	99	6	0	-32	0	15	1	9
6	35,487	3	41,234	21	R	6	41	99	3	0	-39	0	26	1	8
7	33,550	-6	38,030	20	R	6	41	96	-6	0	-28	1	20	1	-1
8	35,417	2	32,486	21	R	9	29	99	2	0	-38	0	1	0	7
9	32,726	-6	39,769	23	U	6	49	97	-6	1	-22	1	19	1	-5
10	38,276	10	39,409	23	R	8	32	99	10	0	-25	0	31	0	28
11	38,539	10	34,338	18	R	9	39	99	10	0	-21	0	26	1	16
12	35,239	2	41,819	29	R	7	43	99	2	0	-28	0	17	0	0
13	36,344	4	32,840	17	R	7	30	99	4	0	-5	0	41	0	0
14	35,394	1	37,945	18	R	5	43	99	1	0	-25	0	23	1	9
15	32,442	-7	38,508	16	R	6	37	98	-7	0	-35	1	19	1	3
16	35,635	3	41,169	20	R	6	43	99	3	0	-36	0	-15	0	5
17	35,322	2	34,292	19	R	8	40	99	2	0	-33	0	10	0	4
18	37,020	4	41,148	19	R	5	43	99	4	0	-33	0	28	0	7
19	37,218	6	44,492	19	R	5	46	97	6	0	-33	1	35	1	8
20	37,719	6	39,965	20	R	7	34	98	6	0	-17	0	25	1	28
21	31,439	-11	35,747	20	U	7	24	97	-11	1	-19	1	11	1	-15
22	34,505	-4	41,747	23	U	6	36	98	-4	0	-12	1	21	0	-3
23	36,230	2	51,895	25	R	4	55	97	1	1	-13	1	28	1	5
24	35,700	3	34,810	19	R	9	33	99	2	0	0	0	6	0	9
25	37,615	6	37,684	24	R	8	36	99	6	0	-21	0	24	0	20
26	39,255	10	57,706	25	S	5	53	99	10	0	-21	0	32	0	15
27	37,099	2	55,643	29	U	5	59	97	2	0	-23	1	31	1	17
28	33,078	-7	37,188	23	U	9	49	94	-8	1	-18	3	24	1	10
29	38,544	8	45,672	22	S	5	44	98	8	0	-9	1	30	0	0
30	35,161	1	59,930	26	S	4	58	98	1	0	-22	1	30	1	16
31	37,572	7	45,188	20	R	6	47	98	7	0	-17	1	34	1	14
32	36,057	4	44,351	16	R	6	41	98	4	0	-6	1	29	1	13
33	35,481	1	39,411	14	R	7	36	97	0	0	-38	2	28	1	5
34	38,544	10	42,129	16	R	6	36	99	10	0	-17	0	38	0	19
35	35,939	6	48,370	15	S	5	50	98	6	1	-5	1	38	1	12

Note: U=urban, S=suburban, R=rural, M=mixed, HH=households.

MAINE
State House Districts

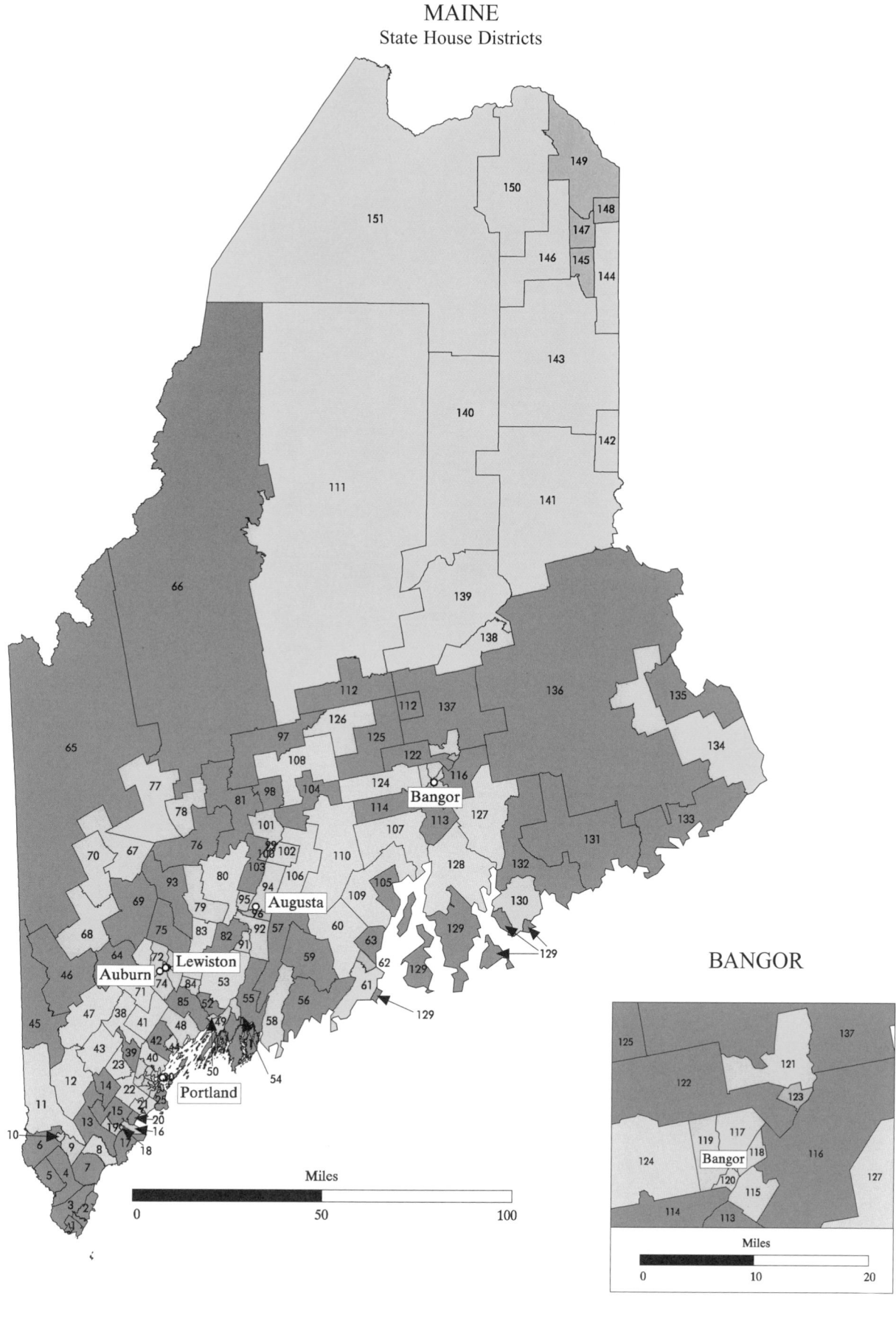

BANGOR

Population Growth ▢ -35% to -12% ▢ -11% to 0% ▢ 1% to 10% ▢ 11% to 26%

LEWISTON

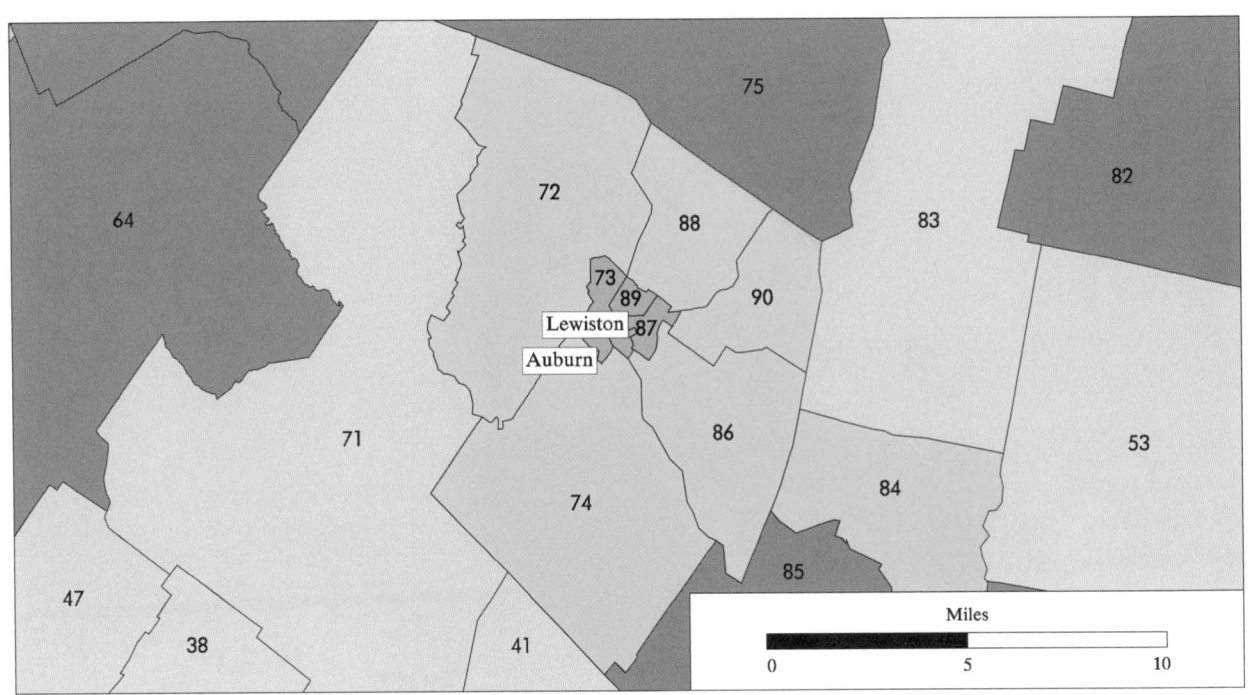

PORTLAND

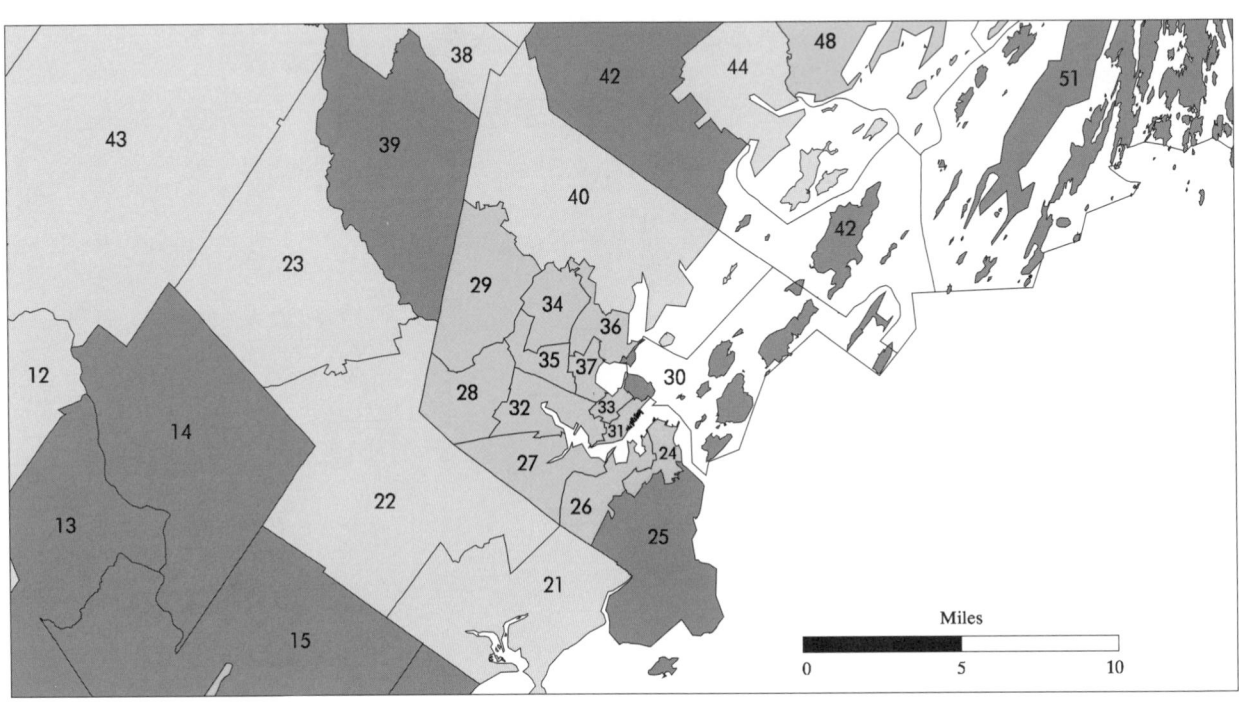

Population Growth ■ -35% to -12%   ▢ -11% to 0%   ■ 1% to 10%   ▢ 11% to 26%

Maine State House Districts: Demographic Data

House District	Population		Average HH Income		District Type	Unempl. Rate	College Educ.	White non-Hispanic		African American		Asian American		Hispanic American	
	1997	+/-	($)	+/-		(%)	(%)	(%)	+/-	(%)	+/-	(%)	+/-	(%)	+/-
Maine	1,244,503	1	40,726	21	R	7	41	98	1	0	-23	1	23	1	7
1	8,212	7	43,804	12	S	4	47	96	6	2	1	1	38	2	26
2	7,797	6	56,722	18	S	5	55	99	6	0	-30	0	33	0	-28
3	10,457	4	46,146	13	S	5	51	98	4	0	-10	1	34	1	9
4	8,666	9	50,495	16	S	6	54	98	9	0	-4	1	32	0	17
5	7,983	4	41,370	14	S	6	38	98	3	0	-30	1	39	0	0
6	9,751	4	41,516	17	R	7	30	97	3	0	-21	2	28	1	26
7	8,301	7	42,870	13	R	7	39	99	7	0	-21	0	39	0	-10
8	9,652	21	55,238	17	R	4	61	98	20	0	0	1	55	1	51
9	9,663	-1	38,280	14	R	6	30	97	-1	0	-37	2	31	1	1
10	5,144	-8	30,241	12	R	10	24	96	-9	0	-67	2	20	1	2
11	9,274	11	37,380	13	R	6	37	99	11	0	-33	0	43	1	12
12	11,448	15	41,996	15	R	6	39	99	15	0	0	0	42	0	0
13	8,474	3	43,994	14	R	6	34	99	3	0	-20	0	14	1	28
14	6,873	7	49,656	18	S	6	40	98	6	0	-10	1	35	0	38
15	10,001	8	45,697	15	R	5	45	99	8	0	-8	0	29	0	26
16	7,016	-3	38,079	16	R	7	47	98	-4	0	-33	1	24	1	16
17	8,647	7	53,520	14	R	7	50	99	7	0	17	0	30	0	-7
18	7,104	-2	29,238	14	R	8	17	98	-2	0	-18	1	19	1	6
19	8,441	-3	36,583	11	R	6	25	98	-3	0	-17	1	23	0	-3
20	7,900	1	37,425	18	S	8	39	98	1	0	-14	0	27	1	8
21	10,118	18	59,054	21	S	5	61	98	17	0	-29	1	55	0	24
22	9,484	16	50,365	23	S	5	49	98	16	0	-3	1	35	0	10
23	9,569	26	52,348	21	S	5	52	99	26	0	17	0	58	0	19
24	7,631	-3	53,863	26	S	3	58	98	-3	0	-44	1	25	0	-18
25	8,670	8	98,290	26	S	2	72	98	8	0	-25	1	35	1	35
26	7,890	-3	44,795	24	S	4	48	97	-4	0	-21	1	24	1	10
27	7,506	-5	39,476	20	S	5	42	96	-5	0	-18	2	30	1	18
28	7,546	-6	37,822	19	S	5	34	98	-6	0	-22	1	25	0	-24
29	7,852	-4	43,502	23	S	5	40	98	-4	1	-18	0	17	0	8
30	7,850	1	35,802	26	U	8	51	95	1	2	-17	1	21	1	31
31	7,532	-10	38,009	29	U	9	50	95	-11	1	-20	2	17	1	-1
32	7,378	-10	49,435	25	U	5	58	96	-10	1	-21	3	25	1	-14
33	7,798	-3	22,323	15	U	14	35	91	-5	2	-15	4	29	2	20
34	7,472	0	49,684	27	U	5	53	97	-1	0	-29	1	32	1	15
35	8,093	-5	51,276	24	U	5	60	96	-5	1	-22	2	27	1	27
36	8,070	-3	45,648	22	U	5	48	97	-4	1	-18	2	28	1	15
37	6,979	-7	48,565	26	U	4	62	98	-8	0	-20	1	23	1	-5
38	9,460	16	53,842	25	S	5	50	99	16	0	-38	0	33	0	-9
39	8,334	2	51,109	22	S	4	47	99	2	0	-21	0	0	0	0
40	9,434	18	79,116	33	S	5	65	99	18	0	-50	1	47	0	33
41	9,468	15	51,184	25	S	6	48	99	15	0	-26	0	55	0	25
42	8,404	7	79,507	27	S	4	70	99	7	0	0	0	24	1	31
43	9,218	14	47,610	16	S	4	43	99	14	0	0	0	47	0	-28
44	8,768	12	62,392	25	S	4	66	98	11	0	-12	0	34	1	59
45	8,237	4	36,794	18	R	7	31	99	4	0	-18	0	9	0	20
46	9,003	10	35,143	22	R	5	41	99	9	0	-26	0	19	1	35
47	9,650	15	40,888	25	R	8	38	99	15	0	-18	0	31	0	57
48	7,940	-3	56,998	26	S	3	55	99	-3	0	-19	0	-7	0	-6
49	8,272	-1	51,650	25	R	5	51	94	0	2	-17	1	26	2	-7
50	7,682	-1	37,316	21	R	5	45	95	-2	1	-9	2	29	1	6

Note: U=urban, S=suburban, R=rural, M=mixed, HH=households.

Maine State House Districts: Demographic Data (cont.)

House District	Population		Average HH Income		District Type	Unempl. Rate	College Educ.	White non-Hispanic		African American		Asian American		Hispanic American	
	1997	+/-	($)	+/-		(%)	(%)	(%)	+/-	(%)	+/-	(%)	+/-	(%)	+/-
Maine	1,244,503	1	40,726	21	R	7	41	98	1	0	-23	1	23	1	7
51	8,583	4	49,247	23	R	4	51	98	4	0	-89	0	41	1	25
52	6,806	3	43,615	18	R	5	47	96	3	1	-28	2	36	1	-15
53	11,118	15	40,772	19	R	5	41	98	16	0	-35	1	32	1	19
54	7,265	-4	38,514	16	R	6	43	97	-4	1	-31	1	26	1	-9
55	8,944	9	45,692	18	R	5	42	98	9	0	-32	0	37	1	25
56	8,556	9	43,640	23	R	5	48	99	9	0	-100	0	25	0	4
57	8,479	3	39,419	20	R	7	37	98	3	0	-33	0	23	1	13
58	8,181	0	42,769	21	R	6	50	99	0	0	-33	0	-54	0	-5
59	8,650	6	37,618	20	R	7	36	100	6	0	-33	0	-50	0	-5
60	10,185	20	36,879	28	R	7	39	99	20	0	0	0	61	0	32
61	8,146	-3	41,746	27	R	5	42	99	-3	0	-25	0	32	0	-35
62	6,971	-13	32,671	24	R	9	30	99	-12	0	-38	0	-58	0	-30
63	8,082	2	55,833	33	R	7	57	99	2	0	-29	0	15	1	19
64	8,243	4	36,566	24	R	7	26	99	4	0	-50	0	50	1	2
65	9,237	5	35,700	21	R	12	39	99	5	0	-25	0	13	0	-5
66	8,623	7	30,186	18	R	9	34	99	7	0	-67	0	37	0	35
67	7,949	0	32,119	16	R	11	28	99	0	0	0	0	3	0	15
68	8,088	-2	36,202	22	R	9	36	99	-2	0	7	0	0	0	-47
69	8,839	7	39,031	22	R	10	37	99	7	0	0	0	24	0	19
70	7,812	-5	32,428	19	R	8	32	99	-6	0	0	0	0	1	0
71	8,911	17	44,175	24	S	5	35	99	17	0	6	0	22	0	8
72	8,397	-5	51,147	21	U	4	52	98	-6	0	-10	1	24	0	-3
73	6,361	-12	28,435	18	U	12	31	97	-12	1	-19	1	16	1	-5
74	7,650	-8	41,910	24	U	6	34	99	-8	0	-16	0	26	1	3
75	8,683	9	44,671	20	R	6	37	97	8	0	-5	0	39	3	48
76	8,262	1	33,681	14	R	8	38	99	1	0	0	0	13	0	-6
77	7,734	-2	35,722	19	R	7	40	99	-2	0	-56	0	-4	0	-4
78	8,157	0	32,516	19	R	7	45	99	0	0	-50	0	6	0	15
79	7,330	-6	47,523	19	R	4	54	99	-6	0	-30	0	16	0	-16
80	9,797	24	48,689	21	R	4	51	99	24	0	-15	0	54	0	25
81	9,610	10	35,244	20	R	9	31	99	10	0	-18	0	55	0	18
82	8,794	8	40,563	16	R	4	34	99	8	0	-50	0	28	0	42
83	9,526	15	38,701	23	R	6	28	99	15	0	-17	0	35	0	17
84	7,672	-3	40,202	21	S	8	36	97	-3	0	-31	1	23	1	13
85	9,503	3	47,594	25	R	5	41	98	3	1	-6	1	34	1	-5
86	7,708	-5	44,779	24	U	7	23	99	-6	0	-20	0	17	1	5
87	6,926	-21	24,751	14	U	11	15	96	-22	1	-19	1	-1	1	-28
88	7,589	-9	46,170	21	U	5	36	98	-10	0	-27	1	20	1	-15
89	5,573	-15	22,238	11	U	11	12	96	-15	1	-17	1	15	1	-23
90	7,621	-2	41,735	19	U	5	26	98	-3	0	-6	0	13	1	17
91	7,551	-2	34,681	16	R	7	37	98	-2	0	-26	0	28	0	-13
92	8,071	-5	39,323	17	R	6	40	98	-5	0	-33	1	31	0	16
93	8,374	4	33,014	17	R	9	27	98	4	0	-7	0	6	1	3
94	8,226	-5	37,548	14	R	5	41	98	-5	0	-57	1	19	1	5
95	7,281	-11	34,313	16	R	6	30	98	-11	0	-26	1	20	1	-4
96	6,936	-16	35,833	13	R	6	36	97	-16	0	-36	1	8	1	-6
97	7,606	3	31,939	18	R	10	23	99	3	0	0	0	33	0	-29
98	8,021	4	31,556	12	R	7	32	99	4	0	-80	0	44	0	0
99	7,258	-8	35,311	11	R	6	47	98	-8	0	-19	1	24	1	0
100	6,285	-16	33,355	20	R	7	39	98	-16	0	-29	1	11	1	-5

Note: U=urban, S=suburban, R=rural, M=mixed, HH=households.

Maine State House Districts: Demographic Data (cont.)

House District	Population		Average HH Income		District Type	Unempl. Rate	College Educ.	White non-Hispanic		African American		Asian American		Hispanic American	
	1997	+/-	($)	+/-		(%)	(%)	(%)	+/-	(%)	+/-	(%)	+/-	(%)	+/-
Maine	1,244,503	1	40,726	21	R	7	41	98	1	0	-23	1	23	1	7
101	8,360	-2	35,549	19	R	6	38	99	-2	0	0	1	32	0	-9
102	7,582	-5	41,541	16	R	4	38	99	-5	0	-60	0	29	0	23
103	8,972	10	39,772	18	R	3	41	99	10	0	-40	0	29	1	21
104	8,746	6	36,667	20	R	7	26	99	6	0	-27	0	-8	1	28
105	8,210	1	35,286	18	R	10	41	99	1	0	-44	0	8	0	-3
106	9,042	16	44,128	18	R	6	41	99	16	0	-40	0	50	0	29
107	9,310	13	38,076	19	R	9	41	99	13	0	-29	0	39	1	25
108	9,212	15	34,687	19	R	9	25	99	15	0	21	0	55	0	-14
109	9,339	11	32,222	16	R	10	38	99	11	0	-8	0	25	1	10
110	9,303	13	30,258	16	R	10	35	99	13	0	-10	0	20	0	13
111	8,127	-3	30,033	16	R	11	30	99	-3	0	-8	0	-9	0	-19
112	8,475	3	31,959	21	R	8	34	98	3	0	0	0	-16	1	26
113	8,214	1	39,576	19	R	7	43	99	1	0	-50	0	26	1	6
114	8,633	4	45,582	24	S	6	46	99	4	0	-57	1	33	0	16
115	7,576	-7	40,031	20	S	6	45	99	-7	0	-47	0	16	1	-13
116	8,595	1	46,038	23	S	6	42	99	1	0	-30	0	26	0	3
117	7,385	-6	46,067	27	U	5	49	96	-6	1	-24	1	18	1	0
118	7,886	-10	40,968	21	U	6	51	97	-10	0	-23	1	23	1	-17
119	8,441	-4	33,716	16	U	6	41	95	-4	1	-16	2	23	1	2
120	7,472	-5	37,540	26	U	6	53	98	-4	1	-33	1	2	0	-16
121	7,978	-4	35,238	20	S	5	43	89	-5	0	-24	3	29	1	2
122	9,025	5	42,269	22	S	6	43	98	5	0	-7	1	18	1	0
123	5,992	-23	43,490	22	R	5	70	95	-23	1	-36	2	8	1	-11
124	9,161	14	40,519	22	R	6	31	99	14	0	0	0	38	1	52
125	8,949	9	40,030	28	R	8	27	99	9	0	-33	0	33	0	10
126	7,961	-3	32,557	19	R	9	23	99	-3	0	-75	0	18	0	6
127	9,410	11	38,203	24	R	6	47	98	11	0	-29	0	33	0	11
128	9,487	14	43,001	27	R	5	52	99	14	0	-42	0	25	1	40
129	8,384	3	34,294	25	R	6	38	99	3	0	-50	0	-33	0	3
130	8,322	0	42,168	25	R	5	57	99	1	0	-60	1	13	0	-18
131	9,025	6	28,830	23	R	11	32	99	7	0	-36	0	6	0	-14
132	8,843	6	36,425	24	R	7	40	98	6	0	-23	0	22	1	22
133	8,048	5	28,521	19	R	9	35	98	5	0	-32	1	8	0	8
134	8,115	0	27,048	20	R	14	27	84	0	0	-38	0	23	0	10
135	8,356	4	34,335	18	R	8	28	99	4	0	-29	0	29	0	18
136	9,016	2	31,115	20	R	13	27	99	2	0	-43	0	14	0	4
137	9,091	9	37,406	21	R	8	30	98	9	0	-20	0	21	0	13
138	7,699	0	33,872	18	R	8	26	99	0	0	-33	0	21	0	17
139	8,241	-4	34,859	20	R	10	32	99	-4	0	-100	0	11	0	-10
140	7,275	-8	40,336	19	R	7	34	99	-8	0	-73	0	19	0	0
141	7,906	-2	30,297	16	R	13	24	98	-3	0	27	0	25	0	68
142	7,875	-3	30,340	12	R	8	37	97	-3	0	-25	0	26	0	-9
143	7,982	-3	32,598	21	R	9	24	97	-3	0	133	0	164	1	55
144	6,863	-8	30,910	16	R	4	29	99	-8	0	-20	0	20	0	19
145	7,876	-13	31,483	9	R	6	37	97	-13	0	-38	1	2	1	39
146	6,400	-6	33,041	20	R	8	31	99	-6	0	-17	0	-25	0	25
147	6,516	-15	29,419	14	R	8	33	96	-15	1	-3	1	30	1	20
148	4,167	-35	30,780	20	R	9	30	88	-35	6	-38	2	-18	3	-44
149	7,549	-28	28,903	21	R	10	21	95	-27	2	-44	1	-24	1	-42
150	7,811	-5	35,457	14	R	6	27	99	-5	0	13	0	-8	0	-20

Note: U=urban, S=suburban, R=rural, M=mixed, HH=households.

Maine State House Districts: Demographic Data (cont.)

House District	Population		Average HH Income		District Type	Unempl. Rate	College Educ.	White non-Hispanic		African American		Asian American		Hispanic American	
	1997	+/-	($)	+/-		(%)	(%)	(%)	+/-	(%)	+/-	(%)	+/-	(%)	+/-
Maine	1,244,503	1	40,726	21	R	7	41	98	1	0	-23	1	23	1	7
151	8,103	-6	31,744	18	R	11	28	99	-6	0	80	0	24	0	43

Note: U=urban, S=suburban, R=rural, M=mixed, HH=households.

MARYLAND

H. L. Mencken usually had a sharp word for everything, and he did not spare his home state. "Maryland," he wrote in the 1920s, "bulges with normalcy. . . . Here, it appears, is the dream paradise of every true Americano, the heaven imagined by the Rotary Club, the Knights of Pythias, and the American Legion. Here is the goal whither all the rest of the Republic is striving and pining to drift."

In some respects, Mencken was right, though he would not have been pleased about it. If the United States is an increasingly suburban country, Maryland is its most suburban state. Almost two-thirds of its people live in a huge suburban "Y" running from the edge of Cumberland in the west and the I-95 corridor in the northeast, through the Annapolis and Washington suburbs, and down the west bank of the Chesapeake almost to its mouth.

Suburban areas tend to be wealthy, and Maryland is—the fifth wealthiest state overall, boasting higher average household income than New York, California, or Massachusetts. It also has the lowest unemployment rate of any state and one of the highest percentages of college graduates (80 percent in Bethesda). With a single exception, every house district that has gained population has been suburban or rural. The lone growing urban district is in Hagerstown; every other one of its urban districts has lost population during the 1990s.

But geography tells something about a state as well as residential patterns. The Mason-Dixon line, which forms the state's border with Pennsylvania, is supposed to divide North from South, although as Mencken also observed, this is untrue geographically, culturally, and historically. If the divide is not there, though, it is someplace close, for Maryland has characteristics of both regions.

It is a northern state, hence its wealth but also its slow rate of economic growth—third-slowest in the nation since 1990 and much more in line with New England than with the New South. It is southern in its atmosphere along the sleepy Eastern Shore and also in the state's high percentage of African Americans—27 percent, higher than Alabama. In keeping with its air of cross-pollination of North and South, though, black districts in Maryland are among the wealthiest black districts in the United States. Prince George's County, in the Washington, D.C., suburbs, boasts one of the strongest and broadest black middle classes anywhere. Average income in the Twenty-sixth House District, which is three-quarters African American, is almost $61,000, making it the third-wealthiest black district in the country and placing it in the top quarter of the state.

The really wealthy districts in Maryland, though, are in Montgomery County, on the other side of Washington, where the percentage of African Americans is much lower. In the Fifteenth and Sixteenth House Districts, around Bethesda and Potomac, average household income is $117,000. Poverty in Maryland is also much more integrated than it is elsewhere. The poorest and third-poorest districts are heavily black neighborhoods in downtown Baltimore. But the second- and fourth-poorest are in Cumberland, in the far western counties where there are very few blacks.

In addition to being one of the most oddly shaped states (at the town of Hancock, on I-70, it is barely two miles wide), Maryland has an odd way of numbering the districts in its House of Delegates. They are organized around the senate districts, but some are subdivided into A, B, and even C house districts while others are not, with no apparent logic.

Politically, this is one of the most Democratic states, one of only six to vote for Jimmy Carter in 1980. Republicans have made some gains in the legislature, but they are still outnumbered by better than two-to-one in both chambers. However, the Maryland congressional delegation is evenly split between the parties, and recent gubernatorial races have been closely contested.

If it is a representative state, Maryland has not pushed its example on the rest of the country. In more than two hundred years of statehood, it has never produced a national political leader, with the possible exception of 1972, when the country was treated to the prospect of not one but two Marylanders (Spiro Agnew and Sargent Shriver) running for vice president. Mencken would have smiled at that.

MARYLAND
State Senate Districts

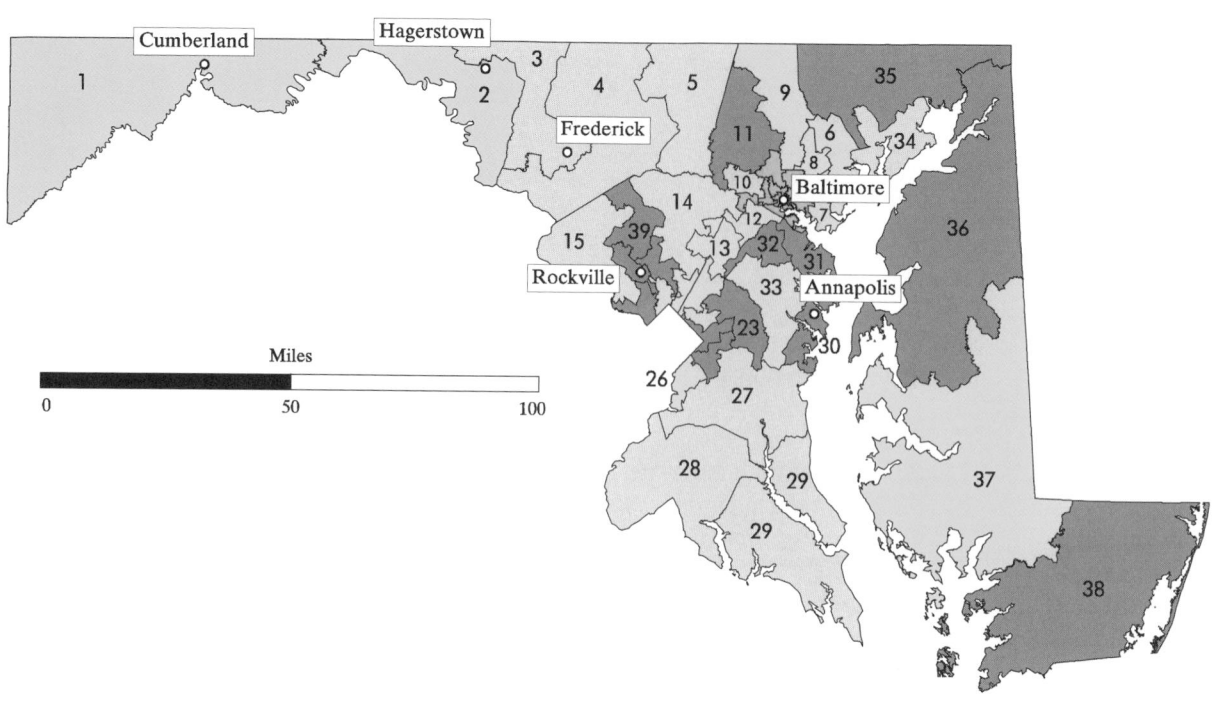

WASHINGTON, D.C. SUBURBS

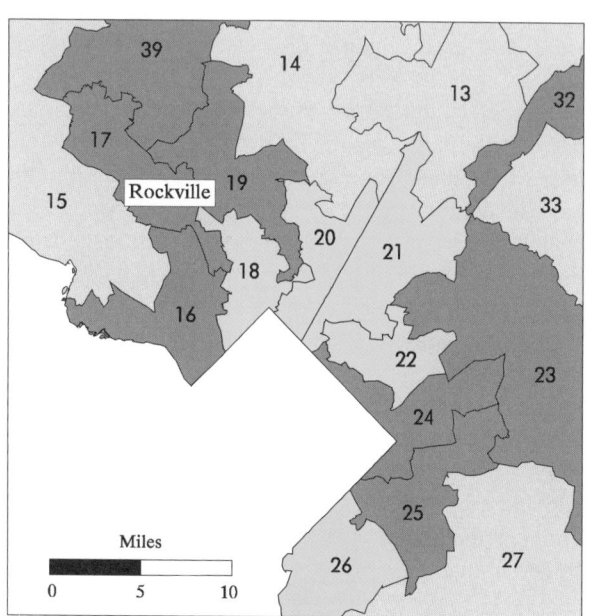

BALTIMORE

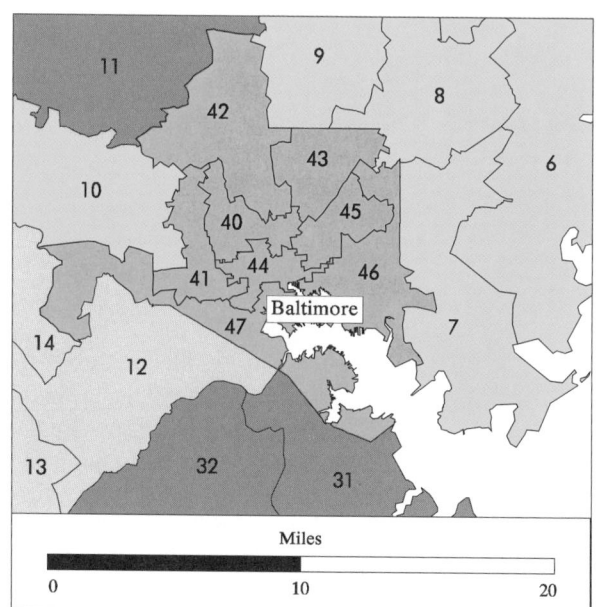

Population Growth   ■ -12% to -4%   □ -1% to 5%   ■ 6% to 12%   □ 14% to 22%

Maryland State Senate Districts: Demographic Data

Senate District	Population 1997	+/-	Average HH Income ($)	+/-	District Type	Unempl. Rate (%)	College Educ. (%)	White (non-Hispanic) (%)	+/-	African American (%)	+/-	Asian American (%)	+/-	Hispanic American (%)	+/-
Maryland	5,099,840	7	59,006	23	S	4	45	65	0	27	16	4	40	4	50
1	102,207	-1	33,506	19	M	8	28	97	-1	2	18	0	21	1	48
2	105,003	5	38,650	18	S	4	25	90	3	8	27	1	36	1	59
3	116,010	19	52,151	19	S	3	43	87	16	8	49	2	65	2	81
4	118,250	20	60,796	25	S	2	38	95	18	4	54	1	54	1	66
5	116,973	18	59,474	26	R	3	40	95	17	3	49	1	59	1	80
6	102,510	4	45,231	20	S	5	22	87	0	10	40	1	34	1	63
7	98,550	1	43,167	17	S	5	20	87	-2	10	27	1	41	1	48
8	98,003	3	53,419	21	S	3	43	86	-1	8	29	4	43	2	55
9	108,632	1	70,465	25	S	2	58	90	-2	4	40	4	41	2	39
10	99,490	4	47,882	17	S	5	41	28	-17	68	13	2	23	2	60
11	114,497	8	81,384	25	S	3	57	81	2	13	48	4	45	2	62
12	121,765	22	61,982	26	S	3	53	79	16	14	52	4	65	3	84
13	123,930	16	64,168	17	S	2	63	71	7	19	46	6	57	4	70
14	124,919	18	84,372	21	S	2	65	78	11	11	43	8	55	3	70
15	116,480	16	116,776	24	S	2	72	76	8	6	44	12	54	5	49
16	102,182	6	117,443	23	S	2	80	81	0	3	33	9	46	7	29
17	116,817	10	66,979	24	S	3	62	62	-5	12	31	12	48	13	63
18	108,271	3	73,889	18	S	3	63	61	-10	15	21	8	32	15	52
19	114,165	9	79,333	23	S	3	65	66	0	14	24	11	38	8	51
20	105,928	2	59,439	19	S	4	61	42	-18	29	12	11	26	17	43
21	109,250	2	56,848	21	S	4	52	46	-15	31	18	8	28	14	42
22	102,901	0	50,594	15	S	4	42	34	-24	50	14	6	23	10	45
23	118,813	12	71,394	24	S	3	56	60	-1	30	37	6	48	3	41
24	113,202	9	49,883	25	S	7	30	10	-22	85	13	1	27	4	46
25	110,330	6	54,641	23	S	4	40	15	-23	80	14	2	23	2	14
26	107,716	1	60,720	18	S	4	42	19	-26	74	10	5	21	2	14
27	126,698	19	69,552	21	S	3	40	61	7	34	43	2	52	2	51
28	114,923	14	61,767	23	S	3	36	73	6	22	38	2	62	3	72
29	123,580	18	53,207	21	R	4	34	78	11	18	46	1	65	2	84
30	112,569	7	65,994	18	S	3	53	77	1	19	33	2	41	2	45
31	109,307	6	55,162	18	S	3	31	89	3	8	33	1	46	1	58
32	109,228	7	52,002	16	S	3	35	77	0	16	32	4	49	3	70
33	125,158	20	75,180	21	S	3	54	80	15	14	42	3	55	3	62
34	128,061	22	51,310	21	S	4	42	79	16	15	43	2	63	3	74
35	115,151	10	55,648	12	R	3	38	94	8	4	44	1	59	1	71
36	112,067	11	51,973	21	R	4	32	85	7	13	37	0	39	1	52
37	112,023	5	43,215	25	R	5	31	66	-2	32	25	0	9	1	37
38	113,393	11	41,640	21	R	6	31	73	3	25	36	1	34	1	50
39	111,002	12	71,577	22	S	2	62	69	1	13	38	9	46	8	73
40	86,284	-10	30,967	25	U	12	22	6	-42	92	-7	1	-13	1	7
41	84,871	-12	36,778	25	U	10	19	12	-38	87	-7	1	-7	1	7
42	89,974	-7	71,745	30	U	4	58	76	-15	19	34	3	33	2	25
43	87,611	-10	49,832	29	U	7	38	30	-31	67	4	1	-4	1	7
44	88,913	-8	28,695	29	U	14	21	14	-34	84	-1	1	-3	1	18
45	84,841	-11	32,500	23	U	11	16	17	-36	81	-3	1	-22	1	16
46	90,298	-8	37,409	26	U	7	19	74	-17	21	27	1	17	3	36
47	97,122	-4	43,491	26	U	6	30	67	-11	29	13	2	29	1	40

Note: U=urban, S=suburban, R=rural, M=mixed, HH=households.

MARYLAND
State House Districts

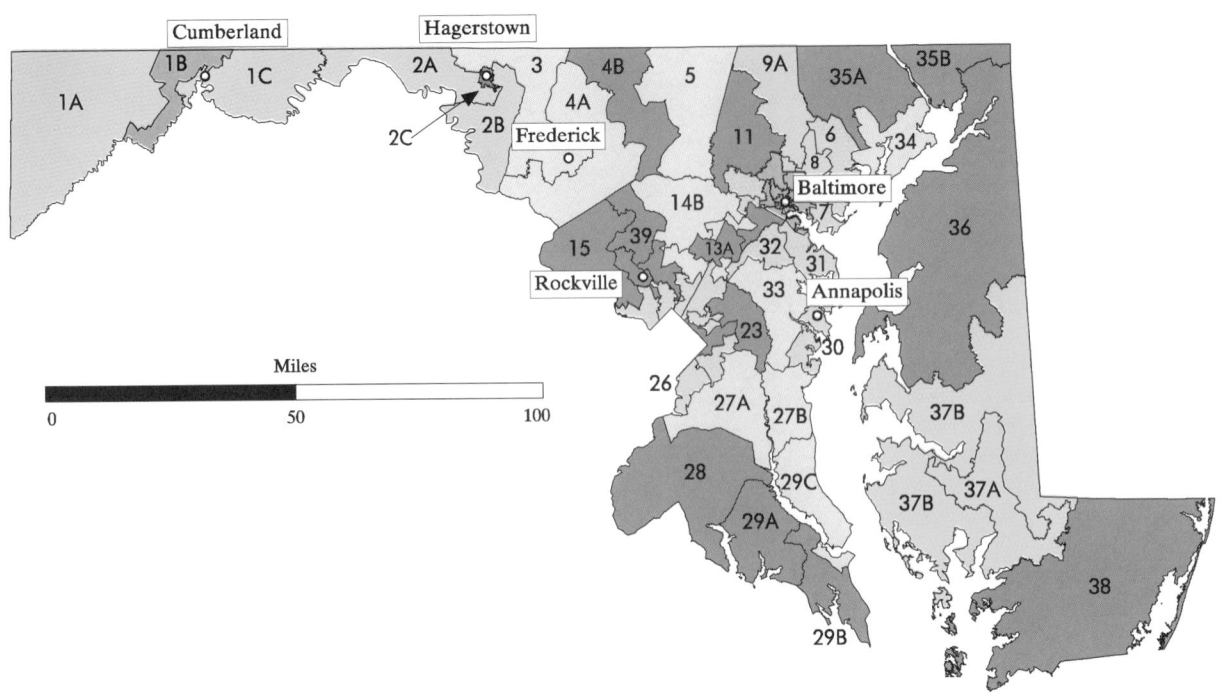

WASHINGTON, D.C. SUBURBS

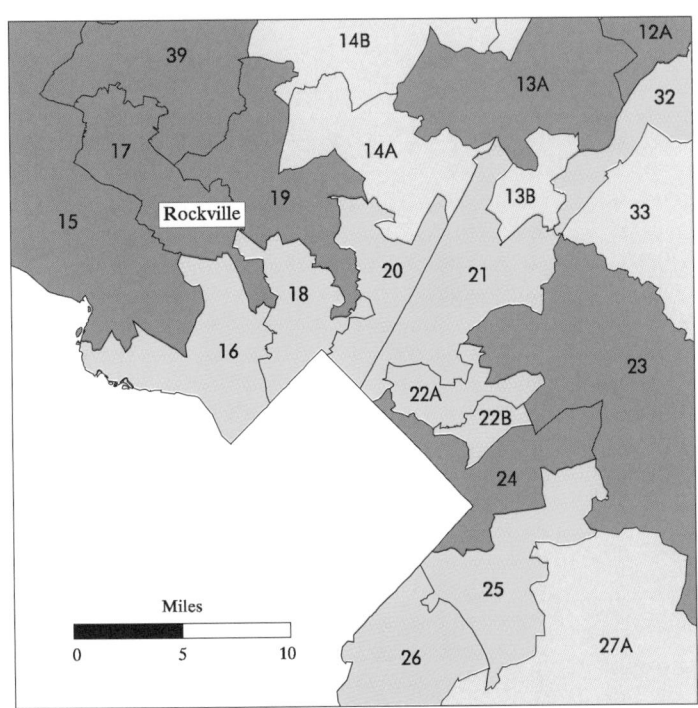

Population Growth · -12% to -6% · -2% to 7% · 8% to 16% · 18% to 35%

BALTIMORE

Population Growth   ▨ -12% to -6%   ▨ -2% to 7%   ▨ 8% to 16%   ▨ 18% to 35%

Maryland State House Districts: Demographic Data

House District	Population		Average HH Income		District Type	Unempl. Rate	College Educ.	White (non-Hispanic)		African American		Asian American		Hispanic American	
	1997	+/-	($)	+/-		(%)	(%)	(%)	+/-	(%)	+/-	(%)	+/-	(%)	+/-
Maryland	5,099,840	7	59,006	23	S	4	45	65	0	27	16	4	40	4	50
1A	34,896	2	32,446	18	R	7	23	99	2	0	-13	0	-38	1	53
1B	33,432	-6	37,695	23	S	7	34	97	-7	2	16	1	23	1	32
1C	33,868	2	30,719	15	U	10	26	95	1	3	22	1	38	1	59
2A	33,957	2	38,877	18	S	4	25	95	1	3	26	1	37	1	62
2B	35,207	4	46,874	20	S	4	28	85	1	13	19	1	21	1	69
2C	35,912	9	32,688	18	U	4	23	90	6	8	40	1	46	1	46
3	116,010	19	52,151	19	S	3	43	87	16	8	49	2	65	2	81
4A	79,433	23	61,891	24	S	2	42	94	21	4	55	1	56	1	65
4B	38,816	15	58,519	29	R	3	31	95	14	3	52	1	48	1	69
5	116,972	18	59,473	26	R	3	40	95	17	3	49	1	59	1	80
6	102,510	4	45,231	20	S	5	22	87	0	10	40	1	34	1	63
7	98,550	1	43,168	17	S	5	20	87	-2	10	27	1	41	1	48
8	98,002	3	53,418	21	S	3	43	86	-1	8	29	4	43	2	55
9A	73,349	2	76,576	27	S	2	56	91	0	3	42	5	40	2	33
9B	35,165	-1	58,533	20	S	3	61	89	-4	6	37	3	42	2	49
10	99,490	4	47,882	17	S	5	41	28	-17	68	13	2	23	2	60
11	114,499	8	81,384	25	S	3	57	81	2	13	48	4	45	2	62
12A	78,083	16	53,634	28	S	3	40	83	11	11	43	4	58	2	82
12B	43,680	35	76,236	20	S	2	72	70	25	19	61	6	74	4	86
13A	81,632	14	67,789	13	S	2	67	73	6	18	40	6	48	3	62
13B	42,253	22	57,971	25	S	3	54	68	9	20	57	7	73	5	80
14A	40,015	18	84,941	19	S	2	67	64	8	17	34	13	48	5	76
14B	84,907	18	84,111	21	S	2	63	84	13	8	55	6	63	2	63
15	116,481	16	116,775	24	S	2	72	76	8	6	44	12	54	5	49
16	102,183	6	117,441	23	S	2	80	81	0	3	33	9	46	7	29
17	116,815	10	66,979	24	S	3	62	62	-5	12	31	12	48	13	63
18	108,271	3	73,889	18	S	3	63	61	-10	15	21	8	32	15	52
19	114,165	9	79,333	23	S	3	65	66	0	14	24	11	38	8	51
20	105,928	2	59,439	19	S	4	61	42	-18	29	12	11	26	17	43
21	109,247	2	56,847	21	S	4	52	46	-15	31	18	8	28	14	42
22A	69,678	1	52,067	15	S	4	45	39	-22	42	17	7	26	12	47
22B	33,278	-2	47,534	17	S	4	37	24	-30	66	10	4	11	6	38
23	118,813	12	71,394	24	S	3	56	60	-1	30	37	6	48	3	41
24	113,203	9	49,883	25	S	7	30	10	-22	85	13	1	27	4	46
25	110,330	6	54,641	23	S	4	40	15	-23	80	14	2	23	2	14
26	107,717	1	60,720	18	S	4	42	19	-26	74	10	5	21	2	14
27A	84,553	18	71,504	21	S	3	42	50	0	44	42	3	49	2	49
27B	42,142	21	65,759	20	S	2	36	82	15	15	52	1	76	1	58
28	114,922	14	61,767	23	S	3	36	73	6	22	38	2	62	3	72
29A	38,324	12	56,233	27	R	4	28	83	7	14	37	1	67	1	73
29B	38,028	9	47,403	23	R	4	36	74	1	20	35	2	58	3	73
29C	47,226	32	55,962	14	R	4	36	76	24	20	64	1	78	2	108
30	112,569	7	65,994	18	S	3	53	77	1	19	33	2	41	2	45
31	109,306	6	55,162	18	S	3	31	89	3	8	33	1	46	1	58
32	109,230	7	52,002	16	S	3	35	77	0	16	32	4	49	3	70
33	125,157	20	75,180	21	S	3	54	80	15	14	42	3	55	3	62
34	128,061	22	51,310	21	S	4	42	79	16	15	43	2	63	3	74
35A	77,061	8	58,657	9	S	3	42	94	6	3	52	1	59	1	70
35B	38,090	13	49,195	19	R	5	28	92	11	6	37	1	57	1	71
36	112,068	11	51,973	21	R	4	32	85	7	13	37	0	39	1	52

Note: U=urban, S=suburban, R=rural, M=mixed, HH=households.

Maryland State House Districts: Demographic Data (cont.)

House District	Population 1997	+/-	Average HH Income ($)	+/-	District Type	Unempl. Rate (%)	College Educ. (%)	White (non-Hispanic) (%)	+/-	African American (%)	+/-	Asian American (%)	+/-	Hispanic American (%)	+/-
Maryland	5,099,840	7	59,006	23	S	4	45	65	0	27	16	4	40	4	50
37A	34,870	3	38,129	28	R	6	26	44	-9	54	16	0	15	1	31
37B	77,147	6	45,392	23	R	4	34	77	0	22	36	0	8	1	40
38	113,395	11	41,640	21	R	6	31	73	3	25	36	1	34	1	50
39	111,001	12	71,577	22	S	2	62	69	1	13	38	9	46	8	73
40	86,284	-10	30,967	25	U	12	22	6	-42	92	-7	1	-13	1	7
41	84,871	-12	36,778	25	U	10	19	12	-38	87	-7	1	-7	1	7
42	89,974	-7	71,745	30	U	4	58	76	-15	19	34	3	33	2	25
43	87,611	-10	49,832	29	U	7	38	30	-31	67	4	1	-4	1	7
44	88,913	-8	28,695	29	U	14	21	14	-34	84	-1	1	-3	1	18
45	84,841	-11	32,501	23	U	11	16	17	-36	81	-3	1	-22	1	16
46	90,299	-8	37,409	26	U	7	19	74	-17	21	27	1	17	3	36
47A	63,311	-7	36,829	29	U	9	19	59	-16	38	10	1	23	1	29
47B	33,811	1	55,333	21	S	2	48	82	-4	12	33	5	32	2	59

Note: U=urban, S=suburban, R=rural, M=mixed, HH=households.

MASSACHUSETTS

Massachusetts has been a fountain of political leaders throughout the nation's history. Although they have represented different factions and parties, a common ideological thread binds them. In the eighteenth and early nineteenth century, Massachusetts Federalists led by John Adams advocated a strong central government and distrusted the masses. During and after the Civil War, Massachusetts Republicans from Charles Sumner to Henry Cabot Lodge also supported a strong Union with a strongly patrician bent. As the twentieth century draws to a close, Massachusetts Democrats, led by Edward M. Kennedy and Thomas P. "Tip" O'Neill, have advocated a powerful federal government, albeit for completely different purposes than their predecessors, but with a familiar distrust for letting people sort things out for themselves.

Massachusetts is bigger and wealthier than its New England neighbors, but like them it is part of a sluggish regional economy. It has the fourth-lowest rate of population growth in the country, though all the states doing worse are in New England, too. What growth there has been has occurred around Foxboro, roughly halfway between Boston and Providence, Rhode Island, where Interstates 95 and 495 intersect. Massachusetts is a very suburban state and getting more so. Almost all its population growth is occurring in house districts classified as suburban, while almost all its population loss is taking place in districts classified as urban. The areas that have lost population fastest are scattered around the state, in Fitchburg, the Connecticut River Valley, Somerville, and Lawrence.

The wealthiest parts of Massachusetts are the outer suburbs of Boston in Middlesex County (and some in Norfolk County): Weston, Newton, Brookline, Concord. Small cities that depended the most on manufacturing have fared the worst: Springfield, Lawrence, Fall River, New Bedford. The poorest districts are all urban, though interestingly, they are not in Boston.

Only 5 percent of Massachusetts residents are African American; by percentages, that puts the state between Wisconsin and Nebraska. Ninety-four of its 160 state house districts are 90 percent or more white. Three of the four districts with an African American majority are located in Boston, the other in Springfield.

Massachusetts may be a predominantly white state, but it is not really a Yankee state anymore, or not nearly as much as it once was. Much of the state is now rich with persons of Irish, Italian, Greek, and Portuguese ancestry. It also has two pockets of Hispanics: the district in downtown Lawrence (79 percent); and the district on the west side of Springfield (54 percent). Two more districts, one in central Boston, the other in Lawrence, are almost 20 percent Asian.

Thanks to a decline in manufacturing, Massachusetts has become one of the country's older states, although a large number of older people tend to live in seaside areas that have little industry. More than 40 percent of the residents of two house districts on the outer end of Cape Cod are over age fifty-five.

The Massachusetts House of Representatives has 160 districts, second only to Pennsylvania but not out of line for New England. The high number is a remnant of the old system, before the days of one-man, one-vote, when each town had its own seat. Democrats dominated it before redistricting, and even more so after. The house, which was 118–37 Democratic in 1990, was 134–25 Democratic in 1996. The party's edge in the senate grew from 25–15 to 34–6. Democrats now also hold every seat in Congress (making it the largest state to have a completely partisan delegation), and readers of a certain age will recall that Massachusetts was the only state George McGovern carried against Richard Nixon in 1972.

A final word needs to be said about education. A greater percentage of Massachusetts's citizens hold college degrees than those of any other state (Massachusetts is the only state to reach 50 percent). In three districts, more than four persons in five have a college degree (the district that includes Beacon Hill, at 85 percent, is the highest in the country). Ironically, the districts that include Harvard, Radcliffe, and MIT rank only eleventh and twelfth statewide, respectively.

MASSACHUSETTS
State Senate Districts

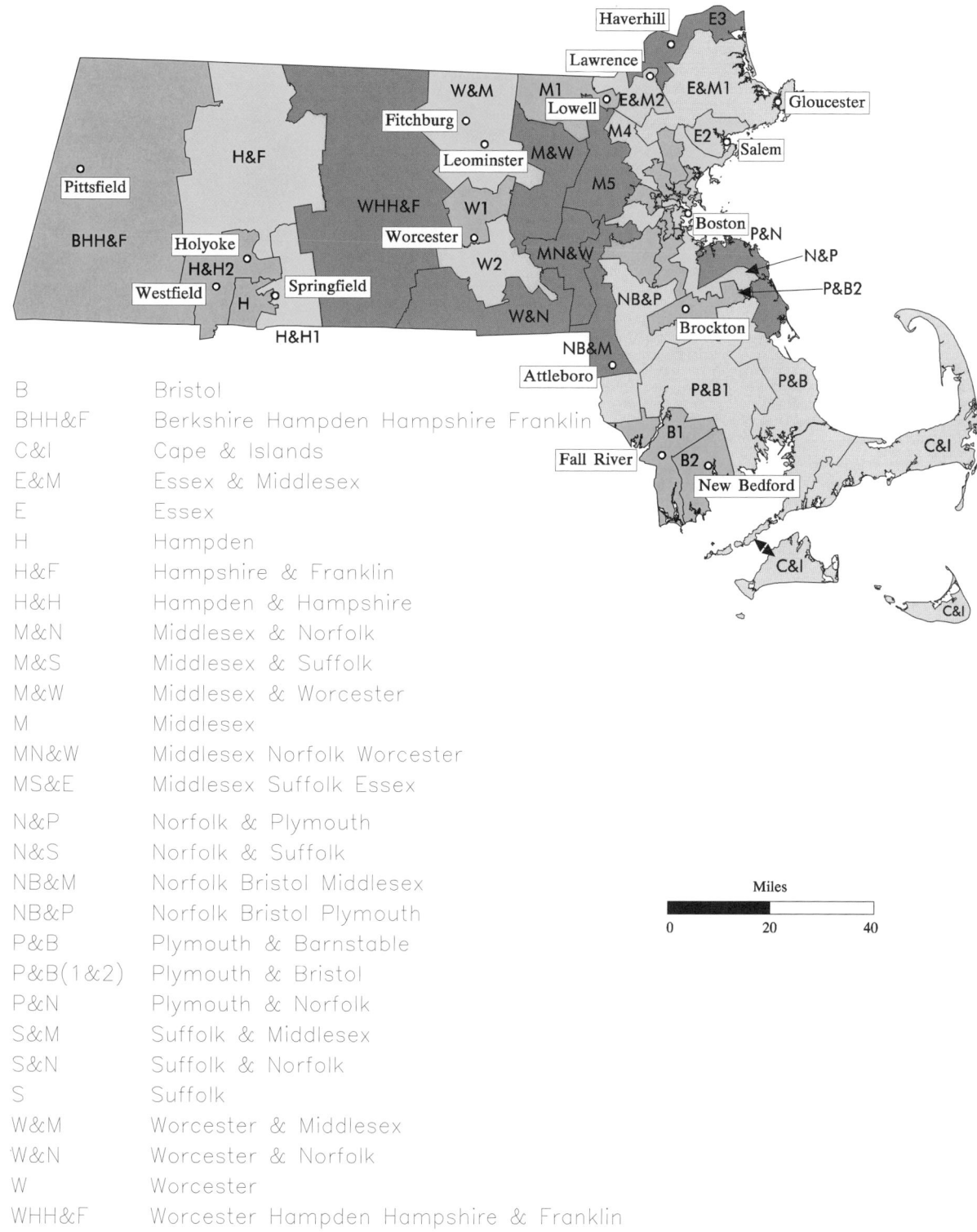

B	Bristol		
BHH&F	Berkshire Hampden Hampshire Franklin		
C&I	Cape & Islands		
E&M	Essex & Middlesex		
E	Essex		
H	Hampden		
H&F	Hampshire & Franklin		
H&H	Hampden & Hampshire		
M&N	Middlesex & Norfolk		
M&S	Middlesex & Suffolk		
M&W	Middlesex & Worcester		
M	Middlesex		
MN&W	Middlesex Norfolk Worcester		
MS&E	Middlesex Suffolk Essex		
N&P	Norfolk & Plymouth		
N&S	Norfolk & Suffolk		
NB&M	Norfolk Bristol Middlesex		
NB&P	Norfolk Bristol Plymouth		
P&B	Plymouth & Barnstable		
P&B(1&2)	Plymouth & Bristol		
P&N	Plymouth & Norfolk		
S&M	Suffolk & Middlesex		
S&N	Suffolk & Norfolk		
S	Suffolk		
W&M	Worcester & Middlesex		
W&N	Worcester & Norfolk		
W	Worcester		
WHH&F	Worcester Hampden Hampshire & Franklin		

Miles
0   20   40

Population Growth	-8% to -2%	-1% to 3%	4% to 8%	10% to 13%

BOSTON

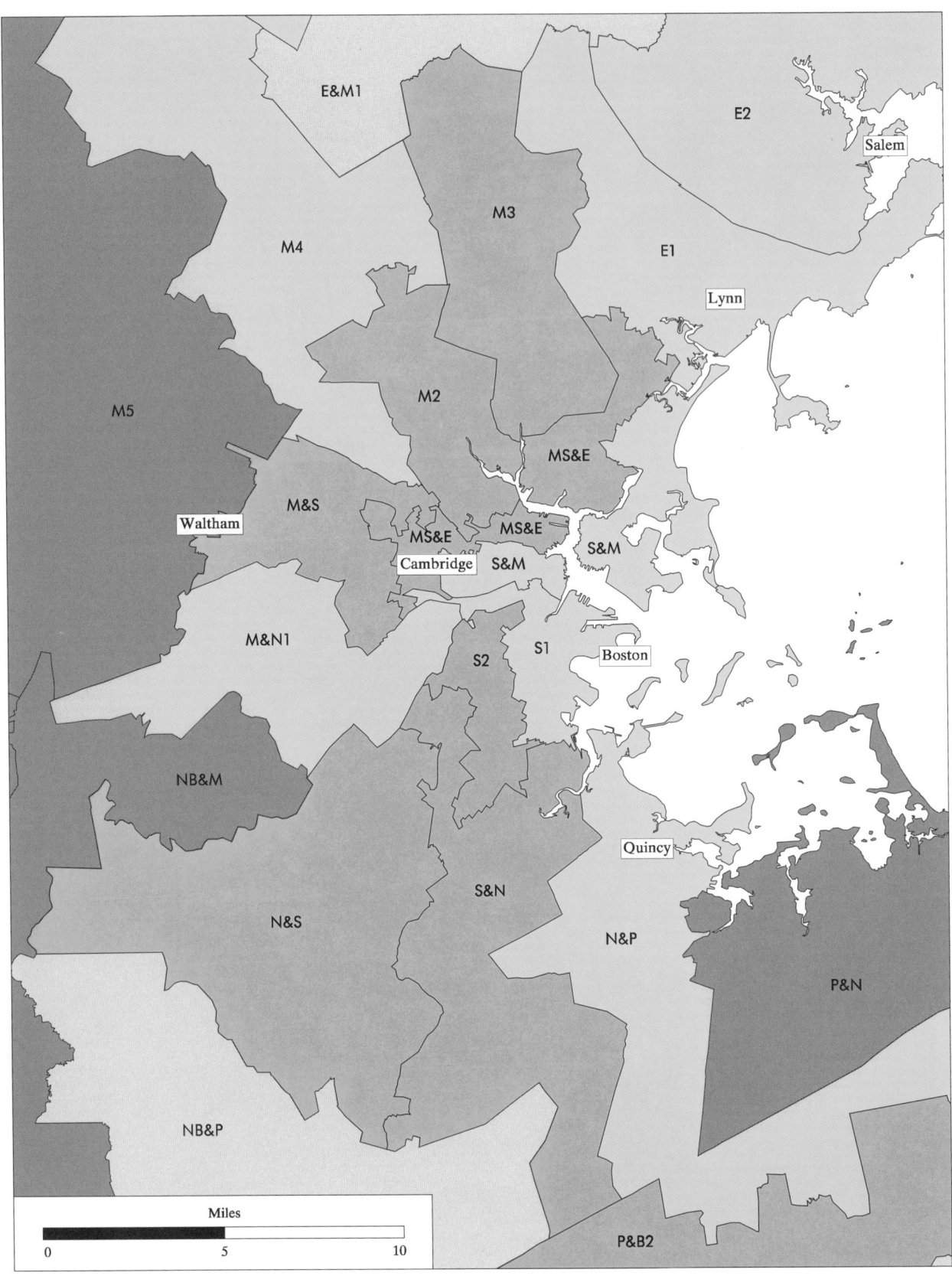

Population Growth   ▢ -8% to -2%   ▢ -1% to 3%   ▢ 4% to 8%   ▢ 10% to 13%

Massachusetts State Senate Districts: Demographic Data

Senate District	Population		Average HH Income		District Type	Unempl. Rate	College Educ.	White (non-Hispanic)		African American		Asian American		Hispanic American	
	1997	+/-	($)	+/-		(%)	(%)	(%)	+/-	(%)	+/-	(%)	+/-	(%)	+/-
Mass.	6,106,155	1	55,803	23	S	7	50	85	-2	5	13	3	35	6	31
BHH&F	144,810	-3	46,328	23	M	6	44	96	-4	2	9	1	23	1	24
B1	143,562	-3	38,734	19	U	8	26	96	-4	1	25	1	29	1	3
B2	146,175	-4	37,329	19	U	10	24	87	-6	3	1	1	7	6	30
P&B1	165,024	11	49,511	17	R	7	38	93	9	2	34	1	45	4	63
C&I	166,064	10	44,888	18	R	7	53	94	9	2	25	1	30	2	44
E1	146,726	0	57,629	22	U	7	49	83	-6	5	25	3	23	9	67
E2	150,098	2	53,702	20	S	6	48	92	-1	1	53	2	50	5	69
E3	159,321	7	51,398	21	S	7	45	91	3	1	51	1	52	6	76
E&M1	166,651	13	69,160	23	S	5	57	97	12	1	73	1	68	1	65
E&M2	150,951	-1	57,378	28	S	9	42	72	-7	1	1	3	35	24	21
H&F	152,672	0	45,257	17	R	5	58	90	-2	2	16	4	32	3	29
H	145,020	-6	35,839	12	U	8	34	63	-15	15	5	1	12	20	24
H&H1	144,809	-1	50,685	13	U	6	45	85	-6	8	28	1	33	6	48
H&H2	145,263	-4	40,337	13	U	6	36	83	-7	2	29	1	28	13	15
M1	145,839	-2	53,283	26	U	9	42	80	-5	2	0	9	17	9	17
M2	139,433	-8	58,763	27	S	6	53	86	-11	4	5	4	33	5	31
M3	147,410	-2	57,529	23	S	6	51	92	-4	2	13	4	39	2	34
M4	154,173	1	66,805	23	S	5	59	92	-1	2	24	4	47	2	31
M5	161,806	4	101,371	26	S	4	72	90	1	2	21	5	52	3	40
M&N1	155,788	2	93,972	24	S	4	78	86	-2	3	22	8	45	3	25
MN&W	164,773	8	66,943	23	S	6	61	89	5	2	17	3	48	5	34
M&S	145,387	-3	58,774	27	U	5	64	80	-9	7	33	7	39	6	31
M&W	160,660	7	67,895	22	S	5	61	90	5	3	11	3	56	4	39
N&P	151,342	0	54,243	20	S	7	49	91	-3	1	24	6	44	2	41
NB&P	169,938	11	67,231	22	S	5	56	95	10	2	33	2	58	1	49
NB&M	163,771	7	70,259	22	S	6	60	93	6	1	26	3	53	2	50
P&N	158,345	5	67,417	18	S	6	60	97	4	1	30	1	50	1	39
P&B2	147,789	-2	48,944	17	U	8	40	82	-6	9	13	2	24	6	41
P&B	170,074	12	50,926	16	R	7	49	95	11	2	37	1	39	2	51
S1	146,860	0	53,707	39	U	9	48	50	-12	22	15	11	20	13	17
S2	143,076	-3	43,805	37	U	11	40	20	-26	57	-1	3	15	19	23
MS&E	153,045	-2	53,016	32	S	7	52	74	-10	6	34	7	32	13	27
S&M	149,805	1	51,353	34	U	7	48	74	-7	7	28	7	39	12	41
N&S	144,198	-2	65,578	28	S	5	57	90	-5	3	43	2	43	4	33
S&N	143,493	-3	61,539	30	U	7	53	70	-11	18	18	4	29	7	29
W1	147,213	-2	44,506	14	U	7	46	80	-7	4	19	3	29	12	29
WHH&F	157,862	6	44,009	15	R	7	40	97	5	1	45	1	47	1	47
W2	153,438	3	49,716	18	S	6	45	90	0	2	30	3	43	5	44
W&M	148,975	-1	48,195	19	U	7	43	88	-5	3	29	2	31	8	33
W&N	156,767	5	48,255	18	S	7	38	94	4	1	41	1	43	4	28

Note: U=urban, S=suburban, R=rural, M=mixed, HH=households.

MASSACHUSETTS
State House Districts

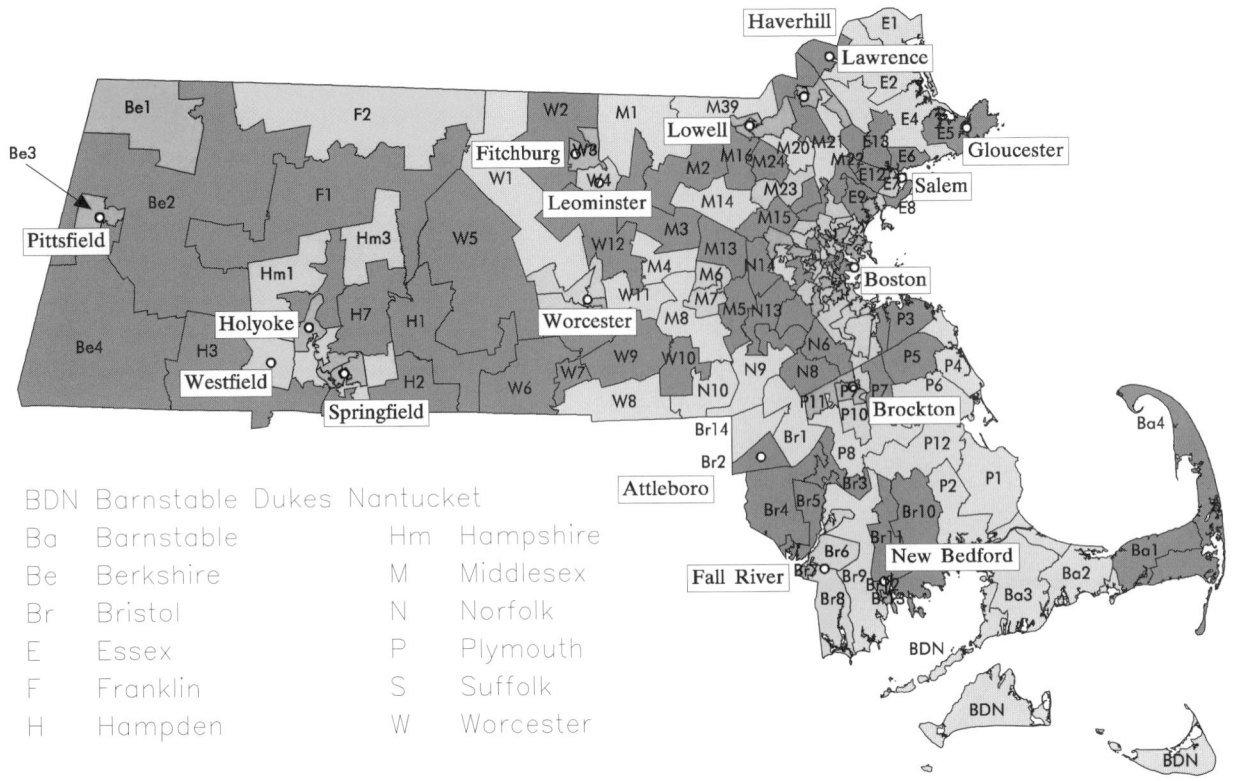

BDN Barnstable Dukes Nantucket
Ba   Barnstable   Hm Hampshire
Be   Berkshire   M   Middlesex
Br   Bristol   N   Norfolk
E   Essex   P   Plymouth
F   Franklin   S   Suffolk
H   Hampden   W   Worcester

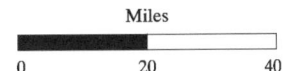

WORCESTER

LOWELL/LAWRENCE

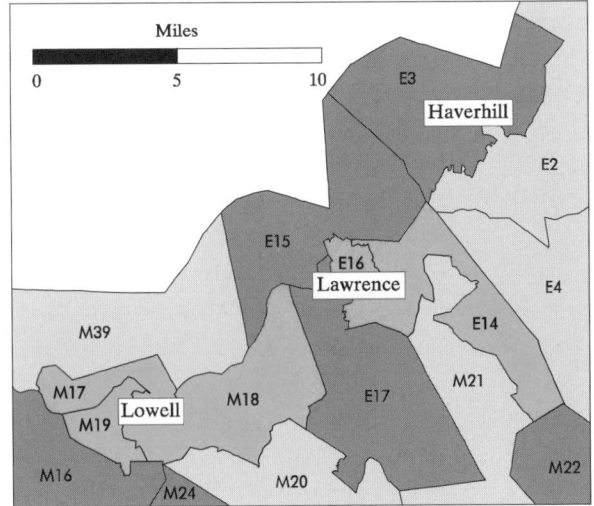

Population Growth   ▢ -17% to -6%   ▢ -5% to 0%   ▢ 1% to 8%   ▢ 9% to 19%

BOSTON

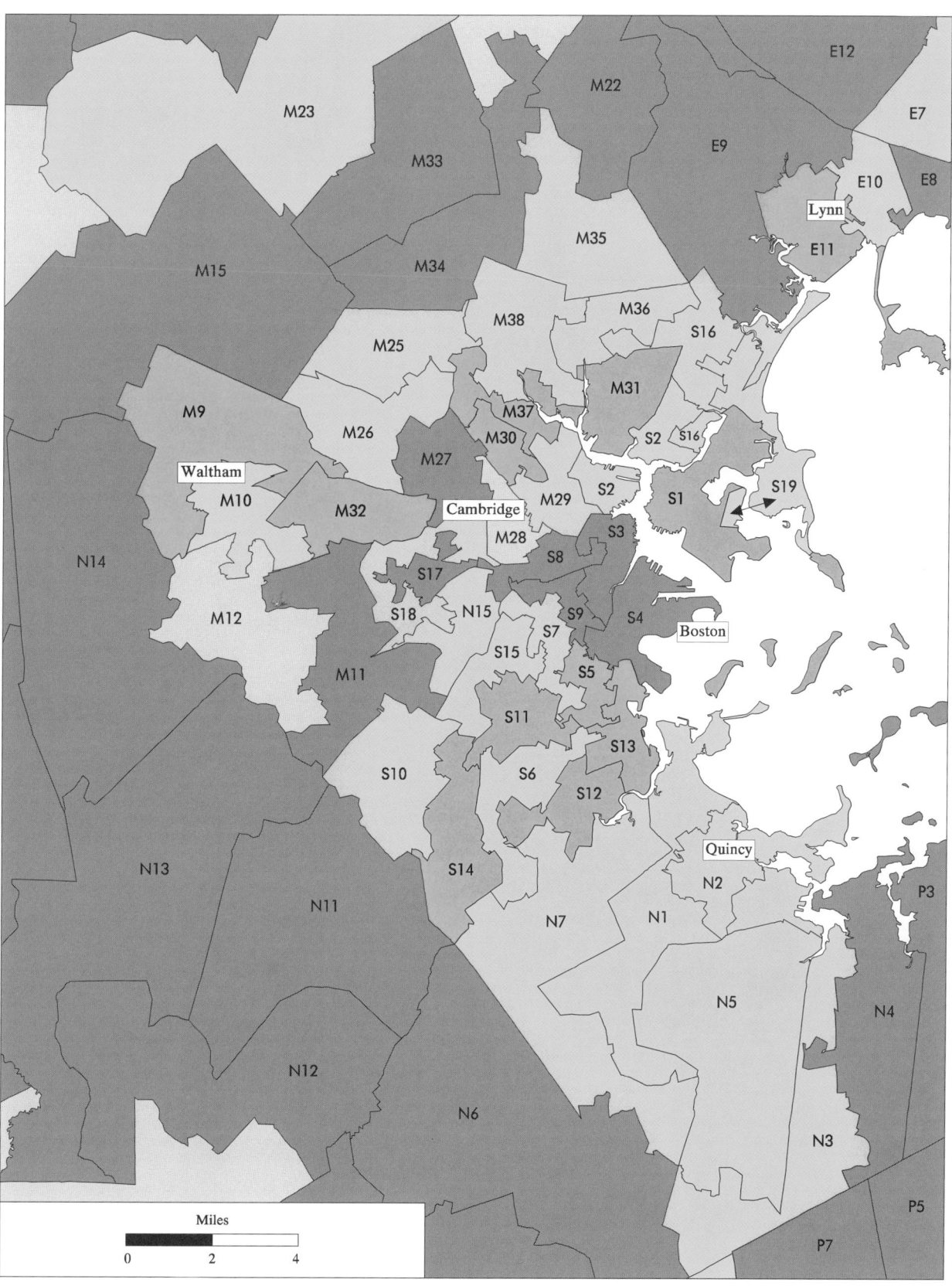

Population Growth ▨ -17% to -6%   ▨ -5% to 0%   ▨ 1% to 8%   ▨ 9% to 19%

SPRINGFIELD

Population Growth   ▨ -17% to -6%   ▢ -5% to 0%   ▨ 1% to 8%

Massachusetts State House Districts: Demographic Data

House District	Population 1997	+/-	Average HH Income ($)	+/-	District Type	Unempl. Rate (%)	College Educ. (%)	White (non-Hispanic) (%)	+/-	African American (%)	+/-	Asian American (%)	+/-	Hispanic American (%)	+/-
Mass.	6,106,155	1	55,803	23	S	7	50	85	-2	5	13	3	35	6	31
Ba1	39,178	6	42,080	18	R	7	51	97	6	1	20	0	37	1	46
Ba2	42,840	9	52,310	19	R	7	55	93	8	2	15	1	43	2	44
Ba3	45,308	16	45,656	15	R	7	52	92	15	2	30	1	27	2	45
Ba4	39,820	6	40,415	16	R	9	54	97	6	1	12	0	25	1	33
BDN	43,093	12	49,570	18	R	6	58	93	11	2	27	1	20	2	37
Be1	34,439	-8	37,719	21	R	8	36	96	-9	2	10	1	20	1	15
Be2	40,124	4	49,684	21	M	5	48	98	3	0	20	0	29	1	30
Be3	35,019	-8	41,792	24	U	8	37	93	-9	4	5	1	10	2	26
Be4	39,142	2	54,048	20	R	5	53	96	1	1	17	1	33	1	25
Br1	46,285	18	60,831	22	S	5	55	95	17	2	56	1	68	2	74
Br2	39,307	3	47,424	18	U	7	42	91	0	1	27	3	41	4	45
Br3	37,784	3	41,384	19	R	9	27	89	0	2	24	1	23	7	61
Br4	39,011	8	58,117	19	S	5	42	96	7	1	32	1	44	1	67
Br5	37,997	2	47,661	19	S	7	36	95	1	1	9	1	44	3	51
Br6	36,863	-3	36,813	20	U	8	25	95	-4	1	28	1	20	2	-2
Br7	33,040	-6	28,824	15	U	11	11	95	-7	1	28	2	34	2	6
Br8	34,849	-4	38,274	19	U	9	24	96	-5	1	17	2	28	1	2
Br9	43,034	11	54,094	19	S	8	38	96	10	1	19	1	33	1	31
Br10	39,091	7	49,358	16	S	8	40	95	6	1	26	0	15	1	36
Br11	38,949	1	42,647	18	U	7	26	95	1	1	17	0	17	2	30
Br12	33,773	-11	29,836	17	U	13	17	75	-18	5	-3	0	-9	14	43
Br13	35,397	-9	30,608	15	U	14	19	78	-13	4	3	0	-10	9	17
Br14	43,038	13	56,582	21	S	7	49	96	11	1	41	1	62	1	77
E1	40,605	9	52,860	23	S	7	47	97	8	1	75	0	38	1	90
E2	44,461	17	60,932	22	S	5	54	97	16	1	70	1	65	1	90
E3	42,916	6	48,591	21	U	7	43	86	0	2	45	1	44	11	80
E4	42,570	12	78,136	21	S	5	65	97	11	1	81	1	67	1	76
E5	41,651	5	48,825	19	U	6	47	98	5	0	76	0	52	1	59
E6	39,328	3	56,329	20	S	5	55	95	1	1	64	2	57	2	83
E7	37,404	-2	46,381	20	U	7	44	85	-8	2	38	2	37	11	64
E8	38,095	4	84,392	24	S	4	70	95	2	1	51	1	51	2	93
E9	38,413	3	57,709	19	S	5	45	96	2	1	65	1	54	2	82
E10	36,369	-4	36,904	16	U	10	32	70	-16	9	23	4	16	17	66
E11	32,869	-7	39,053	16	U	9	33	67	-20	9	22	5	15	18	64
E12	39,841	2	50,428	18	S	6	42	92	-1	1	57	1	54	6	73
E13	39,479	5	69,671	22	S	5	56	96	3	1	73	2	57	2	77
E14	34,259	-7	55,774	28	U	7	45	78	-14	1	4	3	14	18	44
E15	38,995	5	51,608	19	S	7	41	93	2	1	53	2	58	5	93
E16	33,436	-12	23,760	13	U	22	12	18	-55	2	-31	1	-19	79	15
E17	39,135	2	76,870	29	S	6	64	81	-4	1	29	4	54	14	39
F1	40,545	3	43,875	18	R	8	50	96	2	1	25	1	43	2	39
F2	38,847	0	38,770	18	R	7	42	97	-1	1	18	1	37	1	27
H1	37,997	4	42,606	13	R	6	38	97	3	1	47	1	40	1	47
H2	42,367	5	66,549	13	S	5	58	95	3	1	52	2	44	1	56
H3	41,077	4	47,897	14	S	5	43	97	3	1	62	1	47	1	53
H4	39,275	0	43,664	12	U	5	43	92	-2	1	42	1	41	5	37
H5	32,626	-13	32,803	9	U	10	34	54	-24	3	10	1	10	42	4
H6	34,588	-5	40,515	12	S	6	39	88	-10	2	39	1	35	8	65
H7	41,576	8	46,486	16	S	5	36	95	7	1	33	1	49	2	42
H8	33,512	-5	38,266	11	S	5	27	92	-8	3	52	1	24	5	6

Note: U=urban, S=suburban, R=rural, M=mixed, HH=households.

Massachusetts State House Districts: Demographic Data (cont.)

House District	Population		Average HH Income		District Type	Unempl. Rate	College Educ.	White (non-Hispanic)		African American		Asian American		Hispanic American	
	1997	+/-	($)	+/-		(%)	(%)	(%)	+/-	(%)	+/-	(%)	+/-	(%)	+/-
Mass.	6,106,155	1	55,803	23	S	7	50	85	-2	5	13	3	35	6	31
H9	33,758	-8	33,506	10	U	7	28	80	-16	5	37	1	9	14	47
H10	31,946	-13	23,052	7	U	13	22	28	-43	15	8	1	-9	54	12
H11	34,103	-6	39,923	9	U	7	37	72	-16	19	28	1	19	8	60
H12	34,664	-8	30,400	9	U	13	29	23	-42	50	3	1	-7	25	38
H13	36,797	-1	54,378	13	U	6	53	92	-4	4	42	1	41	3	58
Hm1	38,284	0	45,024	16	U	5	55	91	-2	1	11	3	26	4	29
Hm2	37,734	2	47,544	15	S	5	49	95	0	1	14	2	30	2	35
Hm3	37,544	0	47,821	15	R	5	78	79	-5	5	17	10	34	6	29
M1	43,908	13	64,128	22	S	5	53	95	12	2	32	1	59	2	39
M2	41,835	7	75,496	24	S	5	65	91	8	4	-17	3	43	2	2
M3	41,453	7	65,600	22	S	5	51	90	5	3	38	2	58	4	34
M4	42,135	9	60,171	22	S	6	53	89	5	2	29	3	57	6	66
M5	39,572	3	78,979	26	S	5	67	93	1	2	25	3	48	2	37
M6	35,037	-2	74,908	22	U	5	66	88	-5	3	16	4	41	5	45
M7	41,597	0	55,427	22	U	7	52	78	-5	4	10	3	38	14	29
M8	45,402	17	80,049	24	S	5	65	96	16	1	37	2	73	1	48
M9	34,901	-6	62,321	22	U	5	54	87	-9	2	15	6	40	5	34
M10	33,558	-5	51,169	23	U	6	51	82	-10	4	12	5	40	9	31
M11	38,379	3	113,876	21	S	4	80	88	0	2	26	7	50	3	25
M12	39,539	10	105,227	25	S	4	77	89	7	3	32	6	61	2	35
M13	39,088	7	106,633	28	S	3	74	93	5	1	36	4	56	2	22
M14	41,560	9	95,658	22	S	4	77	91	6	2	21	4	62	3	52
M15	38,371	4	109,335	25	S	4	77	87	0	2	23	8	51	2	24
M16	39,452	7	82,852	25	S	5	66	93	5	1	32	5	58	2	55
M17	33,552	-10	42,009	19	U	10	28	77	-17	2	-2	9	24	11	21
M18	35,011	-6	54,465	23	U	9	42	76	-11	2	6	11	20	11	15
M19	32,648	-12	38,177	19	U	11	31	62	-22	3	-6	19	10	15	15
M20	41,697	11	67,320	24	S	7	44	96	10	1	36	2	64	1	44
M21	40,072	9	78,588	24	S	5	62	96	8	1	55	2	64	1	48
M22	39,808	5	69,010	22	S	6	54	97	4	1	48	1	58	1	47
M23	39,539	0	76,486	23	S	5	63	91	-2	2	19	5	45	2	34
M24	40,019	6	63,888	22	S	7	49	95	4	1	28	2	51	2	39
M25	36,603	-3	66,730	23	S	4	65	90	-5	4	5	4	45	2	26
M26	35,675	-3	72,933	23	S	4	71	91	-5	2	19	5	46	2	30
M27	41,226	6	67,046	24	U	5	74	71	-2	14	23	10	45	5	25
M28	43,760	9	50,743	22	U	5	73	61	-2	15	21	14	46	9	37
M29	35,735	-4	44,700	25	S	7	39	69	-13	10	10	6	36	15	31
M30	31,666	-12	48,550	23	S	6	56	81	-17	5	6	5	29	7	28
M31	36,411	-7	42,186	21	S	7	31	88	-10	3	11	3	32	6	41
M32	32,593	-9	59,260	25	S	4	63	92	-11	2	22	3	35	3	12
M33	36,886	2	59,726	24	S	6	51	93	0	1	31	2	50	3	28
M34	37,611	2	85,949	27	S	5	67	95	0	1	25	3	49	1	35
M35	38,046	-3	62,261	22	S	5	55	96	-4	1	22	2	47	1	25
M36	34,695	-5	46,295	22	S	8	43	85	-10	4	15	7	39	4	41
M37	32,244	-11	49,084	25	S	6	46	85	-15	6	6	4	30	5	33
M38	34,116	-4	53,839	23	S	7	43	92	-6	2	17	3	42	3	43
M39	42,014	15	59,918	23	S	8	41	97	14	1	40	2	69	1	53
N1	36,737	-2	54,554	22	S	6	49	83	-7	2	21	13	41	2	44
N2	35,323	-2	47,582	19	S	7	47	89	-6	1	21	7	47	2	35
N3	36,307	-1	50,701	21	S	7	47	94	-2	1	21	3	41	2	31

Note: U=urban, S=suburban, R=rural, M=mixed, HH=households.

Massachusetts State House Districts: Demographic Data (cont.)

House District	Population		Average HH Income		District Type	Unempl. Rate	College Educ.	White (non-Hispanic)		African American		Asian American		Hispanic American	
	1997	+/-	($)	+/-		(%)	(%)	(%)	+/-	(%)	+/-	(%)	+/-	(%)	+/-
Mass.	6,106,155	1	55,803	23	S	7	50	85	-2	5	13	3	35	6	31
N4	37,385	2	56,845	20	S	6	50	96	1	1	23	1	52	1	39
N5	39,150	-1	61,663	20	S	7	51	95	-2	1	14	2	49	1	45
N6	39,906	6	67,902	24	S	6	54	90	4	5	22	3	49	2	46
N7	35,806	-1	68,678	22	S	5	61	88	-4	6	15	4	46	2	34
N8	40,854	5	69,931	22	S	5	60	91	3	4	24	2	56	2	31
N9	45,766	16	69,966	23	S	5	57	94	15	2	20	1	69	3	72
N10	46,504	19	62,744	24	S	6	49	97	19	1	43	1	82	1	44
N11	37,310	2	72,163	21	S	5	60	96	0	1	23	2	53	1	35
N12	37,322	3	65,836	24	S	5	60	95	2	2	26	2	56	1	29
N13	41,181	7	99,782	23	S	4	75	95	5	1	31	3	60	1	33
N14	38,071	3	137,270	24	S	4	83	90	0	2	25	6	52	3	36
N15	35,942	-5	68,318	22	S	5	77	78	-11	4	15	13	36	4	14
P1	41,923	13	50,686	15	R	7	46	94	11	2	57	1	52	2	71
P2	42,463	11	44,478	16	R	8	40	92	10	2	35	0	24	2	48
P3	38,337	4	80,952	19	S	6	65	97	3	1	46	1	57	1	48
P4	41,038	9	66,739	15	S	6	63	97	8	1	39	1	40	1	32
P5	39,255	7	63,582	17	S	6	52	96	5	1	52	1	65	1	56
P6	41,995	12	66,178	12	S	6	59	97	12	1	43	1	58	1	38
P7	40,831	7	51,065	15	S	7	45	98	7	1	42	0	34	1	30
P8	38,988	11	57,476	17	S	5	47	92	9	4	37	1	58	3	71
P9	36,816	-8	44,872	15	U	8	36	71	-16	13	13	2	22	10	42
P10	39,277	-2	47,357	12	U	8	36	85	-6	8	27	1	28	5	50
P11	36,902	-6	47,650	20	U	8	43	75	-11	12	4	2	23	8	37
P12	41,880	11	52,185	15	S	6	43	96	10	2	50	0	30	1	34
S1	32,787	-9	36,841	28	U	11	21	64	-24	5	40	5	23	26	42
S2	36,519	-3	55,986	49	S	10	42	66	-13	4	46	4	22	25	21
S3	35,798	3	68,157	39	U	6	59	64	-5	7	47	22	15	6	21
S4	36,277	1	44,095	41	U	10	34	84	-4	6	54	4	37	4	25
S5	33,208	-6	42,745	35	U	13	24	8	-53	55	2	2	-18	25	10
S6	35,554	-5	48,935	33	U	10	34	16	-32	70	-1	1	-2	12	33
S7	37,105	-3	33,715	35	U	13	33	19	-24	60	-2	3	14	17	33
S8	35,148	4	86,645	39	U	4	85	77	-3	5	59	12	43	5	19
S9	37,218	3	47,367	43	U	7	61	41	-18	33	28	7	29	17	24
S10	35,905	-5	66,873	35	U	5	62	91	-8	2	59	3	42	3	31
S11	33,619	-7	44,221	35	U	11	42	26	-34	43	1	3	6	28	24
S12	32,047	-8	54,332	29	U	10	39	30	-24	62	-1	1	7	6	24
S13	31,574	-9	51,008	36	U	8	38	64	-20	18	24	7	16	9	23
S14	33,420	-7	52,422	33	U	6	44	80	-15	10	60	2	25	8	41
S15	35,769	-3	45,945	32	U	9	44	29	-28	32	11	6	12	33	14
S16	35,200	-5	49,950	35	S	8	32	83	-9	4	23	4	18	8	21
S17	39,102	3	42,739	31	U	7	63	56	-16	13	60	15	37	15	47
S18	38,254	-2	59,322	34	U	5	70	71	-13	7	56	12	34	10	40
S19	36,814	-1	51,206	37	S	6	39	87	-5	2	64	5	26	6	52
W1	43,079	10	54,783	16	S	6	51	97	9	0	51	1	58	1	59
W2	38,689	4	44,828	16	R	8	40	94	2	2	46	1	37	3	62
W3	31,851	-17	35,536	14	U	9	31	77	-24	4	9	4	15	15	24
W4	37,900	0	48,030	18	U	7	40	83	-6	3	37	2	46	11	37
W5	39,234	4	43,003	14	S	7	38	98	3	0	42	0	49	1	29
W6	40,832	4	45,158	18	R	6	37	91	3	0	37	1	35	7	17
W7	40,213	2	49,273	17	S	6	41	97	1	0	38	1	48	1	47

Note: U=urban, S=suburban, R=rural, M=mixed, HH=households.

Massachusetts State House Districts: Demographic Data (cont.)

House District	Population		Average HH Income		District Type	Unempl. Rate	College Educ.	White (non-Hispanic)		African American		Asian American		Hispanic American	
	1997	+/-	($)	+/-		(%)	(%)	(%)	+/-	(%)	+/-	(%)	+/-	(%)	+/-
Mass.	6,106,155	1	55,803	23	S	7	50	85	-2	5	13	3	35	6	31
W8	41,971	11	46,145	17	S	7	35	96	10	1	45	1	53	2	52
W9	40,528	7	53,087	17	S	7	47	97	6	1	41	1	64	1	50
W10	39,658	1	53,410	17	S	7	47	93	-1	2	41	1	39	4	37
W11	43,593	14	61,984	16	S	5	62	91	10	2	57	5	64	2	68
W12	38,732	4	61,396	17	S	5	56	92	2	1	45	2	53	4	30
W13	38,624	0	56,983	11	U	5	59	93	-2	2	28	2	44	3	42
W14	34,628	-4	37,218	12	U	8	41	77	-9	6	23	2	30	14	22
W15	35,322	-6	30,861	12	U	11	31	62	-18	8	11	5	20	24	28
W16	35,843	-3	37,801	16	U	8	34	85	-8	3	36	3	37	8	53
W17	36,759	-4	40,919	16	U	8	34	79	-10	4	21	4	24	12	38

Note: U=urban, S=suburban, R=rural, M=mixed, HH=households.

MICHIGAN

The 1980s could scarcely have been worse for Michigan. The oil shock of 1979 and the ensuing depression (which is what it was here) crushed an economy built on automobile manufacturing and heavy industry. Thousands of unemployed Michigan families, camping in their cars, fled south to Texas where they were known disparagingly as "Black Tag people" for the color of their license plates. Michigan's auto industry shrank from 437,000 employees in October 1978 to 289,000 in October 1982. Detroit, the country's fifth-largest city in 1980, has fallen to tenth today, surpassed by the Sun Belt giants Dallas, Houston, Phoenix, San Antonio, and San Diego.

The 1990s have been better. Autos and heavy industry still have not regained their previous heights and probably never will, but Michigan has found some success in smaller manufacturing and even high tech. The population has grown by 4 percent during this decade—not as fast as Indiana's, but better than any of the other Rust Belt states. That should be enough to keep Michigan where it is; it is the eighth-largest state today and is projected to remain eighth-largest in 2025.

No area of the state could be described as booming; growth is slow but dependable and widespread. Detroit, Ann Arbor, and Lansing are being knit together by a web of fast-growing suburbs, led by the Thirty-eighth House District near Twelve Oaks Mall, the last rural district in the area, which has grown by 22 percent. The city of Detroit, on the other hand, continues to suffer. The One Hundred Ninth District on the Upper Peninsula, which is dependent on timber and mining, has also been hard hit.

Thanks to its glory days at the center of the American economy, Michigan remains one of the wealthier states, and today household income is growing faster here than the national average. Michigan's wealthiest districts are in Detroit's newer suburbs north of the city—Birmingham (average household income, $112,000), Bloomfield Hills, and Auburn Hills—as well as its older, eastern suburbs (Grosse Pointe).

Not surprisingly, downtown Detroit remains desperately poor, one of the poorest parts of the United States. Unemployment in the Fourth District is 27 percent, the highest rate of any house district in the country. It is 26

percent in the Ninth District and 24 percent in the Sixth. In eight house districts, all of them in Detroit and Flint, the unemployment rate is 20 percent or higher.

Racially, Michigan ranks about in the middle: it is twenty-seventh in percentage of white residents; twenty-sixth in percentage of Asians; and twenty-seventh in percentage of Hispanics. Although it ranks fifteenth in percentage of African Americans (the state is 14 percent black), that fits in with other northern industrial states. Blacks migrated to Michigan to find work; hence, the black population is concentrated in the old industrial base and is largely absent elsewhere. Some sixty-five state house districts, more than half the total, are more than 90 percent white. Thirteen house districts, all but one of them in Detroit, have a black majority.

One interesting thing to notice about Detroit's African American population is that the two districts in the city with the highest percentage of African Americans are middle class:

District	% Black	Ave. HH Income	% with College Degree
10	96	$45,839	31
12	95	47,742	32
State Avg.	14	52,098	36

Although Michigan has a very small percentage of Hispanics, the Eighth District along the Detroit River near River Rouge is 25 percent Hispanic. Dearborn is home to the only sizable cluster of Arab Americans in the United States.

The state legislature is one of the most closely contested in the country. The house was 61–49 Democratic in 1990, tied in 1992, 56–54 Republican in 1994, and 58–52 Democratic in 1996. Republicans have held the senate throughout the decade but by a narrow margin (22–16) that has not changed since 1992. Michigan lost one congressional seat after the 1980 census, another after the 1990 census, and is projected to lose still another in 2002.

MICHIGAN
State Senate Districts

DETROIT

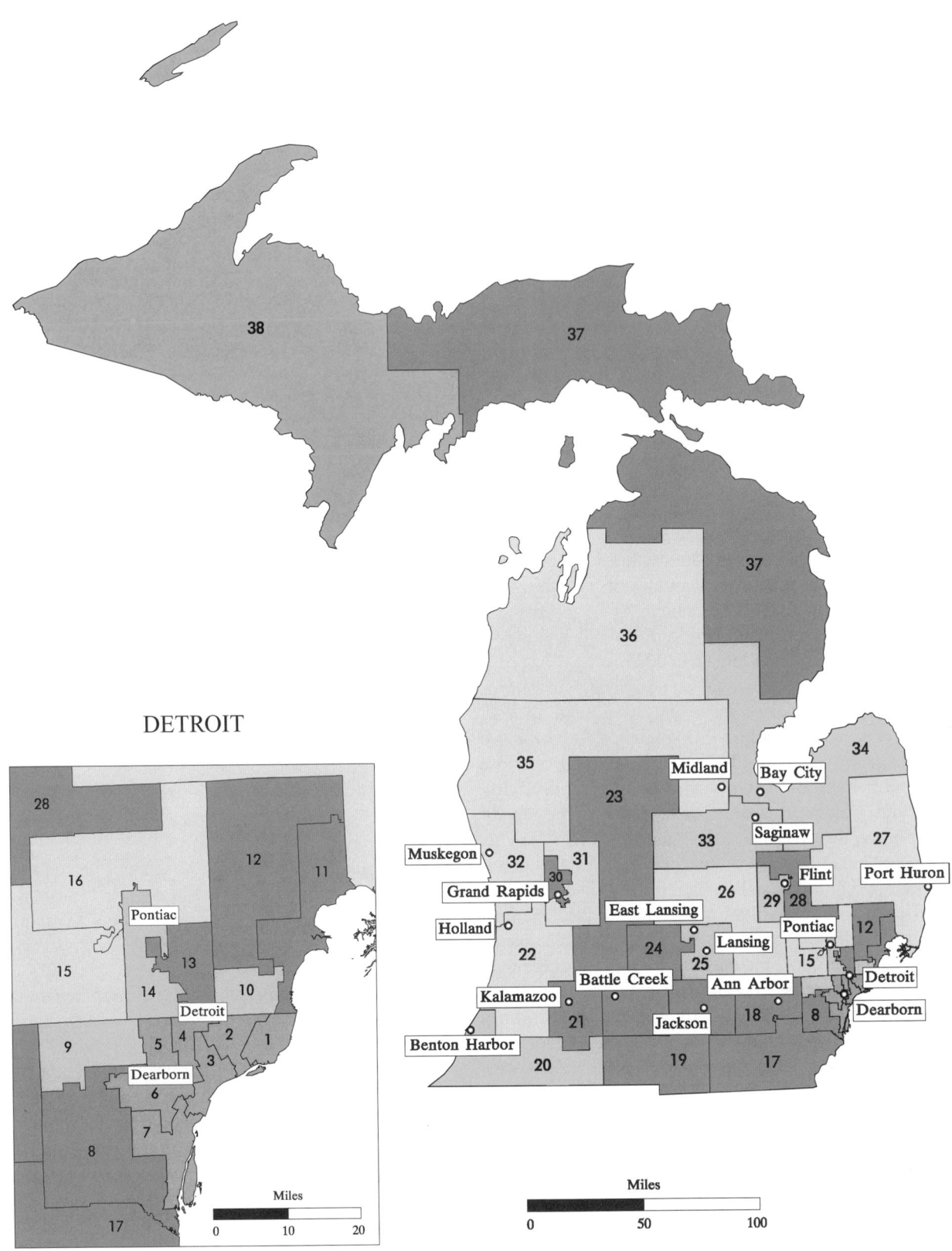

Population Growth   -8% to -3%   -2% to 2%   3% to 7%   9% to 14%

Michigan State Senate Districts: Demographic Data

Senate District	Population		Average HH Income		District Type	Unempl. Rate	College Educ.	White (non-Hispanic)		African American		Asian American		Hispanic American	
	1997	+/-	($)	+/-		(%)	(%)	(%)	+/-	(%)	+/-	(%)	+/-	(%)	+/-
Michigan	9,627,963	4	52,098	37	M	8	36	81	2	14	8	1	28	3	21
1	214,126	-7	53,464	35	U	16	34	40	-15	59	-1	1	9	1	-2
2	212,182	-8	28,565	24	U	21	17	19	-35	79	3	1	-19	1	-3
3	212,540	-7	25,247	27	U	23	19	15	-32	75	-1	1	-5	9	8
4	216,423	-5	37,131	28	U	19	23	8	-36	89	-1	0	-35	3	10
5	218,937	-3	39,417	26	U	14	26	20	-31	78	8	1	-15	1	1
6	229,395	-6	54,412	34	S	7	32	86	-9	10	13	1	29	3	13
7	231,987	-6	51,467	34	S	8	25	89	-8	5	36	1	29	3	11
8	250,812	4	54,278	35	S	7	29	86	-1	9	71	2	42	2	23
9	244,051	2	72,195	39	S	4	46	94	0	2	84	2	45	2	24
10	234,604	-2	48,969	28	S	7	24	96	-3	1	-14	1	27	1	18
11	249,532	5	56,216	32	S	6	32	93	3	4	26	1	52	1	25
12	252,306	6	67,182	33	R	5	38	96	5	0	-13	2	32	1	31
13	270,973	3	69,797	34	S	5	50	93	1	1	47	4	41	1	25
14	261,654	0	74,420	32	S	7	50	63	-8	30	17	3	26	4	17
15	300,719	14	82,254	33	S	4	55	93	12	2	59	3	47	1	40
16	288,367	13	70,867	33	S	5	47	94	11	2	58	2	43	2	43
17	258,763	6	54,159	39	R	7	30	93	5	2	13	1	28	4	27
18	277,116	5	65,538	46	S	4	61	79	1	13	18	5	28	2	24
19	244,431	4	42,999	30	M	8	31	92	3	6	16	0	16	2	25
20	267,516	1	45,867	40	R	7	32	84	-1	12	12	1	20	2	18
21	235,090	3	51,658	35	S	6	48	86	1	10	16	2	25	2	22
22	286,892	12	50,392	41	R	6	33	90	11	3	22	1	37	5	31
23	270,446	7	40,302	32	R	9	31	95	7	2	16	0	17	2	28
24	265,211	6	49,413	37	S	7	37	88	5	8	17	1	30	2	25
25	261,227	0	52,572	43	U	7	50	78	-4	12	13	3	23	6	19
26	276,510	13	59,453	37	R	6	37	97	13	0	11	0	35	2	31
27	286,206	10	47,568	32	R	9	27	95	9	1	20	0	29	2	31
28	236,423	5	55,250	37	S	8	32	88	2	8	32	1	32	2	29
29	249,149	1	46,485	37	U	12	31	66	-3	30	9	1	21	2	14
30	258,105	5	49,726	48	U	6	39	77	1	16	17	1	24	5	26
31	282,223	11	67,406	51	S	4	44	94	10	2	53	1	41	2	32
32	273,126	9	49,844	41	S	7	34	87	7	9	16	1	33	3	30
33	251,550	0	43,287	32	M	10	31	76	-3	16	9	1	20	7	17
34	241,454	2	41,704	36	R	11	25	96	2	1	8	0	11	3	19
35	265,031	12	41,725	35	R	10	33	95	11	1	25	1	29	2	29
36	267,118	14	40,811	38	R	9	35	98	14	0	5	0	10	1	27
37	248,615	5	37,036	40	R	10	29	94	5	1	12	0	-5	1	10
38	237,186	-3	37,178	39	R	9	35	97	-4	1	-6	1	5	1	0

Note: U=urban, S=suburban, R=rural, M=mixed, HH=households.

MICHIGAN
State House Districts

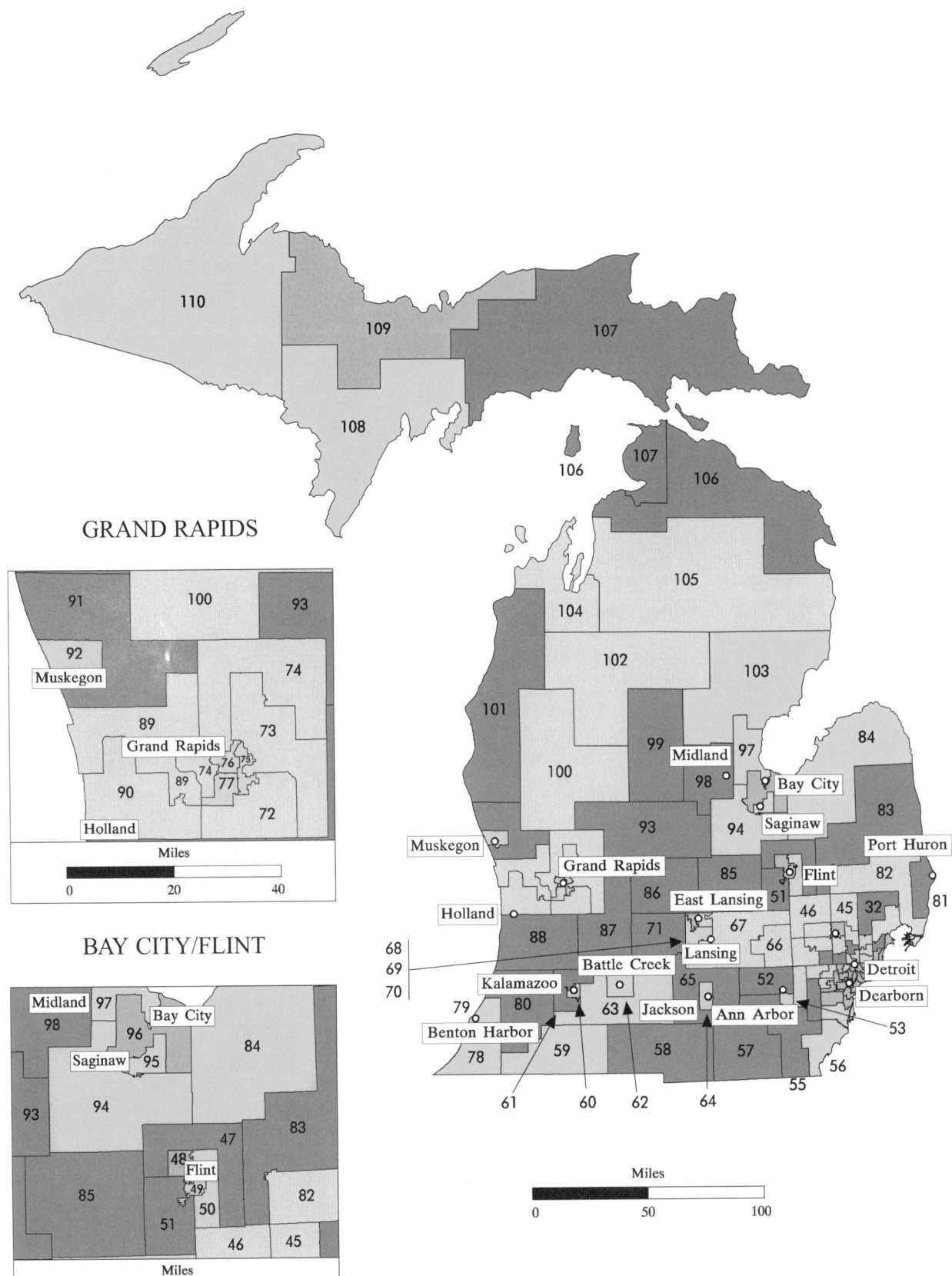

GRAND RAPIDS

BAY CITY/FLINT

Population Growth ▨ -12% to -3% ▨ -2% to 4% ▨ 5% to 11% ▨ 12% to 22%

DETROIT

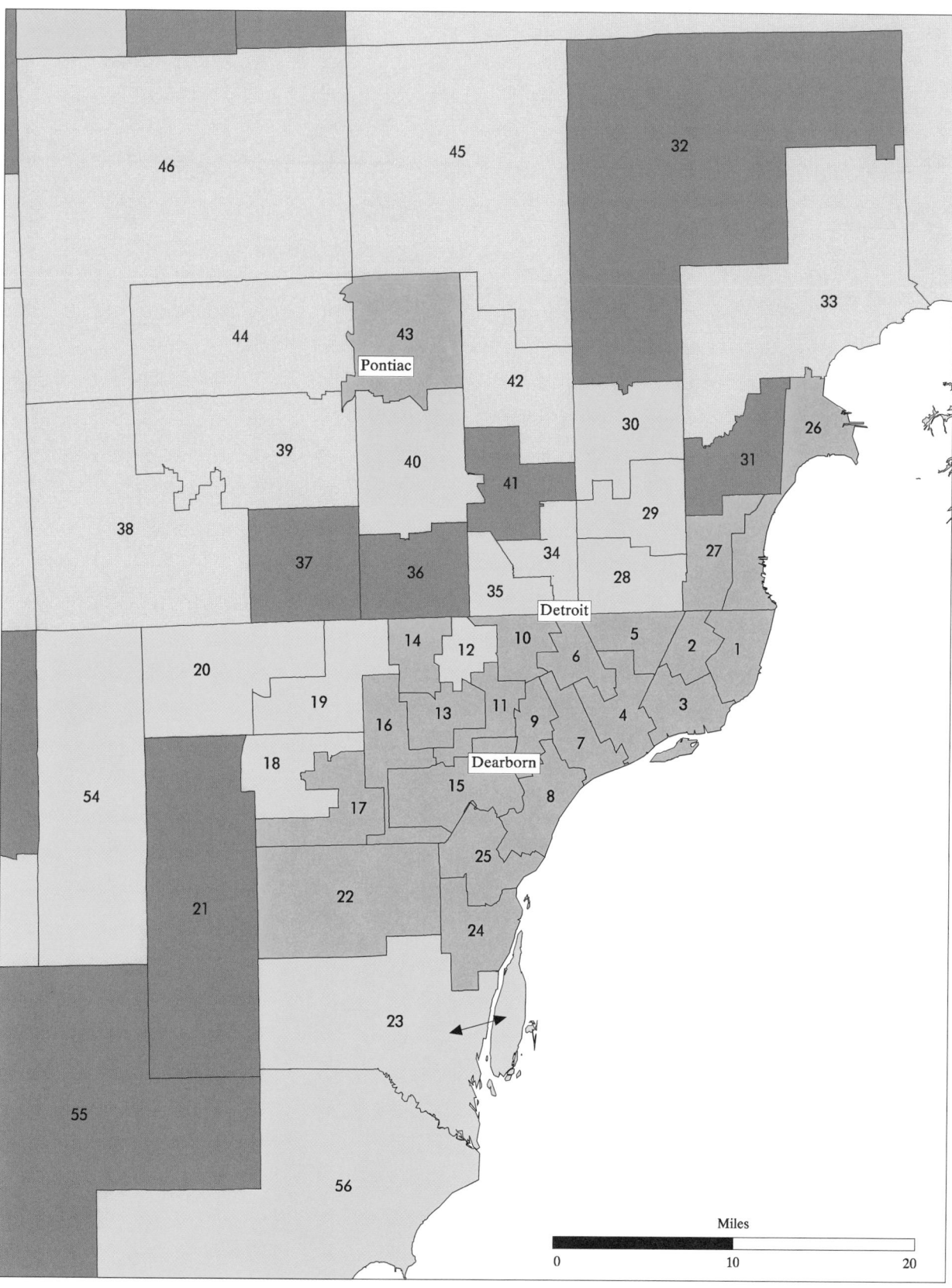

Pontiac

Detroit

Dearborn

Miles

0   10   20

Population Growth   -12% to -3%   -2% to 4%   5% to 11%   12% to 22%

Michigan State House Districts: Demographic Data

House District	Population 1997	+/-	Average HH Income ($)	+/-	District Type	Unempl. Rate (%)	College Educ. (%)	White (non-Hispanic) (%)	+/-	African American (%)	+/-	Asian American (%)	+/-	Hispanic American (%)	+/-
Michigan	9,627,963	4	52,098	37	M	8	36	81	2	14	8	1	28	3	21
1	67,272	-3	92,347	37	S	4	57	87	-7	10	55	2	31	1	14
2	80,381	-6	33,530	21	U	19	20	28	-26	70	6	1	-13	1	1
3	81,947	-10	34,344	32	U	24	23	15	-28	84	-6	0	-3	1	-12
4	72,651	-10	23,828	28	U	27	16	7	-47	91	-4	1	-23	1	-11
5	78,187	-4	31,807	19	U	17	16	16	-41	80	10	2	-19	1	-6
6	74,636	-10	25,223	22	U	24	16	21	-35	77	1	1	-23	1	-8
7	79,770	-4	26,241	35	U	22	27	8	-41	88	2	2	2	2	-1
8	73,635	-9	25,222	20	U	22	11	37	-28	37	5	1	-7	25	9
9	74,923	-8	24,209	22	U	26	13	12	-29	83	-5	0	-36	5	14
10	77,303	-4	45,839	33	U	16	31	3	-51	96	-1	0	-40	1	-10
11	80,762	-4	31,160	24	U	21	17	16	-17	82	-1	0	-6	1	8
12	79,229	-2	47,742	29	U	14	32	4	-51	95	3	0	-40	0	-16
13	77,598	-3	36,273	23	U	15	22	18	-31	79	7	1	-10	2	5
14	75,914	-5	38,686	27	U	14	26	20	-37	79	10	1	-20	1	-13
15	83,754	-6	56,937	35	U	6	39	94	-8	1	88	1	35	3	17
16	84,097	-5	56,366	33	S	6	31	94	-7	1	87	1	34	3	14
17	81,935	-5	46,787	33	S	9	21	65	-13	32	16	1	9	2	10
18	87,690	2	51,697	35	S	6	28	92	-1	3	112	2	45	2	18
19	89,363	-1	61,201	35	S	5	38	96	-2	1	96	1	39	2	21
20	93,538	4	87,914	43	S	3	55	93	2	3	67	2	48	2	32
21	96,832	11	63,742	37	S	6	42	86	6	8	92	4	49	2	24
22	84,515	-4	48,431	34	S	9	17	81	-11	14	60	1	18	3	10
23	93,708	3	65,260	36	S	6	36	93	0	2	95	2	40	2	24
24	78,549	-7	52,029	33	S	7	27	94	-8	1	94	1	30	3	15
25	82,257	-6	44,802	29	S	8	21	86	-9	8	13	1	21	5	11
26	84,666	-6	56,088	31	S	6	32	97	-6	1	-5	1	14	1	18
27	86,925	-3	46,456	29	S	7	22	97	-4	1	-15	1	25	1	13
28	88,255	-2	42,970	25	S	9	20	95	-3	1	-14	2	28	2	25
29	91,012	0	62,478	32	S	5	33	96	-1	0	-13	2	32	1	17
30	92,905	3	64,215	30	R	5	40	94	2	0	-15	4	31	1	31
31	97,697	9	50,531	28	R	7	28	89	7	8	33	2	82	2	25
32	94,779	8	72,137	35	R	5	39	97	7	0	-7	1	40	1	28
33	100,201	13	64,809	33	R	6	36	96	13	1	7	1	35	1	38
34	78,915	-1	45,541	28	R	7	31	95	-2	1	34	2	26	1	20
35	84,956	-2	51,493	28	S	6	41	76	-8	20	23	2	18	2	28
36	85,371	7	62,140	24	S	6	54	59	-6	36	33	3	28	2	55
37	91,793	8	82,656	32	S	4	60	91	6	3	57	5	48	1	34
38	95,855	22	65,851	34	R	4	49	96	21	1	71	2	60	1	43
39	97,893	12	104,683	33	S	4	58	92	10	2	57	4	41	1	41
40	84,017	4	153,234	37	S	2	73	91	2	2	50	5	38	1	21
41	87,739	7	61,451	30	S	4	52	93	5	1	52	4	43	1	33
42	89,362	12	92,442	34	S	4	60	89	9	2	52	7	47	2	39
43	84,117	-6	39,139	27	U	11	26	51	-14	38	4	2	8	8	9
44	100,426	13	57,730	29	S	6	36	95	11	1	57	1	42	2	37
45	93,837	15	76,400	37	S	5	51	95	13	1	62	2	47	2	47
46	96,695	16	69,488	34	S	6	41	96	15	1	58	0	43	2	53
47	92,245	5	57,142	40	S	7	33	95	4	2	86	0	35	2	27
48	79,265	-5	34,960	27	U	20	20	22	-25	75	4	0	-20	2	-5
49	83,304	-1	36,775	32	U	14	26	68	-8	26	22	1	13	4	20
50	88,598	1	56,397	38	S	9	34	89	-2	7	45	1	31	2	29

Note: U=urban, S=suburban, R=rural, M=mixed, HH=households.

Michigan State House Districts: Demographic Data (cont.)

House District	Population 1997	+/-	Average HH Income ($)	+/-	District Type	Unempl. Rate (%)	College Educ. (%)	White (non-Hispanic) (%)	+/-	African American (%)	+/-	Asian American (%)	+/-	Hispanic American (%)	+/-
Michigan	9,627,963	4	52,098	37	M	8	36	81	2	14	8	1	28	3	21
51	93,489	6	60,559	42	S	6	37	91	4	5	53	1	30	2	23
52	87,834	6	79,514	46	U	3	68	84	4	7	23	7	27	2	17
53	87,229	3	58,708	46	U	4	70	77	-2	12	20	7	32	3	28
54	85,403	3	54,813	43	S	6	43	72	-1	23	16	3	21	2	20
55	93,546	9	67,002	44	S	5	37	95	8	2	12	1	40	2	34
56	86,025	4	51,033	35	R	7	25	95	4	2	17	1	27	2	25
57	95,884	7	49,355	37	R	7	31	90	5	2	11	1	23	7	26
58	89,392	5	40,077	32	R	8	28	97	5	1	12	0	2	1	28
59	93,207	4	47,023	41	R	6	27	94	3	4	17	0	17	1	20
60	88,829	-2	40,858	31	U	9	47	74	-7	20	12	2	18	3	18
61	96,986	6	60,629	37	S	4	54	92	5	5	30	2	34	1	28
62	91,564	4	45,041	37	U	9	33	82	1	14	16	1	28	2	27
63	92,880	4	49,386	36	S	7	36	92	3	5	17	0	13	2	17
64	78,940	0	40,693	25	M	8	33	80	-4	17	15	1	26	2	21
65	82,259	8	48,944	33	S	7	31	97	7	1	27	0	9	1	30
66	97,704	21	73,093	37	S	4	43	97	21	1	20	1	53	1	48
67	94,133	16	60,187	39	S	6	41	96	15	1	26	1	48	2	50
68	80,861	2	49,698	41	U	6	36	79	-1	14	11	1	25	6	21
69	83,668	-5	44,875	41	U	8	46	69	-11	17	12	3	24	10	14
70	69,628	1	66,296	48	U	6	75	82	-2	7	20	8	22	3	26
71	94,339	8	54,177	34	S	5	41	92	7	4	20	1	34	3	27
72	99,176	15	69,918	53	S	3	47	92	13	4	59	2	45	2	34
73	98,930	15	80,868	50	S	3	51	97	14	1	61	1	46	1	47
74	96,497	14	56,092	48	S	5	35	97	13	1	62	1	47	1	33
75	79,678	3	55,238	48	U	5	49	73	-2	23	21	2	28	2	23
76	87,389	0	40,601	44	U	9	31	75	-4	16	13	1	17	6	26
77	85,499	0	48,315	44	S	6	33	78	-5	11	17	2	23	8	26
78	79,105	-2	46,577	39	R	6	36	89	-4	7	25	1	18	2	11
79	82,315	2	45,408	39	S	9	34	71	-1	27	8	1	31	2	27
80	94,301	6	40,816	34	R	9	26	87	4	8	19	0	15	3	24
81	94,958	5	45,755	30	S	8	31	93	4	3	20	1	33	2	25
82	101,935	16	52,186	33	R	9	24	96	15	1	26	0	41	2	32
83	89,335	9	44,336	33	R	9	25	97	8	0	8	0	0	2	37
84	93,451	3	40,428	35	R	10	24	97	3	1	10	0	11	2	24
85	81,472	5	45,447	32	R	9	29	97	4	0	-26	0	12	2	22
86	84,768	8	50,450	32	R	6	33	96	7	1	17	0	18	2	31
87	83,452	7	45,307	35	R	7	28	94	6	4	15	0	18	2	24
88	99,976	11	51,540	46	R	6	30	93	10	2	22	1	27	4	30
89	104,609	14	60,211	43	S	4	43	97	14	1	19	1	36	1	39
90	106,922	19	60,050	42	S	4	39	88	17	1	21	2	43	9	37
91	83,584	5	47,559	35	S	7	33	95	4	1	28	0	23	2	22
92	81,903	3	35,081	32	U	11	24	67	-2	29	15	0	18	3	20
93	96,728	9	36,081	24	R	10	26	95	8	2	18	0	-1	3	28
94	81,472	1	50,894	36	S	7	30	93	0	3	18	0	16	4	13
95	82,011	2	30,242	26	U	17	23	44	-7	43	8	0	7	12	18
96	78,420	-4	56,085	40	S	7	41	92	-6	3	27	1	27	4	14
97	80,249	-1	43,795	40	M	11	26	93	-2	1	8	0	17	4	17
98	84,068	7	55,350	33	M	7	49	95	6	1	16	1	41	2	27
99	86,635	9	36,140	32	R	10	34	96	9	1	13	1	26	1	27
100	93,860	12	37,306	40	R	10	30	94	11	3	27	0	6	2	31

Note: U=urban, S=suburban, R=rural, M=mixed, HH=households.

Michigan State House Districts: Demographic Data (cont.)

House District	Population 1997	+/-	Average HH Income ($)	+/-	District Type	Unempl. Rate (%)	College Educ. (%)	White (non-Hispanic) (%)	+/-	African American (%)	+/-	Asian American (%)	+/-	Hispanic American (%)	+/-
Michigan	9,627,963	4	52,098	37	M	8	36	81	2	14	8	1	28	3	21
101	90,104	10	35,056	33	R	11	30	95	10	0	-5	0	-10	3	29
102	88,156	13	34,748	35	R	12	25	98	13	0	-4	0	-2	1	21
103	87,217	2	32,066	32	R	12	21	97	2	1	-9	0	-7	1	12
104	91,516	13	51,545	47	R	6	46	97	13	0	5	0	25	1	33
105	102,000	15	35,897	37	R	9	27	98	15	0	13	0	-9	1	14
106	92,274	6	37,757	39	R	10	29	98	6	0	-40	0	-12	0	11
107	91,693	9	39,711	42	R	10	31	88	9	3	20	0	6	1	17
108	91,040	2	39,310	38	R	8	32	98	2	0	-64	0	-3	0	3
109	70,241	-12	41,076	40	R	9	40	95	-12	2	-1	1	0	1	-2
110	85,917	1	31,602	38	R	10	34	96	1	1	-2	1	12	0	3

Note: U=urban, S=suburban, R=rural, M=mixed, HH=households.

MINNESOTA

The state of Minnesota has been depicted as a place of both oppressive conformity, by Sinclair Lewis, and gentle eccentricity, by Garrison Keillor. It has been a place for hearty pioneers to build a better life, as in Laura Ingalls Wilder's *Little House on the Prairie,* and a place from which jaded sophisticates flee, such as St. Paul's F. Scott Fitzgerald. All four, though, recognized in Minnesotans an earnestness and a dogged sincerity, which may be said to characterize the state's politics as well. Three of its most famous political leaders of recent generations—Harold Stassen, Hubert Humphrey, and Walter Mondale—were, if nothing else, tribunes of the virtues of plugging away.

And so does Minnesota. The state today is clearly above average, as Keillor would say about the children of Lake Wobegon. It grew by 7.4 percent during the 1980s and has grown by 7 percent during the 1990s, slightly ahead of the nation in both cases.

The fastest-growing parts of Minnesota are the Twin City suburbs, and the fastest-shrinking are the Twin City centers. For the most part, growth has occurred to the south and west, if only because the eastern St. Paul suburbs quickly run out of room at the St. Croix River. State house district 37B, south of Bloomington, has grown by 47 percent since 1990. (Minnesota, like several other states, is divided into legislative districts, each of which elects one state senator and two representatives from an "A" and "B" district). On the Minneapolis side, Brooklyn Park, Eden Prairie, and Minnetonka have also grown substantially, as has district 19A northeast toward St. Cloud. Oakdale is the fastest-growing St. Paul suburb. A string of mostly urban districts inside these growing districts—the hole in the metropolitan doughnut, so to speak—are losing population.

Minneapolis is wealthier than St. Paul, and so are its suburbs. Average household income in district 34B (Plymouth) is $106,000. Other wealthy areas include Edina, Minnetonka, St. Louis Park, and the western edge of Bloomington. The poorest sections are in downtown Minneapolis, the Mesabi Iron Range, and the Sioux Indian reservations in north-central Minnesota, where unemployment runs in the double digits.

Elsewhere, little of Minnesota is growing very rapidly. Indeed, the Census Bureau estimates that most of the state's counties will lose population between now and 2020, by which time as much as 68 percent of the state's population will live in the greater Twin Cities area. With a few exceptions already noted, Minnesota's economy is mostly rural, based on mining and logging in the Iron Range and on wheat and dairy farming. Between an urban core pushing out and a hinterland migrating in, the Twin City suburbs have become a magnet drawing from both ends.

Minnesota is homogeneous, though it is a state with racial and ethnic minorities—Indians, Norwegians—one does not find in many other places. It has the smallest percentage of African Americans (3 percent) of any state with even a modicum of heavy industry. The only black neighborhoods are in districts 58B and 61B in Minneapolis. On the other hand, fully 100 of its 134 state house districts are at least 90 percent white. In this respect, Minnesota is much more akin to the Dakotas than to Illinois or the industrial giants to the southeast. Six urban house districts in the Twin Cities are, however, more than 10 percent Asian.

Between Stassen, Humphrey, and Mondale, a Minnesotan either appeared on a national ticket or made a serious bid for a place on it in every presidential election between 1948 and 1984, a feat unparalleled for a state of its size. Minnesota has been strongly Democratic in presidential elections, although Mondale carried it in 1984 by only about 3,700 votes, thus coming within a razor's breadth of losing all fifty states. (Party initials are different here. Democrats belong to the Democratic-Farmer-Labor Party, or DFL; until a few years ago, the Republican Party was known as the Independent Republican Party, or IR). Nevertheless, Republicans have won gubernatorial and senatorial elections. Although Democrats control both chambers of the legislature, their margin in the house has narrowed sufficiently that the GOP could capture it in a strong year.

MINNESOTA
State Senate Districts

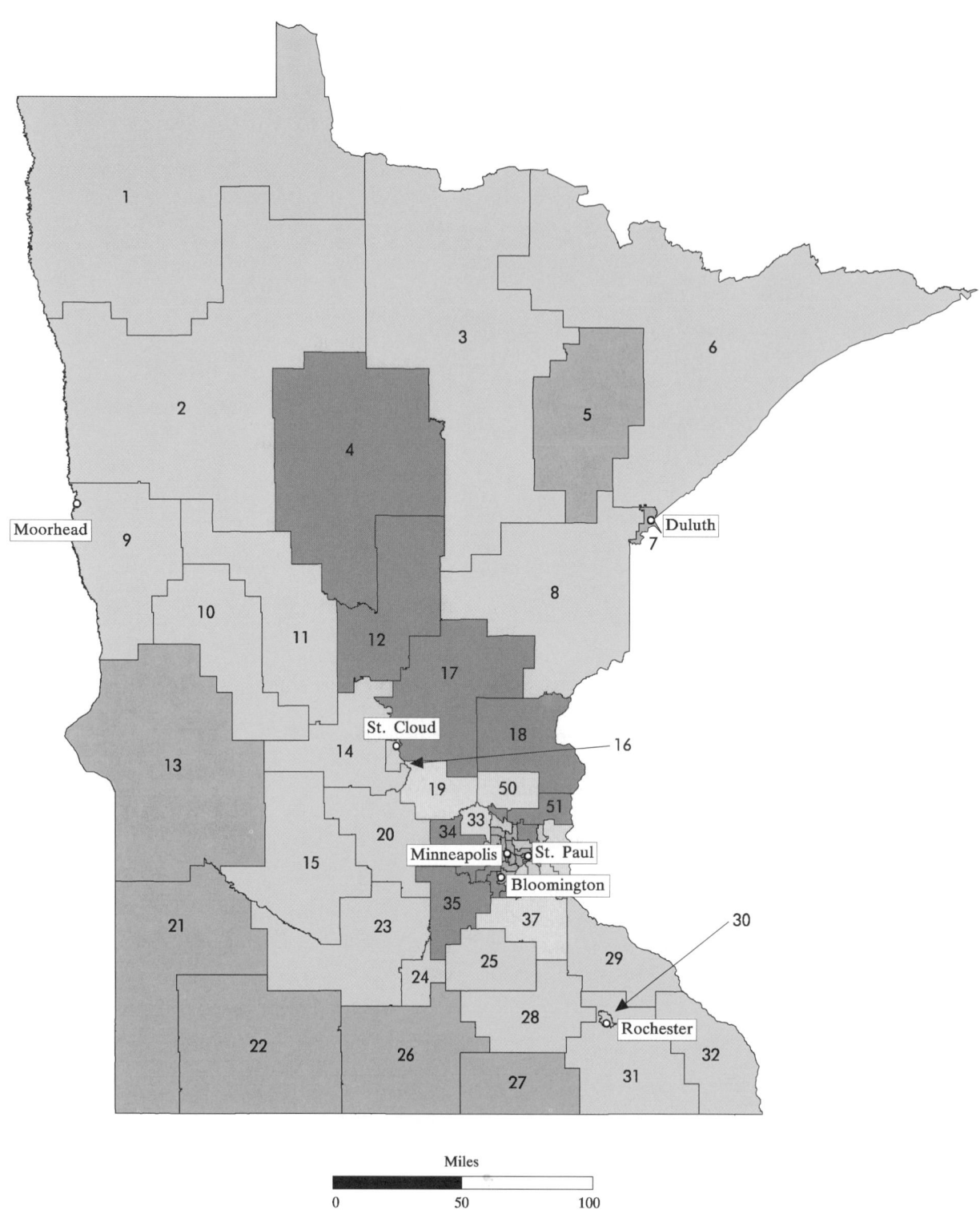

Population Growth   ▨ -9% to 0%   ☐ 1% to 10%   ▨ 12% to 23%   ▨ 29% to 36%

MINNEAPOLIS/ST.PAUL

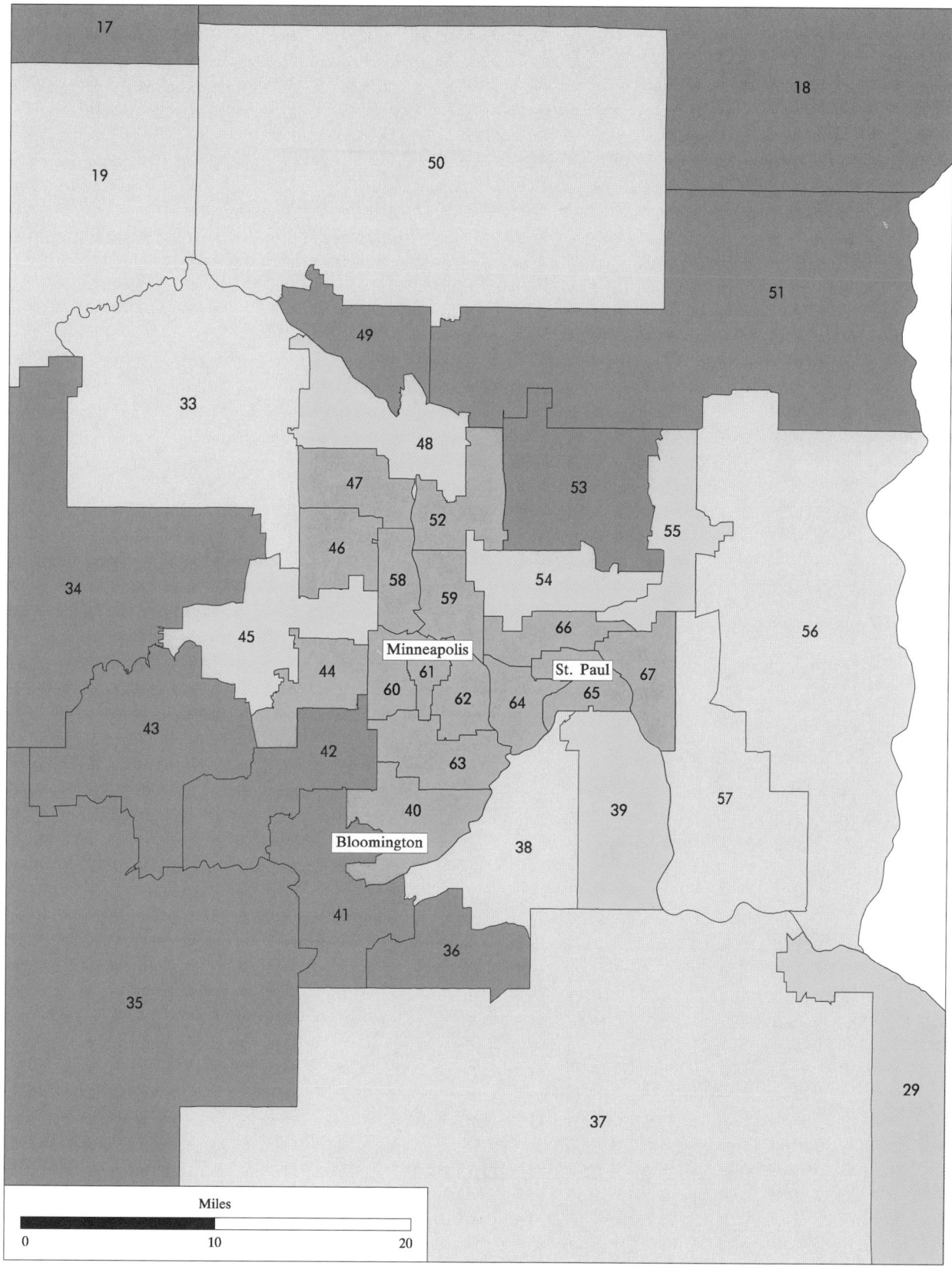

Population Growth ▨ -9% to 0% □ 1% to 10% ▨ 12% to 23% □ 29% to 36%

Minnesota State Senate Districts: Demographic Data

Senate District	Population 1997	+/-	Average HH Income ($)	+/-	District Type	Unempl. Rate (%)	College Educ. (%)	White (non-Hispanic) (%)	+/-	African American (%)	+/-	Asian American (%)	+/-	Hispanic American (%)	+/-
Minn.	4,690,954	7	51,427	36	M	5	46	92	5	3	44	2	43	2	58
1	66,410	3	34,879	28	R	7	33	96	2	0	-10	0	8	2	49
2	66,973	1	32,425	33	R	9	28	86	-1	0	-26	0	-17	1	29
3	67,651	5	36,694	32	R	10	35	96	4	0	-22	0	-6	1	46
4	75,031	14	33,978	38	R	10	38	90	12	0	2	0	24	1	52
5	64,376	-4	35,701	32	R	9	37	97	-4	0	11	0	24	1	42
6	67,241	3	45,007	36	R	8	44	96	2	0	36	1	32	0	31
7	61,415	-4	37,059	39	U	8	37	93	-6	2	37	1	38	1	52
8	71,823	10	39,677	41	R	9	31	95	9	1	36	0	17	1	63
9	67,419	4	41,148	40	M	6	42	95	2	0	36	1	32	3	54
10	70,549	7	37,174	39	R	6	36	99	7	0	-15	0	31	0	49
11	68,656	3	33,438	35	R	6	30	98	3	0	-36	0	-4	1	37
12	72,214	12	38,245	38	R	8	33	98	12	0	-5	0	32	1	65
13	63,687	-3	34,045	35	R	5	33	98	-3	0	-16	0	-6	1	28
14	69,990	8	44,790	34	R	5	36	99	8	0	21	0	39	1	64
15	67,002	3	40,494	37	R	5	37	95	2	0	24	0	12	4	56
16	66,028	9	42,749	31	U	5	47	97	8	1	54	2	55	1	59
17	82,591	14	40,259	31	R	7	33	97	13	1	50	0	40	1	61
18	77,709	20	44,891	32	R	7	31	98	19	0	24	0	49	1	85
19	85,597	31	51,560	31	R	5	39	98	30	0	76	1	79	1	103
20	70,362	8	45,562	37	R	4	32	98	8	0	-10	0	28	1	59
21	65,438	-2	37,658	35	R	4	32	98	-2	0	7	0	5	1	41
22	66,469	-1	34,580	28	R	4	30	97	-2	0	-28	1	28	1	40
23	66,321	2	39,913	35	R	4	31	98	2	0	-26	0	12	1	48
24	67,652	4	46,314	45	R	4	47	96	2	1	31	2	43	1	55
25	68,793	8	45,768	36	R	4	40	97	7	0	34	1	43	1	63
26	62,749	-1	39,091	35	R	4	34	97	-2	0	-33	0	9	2	47
27	63,366	-3	37,374	32	R	7	36	96	-4	0	-13	1	27	3	44
28	69,390	5	46,585	36	R	4	40	97	4	0	11	1	17	2	56
29	65,812	6	47,078	36	R	5	37	98	6	0	21	1	32	1	52
30	51,827	4	53,607	35	U	4	60	91	1	1	48	6	44	2	56
31	85,407	6	53,194	35	M	3	49	96	4	0	53	2	54	1	66
32	66,665	2	43,292	40	R	5	41	98	2	0	20	1	34	1	47
33	86,694	32	73,605	37	S	3	57	95	29	1	139	2	111	1	94
34	75,401	17	89,394	43	S	4	55	95	15	1	130	2	93	1	97
35	82,789	23	56,740	33	R	4	41	97	22	0	61	1	63	1	76
36	77,268	21	67,858	28	S	3	62	93	19	2	72	3	70	2	85
37	88,547	29	59,266	30	S	4	47	97	28	1	93	1	89	1	103
38	85,558	30	69,378	30	S	3	65	91	26	3	81	4	76	2	123
39	67,205	5	52,541	26	S	4	44	93	2	1	51	1	45	5	64
40	59,126	-5	54,008	31	U	4	50	90	-10	3	71	5	49	2	55
41	75,898	19	82,263	38	U	3	64	92	16	2	87	4	74	1	83
42	71,428	12	94,614	35	S	3	69	94	9	2	114	3	86	1	65
43	78,635	22	93,684	39	S	3	64	95	20	1	96	2	86	1	80
44	62,050	-4	55,411	34	S	3	57	91	-7	3	81	3	53	2	54
45	70,940	8	86,915	41	S	3	64	92	4	3	92	3	72	2	78
46	60,580	-5	53,104	34	S	5	45	91	-9	4	77	3	47	2	49
47	65,291	0	51,005	31	S	5	43	83	-7	10	75	4	51	2	49
48	72,253	8	60,877	33	S	4	46	93	5	2	84	3	60	1	65
49	76,139	18	53,844	26	S	4	43	95	17	1	73	2	81	1	83
50	90,063	36	60,375	27	S	5	41	97	35	0	96	1	101	1	99

Note: U=urban, S=suburban, R=rural, M=mixed, HH=households.

Minnesota State Senate Districts: Demographic Data (cont.)

Senate District	Population		Average HH Income		District Type	Unempl. Rate	College Educ.	White (non-Hispanic)		African American		Asian American		Hispanic American	
	1997	+/-	($)	+/-		(%)	(%)	(%)	+/-	(%)	+/-	(%)	+/-	(%)	+/-
Minn.	4,690,954	7	51,427	36	M	5	46	92	5	3	44	2	43	2	58
51	82,150	22	55,328	25	S	4	45	96	21	0	72	1	78	1	79
52	61,982	-5	53,812	33	S	5	47	92	-7	1	56	4	49	2	54
53	77,658	15	80,168	42	S	3	62	93	12	1	86	4	79	2	85
54	68,262	2	58,702	36	S	4	58	88	-3	3	73	6	58	2	61
55	67,140	3	58,049	39	S	4	49	91	0	2	66	3	40	2	67
56	88,228	31	69,512	22	S	3	58	95	29	2	63	2	93	2	113
57	84,345	30	57,287	27	S	4	52	92	26	2	102	2	78	3	93
58	59,537	-9	33,700	24	U	11	29	51	-23	36	18	7	-3	3	30
59	64,049	-4	38,212	34	U	7	49	80	-12	6	60	8	38	4	61
60	61,302	-5	62,551	44	U	4	65	84	-12	9	65	3	46	3	50
61	60,473	-6	27,270	24	U	11	39	39	-31	39	31	7	10	5	53
62	64,325	-6	42,140	28	U	6	48	81	-13	9	64	3	41	3	50
63	60,827	-6	60,693	35	U	3	56	87	-11	6	66	4	49	2	57
64	58,789	-7	65,054	43	U	4	67	90	-11	4	58	3	45	3	60
65	62,104	-5	37,750	36	U	9	38	51	-21	22	19	13	16	12	33
66	61,388	-6	40,306	33	U	6	46	75	-15	8	50	11	27	5	49
67	59,688	-5	38,376	29	U	7	32	76	-14	7	52	9	34	7	56

Note: U=urban, S=suburban, R=rural, M=mixed, HH=households.

MINNESOTA
State House Districts

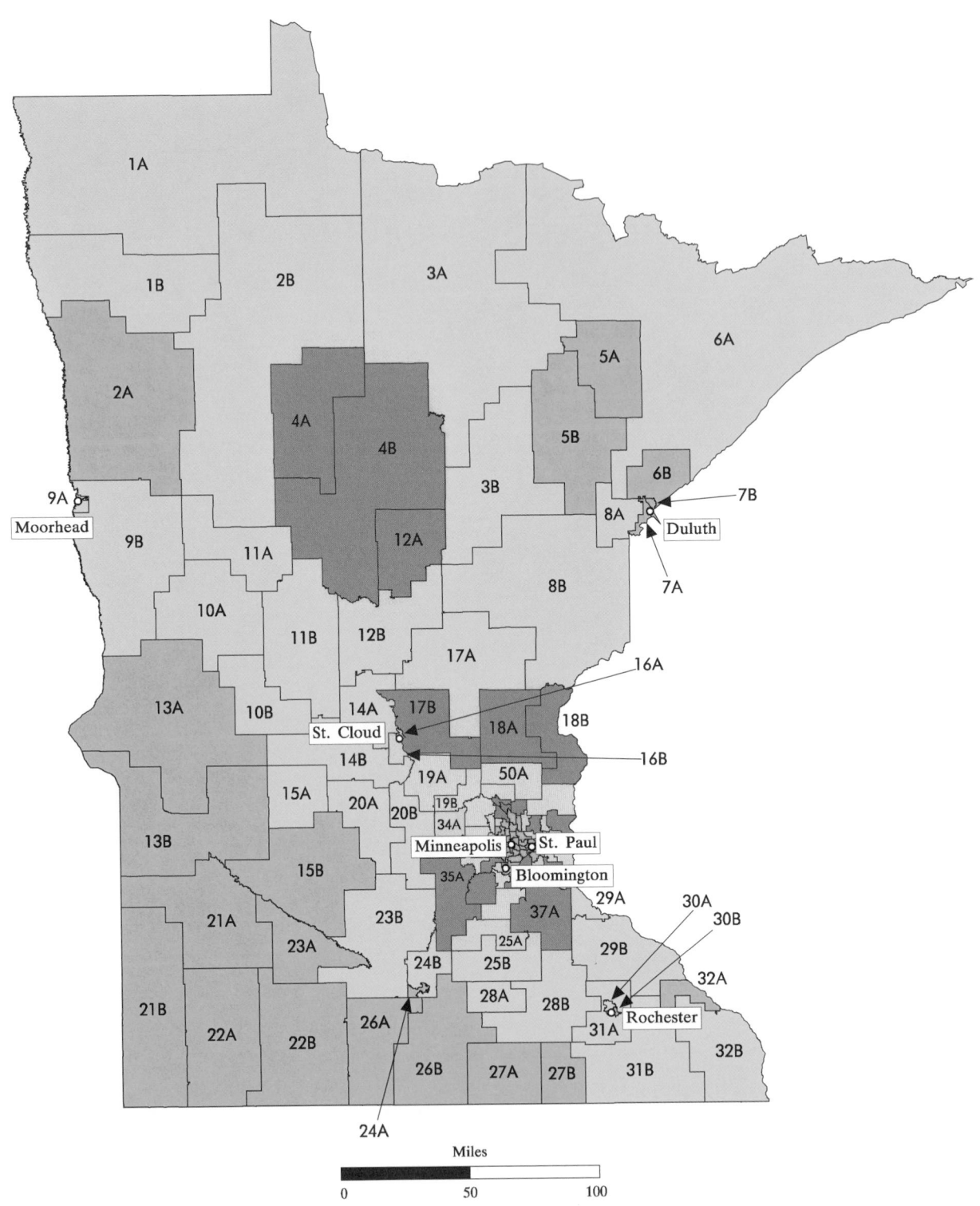

Population Growth ☐ -10% to 1% ☐ 2% to 12% ☐ 13% to 25% ☐ 28% to 47%

MINNEAPOLIS/ST. PAUL

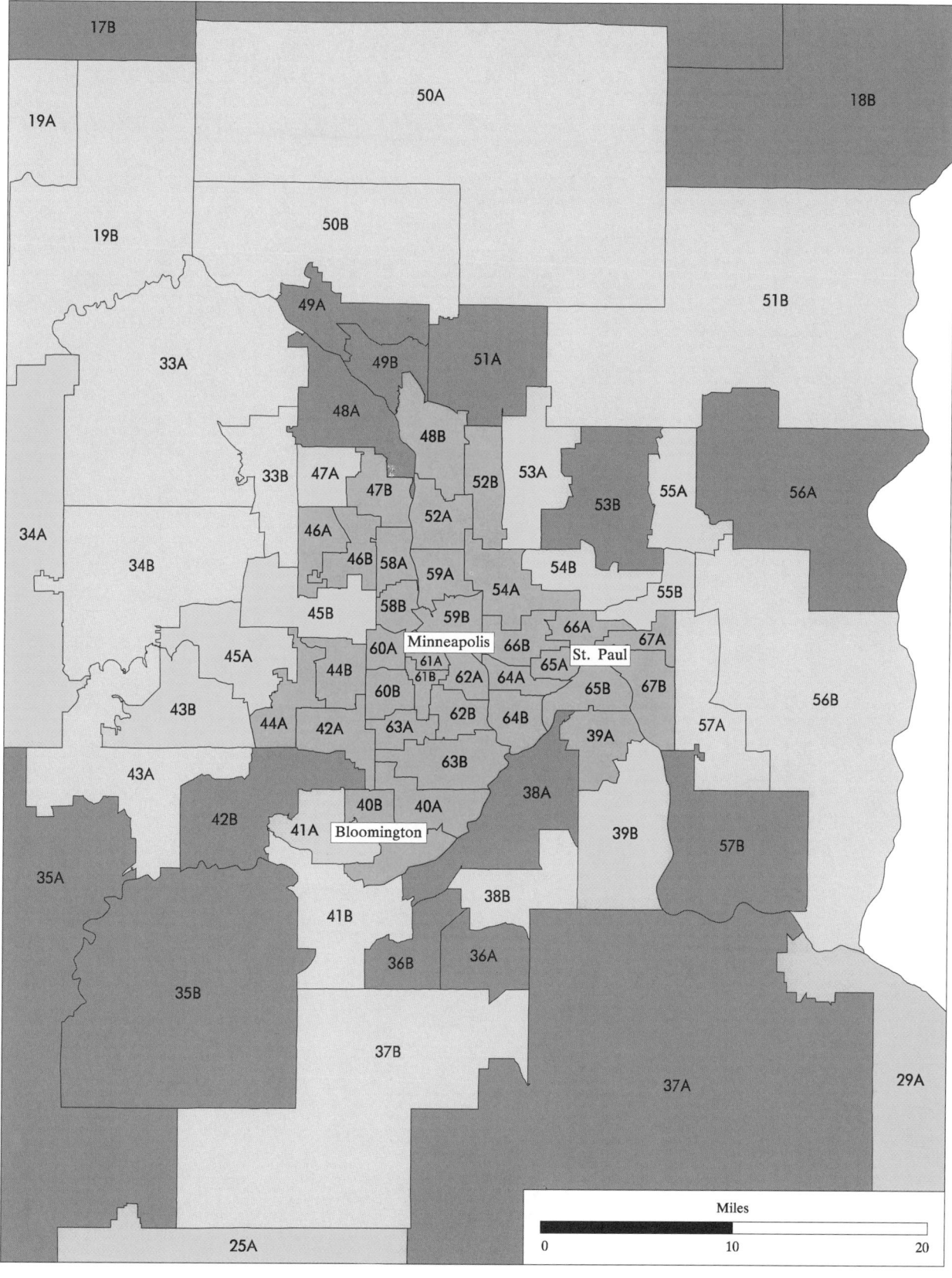

Population Growth   ▨ -10% to 1%   ▨ 2% to 12%   ▨ 13% to 25%   ▨ 28% to 47%

Minnesota State House Districts: Demographic Data

House District	Population		Average HH Income		District Type	Unempl. Rate	College Educ.	White (non-Hispanic)		African American		Asian American		Hispanic American	
	1997	+/-	($)	+/-		(%)	(%)	(%)	+/-	(%)	+/-	(%)	+/-	(%)	+/-
Minn.	4,690,954	7	51,427	36	M	5	46	92	5	3	44	2	43	2	58
1A	33,899	3	34,156	25	R	5	32	98	3	0	-80	0	18	1	19
1B	32,503	2	35,608	31	R	8	34	94	0	0	3	0	-5	4	54
2A	32,988	-2	34,276	29	R	7	31	95	-3	0	-11	0	-9	2	34
2B	33,981	4	30,509	37	R	12	25	77	2	0	-59	0	-24	0	-8
3A	35,117	3	38,807	35	R	9	35	95	3	0	-12	0	-7	1	41
3B	32,527	6	34,556	28	R	11	36	98	6	0	-38	0	-4	1	54
4A	37,063	13	36,188	38	R	8	46	91	11	0	20	1	41	1	59
4B	37,958	15	31,980	39	R	12	29	90	14	0	-36	0	-27	0	42
5A	32,323	-3	34,948	31	R	10	39	98	-4	0	19	0	24	0	36
5B	32,052	-4	36,497	34	R	9	35	97	-4	0	0	0	24	1	46
6A	33,196	5	37,720	39	R	10	35	96	5	0	15	0	5	0	26
6B	34,001	1	52,885	35	U	6	53	97	0	1	41	1	40	1	34
7A	29,965	-4	36,656	37	U	8	29	95	-5	1	40	1	30	1	67
7B	31,566	-5	37,377	41	U	9	43	92	-7	2	36	2	40	1	37
8A	34,335	9	44,180	41	R	8	37	96	8	0	24	0	42	1	44
8B	37,488	10	35,525	40	R	10	26	93	9	1	39	0	-5	2	68
9A	33,093	2	40,897	38	U	6	50	92	0	1	44	1	42	4	52
9B	34,338	5	41,367	42	R	6	35	97	4	0	-29	0	0	2	58
10A	34,946	7	37,329	40	R	6	34	98	6	0	-33	1	32	0	54
10B	35,598	7	37,033	39	R	6	38	99	7	0	4	0	30	0	44
11A	33,027	4	34,614	34	R	6	33	97	4	0	-32	0	6	1	37
11B	35,631	3	32,271	36	R	6	27	99	3	0	-46	0	-18	0	36
12A	37,280	17	37,356	39	R	8	34	98	16	0	4	0	48	1	76
12B	34,939	8	39,275	38	R	7	32	99	7	0	-15	0	8	1	55
13A	31,916	-2	32,971	33	R	5	35	98	-2	0	-4	1	2	1	31
13B	31,779	-4	35,057	37	R	4	31	99	-4	0	-65	0	-20	1	25
14A	35,749	10	47,523	34	S	4	41	98	10	0	40	1	48	1	91
14B	34,254	6	42,155	33	R	6	31	99	6	0	-10	0	18	0	19
15A	34,904	7	43,552	40	R	5	41	93	5	0	38	0	31	6	60
15B	32,097	-1	37,254	33	R	5	32	98	-2	0	-58	0	-6	2	41
16A	30,725	5	37,770	31	U	5	45	96	4	1	42	2	48	1	58
16B	35,356	12	47,192	31	U	5	49	97	11	1	64	2	64	1	63
17A	36,506	9	35,721	32	R	8	25	97	9	0	-7	0	-15	1	41
17B	46,090	19	44,180	30	R	6	39	97	18	1	58	1	62	1	75
18A	37,317	15	45,753	33	R	7	30	98	15	0	24	0	44	1	76
18B	40,359	25	44,117	30	R	7	33	98	24	0	24	0	55	1	97
19A	44,244	33	48,796	29	R	5	37	98	32	0	56	0	71	1	106
19B	41,328	29	54,586	33	R	5	40	98	29	0	100	1	85	1	101
20A	33,860	7	44,852	38	R	4	35	98	6	0	-24	0	29	2	54
20B	36,507	10	46,257	35	R	5	29	99	9	0	19	0	25	1	69
21A	33,619	-1	41,345	42	R	4	36	98	-2	0	25	0	5	1	52
21B	31,820	-2	33,873	27	R	4	27	99	-2	0	-48	0	5	0	14
22A	32,981	-1	34,601	26	R	4	30	96	-2	0	-17	2	33	1	42
22B	33,494	-2	34,559	29	R	4	30	97	-3	0	-75	1	20	1	38
23A	31,516	1	37,961	33	R	4	33	98	1	0	-23	0	17	1	36
23B	34,804	3	41,795	36	R	4	29	98	3	0	-32	0	8	1	54
24A	27,968	-1	40,322	45	R	5	49	94	-2	1	36	3	43	1	46
24B	39,733	7	50,620	44	R	4	46	97	6	0	21	1	44	1	64
25A	32,702	10	46,744	35	R	4	44	97	9	0	49	1	44	1	61
25B	36,095	6	44,962	37	R	4	37	97	5	0	14	1	42	2	63

Note: U=urban, S=suburban, R=rural, M=mixed, HH=households.

Minnesota State House Districts: Demographic Data (cont.)

House District	Population		Average HH Income		District Type	Unempl. Rate	College Educ.	White (non-Hispanic)		African American		Asian American		Hispanic American	
	1997	+/-	($)	+/-		(%)	(%)	(%)	+/-	(%)	+/-	(%)	+/-	(%)	+/-
Minn.	4,690,954	7	51,427	36	M	5	46	92	5	3	44	2	43	2	58
26A	30,287	-1	38,780	35	R	4	34	96	-2	0	-50	0	9	3	47
26B	32,467	0	39,384	35	R	5	34	97	-1	0	-21	0	8	2	47
27A	31,775	-4	34,167	19	R	9	33	94	-5	0	-82	0	2	5	44
27B	31,570	-2	40,457	45	R	4	38	97	-2	0	0	1	38	1	46
28A	34,357	3	45,979	36	R	3	42	97	3	0	22	1	21	2	41
28B	35,037	6	47,239	36	R	4	38	97	5	0	-14	0	11	2	68
29A	28,962	7	49,278	34	R	5	38	97	6	0	32	1	42	1	57
29B	36,847	6	45,269	37	R	5	36	98	5	0	8	1	23	0	46
30A	23,823	10	59,625	33	U	3	65	93	8	1	65	4	59	1	60
30B	27,993	-1	49,153	35	U	4	55	88	-4	2	42	7	38	2	54
31A	51,663	8	62,700	34	U	3	58	95	6	1	59	3	62	1	67
31B	33,736	2	38,923	33	R	4	32	98	1	0	-5	1	13	1	62
32A	29,625	1	41,516	48	R	6	41	96	0	1	34	2	39	1	54
32B	37,061	3	44,748	34	R	5	41	99	3	0	-16	0	22	0	36
33A	43,583	30	74,514	41	S	4	52	96	29	1	132	1	110	1	89
33B	43,063	33	72,884	33	S	3	62	93	29	2	141	3	111	1	100
34A	35,635	7	70,234	40	R	4	44	97	6	0	62	1	67	1	51
34B	39,751	28	106,457	40	S	3	63	94	25	2	149	2	106	2	127
35A	42,335	21	53,031	34	R	4	40	98	21	0	61	1	69	1	88
35B	40,470	24	60,646	31	S	4	43	96	24	1	61	1	56	1	69
36A	38,531	24	73,064	30	S	3	62	94	22	1	78	3	74	2	87
36B	38,770	18	63,519	25	S	3	62	92	15	3	70	3	66	2	83
37A	43,354	15	55,246	30	R	4	43	97	14	1	66	1	62	1	95
37B	45,259	47	63,239	27	S	4	51	96	46	1	115	2	114	1	113
38A	42,784	25	67,648	29	S	4	63	91	22	3	73	4	69	2	122
38B	42,668	35	71,275	30	S	3	67	91	31	3	91	4	82	2	124
39A	31,187	1	55,099	25	S	4	46	91	-3	1	51	1	40	6	65
39B	35,976	8	49,922	27	S	4	42	95	6	1	50	1	53	4	64
40A	29,728	-6	47,836	29	U	4	46	88	-11	4	72	5	45	2	57
40B	29,384	-4	60,641	32	U	3	53	91	-8	2	71	4	53	1	54
41A	35,181	10	95,252	45	U	3	68	92	6	2	98	4	74	1	60
41B	40,772	29	70,369	33	S	3	60	93	27	2	78	3	75	2	102
42A	31,747	1	98,322	36	S	3	69	95	-2	1	89	2	65	1	56
42B	39,711	24	91,451	35	S	3	69	93	20	2	128	4	99	1	75
43A	42,779	35	90,906	37	S	3	64	96	33	1	112	2	100	1	96
43B	35,714	9	96,856	42	S	4	64	95	7	1	84	2	71	1	69
44A	30,874	-2	54,057	33	S	3	55	92	-5	3	84	3	55	2	56
44B	31,284	-5	56,712	34	S	4	58	91	-9	3	77	3	53	2	51
45A	36,545	11	93,650	40	S	3	64	94	8	2	100	2	78	1	80
45B	34,318	4	79,818	40	S	3	64	90	0	4	88	3	66	2	74
46A	29,708	-5	54,064	34	S	4	47	91	-9	4	77	3	48	2	43
46B	30,826	-5	52,242	33	S	5	44	91	-9	4	77	3	48	2	55
47A	32,985	3	49,133	28	S	6	47	81	-6	12	80	4	51	2	54
47B	32,366	-3	53,040	34	S	5	39	85	-9	9	69	4	51	2	44
48A	41,446	19	66,891	40	S	3	50	92	15	3	98	4	73	1	67
48B	30,783	-4	53,713	23	S	5	42	93	-6	1	52	3	43	2	63
49A	37,954	16	55,512	29	S	4	45	96	14	1	66	2	78	1	71
49B	38,184	21	52,170	23	S	4	42	95	20	1	79	1	84	2	92
50A	42,229	28	54,781	25	S	5	38	97	27	0	78	1	83	1	82
50B	47,860	44	65,492	27	S	5	44	97	42	0	115	1	113	1	110

Note: U=urban, S=suburban, R=rural, M=mixed, HH=households.

Minnesota State House Districts: Demographic Data (cont.)

House District	Population		Average HH Income		District Type	Unempl. Rate	College Educ.	White (non-Hispanic)		African American		Asian American		Hispanic American	
	1997	+/-	($)	+/-		(%)	(%)	(%)	+/-	(%)	+/-	(%)	+/-	(%)	+/-
Minn.	4,690,954	7	51,427	36	M	5	46	92	5	3	44	2	43	2	58
51A	38,223	13	51,787	24	S	4	42	95	11	0	71	2	78	1	59
51B	43,845	31	58,488	25	S	4	47	97	30	0	74	1	78	1	103
52A	29,287	-9	44,753	23	S	6	38	92	-12	2	48	3	37	2	55
52B	32,723	0	62,888	41	S	4	54	93	-3	1	68	4	57	1	54
53A	35,814	12	78,397	40	S	3	63	93	9	1	73	4	71	2	78
53B	41,885	18	81,590	44	S	4	61	93	15	2	96	4	85	2	92
54A	34,580	0	59,359	38	S	4	62	86	-6	3	67	8	53	2	52
54B	33,519	4	58,012	35	S	4	53	91	0	3	80	4	71	2	74
55A	33,084	3	65,259	39	S	3	55	96	1	1	71	1	58	2	62
55B	33,989	3	51,505	39	S	5	42	87	-1	4	64	5	37	3	71
56A	39,594	20	66,835	19	S	4	54	95	19	2	37	1	48	1	70
56B	48,652	42	71,712	25	S	3	61	94	39	1	147	2	111	2	141
57A	46,023	38	58,748	30	S	4	57	91	34	3	105	3	94	3	119
57B	38,297	21	55,167	23	S	5	45	94	19	2	97	1	52	3	67
58A	30,977	-8	38,162	24	U	7	31	75	-18	17	54	2	31	3	42
58B	28,765	-10	28,174	24	U	15	26	25	-37	56	9	12	-8	3	19
59A	29,971	-6	38,467	31	U	5	36	88	-10	2	70	3	47	3	63
59B	34,095	-2	37,907	37	U	7	59	72	-13	10	58	12	37	4	59
60A	31,396	-4	61,221	46	U	5	62	79	-13	12	61	3	41	4	51
60B	30,418	-6	63,805	41	U	3	68	88	-11	6	74	3	53	2	47
61A	30,909	-4	23,097	25	U	12	38	41	-28	32	43	8	16	6	55
61B	29,673	-8	32,181	23	U	9	39	37	-34	47	23	6	2	5	51
62A	32,619	-5	37,124	25	U	7	47	78	-13	10	64	4	39	4	53
62B	31,518	-6	47,412	31	U	5	50	85	-12	8	64	2	46	2	47
63A	30,353	-6	73,474	39	U	3	66	89	-10	5	67	3	48	2	59
63B	30,419	-6	48,183	30	S	4	44	86	-12	7	66	4	48	2	58
64A	30,114	-8	63,400	44	U	4	71	90	-11	4	55	3	45	3	52
64B	28,839	-6	66,481	42	U	3	64	90	-10	3	62	4	46	3	71
65A	29,956	-5	39,303	40	U	10	42	37	-27	39	16	16	13	6	38
65B	32,067	-6	36,411	32	U	8	35	64	-18	7	44	10	19	17	32
66A	30,390	-5	36,087	28	U	7	33	68	-16	8	46	16	22	6	50
66B	30,995	-6	44,291	37	U	4	55	81	-13	8	53	6	42	4	47
67A	31,632	-6	35,199	27	U	7	29	75	-15	7	47	10	33	7	56
67B	28,077	-5	41,946	31	U	6	36	76	-14	7	58	8	36	7	55

Note: U=urban, S=suburban, R=rural, M=mixed, HH=households.

MISSISSIPPI

Perhaps no part of Mississippi better exemplifies the progress the state has made in the last thirty years, as well as the limits of that progress, as the town of Tunica, located thirty-five miles south of Memphis. A decade ago, it was a rundown Delta crossroads surrounded by cotton fields and catfish farms. In 1992, the state approved riverboat gambling here. Just a year later, 1.7 million people visited and spent $140 million. Today, the riverbank is lined with at least nine casinos and scores of hotels, conference centers, driving ranges, and restaurants. According to political commentator Michael Barone, the county's casinos now have more square footage than Atlantic City's.

As Atlantic City has demonstrated, gambling will not necessarily lift a place out of poverty, and the county in which Tunica sits remains far from wealthy. But Mississippi may be forgiven for embracing economic development wherever it can find it. Things are better than they have been, but despite the success of gambling in more than a half dozen towns along the river and Gulf Coast, Mississippi remains the nation's poorest and worst educated state.

Like the rest of the South, Mississippi has been growing during the 1990s, but there are really two Souths. States in the eastern South—Virginia, the Carolinas, Georgia, and Florida—have been growing rapidly, being annexed, really, into the wealthy economy of the eastern seaboard. States in the western South—Alabama, Mississippi, Louisiana, and Arkansas—never developed major cities (with the exception of New Orleans, which was already there) or major industry (Birmingham excepted). So Mississippi's growth rate, which is the same as Kentucky's, has been solid but unspectacular, a notch below the national average.

Mississippi has only one large city, Jackson, and its suburbs are the fastest-growing part of the state. The two other rapidly growing areas are the Memphis suburbs, in the northwest corner of the state, and the Gulf Coast, parts of which are suburbs of New Orleans. Mississippi is developing sprawl for the first time, as people are moving into heretofore undeveloped land, which is why four of its ten fastest-growing house districts are classified as rural. The areas that are losing population are central Jackson and Hattiesburg (both heavily black) and white Biloxi, which has lost defense jobs.

The wealthiest sections of the state are in northeast Jackson and the Gulf. The worst pockets of poverty are black areas, mostly rural although centered around small towns: Hattiesburg, Meridian, Greenville, McComb. Unemployment is highest in the Delta, especially south of Vicksburg, and in central Jackson.

Mississippi has the highest percentage of black residents, 36 percent, and the fifth-lowest percentage of whites, 62 percent. The races in Mississippi are not as heavily segregated by region as they are in neighboring Alabama (which actually has more blacks, though they constitute a smaller percentage of the population). Twenty-three house districts are at least 90 percent white in Alabama; only six are in Mississippi. Similarly, Alabama has twenty-six black-majority districts; Mississippi has thirty-eight. Many Mississippi districts are predominantly white, most in the northern half of the state and away from the Delta, but few are exclusively so. Black-majority districts are concentrated in Jackson and the Delta.

Only 28 percent of Mississippians have finished college, the fourth-lowest rate in the nation, though in line with other states in the Cotton South. In only 8 of 122 house districts is the figure higher than 50 percent; in 30 districts, it is below 20 percent. It is worth tweaking Yankee notions of superiority, though, to observe that the rate of college graduation in the worst Mississippi district (the One Hundred Fifteenth, 14 percent) is much better than that in dozens of northern inner city districts and does not rank among the 80 worst districts nationwide.

Like all Southern states, Mississippi must obtain the Justice Department's permission before redrawing any of its legislative districts. In an attempt to maximize black voting strength, U.S. congressional districts were drawn in such a way as to make surrounding districts more Republican. However, the legislature in Mississippi remains comfortably Democratic, as it does in two neighboring southern states, Louisiana and Arkansas. All three now have Republican governors, so the situation may change after the next round of redistricting.

MISSISSIPPI
State Senate Districts

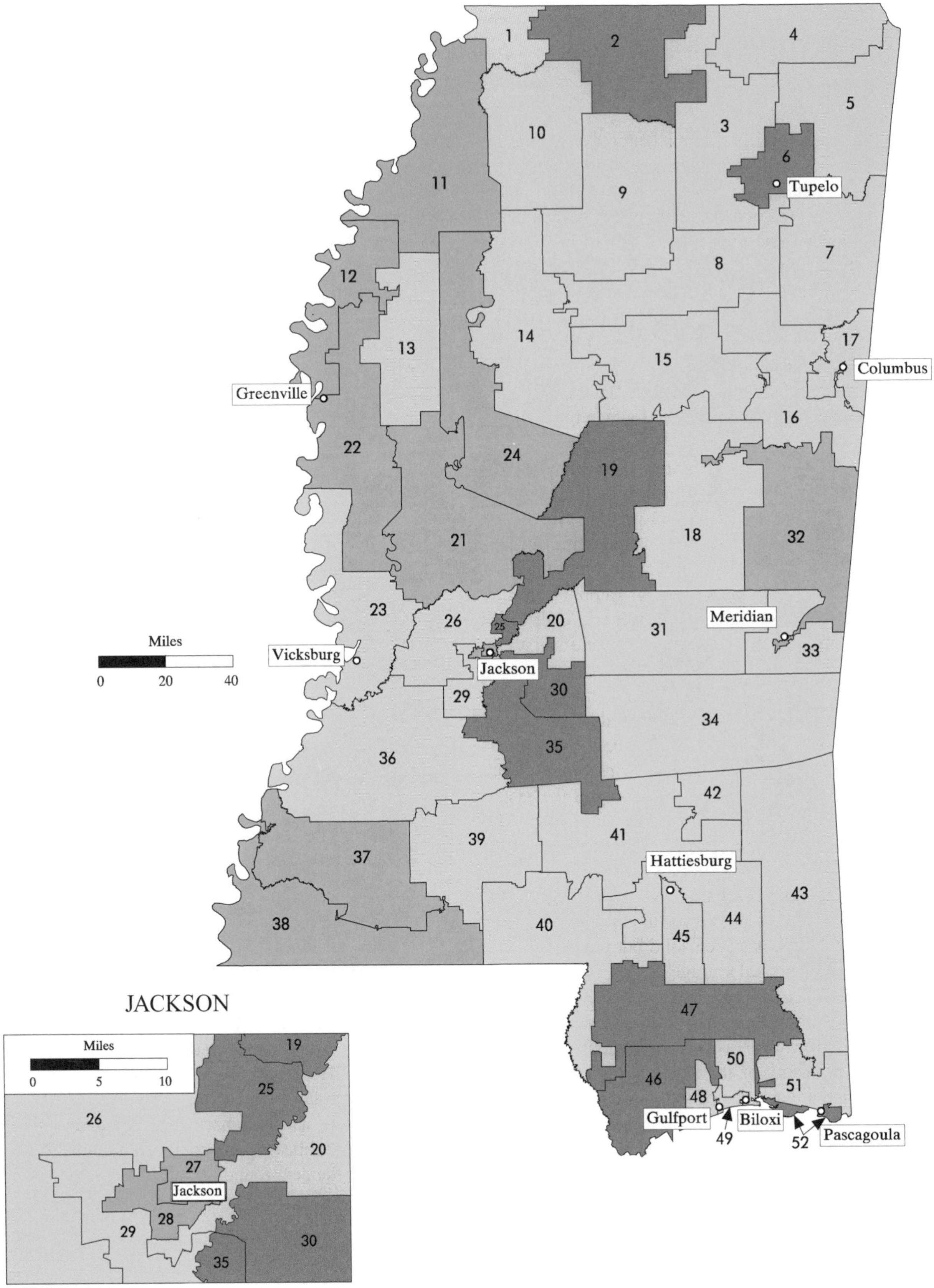

1

2

4

5

10

3

6

○ Tupelo

11

9

7

12

8

13

14

17

15

○ Columbus

Greenville ○

16

22

24

19

21

18

32

23

26

25 20

31

Meridian ○

Vicksburg ○

Jackson ○

33

29

30

34

35

36

42

39

41

37

Hattiesburg ○

43

38

40

44

45

47

46

50

48 ○ 51

Gulfport ○

49

Biloxi ○

52 ○ Pascagoula

JACKSON

Miles
0   5   10

19

25

26

20

27

Jackson

29

28

30

35

Population Growth   ▨ -8% to 1%   ▢ 2% to 10%   ▨ 11% to 20%   ▢ 33%

Mississippi State Senate Districts: Demographic Data

Senate District	Population		Average HH Income		District Type	Unempl. Rate	College Educ.	White non-Hispanic		African American		Asian American		Hispanic American	
	1997	+/-	($)	+/-		(%)	(%)	(%)	+/-	(%)	+/-	(%)	+/-	(%)	+/-
Miss.	2,733,214	6	38,237	42	R	8	28	62	5	36	8	1	23	1	32
1	67,194	33	46,151	29	S	5	22	89	31	10	44	0	50	1	90
2	60,084	16	39,246	41	R	9	19	59	16	40	15	0	1	0	6
3	53,653	7	34,935	43	R	5	19	83	6	16	12	0	-53	0	18
4	53,475	5	32,440	40	R	8	18	87	4	12	13	0	-50	0	29
5	53,555	5	34,160	46	R	6	17	90	4	10	13	0	-15	0	32
6	57,208	13	48,780	47	R	4	31	80	11	19	20	0	7	1	30
7	50,927	4	34,948	39	R	6	17	71	2	28	9	0	-40	1	22
8	51,852	5	33,493	37	R	8	18	63	2	37	9	0	-44	1	23
9	51,850	5	34,198	44	R	6	33	68	2	30	10	2	23	1	31
10	55,923	9	33,394	37	R	9	21	55	6	44	13	0	-17	1	12
11	49,495	-2	32,690	59	R	14	22	33	-5	66	0	0	2	1	-5
12	43,763	-5	29,204	49	R	18	20	20	-11	78	-4	0	7	1	1
13	56,224	7	26,787	29	R	13	19	29	3	70	8	0	16	1	2
14	52,654	3	36,663	41	R	10	22	55	0	44	8	0	-3	0	3
15	44,381	4	34,005	37	R	8	35	69	1	29	8	1	23	1	25
16	51,814	2	32,698	35	R	10	26	38	-3	60	6	1	10	1	15
17	50,892	3	42,249	31	R	6	35	68	0	30	8	1	21	1	41
18	51,938	6	31,755	40	R	7	21	64	4	28	9	0	-41	0	3
19	57,238	13	36,369	49	R	8	31	55	9	43	19	0	29	0	6
20	55,794	10	65,138	44	U	5	49	81	8	17	19	1	35	1	57
21	51,277	1	30,103	42	R	11	19	31	-8	68	5	0	-9	0	-1
22	49,911	-2	46,048	54	R	7	30	59	-6	39	3	1	32	1	4
23	50,813	2	44,047	50	R	8	32	58	-1	41	6	1	18	1	16
24	49,478	-1	26,571	45	R	15	19	22	-6	78	0	0	7	0	-13
25	56,726	17	62,250	36	U	3	63	82	12	16	49	1	43	1	70
26	52,803	4	45,953	38	M	8	40	27	-10	73	10	0	0	0	-27
27	45,376	-8	28,131	29	U	11	30	15	-22	85	-5	0	-2	0	-11
28	45,132	-7	29,313	38	U	15	31	23	-11	76	-6	0	11	0	11
29	50,263	5	56,430	44	S	4	46	76	0	22	27	1	25	0	18
30	54,212	17	49,426	37	S	4	33	80	15	19	24	0	41	1	55
31	51,007	5	34,635	41	R	5	20	64	2	33	10	0	-42	1	26
32	46,189	1	27,536	37	R	13	19	35	-4	64	4	0	-8	0	11
33	49,091	3	45,962	41	R	6	36	76	0	22	9	1	9	1	25
34	50,488	3	32,701	39	R	8	19	62	0	38	7	0	-43	0	13
35	54,589	11	36,737	40	R	6	22	71	9	28	15	0	-3	0	26
36	50,654	2	28,504	35	R	14	24	33	-3	67	5	0	-15	0	-4
37	44,905	-1	36,793	43	R	10	28	64	-3	35	4	0	-19	0	19
38	51,269	1	27,008	37	R	14	20	36	-3	63	3	0	-47	0	13
39	50,440	4	32,707	34	R	9	24	66	2	34	9	0	-26	0	-7
40	54,113	6	31,191	37	R	11	21	69	5	30	9	0	-6	1	27
41	51,477	4	32,105	41	R	8	20	68	2	32	6	0	-23	0	3
42	47,933	3	37,206	39	R	8	27	70	1	29	8	0	7	1	48
43	54,920	9	32,709	45	R	11	19	77	8	22	13	0	-33	0	18
44	55,440	10	41,174	46	R	7	32	85	9	14	20	0	15	1	52
45	53,607	8	35,174	37	R	9	40	59	5	39	12	1	26	1	50
46	58,120	20	36,904	35	S	9	29	85	18	11	24	1	36	2	76
47	58,443	20	34,657	33	R	8	27	81	18	17	27	0	37	1	54
48	52,740	6	42,082	55	S	8	32	68	4	28	9	2	42	2	41
49	53,869	9	47,637	51	U	7	40	77	5	19	25	2	50	3	58
50	53,469	6	35,894	46	U	9	27	74	3	16	6	6	28	3	44

Note: U=urban, S=suburban, R=rural, M=mixed, HH=households.

Mississippi State Senate Districts: Demographic Data (cont.)

Senate District	Population		Average HH Income		District Type	Unempl. Rate	College Educ.	White non-Hispanic		African American		Asian American		Hispanic American	
	1997	+/-	($)	+/-		(%)	(%)	(%)	+/-	(%)	+/-	(%)	+/-	(%)	+/-
Miss.	2,733,214	6	38,237	42	R	8	28	62	5	36	8	1	23	1	32
51	56,691	9	48,058	49	S	8	29	75	9	23	9	1	35	1	50
52	57,665	13	47,603	50	S	9	37	73	8	24	27	1	39	2	64

Note: U=urban, S=suburban, R=rural, M=mixed, HH=households.

MISSISSIPPI
State House Districts

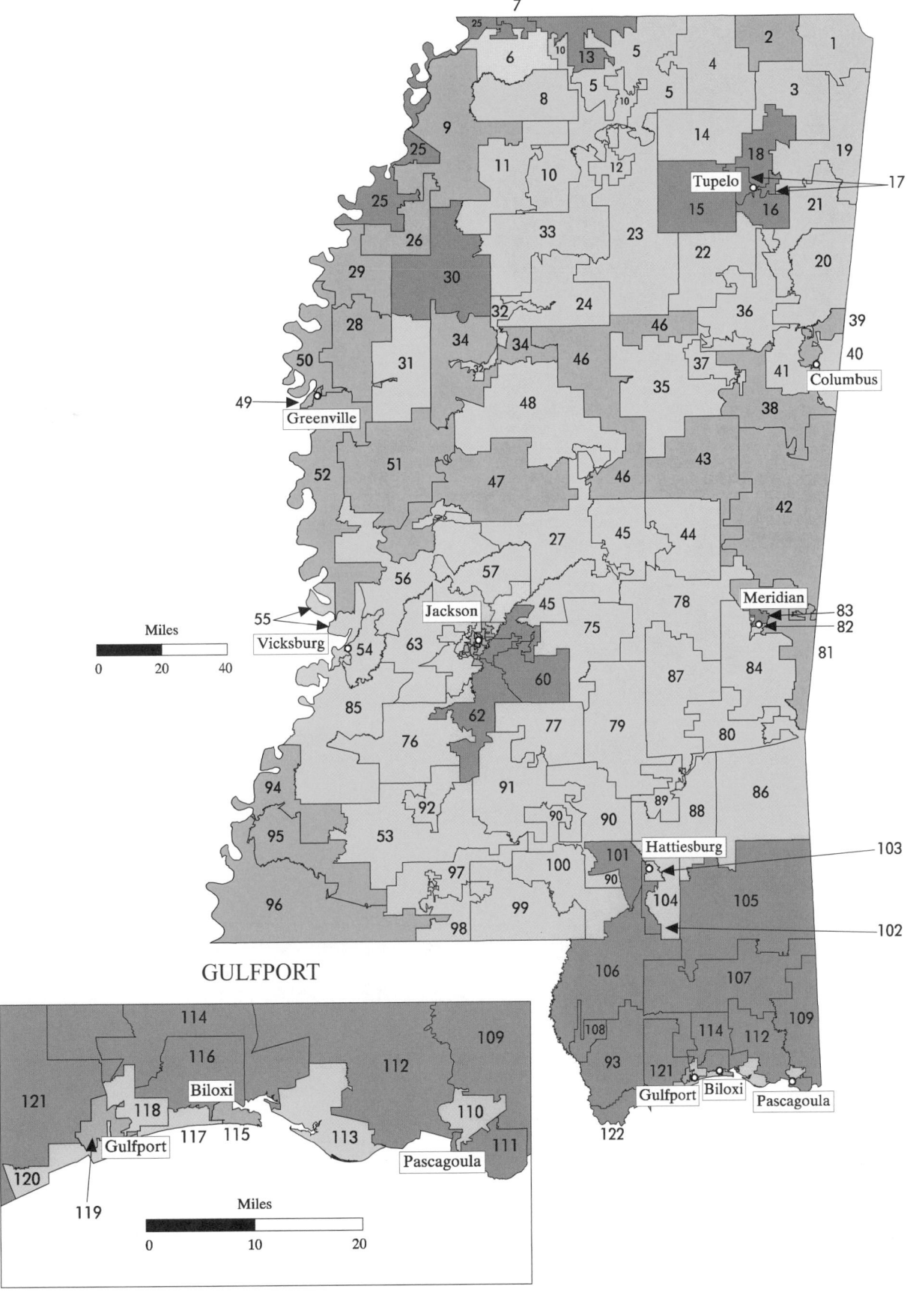

GULFPORT

Miles
0   20   40

Miles
0   10   20

Population Growth ▨ -11% to 0% ▨ 1% to 10% ▨ 12% to 28% ▨ 40% to 58%

JACKSON

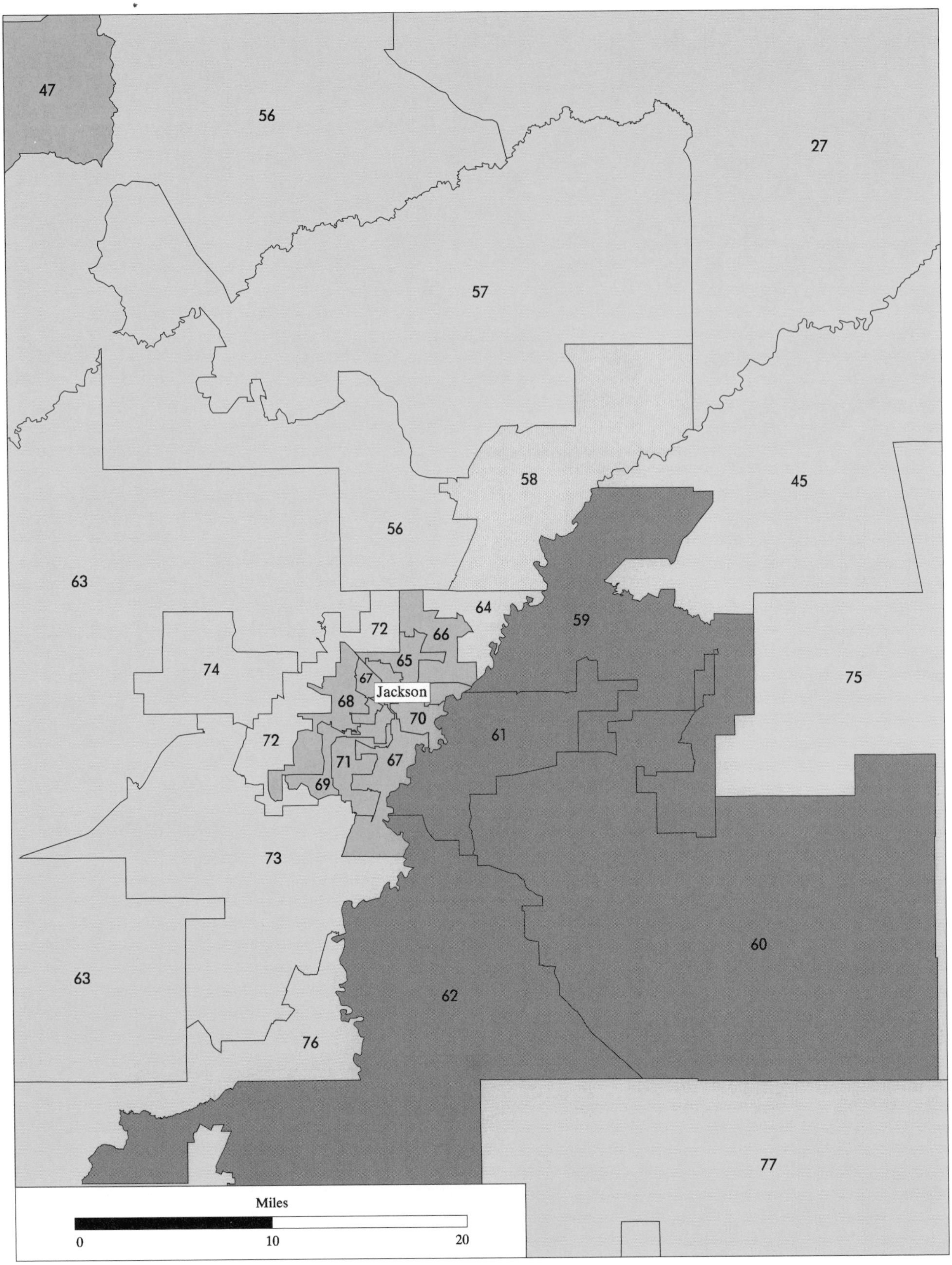

47

56

27

57

58

45

56

63

64

59

72

66

65

74

67

Jackson

68

70

75

72

61

71

67

69

73

60

62

76

77

Miles

0   10   20

Population Growth  -11% to 0%   1% to 10%   12% to 28%   40% to 58%

Mississippi State House Districts: Demographic Data

House District	Population		Average HH Income		District Type	Unempl. Rate	College Educ.	White non-Hispanic		African American		Asian American		Hispanic American	
	1997	+/-	($)	+/-		(%)	(%)	(%)	+/-	(%)	+/-	(%)	+/-	(%)	+/-
Miss.	2,733,214	6	38,237	42	R	8	28	62	5	36	8	1	23	1	32
1	21,361	8	33,612	45	R	8	16	96	8	3	17	0	-31	1	34
2	20,217	-1	31,732	37	R	9	20	82	-2	17	9	0	-71	0	21
3	21,189	3	35,927	49	R	6	18	89	2	10	11	0	-28	1	27
4	22,722	6	31,938	37	R	7	19	81	5	19	12	0	-53	0	7
5	20,546	5	29,713	41	R	13	19	41	1	58	9	0	-19	0	4
6	28,014	40	44,177	30	R	6	21	76	38	24	45	0	54	0	11
7	28,364	22	54,428	34	S	4	28	94	21	5	35	0	44	1	88
8	23,018	7	38,802	40	R	8	24	63	5	36	12	0	-19	1	23
9	19,034	-3	29,927	52	R	14	17	27	-8	72	-1	0	-14	1	-14
10	22,295	10	32,353	34	R	8	21	62	8	37	14	0	6	0	3
11	21,700	8	29,121	38	R	11	19	43	4	56	13	0	-25	0	3
12	18,561	2	37,266	48	R	6	53	73	-1	22	9	4	23	1	45
13	24,750	18	41,190	37	R	8	17	68	17	31	18	0	-8	0	2
14	23,236	5	37,776	48	R	5	20	84	4	15	12	0	-48	1	21
15	24,258	12	33,653	39	R	4	17	84	10	16	20	0	-46	0	27
16	25,260	15	41,102	45	R	6	26	69	12	30	21	0	2	1	63
17	22,514	12	52,344	49	R	4	35	82	10	17	19	0	20	0	24
18	24,442	12	42,647	44	R	6	26	78	10	22	17	0	-26	0	13
19	21,723	7	34,896	48	R	7	15	97	7	3	15	0	-43	0	28
20	21,368	5	35,247	36	R	5	18	82	3	18	11	0	-21	0	15
21	21,882	5	37,481	44	R	6	16	76	3	23	13	0	-30	1	18
22	20,760	3	32,999	36	R	7	17	59	0	40	7	0	-86	1	18
23	21,259	4	34,094	47	R	6	18	74	2	25	7	0	-33	1	17
24	21,000	4	32,809	29	R	10	20	59	1	40	8	0	-14	0	7
25	28,905	27	44,544	44	S	7	20	83	31	16	8	0	19	1	71
26	21,963	0	28,220	57	R	15	24	25	-5	73	1	0	13	1	0
27	20,246	1	25,316	41	R	11	17	29	-8	70	5	0	-29	0	3
28	21,238	-4	38,009	53	R	10	27	51	-6	48	-2	0	30	1	-11
29	21,524	-2	27,808	44	R	18	23	20	-9	79	0	0	0	1	6
30	22,673	13	26,466	43	R	15	14	30	8	69	16	0	21	1	6
31	20,979	3	25,537	22	R	11	21	30	0	69	4	0	16	1	11
32	19,017	1	25,139	34	R	15	18	23	-3	76	2	0	19	0	-13
33	22,463	3	29,724	40	R	9	21	57	0	42	6	0	25	1	6
34	23,066	-1	46,119	47	R	8	27	54	-4	45	2	0	13	0	3
35	22,239	3	30,590	31	R	9	24	69	1	31	9	0	15	0	4
36	21,565	3	31,616	28	R	10	20	39	-1	60	6	0	-27	1	8
37	19,304	5	35,723	35	R	7	50	69	2	27	9	3	24	1	36
38	23,826	-1	34,812	40	R	10	34	42	-5	55	3	2	11	1	24
39	19,055	0	50,899	32	R	5	45	76	-3	20	5	1	22	2	40
40	22,108	5	38,529	29	R	6	30	76	4	23	9	0	21	1	46
41	21,352	7	30,244	34	R	11	20	31	-2	68	11	0	10	1	21
42	21,025	-2	33,849	49	R	13	18	36	-6	63	1	0	-50	0	-7
43	20,724	0	32,242	35	R	9	21	56	-3	43	4	0	-50	0	8
44	23,757	10	32,642	42	R	6	25	68	8	20	16	0	-34	0	9
45	23,511	9	34,052	51	R	8	17	62	6	31	14	0	-67	0	-2
46	21,639	-1	29,777	41	R	9	19	62	-3	38	3	0	-61	0	-2
47	21,279	-1	28,567	50	R	14	17	28	-6	71	1	0	-22	0	1
48	22,075	3	28,820	44	R	12	20	46	1	53	5	0	-13	0	-9
49	19,677	-7	36,422	56	R	16	23	28	-7	71	-7	0	0	1	-4
50	21,902	0	30,850	38	R	15	23	27	-9	72	4	0	15	1	-5

Note: U=urban, S=suburban, R=rural, M=mixed, HH=households.

Mississippi State House Districts: Demographic Data (cont.)

House District	Population 1997	+/-	Average HH Income ($)	+/-	District Type	Unempl. Rate (%)	College Educ. (%)	White non-Hispanic (%)	+/-	African American (%)	+/-	Asian American (%)	+/-	Hispanic American (%)	+/-
Miss.	2,733,214	6	38,237	42	R	8	28	62	5	36	8	1	23	1	32
51	19,458	-4	33,104	58	R	9	18	27	-11	73	-1	0	-2	0	-18
52	22,108	-2	49,444	51	R	5	30	70	-5	29	6	1	36	1	19
53	21,852	4	31,145	37	R	9	20	79	2	21	10	0	-17	0	-2
54	23,397	2	56,779	54	R	6	42	79	0	19	7	1	24	1	20
55	21,190	4	31,205	42	R	10	23	30	-1	69	7	0	-16	1	7
56	24,440	5	40,550	44	R	8	30	56	-3	43	17	0	9	0	0
57	24,431	10	29,613	24	S	12	22	21	-20	78	22	0	3	0	-2
58	34,496	58	52,319	26	S	3	65	82	47	16	154	1	106	1	97
59	28,462	28	70,464	47	S	3	58	89	27	9	36	1	70	1	85
60	27,367	19	45,975	37	S	4	26	67	17	32	24	0	34	1	59
61	24,203	12	45,642	35	S	4	30	91	10	8	28	0	33	1	59
62	24,852	12	39,919	39	R	5	24	76	12	24	14	0	30	0	31
63	23,701	1	44,488	49	R	8	34	32	-12	67	8	0	5	0	-25
64	22,270	4	92,296	54	U	3	66	84	2	14	7	1	37	1	54
65	19,613	-4	40,726	38	U	8	40	23	-11	76	-2	1	14	0	-12
66	19,928	-2	68,663	36	U	4	63	64	-8	34	12	1	19	1	29
67	20,265	-9	26,260	32	U	11	26	27	-15	72	-6	1	-2	0	-17
68	19,360	-5	30,239	27	U	11	31	23	-22	77	1	0	-5	0	-12
69	18,668	-10	33,806	41	U	16	33	30	-8	69	-11	0	2	0	2
70	19,029	-11	32,190	43	U	12	30	22	-16	77	-10	0	-9	1	7
71	19,889	-2	37,276	33	U	9	37	69	-5	30	5	1	23	1	44
72	20,464	3	37,049	27	U	9	38	21	-15	78	9	0	0	0	-13
73	21,174	6	58,905	43	S	4	42	81	2	18	33	0	11	0	31
74	20,530	7	60,803	45	S	3	56	76	2	22	30	1	33	1	9
75	23,722	8	38,309	53	R	5	20	66	5	33	13	0	-15	1	34
76	21,526	4	31,420	42	R	12	24	33	-3	67	7	0	-20	0	-8
77	22,452	6	33,496	43	R	7	19	66	4	33	12	0	-71	0	19
78	22,729	6	32,977	36	R	4	20	68	3	28	11	0	-33	1	26
79	23,303	3	34,216	42	R	6	19	69	0	30	9	0	0	1	15
80	21,516	3	27,467	30	R	10	20	36	-2	63	6	0	5	0	33
81	20,474	-4	39,586	36	R	9	27	72	-7	26	3	1	-2	1	12
82	21,116	3	23,080	29	R	14	18	30	-1	69	5	0	8	0	24
83	22,426	12	50,943	45	R	5	44	75	10	23	16	0	37	1	46
84	21,746	1	36,751	32	R	6	23	76	-2	23	10	0	-16	0	7
85	20,814	2	26,816	32	R	18	24	24	-5	76	4	0	3	0	-3
86	22,469	3	31,760	50	R	11	18	64	1	36	8	0	-12	0	2
87	21,568	3	32,381	42	R	9	22	58	0	41	8	0	-60	0	19
88	21,373	2	36,204	52	R	9	20	82	1	16	6	0	-22	0	10
89	22,653	2	43,971	41	R	6	32	83	1	16	6	0	2	1	49
90	22,281	3	31,623	37	R	7	19	68	1	32	7	0	-53	0	12
91	20,380	2	27,592	28	R	11	20	50	-2	50	5	0	-10	0	-5
92	20,932	4	33,642	31	R	9	29	59	2	41	8	0	-24	0	0
93	26,326	20	41,498	33	R	7	34	93	18	4	32	1	40	2	89
94	19,231	-2	27,185	33	R	17	23	30	-6	70	0	0	-27	0	-6
95	18,655	-3	42,643	46	R	8	29	71	-5	28	4	0	-17	1	31
96	21,792	-1	28,104	39	R	13	18	37	-5	63	2	0	-46	0	-1
97	20,830	3	37,648	45	R	10	29	71	1	28	7	0	-32	1	32
98	21,244	4	25,639	37	R	14	19	37	-1	62	7	0	-40	0	18
99	20,248	2	27,733	34	R	12	17	62	0	38	6	0	-7	0	0
100	22,369	2	32,168	40	R	9	22	71	0	28	8	0	-26	1	34

Note: U=urban, S=suburban, R=rural, M=mixed, HH=households.

Mississippi State House Districts: Demographic Data (cont.)

House District	Population		Average HH Income		District Type	Unempl. Rate	College Educ.	White non-Hispanic		African American		Asian American		Hispanic American	
	1997	+/-	($)	+/-		(%)	(%)	(%)	+/-	(%)	+/-	(%)	+/-	(%)	+/-
Miss.	2,733,214	6	38,237	42	R	8	28	62	5	36	8	1	23	1	32
101	24,538	14	48,819	52	R	6	44	87	13	12	18	1	37	1	49
102	24,562	15	44,523	34	R	7	56	77	9	19	43	2	29	2	61
103	21,002	1	22,338	31	R	14	21	27	-8	72	4	0	-5	1	29
104	23,503	8	36,384	38	R	6	26	87	6	13	27	0	-27	1	60
105	25,480	17	29,677	39	R	10	20	75	15	24	23	0	-82	1	25
106	28,698	19	33,020	32	R	8	25	83	17	16	27	0	10	1	68
107	23,430	15	33,969	42	R	10	25	82	14	17	23	0	-60	0	18
108	24,053	20	33,695	26	R	10	27	79	18	20	26	0	-2	1	56
109	24,723	14	45,143	51	R	7	19	92	12	7	46	0	19	1	33
110	21,225	2	36,313	44	S	16	22	32	-3	67	3	0	50	1	50
111	24,595	16	47,711	49	U	7	37	78	9	19	49	1	43	2	73
112	24,157	15	44,483	42	S	8	30	78	11	20	36	1	36	1	53
113	23,109	8	58,155	53	S	7	46	89	6	6	30	2	34	2	76
114	25,681	21	46,074	48	S	6	31	88	18	8	38	2	57	2	49
115	19,783	-7	28,470	44	U	11	22	56	-14	26	-4	13	22	4	29
116	24,015	16	47,382	55	S	7	36	85	13	9	31	2	60	3	63
117	22,242	6	40,295	44	U	6	40	77	0	17	27	2	46	4	51
118	24,576	10	49,888	50	U	7	39	77	6	19	24	1	52	2	56
119	18,607	0	27,695	45	U	13	20	35	-9	62	5	1	19	2	42
120	23,537	3	48,247	53	S	6	43	78	0	16	12	3	40	2	35
121	24,866	16	44,036	53	S	8	27	82	13	14	31	2	48	2	56
122	25,115	24	32,752	34	S	11	26	84	22	12	30	1	38	3	71

Note: U=urban, S=suburban, R=rural, M=mixed, HH=households.

St. Louis proclaims itself the "Gateway to the West" (from a time when the West began on the far bank of the Mississippi River), but that of course depends on the direction from which one approaches it. Only Tennessee borders as many other states as Missouri, so it is more accurately a gateway to many regions. Across I-70, it is indeed a gateway to the West. Down the river, it is a gateway to the Cotton South. Through Branson, it is a gateway to the Ozarks. Up the Missouri River, it is a gateway to the Rockies. Overland toward Chicago, it is a gateway to the Great Lakes. Across the Mississippi at Cairo, Illinois, junction with the Ohio River, it is a gateway to the Appalachians. And—for Mormons, who believe that the resurrection will occur near Independence—it is a gateway to heaven.

Missouri's two great cities are very different from each other. In 1904, St. Louis was the fourth-largest city in the country, a place capable of hosting the World's Fair, the Democratic National Convention, and the summer Olympics all in the same year. Today, it is the forty-third-largest city and has the third-highest murder rate (behind New Orleans and Washington, D.C.). St. Louis lost more than 7 percent of its population between 1990 and 1994. Kansas City is now the larger of the two and ranks thirty-first in population; it is slightly bigger than Charlotte, North Carolina.

Missouri has grown by 5 percent during the 1990s, a rate that, were it to continue to the end of the decade, would break a fifty-year trend. The state's rate of population growth has fallen in each of the last four decades: 9.2 percent from 1950 to 1960; 8.3 percent from 1960 to 1970; 5.1 percent from 1970 to 1980; and 4.1 percent from 1980 to 1990.

The two fastest-growing state house districts, both of which have grown by more than a third, encompass the southwest suburbs of Springfield. The St. Louis suburbs have also grown, particularly St. Charles. And Branson—country music wonder, retirement mecca, and now the country's second-most-popular tourist destination after Disney World—has grown by almost 30 percent, which is particularly remarkable because it is not served by a large airport or an interstate highway. All of the fast-shrinking districts are in downtown St. Louis.

The greater St. Louis area has huge disparities of wealth. Almost all its western suburbs enjoy high average household incomes; in Chesterfield, it is $117,000. But average income in the Fifty-eighth District, along the Mississippi, is barely $20,000, making it the sixth-poorest district in the United States, and unemployment there in 1997 was 21 percent. Other poor sections include downtown Springfield and two rural districts on the Arkansas border toward the Bootheel.

With the exception of St. Louis County, the ten counties losing population fastest are rural and agricultural areas north of the Missouri River. As it is in Chicago, population is moving out of both city and hinterland simultaneously and meeting in the swelling band of suburbs in between.

Racially, Missouri is closer to Kansas than to Dixie. Of 163 state house districts, 135 are 80 percent or more white. Most of those with the highest percentage of whites are in the vast middle of the state, although the One Hundred Eighth District, which is 90 percent white, lies just south of St. Louis, in Richard Gephardt's congressional district.

Only 11 percent of Missourians are African American. The state has just 15 black-majority house districts, but six of them are at least 90 percent black. The Sixtieth District, in downtown St. Louis, is 99 percent African American, the highest percentage of any house district in the United States. According to Census Bureau estimates, of more than 26,000 people in that district, only 106 are white. Of the ten districts in the country with the highest percentage of blacks, Missouri claims four.

Democrats have held both chambers of the legislature throughout the decade, albeit by narrowing margins. Missouri's most prominent politicians—Thomas Hart Benton, Harry Truman, Stuart Symington, Thomas Eagleton—have all been Democrats. Yet a state's political prominence ebbs and flows. In 2000, Missouri may have two serious presidential candidates: Gephardt and Republican U.S. senator John Ashcroft.

MISSOURI
State Senate Districts

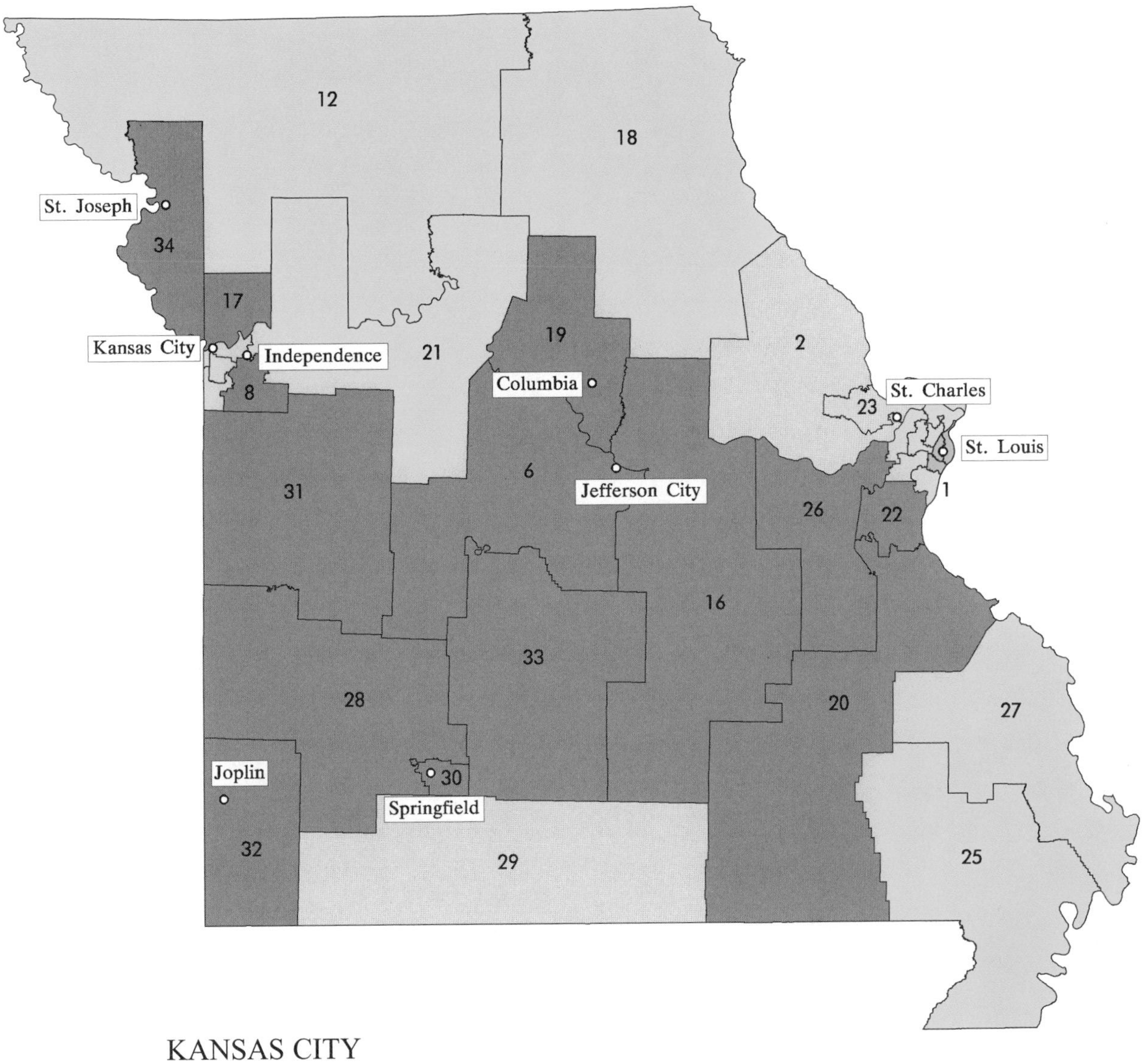

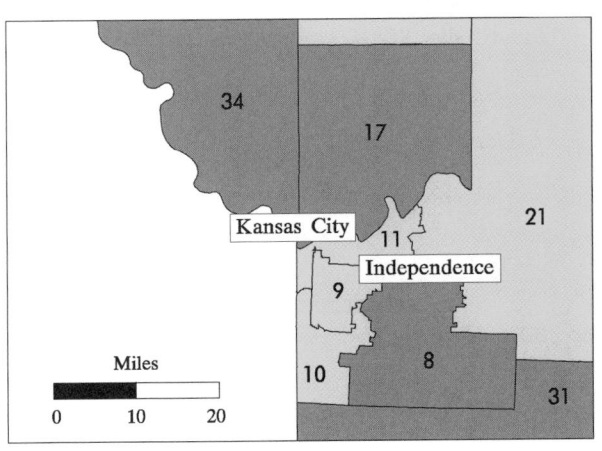

12

18

St. Joseph

34

17

Kansas City

Independence

8

21

19

Columbia

2

23

St. Charles

St. Louis

31

6

Jefferson City

26

22

1

16

33

20

27

28

Joplin

30

Springfield

29

32

25

KANSAS CITY

34

17

Kansas City

21

11

Independence

9

8

10

31

Miles

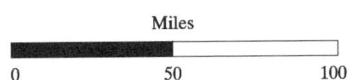

0   50   100

Miles

0   10   20

Population Growth   ▢ -15% to -8%   ▢ -2% to 4%   ▢ 6% to 14%   ▢ 20% to 26%

ST. LOUIS

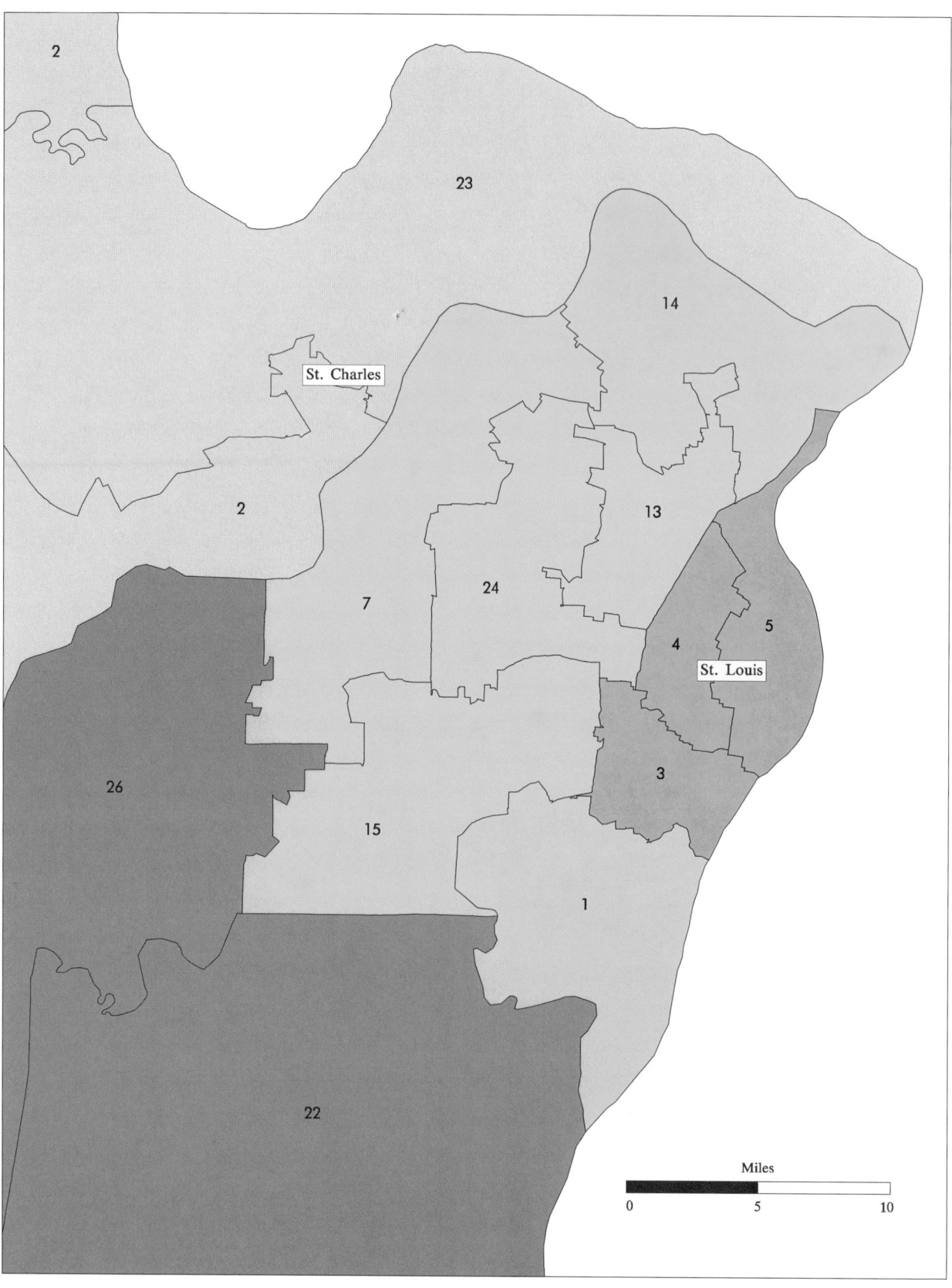

Population Growth   ▢ -15% to -8%   ▢ -2% to 4%   ▢ 6% to 14%   ▢ 20% to 26%

Missouri State Senate Districts: Demographic Data

Senate District	Population 1997	+/-	Average HH Income ($)	+/-	District Type	Unempl. Rate (%)	College Educ. (%)	White (non-Hispanic) (%)	+/-	African American (%)	+/-	Asian American (%)	+/-	Hispanic American (%)	+/-
Missouri	5,387,481	5	44,506	33	M	6	34	86	4	11	9	1	33	1	27
1	153,679	1	58,543	32	S	4	41	97	0	1	41	1	44	1	27
2	175,396	20	45,699	26	R	5	33	95	20	3	38	1	59	1	51
3	136,618	-8	41,109	35	U	5	31	91	-11	5	41	1	29	2	10
4	129,045	-12	37,947	41	U	11	32	31	-22	67	-7	1	15	1	12
5	123,449	-15	29,011	38	U	15	23	25	-36	72	-5	1	-8	2	1
6	163,242	10	38,923	34	R	6	29	94	9	5	21	0	21	1	27
7	152,852	-1	77,213	28	S	3	57	91	-3	4	33	4	38	1	30
8	159,014	6	56,278	34	S	4	45	92	4	5	45	1	50	2	32
9	155,100	1	32,399	26	U	11	25	30	-10	67	7	1	15	2	29
10	154,182	3	58,105	36	U	4	51	81	-3	15	42	1	39	2	29
11	150,765	-2	33,590	29	U	8	29	74	-9	14	33	2	28	9	23
12	153,173	1	34,156	37	R	5	26	97	0	1	14	0	-19	1	16
13	141,839	-1	40,841	32	S	10	29	29	-20	69	10	1	9	1	16
14	150,541	1	55,070	34	S	4	38	81	-4	17	25	1	35	1	28
15	155,458	2	82,284	37	S	3	61	91	0	6	24	2	42	1	22
16	168,683	8	33,634	28	R	6	23	97	7	2	25	1	27	1	24
17	172,559	12	49,979	26	M	4	40	94	11	2	30	1	51	3	43
18	146,620	0	35,082	40	R	7	27	96	-1	3	13	0	11	0	11
19	160,724	10	45,100	44	M	5	51	87	7	9	27	3	48	1	36
20	156,799	8	32,154	28	R	10	18	98	8	1	22	0	4	0	19
21	160,932	3	38,462	29	R	6	27	95	2	3	17	0	29	1	26
22	161,388	12	44,747	25	S	6	25	98	12	1	27	0	55	1	42
23	171,262	20	52,969	21	S	4	41	95	19	3	41	1	62	1	54
24	149,032	0	70,046	34	S	4	51	84	-4	11	30	3	35	2	31
25	158,284	2	30,891	36	R	10	15	89	1	10	14	0	7	1	12
26	170,249	14	53,830	33	R	6	35	96	13	2	37	1	54	1	41
27	160,426	4	36,699	35	R	6	24	92	3	7	17	0	16	1	21
28	169,815	9	35,244	32	R	5	27	98	9	0	19	0	15	1	28
29	197,802	26	34,616	36	R	7	23	98	26	0	-18	0	37	1	53
30	166,261	8	44,823	45	U	5	38	94	7	3	24	1	45	1	38
31	170,117	14	38,502	29	R	6	30	95	13	3	27	1	43	1	39
32	166,521	10	38,049	44	M	6	26	95	9	1	23	1	32	1	36
33	159,872	7	33,293	32	R	7	22	93	8	3	-9	1	7	2	8
34	165,570	6	43,488	28	U	6	36	93	5	3	20	1	50	2	34

Note: U=urban, S=suburban, R=rural, M=mixed, HH=households.

MISSOURI
State House Districts

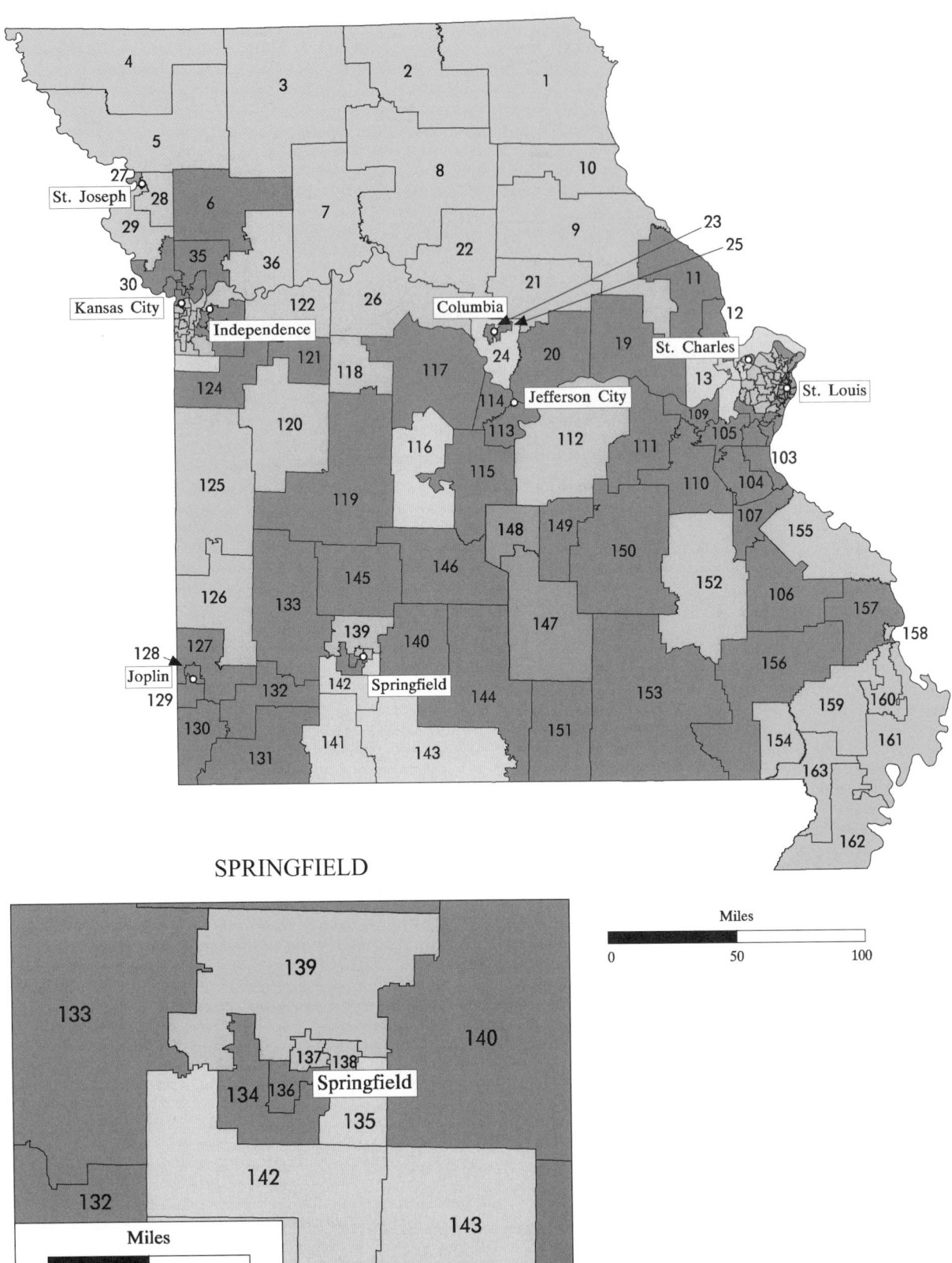

SPRINGFIELD

Miles

0   50   100

Miles

0   10   20

Population Growth   ▢ -19% to -6%   ▢ -5% to 6%   ▢ 7% to 18%   ▢ 19% to 38%

KANSAS CITY

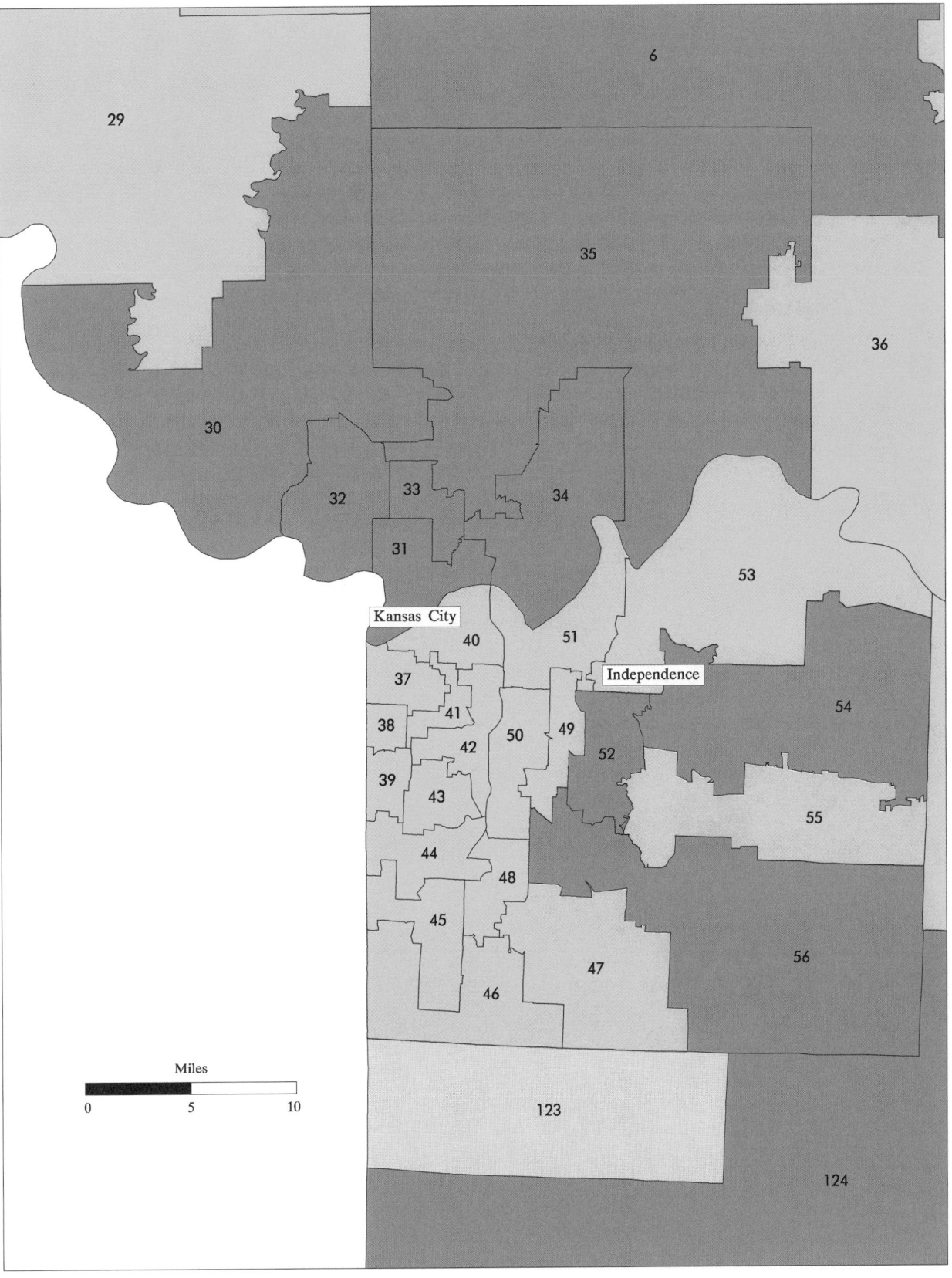

Population Growth

-5% to 6%　　7% to 18%　　19% to 38%

ST. LOUIS

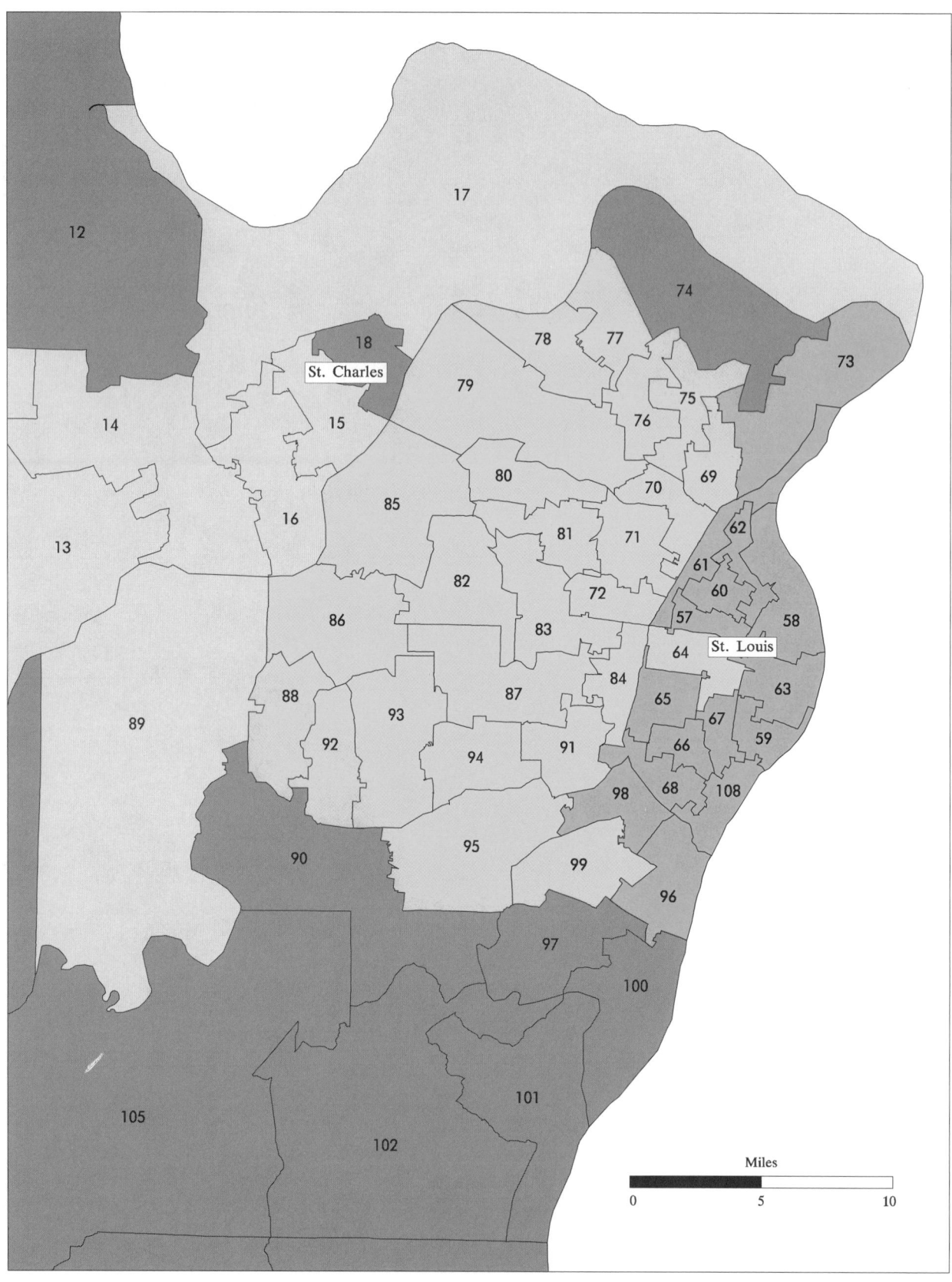

Population Growth | -19% to -6% | -5% to 6% | 7% to 18% | 19% to 38%

Missouri State House Districts: Demographic Data

House District	Population		Average HH Income		District Type	Unempl. Rate	College Educ.	White (non-Hispanic)		African American		Asian American		Hispanic American	
	1997	+/-	($)	+/-		(%)	(%)	(%)	+/-	(%)	+/-	(%)	+/-	(%)	+/-
Missouri	5,387,481	5	44,506	33	M	6	34	86	4	11	9	1	33	1	27
1	31,092	-1	32,793	43	R	7	23	98	-1	1	6	0	-35	0	2
2	32,611	0	32,151	38	R	7	34	97	0	1	6	1	20	1	17
3	32,157	-1	33,028	43	R	6	24	99	-1	0	-64	0	-54	1	2
4	30,588	-3	35,001	42	R	5	33	97	-4	1	2	1	1	1	13
5	33,623	3	35,887	35	R	5	27	97	2	2	19	0	-29	1	27
6	33,838	9	38,403	29	R	6	25	96	9	2	23	0	-28	1	24
7	31,139	-3	35,470	37	R	6	28	97	-3	2	7	0	-29	1	9
8	31,362	0	33,418	38	R	6	25	97	-1	2	12	0	-42	0	13
9	33,574	3	33,943	33	R	7	19	96	2	3	13	0	-47	0	8
10	30,752	0	37,401	48	R	8	27	94	0	5	16	0	20	0	15
11	35,130	14	35,122	22	R	7	22	94	13	5	29	0	-13	1	50
12	38,217	16	48,358	24	S	5	29	97	16	1	38	0	20	1	42
13	38,353	21	56,433	20	R	4	40	92	20	5	42	1	44	2	74
14	40,939	29	57,234	20	S	4	42	96	28	2	52	1	77	1	56
15	40,555	30	51,012	25	U	4	43	94	28	3	53	1	79	2	74
16	39,891	30	59,572	23	S	3	48	95	29	2	51	1	84	1	49
17	37,451	20	51,852	20	S	4	44	95	19	2	46	1	70	1	56
18	32,916	8	47,162	20	U	4	39	95	7	3	29	1	50	1	24
19	35,176	14	37,183	25	R	7	21	96	13	3	31	0	-10	1	35
20	35,303	11	37,499	22	R	4	29	93	10	6	30	0	10	1	34
21	33,844	3	39,990	35	R	5	30	94	3	5	19	0	23	0	9
22	31,489	-1	35,571	33	R	7	28	92	-2	7	12	0	4	1	20
23	32,190	8	58,614	53	U	4	65	82	6	12	19	4	41	1	28
24	42,952	21	50,100	42	M	4	54	88	18	8	42	2	58	1	48
25	33,256	10	34,736	45	U	6	63	82	5	9	35	7	53	2	46
26	32,441	-1	36,576	33	R	6	28	91	-2	7	13	0	-12	1	9
27	30,025	-6	29,138	24	U	10	20	91	-8	6	8	0	-2	3	23
28	31,735	4	46,825	31	U	4	41	94	3	2	26	1	41	2	32
29	32,392	5	38,163	30	U	7	23	95	4	2	17	0	15	2	23
30	37,527	17	57,404	24	U	3	48	93	15	2	32	2	59	3	48
31	36,147	15	43,649	26	U	5	39	91	13	3	34	2	58	4	43
32	36,606	17	48,840	19	U	5	50	91	15	3	33	2	57	3	46
33	35,716	12	53,490	25	S	4	43	94	10	1	30	1	56	3	49
34	35,393	13	51,559	25	S	4	40	94	12	3	31	1	44	2	43
35	38,148	12	56,121	29	M	4	38	96	11	1	25	1	42	2	34
36	30,281	4	35,995	24	S	7	22	96	3	2	17	0	9	1	20
37	30,735	0	26,550	33	U	14	21	15	-22	71	4	1	15	13	15
38	30,495	-2	36,270	38	U	7	51	61	-14	26	31	2	29	10	17
39	31,012	1	84,150	46	U	4	71	78	-3	16	19	2	32	3	26
40	31,674	0	27,575	26	U	9	16	65	-9	18	25	4	22	12	31
41	31,452	0	24,504	24	U	17	14	16	-27	78	6	1	7	5	36
42	32,423	6	28,998	26	U	12	21	25	-6	71	10	1	22	3	31
43	32,073	3	33,452	28	U	13	24	6	-30	92	6	0	-25	1	26
44	31,668	2	39,396	28	U	5	43	70	-8	25	40	1	31	3	26
45	32,693	5	50,946	34	U	4	45	82	-1	13	49	2	45	2	36
46	34,297	5	62,740	34	S	4	46	75	-3	22	35	1	41	2	24
47	33,636	-1	49,632	31	S	4	45	93	-3	5	46	1	41	1	22
48	32,047	0	48,540	30	U	5	37	76	-8	20	42	1	25	2	21
49	32,132	-2	44,315	28	S	5	37	94	-3	2	48	1	45	2	27
50	30,069	-2	39,587	26	U	5	33	80	-8	16	38	1	33	3	27

Note: U=urban, S=suburban, R=rural, M=mixed, HH=households.

Missouri State House Districts: Demographic Data (cont.)

House District	Population 1997	+/-	Average HH Income ($)	+/-	District Type	Unempl. Rate (%)	College Educ. (%)	White (non-Hispanic) (%)	+/-	African American (%)	+/-	Asian American (%)	+/-	Hispanic American (%)	+/-
Missouri	5,387,481	5	44,506	33	M	6	34	86	4	11	9	1	33	1	27
51	33,640	-4	33,326	25	S	7	20	93	-6	2	42	1	36	3	32
52	32,113	8	53,173	34	S	5	41	94	7	2	70	1	58	2	35
53	30,351	0	43,966	29	S	6	25	92	-2	3	51	2	49	3	34
54	34,486	7	54,744	33	S	4	42	94	5	3	53	1	48	2	39
55	33,946	6	60,906	36	S	4	46	94	4	3	53	1	51	2	28
56	37,015	13	63,348	33	S	4	50	94	11	3	66	1	62	2	44
57	25,387	-18	26,038	39	U	18	19	3	-43	96	-17	0	-29	1	-1
58	24,771	-19	20,584	28	U	21	10	9	-51	90	-14	0	-72	0	-41
59	26,029	-17	31,673	35	U	12	27	59	-33	33	36	4	-2	4	10
60	26,224	-16	26,105	31	U	17	16	0	-56	99	-15	0	-69	0	-57
61	26,541	-13	33,107	33	U	14	17	4	-49	95	-10	0	-40	0	-18
62	25,708	-14	31,183	33	U	15	16	5	-48	95	-11	0	-47	0	-30
63	27,324	-13	31,406	49	U	13	34	29	-34	67	0	1	-2	2	-4
64	28,520	-2	50,658	46	U	8	53	38	-29	56	27	3	9	3	35
65	28,309	-7	43,987	39	U	5	34	88	-11	9	54	1	28	2	19
66	28,231	-10	41,326	38	U	5	31	95	-12	2	63	1	27	2	13
67	27,307	-16	32,983	31	U	8	30	66	-28	29	25	3	8	2	3
68	28,147	-6	48,042	39	U	4	35	97	-7	1	73	1	37	2	16
69	28,096	-5	39,292	28	S	8	23	34	-22	64	8	1	6	1	6
70	31,175	0	36,000	35	S	13	20	25	-21	74	9	0	-3	1	0
71	31,038	0	41,431	35	S	10	30	34	-17	64	12	1	10	1	21
72	30,992	1	48,631	36	S	8	46	28	-17	68	9	2	15	1	35
73	31,268	-7	44,859	28	S	5	28	81	-11	17	16	1	10	1	19
74	34,211	10	65,713	34	S	3	49	74	4	24	30	1	49	1	15
75	30,873	-3	51,117	30	S	4	37	65	-11	33	13	1	21	1	26
76	30,218	0	55,514	35	S	4	37	88	-4	9	36	1	31	1	46
77	33,415	4	56,483	34	S	4	39	88	0	9	40	1	39	1	27
78	30,639	0	56,764	37	S	4	39	90	-2	7	33	1	38	2	43
79	30,291	-1	50,057	37	S	7	33	55	-12	43	16	1	18	1	28
80	31,263	2	46,247	35	S	4	28	88	-1	9	36	1	40	1	38
81	34,822	3	41,738	30	S	6	25	85	-1	12	35	2	40	2	37
82	29,558	-3	83,694	30	S	3	62	89	-6	5	29	4	36	1	19
83	31,298	1	92,348	39	S	5	63	79	-4	17	24	3	38	1	31
84	33,397	0	60,225	36	S	4	57	79	-6	15	28	4	33	2	26
85	33,713	3	62,054	23	S	3	60	90	0	3	37	4	44	1	34
86	30,095	-2	106,631	24	S	2	67	90	-5	2	31	6	37	1	25
87	31,921	-2	117,225	36	S	3	68	87	-6	8	26	4	37	1	16
88	27,702	-1	85,365	26	S	2	63	94	-2	2	32	3	39	1	18
89	39,357	22	92,260	30	S	3	58	93	20	4	46	2	68	1	60
90	37,560	14	56,368	34	S	5	39	97	13	1	47	1	63	1	38
91	32,086	0	71,607	40	S	4	63	91	-2	7	14	1	39	1	31
92	31,857	3	72,734	33	S	3	60	93	1	2	39	3	43	1	24
93	34,535	4	91,521	33	S	3	63	92	2	3	43	4	40	1	12
94	29,436	-2	76,847	38	S	3	59	91	-4	7	29	1	36	1	27
95	33,132	-1	66,712	38	S	4	46	93	-2	5	19	1	36	1	24
96	28,415	-8	43,830	30	S	5	24	96	-9	2	34	1	20	1	16
97	35,280	9	63,476	30	S	3	50	97	8	1	46	1	57	1	37
98	28,883	-7	46,810	27	S	3	36	96	-8	1	35	1	36	1	26
99	30,147	0	53,041	27	S	4	37	98	-1	0	28	1	41	1	26
100	34,246	7	68,142	34	S	3	47	97	7	0	25	1	51	1	34

Note: U=urban, S=suburban, R=rural, M=mixed, HH=households.

Missouri State House Districts: Demographic Data (cont.)

House District	Population		Average HH Income		District Type	Unempl. Rate	College Educ.	White (non-Hispanic)		African American		Asian American		Hispanic American	
	1997	+/-	($)	+/-		(%)	(%)	(%)	+/-	(%)	+/-	(%)	+/-	(%)	+/-
Missouri	5,387,481	5	44,506	33	M	6	34	86	4	11	9	1	33	1	27
101	33,889	12	46,887	23	S	5	24	98	12	0	-35	0	63	1	36
102	35,643	15	45,493	23	S	5	26	98	14	0	6	0	57	1	47
103	36,338	9	41,699	24	S	6	24	96	8	3	33	0	39	1	25
104	34,209	8	40,294	26	R	11	20	98	8	1	19	0	42	0	5
105	35,950	13	45,809	26	S	7	24	98	12	1	30	0	56	1	48
106	34,095	8	32,782	27	R	9	21	95	7	3	23	0	25	1	35
107	34,794	12	32,497	30	R	11	18	99	11	0	13	0	16	0	30
108	26,523	-15	31,886	30	U	8	18	90	-18	6	60	1	15	3	-2
109	34,029	12	43,663	27	R	6	27	97	12	1	30	0	46	1	56
110	33,099	13	36,080	28	R	8	17	98	13	1	27	0	31	1	21
111	36,030	12	39,590	31	R	5	20	99	12	0	16	0	13	1	23
112	32,317	4	36,371	37	R	4	20	99	4	0	-23	0	-61	0	1
113	34,383	9	44,776	35	R	4	36	86	7	12	20	0	33	1	39
114	34,270	7	56,739	44	R	4	44	94	6	5	29	1	51	1	27
115	34,532	13	35,211	30	R	7	21	99	13	0	-37	0	-18	1	37
116	35,876	19	34,968	31	R	6	23	98	19	0	-4	0	18	1	46
117	33,975	8	36,552	35	R	5	25	94	7	5	22	0	-20	1	15
118	31,188	4	33,656	26	R	8	29	94	3	4	22	0	30	1	24
119	36,388	15	27,469	24	R	8	17	99	14	0	-7	0	-23	1	25
120	32,847	6	32,260	31	R	7	23	97	6	1	21	0	-15	1	27
121	34,413	11	36,349	30	R	8	45	86	9	8	26	2	45	2	31
122	32,399	4	36,996	24	R	6	26	95	4	3	19	0	2	1	25
123	37,707	24	48,958	25	S	6	34	95	23	2	48	1	69	2	49
124	37,956	18	42,681	25	S	5	28	97	18	1	14	0	43	1	55
125	32,326	4	30,674	29	R	7	21	98	4	1	5	0	-22	1	15
126	31,689	5	38,182	39	R	5	25	97	5	1	17	1	24	1	17
127	37,632	11	39,014	45	S	5	23	97	11	0	23	0	17	1	26
128	32,548	10	39,037	46	U	5	30	94	9	2	25	1	43	1	49
129	33,554	9	40,087	45	U	6	28	95	9	1	30	1	38	1	28
130	33,700	9	35,255	39	R	6	24	95	9	0	5	1	28	1	34
131	35,461	18	30,034	28	R	7	20	98	18	0	-23	0	16	1	51
132	32,846	7	31,745	34	R	6	21	98	7	0	-63	0	-9	1	38
133	33,999	7	30,420	29	R	5	21	98	7	0	-49	0	-19	1	11
134	37,639	15	46,884	37	U	3	45	95	14	2	23	1	55	1	38
135	36,048	21	79,400	50	U	3	54	97	20	0	34	1	67	1	58
136	37,968	16	36,053	38	U	5	35	95	15	2	36	1	50	1	46
137	32,273	1	23,018	31	U	10	16	93	-1	4	24	1	24	1	38
138	32,327	2	36,468	37	U	5	37	92	0	5	23	1	38	1	30
139	33,787	2	42,886	34	M	5	31	98	1	1	25	0	28	1	23
140	35,045	14	36,389	30	R	6	21	98	14	1	27	0	-6	1	31
141	42,436	36	38,756	36	R	9	26	98	36	0	-62	0	48	1	65
142	40,839	38	38,997	30	S	5	27	98	38	0	-3	0	52	1	65
143	40,738	29	36,162	48	R	8	23	98	29	0	-60	0	53	1	58
144	34,437	12	25,535	21	R	7	16	99	12	0	-38	0	-25	1	10
145	35,765	18	28,224	21	R	5	22	98	18	0	-14	0	-7	1	42
146	34,999	12	32,734	37	R	7	17	98	12	0	-16	0	27	1	39
147	33,485	-10	28,537	25	R	10	21	84	-9	9	-20	1	-17	4	3
148	22,675	-11	36,453	43	R	10	27	85	-14	8	12	4	27	3	-7
149	31,781	8	33,483	25	R	7	34	94	7	1	22	3	37	1	32
150	36,069	8	31,623	31	R	8	17	99	8	0	4	0	-8	1	30

Note: U=urban, S=suburban, R=rural, M=mixed, HH=households.

Missouri State House Districts: Demographic Data (cont.)

House District	Population		Average HH Income		District Type	Unempl. Rate	College Educ.	White (non-Hispanic)		African American		Asian American		Hispanic American	
	1997	+/-	($)	+/-		(%)	(%)	(%)	+/-	(%)	+/-	(%)	+/-	(%)	+/-
Missouri	5,387,481	5	44,506	33	M	6	34	86	4	11	9	1	33	1	27
151	35,394	13	30,014	35	R	7	18	98	12	0	-2	0	17	1	39
152	31,626	6	28,090	29	R	12	14	98	5	1	19	0	-65	0	17
153	32,614	8	26,536	37	R	9	16	99	8	0	-58	0	-77	0	3
154	31,201	2	31,191	41	R	9	18	92	1	7	22	0	22	1	25
155	32,729	5	39,095	35	R	5	16	99	5	0	-11	0	10	0	4
156	36,044	12	27,677	29	R	9	13	98	12	1	14	0	-11	1	18
157	35,725	8	43,568	39	R	5	29	97	8	1	27	0	13	1	33
158	31,664	6	39,723	38	R	7	39	88	4	10	24	1	28	1	29
159	32,950	3	29,482	23	R	7	16	97	3	2	15	0	-20	1	16
160	29,907	2	35,050	28	R	7	22	85	0	14	19	0	-9	1	22
161	32,625	-3	31,907	30	R	10	14	81	-5	18	9	0	-27	0	-14
162	31,606	-2	30,162	43	R	11	12	78	-5	21	12	0	-11	1	16
163	32,509	0	31,539	42	R	11	15	89	-1	10	14	0	12	0	4

Note: U=urban, S=suburban, R=rural, M=mixed, HH=households.

MONTANA

There are few sights in North America more impressive than a Montana wheat field in August. Vast rolling hills stretch endlessly under an overwhelming blue sky, the only sound the hum of a thresher. Despite its nickname, "Big Sky Country," few people appreciate how big the fourth-largest state is. As John Gunther notes in *Inside USA,* one of every twenty-five American square miles is Montanan.

Eastern Montana, like eastern Colorado, is a very different place than the mountains across the Continental Divide. Fittingly, the products of the two halves of the state flow in different directions; eastern wheat toward Minnesota, western timber and ore toward Denver or Salt Lake City. In many ways, Montana is emptier now than it once was. Lewis and Clark first crossed it in 1805, and within twenty-five years Fort Union on the Missouri River had grown to become, in author Ian Frazier's phrase, "the Times Square of the Plains," the intersection of a continental fur-trading network. Native Americans stopped roaming not long after they defeated George Armstrong Custer at the Little Big Horn.

In the west, Butte was once the wildest town in the country. Built on huge copper mines (Butte was "a mile high and a mile deep"), it was run by the Anaconda Copper Company, but also home to the International Workers of the World (or "Wobblies," as they were called). Given that explosive combination, Butte was the scene of some of the worst labor violence in American history. More recent violence in the state has come from the militias and from another Montana transplant, Ted Kaczynski, the Unabomber.

The copper mines have closed, though Montana coal is still dug. But the state is not on the way to anywhere, which is why it has not grown. It still does not have a city of 100,000 inhabitants. During the 1980s, Montana had by far the slowest rate of growth in the Rockies. It has picked up considerably during the 1990s, welcoming more young families as well as celebrities like Ted Turner and Jane Fonda, who get all the attention.

This is not to say that there aren't boom areas in Montana, but they are pockets. Two house districts south of Missoula in the Bitterroot Mountains, the Sixty-first and Sixtieth, have grown by 49 and 40 percent, respectively. Bozeman, the Flathead Lake area near Kalispell, and Helena have also done well. Hardly anywhere has done badly. The Ninety-ninth District, which covers a huge expanse of territory centered on Lake Fort Peck, has shrunk by 12 percent during the decade, but no other district has lost half as much.

With large parts of its land owned by the federal government as national parks or Indian reservations, and with an economy built on mining, grazing, and farming, Montana is one of the poorer states. In terms of average income, it is poorer than Maine or Louisiana and just ahead of Arkansas. The wealthiest districts are in the small cities: Billings, Great Falls, Bozeman, and Missoula. The poorest districts are there, too, as well as on the Indian reservations. Montana has one of the highest rates of unemployment—22 percent in the Eighty-fifth District, which includes the Blackfeet reservation on the Canadian border.

With the exception of Native Americans, who comprise about 6 percent of the population, Montana is one of the least diverse states in the country. Eighty-five of one hundred house districts are more than 90 percent white. Two districts just south of Billings have small clusters of Hispanics. The Forty-first District, outside Great Falls, is home to the state's only small concentrations of African Americans or Asians—Montana's Greenwich Village, so to speak.

Given its strong labor background and the orneryness of farmers in bad times, Montana is a Republican state that can go Democratic. The partisan composition of the legislature has been completely reshuffled during the decade. The house has swung from 61–39 Democratic in 1990 to 65–35 Republican in 1996, while the senate switched from 29–21 Democratic to 34–16 Republican. Montana lost a congressional seat after the 1990 census, meaning that its lone representative must run at large. This has produced some bitterly fought races between candidates from the two regions.

MONTANA
State Senate Districts

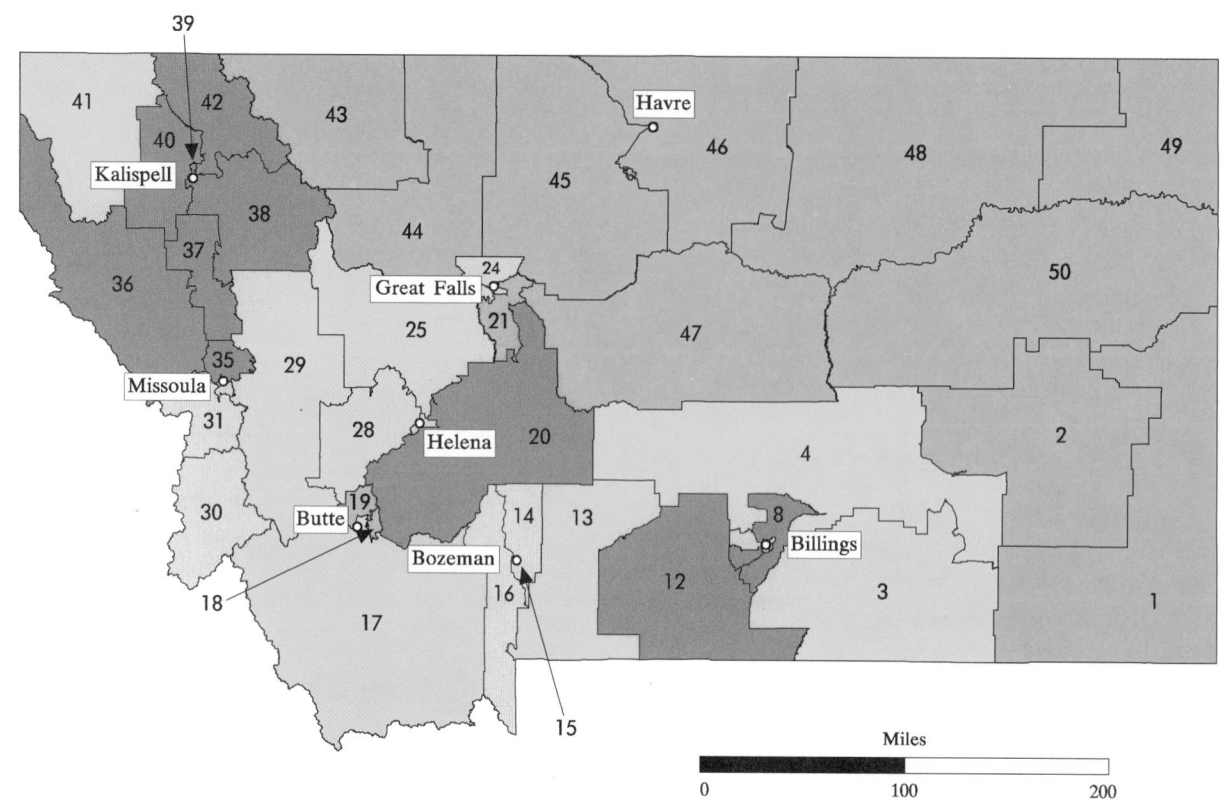

GREAT FALLS

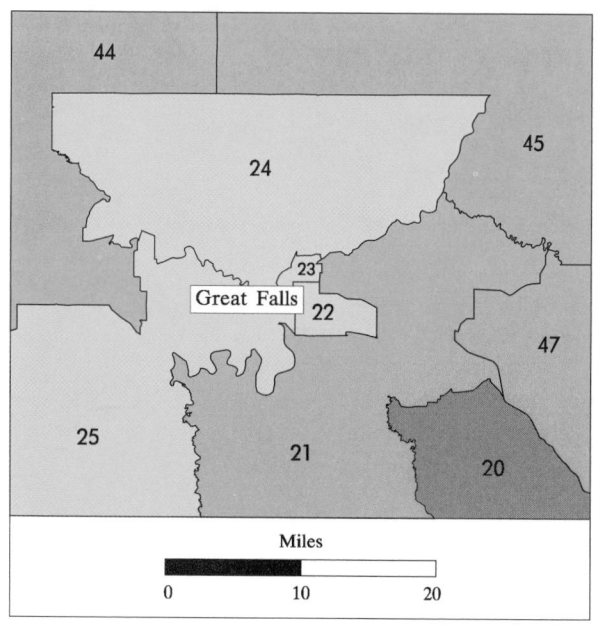

HELENA

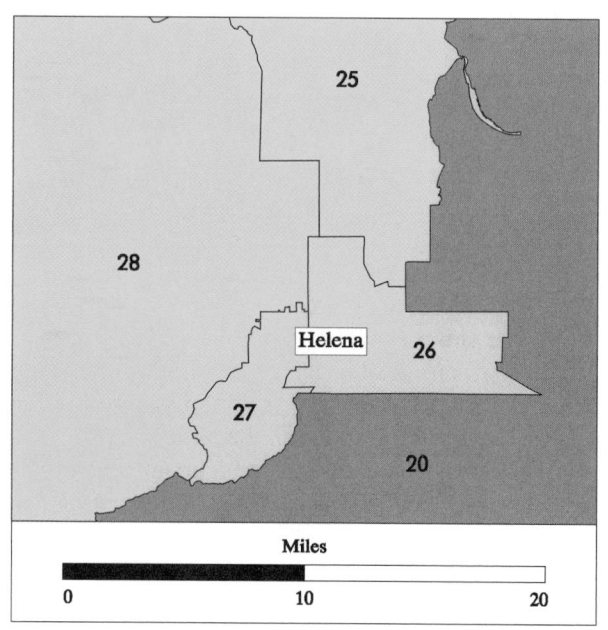

Population Growth   ▨ -7% to 4%   ▨ 5% to 13%   ▨ 16% to 25%   ▨ 26% to 36%

MISSOULA

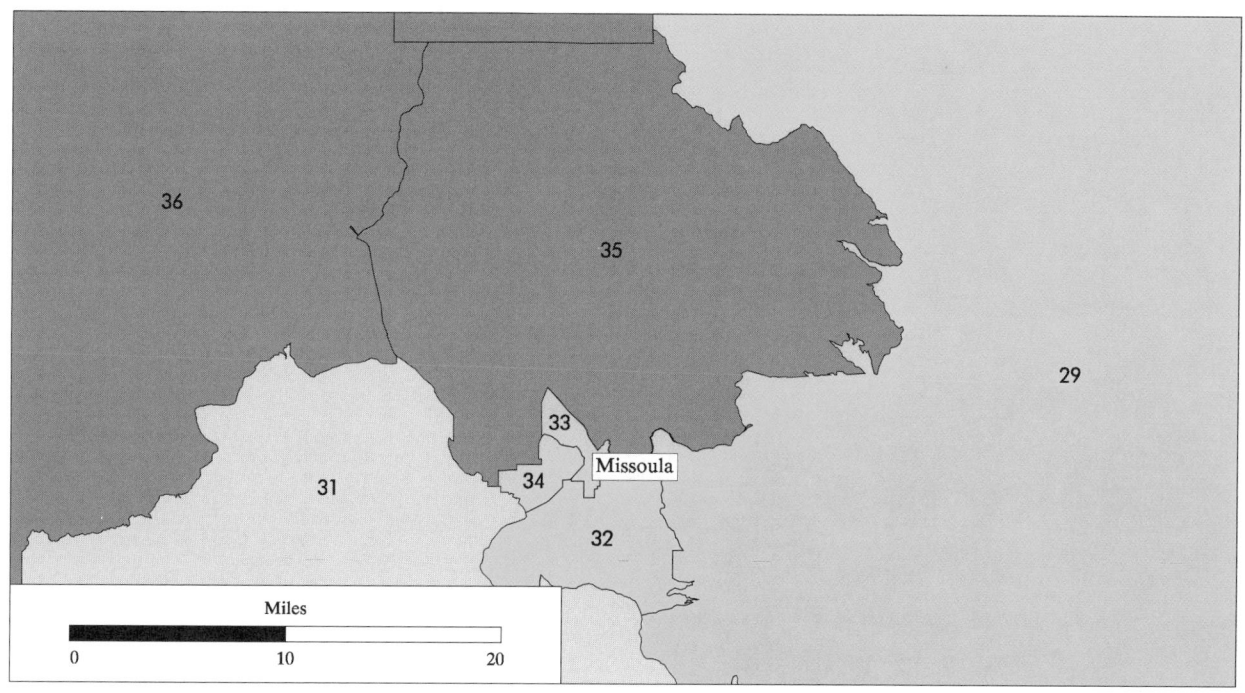

BILLINGS

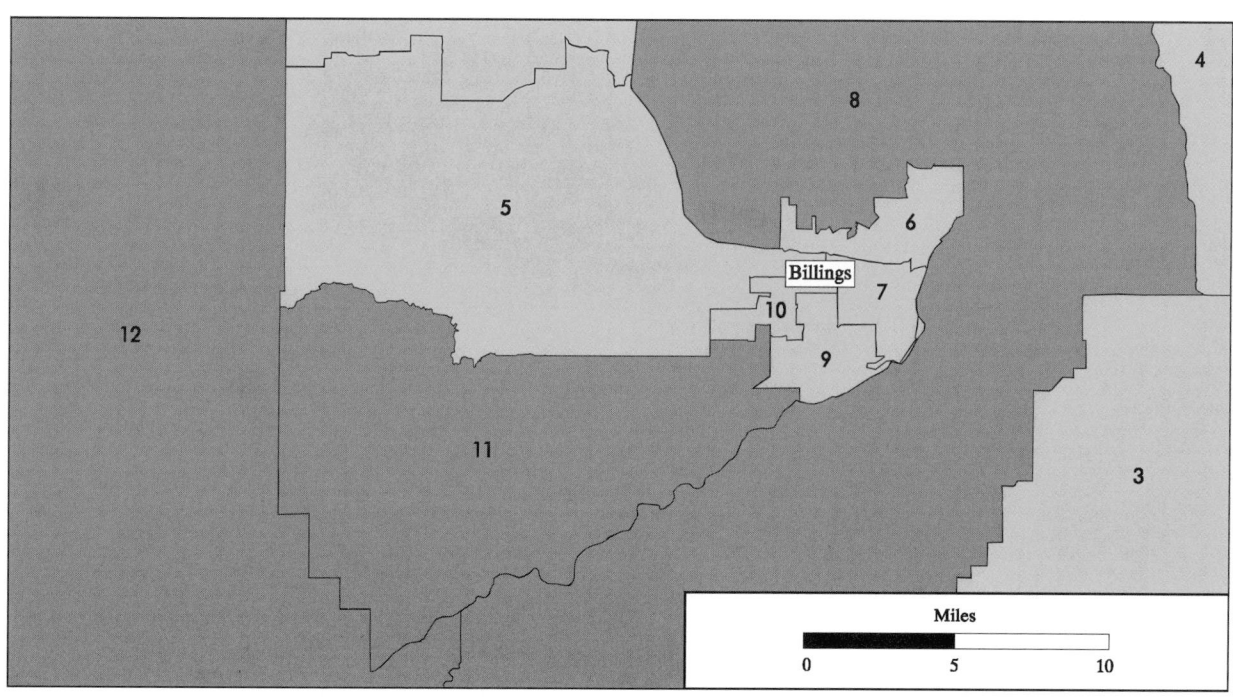

Population Growth   ▢ -7% to 4%   ▢ 5% to 13%   ▢ 16% to 25%   ▢ 26% to 36%

Montana State Senate Districts: Demographic Data

Senate District	Population		Average HH Income		District Type	Unempl. Rate	College Educ.	White (non-Hispanic)		African American		Asian American		Hispanic American	
	1997	+/-	($)	+/-		(%)	(%)	(%)	+/-	(%)	+/-	(%)	+/-	(%)	+/-
Montana	888,752	11	39,636	37	R	7	38	92	11	0	14	1	23	2	32
1	15,493	-4	36,340	29	R	3	30	98	-4	0	0	0	2	1	7
2	16,367	3	34,758	35	R	5	34	96	3	0	24	0	2	1	7
3	17,597	8	31,532	33	R	20	26	43	8	0	-4	0	15	3	11
4	17,411	10	37,215	32	R	5	33	96	10	0	10	0	-8	2	27
5	18,893	13	72,807	50	U	3	54	97	13	0	42	1	33	1	43
6	15,740	11	49,918	47	U	4	44	95	10	0	6	1	21	2	29
7	17,852	9	27,788	33	U	9	34	84	7	2	39	1	28	8	27
8	17,547	19	47,837	41	M	7	38	95	19	0	30	0	26	2	41
9	16,603	6	32,079	29	U	6	29	88	3	1	30	1	21	7	48
10	16,023	6	46,976	40	U	4	45	95	6	0	22	1	24	2	49
11	19,045	21	37,635	37	S	5	33	96	20	0	49	0	33	2	62
12	18,889	17	35,707	29	R	4	36	98	17	0	-30	0	-44	1	38
13	18,169	12	40,848	49	R	7	39	96	11	0	48	0	14	2	45
14	22,832	28	59,429	54	R	4	60	96	28	0	0	1	43	2	51
15	17,155	12	34,129	43	R	6	58	95	11	0	28	2	31	2	35
16	20,044	26	49,367	50	R	5	40	98	26	0	-100	0	34	1	71
17	18,649	12	35,912	34	R	5	39	97	12	0	38	0	-4	2	26
18	16,169	1	43,389	38	R	8	37	97	1	0	-11	0	20	2	4
19	17,525	2	30,141	27	R	11	32	94	1	0	-35	0	17	4	36
20	19,999	19	42,250	33	R	4	38	97	19	0	25	0	-11	1	36
21	16,955	1	39,882	29	M	5	41	89	0	4	7	2	17	3	9
22	15,885	6	39,941	35	U	6	37	91	5	1	11	1	28	2	28
23	15,767	5	27,882	25	U	9	30	88	4	1	14	1	22	3	35
24	17,231	7	37,123	26	U	6	31	94	7	0	14	1	18	1	26
25	18,204	11	56,332	40	R	6	47	96	10	0	3	1	26	1	53
26	17,137	12	49,659	47	R	4	50	95	12	0	22	1	38	1	29
27	17,521	11	38,469	37	R	6	53	95	11	0	14	1	34	2	33
28	18,063	12	39,666	32	R	7	39	95	11	0	-7	1	35	2	29
29	18,492	10	36,767	41	R	9	33	97	9	0	-4	0	15	1	27
30	20,703	32	31,204	29	R	8	34	96	32	0	29	0	33	2	72
31	22,502	36	44,381	44	R	6	38	97	36	0	0	0	44	1	59
32	18,559	9	51,774	46	R	4	55	96	9	0	14	1	37	1	39
33	16,841	9	29,614	34	R	12	51	92	8	1	29	2	31	2	29
34	17,792	8	31,116	35	R	8	38	94	7	0	21	2	34	1	14
35	17,940	23	55,111	45	R	7	44	95	23	0	28	1	50	2	58
36	19,245	16	34,512	29	R	8	31	95	15	0	-47	0	23	1	30
37	19,638	21	32,470	38	R	9	31	76	22	0	58	0	-5	2	19
38	21,584	24	47,794	48	R	8	40	93	23	0	35	0	29	2	47
39	17,023	20	37,165	36	R	5	37	96	20	0	0	1	29	1	44
40	21,223	25	45,772	39	R	8	40	98	25	0	21	0	20	1	36
41	16,784	9	34,857	34	R	17	27	97	9	0	-40	0	11	1	34
42	18,604	20	36,709	34	R	9	29	96	20	0	-13	0	20	2	63
43	16,335	4	29,796	25	R	16	29	51	2	0	-21	0	-29	1	-2
44	15,600	-2	34,261	18	R	3	34	97	-2	0	-69	0	-16	1	8
45	16,824	-1	42,450	32	R	4	41	95	-1	0	-27	0	21	1	0
46	15,913	4	31,074	27	R	11	28	65	3	0	-12	0	13	1	4
47	16,695	4	33,430	18	R	5	34	98	4	0	67	0	-32	1	27
48	15,340	-1	34,229	28	R	5	31	92	-1	0	-45	0	-18	1	-3
49	15,377	-2	30,970	33	R	12	28	63	-4	0	-29	0	-17	1	-8
50	14,807	-7	35,840	35	R	6	32	97	-7	0	-100	0	-16	2	20

Note: U=urban, S=suburban, R=rural, M=mixed, HH=households.

MONTANA
State House Districts

Miles

0   100   200

BOZEMAN

Miles

0   5   10

HELENA

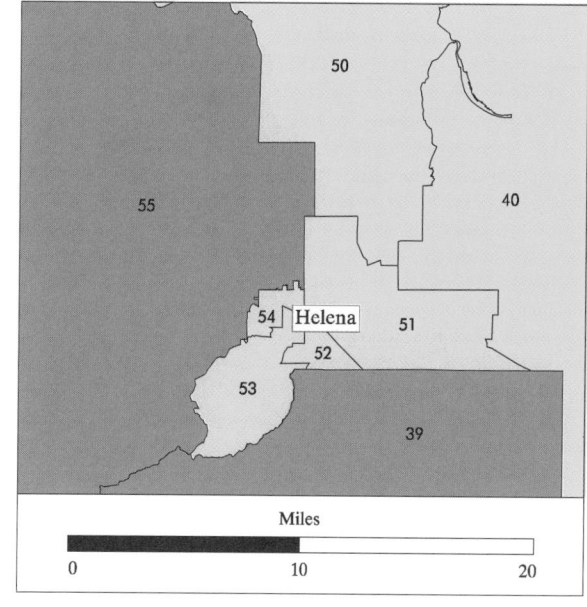

Miles

0   10   20

Population Growth   ▢ -12% to 3%   ▢ 5% to 15%   ▢ 16% to 30%   ▢ 40% to 49%

GREAT FALLS

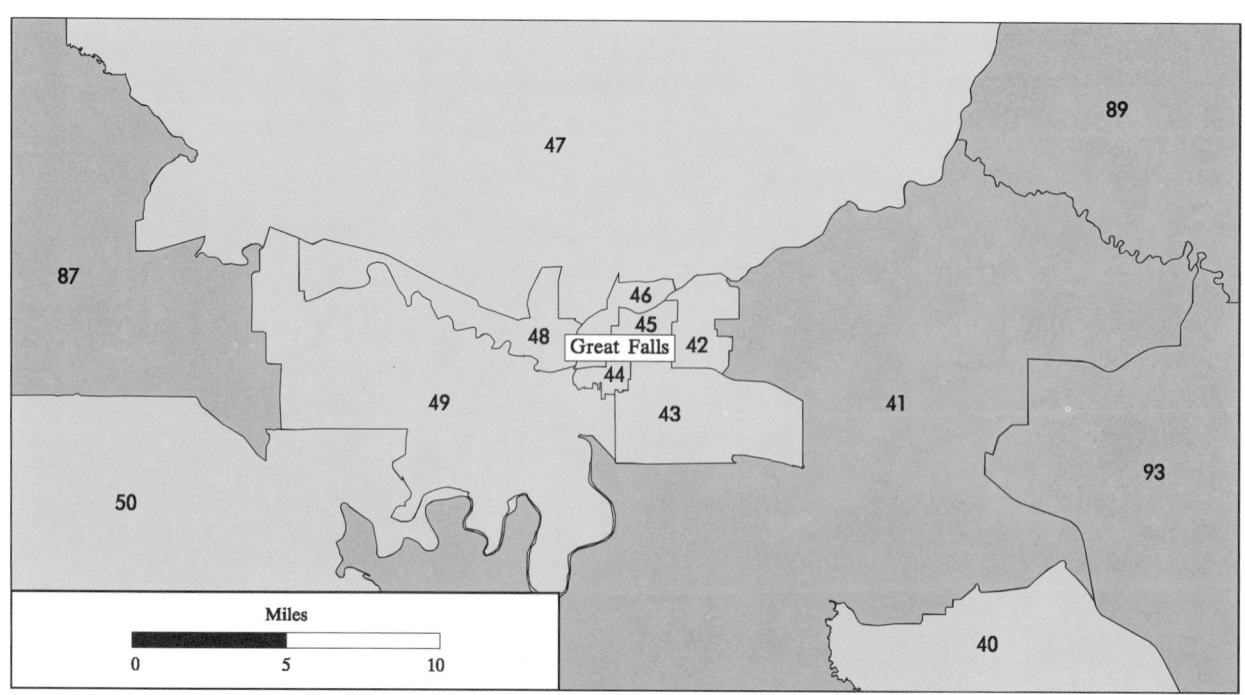

BILLINGS

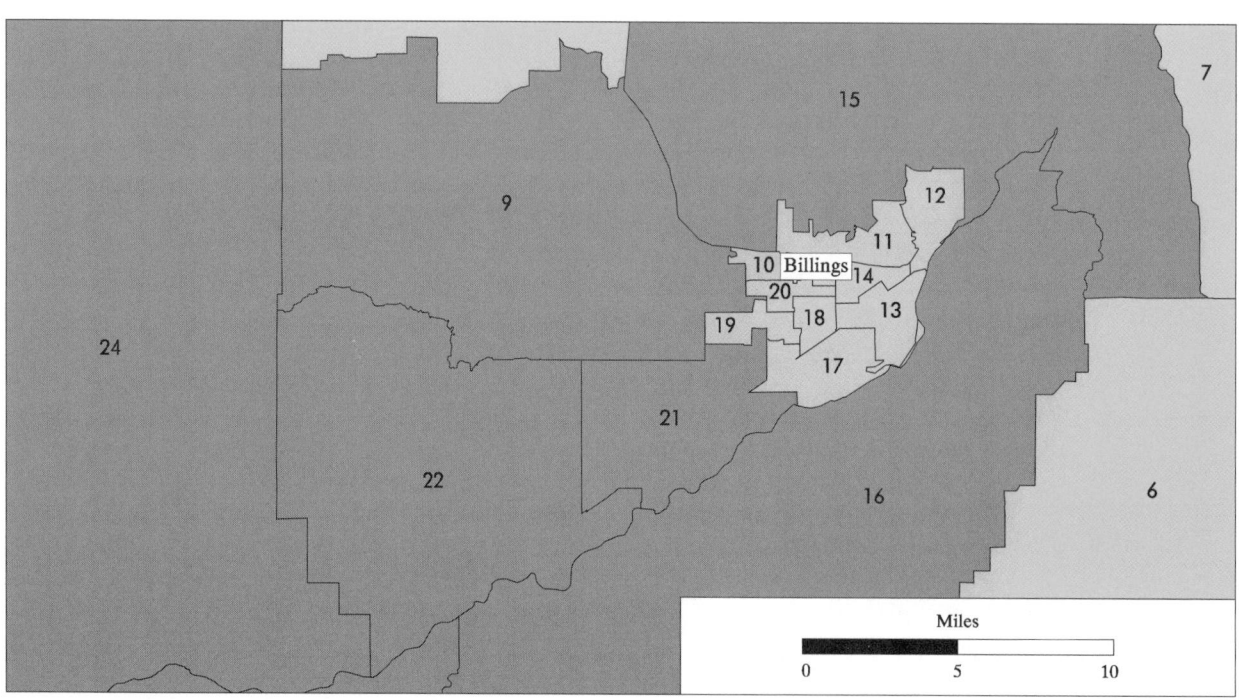

Population Growth   ■ -12% to 3%   □ 5% to 15%   ■ 16% to 30%

MISSOULA

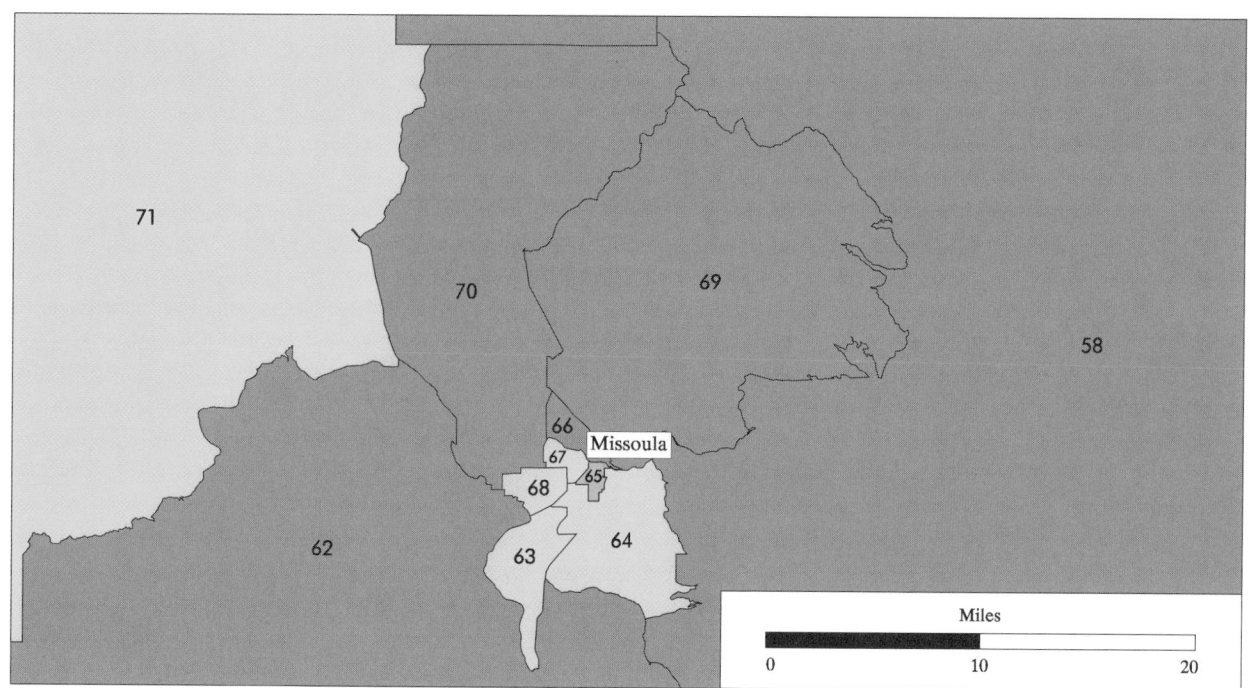

BUTTE

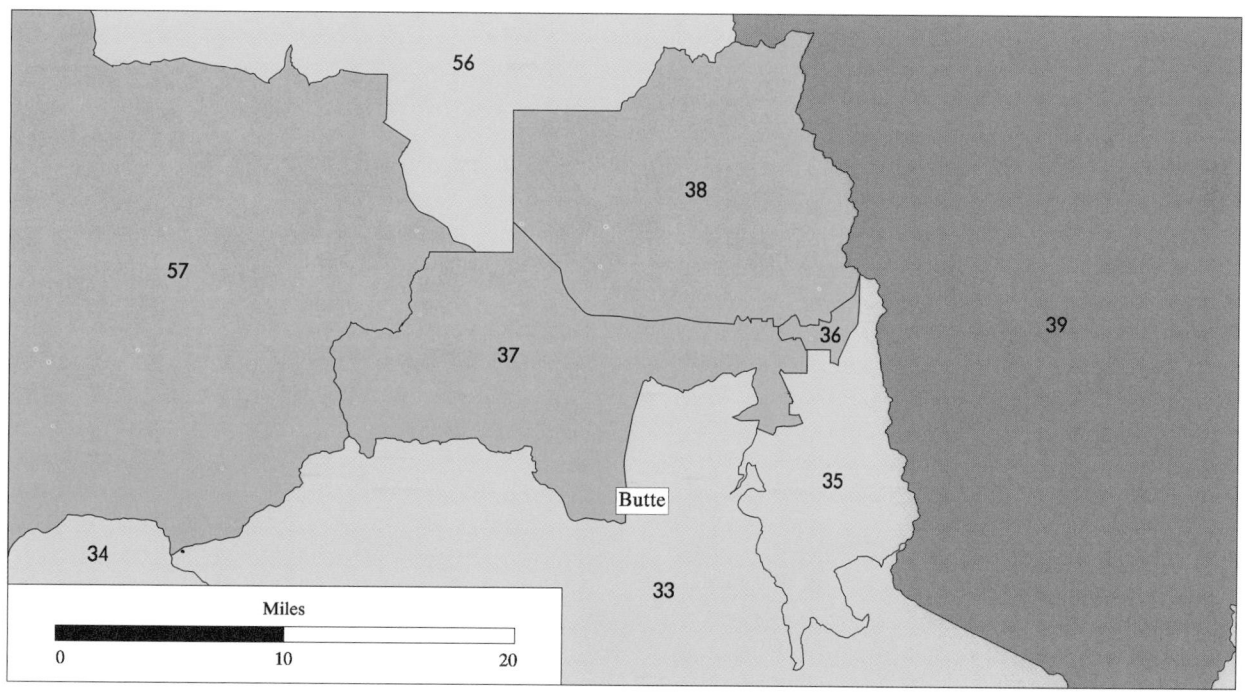

Population Growth   -12% to 3%   5% to 15%   16% to 30%

Montana State House Districts: Demographic Data

House District	Population		Average HH Income		District Type	Unempl. Rate	College Educ.	White (non-Hispanic)		African American		Asian American		Hispanic American	
	1997	+/-	($)	+/-		(%)	(%)	(%)	+/-	(%)	+/-	(%)	+/-	(%)	+/-
Montana	888,752	11	39,636	37	R	7	38	92	11	0	14	1	23	2	32
1	7,524	-5	33,119	18	R	3	28	99	-5	0	0	0	-10	0	-8
2	7,963	-3	39,306	39	R	4	32	98	-3	0	0	0	13	1	18
3	10,601	2	37,663	38	R	4	33	96	2	0	27	1	6	1	3
4	5,760	6	30,276	32	R	6	36	96	6	0	0	0	-22	2	14
5	8,252	3	28,941	30	R	22	25	38	2	0	0	0	7	3	17
6	9,348	11	33,863	35	R	19	26	47	12	0	-6	0	23	2	3
7	8,753	8	47,036	38	R	5	41	94	7	0	18	0	0	4	31
8	8,655	13	28,363	27	R	5	26	98	13	0	-33	0	-15	1	15
9	10,050	21	73,800	54	U	3	52	97	21	0	80	1	42	1	18
10	8,758	5	72,097	46	U	4	55	96	4	0	29	1	25	2	71
11	8,485	8	60,703	53	U	3	54	95	8	0	-4	1	25	2	12
12	7,308	13	39,489	41	U	5	31	94	13	0	38	1	18	3	42
13	8,851	11	21,033	28	U	12	22	77	9	3	42	1	30	12	23
14	9,094	8	34,444	36	U	7	46	91	6	1	33	1	26	3	42
15	9,695	17	53,927	47	R	5	42	96	17	0	13	0	0	2	48
16	7,857	22	40,543	33	S	9	33	93	21	0	31	1	39	2	35
17	8,642	6	32,533	31	U	7	22	84	2	1	35	1	23	8	43
18	7,973	6	31,717	27	U	5	34	91	4	0	18	1	29	4	57
19	8,241	6	49,566	42	U	4	42	96	6	0	23	1	19	2	35
20	7,809	6	44,796	37	U	5	48	95	5	0	40	1	28	3	60
21	8,608	21	38,017	37	U	5	38	95	20	0	46	1	44	2	63
22	10,417	21	37,326	37	S	5	29	97	20	0	46	0	8	2	62
23	9,402	16	33,252	25	R	4	38	98	16	0	-33	0	-53	1	37
24	9,477	17	38,236	33	R	4	35	98	17	0	-29	0	-30	1	39
25	9,981	10	46,806	53	R	6	43	96	10	1	45	0	2	2	42
26	8,218	14	34,520	43	R	8	33	97	13	0	55	0	36	2	48
27	11,923	30	49,351	42	R	5	54	97	30	0	7	1	42	1	58
28	10,965	25	71,293	67	R	4	66	95	25	0	-14	2	43	2	43
29	8,785	9	35,846	50	R	6	55	96	9	0	20	1	22	1	31
30	8,392	15	32,002	35	R	6	61	94	14	1	32	2	36	2	37
31	10,250	28	56,924	55	R	6	43	98	28	0	-100	0	40	1	56
32	9,789	24	40,738	41	R	4	37	98	23	0	-100	0	27	1	87
33	9,882	15	35,953	30	R	5	39	97	15	0	0	0	8	2	27
34	8,765	10	35,850	40	R	5	39	97	9	0	25	0	-11	2	24
35	7,518	5	58,570	47	R	7	47	98	5	0	0	1	26	1	-18
36	8,705	-2	31,544	25	R	9	27	96	-2	0	-25	0	13	2	16
37	9,030	2	31,611	26	R	12	29	95	2	0	0	0	21	3	26
38	8,544	2	28,618	27	R	11	35	92	1	0	-47	0	15	5	43
39	9,961	25	46,307	29	R	4	41	97	24	0	125	0	-33	1	58
40	10,039	14	38,392	37	R	5	34	97	15	0	-75	0	5	1	18
41	8,636	-3	35,463	29	S	7	37	85	-4	6	5	4	15	4	3
42	8,300	6	43,412	29	U	4	45	93	5	2	16	1	21	2	25
43	8,738	6	47,986	38	U	4	42	94	6	1	8	1	30	1	18
44	7,103	6	30,744	31	U	9	30	87	4	1	14	1	25	3	35
45	8,263	5	33,458	26	U	8	35	92	4	1	14	1	26	3	39
46	7,545	5	22,886	23	U	10	25	84	4	1	10	1	22	3	31
47	8,838	8	42,446	27	U	5	34	96	8	0	11	1	21	1	16
48	8,445	6	32,168	25	U	8	28	91	6	0	17	1	18	2	34
49	8,515	7	72,660	43	U	5	58	96	7	0	11	1	31	2	55
50	9,665	14	42,453	39	R	6	36	97	14	0	-40	0	14	1	52

Note: U=urban, S=suburban, R=rural, M=mixed, HH=households.

Montana State House Districts: Demographic Data (cont.)

House District	Population 1997	+/-	Average HH Income ($)	+/-	District Type	Unempl. Rate (%)	College Educ. (%)	White (non-Hispanic) (%)	+/-	African American (%)	+/-	Asian American (%)	+/-	Hispanic American (%)	+/-
Montana	888,752	11	39,636	37	R	7	38	92	11	0	14	1	23	2	32
51	8,476	15	42,890	43	R	5	38	95	14	0	50	1	39	1	28
52	8,660	10	55,325	50	R	4	58	96	10	0	17	1	38	1	30
53	8,730	11	32,389	34	R	7	52	95	10	0	20	1	31	2	31
54	8,829	12	45,255	40	R	4	54	96	11	0	0	1	39	2	35
55	9,805	18	46,353	39	R	7	49	96	18	0	25	1	36	1	38
56	8,252	5	31,058	19	R	7	29	93	5	0	-13	0	33	2	23
57	8,369	-2	30,597	35	R	12	30	96	-2	0	-4	0	0	2	13
58	10,127	21	42,550	43	R	6	36	97	21	0	0	0	26	1	47
59	11,908	27	32,383	31	R	8	32	97	27	0	28	0	38	2	54
60	8,791	40	29,504	26	R	8	38	96	39	0	33	0	25	2	102
61	12,385	49	39,092	39	R	8	36	97	48	0	25	0	45	2	82
62	10,118	23	51,481	52	R	5	40	97	23	0	-10	0	42	1	26
63	6,980	11	53,710	37	R	5	52	96	10	0	0	1	43	1	46
64	11,543	9	50,849	51	R	4	56	96	8	0	14	1	37	1	36
65	7,548	0	42,340	42	R	12	66	93	0	1	22	3	22	1	11
66	9,341	17	22,427	31	R	12	39	91	16	1	37	2	48	2	41
67	8,673	6	27,278	31	R	9	39	93	5	0	25	3	32	1	17
68	9,115	9	35,139	37	R	7	36	95	9	0	23	2	39	1	7
69	8,627	23	65,486	54	R	8	53	97	23	0	8	1	47	1	30
70	9,330	23	44,571	34	R	5	34	93	23	0	43	1	53	2	73
71	8,880	15	38,499	30	R	6	30	92	15	0	-43	1	28	1	14
72	10,361	16	31,117	28	R	11	33	97	15	0	-50	0	16	2	40
73	9,603	16	32,226	39	R	9	32	68	16	0	50	0	-11	2	11
74	10,033	27	32,675	38	R	8	30	84	27	0	67	0	0	1	32
75	10,856	23	46,430	54	R	10	41	88	23	0	33	0	31	2	37
76	10,711	25	49,213	44	R	7	39	97	24	0	36	0	26	1	67
77	8,232	20	48,125	49	R	4	39	97	20	0	14	1	35	1	43
78	8,805	20	28,407	23	R	6	34	96	20	0	-9	1	24	1	47
79	11,872	28	46,711	41	R	9	38	98	28	0	45	0	35	1	47
80	9,354	21	44,711	36	R	7	42	97	21	0	-67	0	10	1	27
81	8,936	13	37,085	38	R	15	30	97	13	0	-29	0	21	1	49
82	7,846	5	32,462	30	R	19	24	96	4	0	-67	0	4	2	25
83	8,138	15	37,120	34	R	10	26	95	14	0	-60	0	21	2	57
84	10,463	25	36,407	33	R	9	31	96	24	0	67	0	19	2	69
85	8,876	8	25,049	23	R	22	26	32	9	0	0	0	-25	0	-11
86	7,484	-1	34,486	28	R	9	33	73	-1	0	-50	0	-29	1	8
87	7,921	0	34,622	19	R	4	33	97	0	0	-50	0	-38	1	8
88	7,669	-3	33,924	17	R	3	34	97	-3	0	-86	0	-4	1	8
89	7,927	-2	34,888	17	R	3	37	97	-2	0	-57	0	0	0	10
90	8,921	-1	49,269	44	R	5	44	93	-1	0	0	1	26	1	-4
91	6,744	0	31,454	28	R	6	29	90	1	0	0	1	19	2	13
92	9,137	8	30,642	27	R	15	27	47	7	0	-25	0	-33	1	-6
93	10,371	3	36,290	20	R	4	35	99	2	0	50	0	-40	1	22
94	6,327	6	29,032	16	R	8	33	97	6	0	71	0	-20	1	35
95	10,114	-1	35,574	23	R	4	33	95	-1	0	-40	0	-22	1	-9
96	5,224	-1	31,737	38	R	6	28	87	-1	0	-100	0	-15	1	8
97	9,162	-4	33,194	36	R	8	29	82	-6	0	-100	0	-30	1	-6
98	6,221	1	27,220	28	R	18	26	36	2	0	-14	0	-7	1	-11
99	7,193	-12	34,845	39	R	4	28	98	-12	0	-100	0	-31	1	7
100	7,612	-2	36,819	31	R	9	35	95	-2	0	-100	0	-5	3	25

Note: U=urban, S=suburban, R=rural, M=mixed, HH=households.

NEBRASKA

Before the Civil War, pioneers moved through Nebraska and kept on going. The vast, treeless prairies reminded many of an ocean, and it intimidated them. There was no wood for shelter, little water for stock or farming, and no hills to break the ceaseless wind. Whether Mormons seeking the Kingdom of God or pioneers on the Oregon Trail seeking more hospitable land in the Willamette Valley, they left Nebraska to the grasshoppers.

In the 1880s, the eastern fringe of Nebraska became a stop for cattle drives moving east toward Chicago and market. Omaha, like Kansas City two hundred miles south, filled with stockyards and slaughter houses. Eastern Nebraska is famous for corn, but west of the one hundredth meridian, there is not enough rain, and it is grazing land. Nebraska produced its radicals, most famously William Jennings Bryan, but never much industry. Little of Nebraska west of Lincoln has been developed.

Demographically, Nebraska remains Omaha, Lincoln, and everywhere else. Population growth was slow in the 1980s due to the farm crisis, but it has picked up in the 1990s to a steady 5 percent. There are few extremes at either end of the growth scale; the fast are not very fast here, nor the slow very slow. Only four Nebraska districts have grown by even 15 percent since 1990: all in the suburbs of Omaha and Lincoln. The only district to have lost even 4 percent of its population is the Fortieth, home to the Santee Sioux reservation, across the Missouri River from Yankton, South Dakota.

Omaha and Lincoln are pretty much the story when it comes to income, too. The suburbs are wealthy; the Omaha city districts are the poorest. Nebraska has one district that is much wealthier than the rest: the Fourth District, on the western edge of Omaha (average household income, $94,000). By far its poorest district is the Eleventh, across town and along the river, where average income is only $23,000. In a state that has not developed many deep suburbs (Lincoln, for example, has no buffer at all between its urban and rural districts), wealth is still found in the city neighborhoods. Seven of the ten richest districts are classified as urban. Most of the poorest are

rural, although the bottom four are urban, too.

Nebraska is overwhelmingly white; in thirty-eight of its forty-nine districts, the population is at least 90 percent white. This is not to say that it lacks all ethnic diversity. Many Scandinavian families followed the land speculators to Nebraska, and perhaps a tenth of the state is of Czech extraction. The heroine in Willa Cather's *My Antonia,* recall, was Bohemian. The state is 4 percent black (the same percentage as Rhode Island), most of whom are drawn into three districts in northeast Omaha: the Eleventh (76 percent African American), Thirteenth (32 percent), and Eighth (16 percent). Two districts at opposite ends of the state have sizable Hispanic communities: the Forty-eighth, around Scottsbluff (21 percent), and the Seventh, in Omaha (18 percent).

Nebraska's legislature is unicameral and nonpartisan, the only one of either in the country. The single legislative chamber is called the senate. The unique system was adopted as an experiment, pushed through in 1934 by U.S. senator George Norris, who thought the bicameral system produced too much stalemate. This method of organization, though uncommon, was not unprecedented. Pennsylvania and Georgia had unicameral legislatures before 1789, and Minnesota's legislature was nonpartisan (though bicameral) until 1972. Nor is this the only way in which supposedly bland Nebraska has shown itself unafraid to do things differently. It is one of three states (Louisiana and North Dakota are the others) whose capitol is a skyscraper.

Lack of party affiliation does not appear to make it difficult for members to run for higher office under a party flag. Two members of the state's congressional delegation, both Republicans, served in the senate. Legislative districts in the sparsely populated western part of Nebraska are geographically large, much bigger than in Kansas, to the south. The Third Congressional District, for example, takes in the western four-fifths of the state; geographically, it is one of the largest districts in the country.

NEBRASKA
State Legislative Districts

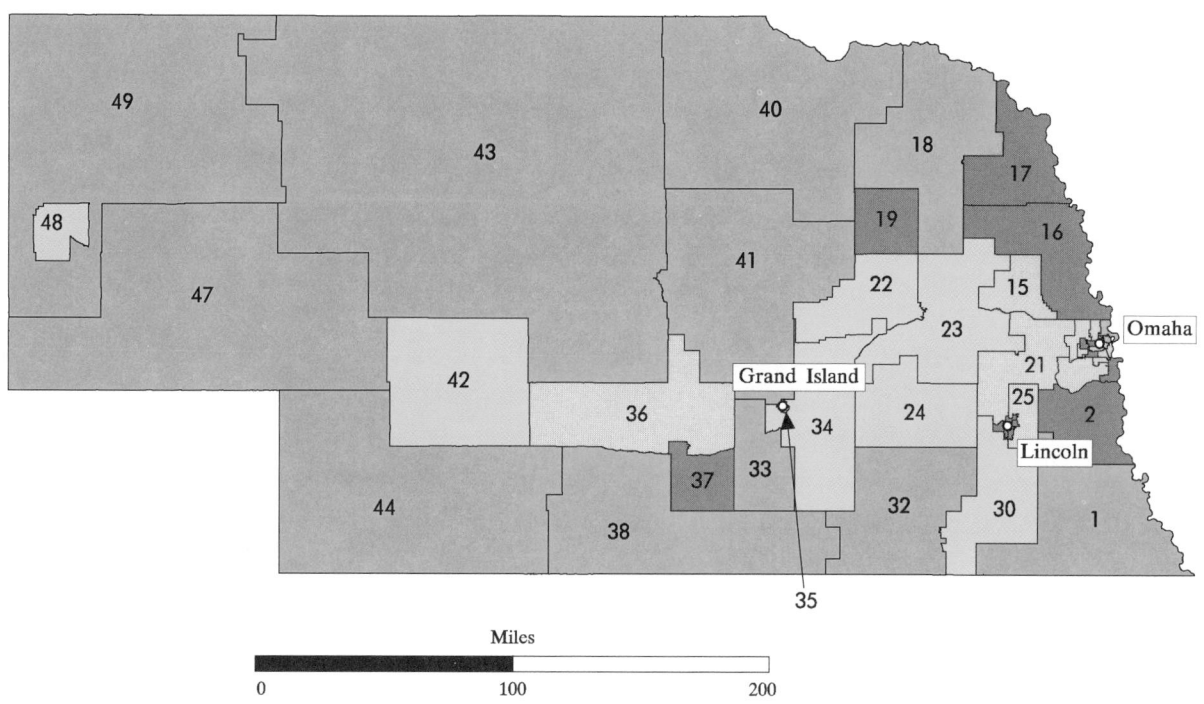

LINCOLN

OMAHA

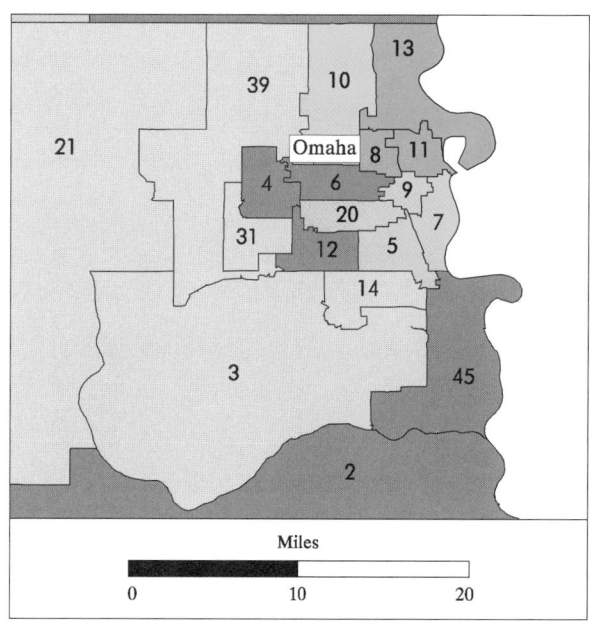

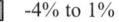

Population Growth   ▨ -4% to 1%   ▨ 2% to 5%   ▨ 6% to 11%   ▨ 12% to 21%

Nebraska State Legislative Districts: Demographic Data

Legis. District	Population		Average HH Income		District Type	Unempl. Rate	College Educ.	White (non-Hispanic)		African American		Asian American		Hispanic American	
	1997	+/-	($)	+/-		(%)	(%)	(%)	+/-	(%)	+/-	(%)	+/-	(%)	+/-
Nebraska	1,660,023	5	45,966	43	R	4	41	91	3	4	13	1	41	3	55
1	32,088	-1	37,020	45	R	4	32	98	-2	0	-11	0	14	1	13
2	35,332	8	44,845	49	R	4	33	98	8	0	-21	0	16	1	60
3	43,029	21	58,939	42	S	4	53	87	18	5	26	2	66	4	84
4	31,620	8	94,319	52	U	2	65	95	6	2	30	2	60	2	53
5	32,224	3	37,574	34	U	5	24	83	-2	6	20	1	31	9	57
6	35,081	10	76,536	49	U	3	59	94	8	2	39	2	65	2	74
7	32,812	3	29,838	31	U	7	23	74	-5	5	27	1	41	18	53
8	31,489	0	40,521	36	U	4	38	79	-5	16	17	1	29	3	66
9	33,114	3	31,859	34	U	5	47	81	-2	9	21	3	39	5	69
10	33,081	4	57,792	42	U	2	48	92	2	5	27	1	46	1	52
11	30,535	-1	23,044	27	U	14	15	19	-21	76	4	0	-8	3	46
12	37,215	8	65,299	47	U	2	55	93	6	2	31	1	44	3	78
13	32,043	0	44,137	38	U	8	28	64	-7	32	14	0	16	2	55
14	31,681	13	52,831	31	S	3	45	91	10	2	27	1	65	5	83
15	33,011	2	40,442	40	R	5	32	98	2	0	24	0	34	1	51
16	34,375	6	42,242	37	R	3	35	98	6	0	-4	0	-21	1	44
17	34,229	8	39,539	46	R	5	31	83	6	0	-3	1	27	5	54
18	34,056	0	38,016	48	R	2	30	99	0	0	-15	0	-58	0	2
19	34,978	7	42,406	48	R	3	35	96	6	1	7	0	22	3	55
20	32,607	5	62,565	44	U	3	53	94	3	1	33	1	49	3	74
21	37,048	12	50,639	40	R	3	39	96	11	1	21	1	51	2	70
22	30,566	2	41,728	41	R	2	34	98	2	0	-2	0	29	1	35
23	35,416	5	41,461	41	R	3	29	98	5	0	-54	0	-54	2	55
24	33,340	3	42,734	42	R	3	39	98	3	0	-5	0	-28	1	39
25	44,624	15	81,337	54	U	2	63	96	14	1	23	1	65	1	68
26	29,504	6	43,099	40	U	3	45	95	4	1	21	1	47	3	65
27	34,875	10	45,092	41	U	4	44	89	7	3	16	2	50	4	60
28	32,681	1	38,843	41	U	5	52	90	-2	4	15	3	37	3	56
29	30,633	10	59,351	49	U	2	59	95	9	1	21	2	59	2	63
30	37,979	3	45,284	44	R	3	38	97	2	1	2	0	11	1	55
31	33,931	17	73,444	52	S	2	54	96	16	1	40	1	64	2	80
32	32,001	-2	35,921	33	R	3	32	98	-2	0	-31	0	4	1	18
33	33,051	0	44,668	41	R	4	36	97	-1	1	5	0	17	2	37
34	35,577	4	35,989	26	R	3	33	96	3	0	-28	0	7	4	63
35	31,613	7	40,401	43	R	4	34	91	4	0	-5	2	48	6	53
36	40,615	13	39,895	40	R	3	36	95	11	0	-34	0	-14	4	68
37	30,626	6	41,957	42	R	4	46	95	5	0	3	1	33	4	50
38	31,688	0	36,540	40	R	3	33	99	0	0	-82	0	-15	1	27
39	43,128	21	65,792	47	S	3	53	94	19	3	43	1	71	2	89
40	30,840	-4	36,306	45	R	3	30	98	-4	0	-80	0	-63	0	5
41	31,462	0	35,782	37	R	3	30	99	0	0	-36	0	-8	0	8
42	33,738	4	43,174	41	R	4	35	92	1	0	-4	0	23	7	53
43	32,438	-1	33,225	30	R	2	31	98	-1	0	-91	0	-57	1	11
44	30,710	-3	37,059	41	R	4	36	98	-4	0	-60	0	-53	2	24
45	37,820	11	48,754	29	S	4	47	82	6	8	20	4	56	6	67
46	31,654	7	32,308	39	U	6	43	85	4	5	16	4	43	4	60
47	32,508	-1	36,025	36	R	3	33	93	-3	0	-30	0	-30	6	40
48	32,490	2	35,047	29	R	5	33	77	-5	0	8	1	44	21	43
49	32,867	-1	39,168	40	R	6	35	90	-3	0	-12	1	10	6	37

Note: U=urban, S=suburban, R=rural, M=mixed, HH=households.

NEVADA

Nevada, a state built on silver mining, is no stranger to boom and bust cycles. It was born on a boom, with the discovery of the Comstock Lode in 1859, and was admitted to the Union six years later with only about ten thousand inhabitants in order to provide Abraham Lincoln with votes in the Senate to pass the Thirteenth Amendment. By the end of the century, many of the mines had been played out.

It took a while for Nevada to settle on sin as an economic base. Slot machines were banned in 1901, and a quickie, six-month divorce law was repealed in 1913. Nevada lowered the wait for a divorce to three months in 1927, then reduced it to six weeks in 1931, when it also legalized gambling.

As late as the 1960s, Las Vegas was still more a tourist destination than a city. The real Las Vegas boom, and hence the Nevada boom, has come more recently, when the city started becoming a destination for young families fed up with the congestion of Southern California and for northeasterners seeking a warmer climate. During the 1980s, Nevada's population swelled by more than 50 percent and was growing at a rate of 6,000 new residents each week. That boom has continued into its second decade, for Nevada remains the nation's fastest-growing state. Its population has grown another 38 percent since 1990, more than half again as fast as the next-fastest-growing state, Arizona. Overall, it has risen from thirty-ninth in population to thirty-seventh in just seven years.

Growth continues to be centered on Las Vegas (as well as the neighboring city of Henderson), and to a much lesser extent on Reno. Take those cities away, and the state becomes Wyoming. Las Vegas is adjusting to its new size, yet it comes as a surprise to discover that it is still only the forty-ninth-largest city in the United States and has almost the same number of inhabitants as Toledo, Ohio.

The growth in Las Vegas has been to the west and south. The Fourth House District, in northwest Las Vegas, has grown by 168 percent in just seven years, the fastest rate of growth of any district in the country. (Nevada has ten of the fifty fastest-growing districts in the country.) The Twentieth District, slightly farther out into the desert, has grown by 159 percent; the Twenty-first District, southeast toward Henderson, by 124 percent; and the Thirteenth District, southwest of the city, by 103 percent. The Ninth House District, in the middle of the city, has lost 5 percent of its population as people cleared out for the suburbs, but it is the only district in the state to have shrunk at all.

Nevada does not show the extreme aggregations of wealth suggestive of a boom or of persons making their fortunes overnight. The wealthy districts are not really that wealthy, and average income figures quickly level off from both ends of the scale into a broad middle, which suggests stable and sustainable growth. Furthermore, three of the six wealthiest districts are not in Las Vegas at all, but in Reno and Carson City. Nevada is a predominantly white state. African Americans come close to a majority only in two North Las Vegas districts: the Seventh District (54 percent) and the Sixth (48 percent). Although there are almost twice as many Nevada Hispanics as blacks, they are much more dispersed. Only one district, the Twenty-eighth (52 percent), has a Hispanic majority. These three minority districts are the only ones in the state with double-digit unemployment, exceeding even the mining areas.

Given that Las Vegas and Reno account for thirty-one of the forty-two seats in the state assembly, it is surprising that the influx of huge numbers of new residents has not shaken up the state's political system more than it has. Nevada has a Democratic governor and two Democratic U.S. senators and voted for Bill Clinton twice. But it has elected Republicans to the U.S. House, and the GOP has captured both chambers of the legislature. Most of the rapidly growing areas are Republican, which may influence a number of races in the years to come.

NEVADA
State Senate Districts

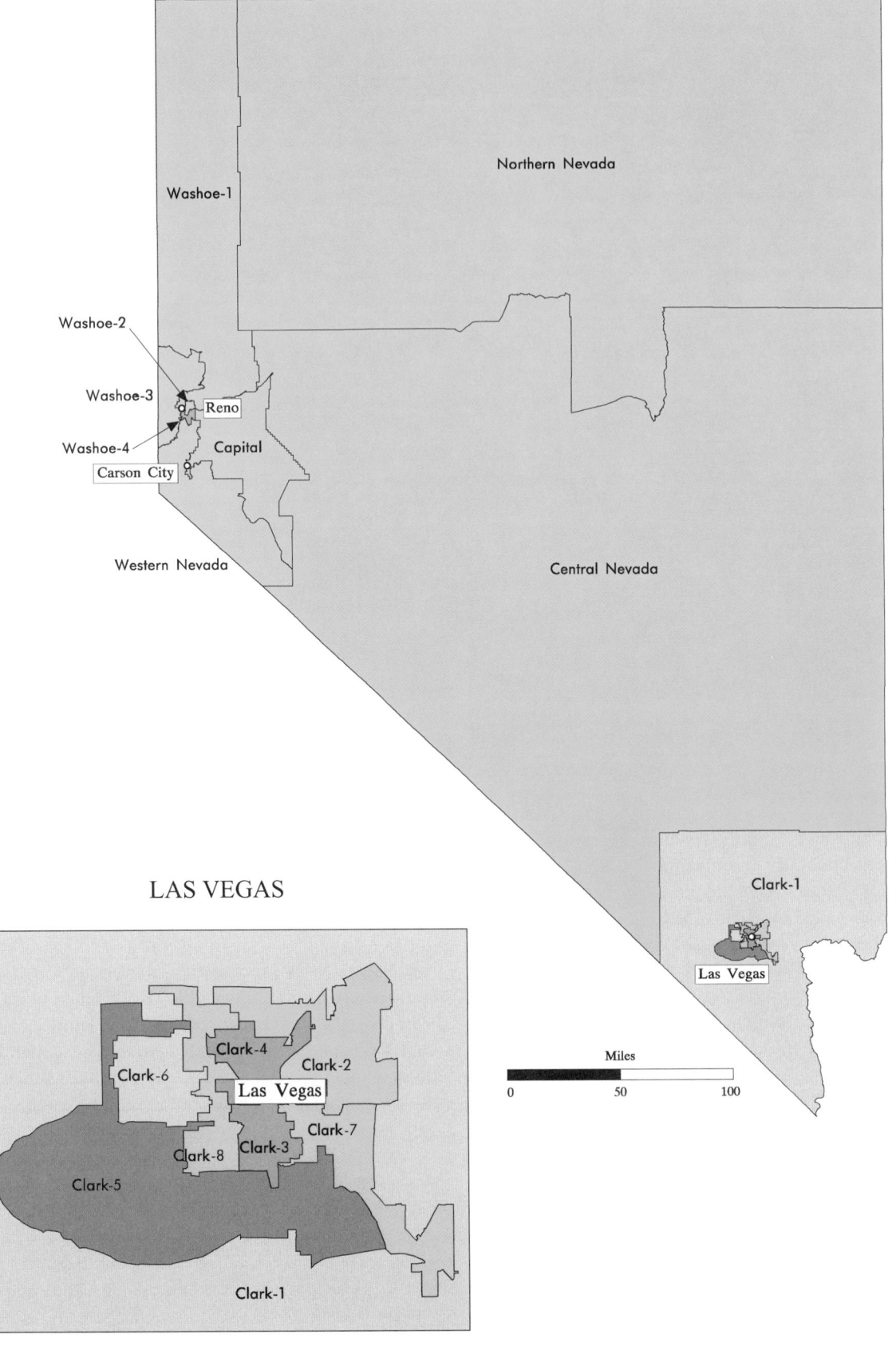

Northern Nevada

Washoe-1

Washoe-2

Washoe-3

Reno

Washoe-4

Capital

Carson City

Western Nevada

Central Nevada

Clark-1

Las Vegas

LAS VEGAS

Clark-4

Clark-6

Clark-2

Las Vegas

Clark-7

Clark-8 Clark-3

Clark-5

Clark-1

Miles

0   50   100

Population Growth   6% to 11%   20% to 31%   84%   119% to 122%

Nevada State Senate Districts: Demographic Data

Senate District	Population		Average HH Income		District Type	Unempl. Rate	College Educ.	White (non-Hispanic)		African American		Asian American		Hispanic American	
	1997	+/-	($)	+/-		(%)	(%)	(%)	+/-	(%)	+/-	(%)	+/-	(%)	+/-
Nevada	1,652,849	38	51,973	34	M	6	32	75	31	7	50	4	69	13	75
Clark-1	138,499	122	57,818	35	M	6	30	82	109	5	192	2	221	10	239
Clark-2	134,936	21	42,121	27	S	7	22	58	4	15	52	5	39	2	71
Clark-3	122,511	6	35,323	16	S	8	25	56	-12	10	39	6	33	27	51
Clark-4	62,598	9	38,115	22	U	12	18	28	-15	52	15	2	13	17	59
Clark-5	216,052	84	74,481	40	S	5	42	81	75	4	137	5	147	9	138
Clark-6	121,228	119	59,737	34	U	4	36	82	110	6	174	3	171	8	184
Clark-7	149,635	31	45,465	25	S	7	25	77	23	5	83	4	76	13	65
Clark-8	141,503	31	48,699	25	U	5	30	75	21	8	79	4	61	12	82
Washoe-1	72,199	21	45,207	33	U	5	34	73	14	4	22	6	43	14	49
Washoe-2	66,586	20	47,400	30	S	5	31	77	15	3	34	5	53	13	49
Washoe-3	73,365	24	70,528	39	U	5	46	88	22	1	37	3	59	6	48
Washoe-4	63,593	11	42,888	26	U	6	37	77	5	2	23	5	39	14	47
Northern	73,122	28	46,674	22	R	6	30	75	22	1	19	1	43	18	59
Central	72,623	25	38,920	19	R	7	25	84	22	2	21	1	48	9	56
Capital	69,567	27	42,050	26	R	5	30	85	24	1	23	1	53	10	60
Western	74,876	27	70,879	40	R	4	44	90	24	1	23	1	62	7	56

Note: U=urban, S=suburban, R=rural, M=mixed, HH=households.

NEVADA
State Assembly Districts

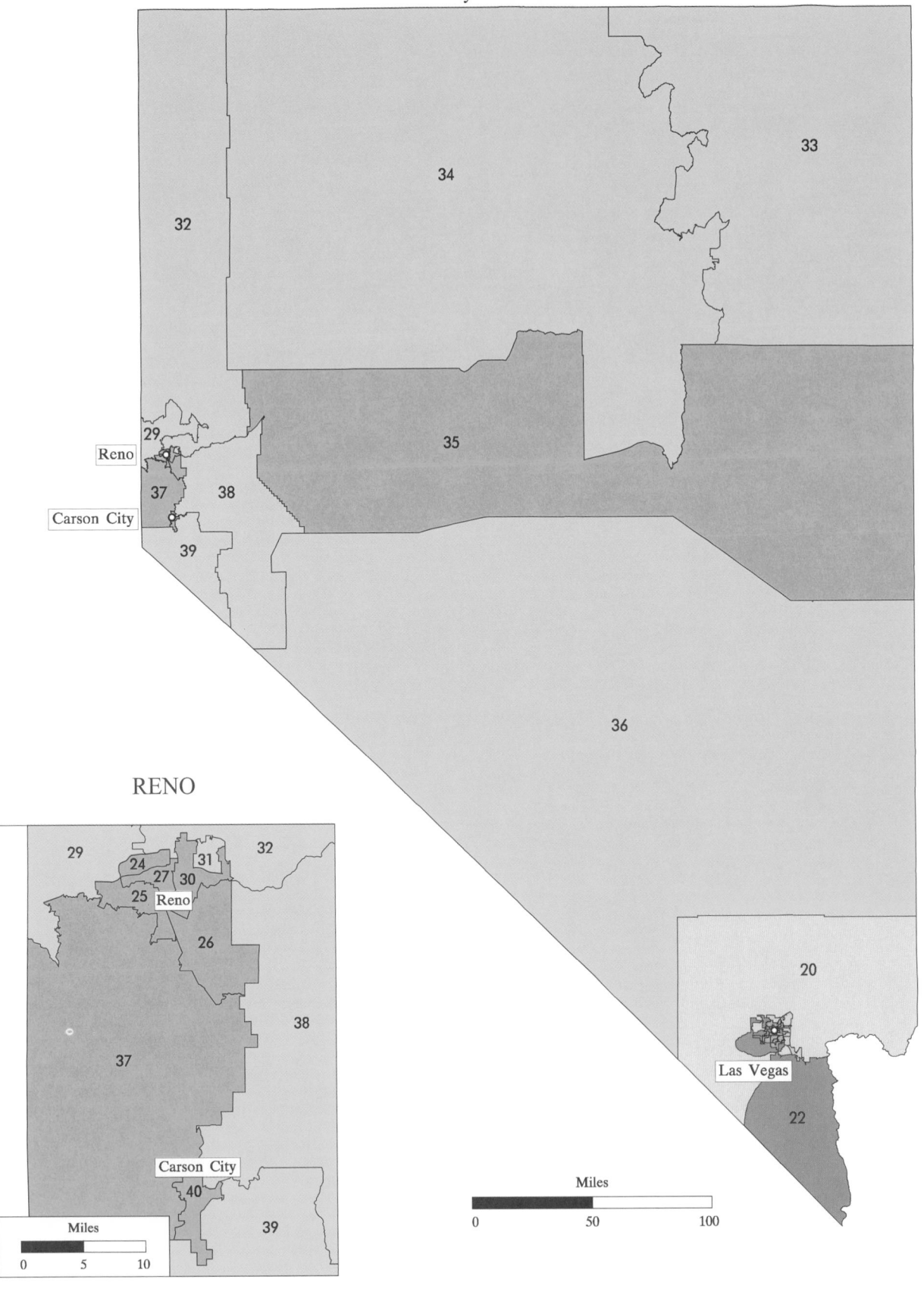

RENO

Population Growth ◼ -5% to 21%   ◻ 24% to 47%   ◼ 71% to 103%   ◻ 124% to 168%

LAS VEGAS

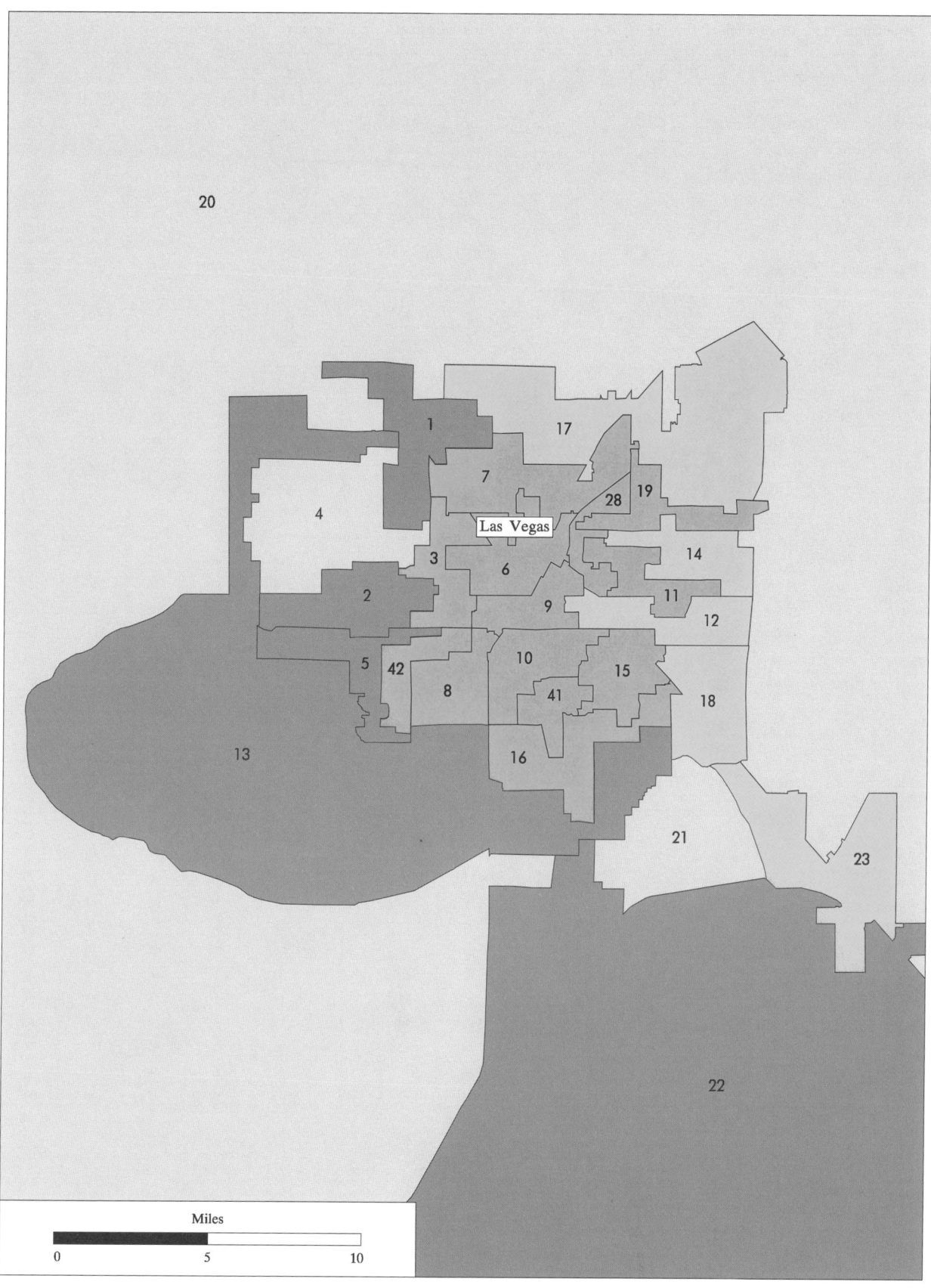

Population Growth ▢ -5% to 21%　　▢ 24% to 47%　　▢ 71% to 103%　　▢ 124% to 168%

Nevada State Assembly Districts: Demographic Data

Assembly District	Population 1997	+/-	Average HH Income ($)	+/-	District Type	Unempl. Rate (%)	College Educ. (%)	White (non-Hispanic) (%)	+/-	African American (%)	+/-	Asian American (%)	+/-	Hispanic American (%)	+/-
Nevada	1,652,849	38	51,973	34	M	6	32	75	31	7	50	4	69	13	75
1	47,737	86	56,046	32	U	5	30	80	76	8	146	2	127	9	147
2	48,029	71	64,443	36	U	5	35	82	63	5	128	3	120	9	124
3	31,906	11	42,727	13	U	5	31	76	2	8	57	3	49	12	63
4	73,196	168	56,865	34	U	4	37	82	158	6	210	3	226	8	247
5	52,231	98	84,819	47	S	6	42	81	86	4	155	6	176	8	170
6	28,538	1	40,366	22	U	11	22	32	-23	48	10	2	16	17	59
7	34,201	16	35,830	24	S	12	15	25	-5	54	18	2	10	18	58
8	34,763	21	39,898	21	S	6	29	70	7	8	62	7	57	15	81
9	25,933	-5	40,343	22	U	9	24	57	-19	8	15	6	20	28	32
10	37,663	11	36,422	18	S	7	25	65	-5	9	51	6	45	20	65
11	34,860	11	37,780	16	U	6	23	55	-8	12	42	6	38	26	56
12	41,629	47	44,366	25	S	8	25	69	31	7	111	7	98	16	100
13	72,306	103	77,161	33	S	4	43	82	93	4	169	5	165	9	170
14	34,919	27	47,561	23	S	7	26	63	11	12	65	7	56	18	77
15	31,557	5	54,620	21	S	6	35	78	-3	5	55	4	45	12	50
16	33,515	14	51,643	28	S	6	37	77	5	5	52	5	56	12	56
17	40,880	36	41,404	37	S	7	20	59	16	19	65	4	30	17	135
18	38,192	28	39,002	22	S	7	20	80	23	5	77	3	69	11	46
19	29,807	14	37,636	25	S	9	21	60	-1	16	48	3	30	19	53
20	81,441	159	60,350	30	R	5	28	79	143	6	214	2	218	12	290
21	58,041	124	75,778	34	S	4	44	84	114	3	214	4	210	8	188
22	56,911	84	57,632	36	S	6	34	87	76	2	163	2	208	8	167
23	40,205	45	49,457	41	S	6	24	82	42	3	80	1	82	11	58
24	32,257	16	46,785	34	U	5	40	68	7	5	18	9	39	17	49
25	29,317	15	74,456	36	U	5	55	88	12	1	27	3	49	6	47
26	32,591	16	45,521	26	U	4	42	82	12	2	29	4	47	11	45
27	30,596	7	30,403	19	U	7	27	69	-2	3	18	5	31	20	46
28	27,552	4	24,362	6	U	11	11	26	-40	18	29	4	7	52	46
29	43,129	32	59,615	40	M	5	38	87	29	2	38	3	65	7	55
30	34,488	17	39,136	23	S	6	28	71	9	3	29	5	44	18	51
31	32,026	24	57,161	35	S	4	35	83	20	2	43	6	63	8	45
32	37,677	28	46,682	34	M	6	28	80	24	2	36	3	57	10	51
33	35,033	33	48,531	24	R	6	33	75	25	1	8	1	56	19	70
34	38,080	24	44,952	20	R	6	28	76	19	1	31	0	24	17	50
35	34,474	20	40,967	24	R	7	28	84	17	1	13	2	49	9	50
36	38,149	30	37,125	14	R	6	22	84	28	2	26	1	45	9	62
37	37,405	20	89,350	43	M	3	53	92	18	0	33	2	56	5	37
38	39,329	35	38,356	20	R	5	27	87	32	0	12	1	55	9	70
39	39,851	31	65,003	42	R	5	38	88	28	1	17	1	64	8	66
40	31,480	18	46,039	32	R	5	34	84	15	2	25	2	51	10	50
41	23,812	11	30,237	10	S	7	32	63	-7	8	52	6	44	23	71
42	27,098	8	58,336	28	S	5	31	72	-2	6	47	6	43	15	56

Note: U=urban, S=suburban, R=rural, M=mixed, HH=households.

NEW HAMPSHIRE

New Hampshire, a most atypical state, offers in some ways a picture of the nation at both extremes in that it has one of the most rapidly growing districts in the United States and several of the fastest shrinking. This reflects the split in a state that borders both high-tech Massachusetts and low-tech Maine and shares attributes, both good and bad, with each.

First, let's say a word about New Hampshire's unusual legislature. Its upper chamber has only twenty-four members, making it the second-smallest state senate in the country. Its lower chamber has four hundred members, making it the third-largest deliberative body in the world, behind the House of Commons in London and the House of Representatives in Washington.

Members of the New Hampshire house may represent districts with as few as 1,832 people. The districts are small enough that it is possible to know a large share of voters personally, to keep one's telephone number listed, and to campaign on foot. By contrast, one member of the California house of representatives represents more than a half-million people, making TV advertising the only effective way to campaign. Such are the quirks of democracy in different corners of the United States.

This remains mostly a rural state; all of New Hampshire's urban and suburban districts are located in the southeastern corner, between the Piscataqua and Merrimack Rivers along the state's southern border, where it has attracted many expatriates from Massachusetts.

The New Hampshire that has embraced high tech is doing quite well. The New Hampshire that has been dependent on manufacturing, logging, and ship building is doing very poorly. The Third District of Belknap County, around the town of Franklin, and the Eighth District of Merrimack County, around Laconia, have grown by 49 and 46 percent, respectively, since 1990, ranking them among the fastest-growing districts in the country.

The Thirty-second District of Rockingham County, on the other hand, located just outside Portsmouth and many of whose residents work at the naval shipyard there, has lost 42 percent of its population in that period, making it the single fastest-shrinking district in the United States. Six other Portsmouth area districts are also among the bottom fifty nationwide.

The sluggish economy has left income levels stagnant. The state, and indeed New England as a whole, has been left behind in the boom of the 1990s. New Hampshire ranked ninth in average household income in 1990 and fifteenth in 1997, and its rate of income growth is the second-slowest behind distressed Maine. The wealthiest districts are those west and northwest of Manchester, reaching as far down as Nashua and over to Derry, areas in which many Massachusetts tax refugees live and home to a growing number of high-tech businesses. The poorest districts, and the slowest growing, are concentrated in central Manchester, where most of the old textile mills have closed. Here, and in several more districts in Portsmouth and the ski country along the Maine border, unemployment remains in double digits. By contrast, in districts around Hillsborough, unemployment is just 2 to 3 percent.

Racially, New Hampshire is one of the most homogeneous states. It is 97 percent white, and although some of its districts are as small as neighborhoods, none is more than 8 percent African American or Asian, and only one is more than 8 percent Hispanic.

Incongruously, considering its sluggish manufacturing economy and loss of jobs, New Hampshire is one of the younger states by population. It also has the fourth-highest percentage of college graduates (the top four are all in New England).

The legislature is controlled by Republicans and has been throughout the decade. They have lost seats in the house but still control it by more than one hundred seats. Republicans had a narrow 13–11 advantage in the senate in 1990, but it had grown to 15–9 by 1996. Democrats can still be competitive here. In 1996, the state voted for Bill Clinton (for a second time), elected a Democratic governor, and almost elected a Democratic U.S. senator. New Hampshire's governor, one of two in the country to serve a two-year term (Vermont's is the other), is officially known as "Your excellency."

NEW HAMPSHIRE
State Senate Districts

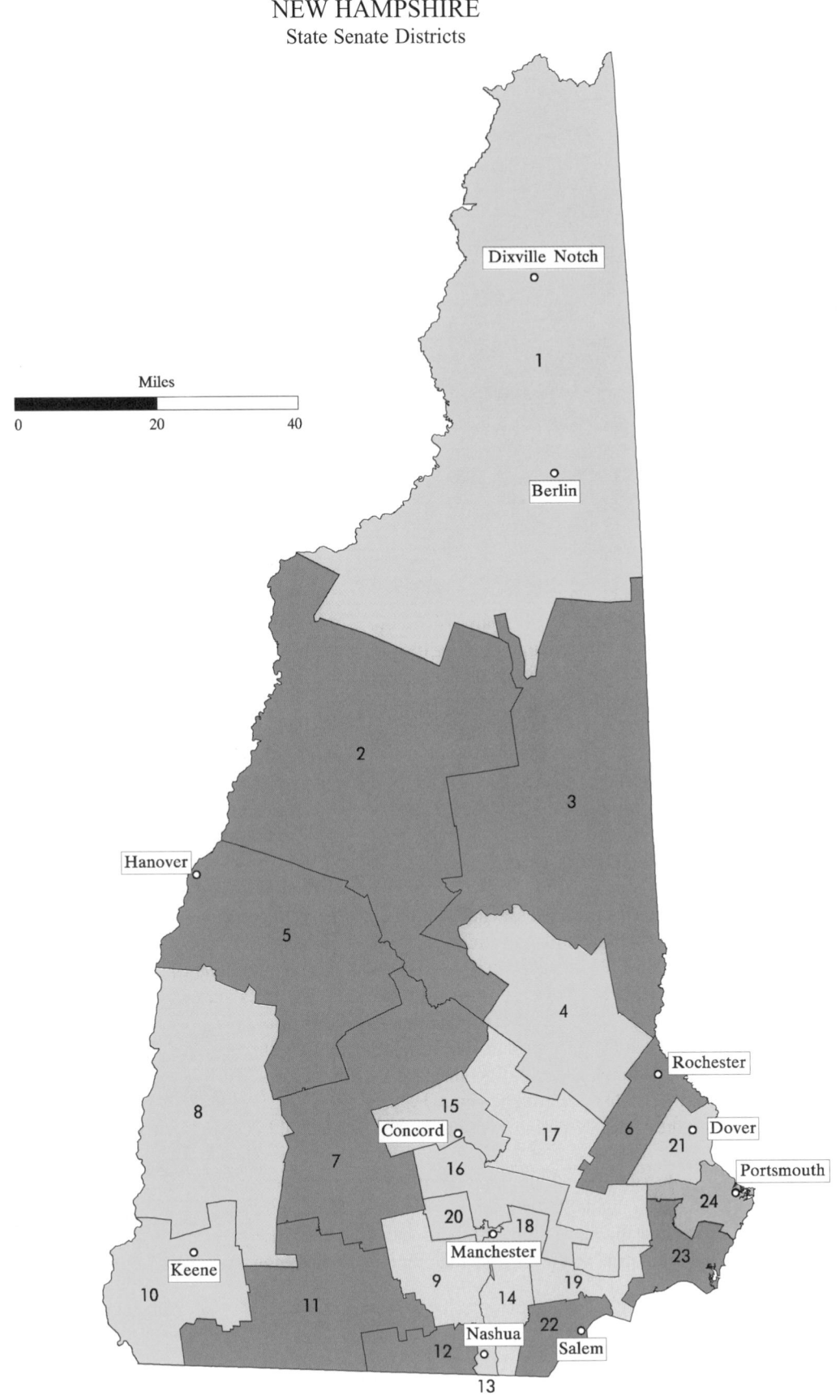

Population Growth   ▨ -11%   ▨ -3% to 4%   ▨ 6% to 11%   ▨ 13% to 17%

New Hampshire State Senate Districts: Demographic Data

Senate District	Population		Average HH Income		District Type	Unempl. Rate	College Educ.	White (non-Hispanic)		African American		Asian American		Hispanic American	
	1997	+/-	($)	+/-		(%)	(%)	(%)	+/-	(%)	+/-	(%)	+/-	(%)	+/-
New Hamp.	1,465,475	6	51,889	21	M	6	48	97	5	1	2	1	23	1	32
1	44,640	-2	36,188	19	R	8	33	99	-2	0	-35	0	1	1	20
2	48,896	6	42,269	24	R	8	42	99	6	0	-25	0	8	1	23
3	50,842	10	39,581	14	R	7	47	99	10	0	-18	0	21	0	23
4	45,362	1	43,249	15	R	7	41	99	1	0	-34	0	11	1	17
5	49,816	10	57,672	34	R	5	59	96	10	1	-11	2	9	1	34
6	50,858	8	43,404	21	U	6	37	98	8	0	1	1	30	1	41
7	48,232	6	48,224	23	R	5	45	99	6	0	-3	0	12	1	18
8	45,075	3	41,451	25	R	7	39	99	3	0	-2	0	12	1	31
9	56,470	16	77,118	16	S	5	64	97	15	1	20	1	36	1	37
10	47,003	1	44,523	24	R	5	45	98	1	0	-18	1	22	1	22
11	47,814	7	50,005	14	R	6	51	98	7	1	3	1	24	1	20
12	49,131	6	60,663	15	U	5	57	94	5	1	10	2	27	3	36
13	44,605	0	48,246	13	U	7	45	91	-2	1	3	2	22	5	37
14	52,920	17	64,945	19	S	6	55	97	17	1	28	1	42	1	51
15	49,425	4	53,036	26	R	6	53	98	4	0	4	1	19	1	36
16	50,048	4	58,124	19	U	5	54	97	4	1	9	1	27	1	16
17	53,391	16	52,168	25	R	7	39	98	15	0	24	0	32	1	43
18	44,735	0	43,560	13	U	7	36	96	-1	1	3	1	24	2	28
19	55,593	13	59,425	23	S	6	50	96	12	1	43	1	46	2	65
20	47,978	1	38,155	14	U	7	35	95	1	1	0	1	13	3	22
21	43,382	-3	51,361	24	U	6	55	96	-3	1	-7	2	17	1	22
22	54,814	11	70,187	24	S	6	51	96	10	1	32	2	40	1	50
23	48,404	9	56,922	25	S	7	49	98	8	0	34	1	39	1	43
24	41,768	-11	56,774	28	U	5	57	94	-12	3	-15	2	4	2	0

Note: U=urban, S=suburban, R=rural, M=mixed, HH=households.

NEW HAMPSHIRE
State House Districts

*Be6 is comprised of B2-5
Ca3 contains Ca1 & 2
Ca8 contains Ca6 & 7
Ca10 contains Ca9
Ch2 contains Ch1
Ch6 is comprised of Ch3-5
Ch13 is comprised of Ch10-12
Ch19 is comprised of Ch14-18
Co4 is comprised of Co2 & 3
Gr13 is comprised of Gr12 & 14
Hi3 is comprised of Hi1 & 2
Hi6 is comprised of Hi4 & 5
Hi12 is comprised of Hi9-11
Hi16 is comprised of Hi 14 & 15
Hi21 is comprised of Hi19-20
Hi25 is comprised of Hi23 & 24
Hi35 is comprised of Hi29, 31-34
Hi36 is comprised of Hi26-28 & 30
Me7 contains Me4-6
Me9 contains Me8
Me24 is comprised of Me14-23
Ro4 is comprised of Ro1-3
Ro8 is comprised of Ro5-7
Ro11 is comprised of Ro9 & 10
Ro17 is comprised of Ro14-16
Ro28 is comprised of Ro26 & 27
Ro34 is comprised of Ro30, 32, & 33
Ro36 is comprised of Ro31 & 35
St5 is comprised of St1-4
St9 is comprised of St6-8
St13 is comprised of St11 & 12
Su3 is comprised of Su1 & 2
Su7 is comprised of Su5 & 6
Su11 is comprised of Su8-10

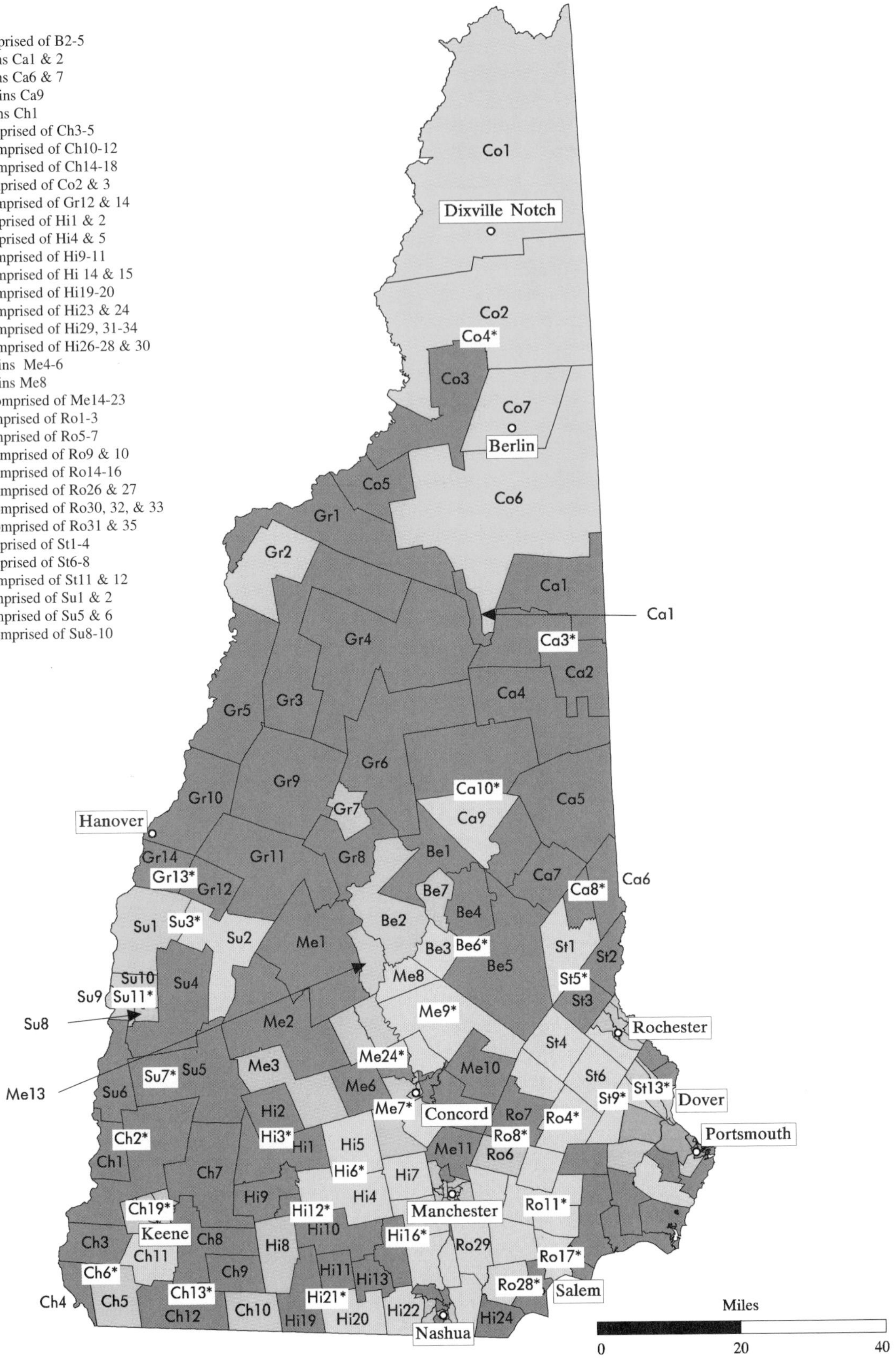

Co1

Dixville Notch

Co2

Co4*

Co3

Co7

Berlin

Co5

Gr1

Co6

Ca1

Gr2

Ca1

Ca3*

Ca2

Gr4

Ca4

Gr5   Gr3

Ca10*

Ca5

Gr6

Ca9

Gr9

Gr10

Hanover

Ca7

Ca8*   Ca6

Gr14

Gr11   Gr8   Be1

Gr13*   Gr12

Be7

Be4

St1

St2

Su1   Su3*

Su2   Me1

Be2

Be3 Be6*

Be5

St5*

St3

Su10

Su4

Me8

Me9*

St4

Rochester

Su9   Su11*

Su8

Me2

Me24*

Me10

St6

St9*   St13*   Dover

Me13

Su7*   Su5

Su6

Me3

Me6

Me7*

Concord

Ro7

Ro4*

Portsmouth

Hi2

Hi3*

Hi1   Hi5

Me11

Ro8*

Ro6

Ch2*

Ch1

Ch7

Hi9

Hi6*

Hi7

Hi4

Manchester

Ro11*

Ch19*

Keene   Ch8

Hi12*

Hi10

Hi16*

Ro29

Ro17*

Ch6*

Ch3

Ch11

Ch9

Hi8

Hi11 Hi13

Ro28*

Salem

Ch4   Ch5

Ch13*

Ch12   Ch10

Hi21*

Hi19   Hi20

Hi22

Hi24

Nashua

Miles

0   20   40

Population Growth   ▢ -42% to -17%   ▢ -14% to 1%   ▢ 2% to 13%   ▢ 14% to 49%

CONCORD/MANCHESTER

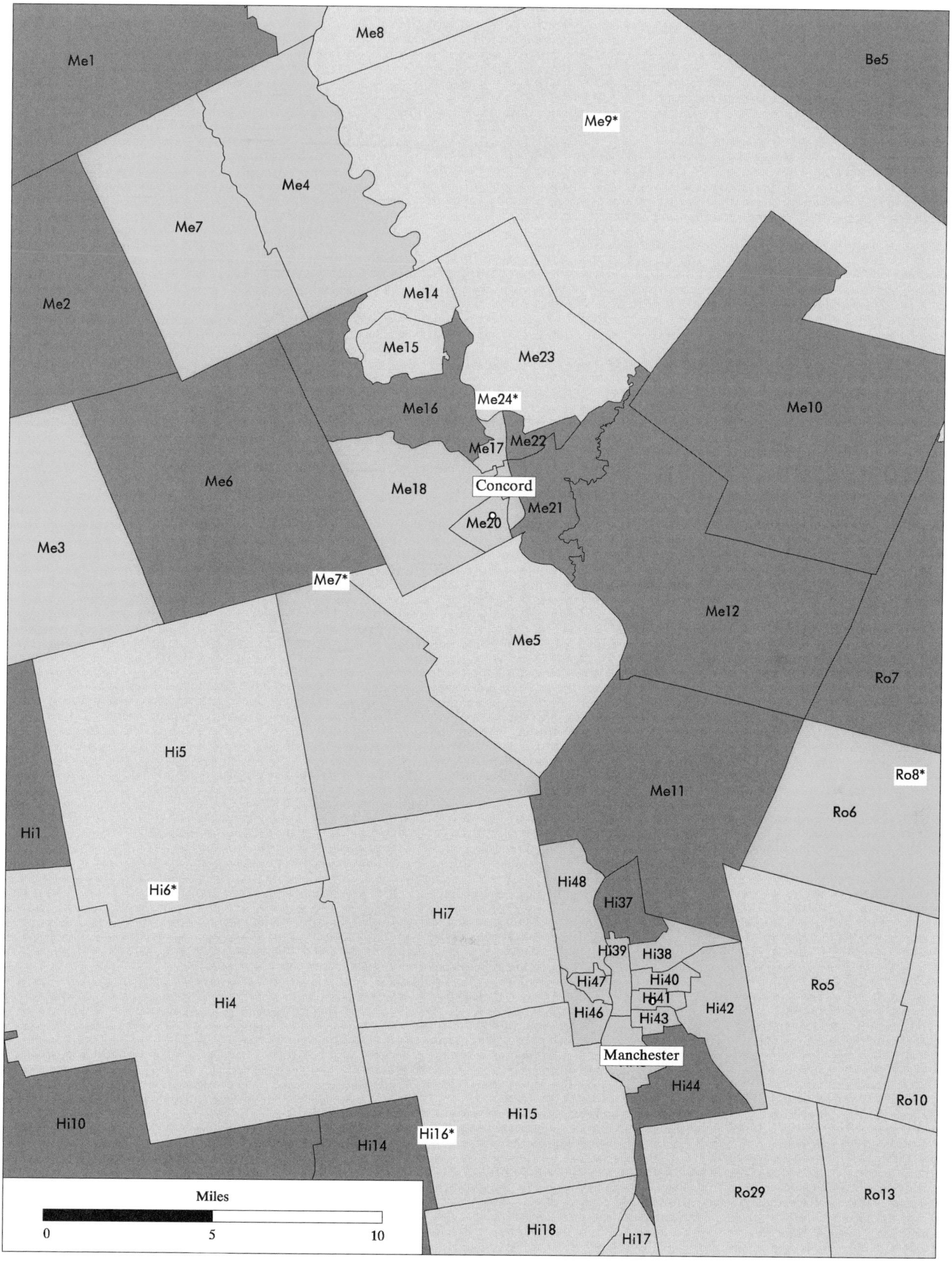

Me8

Me1

Be5

Me9*

Me4

Me7

Me2

Me14

Me15

Me23

Me6

Me16

Me24*

Me10

Me17 Me22

Me3

Me18 Concord

Me20 Me21

Me7*

Me12

Me5

Ro7

Ro8*

Hi5

Ro6

Hi1

Me11

Hi6*

Hi48

Hi37

Hi7

Hi39 Hi38

Hi4

Hi47 Hi40

Ro5

Hi41

Hi46 Hi42

Hi43

Manchester

Hi44

Hi10

Hi15

Ro10

Hi16*

Hi14

Ro29 Ro13

Hi18 Hi17

Miles

0   5   10

Population Growth   ☐ -14% to 1%   ■ 2% to 13%   ☐ 14% to 49%

PORTSMOUTH/ROCHESTER

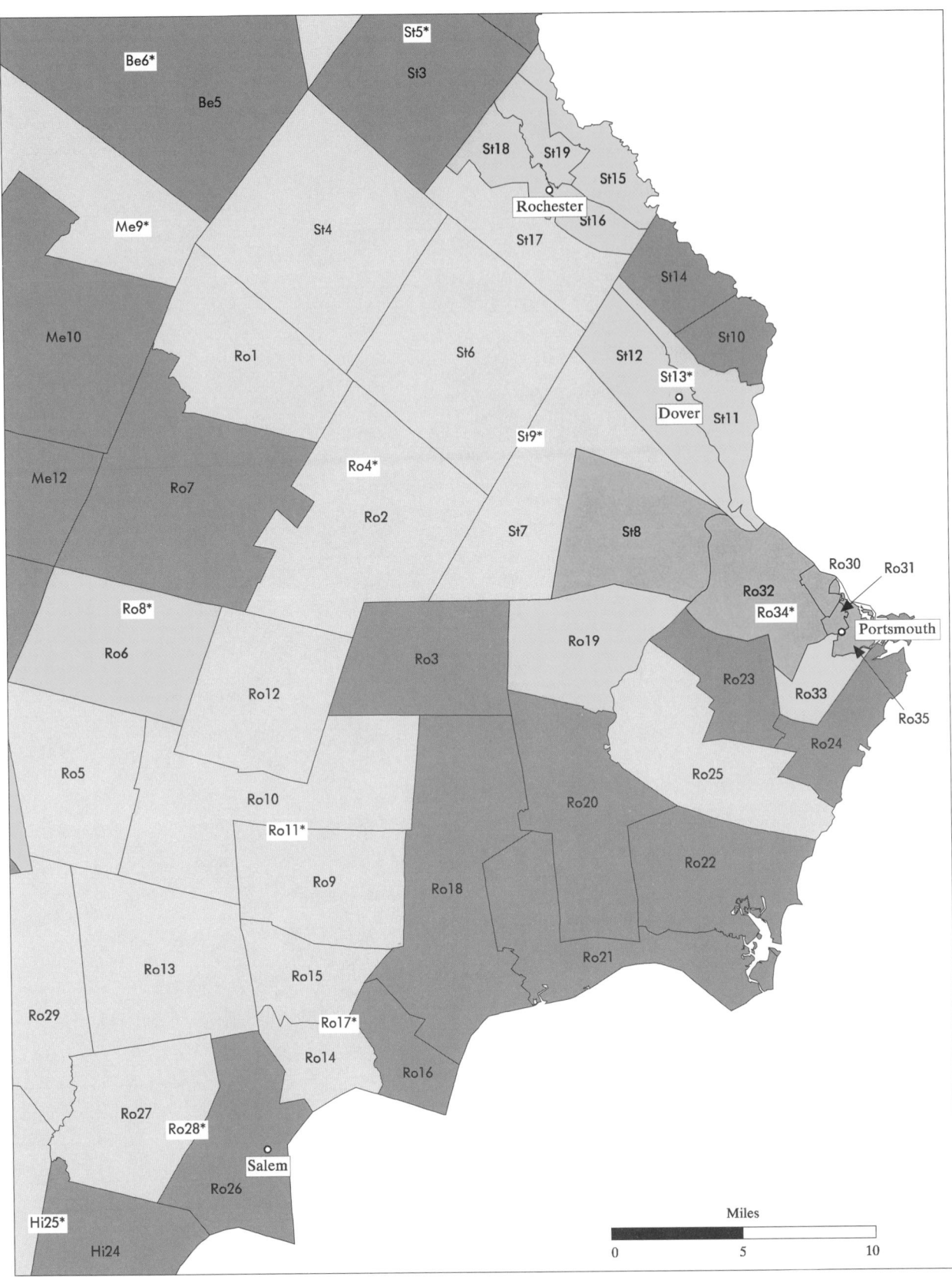

Population Growth

-42% to -17%   -14% to 1%   2% to 13%   14% to 49%

Miles

0   5   10

KEENE

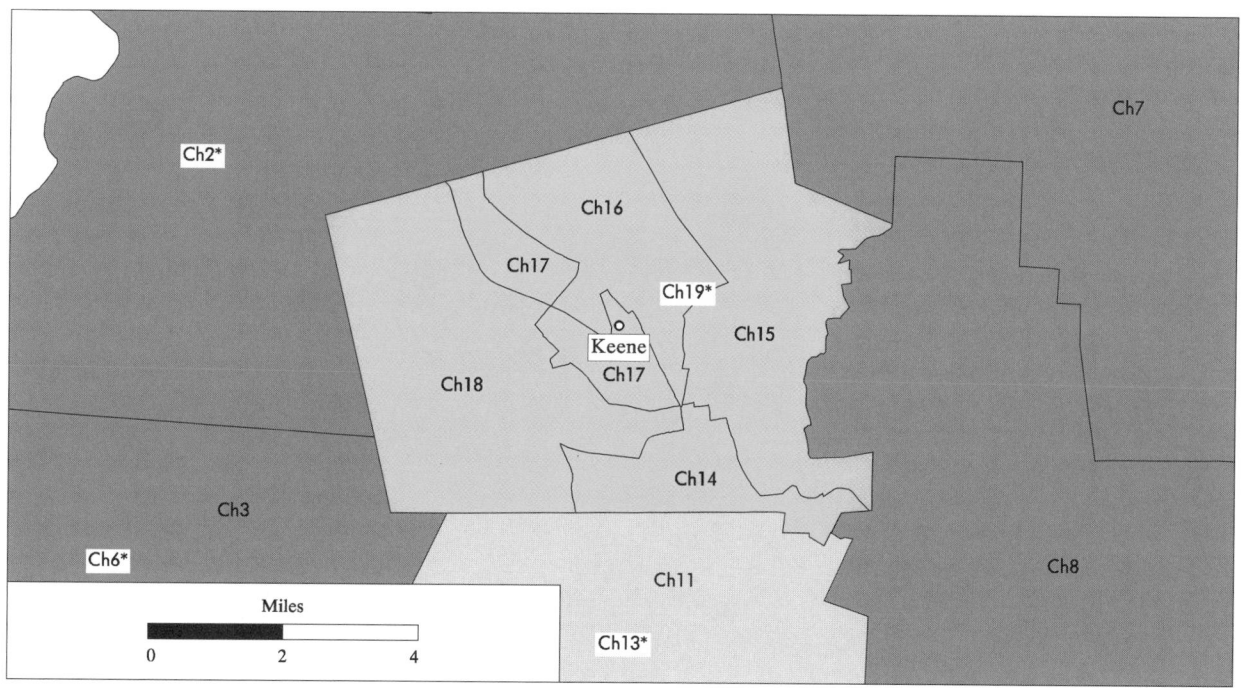

NASHUA

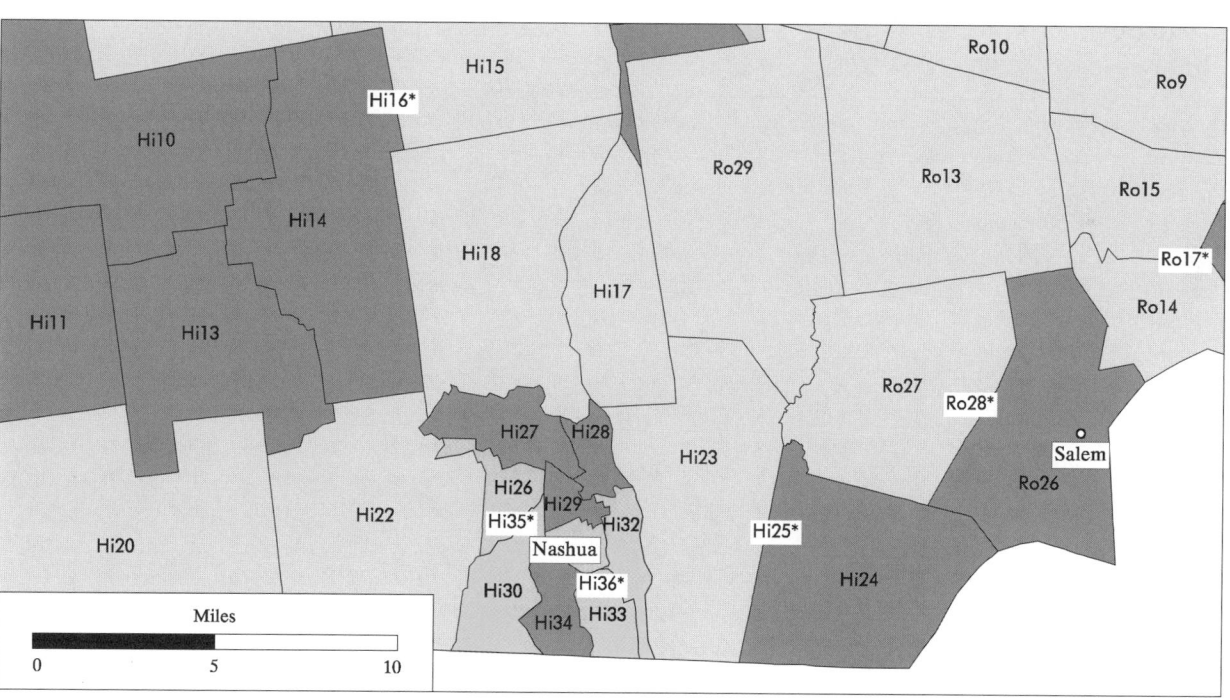

Population Growth   ☐ -14% to 1%   ☐ 2% to 13%   ☐ 14% to 49%

New Hampshire State House Districts: Demographic Data

House District	Population		Average HH Income		District Type	Unempl. Rate	College Educ.	White (non-Hispanic)		African American		Asian American		Hispanic American	
	1997	+/-	($)	+/-		(%)	(%)	(%)	+/-	(%)	+/-	(%)	+/-	(%)	+/-
New Hamp.	1,465,475	6	51,889	21	M	6	48	97	5	1	2	1	23	1	32
Be1	6,571	9	39,939	14	R	5	50	99	9	0	-17	0	33	0	-14
Be2	6,317	-9	41,005	15	R	6	40	99	-10	0	0	0	-5	0	15
Be3	8,672	49	40,462	12	R	8	37	98	49	0	30	0	78	1	142
Be4	6,015	3	45,401	8	R	7	54	99	2	0	-50	1	35	1	31
Be5	9,993	11	42,767	12	R	7	49	99	11	0	0	0	29	0	13
Be6*	30,997	12	42,313	12	R	7	45	99	12	0	6	0	32	1	44
Be7	14,233	-9	42,950	16	R	8	37	98	-9	0	-32	1	7	1	7
Ca1	1,832	8	42,979	10	R	6	51	99	8	0	0	0	33	1	43
Ca2	7,906	5	39,029	15	R	6	48	98	5	0	-22	1	20	0	13
Ca3*	12,061	8	39,829	15	R	7	50	99	8	0	-17	1	22	0	30
Ca4	2,866	10	39,887	14	R	7	53	99	10	0	0	0	-50	0	30
Ca5	5,380	4	35,960	11	R	12	37	99	4	0	-24	0	-9	0	-23
Ca6	3,182	9	39,225	10	R	7	36	99	9	0	-27	0	30	0	67
Ca7	5,221	9	38,086	11	R	2	54	99	8	0	0	0	-33	1	64
Ca8*	9,166	9	38,941	11	R	4	49	99	9	0	-23	0	6	1	64
Ca9	3,591	21	38,253	14	R	8	51	99	22	0	0	0	40	0	-17
Ca10*	9,110	14	40,079	13	R	7	51	99	14	0	-10	0	33	0	10
Ch1	3,380	5	42,928	17	R	7	59	99	5	0	0	0	38	0	-20
Ch2*	9,291	8	46,273	24	R	5	51	99	8	0	-9	0	38	0	20
Ch3	3,244	4	51,320	27	R	3	52	98	4	0	0	0	18	1	62
Ch4	4,058	3	35,630	20	R	3	27	98	3	0	-13	1	25	0	67
Ch5	3,774	-7	36,356	20	R	6	27	98	-7	0	-38	1	11	0	13
Ch6*	11,074	0	40,491	23	R	4	36	98	0	0	-23	1	18	1	47
Ch7	2,885	6	51,364	31	R	6	49	99	6	0	-33	0	20	0	0
Ch8	6,279	7	47,175	26	R	4	47	99	7	0	-30	0	33	0	-21
Ch9	5,445	2	44,628	21	R	6	41	98	1	0	-7	1	31	1	52
Ch10	5,005	1	46,642	9	R	6	48	97	1	1	-15	1	12	1	27
Ch11	7,179	15	45,448	22	R	5	40	99	15	0	0	0	33	0	75
Ch12	3,032	5	48,552	23	R	4	49	99	5	0	-11	0	-50	0	25
Ch13*	15,216	8	46,419	18	R	5	44	99	8	0	-13	0	15	1	39
Ch14	3,596	-9	41,801	21	R	6	49	98	-10	0	-27	1	24	1	11
Ch15	4,746	-2	45,340	26	R	6	47	98	-2	0	-19	1	22	1	13
Ch16	3,961	-2	43,315	24	R	6	53	98	-2	0	-6	1	22	1	0
Ch17	4,063	-3	45,780	25	R	5	53	99	-3	0	-14	0	21	0	-6
Ch18	5,105	-4	51,584	26	R	9	57	98	-4	0	-11	1	25	1	19
Ch19*	21,504	-4	46,074	25	R	6	52	98	-4	0	-16	1	23	1	11
Co1	5,453	-1	32,388	14	R	8	27	99	-1	0	-50	0	-8	1	29
Co2	4,095	-1	32,658	11	R	7	25	99	-1	0	-25	0	-17	0	0
Co3	3,876	2	38,634	19	R	8	47	99	1	0	-100	0	0	1	38
Co4*	7,972	0	35,538	15	R	8	37	99	0	0	-50	0	-6	0	21
Co5	2,861	5	33,296	15	R	10	35	99	5	0	-100	0	11	0	27
Co6	6,116	0	37,856	16	R	9	35	99	0	0	0	1	6	0	12
Co7	10,957	-12	32,696	13	R	8	24	99	-12	0	-40	1	-2	1	-2
Gr1	8,942	7	39,884	30	R	8	39	98	7	0	-21	0	2	1	33
Gr2	3,053	-1	40,353	34	R	6	35	100	-1	0	-100	0	-100	0	29
Gr3	3,042	2	49,549	31	R	7	49	98	2	0	-50	0	0	1	32
Gr4	2,868	2	40,125	30	R	10	39	99	2	0	-20	0	0	0	-19
Gr5	5,912	2	40,935	30	R	6	39	99	2	0	-25	0	0	1	3
Gr6	5,904	4	47,598	29	R	8	52	99	4	0	-67	0	0	0	13
Gr7	5,839	1	37,203	29	R	10	46	98	1	0	-26	1	9	1	14

Note: U=urban, S=suburban, R=rural, M=mixed, HH=households.

New Hampshire State House Districts: Demographic Data (cont.)

House District	Population 1997	+/-	Average HH Income ($)	+/-	District Type	Unempl. Rate (%)	College Educ. (%)	White (non-Hispanic) (%)	+/-	African American (%)	+/-	Asian American (%)	+/-	Hispanic American (%)	+/-
New Hamp.	1,465,475	6	51,889	21	M	6	48	97	5	1	2	1	23	1	32
Gr8	5,773	2	40,697	32	R	7	41	99	2	0	-31	0	-12	0	18
Gr9	2,657	5	42,372	30	R	7	39	99	5	0	-25	0	-50	0	11
Gr10	11,542	8	82,454	35	R	6	85	91	8	2	-11	4	10	2	32
Gr11	6,048	12	43,070	27	R	6	41	99	12	0	0	0	-27	1	16
Gr12	4,424	11	46,959	30	R	6	42	99	11	0	-50	0	-6	1	55
Gr13	17,151	6	46,741	32	R	4	48	97	6	0	-23	1	7	1	37
Gr14	12,72	4	46,669	33	R	3	51	97	4	0	-22	2	8	1	33
Hi	4,828	9	45,528	14	R	8	41	99	9	0	0	0	24	0	-8
Hi	4,360	3	38,365	9	R	2	45	98	3	0	-57	1	19	1	33
Hi3	9,188	6	42,073	12	R	5	43	98	6	0	-29	1	21	1	18
Hi4	5,230	18	63,082	16	R	7	56	99	18	0	18	0	-20	0	14
Hi5	7,375	19	52,995	17	R	5	49	99	19	0	-8	0	40	1	61
Hi6	12,605	19	57,138	16	R	6	53	99	19	0	4	0	20	0	45
Hi7	17,790	22	49,478	11	S	6	44	98	21	0	23	0	37	1	59
Hi8	5,884	1	52,865	10	R	5	62	98	1	0	-27	1	17	0	-21
Hi9	3,162	11	46,749	9	R	4	51	98	11	0	0	0	30	1	32
Hi10	5,030	9	59,424	16	R	6	55	99	9	0	-5	0	19	0	31
Hi11	3,406	9	51,514	10	S	8	53	98	9	0	-10	1	17	0	-20
Hi12	11,599	10	53,187	12	R	6	53	98	10	0	-6	1	20	0	25
Hi13	13,291	13	48,741	12	S	6	48	98	12	1	23	1	32	1	37
Hi14	9,835	8	90,367	16	S	5	73	98	8	0	-8	1	18	1	32
Hi15	15,223	21	95,694	18	S	4	66	98	21	0	13	1	47	1	22
Hi16	25,092	16	93,490	18	S	4	69	98	16	0	2	1	37	1	27
Hi17	7,500	36	59,278	12	S	6	54	98	36	1	43	1	55	1	65
Hi18	25,532	15	64,584	14	S	5	60	96	15	1	25	1	36	1	44
Hi19	5,372	9	51,125	13	R	5	43	99	9	0	14	0	33	0	-35
Hi20	6,819	16	57,004	17	R	5	48	98	16	0	17	0	33	1	42
Hi21	12,191	13	54,638	16	R	5	46	99	13	0	16	0	33	1	17
Hi22	6,667	18	90,257	19	S	5	63	97	17	0	16	2	46	1	50
Hi23	22,579	16	59,368	14	S	7	51	97	15	1	23	1	40	1	52
Hi24	10,334	10	67,088	16	S	6	44	97	10	0	12	1	26	1	37
Hi25	32,913	14	61,641	15	S	6	49	97	13	0	20	1	36	1	48
Hi26	9,115	0	63,299	11	U	4	62	94	0	1	10	3	22	2	15
Hi27	9,681	8	53,103	11	U	4	64	90	5	2	14	3	31	4	46
Hi28	9,129	2	51,740	11	U	9	47	91	0	2	9	1	22	6	38
Hi29	8,733	4	30,676	10	U	12	22	85	-1	2	9	1	19	11	50
Hi30	7,717	-1	58,909	20	U	4	55	94	-2	1	6	2	21	2	27
Hi31	8,456	-4	41,562	9	U	5	35	95	-5	1	1	1	13	2	27
Hi32	10,724	-4	42,153	9	U	7	41	92	-5	1	-2	2	15	4	32
Hi33	7,196	-1	59,133	13	U	6	62	89	-3	2	0	5	23	3	31
Hi34	9,799	4	72,327	20	U	4	63	94	3	1	9	3	30	2	8
Hi35	35,643	2	56,485	13	U	5	57	92	1	2	9	2	25	4	36
Hi36	44,605	0	48,246	13	U	7	45	91	-2	1	3	2	22	5	37
Hi37	9,415	5	71,545	7	U	5	64	96	4	0	2	2	26	1	30
Hi38	8,322	-1	46,202	12	U	5	53	95	-2	1	8	1	32	2	22
Hi39	7,393	-10	28,316	14	U	12	35	88	-12	2	-4	2	10	8	19
Hi40	8,068	-7	34,609	9	U	9	33	95	-8	2	-2	1	3	3	17
Hi41	7,564	-11	31,001	7	U	13	22	93	-12	1	-8	1	0	5	25
Hi42	8,470	1	49,454	14	U	5	40	97	1	1	12	1	31	2	36
Hi43	6,966	-7	37,043	8	U	7	33	96	-7	1	4	1	3	3	26

Note: U=urban, S=suburban, R=rural, M=mixed, HH=households.

New Hampshire State House Districts: Demographic Data (cont.)

House District	Population 1997	+/-	Average HH Income ($)	+/-	District Type	Unempl. Rate (%)	College Educ. (%)	White (non-Hispanic) (%)	+/-	African American (%)	+/-	Asian American (%)	+/-	Hispanic American (%)	+/-
New Hamp.	1,465,475	6	51,889	21	M	6	48	97	5	1	2	1	23	1	32
Hi44	9,184	9	47,443	10	U	6	43	96	8	1	22	2	39	2	30
Hi45	7,575	-3	40,019	10	U	7	32	96	-4	1	-4	1	14	3	31
Hi46	7,730	-7	37,685	9	U	5	29	95	-8	1	0	1	10	2	21
Hi47	7,136	-8	32,241	10	U	7	24	96	-8	1	-2	1	5	2	7
Hi48	8,235	-2	37,842	8	U	5	46	95	-2	1	9	2	23	2	-1
Me1	5,957	7	48,759	28	R	6	46	98	7	0	0	0	5	1	34
Me2	8,956	9	73,678	37	R	4	61	99	9	0	14	0	11	0	0
Me3	5,502	-1	52,365	24	R	4	59	98	-1	0	-5	0	-5	1	28
Me4	3,347	-7	40,824	23	R	5	31	98	-7	0	-8	0	7	1	10
Me5	6,669	21	76,431	29	R	4	64	99	21	0	11	1	35	0	29
Me6	5,243	9	85,557	32	R	5	72	99	9	0	20	0	27	0	-10
Me7	17,757	4	70,500	33	R	5	60	99	4	0	0	0	20	0	5
Me8	6,183	46	46,140	29	R	5	41	99	46	0	46	0	63	0	31
Me9	16,617	21	48,869	26	R	5	40	99	21	0	15	0	8	0	27
Me10	5,865	6	53,225	29	R	8	45	99	6	0	-29	0	7	1	74
Me11	9,366	7	67,210	33	S	7	45	98	7	1	9	1	26	1	38
Me12	11,617	3	50,742	29	R	6	41	98	3	0	2	0	8	1	13
Me13	7,143	-14	39,651	24	R	8	31	98	-14	0	-20	0	0	1	0
Me14	3,275	20	49,385	28	R	5	47	98	20	0	25	0	30	1	75
Me15	2,357	15	49,170	29	R	7	48	96	14	1	13	1	21	2	67
Me16	6,618	6	48,865	24	R	5	48	96	6	1	0	1	31	2	52
Me17	3,290	-9	43,577	24	R	7	52	96	-10	0	-14	1	8	2	48
Me18	4,056	-2	81,660	28	R	5	61	97	-3	1	10	1	13	1	42
Me19	2,648	-10	35,719	20	R	10	37	97	-10	0	-11	1	0	1	12
Me20	3,460	-4	47,879	16	R	5	58	99	-4	0	0	1	21	0	-6
Me21	4,061	3	37,712	22	R	8	45	98	3	0	6	1	30	1	-8
Me22	2,785	4	38,655	21	R	8	46	97	4	1	-4	1	27	1	5
Me23	4,740	15	51,602	21	R	4	61	97	14	1	13	1	27	1	53
Me24	37,254	3	48,537	23	R	6	51	97	3	1	3	1	20	1	38
Ro1	3,631	16	41,751	21	R	9	44	97	15	0	13	1	50	1	68
Ro2	3,640	24	56,405	27	R	5	49	98	24	0	56	1	55	0	21
Ro3	5,521	7	46,401	20	R	6	36	98	7	0	0	0	-12	1	32
Ro4	12,792	14	47,845	23	R	7	42	98	14	0	21	1	35	1	40
Ro5	4,700	15	68,257	25	S	4	45	98	15	0	27	1	43	0	12
Ro6	3,516	-1	60,124	23	S	8	49	99	-1	0	17	0	0	1	12
Ro7	3,506	12	61,877	27	R	5	52	99	12	0	29	0	40	0	55
Ro8	11,722	9	63,881	25	S	5	48	99	9	0	23	0	35	0	22
Ro9	8,470	28	58,724	22	S	5	45	99	28	0	53	0	62	0	4
Ro10	6,490	23	57,169	23	R	5	45	98	23	0	44	1	43	1	74
Ro11	14,960	26	58,057	23	S	5	45	99	26	0	48	0	49	1	46
Ro12	10,006	15	50,446	27	R	9	33	99	15	0	44	0	43	1	33
Ro13	33,641	15	56,945	22	S	5	50	96	13	1	47	1	45	2	68
Ro14	6,030	18	79,736	28	S	5	60	98	17	0	13	1	49	0	0
Ro15	8,034	18	64,213	24	S	6	58	97	17	0	25	1	58	1	72
Ro16	7,986	9	58,124	24	S	6	42	97	8	0	30	1	46	1	60
Ro17	22,048	15	66,227	26	S	6	53	98	14	0	24	1	52	1	60
Ro18	13,115	13	64,871	26	S	6	42	98	12	1	31	0	42	1	64
Ro19	7,917	-2	47,707	25	S	5	55	94	-3	1	27	4	27	1	40
Ro20	14,664	4	57,496	25	S	6	54	98	4	0	31	1	34	0	8
Ro21	9,312	8	44,744	19	S	7	30	98	8	0	35	1	36	1	54

Note: U=urban, S=suburban, R=rural, M=mixed, HH=households.

New Hampshire State House Districts: Demographic Data (cont.)

House District	Population		Average HH Income		District Type	Unempl. Rate	College Educ.	White (non-Hispanic)		African American		Asian American		Hispanic American	
	1997	+/-	($)	+/-		(%)	(%)	(%)	+/-	(%)	+/-	(%)	+/-	(%)	+/-
New Hamp.	1,465,475	6	51,889	21	M	6	48	97	5	1	2	1	23	1	32
Ro22	15,361	11	58,056	25	S	8	54	98	11	0	41	1	53	1	47
Ro23	2,964	12	66,615	27	S	6	63	96	10	0	18	1	26	2	94
Ro24	5,666	6	84,202	27	S	4	65	99	6	0	30	0	35	0	-18
Ro25	10,132	18	80,560	30	S	5	61	98	17	0	43	1	52	1	56
Ro26	27,810	8	61,490	23	S	6	45	95	7	1	35	2	39	2	54
Ro27	10,626	18	93,531	28	S	6	65	97	17	1	45	1	54	1	56
Ro28	38,436	11	69,430	25	S	6	51	95	9	1	36	2	41	2	54
Ro29	22,841	14	72,665	25	S	5	58	97	13	0	28	1	42	1	46
Ro30	1,91	-31	41,823	21	U	10	46	90	-32	7	-17	1	-29	1	-29
Ro31	3,70	-20	41,129	15	U	7	51	95	-20	3	5	1	-5	2	-7
Ro32	4,852	-42	43,471	27	U	7	41	85	-43	8	-38	2	-40	4	-31
Ro33	5,917	-5	46,523	12	U	4	54	92	-7	4	21	3	19	2	21
Ro34	12,671	-27	44,764	20	U	6	48	89	-28	6	-23	2	-17	3	-21
Ro35	4,054	-18	50,360	20	U	4	61	94	-19	3	6	1	2	2	23
Ro36	7,756	-19	45,837	18	U	6	56	94	-20	3	6	1	0	2	8
St1	4,004	27	43,283	21	R	7	32	99	27	0	0	0	57	0	12
St2	4,014	9	42,423	24	S	7	31	99	9	0	0	1	24	0	43
St3	5,933	3	42,169	22	S	11	21	98	3	0	-100	0	0	1	5
St4	3,405	15	47,466	17	R	5	54	99	15	0	0	0	25	1	62
St5	17,354	12	43,486	21	S	8	33	99	12	0	-53	0	21	1	19
St6	7,341	19	47,431	21	S	5	49	98	19	0	6	0	14	1	83
St7	6,022	17	60,548	24	S	6	65	97	17	0	5	2	47	1	64
St8	9,770	-17	72,993	33	S	7	80	96	-18	1	-22	2	-3	1	5
St9	23,133	0	58,572	23	S	6	65	97	0	0	-13	1	9	1	39
St10	2,841	7	57,593	26	S	7	38	98	7	0	0	1	23	1	-5
St11	12,038	-4	45,707	24	U	5	47	96	-4	1	-7	2	26	2	28
St12	12,668	1	44,670	22	U	7	47	96	1	1	-1	1	29	1	17
St13	24,743	-1	45,175	23	U	6	47	96	-2	1	-3	1	27	1	24
St14	12,210	9	41,913	20	S	5	34	97	8	1	-1	1	37	1	25
St15	6,072	-2	45,914	17	U	5	34	98	-2	0	-13	1	16	1	51
St16	5,341	1	44,982	24	U	7	45	98	0	0	-11	1	22	1	22
St17	6,874	21	42,322	20	U	6	35	97	20	0	11	1	36	1	76
St18	4,897	-2	35,758	16	U	10	27	98	-2	0	-4	0	30	1	10
St19	4,470	0	37,063	26	U	7	24	98	0	0	-7	1	14	0	0
Su1	3,745	1	54,204	29	R	3	58	99	1	0	0	0	23	0	-18
Su2	5,531	23	53,543	28	R	4	54	99	23	0	25	0	9	1	85
Su3	9,276	13	53,796	28	R	4	55	99	13	0	10	0	17	0	48
Su4	8,635	6	40,828	27	R	9	32	99	5	0	13	0	21	0	61
Su5	3,524	12	41,226	25	R	10	40	99	11	0	0	0	0	1	71
Su6	5,489	7	46,648	30	R	5	40	99	6	0	-11	0	-88	1	42
Su7	9,014	9	44,627	28	R	7	40	99	8	0	-11	0	-64	1	56
Su8	3,860	-5	30,528	20	R	7	30	98	-5	0	-8	1	15	1	4
Su9	4,683	-5	40,213	22	R	3	37	97	-5	0	0	1	18	1	23
Su10	4,663	-5	31,762	19	R	12	22	98	-5	0	7	1	26	0	24
Su11	13,205	-5	34,303	21	R	7	30	98	-5	0	0	1	19	1	17

Note: U=urban, S=suburban, R=rural, M=mixed, HH=households.

NEW JERSEY

Benjamin Franklin's description of New Jersey as "a vale of humility between two mountains of conceit" is often invoked by New Jerseyites, but rather defensively. To New Yorkers or Philadelphians, the state can seem like one vast expanse of exit signs along the Turnpike or Garden State Parkway. On weekday mornings, the Lincoln Tunnel is jammed with commuters trying to get into Manhattan, just as the Walt Whitman Bridge is likely to be backed up with people from the Gloucester County subdivisions crossing the Delaware River into Philadelphia.

As essayist and literary critic Edmund Wilson wrote in the 1920s, "Almost every characteristic phase of New Jersey takes its function from the nearness of the cities." The dividing line is roughly at Trenton; north, people get New York TV and read the New York papers; south, they receive Philadelphia TV and the *Inquirer*. Newark, the state's largest city (though part of a mighty manufacturing and transportation strip running from Elizabeth to Paramus), is about the same size as St. Paul, Minnesota, and as thoroughly overshadowed by its cross-river neighbor.

With the exception of the Pine Barrens in the middle and the rural areas along the upper Delaware, New Jersey is essentially a suburban state; the suburbs run in one long "S" from the George Washington Bridge to Atlantic City. As those suburban areas have grown more established, they have developed their own identities. New Jersey now roots for particularly New Jersey sports teams as well as those from New York and Philadelphia. It has also developed an independent pride at being a safer, less hectic place to live.

This suburban agglomeration has made New Jersey the ninth-most-populous state and given it a steady, if unremarkable, rate of growth: 5 percent in the 1980s, 4 percent in the 1990s. Few places are expanding or shrinking very quickly. Four state house districts around Monmouth County in the north, Somerset County in the middle, and Gloucester County in the south are the only ones that have grown by even 10 percent since 1990. Likewise, Newark and Camden are the only places to have lost much.

The development of the metropolitan doughnut—the phenomenon seen in Chicago, St. Louis, and elsewhere in which people are moving out of both the cities and the rural areas for the suburbs—is taking place here, as well. In New Jersey, though, it is masked by the fact that the two big cities are in other states. People are moving out of Camden and Newark, too, and the ring of suburbs is creeping farther out toward Morristown and Glassboro, with more suburb-to-suburb commuting.

Because large parts of the state are suburbs of two wealthy cities, New Jersey is the second-richest state in terms of average household income, trailing only Connecticut, an even more suburban state. The wealthiest neighborhoods are all in the New York half, around Montclair, Livingston, Saddle River (where Richard Nixon eventually retired), Parsippany, and Passaic County. The poorest parts include the two big cities as well as the rural Ninth District, which includes much of the Pine Barrens. For all the squalor of Camden and Newark, they are fairly well-to-do by national standards, with average household income around $40,000. Unemployment runs as high as 14 percent in Newark—high, but not nearly as bad as it is across the Hudson.

New Jersey is 70 percent white and is one of six states, all in the Northeast, in which the percentage of white residents is falling. Only three house districts, all in Newark, have a black majority. Many other suburbs are racially integrated.

Four districts around Newark are more than one-third Hispanic, including the Thirty-third District, which is 60 percent Hispanic and home to the largest concentration of Cuban Americans outside Miami. New Jersey also has the fourth-highest percentage of Asians, after (but far after) Hawaii, California, and New York.

Over the last generation, New Jersey has alternated between Democratic and Republican governors. It currently has two Democratic U.S. senators, but the race for an open seat in 1996 was very close. Republicans hold both chambers of the legislature by comfortable margins, although Democrats have made gains in the house.

NEW JERSEY
State Legislative Districts

NEWARK

Population Growth · -10% to 0% · 1% to 6% · 7% to 11% · 14% to 18%

New Jersey State Legislative Districts: Demographic Data

Legis. District	Population		Average HH Income		District Type	Unempl. Rate	College Educ.	White (non-Hispanic)		African American		Asian American		Hispanic American	
	1997	+/-	($)	+/-		(%)	(%)	(%)	+/-	(%)	+/-	(%)	+/-	(%)	+/-
New Jersey	8,016,993	4	65,349	28	M	6	44	70	-2	13	8	5	45	12	29
1	197,848	2	47,941	27	M	7	29	77	-3	9	13	1	43	12	27
2	202,922	5	48,589	16	S	5	35	68	-2	20	14	3	46	9	43
3	201,475	4	51,635	32	M	6	32	78	0	16	12	1	45	4	42
4	209,838	8	55,464	27	S	5	41	84	3	11	33	3	62	3	58
5	181,160	-5	40,818	27	M	9	22	51	-13	28	-7	1	-21	20	26
6	190,023	-1	71,152	28	S	3	55	86	-6	5	42	6	53	3	65
7	196,327	4	56,003	26	S	5	38	67	-6	24	23	2	53	6	65
8	216,764	14	72,250	30	S	4	52	85	9	9	56	3	81	3	60
9	214,502	10	44,695	27	R	6	27	93	8	2	32	1	65	3	46
10	213,926	11	60,084	28	R	5	42	94	8	1	37	1	65	3	66
11	197,073	2	63,774	25	R	6	48	75	-2	16	11	2	36	6	31
12	228,252	18	80,768	24	S	4	56	82	12	7	35	6	68	5	61
13	203,240	4	67,555	23	S	5	45	85	-1	4	29	5	53	6	47
14	204,139	7	66,311	29	S	4	53	82	1	7	39	6	58	5	58
15	190,129	0	69,859	35	M	6	49	55	-9	30	7	5	45	11	28
16	225,854	15	90,733	31	R	3	63	82	10	7	27	6	67	4	54
17	192,299	0	58,224	24	R	6	44	50	-11	27	0	7	39	15	37
18	207,599	5	74,840	25	S	4	56	74	-3	6	21	13	45	7	64
19	200,630	2	56,130	23	S	6	34	68	-7	6	13	5	49	21	25
20	186,154	-3	45,851	21	U	8	26	41	-22	23	9	3	23	33	22
21	202,520	3	102,420	32	S	4	58	83	-2	5	30	6	47	5	55
22	203,861	5	94,650	29	S	3	62	86	1	4	29	5	53	5	50
23	216,539	10	72,342	28	R	3	52	94	8	2	21	2	64	2	49
24	213,055	8	73,339	25	R	4	53	94	7	1	19	2	58	3	46
25	206,842	6	87,985	29	R	4	57	82	2	5	17	5	56	9	35
26	210,204	9	92,119	30	R	3	58	87	4	2	24	7	60	4	55
27	189,539	-1	62,290	31	S	8	44	31	-18	56	4	3	31	9	45
28	185,444	-3	54,159	32	M	10	34	19	-34	57	5	2	2	21	19
29	172,775	-10	37,984	31	U	14	17	15	-31	53	-12	1	-1	30	11
30	196,049	2	53,518	27	R	5	35	76	-1	13	5	3	36	8	30
31	185,363	-1	46,962	28	U	9	33	40	-14	30	-4	8	22	22	32
32	196,889	3	52,200	28	S	8	34	50	-16	4	6	10	32	35	36
33	184,500	-3	48,823	32	S	9	33	31	-23	3	12	6	27	60	7
34	202,933	5	66,682	22	S	5	46	83	-2	3	67	5	57	8	80
35	187,270	-1	45,057	18	U	9	23	31	-27	26	5	2	24	41	28
36	190,824	-1	52,426	23	S	7	35	61	-13	7	20	7	31	24	25
37	196,392	1	70,310	20	S	5	52	59	-9	17	10	11	40	12	28
38	200,323	1	59,833	19	S	5	40	79	-6	2	16	9	50	10	41
39	205,100	4	101,339	23	S	3	61	83	-1	1	22	12	50	4	29
40	210,417	8	92,680	22	S	4	60	89	4	2	38	5	58	4	49

Note: U=urban, S=suburban, R=rural, M=mixed, HH=households.

NEW MEXICO

The United States seized the territory that is now New Mexico as one of the spoils of the Mexican War, although New Mexico was never considered as attractive as the real prizes, Texas and California. Its southern quarter (as well as the southern quarter of Arizona) was not annexed until 1853, as part of the Gadsden Purchase, and New Mexico itself was the next to last of the lower forty-eight states to be admitted to the Union. In some respects, it has also been the last part of the contiguous United States to be integrated into American society.

New Mexico is, to start, one of only two states in which whites do not constitute a majority of the population (Hawaii is the other). It is almost 40 percent Hispanic, by far the highest percentage in the country. Much of the Hispanic population of New Mexico, unlike, for example, that of Texas or California, is of ancient stock and has been here since the early sixteenth century, when Coronado passed through on his way toward Kansas in search of the City of Gold. Another 9 percent of the population is Native American, again the highest percentage of any state, and much of the Native American population is living in poverty on all but inaccessible reservations.

For the past two decades, New Mexico has been fully a part of the Mountain time zone boom. The six fastest-growing states in the country are all located more or less in a line along the Rockies: Nevada, Arizona, Idaho, Utah, Colorado, and New Mexico, which ranks sixth but has nonetheless grown by 15 percent since 1990. Less well appreciated is that this regional boom has been going on for some time. The Mountain West was the fastest-growing part of the country in the 1980s, as well. The Census Bureau anticipates that the growth will continue and projects New Mexico as the second-fastest-growing state over the next twenty-five years, behind California.

That growth has occurred primarily in the two largest cities, Albuquerque and Santa Fe, located sixty miles apart. As they have grown, their suburbs have expanded into previously rural areas, a phenomenon seen repeatedly around the country. It should be noted that as many of these growing suburbs are predominantly Hispanic as are predominantly white. There has also been some rapid growth in Las Cruces, on the border with El Paso and Juarez. Only two districts have lost population, both of them rural: the Sixty-seventh District (Clovis), in the northeast corner of the state, and the Sixty-first District (Hobbs), in the southeast corner.

New Mexico is a poor state, particularly its rural areas. Average household income on the Navajo and Zuni Indian reservations in the northwest corner is less than $28,000 a year, and the unemployment rate is as high as 26 percent. Income levels are also depressed in the eastern grazing lands and near the border in Las Cruces. New Mexico as a whole has the fifth-highest rate of unemployment, ranking between Mississippi and Michigan. There are, however, pockets of considerable wealth, almost evenly split between Albuquerque and Santa Fe and almost all in the residential neighborhoods and older suburbs closer to the center of town.

Although a minority, whites are the largest racial group and predominate in the wealthier parts of Albuquerque as well as the rural east (which is spiritually more a part of the Texas panhandle, which it borders). In the Ninth District, a Navajo reservation, whites make up just 5 percent of the population.

Eight New Mexico districts are more than 70 percent Hispanic. The Sixty-third District, centered around Clovis and Portales, is 11 percent African American, the only sizable concentration in the state.

Its high Hispanic and Native American populations make New Mexico one of the most Democratic states in a heavily Republican region. The party holds both chambers of the legislature, although the Republicans have closed the gap in the senate. But Hispanic population is growing faster than white population, and Democrats currently represent eight of the ten fastest-growing districts. Races in several of those districts have been very close, but Democrats would seem to be in a strong position for the future.

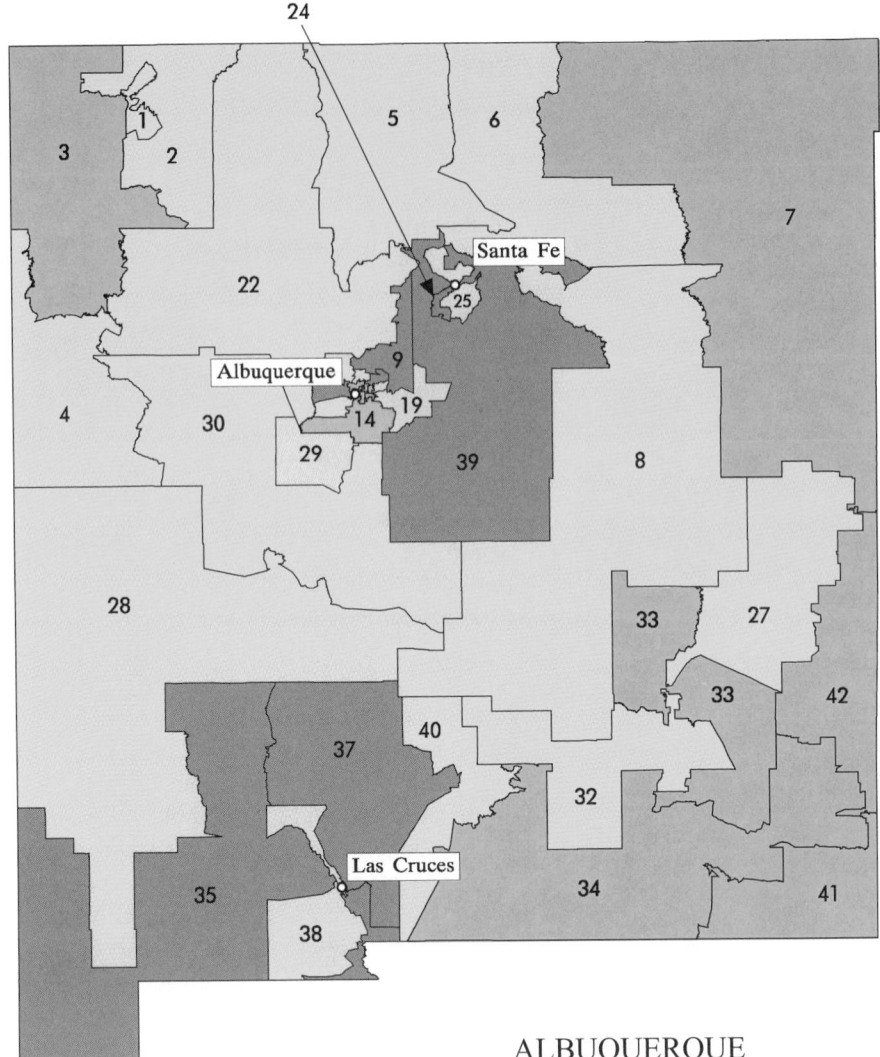

NEW MEXICO
State Senate Districts

Santa Fe

Albuquerque

Las Cruces

ALBUQUERQUE

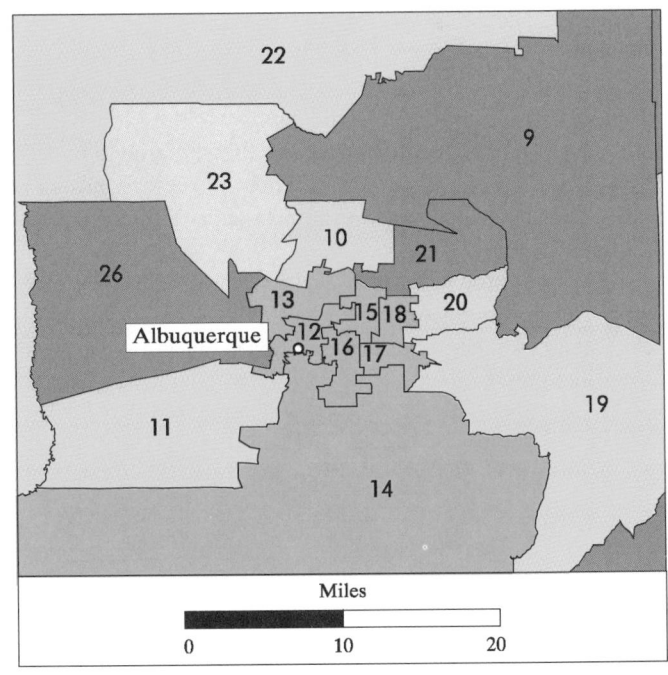

LAS CRUCES

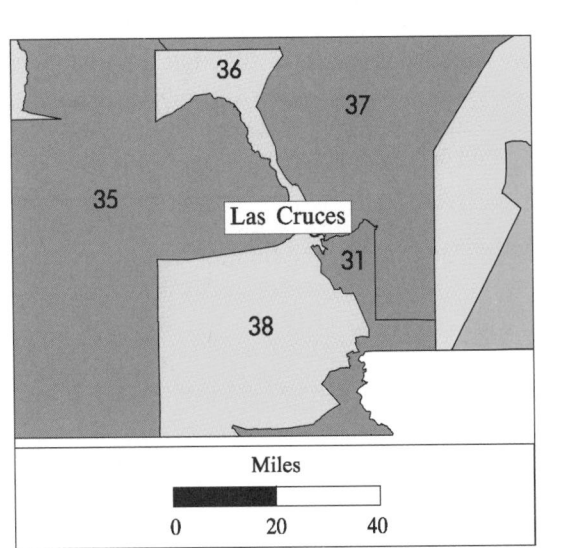

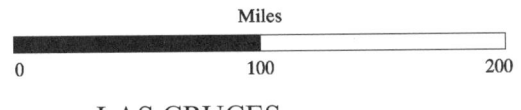

Miles

0   100   200

Population Growth   ▨ 1% to 9%   ▢ 10% to 19%   ▨ 21% to 31%   ▢ 37% to 45%

New Mexico State Senate Districts: Demographic Data

Senate District	Population		Average HH Income		District Type	Unempl. Rate	College Educ.	White (non-Hispanic)		African American		Asian American		Hispanic American	
	1997	+/-	($)	+/-		(%)	(%)	(%)	+/-	(%)	+/-	(%)	+/-	(%)	+/-
N.Mexico	1,736,796	15	42,911	38	R	8	36	49	11	2	39	1	47	39	18
1	42,989	19	52,555	53	R	7	36	68	15	1	40	0	62	15	20
2	39,042	17	40,022	48	R	9	22	56	11	0	28	0	28	20	19
3	39,001	5	26,310	44	R	22	14	5	3	0	5	0	-2	10	19
4	42,904	15	35,480	37	R	11	24	20	14	1	22	1	56	13	21
5	41,328	13	41,947	42	R	10	33	22	9	0	14	1	34	69	13
6	40,956	16	33,983	40	R	12	31	24	13	0	40	0	5	71	17
7	41,978	7	36,492	33	R	6	30	63	7	2	65	1	65	33	5
8	43,413	16	33,027	42	R	9	29	38	19	1	43	0	39	60	14
9	46,515	31	51,591	44	R	6	43	60	29	2	86	1	80	30	30
10	37,419	12	55,951	38	U	5	44	61	9	1	49	1	52	35	17
11	38,571	11	33,641	31	S	10	18	19	-8	2	40	0	17	76	17
12	32,919	4	34,749	41	U	9	37	40	1	3	45	1	34	52	3
13	38,688	7	40,220	34	U	8	35	36	5	2	45	1	36	57	8
14	37,748	3	33,424	35	U	12	25	29	-9	8	26	2	8	52	5
15	39,997	3	47,400	33	U	6	51	65	-2	2	47	2	43	28	13
16	36,106	1	40,380	32	U	6	60	65	-4	5	38	3	39	24	9
17	35,996	3	28,235	27	U	9	29	42	-8	6	39	3	35	44	13
18	36,883	5	49,621	35	U	5	46	70	0	3	46	3	48	23	15
19	40,660	14	56,876	44	U	6	47	70	13	3	50	2	49	23	14
20	41,536	13	62,604	40	U	4	57	74	9	3	56	2	57	20	21
21	44,920	22	89,031	54	U	3	66	80	20	2	64	3	74	14	20
22	42,445	14	39,901	29	R	13	30	26	11	0	33	1	28	12	1
23	51,203	45	53,314	36	M	4	49	64	35	3	95	2	93	29	66
24	44,886	24	44,721	39	U	5	39	31	13	1	67	1	63	65	30
25	43,402	18	75,811	55	U	4	61	67	21	0	60	1	75	30	9
26	42,804	25	43,384	36	U	6	35	31	23	4	67	1	67	63	24
27	38,423	10	28,788	22	R	10	23	56	2	8	27	2	37	33	21
28	39,273	11	32,727	29	R	11	28	46	10	0	27	0	5	50	13
29	51,746	37	43,226	44	R	9	25	42	31	1	72	0	92	55	42
30	42,920	13	32,093	30	R	12	26	39	15	1	49	1	25	40	15
31	46,413	25	30,619	27	S	10	27	28	21	1	51	1	56	70	26
32	35,762	11	27,402	24	R	12	15	39	8	3	38	0	30	50	13
33	42,454	8	41,882	24	R	4	34	70	7	2	38	0	31	27	11
34	43,344	9	43,067	34	R	6	29	72	8	1	27	1	56	25	11
35	44,341	21	29,413	21	R	11	23	55	19	1	78	0	22	43	24
36	39,918	17	34,330	24	U	9	33	38	15	2	45	1	59	58	17
37	47,950	24	39,686	30	R	9	42	57	14	4	15	2	39	36	43
38	39,558	17	31,770	24	U	10	35	39	13	1	48	1	53	58	19
39	45,821	22	50,308	42	R	7	39	46	17	0	50	1	29	50	27
40	41,802	14	39,079	35	R	9	33	65	10	5	34	2	66	27	17
41	32,946	1	28,962	31	R	10	11	42	-7	7	17	0	-8	49	6
42	39,578	8	40,730	31	R	6	31	75	6	4	28	1	60	19	11

Note: U=urban, S=suburban, R=rural, M=mixed, HH=households.

NEW MEXICO
State House Districts

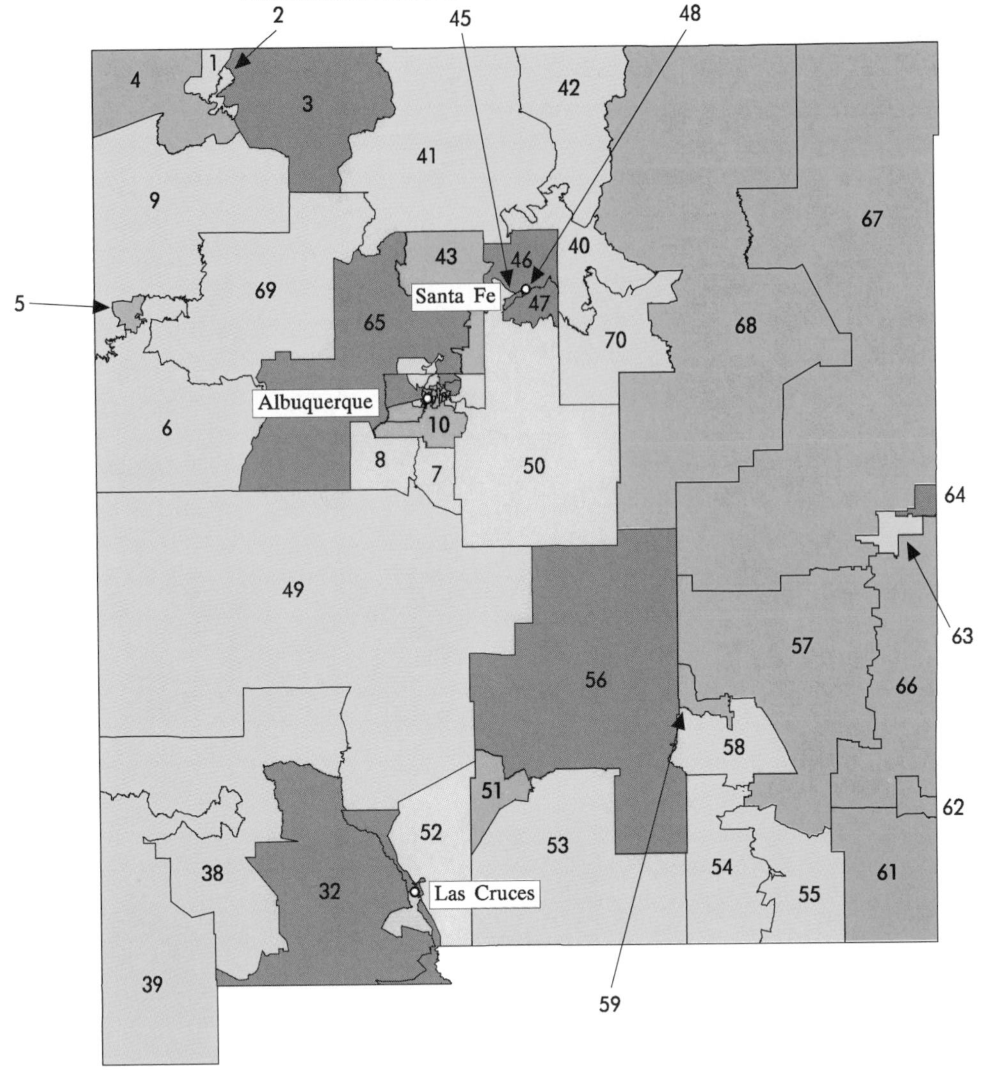

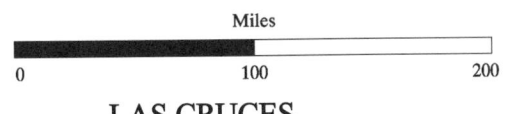

LAS CRUCES

Miles

0   100   200

LAS CRUCES

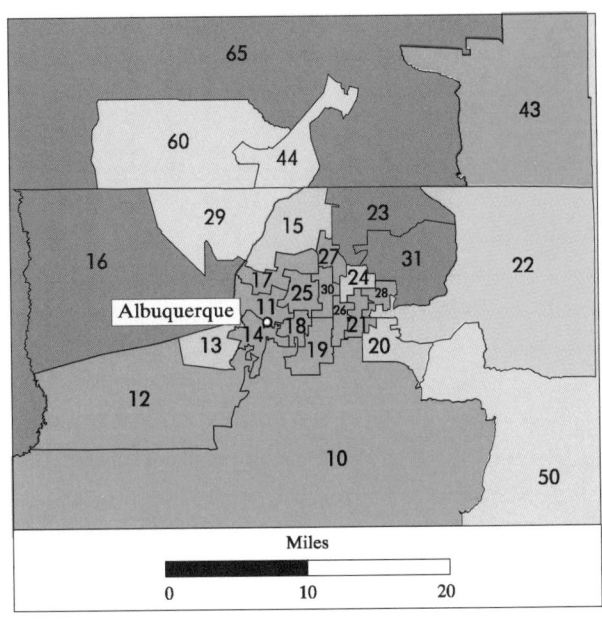

ALBUQUERQUE

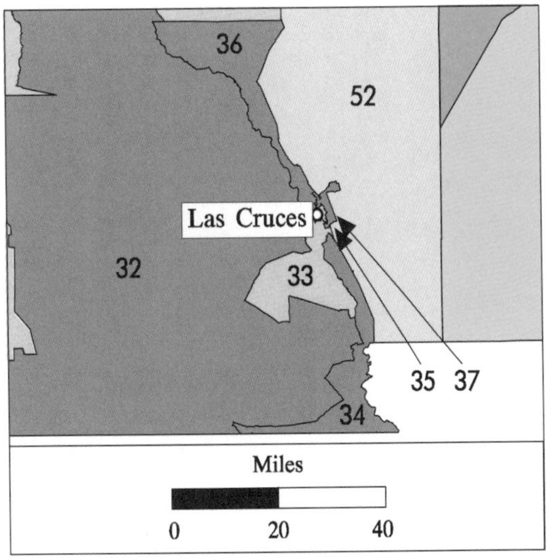

Population Growth   ■ -2% to 8%   □ 9% to 17%   ■ 19% to 30%   □ 33% to 48%

New Mexico State House Districts: Demographic Data

House District	Population 1997	+/-	Average HH Income ($)	+/-	District Type	Unempl. Rate (%)	College Educ. (%)	White (non-Hispanic) (%)	+/-	African American (%)	+/-	Asian American (%)	+/-	Hispanic American (%)	+/-
N.Mexico	1,736,796	15	42,911	38	R	8	36	49	11	2	39	1	47	39	18
1	24,915	17	56,755	57	R	6	40	69	14	1	33	0	60	14	14
2	25,194	16	44,955	45	R	9	29	66	11	1	38	0	53	19	20
3	24,241	19	38,652	46	R	9	23	58	19	0	45	0	18	22	18
4	22,322	3	38,129	72	R	18	17	18	-2	0	3	0	15	4	4
5	18,998	8	40,768	33	R	7	29	31	4	1	20	1	54	37	24
6	30,159	16	27,705	33	R	13	19	17	16	0	18	0	16	18	17
7	31,460	42	45,946	48	R	9	28	55	44	1	100	1	115	42	37
8	25,713	34	40,770	42	R	9	23	35	19	1	62	0	76	62	43
9	23,779	9	22,882	34	R	26	13	5	13	0	-17	0	75	1	-3
10	23,279	3	34,399	36	S	10	26	30	-12	6	26	1	10	47	7
11	22,104	4	36,628	41	U	9	33	35	8	3	46	1	26	59	1
12	23,181	7	35,055	33	S	10	19	24	-7	2	34	0	21	73	13
13	25,157	14	33,576	29	U	9	17	14	-9	3	45	0	12	79	19
14	21,330	2	36,617	45	U	12	24	21	-2	5	27	0	13	71	2
15	23,307	11	51,890	39	S	6	38	50	8	1	45	1	39	47	15
16	28,519	30	43,501	33	U	6	39	35	25	3	76	1	72	58	32
17	22,197	7	37,448	30	U	8	33	37	2	2	42	1	34	57	9
18	20,396	1	35,147	31	U	7	59	61	-4	5	32	4	30	26	3
19	22,405	1	35,617	30	U	7	49	58	-7	7	35	3	36	29	12
20	23,243	9	51,293	43	U	7	43	60	2	6	48	3	48	29	18
21	22,692	5	38,686	33	U	6	37	60	-2	4	44	3	44	31	14
22	25,951	14	57,913	42	U	5	53	74	12	2	52	2	51	20	13
23	26,729	21	93,128	56	U	3	64	82	20	1	65	3	68	14	17
24	24,481	12	56,244	36	U	4	55	74	7	2	57	3	55	20	23
25	21,906	5	43,156	31	U	6	52	57	0	3	48	2	44	35	10
26	21,948	1	31,806	28	U	10	31	42	-11	5	34	3	29	44	11
27	23,166	7	52,474	31	U	6	53	69	2	2	47	2	47	26	17
28	22,321	7	54,015	36	U	5	52	70	2	3	49	2	45	23	15
29	30,913	42	59,570	33	U	4	55	63	36	3	100	2	90	30	51
30	23,245	2	45,523	33	U	6	48	65	-4	2	46	2	44	28	14
31	29,133	25	89,864	50	U	3	66	81	23	2	73	3	78	13	24
32	27,401	25	30,495	23	R	11	25	47	23	1	74	0	42	50	26
33	25,762	14	31,598	26	S	10	39	43	13	2	43	1	40	53	14
34	25,355	25	27,337	20	S	10	16	15	20	0	51	0	74	84	26
35	23,313	13	30,133	24	U	11	30	35	18	2	41	1	51	61	9
36	23,263	23	38,081	21	U	9	39	43	15	1	56	1	65	54	29
37	21,133	21	40,297	25	U	8	56	61	16	3	61	2	73	33	25
38	27,365	16	31,207	25	R	9	27	62	14	1	60	0	9	36	17
39	24,150	11	33,975	30	R	10	25	40	9	0	13	0	13	59	13
40	25,605	16	36,758	49	R	11	25	13	14	0	39	0	90	80	16
41	23,587	11	32,248	42	R	12	23	16	10	0	8	0	13	75	10
42	23,493	14	33,719	36	R	11	34	29	12	0	44	0	5	64	15
43	24,383	6	69,283	28	R	3	65	74	3	0	15	2	28	12	-2
44	27,353	33	50,440	45	R	7	38	59	29	2	88	1	89	36	35
45	27,650	29	39,915	29	U	4	35	27	8	1	68	0	61	70	40
46	26,686	21	72,326	57	M	6	48	41	14	0	43	0	56	54	26
47	29,677	27	78,653	57	U	3	62	65	29	1	71	1	79	32	22
48	22,773	8	45,907	39	U	5	48	46	13	1	55	1	68	50	3
49	25,949	13	29,346	21	R	11	27	46	9	1	32	1	5	46	17
50	30,142	35	41,771	40	R	7	33	62	36	1	82	0	43	36	32

Note: U=urban, S=suburban, R=rural, M=mixed, HH=households.

New Mexico State House Districts: Demographic Data (cont.)

House District	Population 1997	+/-	Average HH Income ($)	+/-	District Type	Unempl. Rate (%)	College Educ. (%)	White (non-Hispanic) (%)	+/-	African American (%)	+/-	Asian American (%)	+/-	Hispanic American (%)	+/-
N. Mexico	1,736,796	15	42,911	38	R	8	36	49	11	2	39	1	47	39	18
51	21,396	1	33,556	35	R	10	26	59	-4	8	6	3	25	28	9
52	38,266	41	37,938	31	M	10	32	40	33	2	43	1	77	56	47
53	25,005	16	43,048	33	R	8	39	70	11	5	37	2	68	21	27
54	25,699	10	32,494	34	R	10	14	49	5	3	45	0	2	47	13
55	21,663	11	44,639	37	R	6	31	72	10	1	56	1	60	26	11
56	26,630	19	33,944	33	R	10	28	61	21	1	53	0	5	28	21
57	27,132	8	46,363	28	R	5	37	74	7	1	43	0	43	24	10
58	20,293	14	26,952	24	R	9	13	36	12	4	37	0	31	59	14
59	22,046	7	32,224	16	R	5	30	65	4	3	37	1	28	31	10
60	30,676	48	48,205	40	R	5	41	64	33	3	90	1	92	30	87
61	22,131	-1	27,974	29	R	10	11	47	-7	9	9	0	-6	43	5
62	22,705	5	49,643	37	R	5	35	81	5	3	19	1	48	15	3
63	23,734	10	24,280	18	R	13	15	43	-5	11	27	2	30	43	26
64	24,879	20	40,872	33	R	5	35	78	17	4	54	3	78	15	21
65	27,986	20	35,091	44	R	14	23	16	32	1	41	0	45	18	12
66	26,090	7	34,631	26	R	8	28	68	7	2	22	1	58	28	3
67	21,024	-2	29,962	20	R	6	23	64	-4	1	51	0	-19	34	1
68	22,461	8	32,687	41	R	8	25	38	6	0	71	0	-10	61	9
69	24,376	11	28,522	36	R	19	19	22	13	1	23	0	31	17	9
70	23,417	12	33,752	54	R	12	29	15	5	1	32	1	51	83	13

Note: U=urban, S=suburban, R=rural, M=mixed, HH=households.

NEW YORK

New York City's history is inseparable from its geography. Manhattan, of course, is an island, and a narrow one at that. With no way to grow beyond Manhattan before the bridges and tunnels were built, the city built vertically, stacking office workers in skyscrapers and erecting apartments instead of row houses.

Given an opportunity to do so, the city also expanded outward. The population of Brooklyn increased 40 percent in the decade after the bridge was opened in 1883. Automobiles made it possible for Queens to grow by 177 percent between 1920 and 1940. With the opening of the Verrazano Narrows Bridge in 1964, Staten Island's population grew by one-third.

The population also spilled beyond the city's borders. Commuting out across Long Island and up the Hudson on freeways built by Parks Commissioner Robert Moses, New Yorkers began to spread out. Canarsie gave way to Levittown, which gave way to West Babylon, just as Mount Vernon gave way to White Plains.

Outward expansion of the city continues in our own time. The fastest-growing parts of the state, indeed the only rapidly growing parts, are farther up the Hudson, to places like Peekskill and Tarrytown; out the Long Island Expressway to Suffolk County; across to Staten Island; or northwest to Sullivan and Orange Counties, along the Delaware River. Brooklyn and the Bronx are less crowded today than they were in the 1920s, while Manhattan has fewer people than it did in 1900.

As political commentator Michael Barone has observed, this transformation has enormous implications, not the least of which are political. In the 1940s, New York City cast more than half of the state's votes; today it dominates just twenty-five of the state's sixty-one senate districts, meaning that Gov. George Pataki need pay far less attention to the city's opinion than Gov. Thomas Dewey (1943–1955) or even Gov. Nelson Rockefeller (1959–1973) did. It also makes it more likely that there will *be* a Governor Pataki—a little-known, upstate social conservative.

New York State has changed as well. It began the decade as the country's second-largest state but ends it as the third-largest, having fallen behind Texas. The Census Bureau predicts that the state will have one of the lowest rates of growth over the next quarter century and will slip behind Florida in total population by 2025.

Within New York City, disparities of wealth appear to be growing greater, perhaps approaching conditions of the late nineteenth century, before the ameliorative effects of social welfare programs. Income is growing fastest in the Upper West Side, Greenwich Village, and Park Avenue, where the fruits of the stock market and law firm booms have been reaped. In some places, disparities of wealth can be striking within a short distance. The Seventy-third Assembly District is the state's wealthiest; average income is almost $178,000 a year. The district is 84 percent white, and 77 percent of its residents have a college degree. The Seventy-fourth District is the state's poorest; average income here is barely $21,000. It is 71 percent Hispanic and 27 percent African American, and only 11 percent have finished college. The Seventy-third District is the Upper East Side of Manhattan. The Seventy-fourth District, perhaps a mile and a half away, is the South Bronx.

Not only is the population of New York shifting, its face is changing as well. New York is one of two states (Florida is the other) in which Hispanics have surpassed blacks as the largest minority group. New York remains the country's melting pot, and one in perpetual metamorphosis. The state assembly district comprising the Lower East Side of Manhattan, where Gov. Al Smith once worked in the Fulton Fish Market, is now almost half Chinese. Not far away, in Flushing, Queens, lives the country's largest Korean community. But it is worth noting that ethnic concentration does not immediately translate into political power. The Koreans in Queens have an assembly member named McLaughlin, while the Chinese on the Lower East Side are represented in Albany by the Jewish assembly speaker, Sheldon Silver.

As they have for years, Democrats control the state assembly and Republicans the senate. Their numbers in both chambers have scarcely budged since 1990.

NEW YORK
State Senate Districts

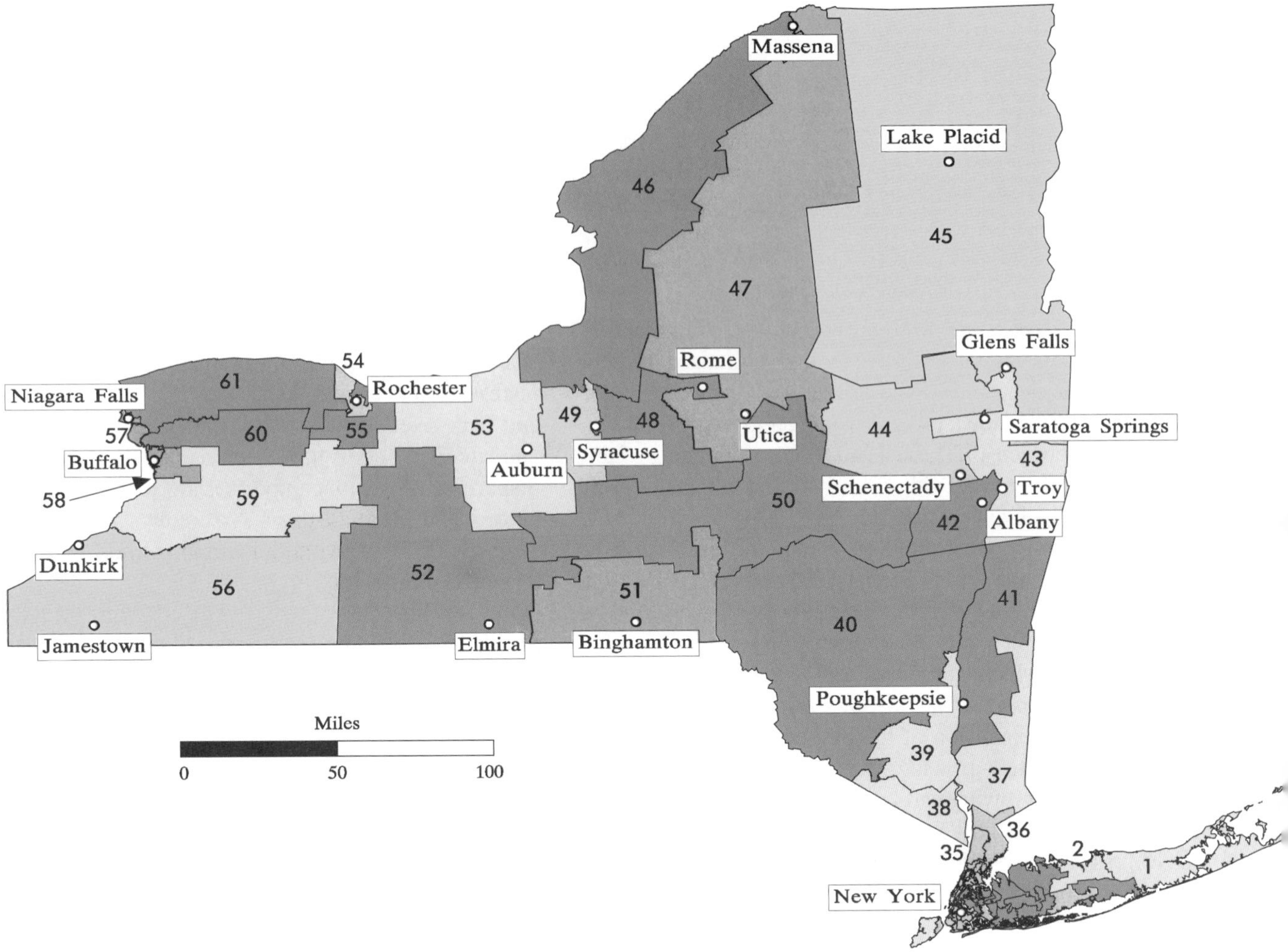

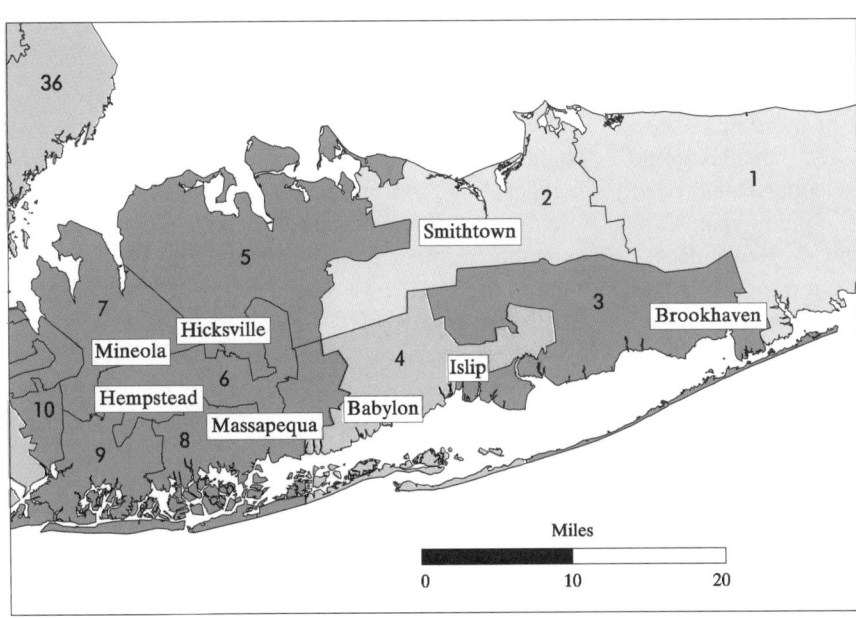

Massena

Lake Placid

46

45

47

Rome

Glens Falls

Niagara Falls

54

61

Rochester

53

49

48

Utica

44

Saratoga Springs

57

60

55

43

Buffalo

Auburn

Syracuse

Schenectady

Troy

58

50

Albany

59

42

Dunkirk

41

56

52

51

40

Jamestown

Elmira

Binghamton

Poughkeepsie

39

37

38

36

35

2

1

New York

Miles

0   50   100

LONG ISLAND

36

1

2

Smithtown

5

3

7

Brookhaven

Hicksville

Mineola

4

Islip

6

Hempstead

Babylon

10

Massapequa

9

8

Miles

0   10   20

Population Growth   ▮ -7% to -4%   ▯ -2% to 0%   ▮ 1% to 3%   ▯ 4% to 12%

NEW YORK CITY

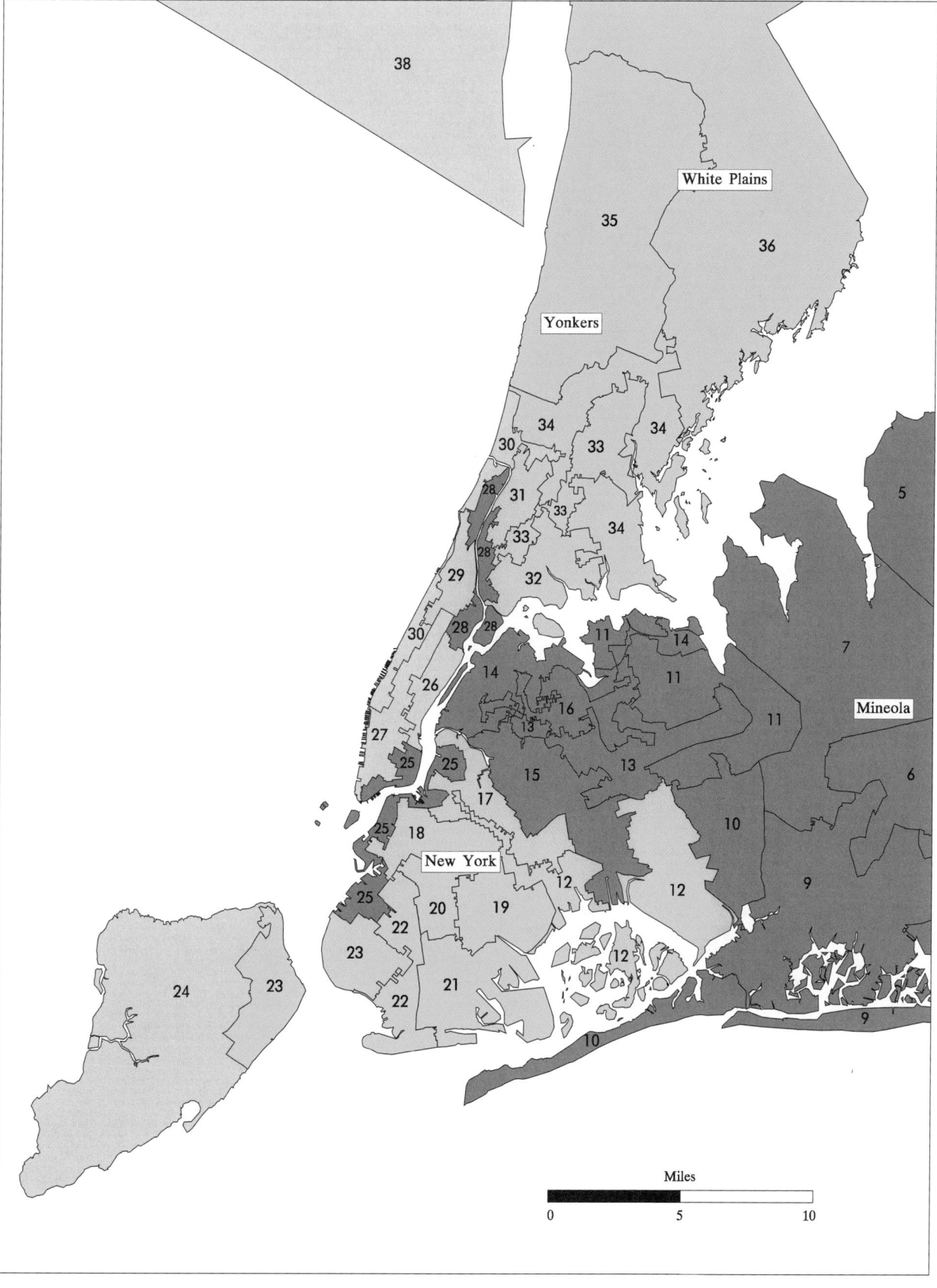

Population Growth

☐ -2% to 0%   ■ 1% to 3%   ☐ 4% to 12%

New York State Senate Districts: Demographic Data

Senate District	Population 1997	+/-	Average HH Income ($)	+/-	District Type	Unempl. Rate (%)	College Educ. (%)	White (non-Hispanic) (%)	+/-	African American (%)	+/-	Asian American (%)	+/-	Hispanic American (%)	+/-
NewYork	18,225,862	1	57,069	29	M	7	42	65	-4	15	3	5	27	15	22
1	313,195	8	63,387	28	R	4	44	86	4	6	30	2	45	6	46
2	301,444	4	87,273	30	R	4	55	90	1	2	17	4	43	4	37
3	297,142	2	66,590	28	R	5	39	78	-3	6	13	2	35	14	35
4	287,691	-1	69,536	29	S	5	37	78	-5	9	7	2	32	12	30
5	291,836	1	99,420	28	S	4	58	85	-3	4	18	4	42	6	36
6	294,148	1	74,480	24	S	4	47	72	-4	16	4	3	38	9	29
7	293,475	1	95,912	23	S	4	55	77	-5	7	20	7	39	9	38
8	291,985	1	77,988	24	S	5	48	73	-5	16	10	2	36	9	33
9	292,715	2	81,331	24	S	4	53	86	-2	4	29	3	41	7	33
10	301,890	1	52,662	25	U	9	31	17	-14	67	3	2	17	13	20
11	304,290	1	60,875	21	U	5	45	59	-10	7	4	18	29	15	28
12	300,542	0	39,266	26	U	13	20	8	-21	64	-2	4	12	24	17
13	304,096	2	53,201	20	U	6	50	57	-10	5	6	21	28	17	21
14	305,220	2	44,750	22	U	8	37	50	-12	6	1	15	29	28	21
15	304,272	1	48,682	23	U	7	28	65	-10	2	1	9	29	24	37
16	299,633	2	40,108	17	U	9	33	16	-30	12	-8	26	19	45	14
17	294,284	-1	29,673	28	U	15	12	6	-44	23	-9	3	-12	67	10
18	293,432	-2	43,897	41	U	12	33	11	-25	66	-3	2	10	20	22
19	291,500	-2	46,142	30	U	10	29	18	-21	67	0	3	14	12	26
20	291,155	-2	47,636	33	U	10	37	14	-25	66	1	3	4	15	16
21	293,103	-1	54,045	30	U	7	40	78	-8	4	25	8	28	9	49
22	296,564	-1	39,435	27	U	10	27	61	-12	9	11	10	27	19	32
23	300,034	0	50,520	29	U	7	32	68	-9	5	17	11	28	15	39
24	315,060	6	66,006	24	U	6	41	79	1	6	15	6	45	9	40
25	304,668	2	46,691	37	U	9	34	39	-17	9	38	12	23	40	13
26	309,134	4	135,470	42	U	4	77	82	-2	3	44	7	48	7	48
27	313,849	6	84,209	42	U	6	64	60	-5	7	47	20	22	12	28
28	304,092	1	38,315	32	U	14	25	9	-39	20	-9	2	3	68	16
29	294,888	0	34,140	33	U	14	29	4	-54	50	-9	2	5	44	30
30	307,935	4	82,523	42	U	6	65	57	-11	12	42	6	35	24	35
31	297,295	-2	27,385	20	U	15	17	6	-41	24	-15	4	-1	65	11
32	300,454	0	28,148	22	U	15	15	2	-49	29	-7	1	1	66	7
33	288,324	-2	39,726	25	U	11	26	12	-26	56	-3	2	10	30	16
34	302,457	-1	53,731	29	U	6	33	60	-10	11	-1	4	17	25	24
35	293,039	-1	74,780	28	S	6	51	61	-11	15	9	6	35	17	27
36	298,425	0	108,141	31	S	4	59	71	-7	10	14	5	36	13	30
37	323,806	12	90,037	28	S	4	56	87	9	5	28	2	56	5	48
38	315,599	6	76,578	25	S	4	53	77	0	9	15	5	45	8	38
39	315,756	5	52,262	20	R	6	39	81	1	8	17	2	41	9	38
40	305,244	2	42,683	19	R	6	37	88	-1	5	11	1	31	6	38
41	290,015	1	54,010	16	M	4	47	85	-3	8	14	3	39	4	35
42	299,371	1	54,438	34	S	4	52	86	-2	9	14	2	36	2	34
43	305,537	4	51,963	30	S	5	48	94	3	3	16	1	36	2	39
44	293,720	0	46,203	31	M	6	42	93	-1	3	11	1	37	3	34
45	294,539	0	41,341	29	R	8	36	93	-1	3	7	1	26	3	31
46	301,678	3	40,040	26	R	9	35	93	2	3	10	1	33	2	37
47	280,167	-4	40,686	28	M	7	37	93	-5	4	3	1	27	2	23
48	295,583	1	45,856	28	M	6	46	82	-2	13	8	2	32	3	30
49	287,303	-2	48,599	25	S	4	48	93	-4	3	32	1	35	2	35
50	295,401	1	40,966	29	R	6	46	94	-1	2	10	3	30	2	34

Note: U=urban, S=suburban, R=rural, M=mixed, HH=households.

New York State Senate Districts: Demographic Data (cont.)

Senate District	Population		Average HH Income		District Type	Unempl. Rate	College Educ.	White (non-Hispanic)		African American		Asian American		Hispanic American	
	1997	+/-	($)	+/-		(%)	(%)	(%)	+/-	(%)	+/-	(%)	+/-	(%)	+/-
New York	18,225,862	1	57,069	29	M	7	42	65	-4	15	3	5	27	15	22
51	279,033	-4	41,586	20	M	6	45	95	-5	2	5	2	27	1	27
52	296,143	1	42,234	30	R	7	39	95	0	3	10	1	31	1	32
53	303,833	4	48,238	29	R	5	40	94	2	3	17	1	44	2	38
54	291,467	-1	42,986	21	U	7	44	63	-9	26	9	2	28	9	32
55	297,860	1	59,365	25	S	4	56	89	-2	5	30	3	42	3	42
56	293,671	0	37,974	30	R	7	35	95	0	1	7	1	30	2	34
57	270,126	-7	34,447	32	U	12	34	53	-16	38	3	1	6	7	33
58	275,105	-7	39,640	30	S	7	33	90	-10	6	43	1	7	2	26
59	310,464	5	50,313	31	S	5	43	95	4	2	28	0	38	2	36
60	308,706	3	56,945	34	S	5	53	93	1	3	78	3	47	1	38
61	302,963	3	47,947	27	S	5	39	94	2	3	28	1	39	2	42

Note: U=urban, S=suburban, R=rural, M=mixed, HH=households.

NEW YORK
State Assembly Districts

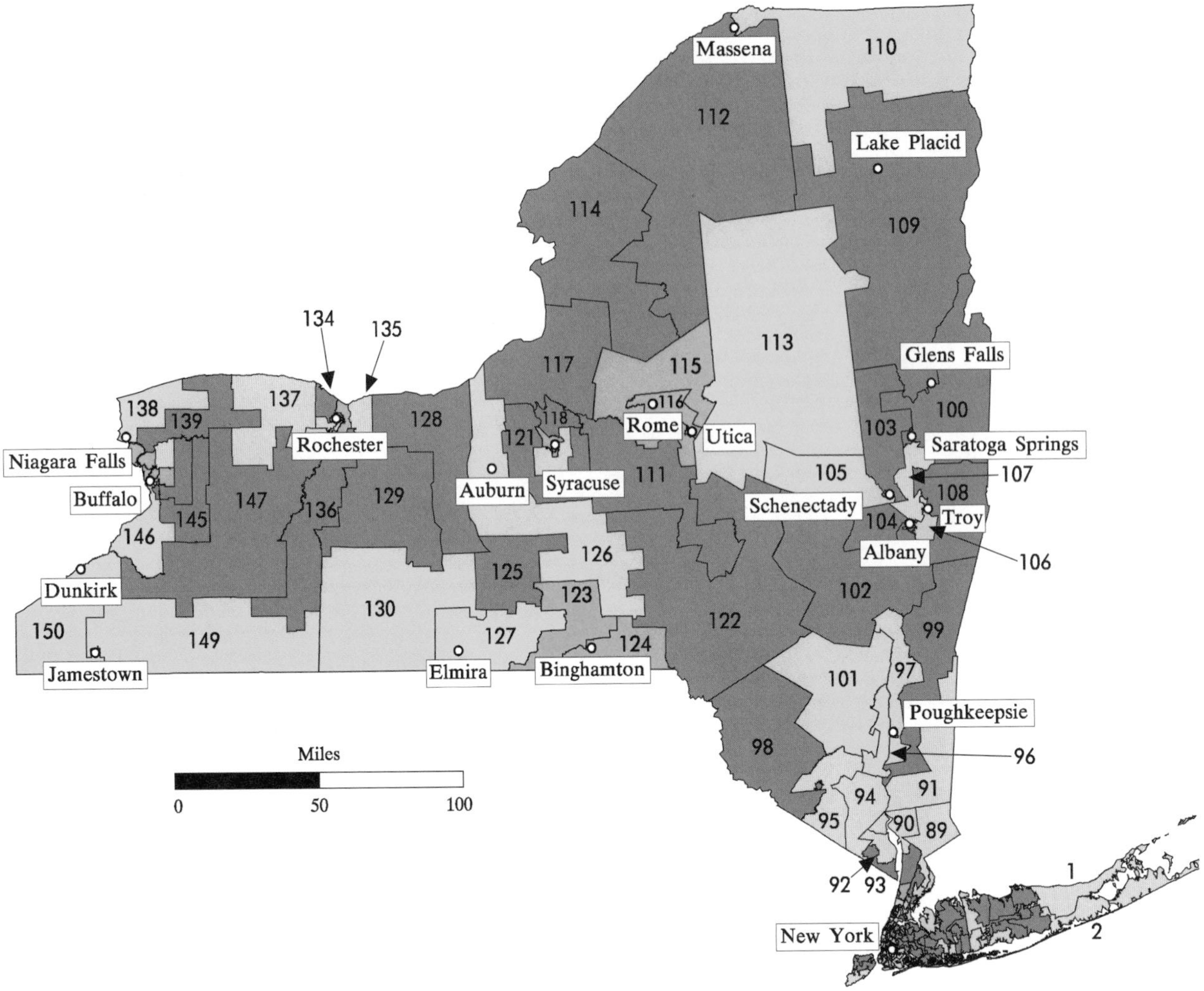

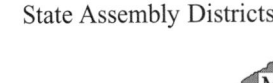

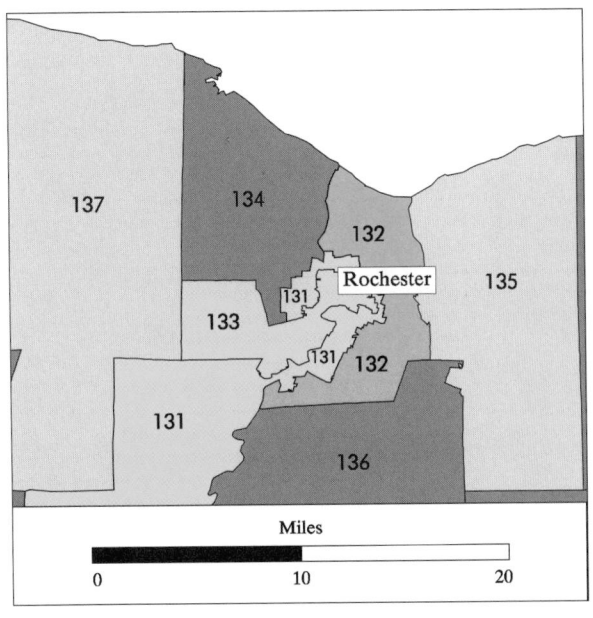

ROCHESTER

SYRACUSE

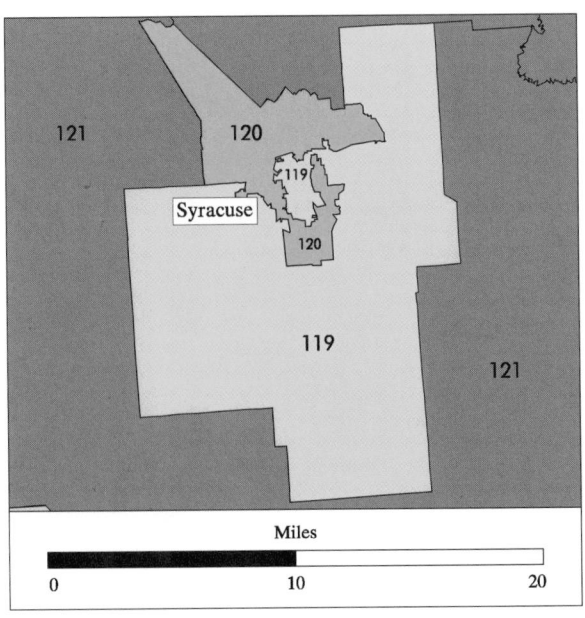

Population Growth ▨ -12% to -4% ▨ -3% to 0% ▨ 1% to 5% ▨ 6% to 12%

NEW YORK CITY

Population Growth ☐ -12% to -4%   ☐ -3% to 0%   ■ 1% to 5%   ☐ 6% to 12%

BUFFALO

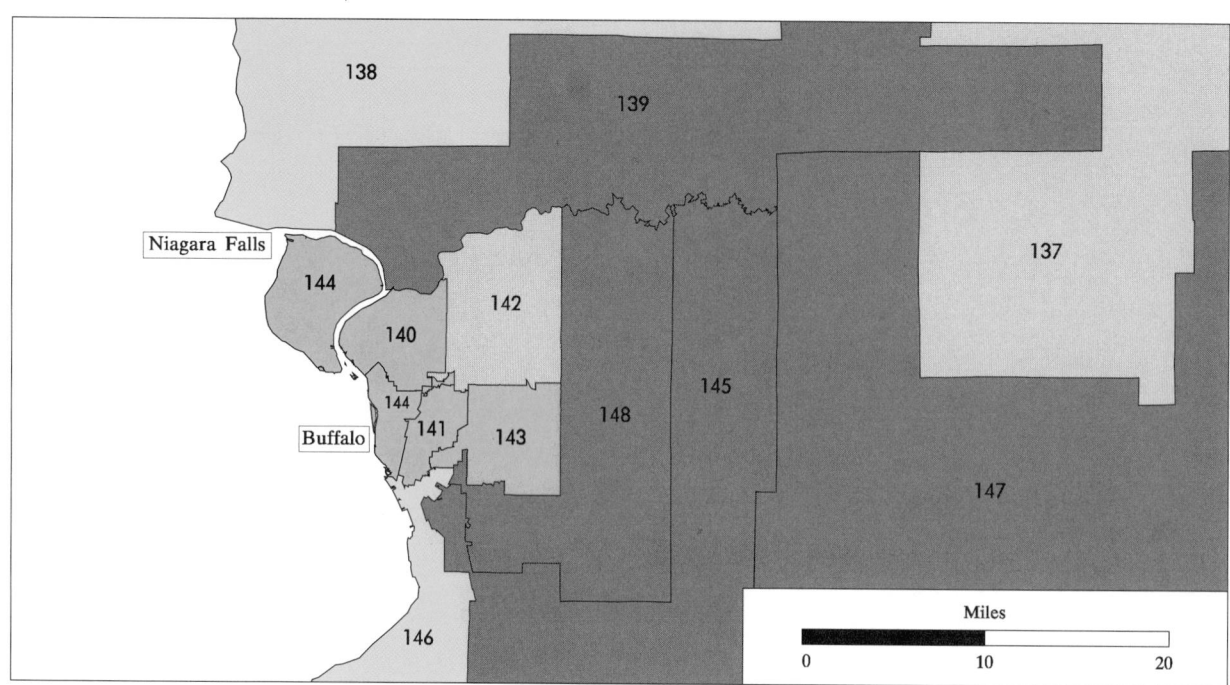

LONG ISLAND

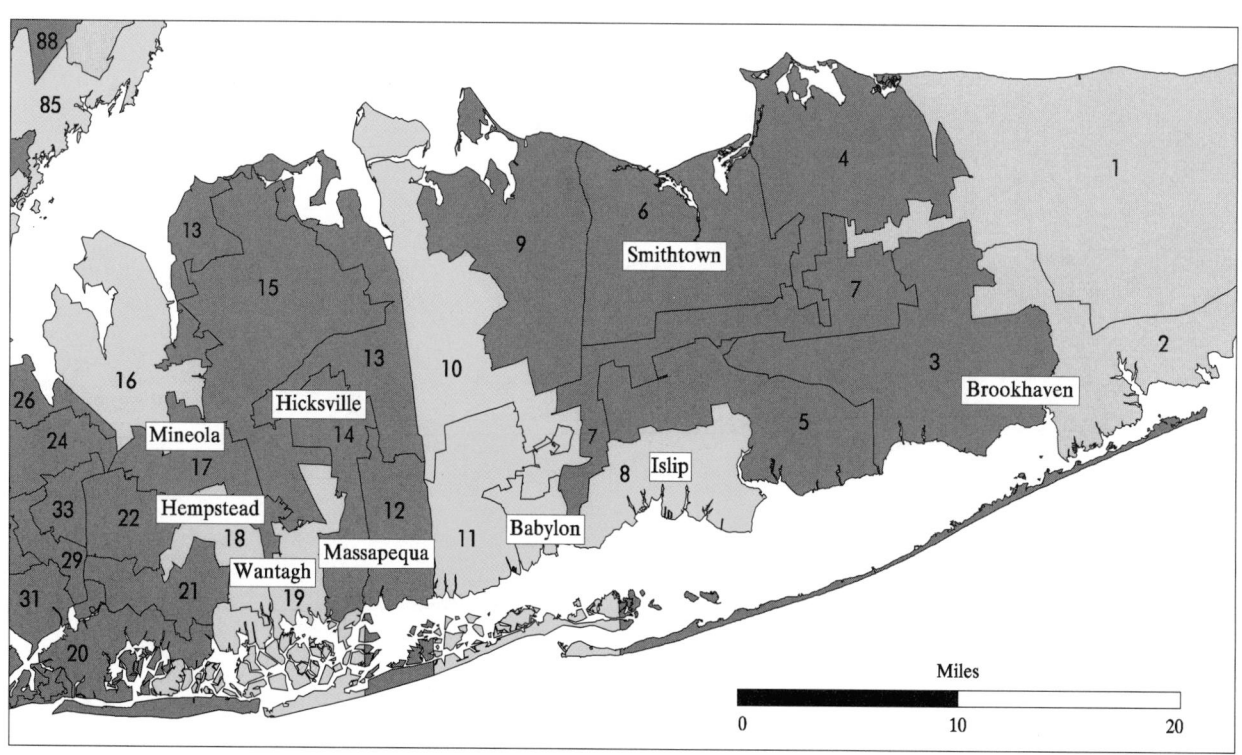

Population Growth   ▨ -12% to -4%   ▨ -3% to 0%   ▨ 1% to 5%   ▨ 6% to 12%

New York State Assembly Districts: Demographic Data

Assembly District	Population 1997	+/-	Average HH Income ($)	+/-	District Type	Unempl. Rate (%)	College Educ. (%)	White (non-Hispanic) (%)	+/-	African American (%)	+/-	Asian American (%)	+/-	Hispanic American (%)	+/-
New York	18,225,862	1	57,069	29	M	7	42	65	-4	15	3	5	27	15	22
1	130,793	8	57,810	26	R	4	43	89	5	5	32	1	47	4	44
2	131,811	10	62,918	29	R	5	41	86	6	6	30	1	46	7	50
3	125,255	4	63,107	28	R	6	39	81	0	7	20	2	39	9	31
4	125,401	5	80,007	29	R	4	56	86	1	3	18	5	41	6	34
5	119,801	1	66,833	27	R	5	36	60	-10	11	10	2	26	27	30
6	124,823	4	87,139	30	R	4	54	93	2	1	14	3	46	4	45
7	123,912	2	68,078	29	R	5	37	85	-1	3	15	2	39	10	33
8	120,041	0	75,246	29	R	4	44	86	-4	4	18	2	37	8	38
9	121,119	1	94,837	29	S	4	61	89	-2	3	18	3	41	4	42
10	114,327	-1	89,087	30	S	5	51	84	-6	5	10	3	35	8	38
11	120,720	0	64,612	27	S	6	33	65	-7	23	7	1	24	10	42
12	119,253	1	76,566	23	S	4	48	90	-2	3	26	2	43	4	30
13	121,135	4	103,877	27	S	4	59	78	-1	10	16	5	43	7	37
14	118,473	1	72,304	23	S	4	47	91	-1	0	28	4	45	5	30
15	121,135	3	102,904	26	S	4	54	84	-1	4	23	6	44	6	35
16	117,454	0	126,020	24	S	3	67	80	-6	4	31	9	40	7	33
17	119,457	2	79,908	25	S	3	52	83	-3	5	24	5	44	6	33
18	115,045	-1	58,023	21	S	6	35	17	-35	58	4	1	4	23	30
19	117,481	-1	84,625	26	S	4	52	90	-3	2	29	2	42	5	25
20	118,006	2	93,585	25	S	4	57	84	-2	6	30	2	42	7	31
21	119,649	3	72,166	23	S	4	52	88	-1	2	37	3	46	7	34
22	118,083	1	68,945	23	S	4	45	79	-5	7	22	5	34	9	39
23	126,882	1	52,446	25	U	7	32	66	-7	11	8	5	28	17	34
24	125,270	1	62,531	20	U	5	52	68	-8	4	10	17	32	10	35
25	125,937	2	44,439	15	U	7	43	30	-22	7	-1	39	21	24	20
26	122,121	2	66,937	23	U	5	49	76	-5	2	7	12	36	9	38
27	125,693	1	53,454	20	U	6	45	57	-11	8	8	16	29	19	31
28	122,247	1	56,107	22	U	6	53	72	-5	2	11	15	33	11	19
29	121,041	2	52,777	22	U	8	33	10	-22	64	3	8	18	17	16
30	128,492	2	46,139	21	U	7	35	48	-14	2	1	20	28	29	23
31	122,881	1	47,989	25	U	10	24	13	-25	60	3	5	17	21	16
32	122,428	2	44,973	22	U	10	28	11	-20	59	2	6	19	23	17
33	124,065	1	59,336	23	U	8	34	16	-16	65	2	6	25	12	16
34	125,914	2	40,844	18	U	10	27	16	-34	3	-18	19	18	62	13
35	125,510	2	41,734	18	U	8	35	11	-34	21	-8	30	19	38	15
36	137,991	2	42,819	24	U	7	32	57	-8	4	-22	11	33	29	22
37	121,770	1	37,036	21	U	10	27	37	-18	11	-1	14	26	37	21
38	124,914	1	46,923	23	U	7	27	69	-10	1	-1	7	29	23	44
39	113,751	-2	57,624	32	U	7	34	79	-8	6	21	5	28	10	49
40	115,087	-1	32,375	30	U	16	16	1	-61	65	-4	1	-12	31	17
41	114,113	-2	54,512	27	U	7	41	50	-15	34	7	5	23	11	50
42	114,754	-2	43,238	28	U	11	31	6	-39	73	0	3	-5	17	15
43	111,816	-2	40,517	29	U	10	29	7	-34	82	-1	1	-8	10	21
44	120,331	0	63,359	37	U	7	53	53	-14	18	24	10	21	18	21
45	114,052	-1	49,083	28	U	7	41	77	-9	3	30	10	28	9	48
46	115,857	0	37,845	30	U	11	29	52	-13	19	3	7	24	22	36
47	114,975	-1	44,380	29	U	8	26	73	-11	1	31	13	30	12	55
48	118,118	-1	44,228	26	U	8	28	66	-11	3	42	14	22	17	24
49	115,993	-1	44,028	27	U	9	23	77	-10	3	35	12	30	11	57
50	114,063	0	39,640	36	U	10	24	50	-10	21	6	3	18	26	17

Note: U=urban, S=suburban, R=rural, M=mixed, HH=households.

New York State Assembly Districts: Demographic Data (cont.)

Assembly District	Population 1997	+/-	Average HH Income ($)	+/-	District Type	Unempl. Rate (%)	College Educ. (%)	White (non-Hispanic) (%)	+/-	African American (%)	+/-	Asian American (%)	+/-	Hispanic American (%)	+/-
New York	18,225,862	1	57,069	29	M	7	42	65	-4	15	3	5	27	15	22
51	120,641	-1	38,045	33	U	12	23	15	-41	14	17	9	18	62	11
52	122,219	0	72,804	41	U	6	54	67	-8	8	36	8	29	18	16
53	117,375	-1	27,466	27	U	15	12	9	-44	10	-7	4	-4	76	9
54	113,828	-2	30,549	27	U	14	11	1	-82	24	-11	2	-24	71	9
55	111,250	-4	27,789	28	U	19	14	0	-68	77	-9	0	-33	22	27
56	113,373	-3	32,650	34	U	15	18	0	-83	82	-7	0	-24	17	34
57	117,528	-2	46,662	40	U	10	39	9	-32	73	0	2	7	16	20
58	112,671	-2	48,423	34	U	11	27	4	-40	86	0	2	5	8	10
59	128,899	2	52,869	22	U	8	38	57	-9	21	13	5	33	17	34
60	129,983	3	63,769	22	U	6	41	79	-3	3	21	9	42	9	41
61	141,313	11	70,439	25	U	5	40	89	8	1	21	4	59	6	45
62	125,266	5	40,754	32	U	8	27	20	-26	8	40	48	15	24	14
63	127,881	3	67,839	36	U	7	60	50	-12	11	28	9	36	30	18
64	129,681	6	79,759	40	U	6	66	63	-7	9	45	8	48	19	32
65	132,233	5	108,782	43	U	4	76	79	-2	5	44	7	49	9	48
66	136,833	6	91,364	44	U	5	73	74	-3	6	52	9	49	10	31
67	134,433	7	103,328	46	U	6	72	69	-4	9	57	5	47	16	36
68	121,725	0	40,165	42	U	16	22	5	-48	31	-14	1	-11	62	18
69	130,004	4	74,652	45	U	7	63	39	-21	25	31	8	37	27	30
70	121,631	-3	26,380	28	U	17	20	0	-83	63	-13	0	-38	36	33
71	127,632	1	35,872	25	U	12	32	10	-46	33	-11	2	14	54	34
72	125,237	3	30,527	21	U	15	18	3	-72	8	-3	2	-14	86	15
73	133,379	4	177,794	43	U	4	77	84	-1	3	45	6	49	7	40
74	123,452	0	21,129	19	U	17	11	1	-59	27	-10	1	-18	71	6
75	107,567	1	29,387	24	U	16	14	1	-52	31	-4	1	-3	66	5
76	120,387	-1	34,551	20	U	11	21	7	-44	22	-9	5	3	65	11
77	116,560	-2	25,185	21	U	17	15	1	-65	37	-16	1	-9	60	13
78	121,216	-1	27,607	19	U	16	17	4	-50	24	-14	4	-2	67	11
79	120,265	-1	22,478	21	U	19	12	4	-36	40	-10	1	-4	55	12
80	120,946	-1	40,432	25	U	9	30	49	-16	11	0	6	14	34	27
81	117,984	-2	52,798	25	U	6	44	52	-12	11	-3	6	11	30	20
82	118,190	-1	49,874	29	U	6	28	56	-9	17	-2	2	15	24	23
83	120,425	-1	47,420	26	U	9	29	12	-20	64	1	2	12	21	7
84	120,810	-4	43,191	23	S	9	31	25	-28	45	2	3	10	26	21
85	124,935	0	106,379	31	S	4	59	74	-8	7	21	5	37	15	32
86	127,254	2	101,060	31	S	4	63	71	-4	11	12	8	42	9	25
87	117,520	-5	64,668	25	S	5	46	79	-11	6	14	4	32	11	30
88	140,297	1	100,405	29	S	5	59	63	-10	17	15	7	36	13	36
89	126,268	12	134,968	31	S	3	67	87	8	3	31	4	51	6	51
90	138,007	11	82,576	30	S	4	55	78	6	10	26	3	51	9	39
91	144,236	9	68,436	20	S	4	47	92	7	2	12	1	52	4	38
92	126,288	6	85,272	28	S	3	55	74	0	8	14	6	50	12	35
93	118,398	4	73,254	21	S	4	52	73	-2	14	14	6	39	6	39
94	131,557	9	63,163	22	R	5	48	88	6	4	29	2	47	6	51
95	112,651	8	56,539	21	R	5	39	85	5	5	22	1	46	8	49
96	119,343	-1	45,279	16	R	7	36	65	-8	20	11	1	30	13	30
97	119,535	-2	55,055	15	S	4	50	88	-5	5	13	4	36	3	34
98	124,126	3	43,256	22	R	6	33	81	-2	8	17	1	37	10	38
99	122,354	2	56,496	18	R	4	47	90	0	4	12	2	45	3	34
100	128,756	5	45,130	27	R	6	39	94	4	3	12	0	34	2	43

Note: U=urban, S=suburban, R=rural, M=mixed, HH=households.

New York State Assembly Districts: Demographic Data (cont.)

Assembly District	Population 1997	+/-	Average HH Income ($)	+/-	District Type	Unempl. Rate (%)	College Educ. (%)	White (non-Hispanic) (%)	+/-	African American (%)	+/-	Asian American (%)	+/-	Hispanic American (%)	+/-
New York	18,225,862	1	57,069	29	M	7	42	65	-4	15	3	5	27	15	22
101	140,268	0	45,290	16	R	5	42	87	-2	5	11	2	30	6	33
102	123,169	3	50,976	28	R	5	45	94	2	2	11	1	37	3	35
103	123,728	2	53,302	31	S	5	51	92	1	4	9	2	40	2	36
104	122,528	1	54,075	34	U	4	58	87	-2	7	17	3	35	3	38
105	119,948	-1	42,843	31	M	6	37	93	-3	2	14	1	32	4	34
106	114,660	-2	39,204	30	S	7	36	78	-7	17	13	2	24	3	34
107	134,536	7	65,490	32	S	3	58	94	6	2	18	3	46	1	36
108	121,708	2	49,811	29	S	5	45	96	1	1	20	1	32	1	34
109	123,756	2	43,154	28	R	7	40	96	1	1	10	1	33	2	34
110	118,003	-3	39,032	32	R	8	32	89	-4	4	6	1	25	3	27
111	119,164	1	44,932	29	R	5	45	96	1	1	7	1	34	1	36
112	120,670	3	38,403	31	R	9	37	96	2	1	9	1	34	1	33
113	124,918	0	36,655	30	R	8	34	98	-1	1	5	0	33	1	32
114	121,835	2	36,049	17	R	11	35	89	1	6	11	1	31	3	34
115	111,937	-4	47,907	29	S	5	43	97	-4	1	14	1	34	1	20
116	102,971	-11	34,069	27	U	9	29	81	-15	12	2	1	19	6	24
117	125,619	3	43,732	31	R	8	34	97	2	1	9	0	35	1	43
118	124,052	3	51,447	25	S	3	49	94	1	3	43	2	42	1	35
119	105,813	-3	46,314	27	U	8	49	67	-8	25	5	3	24	4	32
120	115,089	-5	35,584	21	U	6	40	85	-9	9	26	2	32	3	35
121	119,859	2	60,120	27	S	4	57	97	1	1	38	1	47	1	39
122	117,180	1	38,135	23	R	7	36	97	1	1	7	0	28	1	36
123	114,091	-6	43,161	18	S	5	47	96	-7	1	4	2	22	1	17
124	111,359	-5	41,664	21	M	6	45	92	-7	3	5	3	30	2	31
125	123,473	1	45,346	31	R	5	60	88	-1	3	14	6	30	3	33
126	116,936	0	41,663	29	R	7	35	95	-1	3	10	0	32	2	30
127	118,898	-2	41,284	30	M	7	36	93	-3	5	8	1	26	2	24
128	127,100	4	46,273	29	R	6	36	94	2	3	17	1	35	2	40
129	133,700	5	48,087	30	R	5	43	96	4	2	18	1	43	2	42
130	118,224	0	39,447	27	R	7	37	97	0	1	11	1	34	1	34
131	119,399	0	37,461	22	U	7	42	70	-9	17	22	3	30	9	42
132	108,212	-7	55,060	22	S	4	57	90	-10	4	27	2	29	3	40
133	111,922	-2	34,521	20	U	10	26	35	-16	50	5	1	13	13	24
134	120,097	2	49,774	21	S	4	44	91	-1	4	35	2	43	3	56
135	119,731	7	66,885	26	S	3	63	94	5	2	43	3	51	1	44
136	126,541	5	64,076	27	S	4	57	91	3	4	27	3	43	2	44
137	127,680	6	47,630	22	S	5	41	93	4	4	26	1	37	2	52
138	117,205	-1	41,370	32	U	8	33	87	-3	10	11	0	34	1	32
139	121,774	2	44,652	31	R	6	37	95	0	3	27	1	42	1	33
140	111,290	-7	44,092	30	S	5	46	95	-9	2	67	1	24	1	35
141	104,086	-12	26,747	27	U	16	26	16	-43	80	-2	1	-20	3	23
142	131,885	10	69,686	36	S	4	64	87	5	6	89	5	46	2	42
143	111,450	-7	39,043	30	S	5	29	95	-9	4	57	0	21	1	26
144	113,511	-5	40,168	35	U	9	42	69	-16	14	51	2	13	14	35
145	121,576	1	50,304	35	S	6	43	96	0	1	52	1	39	2	26
146	119,953	0	45,709	30	S	7	38	91	-2	4	45	0	11	3	27
147	126,493	5	41,567	26	R	6	32	95	4	2	14	0	31	2	36
148	124,080	4	53,696	35	S	5	43	98	4	1	88	1	41	1	34
149	119,785	0	37,273	28	R	8	37	96	-1	1	10	1	32	1	28
150	119,924	0	38,267	32	M	7	35	93	-2	2	6	0	29	4	35

Note: U=urban, S=suburban, R=rural, M=mixed, HH=households.

NORTH CAROLINA

North Carolina has never received the attention it deserves. Unlike Virginia and South Carolina, its neighbors to the north and south, it never developed a great port on the Atlantic Ocean. It initially declined to ratify the Constitution and later voted against secession, relenting only after Virginia had been invaded. As one writer put it, North Carolina "got into the Union too late to vote for George Washington and got out of it too late to vote for Jefferson Davis."

It still does not receive its due. Charlotte is a major banking center and one of the wonder cities of the country, but it is little noticed. North Carolina has enjoyed the surge in population and prosperity that have swept through the South, but not quite to the same extent. Its population has grown by more than 12 percent in each of the last two decades, yet it has slipped from being the tenth-biggest state in 1990 to the eleventh-biggest in 1998 because Georgia has grown even faster. Indeed, North Carolina may be overshadowed by Georgia today as much as it has been by Virginia traditionally.

It is a state of broad prosperity but not of tremendous wealth. Its economy is based on tobacco, of course, but also on peanuts, textiles, and furniture-making, as well as banking and high-tech endeavors in the Research Triangle. It has several large cities in Charlotte, Raleigh, Durham, Greensboro, and Winston-Salem, but many of them are clustered together, making it hard for any one to achieve real prominence.

Even in these cities, though, one finds growth concentrated toward the outer suburbs. The areas of the state that are gaining population fastest form a ring around Raleigh. They include the suburban Sixty-second House District southwest of the city (48 percent growth), the nominally urban Sixty-third District linking Raleigh and Durham (including the Research Triangle), and also rural districts such as the Ninety-fifth, southeast of Raleigh, toward which the suburbs seem to be encroaching. The only areas in the state that have lost population are parts of Fayetteville, Rocky Mount, and along the coast above Wilmington.

North Carolina does not have the great concentrations of wealth or poverty found in Georgia or South Carolina.

In only one house district is average household income greater than $78,000 (the Fifty-seventh District in southeast Charlotte) or less than $30,000 (the Seventieth District around Rocky Mount). Of the twenty poorest districts in the state, fifteen are classified as rural, most in tobacco country and in the western mountains. Unemployment rates are low; the Seventeenth District northwest of Fayetteville is the only place where it exceeds 10 percent.

The state population is 74 percent white; that figure is low for what might be called the fringe South and is more in line with states further down the coast. Districts in the mountains near Tennessee and north along the Virginia border in the Appalachians are almost entirely white. There are fifteen black-majority districts, almost evenly split between downtown urban areas (Greensboro, Winston-Salem, Charlotte) and rural areas (tobacco country around Rocky Mount). Like most of the states of the old Confederacy, there is hardly any other racial or ethnic diversity, and there are no pockets of Asian or Hispanic residents.

No state had a harder time reapportioning its congressional districts in this decade. The state tried to create a second black-majority congressional seat, which proved difficult because African Americans are not clustered in any one place. Using sophisticated computer mapping technology, reapportioners constructed an ungainly district that ran from west of Charlotte all the way to Durham, snaking through Winston-Salem and Greensboro, in places no wider than a single lane on I-85. It was joked at the time that a motorist driving down the highway with the door open could kill half the members of the district. The Supreme Court was not amused and ruled in 1993 that the district was unconstitutional based on race. It has since been redrawn twice. The battle will certainly spill over to the next round of reapportionment.

Aided by gerrymandering and the general Republican tide in the South, the GOP captured control of the state house in 1994 and now controls both chambers of the legislature.

NORTH CAROLINA
State Senate Districts

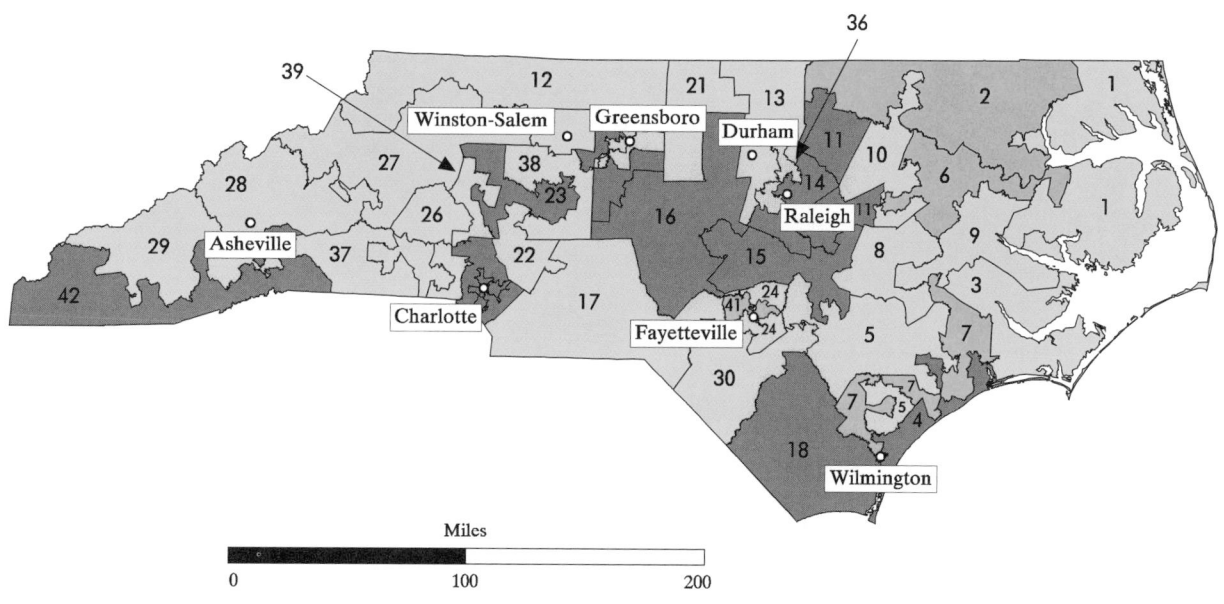

CHARLOTTE

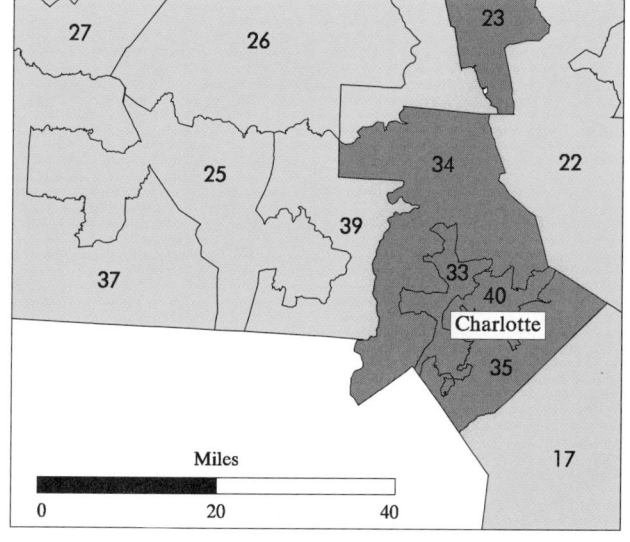

WINSTON-SALEM/GREENSBORO

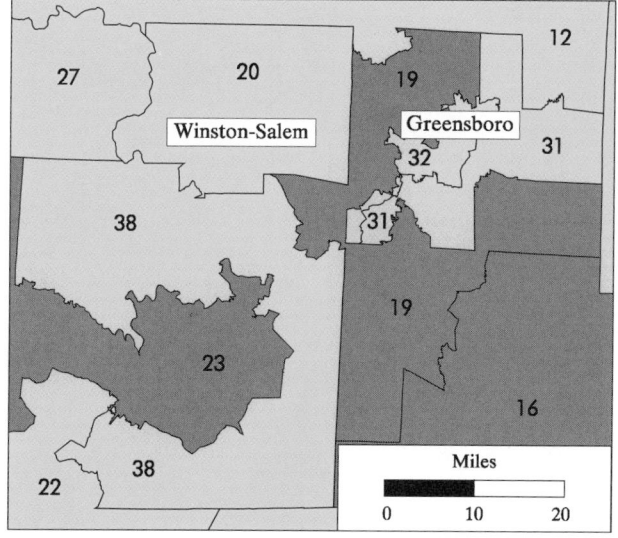

Population Growth   -4% to 2%   5% to 13%   14% to 24%   51%

North Carolina State Senate Districts: Demographic Data

Senate District	Population 1997	+/-	Average HH Income ($)	+/-	District Type	Unempl. Rate (%)	College Educ. (%)	White (non-Hispanic) (%)	+/-	African American (%)	+/-	Asian American (%)	+/-	Hispanic American (%)	+/-
N. Carolina	7,411,047	12	45,528	37	R	5	35	74	11	22	12	1	51	1	45
1	144,082	10	39,936	34	R	6	29	73	11	25	7	0	24	1	39
2	127,467	2	32,821	38	R	7	19	37	0	60	3	0	-9	0	4
3	145,475	7	41,346	38	R	6	32	76	6	21	9	1	38	2	34
4	163,262	21	50,681	40	S	5	43	88	20	9	33	1	55	2	49
5	149,962	10	40,552	49	R	6	25	67	7	28	11	1	43	4	44
6	131,320	2	33,144	34	R	7	21	41	0	58	3	0	21	1	11
7	123,470	-4	31,317	38	R	9	25	49	-9	45	1	1	16	4	-2
8	142,601	8	36,945	33	R	6	28	65	6	32	10	1	44	2	47
9	148,939	10	44,208	40	R	5	37	71	8	27	15	1	50	1	39
10	154,427	12	41,086	30	R	5	29	66	10	33	14	0	40	1	45
11	157,384	17	43,181	38	R	5	29	69	16	29	17	0	25	1	51
12	283,800	8	38,785	34	R	5	24	89	7	9	8	0	16	1	48
13	300,494	12	50,137	38	U	4	48	62	11	34	12	2	51	1	47
14	316,053	17	49,622	30	U	4	49	68	13	28	22	2	53	2	56
15	160,219	18	40,292	45	R	6	27	75	17	22	19	0	51	2	50
16	304,349	15	48,968	39	R	4	46	81	13	16	18	1	54	2	58
17	299,200	12	39,223	29	R	5	25	73	11	24	11	0	37	1	42
18	155,399	15	37,224	39	R	7	24	72	15	26	14	0	6	1	49
19	165,467	16	57,845	35	S	3	43	92	15	5	26	1	67	1	56
20	279,324	8	50,519	29	U	5	44	72	7	26	9	1	47	1	48
21	147,978	9	42,958	32	M	3	30	76	8	23	10	0	38	1	50
22	154,593	13	45,693	34	S	4	27	87	13	12	15	0	50	1	51
23	154,169	16	40,868	34	R	4	28	76	15	22	16	1	58	1	63
24	148,629	9	50,777	54	S	6	38	69	6	22	9	2	50	5	45
25	142,172	9	42,410	34	M	5	25	82	8	17	10	1	47	1	58
26	149,758	10	47,812	38	S	3	30	88	9	9	11	1	52	1	60
27	276,450	7	37,999	32	R	4	20	94	6	4	9	0	11	1	52
28	285,291	10	40,537	36	M	4	33	91	9	8	12	1	47	1	50
29	146,988	11	36,576	29	R	6	32	90	10	3	12	0	27	1	57
30	149,577	11	38,005	48	R	8	22	39	7	27	11	0	32	1	30
31	129,214	5	37,995	31	U	6	28	45	3	53	7	1	36	1	13
32	138,361	11	54,743	35	U	3	49	78	8	17	19	2	48	2	59
33	141,828	17	47,862	39	U	5	39	41	17	55	15	2	68	1	53
34	165,116	24	53,811	38	S	4	38	71	21	26	28	2	63	1	71
35	162,890	20	87,937	44	U	3	64	92	19	4	27	2	71	1	64
36	205,428	51	69,440	32	S	3	66	84	47	10	71	4	105	2	112
37	139,336	8	39,184	30	R	5	25	82	7	16	9	0	37	1	50
38	148,086	9	44,536	29	S	3	28	92	9	7	8	0	30	1	46
39	143,552	7	48,953	37	S	4	27	90	6	9	9	1	41	1	45
40	145,931	15	49,546	37	U	4	46	71	10	23	22	3	56	3	69
41	128,220	-1	41,878	49	M	11	37	45	-8	43	1	3	32	8	24
42	154,999	14	41,332	33	R	5	34	96	13	2	13	0	37	1	66

Note: U=urban, S=suburban, R=rural, M=mixed, HH=households.

NORTH CAROLINA
State House Districts

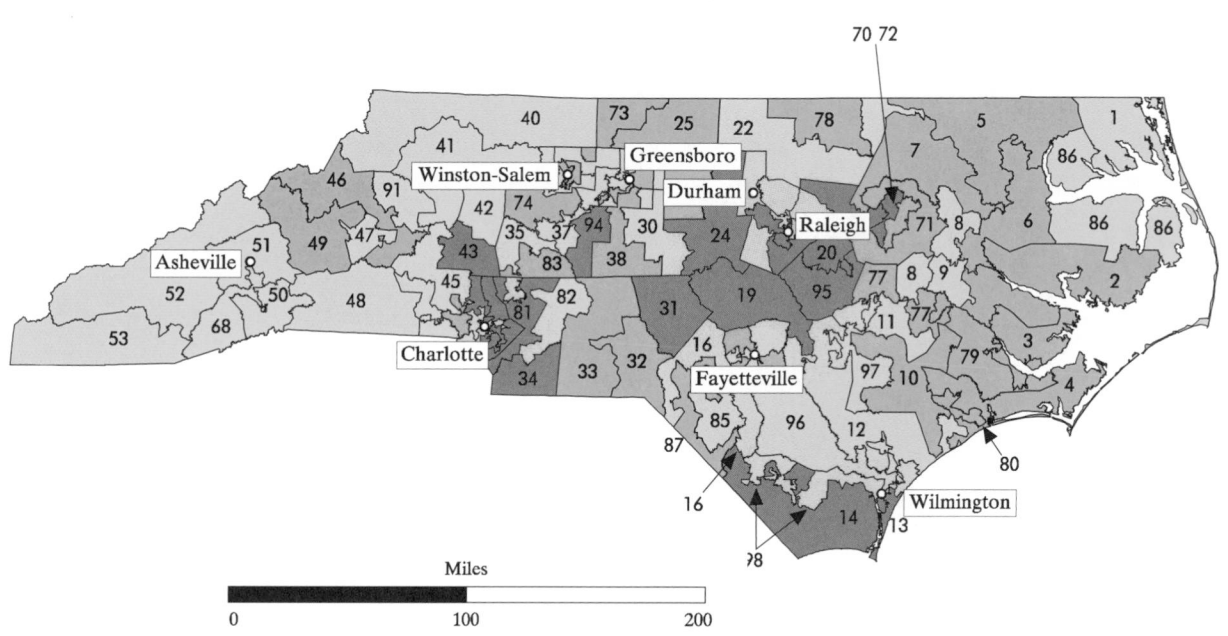

RALEIGH

FAYETTEVILLE

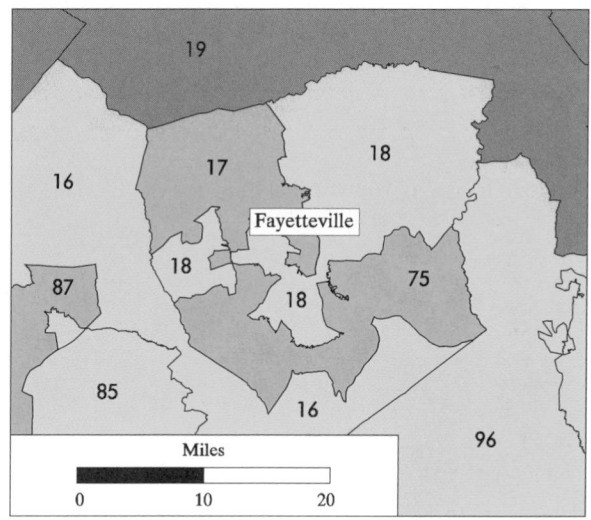

| Population Growth | | -6% to 7% | | 8% to 16% | | 17% to 29% | | 38% to 48% |

WINSTON-SALEM/GREENSBORO

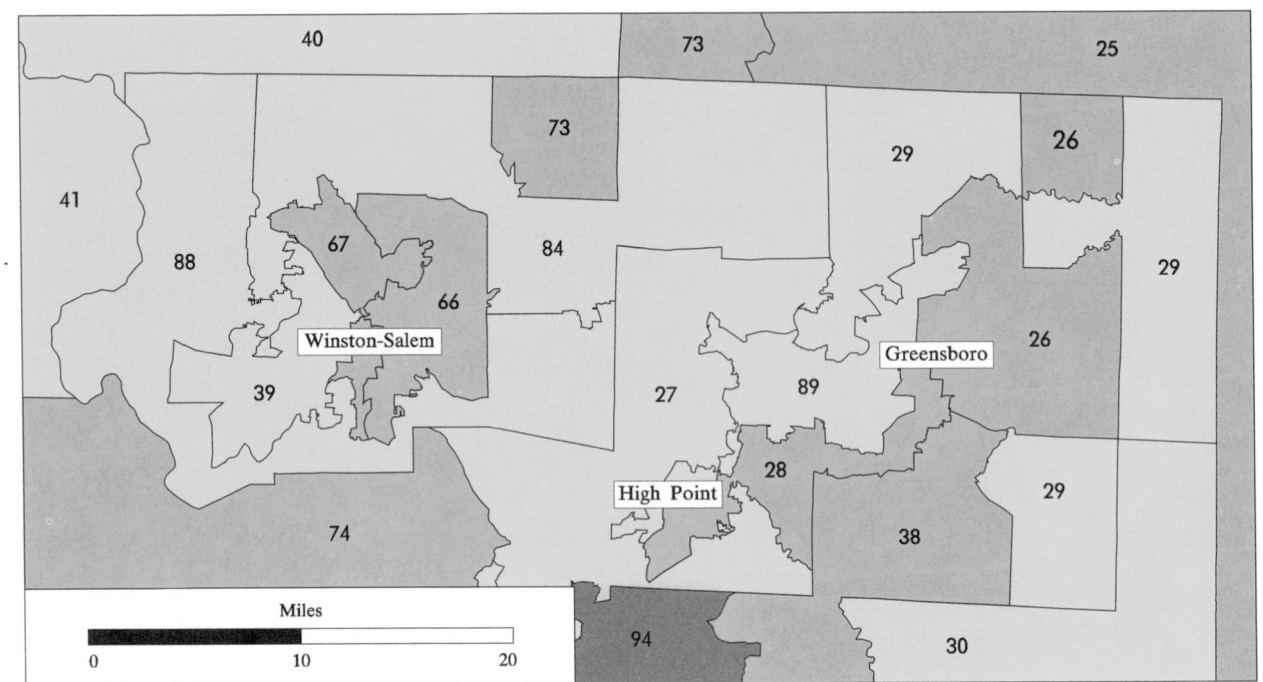

CHARLOTTE

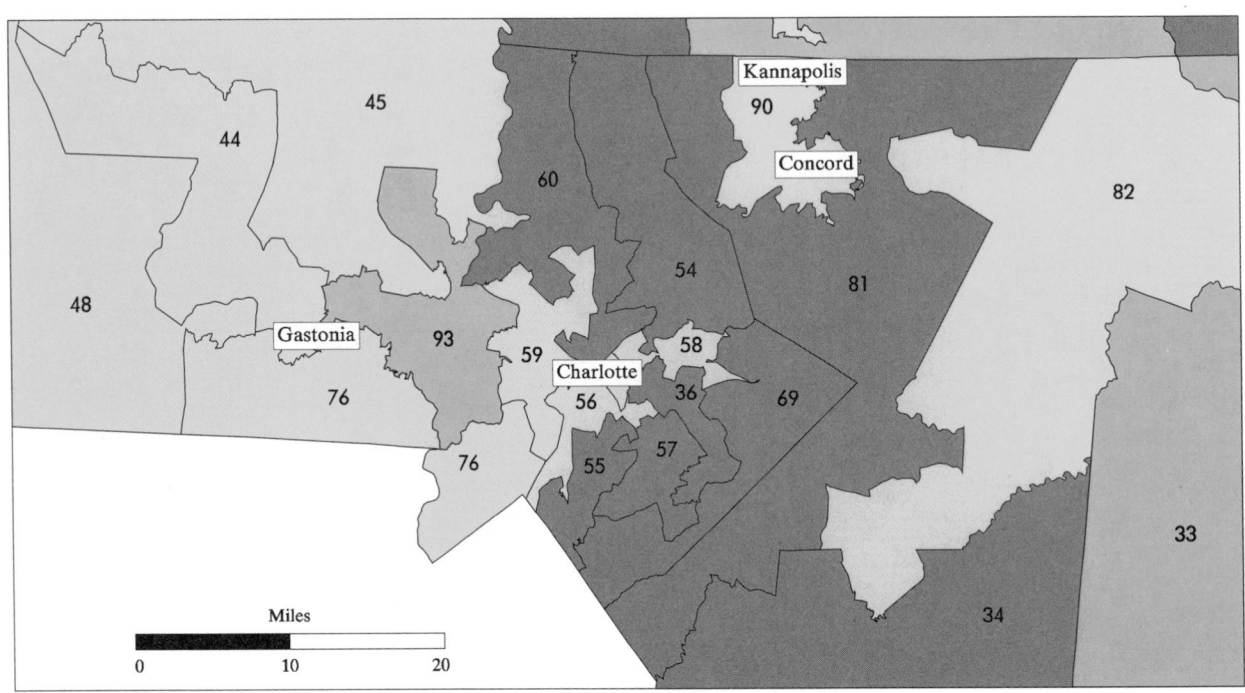

Population Growth   ▨ -6% to 7%   ▨ 8% to 16%   ▨ 17% to 29%

North Carolina State House Districts: Demographic Data

House District	Population 1997	+/-	Average HH Income ($)	+/-	District Type	Unempl. Rate (%)	College Educ. (%)	White (non-Hispanic) (%)	+/-	African American (%)	+/-	Asian American (%)	+/-	Hispanic American (%)	+/-
N. Carolina	7,411,047	12	45,528	37	R	5	35	74	11	22	12	1	51	1	45
1	60,155	13	39,297	33	R	6	26	70	13	28	11	1	43	1	51
2	62,016	5	38,204	36	R	6	25	69	4	30	6	0	-15	1	28
3	54,118	7	43,252	38	R	7	33	78	5	17	8	1	37	3	33
4	120,758	5	42,339	40	R	7	34	78	5	16	1	2	40	4	24
5	56,308	2	33,870	41	R	7	20	40	2	59	3	0	-1	0	1
6	60,931	6	35,569	35	R	6	28	60	6	39	6	0	33	1	23
7	56,734	3	31,078	37	R	8	15	33	0	63	4	0	-38	0	11
8	58,174	9	32,774	31	R	7	23	39	6	60	10	0	40	1	27
9	62,122	12	47,949	42	R	5	46	73	10	24	16	1	58	1	45
10	57,378	1	36,731	52	R	5	19	74	-1	21	3	1	17	4	15
11	57,940	9	39,968	34	R	5	33	67	6	30	14	1	44	2	54
12	64,748	14	38,233	44	R	6	25	64	13	32	15	0	13	2	34
13	66,001	23	50,637	35	S	4	44	90	20	8	49	1	64	1	68
14	126,325	20	41,001	39	R	6	30	80	19	17	20	0	53	1	56
15	68,788	25	57,896	39	S	2	46	81	23	16	31	1	83	1	62
16	62,460	13	38,514	40	R	7	25	62	10	26	17	0	29	1	44
17	99,928	-6	38,926	47	M	13	35	41	-13	47	-2	3	21	8	11
18	122,290	13	52,208	53	S	7	42	65	8	24	13	3	55	6	58
19	134,855	18	42,026	47	R	6	28	74	16	22	19	1	52	2	48
20	63,538	20	42,819	36	R	4	27	77	19	20	20	0	26	2	67
21	62,587	16	39,989	27	U	5	40	42	15	54	15	2	55	2	71
22	124,736	11	40,914	36	R	6	26	65	9	33	13	0	10	1	40
23	176,794	9	50,064	37	U	4	54	56	7	40	10	2	47	1	41
24	136,396	18	54,515	41	M	4	63	78	16	17	22	3	58	2	59
25	177,982	7	42,486	33	M	4	28	75	6	24	7	0	34	1	44
26	55,087	4	34,438	27	U	6	27	39	-1	59	8	1	37	1	23
27	69,412	15	57,161	36	U	3	45	90	13	8	24	1	65	1	58
28	56,212	6	40,097	33	U	7	30	40	6	58	5	1	38	1	14
29	65,483	12	65,839	30	U	2	57	87	10	10	22	2	59	1	51
30	62,227	8	38,767	32	R	4	22	84	6	14	12	0	19	2	65
31	67,199	18	49,519	36	R	4	41	80	18	19	19	0	40	1	57
32	54,573	3	34,154	31	R	6	22	67	2	29	4	0	30	1	39
33	54,433	3	37,160	35	R	4	20	64	1	34	4	0	3	2	31
34	68,629	25	41,398	19	R	3	29	77	24	21	27	0	68	1	58
35	61,965	16	41,334	35	R	4	32	71	16	27	15	1	68	1	54
36	65,864	17	46,480	32	U	3	46	73	13	20	21	3	58	3	78
37	58,380	12	38,296	29	R	4	23	80	11	18	12	1	50	1	54
38	62,801	7	46,857	35	S	3	27	94	7	5	13	0	22	1	27
39	53,414	9	63,134	27	U	3	59	90	7	8	29	1	51	1	52
40	183,682	10	38,057	35	R	5	25	95	9	4	11	0	19	1	53
41	123,582	8	36,772	27	R	4	20	94	8	5	11	0	2	1	52
42	58,046	10	44,396	36	R	4	28	78	9	20	10	1	44	1	66
43	69,083	17	49,451	40	R	4	27	88	15	11	27	0	57	1	32
44	61,079	9	36,854	31	M	6	17	77	9	21	10	0	39	1	61
45	126,189	11	46,155	37	S	3	25	90	10	8	13	1	53	1	71
46	117,373	4	41,043	35	R	4	25	93	3	6	5	1	36	1	38
47	57,788	11	40,441	35	S	4	27	88	10	9	12	2	53	1	55
48	180,227	9	39,459	30	R	5	26	82	8	17	10	0	37	1	50
49	57,499	7	35,511	35	R	5	22	95	7	4	7	1	42	0	37
50	65,923	13	42,828	31	R	4	38	96	13	1	7	0	52	2	61

Note: U=urban, S=suburban, R=rural, M=mixed, HH=households.

North Carolina State House Districts: Demographic Data (cont.)

House District	Population		Average HH Income		District Type	Unempl. Rate	College Educ.	White (non-Hispanic)		African American		Asian American		Hispanic American	
	1997	+/-	($)	+/-		(%)	(%)	(%)	+/-	(%)	+/-	(%)	+/-	(%)	+/-
N. Carolina	7,411,047	12	45,528	37	R	5	35	74	11	22	12	1	51	1	45
51	173,362	10	42,110	37	S	4	36	89	9	9	12	1	44	1	59
52	116,101	9	35,155	33	R	8	29	91	8	1	6	0	10	1	46
53	60,953	14	32,747	31	R	6	26	96	14	1	8	0	8	1	63
54	65,835	22	52,998	42	S	4	46	65	18	30	26	2	58	2	67
55	64,729	17	76,046	43	U	3	63	87	14	8	30	3	71	2	69
56	61,669	16	54,961	41	U	4	48	63	14	32	15	2	59	2	59
57	67,937	22	93,089	42	U	3	68	90	19	5	28	3	74	2	76
58	63,160	14	54,558	40	U	5	41	60	8	34	21	3	53	2	57
59	62,470	16	39,617	31	U	6	23	42	14	55	17	1	57	1	31
60	68,087	25	43,799	40	U	6	29	45	34	53	17	1	69	1	56
61	61,109	15	67,002	30	U	3	70	84	11	11	28	3	56	2	55
62	80,224	48	67,226	36	S	2	61	81	45	13	50	3	111	2	100
63	78,518	29	49,355	31	U	4	62	76	24	16	34	6	70	3	78
64	64,126	17	48,429	33	U	4	50	68	14	29	22	2	61	2	54
65	74,736	41	53,813	28	S	4	50	74	34	23	61	1	84	1	84
66	54,082	1	33,612	26	U	8	24	41	-4	57	3	0	28	1	34
67	51,296	3	36,647	22	U	7	42	47	-3	51	7	1	44	1	31
68	64,931	13	47,377	32	R	4	43	92	12	6	17	1	44	1	65
69	67,554	22	76,791	45	S	2	56	91	20	5	30	2	82	1	58
70	54,411	-1	28,933	28	R	9	17	34	-2	65	-1	0	11	0	-3
71	59,461	3	40,810	37	R	4	24	64	0	34	7	0	9	1	24
72	65,888	19	52,436	32	R	4	43	78	17	20	25	1	55	1	54
73	61,031	7	40,420	33	R	5	21	82	6	16	11	0	23	1	46
74	61,488	7	48,718	32	S	4	32	92	7	6	8	0	15	1	56
75	57,050	7	47,330	53	S	6	29	73	5	18	7	2	43	4	50
76	64,812	11	56,569	38	S	4	39	86	9	12	19	1	54	1	66
77	61,878	4	43,843	39	R	4	28	78	3	21	9	0	29	1	28
78	54,491	5	32,103	29	R	8	19	45	4	54	7	0	-30	1	26
79	63,107	3	35,452	39	R	7	27	48	3	50	2	1	36	1	13
80	53,571	-3	42,835	48	M	9	37	70	-6	19	-4	3	26	7	15
81	73,857	22	54,942	30	S	2	34	93	22	5	23	0	53	1	61
82	62,272	10	37,795	24	R	4	23	88	9	10	11	1	46	1	45
83	61,350	7	40,806	32	R	3	24	94	7	5	-1	1	41	1	49
84	69,166	16	56,193	33	S	4	42	90	15	8	30	1	51	1	73
85	61,283	12	43,101	54	R	8	25	25	6	15	12	0	45	1	17
86	61,066	10	41,613	36	R	6	31	76	12	23	5	0	-2	1	36
87	51,942	7	31,803	42	R	9	18	30	5	51	9	0	-12	0	-2
88	67,677	10	62,568	30	S	3	50	90	8	8	26	1	52	1	53
89	114,308	11	51,891	36	U	4	46	76	7	19	18	2	47	2	58
90	62,778	14	43,766	35	S	5	26	79	13	19	17	1	52	1	76
91	60,026	9	44,925	37	R	3	25	93	9	6	10	0	21	1	62
92	80,241	38	77,026	36	S	3	65	86	36	9	40	3	97	1	93
93	59,927	3	44,408	35	S	4	23	89	3	8	6	1	43	1	49
94	65,019	19	40,632	31	S	4	20	95	19	4	18	0	84	0	48
95	68,857	26	40,913	40	R	4	27	80	24	18	30	0	53	2	65
96	63,676	15	43,860	45	R	5	30	71	15	27	12	0	32	1	44
97	57,809	10	34,459	44	R	8	25	49	9	47	10	1	48	2	39
98	61,301	12	34,595	42	M	8	26	46	8	52	15	0	33	1	62

Note: U=urban, S=suburban, R=rural, M=mixed, HH=households.

NORTH DAKOTA

North Dakota was founded and settled by optimists. It took optimism to come here at all, to look across the lonely plains and imagine something grander. The first whites to cross it were Lewis and Clark, who spent the winter of 1804–1805 near Mandan before continuing in search of a water route across the continent. Theodore Roosevelt fancied himself a cowboy and built a ranch in the Bad Lands before blizzard and drought drove him out. In *The American Commonwealth,* Lord Bryce describes attending a ceremony for laying the cornerstone of the territorial capitol in Bismarck in 1883. The lot was a mile or so outside of town, and he asked whether a park was planned around it. No, he was told; this is where the center of the city is destined to be someday. When a later generation built a bigger capitol, they put up a skyscraper.

Optimism also infected the Nonpartisan League, which dominated North Dakota politics from 1915 until 1960. The league was built by the northern European farmers who had been conned into moving there by railroad speculators (Bismarck was given its name to help sell the place to Germans). They advocated socialism, railed against the Minnesota mill owners and railroad magnates who dominated the state economy, and whipped up a frenzy of enthusiasm for cooperative agriculture. When World War I came, many sided with the kaiser.

Although the state's politics have become tamer, its commercial outline would be familiar to an earlier generation. The western part of the state is better suited to grazing; the eastern part is where much of the country's durum (pasta) wheat is grown. It remains a state of small farmers and ranchers. Fargo and Grand Forks, the only cities of any size (though neither has more than 100,000 residents), hug I-29 and the Red River on the state's eastern border.

Periodic farm crises over the last seventy-five years have thrown ever more people off the land. Political commentator Michael Barone writes that the counties comprising Fargo, Grand Forks, Minot, and Bismarck grew in population from 134,000 in 1930 to 310,000 in 1996,

while the population of the remaining 48 counties fell from 546,000 to 333,000. Much of North Dakota, in other words, is emptier today than at any time since the Indians roamed there. North Dakota was the forty-sixth-most-populous state in 1980 and the forty-seventh-most-populous in 1990, having lost more than 2 percent of its residents to the farm crisis. It has grown only about 1 percent since 1990.

Fargo, which has a thriving partnership with its sister city, Moorhead, Minnesota, across the Red River, is the only place to have grown at all this decade. The Forty-first District, which has grown by 35 percent since 1990, is by far the biggest gainer. Several rural districts, many along the Canadian border, have lost population.

The cities are also the only places of real wealth in the state, though even that is modest by national standards. Average household income is $59,000 in Grand Forks's Seventeenth House District. Districts in Fargo and Bismarck are not far behind. The poorest parts of the state are the rural wheat-growing districts along the Canadian or South Dakota borders, as well as the Indian reservations. Unemployment on the reservations still runs as high as 18 percent, but ironically, income there is rising faster than anywhere else in the state, thanks to gambling. Casinos at the Turtle Mountain, Standing Rock, and Fort Berthhold reservations are now among the state's biggest private employers.

Native Americans, who make up about 4 percent of the state population, are the only large minority group. Forty-three of North Dakota's forty-nine state house districts are at least 90 percent white. The only districts that have any sizable numbers of African Americans, Asians, or Hispanics are those around the Minot or Grand Forks Air Force Bases.

Although North Dakota's two U.S. senators and lone representative are Democrats, Republicans have captured the governorship and made great gains in the legislature. They have increased their majority in the house from 58–48 in 1990 to 72–26 in 1996. Democrats held the senate in 1990, 27–26, but by 1996 the GOP controlled it, 30–19.

NORTH DAKOTA
State Legislative Districts

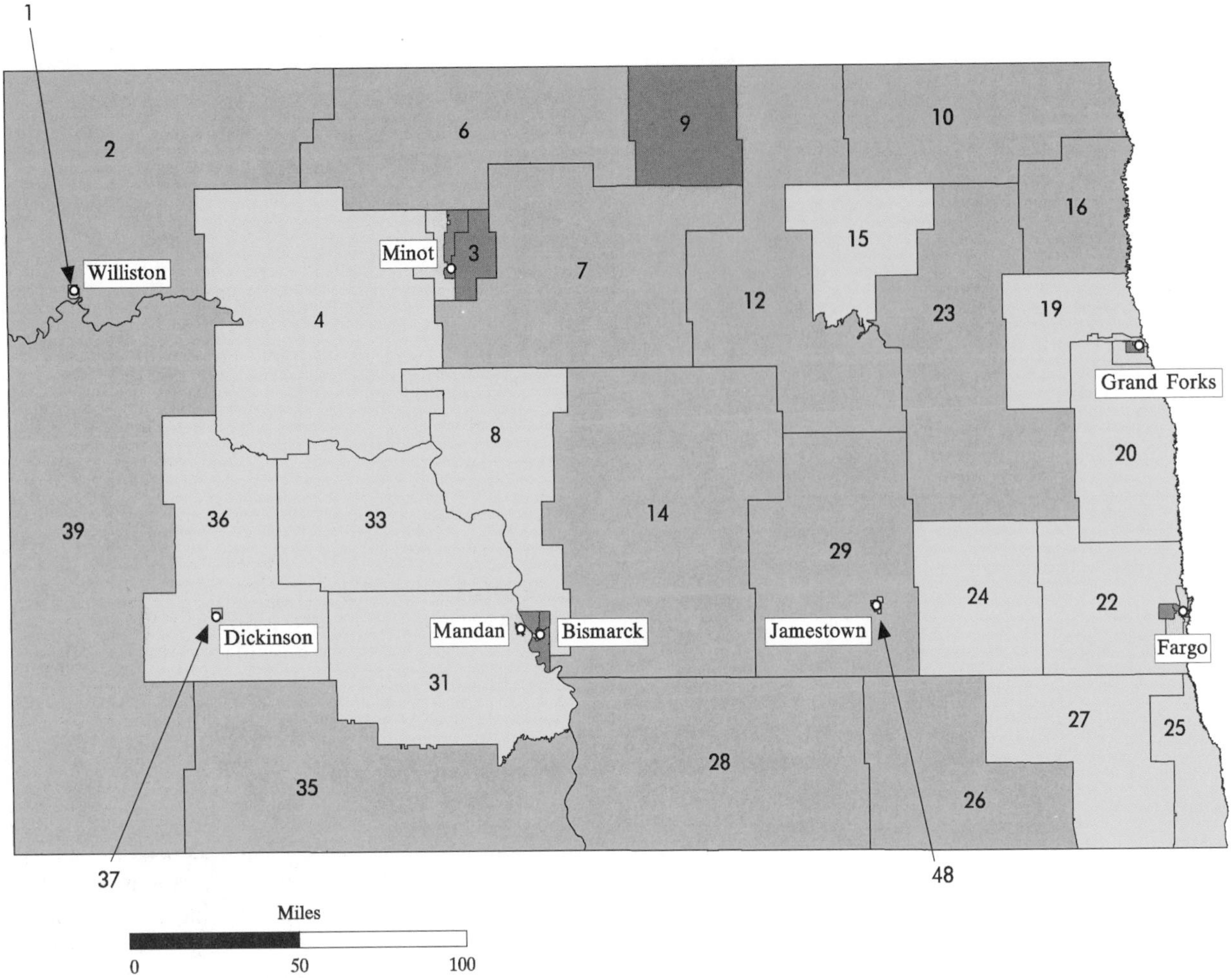

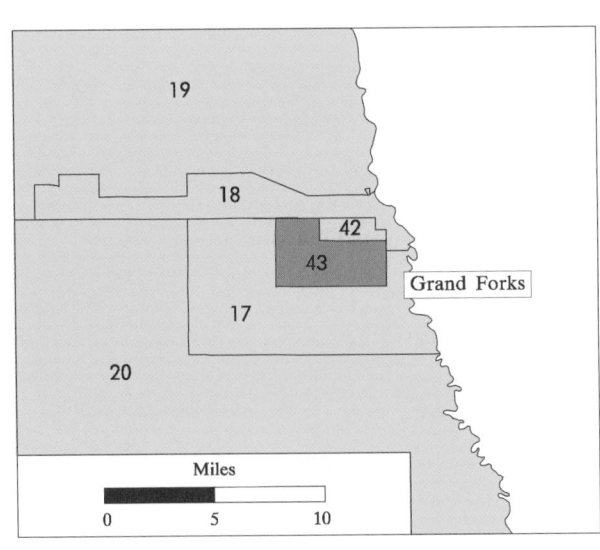

1

2

6

9

10

Williston

Minot 3

15

16

7

12

23

19

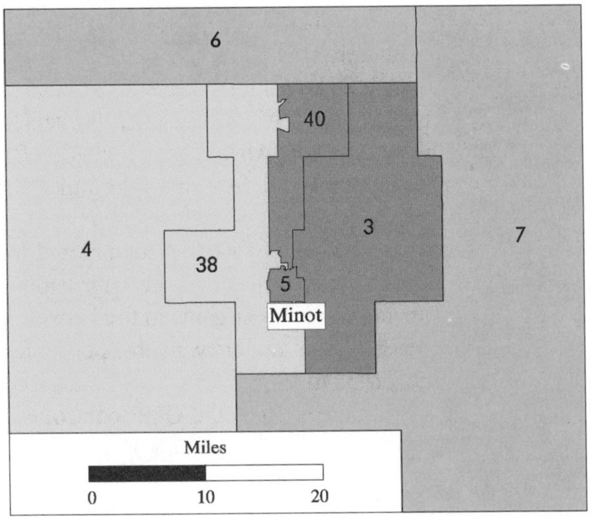

Grand Forks

4

20

39

36

33

8

14

29

24

22

Fargo

Dickinson

Mandan Bismarck

Jamestown

31

27

25

37

35

28

26

48

Miles

0   50   100

MINOT

6

40

4

38

3

5

Minot

7

Miles

0   10   20

GRAND FORKS

19

18

42

43

17

Grand Forks

20

Miles

0   5   10

Population Growth   -11% to -5%   -4% to 3%   5% to 17%   23% to 35%

FARGO

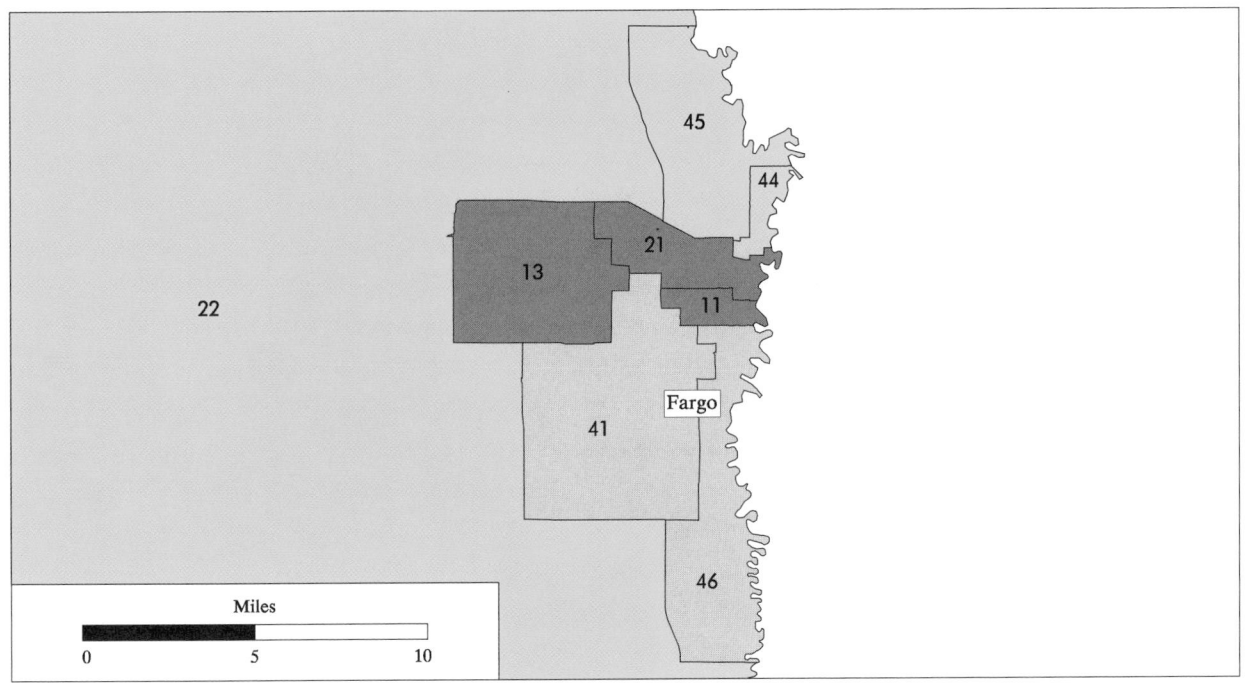

BISMARCK

Population Growth ■ -11% to -5%   ■ -4% to 3%   ■ 5% to 17%   □ 23% to 35%

North Dakota State Legislative Districts: Demographic Data

Legis. District	Population		Average HH Income		District Type	Unempl. Rate	College Educ.	White (non-Hispanic)		African American		Asian American		Hispanic American	
	1997	+/-	($)	+/-		(%)	(%)	(%)	+/-	(%)	+/-	(%)	+/-	(%)	+/-
N.Dakota	644,760	1	41,290	44	R	6	40	94	0	1	1	1	40	1	13
1	11,397	-3	37,983	33	R	6	40	95	-3	0	75	0	11	1	18
2	13,993	-9	38,943	45	R	5	33	95	-9	0	-13	0	-15	1	17
3	14,166	6	34,753	31	R	8	35	95	5	1	10	1	52	1	42
4	13,646	-2	38,531	59	R	10	33	79	-2	0	-13	0	-24	1	15
5	14,351	9	45,438	50	R	5	44	96	8	1	28	1	66	1	16
6	12,002	-8	36,652	40	R	7	35	99	-8	0	-20	0	-20	0	-3
7	12,855	-5	34,502	47	R	7	33	99	-5	0	20	0	-77	0	20
8	12,945	1	46,534	53	R	5	37	97	1	0	100	0	33	0	3
9	14,202	11	28,560	37	R	18	28	32	7	0	-7	0	-31	0	-22
10	11,364	-9	44,047	56	R	5	32	98	-9	0	-18	0	-40	1	10
11	13,367	6	46,233	42	U	3	47	96	5	0	14	2	60	1	27
12	12,279	-6	33,808	57	R	9	28	77	-7	0	-100	0	-90	0	-6
13	13,729	17	46,055	47	S	4	46	98	17	0	13	0	67	1	25
14	14,515	-7	38,806	54	R	6	29	99	-7	0	-25	0	-29	0	-3
15	12,979	-3	37,265	35	R	5	36	94	-4	0	-32	0	8	0	2
16	12,750	-7	44,860	56	R	5	34	95	-7	0	6	0	0	4	-2
17	13,489	-1	59,026	46	U	3	55	96	-1	0	-21	1	36	1	14
18	12,228	-1	32,331	33	R	7	37	90	-3	3	1	1	47	3	16
19	13,917	-2	38,409	46	R	8	38	89	-4	5	5	2	52	2	8
20	13,030	-2	40,816	37	R	5	37	98	-2	0	-29	0	-4	1	3
21	14,936	5	30,132	36	U	6	41	95	4	0	-6	1	53	1	14
22	13,696	2	53,554	45	R	4	42	99	2	0	-100	0	18	1	15
23	11,650	-11	34,078	43	R	7	29	99	-11	0	-100	0	-93	0	0
24	12,119	-3	37,383	49	R	6	37	99	-4	0	26	0	16	0	0
25	13,740	1	44,008	51	R	7	43	96	1	0	-26	1	29	0	0
26	12,112	-6	36,734	45	R	4	33	99	-6	0	-38	0	6	0	6
27	11,679	-3	40,163	45	R	3	31	99	-3	0	-57	0	-81	0	-12
28	11,779	-11	31,822	38	R	4	20	100	-11	0	-100	0	-55	0	-4
29	14,852	-5	42,086	46	R	5	33	99	-6	0	-15	0	3	0	11
30	15,284	10	40,755	39	U	5	44	95	9	0	17	0	45	1	12
31	15,492	0	39,402	35	R	4	31	98	0	0	33	0	-12	0	-12
32	12,951	2	39,609	34	U	5	43	94	2	0	-24	1	49	1	8
33	12,592	-4	47,083	46	R	6	33	96	-4	0	25	0	13	0	-4
34	10,175	7	35,955	35	S	7	32	97	6	0	33	0	43	1	19
35	11,819	-7	34,344	49	R	10	28	72	-12	0	-29	0	-43	0	2
36	14,387	-2	36,527	42	R	5	30	98	-2	0	0	0	7	1	20
37	10,934	-1	34,680	25	R	4	37	98	-1	0	-18	0	37	0	-4
38	14,240	-3	43,898	48	R	6	45	86	-4	6	-4	3	42	4	7
39	12,219	-8	37,358	43	R	4	33	98	-8	0	0	0	-60	0	-19
40	9,518	6	39,818	46	R	8	42	91	5	3	12	2	60	2	24
41	18,096	35	54,304	37	U	4	60	97	34	0	46	1	91	1	61
42	12,651	1	35,548	38	U	7	57	91	-1	1	-13	3	41	2	34
43	15,848	11	43,543	43	U	5	55	95	10	1	4	1	65	1	21
44	12,711	2	51,798	50	U	4	56	96	1	0	-6	2	56	1	32
45	13,010	3	44,827	36	U	5	59	94	1	0	2	4	54	1	25
46	14,011	23	54,829	39	U	3	60	98	23	0	34	1	82	1	31
47	14,420	16	58,866	38	U	5	64	97	15	0	17	1	71	1	26
48	10,245	-3	37,119	38	R	4	36	97	-3	0	3	1	46	1	26
49	14,390	13	46,017	34	U	4	51	97	12	0	-88	0	66	1	24

Note: U=urban, S=suburban, R=rural, M=mixed, HH=households.

OHIO

Ohio can be divided into three broad latitudinal bands, each with its representative big city. In the north is Cleveland, with its industry and lake traffic, as well as Toledo, Youngstown, and Akron. In the middle of the state is Columbus, now the biggest of the three and a growing corporate headquarters and distribution center. In the south, Cincinnati, the oldest and wealthiest of the three, looks across the Ohio River at Kentucky. In a sense, Ohio, rather than Pennsylvania, might better be called the Keystone State, linking the eastern seaboard with the Midwest, and the Border South with the Great Lakes.

The state's industrial luster has dimmed, though it is making some strides in light manufacturing. It was the sixth-largest state in 1980 and is now the seventh-largest, having been pushed aside by Florida. Population grew by less than 1 percent in the 1980s but has grown by 3 percent in this decade—ninth-slowest overall, but ahead of its traditional rivals, New York, Pennsylvania, Michigan, and Illinois. Although Ohio remains an important state in presidential years, its political clout has fallen. It had twenty-four electoral votes in 1970; by 2002, it most likely will have only eighteen.

Ohio's industrial cities have shrunk. Cleveland and Cincinnati are as small as they have been since 1910 (see Table 1); Akron, Canton, and Dayton, since the 1920s. Only Columbus has grown—by 12 percent from 1980 to 1990. As Ohio's cities have lost population, its suburbs have grown, particularly its outer suburbs. The fastest-

growing districts are all on the outskirts of Columbus or the corridor between Dayton and Cincinnati. The areas losing population fastest are distributed evenly among the downtown areas of the big cities: Cleveland, Cincinnati, Youngstown, Toledo, and Columbus. Of the twenty fastest-growing house districts in the state, eleven are suburban, six are rural, one is urban, and two are of mixed composition. Of the twenty fastest-shrinking, fifteen are urban and five suburban (and all are close-in to the cities).

After a tough time in the 1980s, Ohio's unemployment rate is now about the national average, and it ranks in the middle of the other Rust Belt states. It is highest in the central cities—22 percent in Cleveland's Tenth District. Average household income in the Tenth District is just $21,000 a year, among the lowest in the country. The wealthiest districts are the older suburbs: Shaker Heights on the east side of Cleveland and Rocky River on the west side; districts northwest, north, and southeast of Cincinnati; Akron; Trumbull County.

Ohio is 86 percent white and 11 percent African American; it has fewer blacks and more whites than New York, Michigan, or Illinois, but not Pennsylvania. The percentage of whites is highest in the rural farming counties scattered throughout the state but is 90 percent or greater in sixty-two of the ninety-nine house districts. There are ten black-majority house districts in the state: five in Cleveland, two in Cincinnati, two in Columbus, and one in Toledo.

A word should be said about the Eleventh District outside Cleveland, which is exactly half African American. It is suburban and one of only twelve suburban black-majority districts north of the Mason-Dixon line (there are forty-eight in all). It is also the wealthiest black-majority district in the country—average household income of $65,488—and one of only two in the country in which at least half the people have finished college. It should also be noted that this district borders the Tenth District, which as already mentioned is one of the poorest districts in the country, with one of the highest rates of unemployment.

Republicans control both houses of the legislature, although the stories are very different in the chambers. The senate has changed hardly at all in this decade, but the house has changed dramatically, flipping from a 61–38 Democratic majority in 1990 to a 60–39 Republican majority six years later.

Table 1 Twentieth-Century Populations of Cleveland and Cincinnati

Year	Cleveland Population	Cincinnati Population
1900	381,768	325,902
1910	560,663	363,591
1920	796,841	401,247
1930	900,429	451,160
1940	878,336	455,610
1950	914,808	503,998
1960	876,050	502,550
1970	750,879	453,514
1980	573,822	385,409
1990	505,616	364,040

OHIO
State Senate Districts

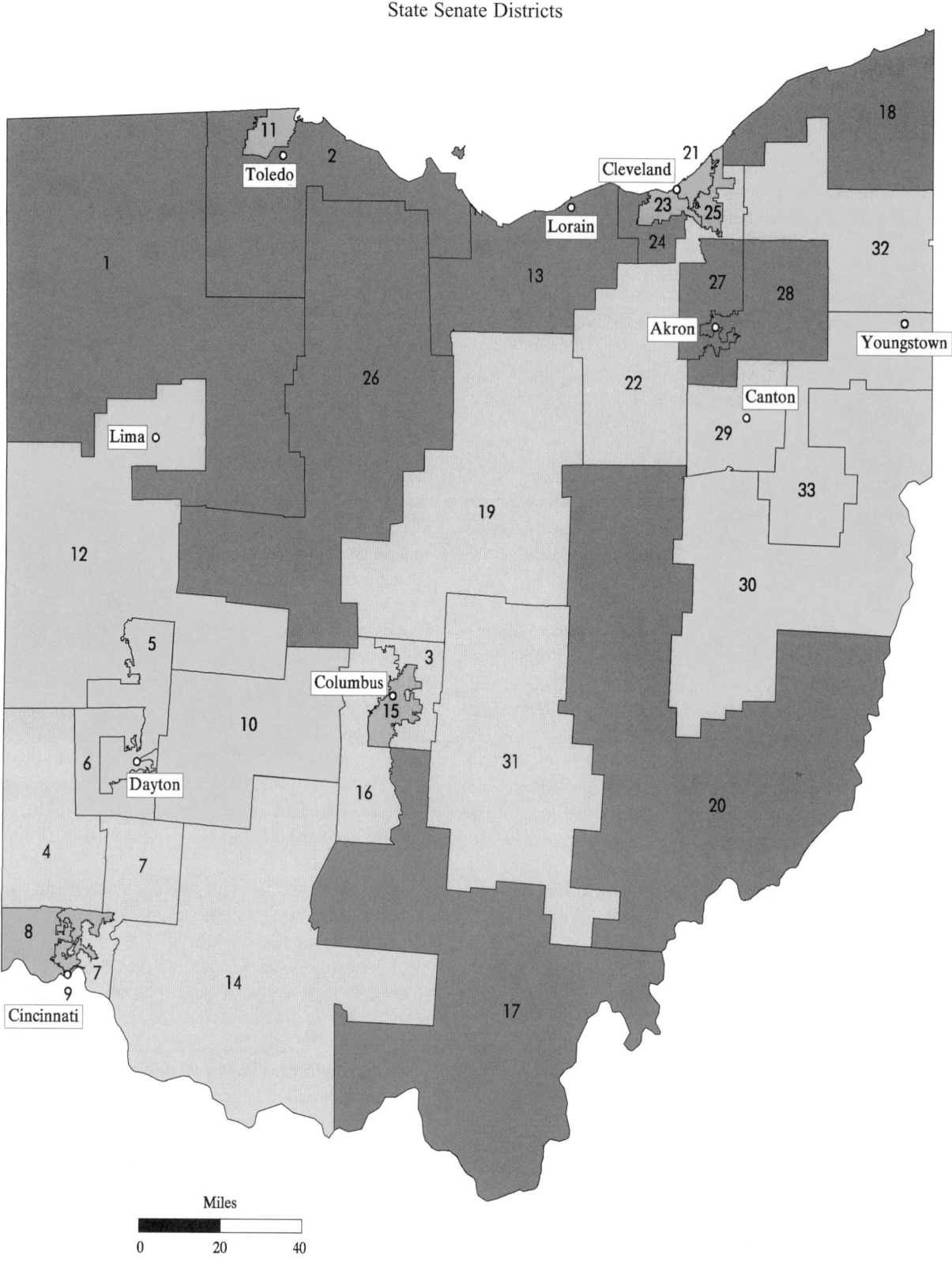

Population Growth   ▨ -6% to -2%   ▨ -1% to 2%   ▨ 3% to 6%   ▨ 9% to 12%

Ohio State Senate Districts: Demographic Data

Senate District	Population		Average HH Income		District Type	Unempl. Rate	College Educ.	White (non-Hispanic)		African American		Asian American		Hispanic American	
	1997	+/-	($)	+/-		(%)	(%)	(%)	+/-	(%)	+/-	(%)	+/-	(%)	+/-
Ohio	11,202,822	3	47,732	35	M	6	36	86	2	11	10	1	23	2	21
1	356,252	4	45,659	33	R	6	32	95	3	1	4	0	8	4	23
2	348,288	4	54,300	33	S	6	41	92	3	4	20	1	26	3	25
3	355,949	12	58,543	35	U	3	52	87	8	9	52	2	40	1	39
4	370,257	12	49,894	33	M	5	37	94	11	4	24	1	37	1	33
5	315,863	-1	39,962	33	U	8	30	67	-4	31	5	1	13	1	19
6	320,701	0	57,271	35	S	4	46	94	-2	4	34	2	25	1	19
7	373,557	9	66,846	40	S	4	47	94	8	4	26	1	35	1	29
8	316,856	-2	50,677	34	S	4	38	90	-4	8	22	1	16	1	18
9	302,095	-3	43,038	38	U	8	39	47	-11	51	4	2	17	1	18
10	329,025	2	49,943	39	S	6	37	89	1	9	12	1	25	1	20
11	311,489	-6	41,201	30	U	10	33	72	-9	22	5	1	10	5	12
12	341,514	2	45,929	35	R	6	29	94	1	5	8	1	19	1	18
13	359,081	4	47,692	33	M	6	31	87	3	7	13	1	20	6	23
14	374,423	12	42,994	34	R	6	26	98	12	1	21	0	23	0	26
15	320,936	-3	34,726	34	U	8	28	57	-10	40	7	2	5	1	13
16	361,566	10	59,177	38	U	3	54	90	7	5	40	3	37	1	39
17	355,308	5	35,891	36	R	11	22	96	5	3	16	0	13	0	12
18	326,520	4	48,770	31	R	6	34	96	3	2	13	1	31	1	24
19	360,584	10	47,760	36	R	6	34	95	10	4	14	1	25	1	26
20	352,071	3	37,483	35	R	8	25	97	3	2	11	0	-2	0	15
21	299,487	-6	31,895	30	U	15	26	28	-20	69	1	1	-3	2	2
22	360,017	12	67,517	36	S	4	44	95	11	3	48	1	41	1	31
23	333,014	-4	38,933	30	U	8	28	85	-8	5	56	1	18	7	19
24	346,534	6	63,555	37	S	4	46	96	4	1	77	2	43	1	25
25	310,832	-4	50,974	34	S	7	38	54	-12	44	8	1	10	1	8
26	342,618	4	42,415	33	R	7	28	95	3	2	12	0	13	2	20
27	342,083	5	54,216	33	S	5	44	92	3	6	31	1	29	1	31
28	340,601	3	42,791	32	M	7	31	82	2	16	8	1	20	1	23
29	335,628	2	45,827	33	S	7	33	91	1	7	12	0	22	1	26
30	333,218	2	36,497	31	R	9	24	97	1	2	7	0	11	0	15
31	365,777	10	45,466	37	M	7	34	97	10	2	17	1	24	1	28
32	313,106	1	51,230	33	S	6	33	93	1	6	10	1	24	1	21
33	327,452	-1	39,566	32	S	9	30	83	-3	14	7	0	15	2	17

Note: U=urban, S=suburban, R=rural, M=mixed, HH=households.

OHIO
State House Districts

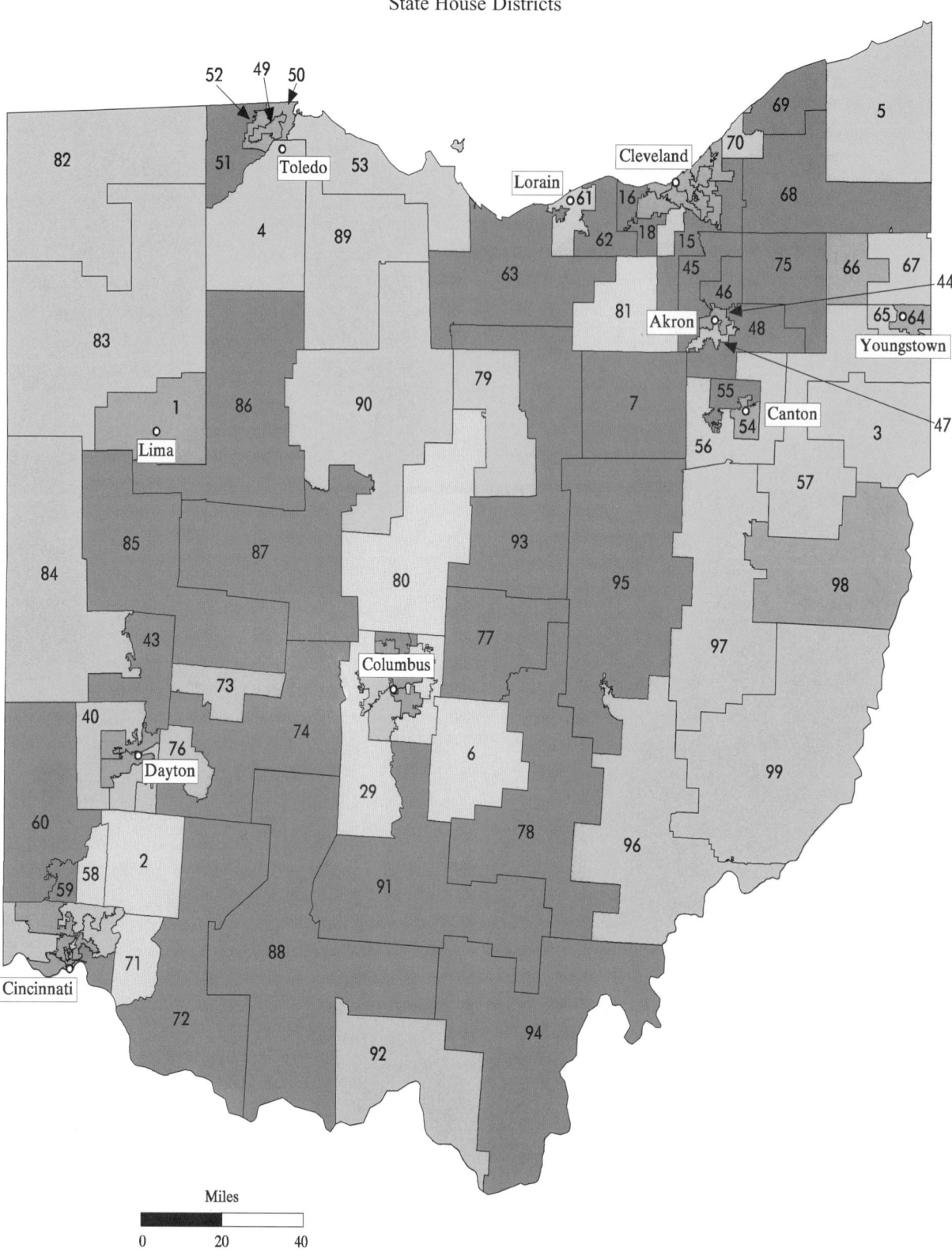

Population Growth   ■ -9% to -2%   ■ -1% to 4%   ■ 5% to 12%   □ 13% to 29%

CLEVELAND

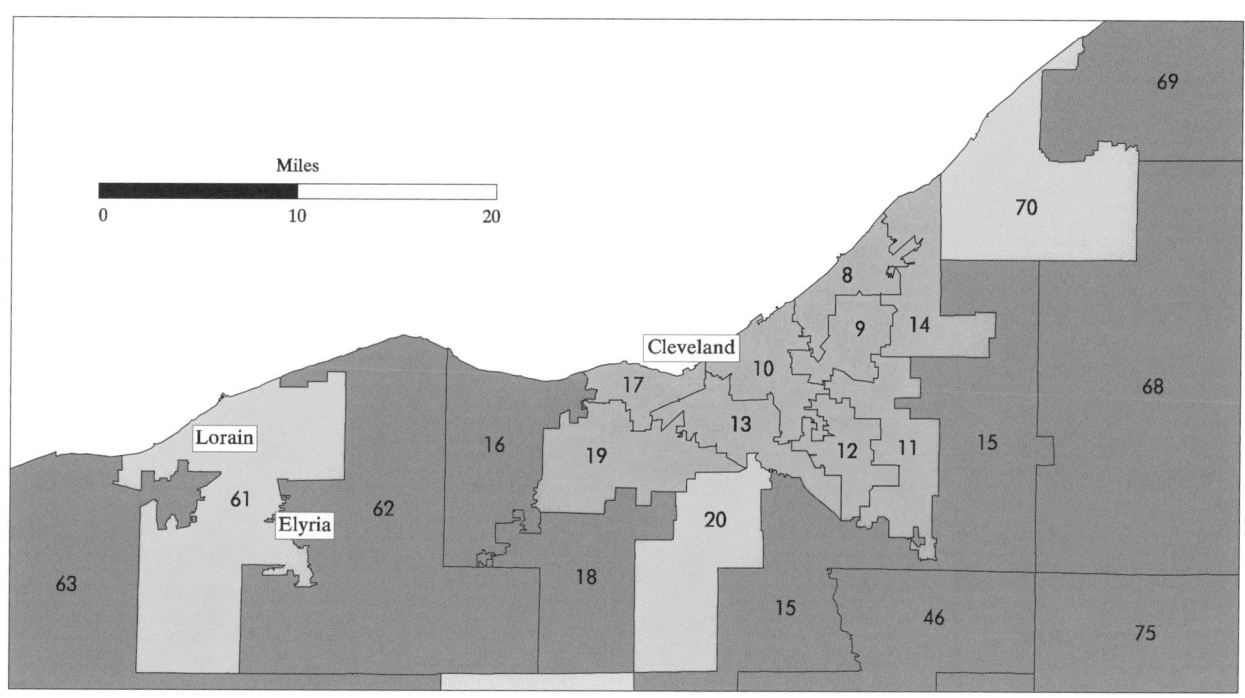

CINCINNATI

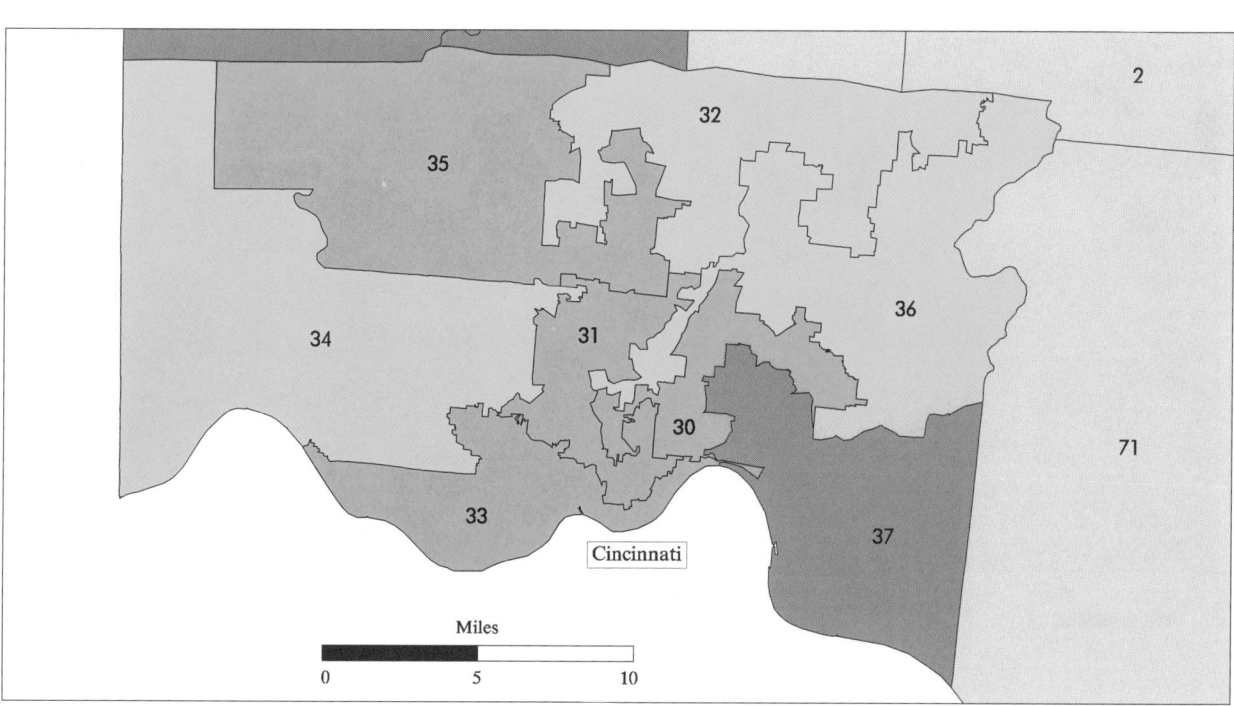

Population Growth   ▨ -9% to -2%   ☐ -1% to 4%   ▨ 5% to 12%   ☐ 13% to 29%

COLUMBUS

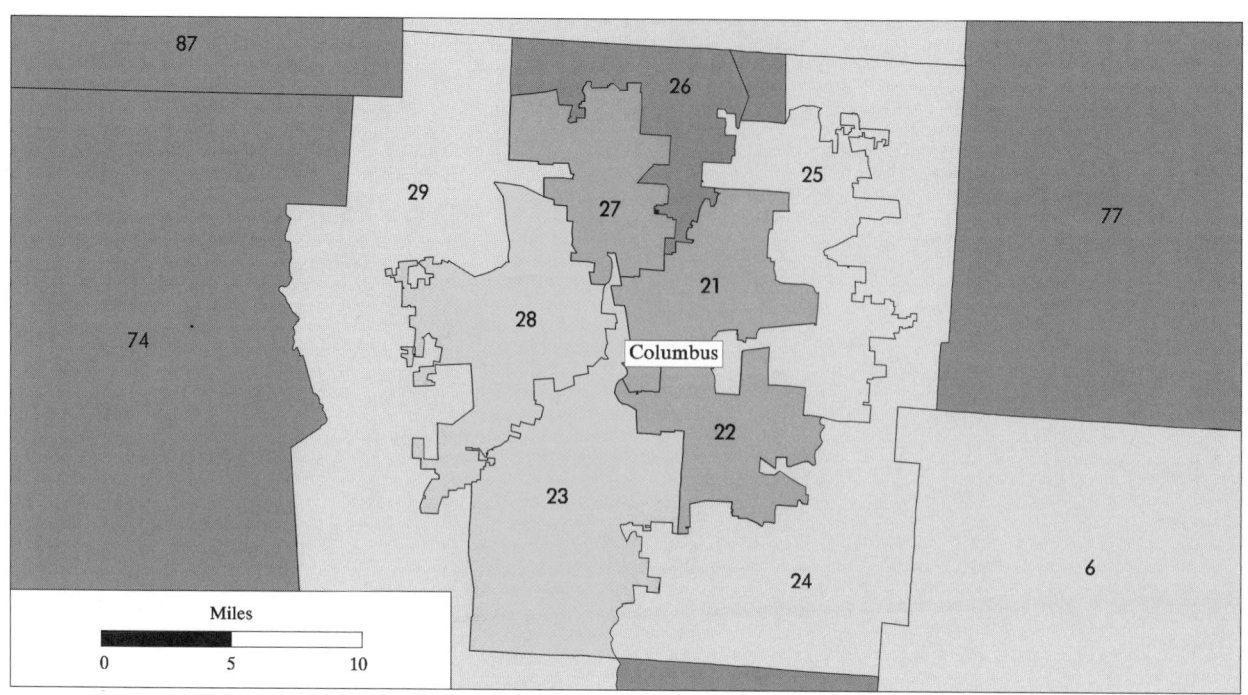

DAYTON

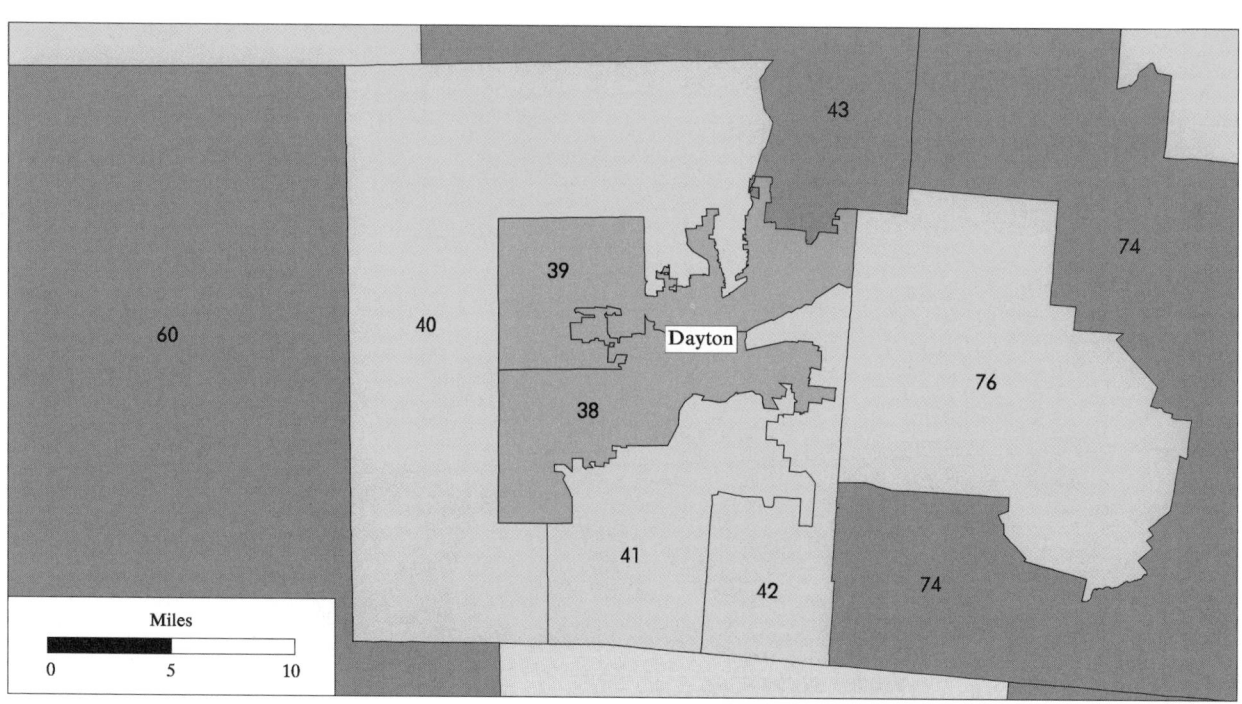

Population Growth   ☐ -9% to -2%   ☐ -1% to 4%   ☐ 5% to 12%   ☐ 13% to 29%

Ohio State House Districts: Demographic Data

House District	Population		Average HH Income		District Type	Unempl. Rate	College Educ.	White (non-Hispanic)		African American		Asian American		Hispanic American	
	1997	+/-	($)	+/-		(%)	(%)	(%)	+/-	(%)	+/-	(%)	+/-	(%)	+/-
Ohio	11,202,822	3	47,732	35	M	6	36	86	2	11	10	1	23	2	21
1	108,097	-2	43,373	34	M	8	31	86	-3	12	8	1	17	1	17
2	137,525	21	57,595	37	S	4	38	96	20	2	31	1	48	1	44
3	111,593	3	36,892	32	R	8	24	98	3	1	12	0	11	0	19
4	118,125	4	51,806	33	S	6	47	95	4	1	7	1	26	3	26
5	102,429	3	37,843	32	R	9	24	94	2	3	11	0	14	2	22
6	121,072	17	51,168	35	S	6	37	98	17	1	23	0	43	1	38
7	109,395	8	46,338	34	R	5	31	97	7	2	17	1	28	0	24
8	100,657	-4	30,383	27	U	15	21	30	-14	69	1	1	-8	1	-3
9	103,046	-5	43,242	32	S	10	42	27	-26	70	7	2	-2	1	-5
10	95,721	-9	21,139	27	U	22	12	25	-19	70	-5	1	-1	3	5
11	101,820	-3	65,488	36	S	6	50	47	-16	50	14	1	0	1	11
12	101,699	-3	36,141	29	U	12	17	28	-13	71	1	0	-4	1	-3
13	111,786	-3	32,060	27	U	10	17	80	-8	5	65	1	15	13	19
14	107,299	-5	49,797	33	S	4	43	85	-10	12	38	2	21	1	11
15	123,461	12	96,865	39	S	3	56	92	10	5	65	2	43	1	31
16	115,055	8	74,745	38	S	3	56	96	6	1	93	2	46	1	30
17	101,964	-5	40,574	31	S	7	36	86	-9	5	68	2	17	7	21
18	114,795	6	61,455	37	S	4	45	94	4	2	71	2	44	1	27
19	119,394	-3	43,521	31	U	5	30	90	-6	6	44	1	21	2	17
20	116,665	3	54,387	36	S	4	36	97	2	1	84	2	37	1	18
21	102,887	-7	28,380	33	U	10	28	38	-18	58	1	2	1	1	8
22	103,402	-6	37,922	33	U	8	28	46	-17	51	8	1	-7	1	11
23	114,601	2	37,429	35	U	7	27	84	-2	12	34	2	16	1	21
24	91,051	13	56,327	35	S	4	41	91	11	6	62	1	40	1	31
25	120,320	14	60,639	37	S	4	51	86	10	11	56	2	34	1	38
26	144,553	10	58,112	35	U	3	58	85	6	10	44	3	43	1	42
27	105,050	-4	52,745	34	U	3	60	89	-6	5	38	4	22	1	19
28	111,284	3	60,781	38	U	4	53	89	0	7	39	3	26	1	24
29	145,367	29	63,346	39	M	3	50	91	27	4	44	3	68	1	71
30	96,197	-5	34,987	28	U	8	37	33	-17	65	2	1	8	1	11
31	95,885	-8	26,140	29	U	13	28	34	-20	63	-1	1	8	1	3
32	109,679	4	66,602	42	S	5	48	69	-3	28	21	2	30	1	38
33	108,823	-4	43,397	33	U	5	35	88	-7	10	23	1	16	1	14
34	108,326	3	54,926	34	S	3	39	95	2	3	28	1	21	0	21
35	100,167	-5	54,647	34	S	4	40	86	-8	12	20	1	13	1	20
36	117,426	1	75,442	41	S	4	50	89	-1	8	19	2	31	1	21
37	118,567	5	67,916	44	S	4	53	95	3	3	43	1	33	1	26
38	103,238	-4	30,339	30	U	11	22	53	-6	45	-2	1	5	1	15
39	100,392	-6	38,220	30	U	9	32	51	-17	47	9	1	-5	1	8
40	107,292	0	51,660	32	S	4	37	93	-1	6	32	1	20	1	16
41	105,250	-1	57,669	32	S	4	49	96	-2	2	38	1	25	1	19
42	108,206	0	62,329	39	S	4	50	93	-2	3	34	3	26	1	20
43	112,298	6	51,233	35	S	5	35	93	4	5	37	1	30	1	34
44	101,830	-2	31,857	30	U	12	22	51	-10	47	7	1	9	1	19
45	114,479	8	69,215	31	S	4	51	91	6	7	41	1	30	1	31
46	113,705	7	62,725	37	S	4	54	96	6	2	38	1	39	1	44
47	113,856	-1	31,601	25	U	9	21	88	-3	10	24	1	18	1	19
48	120,616	6	49,524	32	S	5	33	97	5	1	27	1	26	1	27
49	93,773	-8	30,494	28	U	15	22	39	-18	54	-2	1	2	5	4
50	107,759	-6	36,130	29	U	10	22	84	-10	9	23	1	3	7	14

Note: U=urban, S=suburban, R=rural, M=mixed, HH=households.

Ohio State House Districts: Demographic Data (cont.)

House District	Population 1997	+/-	Average HH Income ($)	+/-	District Type	Unempl. Rate (%)	College Educ. (%)	White (non-Hispanic) (%)	+/-	African American (%)	+/-	Asian American (%)	+/-	Hispanic American (%)	+/-
Ohio	11,202,822	3	47,732	35	M	6	36	86	2	11	10	1	23	2	21
51	118,122	7	64,533	35	S	5	46	93	5	3	43	1	32	2	32
52	110,265	-2	54,231	31	U	5	49	88	-5	7	36	2	18	2	23
53	112,011	1	46,433	31	R	7	30	89	-1	7	13	0	7	3	19
54	104,035	-2	34,468	30	U	10	23	82	-4	16	9	0	4	1	17
55	115,103	5	53,232	31	S	5	44	93	4	5	20	1	33	1	30
56	116,527	3	49,125	35	S	6	31	97	3	2	19	0	11	1	33
57	117,859	4	41,579	32	S	8	28	96	3	3	14	0	9	1	31
58	129,980	21	58,325	35	S	5	44	92	20	6	29	1	53	1	54
59	116,081	7	44,636	29	U	6	33	92	7	6	19	1	17	1	21
60	124,175	7	45,982	30	R	5	32	97	6	2	28	1	31	0	23
61	116,030	0	39,022	29	U	9	25	70	-5	15	12	1	17	14	20
62	122,163	6	54,081	36	S	5	36	93	5	4	15	1	25	2	42
63	120,800	7	49,735	33	R	6	33	97	7	1	23	0	13	2	33
64	97,933	-8	27,660	25	U	15	20	55	-16	40	4	0	-11	5	11
65	111,675	1	47,975	34	S	6	40	95	-1	3	58	1	29	2	37
66	104,822	-2	44,359	32	S	9	26	85	-4	13	8	1	20	1	18
67	101,336	0	44,624	31	S	7	30	96	-1	3	13	1	26	1	23
68	106,966	7	66,383	34	R	4	41	98	6	1	21	0	29	0	22
69	128,639	8	56,147	31	R	5	39	96	7	2	17	1	39	1	33
70	95,566	-1	50,558	29	S	4	36	97	-1	1	8	1	31	1	12
71	127,036	15	52,132	31	S	4	35	98	15	1	26	0	43	1	44
72	123,713	12	41,834	35	R	6	21	98	12	1	21	0	5	0	13
73	108,171	0	43,224	39	U	7	27	86	-2	13	10	0	14	1	9
74	113,927	7	52,542	38	S	5	35	94	6	5	21	1	24	1	31
75	117,904	5	46,139	31	M	6	37	94	4	3	16	1	27	1	25
76	106,922	1	54,488	38	S	5	47	88	-1	8	10	2	27	1	20
77	122,025	8	48,902	40	M	6	33	97	7	2	19	0	27	1	25
78	122,697	7	36,118	32	R	9	33	96	7	2	11	1	17	1	24
79	113,444	2	38,663	22	M	7	27	89	1	10	11	1	24	1	17
80	130,961	19	61,938	42	S	4	43	97	19	2	34	1	32	1	42
81	127,149	15	55,685	32	S	5	39	98	15	1	26	1	45	1	37
82	119,624	4	46,410	35	R	6	31	93	3	1	7	0	1	5	23
83	116,206	2	44,501	32	R	5	29	95	1	0	-3	0	-11	4	22
84	120,786	2	46,504	35	R	5	28	98	2	1	4	0	20	1	22
85	112,619	5	47,769	34	R	5	29	97	4	2	13	1	21	1	16
86	120,396	5	45,987	32	R	6	36	96	4	1	6	1	19	2	26
87	120,729	9	44,045	39	R	7	27	95	9	3	16	1	27	1	20
88	123,653	10	34,867	37	R	10	19	98	10	2	19	0	4	0	10
89	112,851	1	40,969	27	R	8	29	92	0	3	9	0	3	5	20
90	109,007	1	42,072	33	R	7	28	97	1	2	9	0	4	1	18
91	120,212	8	40,563	36	R	9	23	94	7	5	18	0	24	0	14
92	112,285	1	33,275	36	R	12	21	96	1	3	11	0	6	0	15
93	116,181	9	41,564	37	R	6	30	98	9	1	14	0	18	1	24
94	122,786	7	33,934	36	R	11	21	97	6	2	17	0	4	0	8
95	122,599	6	41,698	38	R	6	22	98	6	1	10	0	-7	0	19
96	114,308	4	37,032	37	R	9	28	95	3	4	13	0	-2	0	13
97	116,797	4	37,727	32	R	8	26	98	4	1	10	0	23	0	16
98	104,899	-3	34,759	29	M	10	23	94	-3	5	5	0	-1	1	12
99	115,090	-1	34,002	31	R	10	26	98	-1	1	7	0	5	0	12

Note: U=urban, S=suburban, R=rural, M=mixed, HH=households.

OKLAHOMA

Oklahomans, as everyone knows, are called "Sooners" because of the many who jumped the start of the claims period to grab homesteads (and thus got there "sooner" than they were supposed to). The fight song of the University of Oklahoma is "Boomer Sooner," and that too is appropriate. As historian and editor Burton Rascoe wrote in *The Nation* more than sixty years ago, "Oklahoma has been, from the first, a boomer State, even before it was a State—when old Oklahoma Territory was thrown open to settlers. It was peopled by and large by land gamblers instead of home seekers."

Any state with working oil rigs on the grounds of the state capitol will likely thrive and fail on the boom and bust cycle of that most speculative industry. The 1980s were a time of bust in the oil business, when Oklahoma grew by just 4 percent and slipped in population from twenty-sixth to twenty-eighth. The 1990s have been a more prosperous time, not only in oil but in wheat and livestock grazing, two of the state's other leading industries. The result has been a slightly more robust 6 percent growth in population, pushing Oklahoma back up to twenty-seventh overall.

Growth has been centered around the two largest metropolitan centers, Oklahoma City in the middle of the state (and planned that way) and Tulsa in the northeast. Districts within the cities (the Eighty-second House District in Oklahoma City and Sixty-seventh in Tulsa) and in the suburbs (the Ninety-eighth and Fifty-third Districts south of Oklahoma City and the Seventy-sixth and Ninth districts east of Tulsa) have experienced growth.

No area of the state is losing population with any great intensity. The Fifty-ninth House District around Woodward, which has lost 5 percent, is as bad as it gets. Nevertheless, Oklahoma is growing poorer, at least in relative terms. It ranked forty-first in average household income at the beginning of the decade and forty-fourth at the end, though its rate of growth is slightly above average. The only really wealthy district is the Sixty-seventh, in southeast Tulsa ($92,000). Nowhere else is average income more than $73,000. There are poor districts, but

with the exception of one in "Little Dixie" along the Red River, all are in central Oklahoma City or Tulsa. The districts comprising the Osage reservation in the northeast part of the state are not especially poor, nor do they have unusually high rates of unemployment.

Native Americans remain the state's largest minority group—more than 8 percent of the population, although that figure does not include the many who are not full-blooded. (The state was only 5.3 percent Indian when it was admitted to the Union in 1907.) What is now eastern Oklahoma was originally Indian Territory, where whites were forbidden to enter. Indians were also relocated to the western part of the state, known as Oklahoma Territory, but whites were permitted there too. Eighty percent of the population today is white, with the highest concentrations in the old Oklahoma Territory. Eight percent of the population is African American, most of whom live in three large black-majority districts, two in Oklahoma City, one in Tulsa.

Oklahoma is a Republican state with a Democratic legislature. The governor, both U.S. senators, and all six congressional representatives belong to the GOP. But the Democrats control both the state house and senate by substantial margins, which have not changed much during the decade.

One curiosity is that the state senate districts are not numbered sequentially, although the house districts are. There is no Twenty-fifth, Twenty-seventh, Twenty-eighth, Thirtieth, Thirty-sixth, or Fifty-third senate district. The official explanation is that less-populated districts are sometimes collapsed together, but numbers can disappear from the map and then reappear decades later in a different part of the state. Influential members of the senate can sometimes choose their new district number, rather like selecting a uniform number on a baseball team.

In a short span of statehood, Oklahoma has also produced a few political leaders of note, in particular former senator Robert Kerr, former House speaker Carl Albert, and—one of the great American incongruities—New York's Daniel Patrick Moynihan, born in Tulsa in 1927.

OKLAHOMA
State Senate Districts

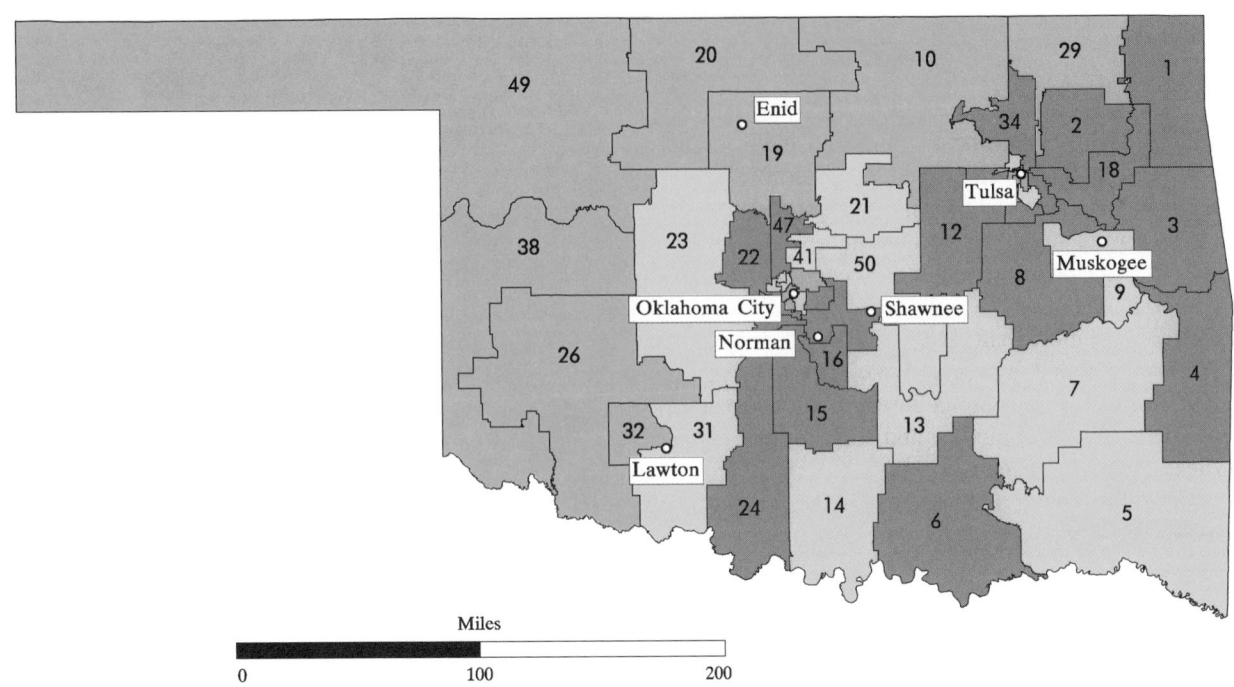

OKLAHOMA CITY

TULSA

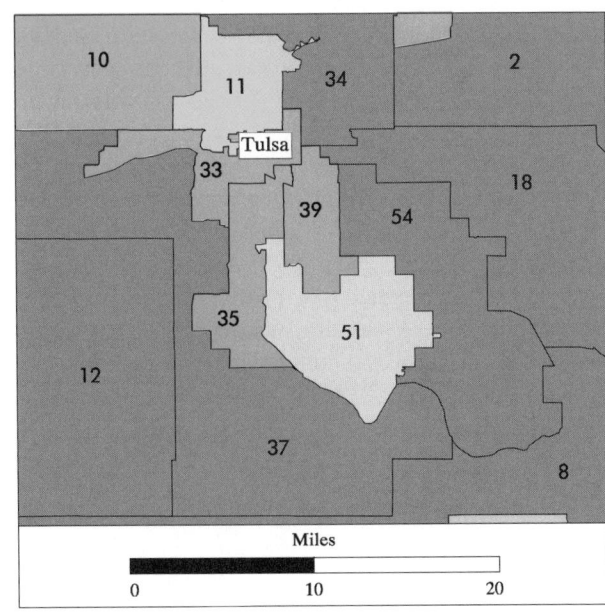

Population Growth   ▨ -3% to 1%   ▨ 2% to 6%   ▨ 7% to 15%   ▨ 24% to 26%

Oklahoma State Senate Districts: Demographic Data

Senate District	Population 1997	+/-	Average HH Income ($)	+/-	District Type	Unempl. Rate (%)	College Educ. (%)	White (non-Hispanic) (%)	+/-	African American (%)	+/-	Asian American (%)	+/-	Hispanic American (%)	+/-
Oklahoma	3,318,854	6	41,197	35	M	7	33	80	5	8	8	1	26	3	29
1	72,436	8	33,006	40	R	7	24	77	8	1	-1	0	-14	1	18
2	75,080	15	43,774	37	S	6	31	85	15	1	19	0	17	1	43
3	69,785	10	32,162	37	R	9	27	63	11	1	7	0	-1	1	20
4	71,959	8	33,331	38	R	8	22	83	8	3	11	0	1	1	31
5	66,505	3	28,894	40	R	11	18	75	3	9	7	0	-1	1	8
6	68,945	8	31,322	40	R	9	25	83	8	2	9	0	-13	2	24
7	67,325	4	32,401	36	R	10	23	83	4	3	6	0	-6	1	19
8	69,575	8	31,020	34	R	9	22	75	8	10	10	0	-28	1	20
9	69,369	2	33,942	30	R	7	29	71	1	15	6	0	10	1	18
10	67,874	1	40,480	38	R	6	30	86	1	2	9	0	-7	1	19
11	65,165	3	25,719	27	U	12	20	37	-3	53	6	1	27	4	37
12	74,643	8	37,380	35	S	6	23	86	7	4	9	0	-5	1	28
13	66,220	2	32,997	37	R	9	24	81	2	3	7	0	-3	1	12
14	67,340	4	37,339	36	R	7	25	82	3	7	8	0	-1	2	24
15	75,106	11	46,246	42	R	6	38	88	10	2	12	1	42	3	45
16	71,947	10	35,671	27	U	7	44	84	8	4	13	3	29	3	40
17	76,479	12	43,472	32	U	7	31	87	11	3	12	1	30	2	34
18	72,793	9	39,310	30	M	6	26	82	8	3	17	1	28	2	29
19	67,198	1	37,801	32	U	6	33	91	0	3	4	1	11	3	26
20	59,955	-3	38,074	32	R	5	34	91	-4	2	0	0	7	2	13
21	70,751	6	36,791	39	R	7	45	84	5	7	10	3	16	2	36
22	72,203	8	46,691	35	M	6	35	87	7	4	13	2	26	3	43
23	70,375	5	36,013	38	R	8	24	81	6	5	9	0	6	4	11
24	71,591	8	40,539	37	R	6	28	90	7	2	11	1	31	3	41
26	64,767	0	33,841	41	R	8	23	84	-1	4	-5	0	-16	7	19
29	62,900	0	44,589	26	R	5	40	86	0	2	5	1	24	2	18
31	69,056	3	35,999	30	M	9	30	75	1	13	3	2	25	6	30
32	62,673	-2	37,245	25	U	11	36	67	-5	17	-2	4	21	8	20
33	64,128	0	46,648	36	U	5	42	86	-2	5	13	1	24	3	23
34	70,175	8	37,437	31	M	7	24	84	8	4	11	0	26	2	27
35	64,705	1	57,929	33	U	5	55	86	-1	6	13	2	28	3	33
37	65,215	9	42,427	35	S	6	30	84	8	5	17	1	26	2	41
38	64,208	-1	36,686	37	R	8	32	79	-4	6	2	1	10	11	25
39	64,256	0	52,615	32	U	4	53	86	-2	5	18	2	33	3	37
40	68,088	2	50,427	28	U	5	42	84	-1	7	20	3	32	4	35
41	81,694	26	63,375	34	S	4	58	90	25	3	39	2	49	2	55
42	72,025	7	47,130	34	S	6	35	80	5	10	20	2	33	3	23
43	69,957	3	34,749	28	U	9	23	71	-1	14	12	2	26	8	30
44	65,361	1	32,942	27	U	8	19	78	-3	4	17	2	26	10	37
45	68,425	12	52,317	35	S	4	36	87	10	2	17	3	42	4	40
46	66,094	-1	29,725	29	U	12	27	56	-8	21	4	4	23	13	29
47	76,248	11	58,850	33	U	4	54	84	9	9	19	2	42	2	38
48	67,014	1	38,070	33	U	11	30	32	-3	63	3	1	17	2	20
49	64,701	-2	39,041	40	R	4	29	91	-3	0	-12	0	-9	6	25
50	69,149	3	37,154	38	R	8	23	82	3	5	8	0	-19	2	22
51	76,975	24	82,831	41	S	3	60	92	23	2	41	1	55	2	53
52	66,132	2	53,137	31	U	5	47	84	-1	7	18	2	30	3	32
54	74,253	8	43,539	27	U	5	40	84	6	5	21	3	32	4	43

Note: U=urban, S=suburban, R=rural, M=mixed, HH=households.

OKLAHOMA
State House Districts

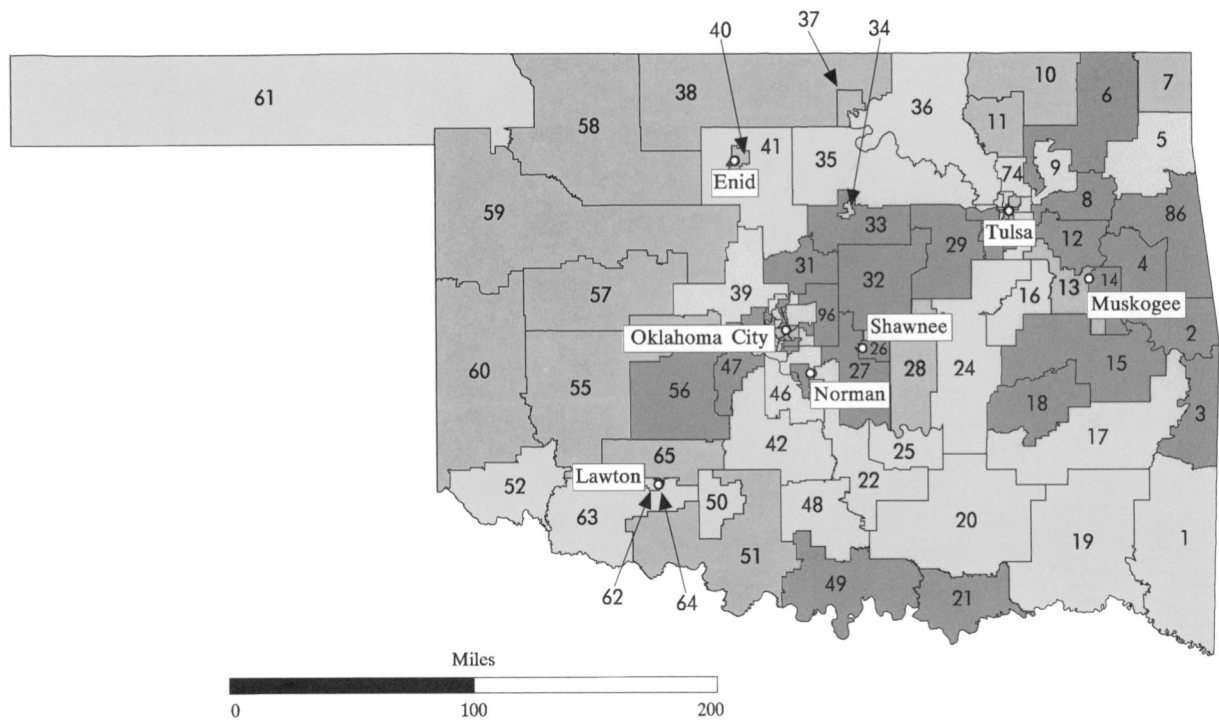

OKLAHOMA CITY

TULSA

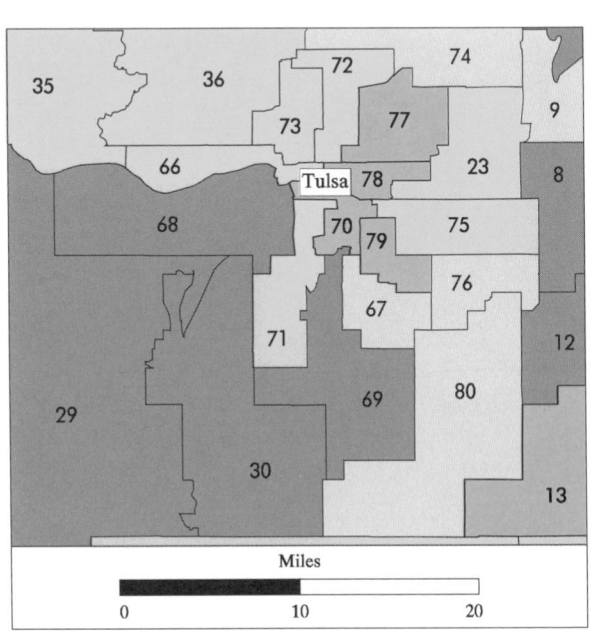

Population Growth | ▨ -5% to 0% | ▨ 1% to 5% | ▨ 6% to 13% | ▨ 14% to 26%

Oklahoma State House Districts: Demographic Data

House District	Population		Average HH Income		District Type	Unempl. Rate	College Educ.	White (non-Hispanic)		African American		Asian American		Hispanic American	
	1997	+/-	($)	+/-		(%)	(%)	(%)	+/-	(%)	+/-	(%)	+/-	(%)	+/-
Oklahoma	3,318,854	6	41,197	35	M	7	33	80	5	8	8	1	26	3	29
1	32,058	4	31,317	45	R	11	18	72	3	11	9	0	12	2	10
2	34,334	10	34,957	42	R	8	19	76	10	2	14	0	14	1	35
3	32,961	8	32,817	36	R	8	24	86	8	3	9	0	-3	1	33
4	33,886	13	32,978	29	R	9	35	66	13	1	9	0	3	2	27
5	38,319	19	34,647	41	R	7	22	76	20	0	-21	0	-10	1	16
6	35,443	8	41,059	36	R	7	27	83	9	2	8	0	-2	1	18
7	30,318	-1	31,151	38	R	8	26	80	-1	1	-13	0	-11	1	15
8	35,731	11	41,373	30	R	6	30	87	11	0	6	0	22	2	38
9	37,487	19	45,183	38	S	5	33	83	19	1	23	0	29	2	57
10	28,604	-3	31,193	24	R	6	24	82	-3	4	1	0	9	2	9
11	32,145	0	54,274	25	R	4	52	88	-1	2	6	1	30	2	29
12	36,568	11	39,842	26	S	6	25	83	11	5	18	0	15	1	32
13	32,670	0	34,290	28	R	7	29	63	-1	25	4	0	5	1	18
14	33,298	7	35,402	33	R	6	30	79	6	4	17	0	20	2	26
15	33,588	7	28,629	32	R	10	20	78	7	4	14	0	-31	1	9
16	31,476	3	30,087	35	R	9	22	74	2	13	9	0	-27	2	18
17	31,084	2	31,395	38	R	10	24	82	2	1	-5	0	-16	1	13
18	34,118	8	34,200	34	R	9	23	83	8	4	10	0	1	1	30
19	31,469	3	27,203	36	R	11	18	77	3	7	4	0	-26	1	8
20	32,295	5	27,480	38	R	11	20	81	5	3	7	0	-41	1	3
21	31,860	7	31,693	37	R	9	29	83	7	1	4	0	-1	2	31
22	31,639	4	34,379	31	R	8	21	84	4	4	3	0	4	2	27
23	34,106	5	41,939	31	U	5	33	82	3	6	19	3	32	4	37
24	32,509	1	32,650	44	R	9	19	75	2	7	10	0	-30	1	7
25	31,193	3	34,675	37	R	8	30	82	3	3	5	0	0	1	17
26	33,432	9	35,327	31	U	9	29	82	9	3	10	1	25	2	24
27	34,067	6	38,102	31	M	8	22	87	6	1	10	0	6	2	16
28	30,071	-2	33,773	41	R	9	21	74	-2	9	1	0	-24	2	12
29	40,042	9	35,764	33	S	6	22	86	9	4	15	0	-14	1	21
30	29,015	9	43,586	35	S	6	28	86	8	3	16	0	19	2	53
31	33,348	12	56,326	43	S	6	38	87	12	7	-2	1	20	3	43
32	33,272	7	34,940	36	R	8	21	90	7	3	12	0	-26	1	33
33	37,052	8	39,006	36	R	6	41	84	6	8	20	2	5	2	41
34	28,499	3	35,949	43	R	6	58	87	2	4	8	4	27	2	28
35	32,986	3	38,663	35	R	6	27	89	3	1	0	0	-5	1	13
36	33,435	3	36,511	41	R	8	23	68	2	16	11	0	-48	2	20
37	30,140	-3	46,664	36	R	5	42	88	-3	3	2	1	17	2	12
38	30,710	-2	32,936	28	R	5	31	91	-2	1	-4	0	-13	2	16
39	38,926	15	47,692	34	R	5	40	87	14	4	17	0	30	3	46
40	29,929	-1	28,100	25	U	9	25	87	-2	6	3	1	12	3	25
41	31,981	2	45,961	35	U	4	41	95	2	1	3	1	14	1	26
42	34,098	5	35,124	34	R	7	20	90	5	1	7	0	6	2	31
43	35,035	10	54,876	33	S	4	41	91	9	2	30	2	42	2	39
44	30,396	6	37,280	26	U	7	57	84	4	4	10	5	28	3	37
45	34,811	13	37,577	32	U	6	42	86	12	4	20	1	37	3	39
46	39,168	14	42,977	33	M	5	39	88	13	2	13	2	29	3	47
47	33,751	11	41,352	39	R	7	29	88	11	5	12	0	20	2	34
48	32,271	4	39,538	41	R	8	26	78	3	11	7	0	11	3	34
49	34,074	8	37,187	37	R	6	24	86	8	3	9	0	-15	3	21
50	31,573	3	37,195	29	R	8	31	90	2	3	6	0	11	4	37

Note: U=urban, S=suburban, R=rural, M=mixed, HH=households.

Oklahoma State House Districts: Demographic Data (cont.)

House District	Population 1997	+/-	Average HH Income ($)	+/-	District Type	Unempl. Rate (%)	College Educ. (%)	White (non-Hispanic) (%)	+/-	African American (%)	+/-	Asian American (%)	+/-	Hispanic American (%)	+/-
Oklahoma	3,318,854	6	41,197	35	M	7	33	80	5	8	8	1	26	3	29
51	29,486	-1	29,890	34	R	8	17	91	-1	1	-6	0	-35	3	16
52	31,903	4	37,919	42	R	10	32	73	0	9	4	1	16	15	33
53	37,575	19	64,974	43	S	5	47	88	17	2	22	2	46	4	65
54	33,188	7	45,439	34	S	5	36	87	5	2	12	2	38	4	38
55	29,635	-1	32,248	32	R	6	22	87	-1	3	1	0	-12	5	15
56	33,241	9	34,448	42	R	10	22	74	12	3	9	0	0	4	1
57	30,157	-4	35,941	33	R	6	34	84	-5	4	-2	1	1	6	11
58	29,504	-4	37,138	34	R	5	29	94	-5	0	-10	0	-14	3	20
59	29,352	-5	37,029	34	R	4	28	91	-5	2	-2	0	-25	3	15
60	30,217	-2	36,993	47	R	7	24	89	-3	3	0	0	-14	6	23
61	30,916	2	42,196	46	R	4	30	88	0	0	-13	0	-8	10	29
62	32,186	2	44,149	27	U	8	43	66	-2	20	3	5	27	7	34
63	31,483	1	35,451	32	M	11	29	70	-1	13	4	2	30	10	25
64	29,198	-3	29,106	23	U	13	28	67	-7	17	1	3	23	9	20
65	28,969	-4	39,626	30	R	11	34	69	-5	17	-9	2	4	8	14
66	31,485	2	36,431	35	U	7	31	83	1	7	15	1	22	3	25
67	37,342	18	91,613	46	U	3	69	92	17	2	29	2	51	2	48
68	33,963	6	41,939	36	S	6	26	84	5	6	16	1	21	2	22
69	35,554	11	72,978	42	U	5	53	86	9	5	8	2	30	4	45
70	31,671	0	71,614	36	U	4	58	90	-2	4	20	1	31	2	31
71	32,388	2	47,489	34	U	5	51	81	0	10	15	1	27	3	36
72	32,346	4	24,554	25	U	9	19	59	-2	28	12	1	37	6	41
73	30,785	1	27,378	29	U	14	24	22	-7	72	3	0	-3	3	29
74	35,536	15	44,369	35	S	5	30	88	15	2	21	0	45	1	40
75	31,856	2	43,777	30	U	5	44	83	-1	6	16	3	29	4	37
76	36,131	21	54,320	36	S	4	47	89	20	4	36	1	53	3	50
77	30,564	-1	32,147	25	U	8	23	85	-2	4	17	1	22	3	17
78	31,467	-1	41,718	29	U	4	43	87	-3	4	17	2	24	3	29
79	31,515	-1	53,173	29	U	4	57	85	-4	6	13	3	31	4	40
80	37,635	17	54,142	28	S	4	46	90	16	3	36	1	37	2	46
81	36,893	16	65,483	43	S	4	59	88	14	4	31	3	42	2	46
82	38,168	26	67,631	25	U	3	63	89	24	4	37	2	52	2	58
83	33,479	8	61,184	28	U	3	58	81	6	13	22	2	37	2	38
84	31,289	0	42,811	30	U	6	39	85	-2	6	16	2	31	4	29
85	32,439	3	64,639	31	U	5	55	87	1	6	19	2	32	2	31
86	34,952	11	31,732	42	R	8	19	60	12	0	-15	0	-33	1	8
87	31,517	1	36,916	27	U	6	37	79	-3	8	19	4	32	6	35
88	30,371	-1	31,187	28	U	11	33	56	-8	20	8	8	24	12	22
89	30,783	-1	23,673	22	U	13	11	61	-10	9	12	1	10	22	38
90	32,642	2	40,100	32	U	8	29	78	-1	10	14	3	26	5	30
91	31,803	5	48,582	35	U	5	33	84	3	4	14	4	32	5	31
92	33,052	8	40,448	35	U	7	28	71	4	15	18	4	30	6	33
93	31,002	0	26,544	22	U	11	11	73	-5	4	10	1	18	16	32
94	30,951	0	34,814	28	S	8	22	74	-4	15	14	2	26	5	21
95	31,869	2	43,434	30	S	6	34	82	0	8	18	2	30	3	18
96	33,924	10	47,862	30	S	6	31	87	10	4	15	0	21	2	36
97	32,041	2	48,013	41	U	9	34	33	5	63	0	0	14	1	23
98	36,596	24	55,206	36	U	3	37	88	22	1	37	4	50	3	57
99	30,603	-1	27,315	22	U	13	24	23	-9	71	2	1	15	3	20
100	32,831	8	47,438	30	U	4	46	84	5	7	24	3	39	4	41

Note: U=urban, S=suburban, R=rural, M=mixed, HH=households.

Oklahoma State House Districts: Demographic Data (cont.)

House District	Population		Average HH Income		District Type	Unempl. Rate	College Educ.	White (non-Hispanic)		African American		Asian American		Hispanic American	
	1997	+/-	($)	+/-		(%)	(%)	(%)	+/-	(%)	+/-	(%)	+/-	(%)	+/-
Oklahoma	3,318,854	6	41,197	35	M	7	33	80	5	8	8	1	26	3	29
101	33,196	7	41,944	35	S	8	32	65	4	28	14	2	32	3	25

Note: U=urban, S=suburban, R=rural, M=mixed, HH=households.

OREGON

"Welcome to Oregon. While you're here, I want you to enjoy yourselves. Travel, visit, drink in the great beauty of our state. But for God's sake, don't move here."

So declared Gov. Tom McCall to the national Jaycee convention in 1971. His attitude, conveying pride in the state's unappreciated beauty and a determination to keep it unappreciated, says a lot about Oregon and its development. People were moving to the Willamette Valley on the Oregon Trail in the 1840s with a vision of re-creating an orderly New England society in the wilderness. (A delegation from Maine that wanted to name the big city "Portland" won out over a contingent from Massachusetts that wanted to call it "Boston.") When gold was discovered in California a few years later, the nation's attention turned south, where it has stayed ever since.

Starting in the 1970s, though, people began to look again to Oregon. The state's unspoiled beauty and strict zoning laws to control development appealed to a nation growing more environmentally conscious. Harried suburbanites from Seattle and Southern California found here a less crowded, less polluted way of life. International attention came a few years later after entrepreneur Phil Knight won a following at track meets selling a new brand of sneaker, called Nike for the Greek goddess of victory, out of the back of his car.

Oregon's population grew by 8 percent during the 1980s and another 14 percent in the 1990s, a faster pace than Texas's. It is now the twenty-ninth biggest state (up from thirtieth in 1980), has already added one new congressional district, and will likely get another in 2002.

The Oregon of popular imagination is that part of the state west of the Cascades, lush with trees and rain. East of the cascades, however, the trees turn to sagebrush and the land is flat. Almost all the state's big cities—Portland, Salem, Eugene, Corvallis, Medford—are located in a line along I-5 at the western edge of the mountains. First among them, of course, is Portland, which has been described as an undeveloped Seattle, although John Gunther once wrote in *Inside USA* that the two were as different as tea and gin. Nevertheless, traditionally staid Portland has adopted some of Seattle's grunge during the decade, as well as some of its growth. Expansion has been fastest in the city's suburbs, which despite efforts to curtail them have spread ever farther from the city. Five suburban House districts have all grown by at least 25 percent since 1990, as have two rural districts slightly farther west along the edge of the Cascades. No house district in the state has lost population.

Lacking the diversity of California or a port the size of Seattle's, Oregon is not an especially wealthy state—it is the poorest of the Pacific Rim states (Alaska included)—but its rate of income growth recently has been faster. There are a few wealthy districts, all in the Portland suburbs, but household income levels off into relative prosperity. The poorest districts are in the logging regions along the southern coast and around Klamath Falls.

The population is 89 percent white overall and is at least 75 percent white in every state house district but one. That lone exception, the Eighteenth District in downtown Portland, is 48 percent African American and is also the third-poorest district in the state. The Fourteenth District, on the east bank of the Willamette River in downtown Portland, is 10 percent Asian. The Thirty-eighth District, northeast of Salem, is 22 percent Hispanic.

Republicans have controlled the state senate throughout the 1990s, with little change in their majority, while the house has been turned inside-out. Democrats began the decade with a majority of 20–10, which was exactly the size of the Republican majority six years later.

Perhaps true to its reputation for simplicity, Oregon is also the only state that does not have an office of lieutenant governor.

OREGON
State Senate Districts

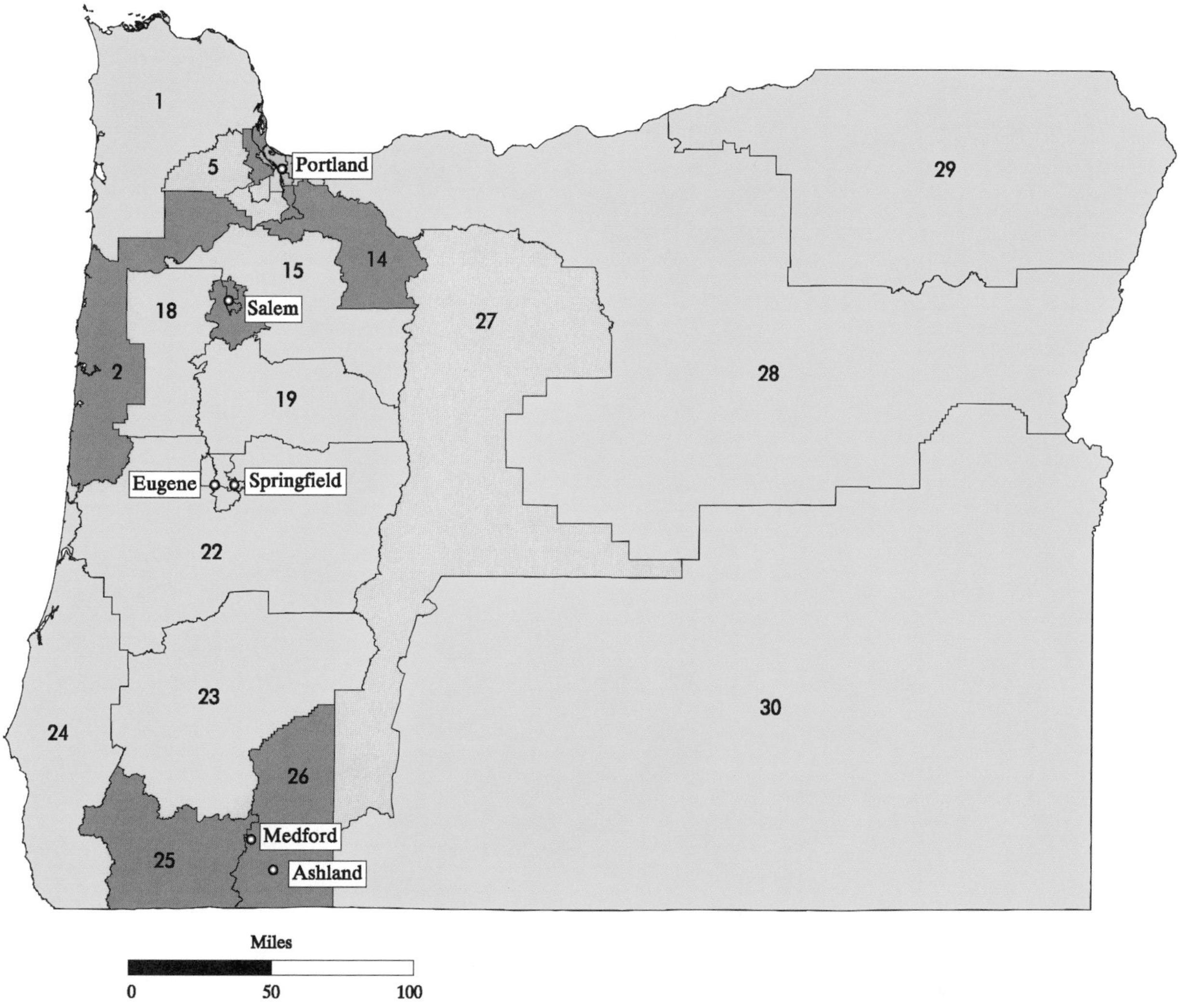

Portland

1

5

15

14

18

Salem

2

19

27

29

28

Eugene Springfield

22

23

26

24

Medford

25

Ashland

30

Miles

0   50   100

EUGENE

19

21

Eugene Springfield

22

20

22

Miles

0   10   20

SALEM

17

Salem

15

18

16

19

Miles

0   10   20

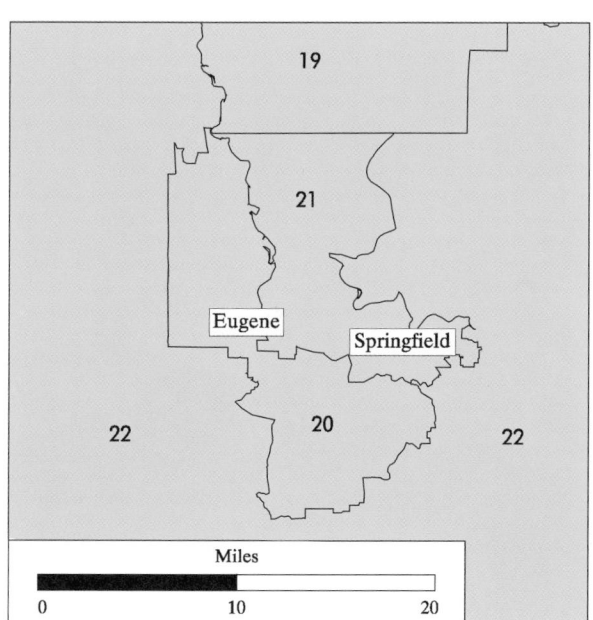

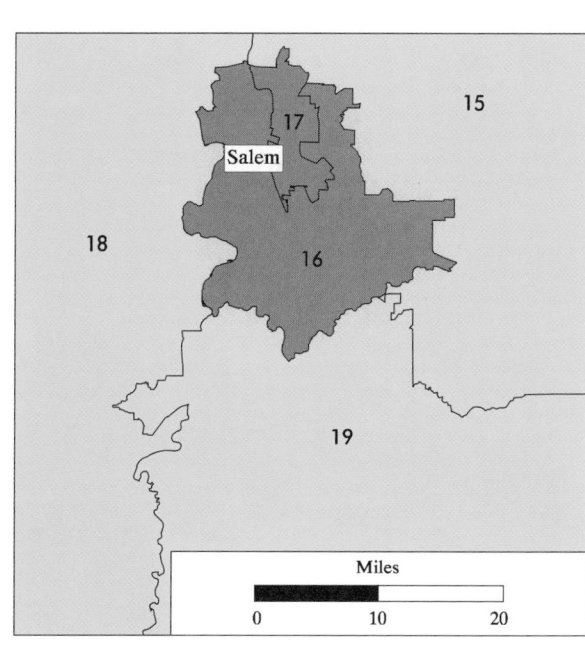

Population Growth   ▦ 1% to 3%   ▦ 7% to 13%   ▦ 16% to 20%   ▦ 25% to 32%

PORTLAND

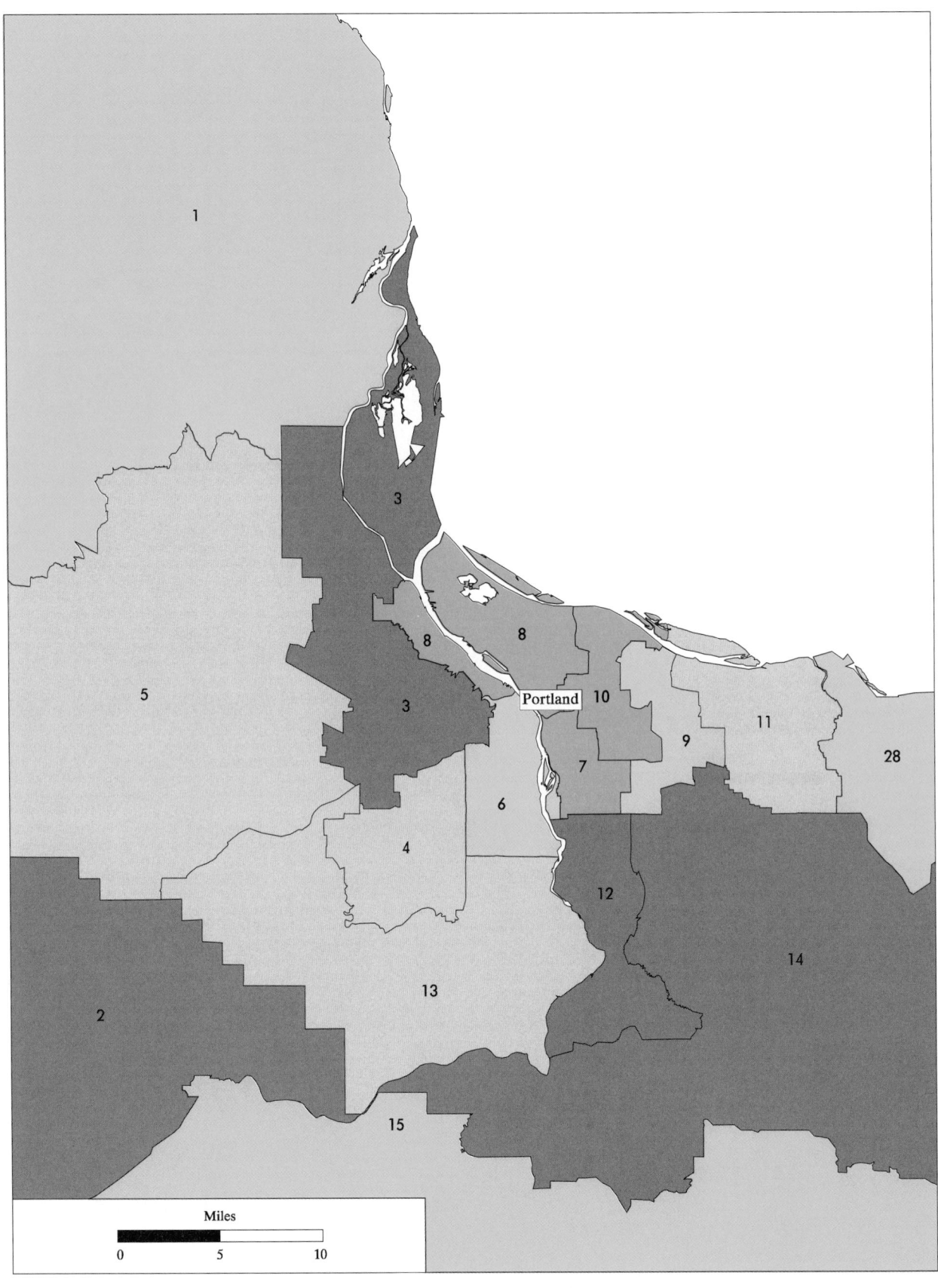

Portland

Population Growth   ▢ 1% to 3%   ▢ 7% to 13%   ▢ 16% to 20%   ▢ 25% to 32%

Oregon State Senate Districts: Demographic Data

Senate District	Population 1997	+/-	Average HH Income ($)	+/-	District Type	Unempl. Rate (%)	College Educ. (%)	White (non-Hispanic) (%)	+/-	African American (%)	+/-	Asian American (%)	+/-	Hispanic American (%)	+/-
Oregon	3,245,193	14	46,602	37	M	6	39	89	12	2	25	3	39	5	45
1	106,424	12	41,579	31	R	6	30	95	11	0	8	1	34	2	41
2	116,092	20	43,791	33	R	5	34	92	19	0	27	1	46	5	54
3	111,206	18	67,898	43	S	4	55	88	15	1	41	8	50	3	42
4	120,380	26	58,318	36	S	4	54	90	24	1	55	6	62	3	52
5	120,583	28	52,171	38	S	5	38	84	23	0	45	3	66	11	63
6	103,333	9	69,484	51	U	4	61	89	6	2	43	5	37	3	39
7	95,959	3	39,021	40	U	6	39	83	-1	3	34	8	28	4	29
8	96,038	1	36,252	37	U	10	28	58	-8	30	17	5	20	6	36
9	101,696	10	42,290	40	U	6	29	88	7	2	43	5	38	4	54
10	96,638	3	48,013	42	U	5	44	83	-2	4	29	8	30	4	41
11	114,228	25	46,549	27	S	4	35	89	22	2	61	3	57	5	73
12	110,951	17	48,341	37	S	4	35	94	15	1	37	2	45	3	45
13	121,458	27	76,697	37	S	3	57	93	26	1	44	3	57	3	62
14	117,722	20	59,091	38	S	4	38	93	18	0	32	2	54	4	54
15	105,078	11	46,245	38	R	6	28	84	7	0	34	1	27	14	39
16	110,244	18	52,581	37	S	5	43	91	16	1	46	2	40	5	50
17	111,440	18	38,866	36	U	7	34	84	14	2	39	3	39	9	51
18	107,481	12	43,560	39	R	6	50	89	10	1	23	5	25	5	38
19	105,858	13	43,128	37	R	7	30	95	12	0	6	1	41	3	42
20	102,738	8	44,558	33	U	6	49	91	6	1	24	3	28	3	43
21	99,956	8	39,631	35	U	8	39	92	7	1	24	3	28	4	44
22	109,256	12	43,424	33	R	8	32	95	11	0	16	1	32	2	30
23	107,005	10	34,968	24	R	8	28	94	9	0	6	1	35	3	39
24	100,791	7	34,833	27	R	8	29	94	6	0	-7	1	30	3	39
25	108,338	17	35,100	25	R	9	27	94	15	0	12	1	41	4	50
26	110,095	16	42,737	32	M	7	38	91	15	0	32	1	40	6	47
27	123,674	32	44,650	35	R	6	36	91	32	0	25	1	53	4	59
28	103,706	7	39,255	28	R	8	32	91	6	0	7	1	21	7	36
29	103,844	10	35,762	28	R	9	32	88	8	1	14	1	22	9	36
30	102,913	8	36,067	28	R	9	30	84	5	1	23	2	26	11	33

Note: U=urban, S=suburban, R=rural, M=mixed, HH=households.

OREGON
State House Districts

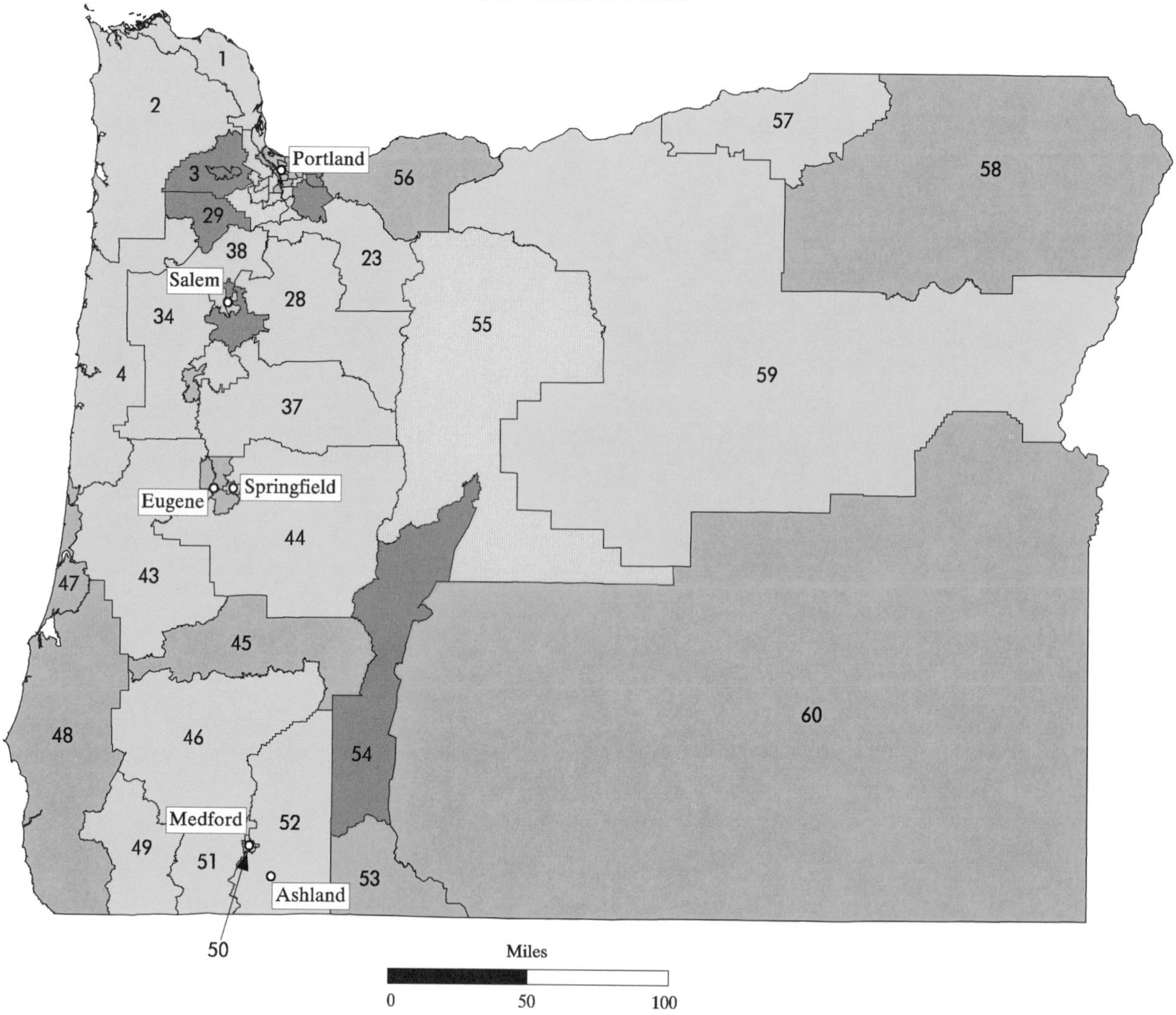

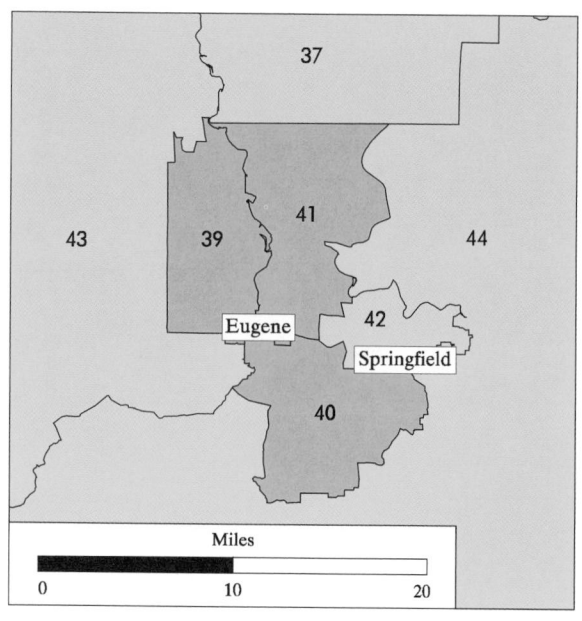

EUGENE

SALEM

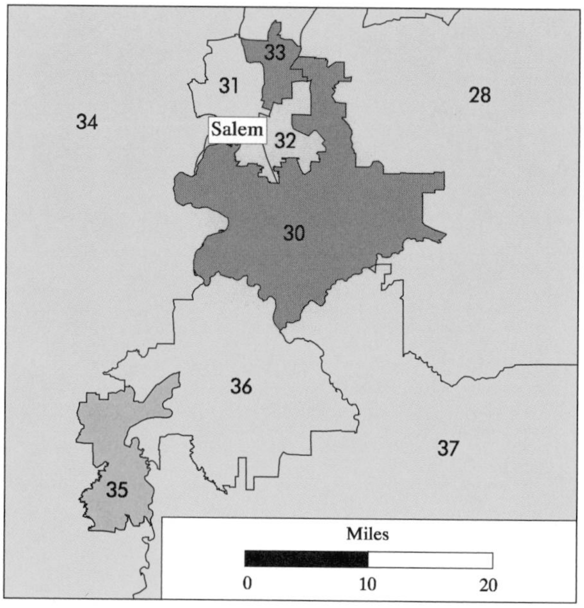

Population Growth ▨ 1% to 9% ▨ 11% to 19% ▨ 20% to 29% ▢ 35% to 40%

PORTLAND

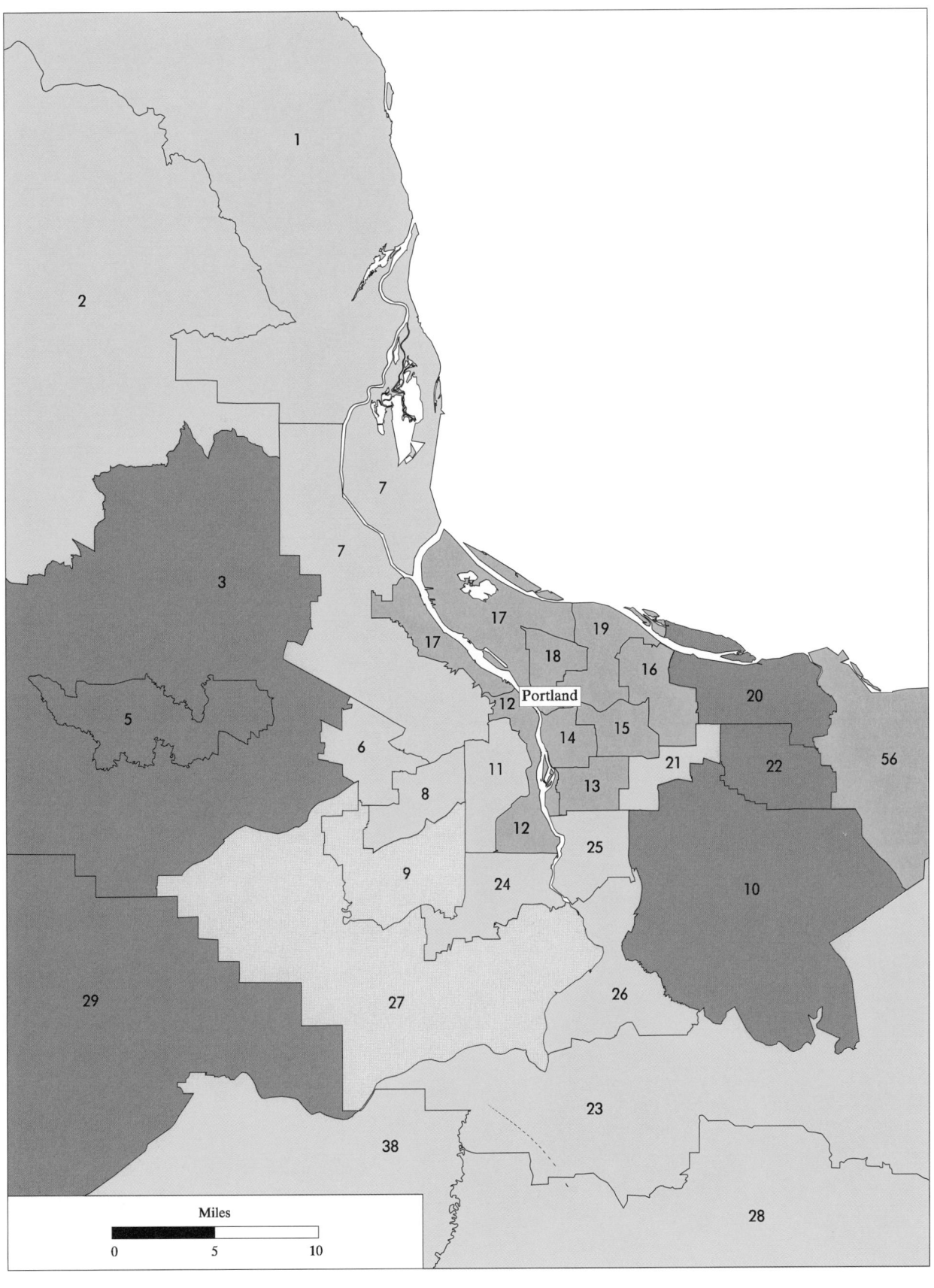

Population Growth ☐ 1% to 9%   ☐ 11% to 19%   ☐ 20% to 29%   ☐ 35% to 40%

Oregon State House Districts: Demographic Data

House District	Population 1997	+/-	Average HH Income ($)	+/-	District Type	Unempl. Rate (%)	College Educ. (%)	White (non-Hispanic) (%)	+/-	African American (%)	+/-	Asian American (%)	+/-	Hispanic American (%)	+/-
Oregon	3,245,193	14	46,602	37	M	6	39	89	12	2	25	3	39	5	45
1	51,039	11	43,638	30	R	6	29	94	10	0	13	1	33	3	46
2	55,383	12	39,790	31	R	6	31	96	11	0	1	1	37	2	36
3	65,451	29	59,466	40	S	5	41	88	26	0	42	4	72	6	62
4	55,990	17	37,452	31	R	6	32	94	17	0	-5	1	45	2	53
5	55,183	26	43,847	34	R	5	34	79	19	0	47	2	53	17	63
6	55,548	18	52,461	35	S	4	49	85	14	1	46	9	49	4	48
7	55,744	18	82,910	47	S	4	61	91	15	1	33	6	50	2	30
8	52,438	12	59,540	38	S	4	58	87	9	1	41	7	46	4	41
9	67,910	40	57,420	36	S	4	51	92	37	1	73	4	88	3	68
10	64,560	25	61,600	36	S	4	40	93	24	1	49	3	60	2	56
11	53,188	12	84,087	54	U	3	65	91	10	1	44	4	42	3	51
12	50,027	5	56,985	47	U	6	57	86	2	4	43	5	33	4	30
13	48,453	3	43,188	40	U	5	35	87	0	2	36	7	30	4	36
14	47,522	2	35,266	39	U	6	43	80	-2	4	33	10	27	4	24
15	48,893	4	45,356	39	U	5	41	84	0	2	34	9	32	4	40
16	50,461	7	44,417	39	U	5	32	87	4	2	38	7	37	3	47
17	47,726	1	38,956	35	U	9	25	75	-6	11	29	6	24	6	33
18	48,312	2	33,464	39	U	12	30	41	-12	48	15	3	13	6	39
19	47,745	2	50,664	45	U	5	47	81	-3	7	28	7	28	4	41
20	58,559	23	47,004	32	S	5	34	88	20	3	61	3	54	5	70
21	51,235	14	40,082	43	S	7	26	88	10	2	48	4	41	5	59
22	55,669	27	46,070	22	S	4	37	90	24	1	62	3	60	4	77
23	53,157	13	55,971	39	S	5	35	92	11	0	3	1	33	5	54
24	48,210	16	83,269	35	S	3	64	94	15	1	37	3	45	2	45
25	55,070	15	45,907	35	S	5	36	93	14	1	34	3	43	3	44
26	56,020	18	51,053	40	S	4	35	94	17	0	40	2	49	3	45
27	73,274	36	71,781	41	S	3	52	93	34	1	49	3	67	3	71
28	53,652	11	49,393	41	R	6	31	92	9	0	11	1	33	6	51
29	60,102	23	50,745	34	R	5	36	89	21	0	54	1	48	8	54
30	57,037	20	49,808	36	S	6	35	91	18	1	50	2	41	6	52
31	53,204	17	55,301	37	U	4	51	92	15	1	40	2	39	4	48
32	52,267	12	36,971	34	U	7	33	84	9	3	31	3	37	8	42
33	59,132	23	40,446	38	S	7	34	84	20	1	58	3	41	10	59
34	58,063	18	42,817	35	R	7	38	91	16	0	4	1	33	6	41
35	49,418	6	44,372	44	R	5	63	86	3	1	30	9	23	3	33
36	52,450	13	45,987	38	R	6	35	94	12	0	18	2	43	3	42
37	53,410	13	40,224	37	R	9	24	95	13	0	-19	1	37	2	43
38	51,437	11	42,724	35	R	6	25	75	5	1	38	1	23	22	36
39	52,016	9	39,884	33	S	7	33	93	8	1	23	1	30	4	47
40	50,722	6	49,221	34	U	6	62	90	4	1	25	5	28	3	38
41	49,568	6	42,787	37	U	7	49	91	4	1	24	4	26	4	42
42	50,388	11	36,065	33	U	8	28	93	9	1	24	2	35	4	46
43	53,358	11	44,043	32	R	7	33	95	10	0	19	1	32	2	34
44	55,901	12	42,829	34	R	9	32	95	12	0	11	1	32	2	27
45	50,819	8	36,966	24	R	7	31	94	7	0	7	1	35	3	42
46	56,183	12	33,119	25	R	10	25	94	11	0	6	1	36	3	36
47	48,938	7	34,054	27	R	9	29	93	6	0	-6	1	32	3	39
48	51,852	7	35,560	27	R	7	29	94	7	0	-7	1	27	2	39
49	54,914	17	31,407	19	R	10	27	94	16	0	8	1	44	4	52
50	50,826	19	43,905	32	U	7	35	90	16	0	37	1	47	7	63

Note: U=urban, S=suburban, R=rural, M=mixed, HH=households.

Oregon State House Districts: Demographic Data (cont.)

House District	Population		Average HH Income		District Type	Unempl. Rate	College Educ.	White (non-Hispanic)		African American		Asian American		Hispanic American	
	1997	+/-	($)	+/-		(%)	(%)	(%)	+/-	(%)	+/-	(%)	+/-	(%)	+/-
Oregon	3,245,193	14	46,602	37	M	6	39	89	12	2	25	3	39	5	45
51	53,422	17	39,252	30	S	8	27	94	15	0	17	1	37	4	49
52	59,269	14	41,725	32	S	7	41	93	14	0	29	1	34	5	30
53	49,246	7	34,950	25	R	9	30	88	5	1	31	1	23	7	39
54	58,196	29	42,054	32	R	5	39	95	28	0	25	1	59	3	64
55	65,485	35	47,177	38	R	6	33	88	35	0	27	1	46	5	57
56	50,707	4	40,998	25	R	8	34	86	0	0	13	2	26	11	37
57	52,495	13	36,102	27	R	9	30	85	10	1	22	1	29	12	36
58	51,351	7	35,427	28	R	8	33	91	6	0	-5	1	11	5	36
59	52,998	11	37,547	31	R	8	30	96	10	0	-9	0	0	3	34
60	53,667	8	37,169	31	R	9	30	81	5	0	-1	2	27	14	30

Note: U=urban, S=suburban, R=rural, M=mixed, HH=households.

PENNSYLVANIA

Pennsylvania is a state often ignored by its own great cities. Philadelphia scarcely admits it belongs there and faces toward New York. Pittsburgh looks down the Ohio River toward West Virginia and the Midwest. In between is a state of great natural beauty and once-great industrial might. Previous generations of Americans mastered the continent riding locomotives built in Philadelphia, made of steel forged in Pittsburgh, fired by coal mined in Scranton. Too insular to achieve the political influence its economic status accorded it, Pennsylvania for more than a century was, nevertheless, the nation's indispensable state.

It is much less indispensable today. Most of the mines, mills, and factories have closed. Pittsburghers no longer peer at the sun through a cloud of soot but try to build a new reputation for the city as a medical center. Philadelphia struggles to lure shipbuilders and computer firms but has lost its last major bank headquarters.

Pennsylvania began the 1980s as the fourth-largest state, ends the 1990s as the fifth-largest (having been passed by Florida), and is projected to fall to sixth by 2025, behind Illinois. Despite the well-publicized problems in rural coal country, most of the state's population loss is occurring in its cities, particularly Philadelphia and Pittsburgh. Eighty-six percent of the state's urban house districts have lost population since 1990, while 71 percent of its suburban districts and 82 percent of its rural districts have gained population.

Most of the suburbs losing population are those on the cities' edges—older suburbs filled a generation ago and now beginning to experience urban problems of their own. The suburbs that are growing now are those farther from the cities. Thus, the One Hundred Ninety-second District in the Overbrook section of Philadelphia has lost 9 percent of its population; the One Hundred Forty-eighth District, which includes the Main Line just beyond the city limits, has grown by only 1 percent; but the Sixty-first District, near Norristown, has grown by 10 percent. A similar pattern has occurred around Pittsburgh as well.

Often, what is left in the cities is poverty on a scale far exceeding that in the poorest parts of the rural South.

Average household income in the heavily Hispanic One Hundred Eightieth House District in North Philadelphia is less than $20,000, making it the third-poorest district in the country. It also has the nation's lowest rate of college graduation—4 percent. In the neighboring One Hundred Ninety-seventh District, which is 98 percent African American (the second-highest percentage in the country), average income is $26,000, and only 10 percent have finished college. Unemployment in both districts is 20 percent, which is lower than in any of the state's coal-mining districts.

Still stocked with German, Irish, and Slavic immigrants, Pennsylvania is 87 percent white, considerably higher than either New York (65 percent) or New Jersey (70 percent). Nine urban districts are more than 70 percent black, and there are pockets of Koreans in Cheltenham, Vietnamese in South Philadelphia, and Hispanics in Reading and Lancaster. But most of the state is white, poor, and conservative (it has more members of the National Rifle Association than any state except California). Another important factor in Pennsylvania politics is age. A quarter of the population is age fifty-five or older. In non-presidential election years, seniors account for half the electorate, giving them political influence disproportionate to their share of the population. Pennsylvania is, for example, one of the only states that devotes all of its lottery proceeds to senior citizen programs rather than to economic development or education.

The state legislature has an undistinguished history. It was historically in the pocket of the Pennsylvania Railroad, and muckraker Henry Demarest Lloyd once remarked that the Standard Oil Company "did everything to the Pennsylvania legislature except refine it." More recently, house Democrats staged a coup against a speaker of their own party who pushed reform too quickly. They have not been rewarded for their efforts; a thirteen-seat Democratic majority in 1990 became a five-seat Republican majority in 1996. Republicans, who controlled the senate by two seats in 1990, controlled it by ten six years later.

PENNSYLVANIA
State Senate Districts

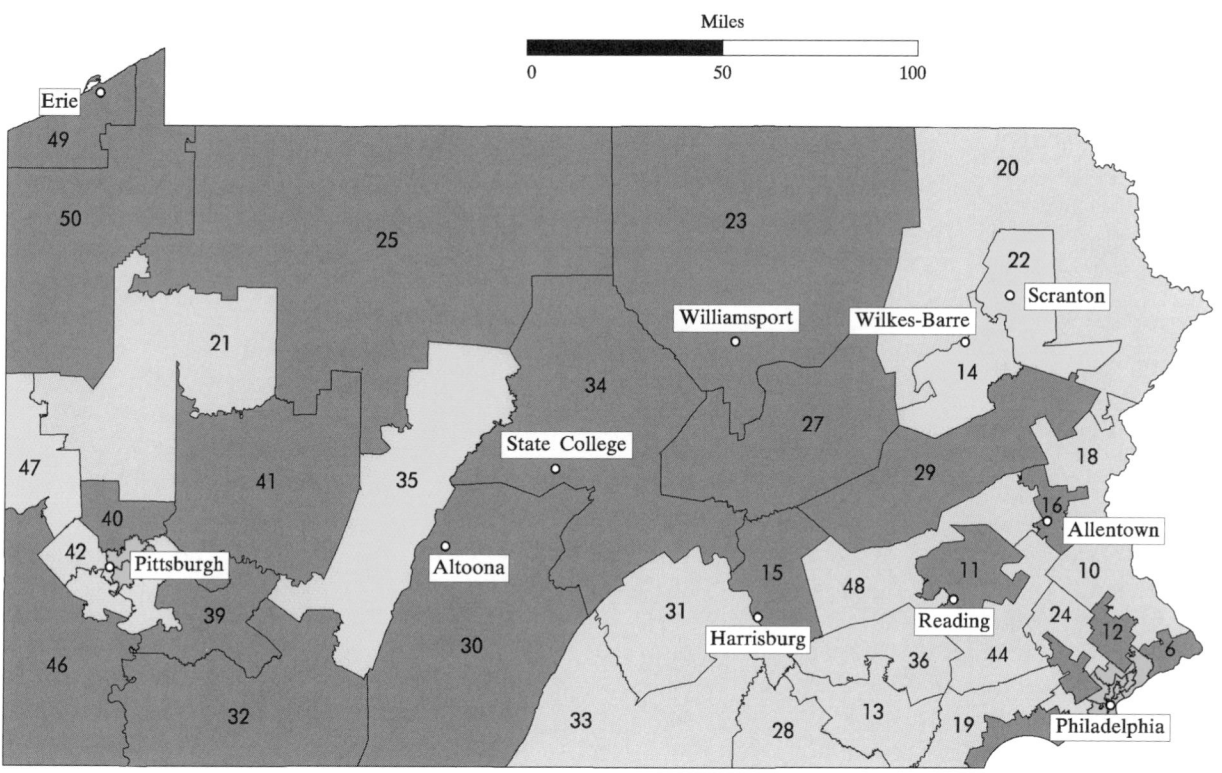

PITTSBURGH

PHILADELPHIA

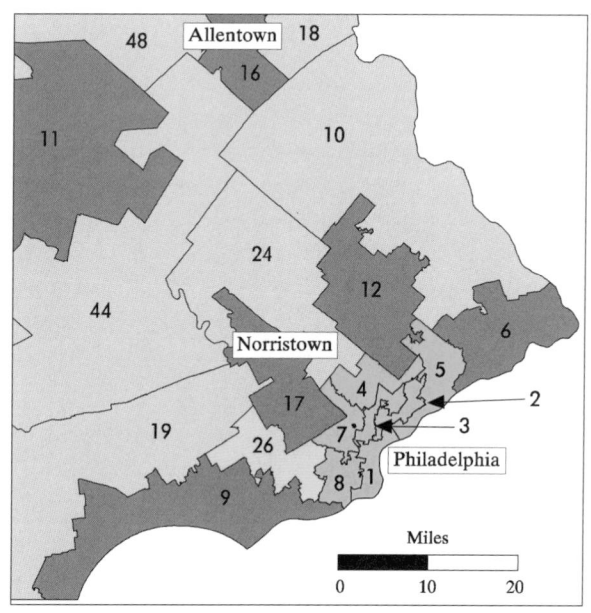

Population Growth | -10% to -6% | -3% to 0% | 1% to 5% | 6% to 12%

Pennsylvania State Senate Districts: Demographic Data

Senate District	Population 1997	+/-	Average HH Income ($)	+/-	District Type	Unempl. Rate (%)	College Educ. (%)	White (non-Hispanic) (%)	+/-	African American (%)	+/-	Asian American (%)	+/-	Hispanic American (%)	+/-
Penn.	12,049,031	1	48,834	33	M	6	38	87	0	9	5	1	32	2	26
1	215,464	-7	45,018	31	U	9	37	71	-14	19	9	6	26	5	10
2	214,349	-10	33,821	23	U	10	18	58	-18	11	-3	3	8	27	8
3	213,031	-10	31,739	24	U	14	19	25	-26	62	-6	5	10	8	23
4	221,332	-6	53,357	29	U	8	43	32	-16	64	-2	2	14	2	13
5	223,189	-6	49,549	28	U	6	30	90	-9	4	11	3	39	2	28
6	243,952	2	53,287	24	S	5	39	89	0	6	20	3	41	3	39
7	220,140	-7	36,482	26	U	11	31	31	-17	65	-2	3	10	1	13
8	221,574	-6	35,170	27	U	11	26	30	-21	65	2	3	12	1	9
9	246,341	3	62,668	38	S	5	44	79	1	17	8	1	41	3	37
10	263,983	12	77,988	30	R	3	57	96	10	1	30	2	59	1	45
11	249,934	4	45,159	27	S	5	31	87	1	4	16	1	25	9	34
12	248,814	5	73,570	30	S	3	56	91	3	5	18	3	48	2	34
13	249,952	6	50,257	30	S	4	36	87	4	4	17	1	41	7	38
14	217,677	-3	37,860	31	S	6	30	97	-4	1	7	1	28	1	20
15	247,484	4	50,663	38	S	5	41	79	0	16	17	1	37	3	32
16	240,337	1	47,156	30	U	5	37	88	-2	3	11	1	32	8	31
17	239,653	1	92,660	33	S	3	64	91	-1	4	27	3	43	1	25
18	255,371	7	48,244	28	M	5	36	90	4	3	19	1	37	6	35
19	261,289	9	83,714	44	R	3	59	86	7	10	24	2	47	3	37
20	273,035	9	41,281	24	R	6	36	97	9	1	17	1	46	1	55
21	248,403	6	41,515	32	R	7	34	98	5	1	18	0	40	0	37
22	238,718	0	41,167	30	S	6	35	97	-1	1	19	1	36	1	52
23	242,700	1	38,597	31	R	7	33	97	1	2	16	0	34	1	33
24	263,344	11	65,677	30	R	3	49	88	8	7	22	3	55	2	43
25	239,484	1	38,637	35	R	8	31	99	1	0	6	0	26	1	19
26	235,857	-1	59,652	33	S	4	47	90	-4	5	26	4	34	1	27
27	242,730	2	40,071	36	R	6	29	98	2	0	9	0	28	1	30
28	260,276	10	47,472	27	S	4	31	92	8	5	25	1	46	2	43
29	247,910	4	37,466	27	R	6	27	98	4	1	14	0	44	1	42
30	240,208	2	38,686	38	R	7	27	98	1	2	12	0	20	0	27
31	255,085	7	51,532	31	S	3	43	96	6	1	17	1	45	1	37
32	235,190	1	35,267	34	R	11	25	96	1	3	15	0	32	0	35
33	253,278	7	46,988	30	R	4	33	96	6	2	21	1	45	1	36
34	249,509	4	40,413	32	R	6	43	95	3	1	14	2	43	1	30
35	231,134	-2	33,959	29	M	9	26	97	-3	2	9	0	26	1	26
36	259,436	8	52,212	30	R	3	32	96	7	1	32	1	48	2	41
37	234,270	-1	67,119	40	S	4	57	96	-2	2	46	1	35	1	30
38	221,409	-6	41,843	39	U	10	38	60	-11	37	1	2	23	1	28
39	246,159	2	43,344	36	R	7	37	98	1	1	19	0	31	0	31
40	244,419	2	60,878	41	S	4	51	96	1	2	31	1	41	1	31
41	239,192	1	36,906	30	R	8	30	98	0	1	14	0	23	0	24
42	232,178	-3	47,972	38	S	6	39	88	-5	10	17	1	26	1	29
43	222,536	-6	49,675	38	S	6	47	83	-10	14	16	2	28	1	25
44	256,558	7	65,277	37	R	4	46	94	6	3	30	1	46	1	40
45	229,993	-3	44,480	37	S	7	40	89	-6	9	26	1	32	1	21
46	238,987	1	40,213	35	R	9	29	95	0	4	14	0	13	1	29
47	236,620	0	38,021	33	R	8	30	92	-1	6	15	0	27	1	31
48	251,515	6	53,711	32	S	3	38	96	5	1	24	1	46	2	39
49	240,645	2	45,094	35	M	7	38	90	0	7	17	1	31	2	33
50	243,932	2	38,639	31	R	7	31	96	1	3	15	0	30	1	25

Note: U=urban, S=suburban, R=rural, M=mixed, HH=households.

PENNSYLVANIA
State House Districts

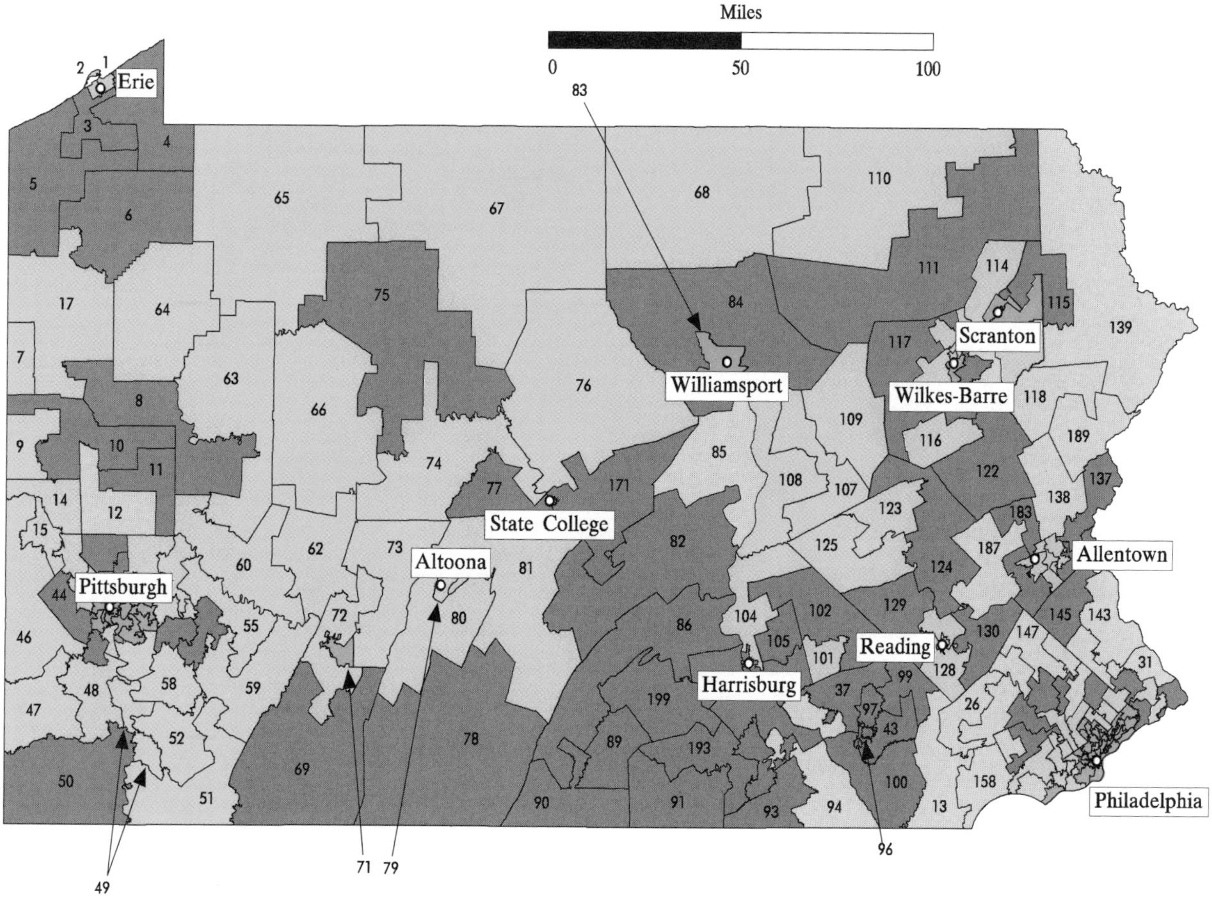

Miles

0   50   100

Erie

83

Williamsport

Scranton

Wilkes-Barre

State College

Altoona

Pittsburgh

Reading

Allentown

Harrisburg

Philadelphia

49

71 79

96

HARRISBURG/YORK

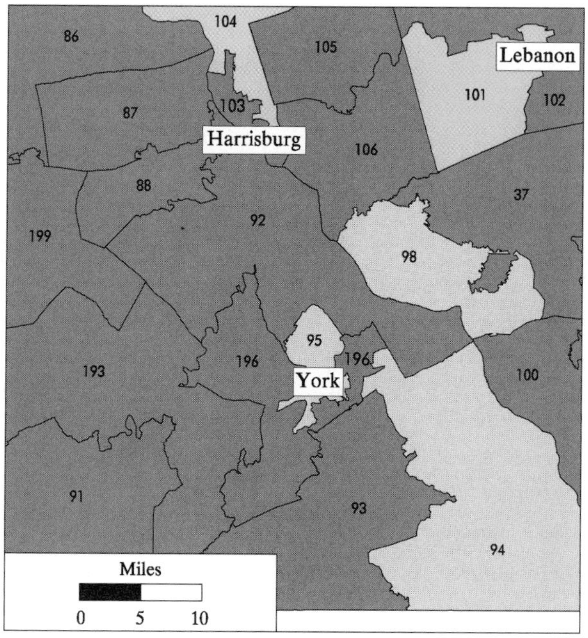

Lebanon

Harrisburg

York

Miles

0   5   10

WILKES-BARRE/SCRANTON

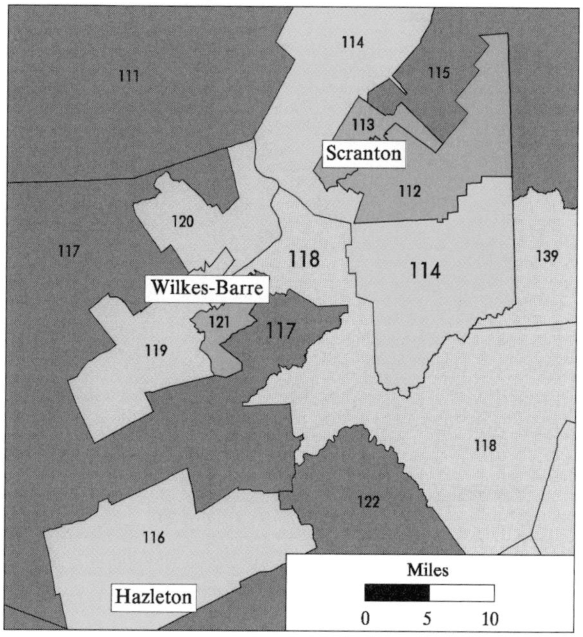

Scranton

Wilkes-Barre

Hazleton

Miles

0   5   10

Population Growth   -11% to -4%   -3% to 2%   3% to 9%   10% to 25%

ALLENTOWN-READING

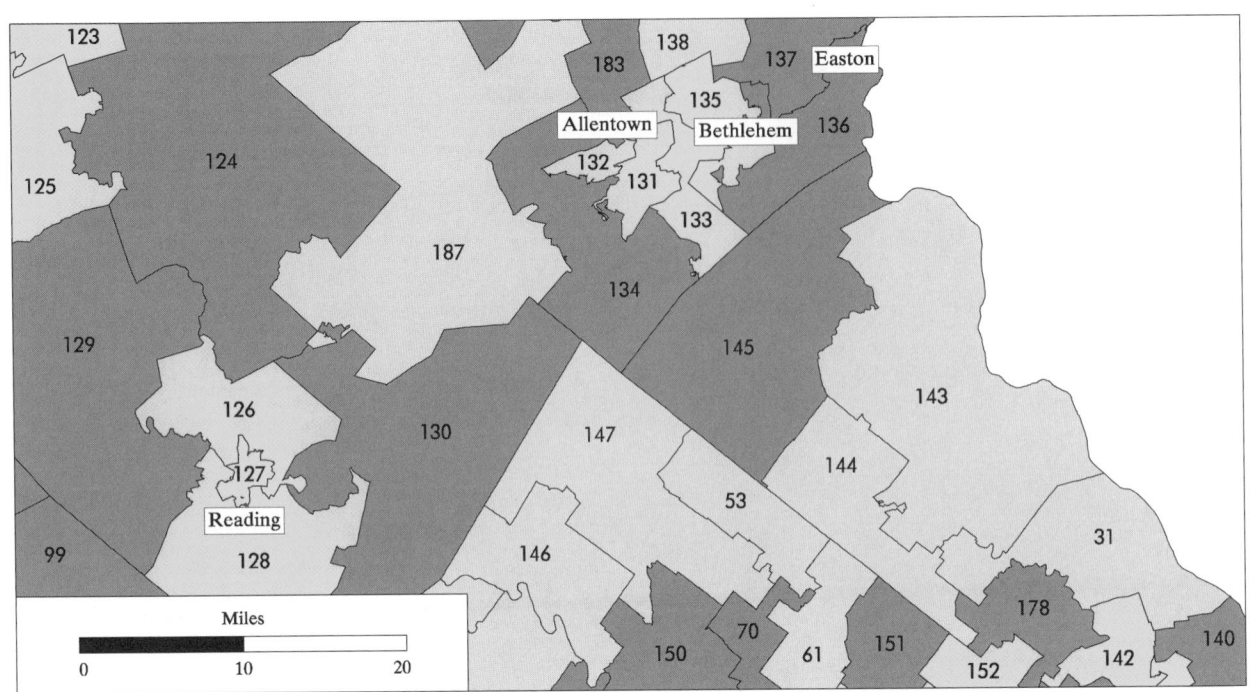

PITTSBURGH

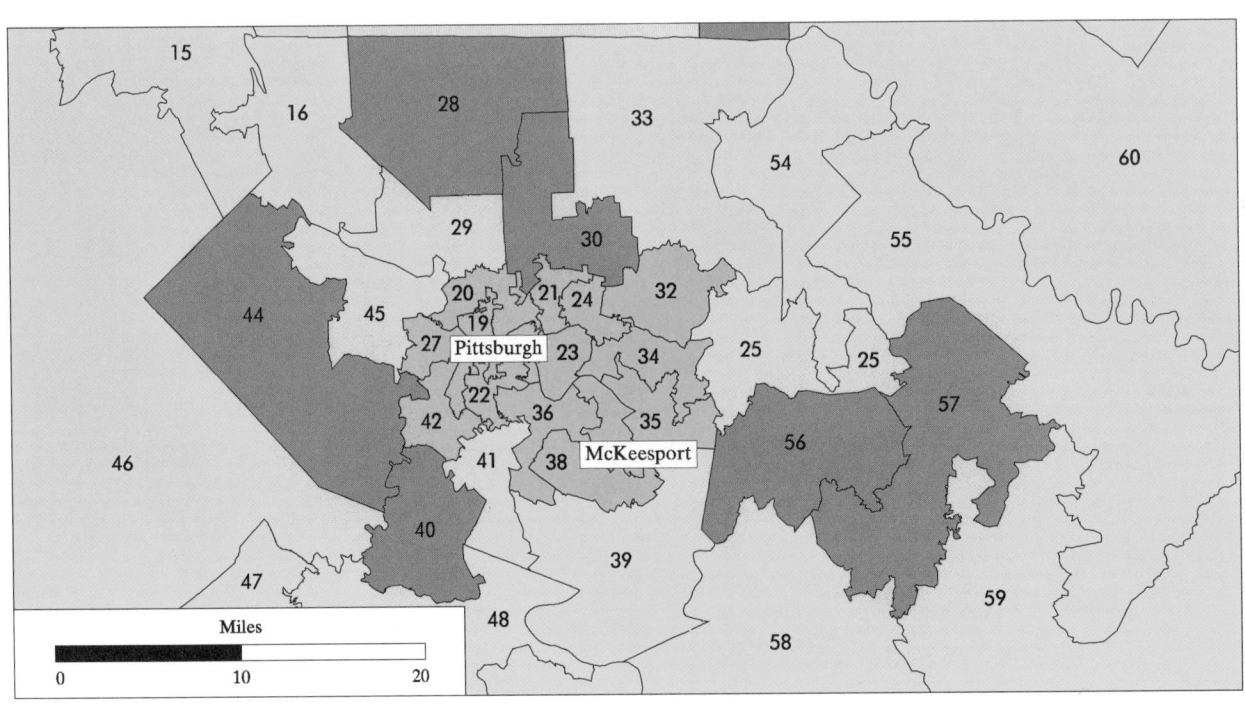

Population Growth   ▢ -11% to -4%   ▢ -3% to 2%   ▢ 3% to 9%   ▢ 10% to 25%

PHILADELPHIA 1

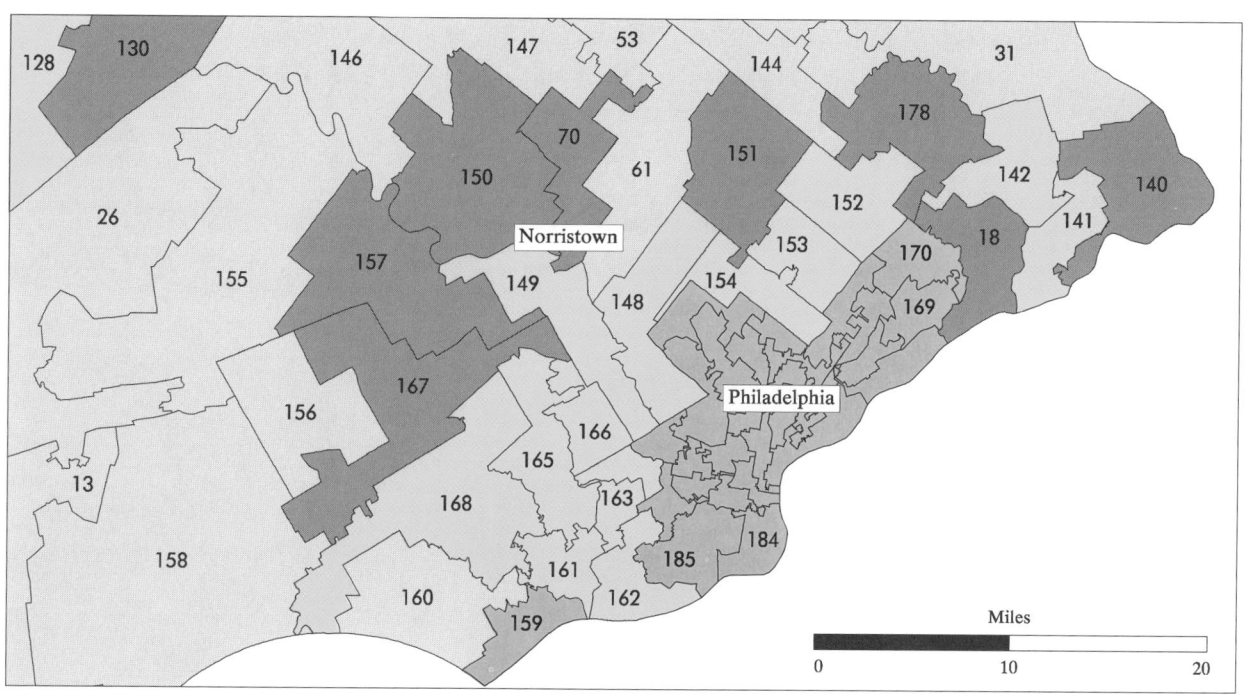

PHILADELPHIA 2

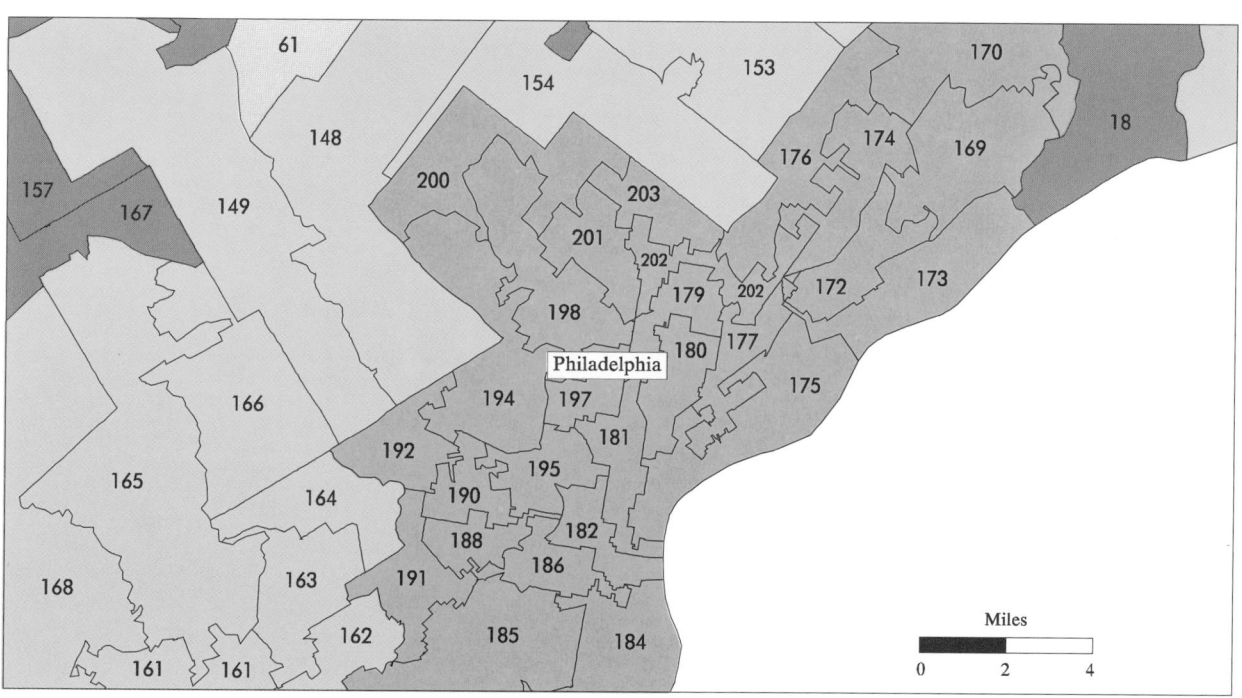

Population Growth   ▨ -11% to -4%   ☐ -3% to 2%   ▨ 3% to 9%   ☐ 10% to 25%

Pennsylvania State House Districts: Demographic Data

House District	Population 1997	+/-	Average HH Income ($)	+/-	District Type	Unempl. Rate (%)	College Educ. (%)	White (non-Hispanic) (%)	+/-	African American (%)	+/-	Asian American (%)	+/-	Hispanic American (%)	+/-
Penn.	12,049,031	1	48,834	33	M	6	38	87	0	9	5	1	32	2	26
1	58,071	-2	32,587	28	U	10	24	79	-7	16	16	0	12	4	41
2	56,567	-1	39,244	34	U	8	39	87	-3	10	15	1	16	2	28
3	61,317	6	55,926	37	S	4	48	97	5	1	34	1	47	0	20
4	59,544	3	42,427	31	S	7	31	98	3	1	22	0	30	1	19
5	62,268	5	48,926	35	R	7	40	98	5	1	28	0	33	0	6
6	59,118	3	37,598	31	R	8	30	97	2	2	15	0	31	1	34
7	57,998	1	36,769	29	S	8	31	89	-1	10	14	0	36	1	28
8	63,461	6	36,263	30	R	7	35	97	5	2	29	1	72	0	40
9	56,310	-2	36,338	28	R	8	29	94	-3	5	13	0	29	0	23
10	60,178	4	38,885	31	R	7	32	98	4	1	24	0	23	0	32
11	64,141	8	41,135	31	R	6	33	98	8	1	22	0	12	0	45
12	66,457	13	55,239	38	R	5	45	99	13	0	20	0	31	1	54
13	65,628	14	59,128	42	R	3	34	91	13	6	24	0	50	2	52
14	58,852	1	35,572	34	R	9	26	92	0	7	19	0	16	1	34
15	58,951	1	49,691	40	R	6	40	97	0	2	22	0	41	1	44
16	57,961	-1	49,235	35	R	7	37	87	-3	12	15	0	25	1	25
17	57,672	0	40,670	34	R	6	30	99	0	1	17	0	26	0	10
18	60,865	3	54,228	26	S	5	43	85	0	7	18	5	41	3	38
19	53,201	-10	26,866	31	U	16	29	35	-19	62	-4	1	15	1	22
20	53,640	-7	35,266	34	U	8	25	84	-11	14	19	1	19	1	31
21	54,916	-4	41,109	35	U	6	44	77	-8	18	13	3	32	2	30
22	53,914	-5	34,998	33	U	7	27	91	-7	8	13	1	15	1	20
23	54,327	-5	65,191	42	U	6	65	81	-11	10	27	7	29	2	34
24	51,772	-8	34,390	34	U	13	37	25	-23	72	-2	1	1	1	30
25	59,187	0	62,362	43	S	4	57	91	-2	5	40	3	35	1	33
26	63,046	10	59,437	40	R	4	37	80	6	16	22	1	44	3	55
27	54,565	-6	45,563	37	U	7	40	87	-9	11	14	1	24	1	15
28	59,393	3	86,151	43	S	3	64	96	1	1	60	2	46	1	42
29	55,884	-2	53,196	36	S	4	50	97	-3	2	49	1	36	0	16
30	61,066	3	90,182	46	S	3	56	97	2	1	49	2	42	1	24
31	70,039	21	97,648	28	S	3	70	94	19	2	42	3	72	2	75
32	57,284	-6	48,210	36	S	6	44	83	-10	16	13	1	18	1	29
33	58,917	-1	47,236	36	S	5	40	98	-2	1	47	0	22	0	13
34	55,374	-6	50,075	37	S	5	53	82	-11	16	21	1	16	1	32
35	52,448	-10	28,385	28	S	11	22	69	-18	29	16	0	-4	1	9
36	56,289	-6	42,811	32	S	5	37	97	-7	1	31	0	16	1	24
37	60,962	6	59,492	33	S	3	43	96	5	1	27	1	49	1	50
38	54,026	-4	34,988	30	S	9	28	88	-8	11	38	0	4	1	12
39	58,420	-1	42,878	32	S	7	37	91	-3	8	24	0	33	1	11
40	60,269	5	94,533	43	S	3	68	96	4	1	46	2	40	1	49
41	58,722	-1	51,918	34	S	4	47	97	-2	2	49	1	33	1	29
42	56,159	-5	75,340	39	S	3	63	96	-6	1	38	2	32	1	27
43	57,583	6	55,933	33	S	2	32	95	5	1	26	2	47	2	35
44	58,873	3	51,484	39	S	5	43	93	1	5	50	1	36	1	33
45	57,765	-1	47,959	40	S	6	40	92	-4	6	34	1	34	1	26
46	58,366	-2	44,703	37	R	7	30	95	-2	3	17	0	11	1	24
47	58,621	1	39,790	33	R	8	31	93	0	6	16	0	15	1	41
48	58,387	2	43,421	33	R	7	30	96	1	3	23	0	22	1	43
49	57,801	-3	35,143	33	R	11	29	94	-4	5	13	0	32	1	22
50	60,444	3	34,505	36	R	13	25	97	3	2	13	0	7	1	31

Note: U=urban, S=suburban, R=rural, M=mixed, HH=households.

Pennsylvania State House Districts: Demographic Data (cont.)

House District	Population 1997	+/-	Average HH Income ($)	+/-	District Type	Unempl. Rate (%)	College Educ. (%)	White (non-Hispanic) (%)	+/-	African American (%)	+/-	Asian American (%)	+/-	Hispanic American (%)	+/-
Penn.	12,049,031	1	48,834	33	M	6	38	87	0	9	5	1	32	2	26
51	54,700	1	35,180	37	R	14	23	95	0	4	15	0	32	1	43
52	63,327	-1	32,941	34	R	13	25	97	-1	3	17	0	20	0	25
53	61,224	10	54,561	27	R	3	41	91	8	2	39	5	54	2	31
54	58,807	0	44,071	40	R	6	37	94	-1	5	18	1	34	1	38
55	59,421	1	40,397	35	R	8	30	98	0	1	21	0	16	0	26
56	60,082	3	45,424	37	R	6	40	98	3	1	17	0	31	0	24
57	59,940	3	40,168	35	R	6	38	96	2	3	22	1	35	1	54
58	59,956	-1	37,915	33	R	9	31	96	-2	3	9	0	20	0	11
59	60,625	2	49,817	41	R	7	39	99	1	0	14	1	38	0	20
60	59,830	0	35,610	28	R	8	25	98	0	1	14	0	10	0	23
61	66,764	10	86,643	32	S	3	63	88	7	4	19	6	55	1	31
62	58,602	-1	36,454	28	R	9	37	96	-2	2	10	1	28	1	25
63	59,695	2	34,176	27	R	9	28	99	1	0	4	0	29	0	11
64	58,656	-1	36,975	33	R	8	29	98	-1	1	12	0	16	0	21
65	59,856	-1	40,470	33	R	6	30	98	-2	1	13	0	23	1	28
66	58,367	2	34,639	28	R	9	25	99	1	0	-12	0	1	0	9
67	60,404	2	37,330	37	R	9	31	99	2	0	-1	0	15	0	7
68	59,380	2	37,807	38	R	7	32	99	2	0	2	0	24	0	18
69	59,919	4	36,407	30	R	8	23	99	3	0	-2	0	35	0	41
70	58,947	6	52,988	30	U	4	38	76	0	18	24	3	52	3	50
71	59,911	-4	34,686	29	S	9	33	93	-5	5	6	0	29	1	26
72	53,826	-2	36,057	29	S	7	28	99	-2	1	16	0	22	0	11
73	58,765	-2	32,755	27	R	8	25	98	-3	1	23	0	26	1	40
74	61,030	2	37,125	33	R	11	32	98	1	1	9	1	39	0	27
75	60,866	3	40,398	39	R	8	33	99	2	0	-20	0	46	0	23
76	60,449	1	38,904	35	R	8	32	97	0	2	20	1	40	1	33
77	61,643	6	42,237	35	U	7	69	88	4	3	12	7	44	2	31
78	61,481	3	36,917	38	R	8	22	99	3	0	1	0	16	0	28
79	59,959	0	36,634	38	U	8	27	97	0	2	13	0	24	1	38
80	58,187	1	43,604	41	S	6	32	99	1	0	7	0	35	0	21
81	60,597	2	37,912	36	R	7	27	95	1	4	14	0	-13	0	19
82	61,872	4	36,866	25	R	6	21	99	4	0	-12	0	15	0	15
83	57,104	-4	38,861	30	U	8	35	94	-5	5	13	1	35	1	17
84	61,584	4	39,832	29	S	6	32	98	3	1	17	0	33	1	41
85	65,248	10	43,698	33	R	4	34	96	9	2	30	1	35	2	43
86	63,200	7	45,511	35	S	4	29	98	7	1	19	0	32	1	38
87	63,241	7	60,860	32	S	3	52	96	6	1	11	2	46	1	30
88	64,539	8	57,759	32	S	2	52	95	7	2	17	2	46	1	47
89	62,250	6	43,740	31	R	4	32	94	5	3	20	1	54	1	38
90	62,620	5	45,530	33	R	4	28	96	4	2	23	1	38	1	36
91	65,101	9	44,460	25	R	4	31	96	8	1	24	1	47	2	42
92	64,316	9	49,990	29	S	3	35	98	8	1	17	1	43	1	30
93	61,684	6	53,930	29	S	2	37	98	5	0	17	1	43	1	14
94	68,860	18	49,308	26	S	4	31	97	17	1	30	1	55	1	46
95	64,982	11	36,451	25	S	7	24	74	5	17	25	1	44	8	48
96	62,449	5	36,907	30	U	6	26	61	-6	11	15	2	35	25	37
97	62,468	7	60,835	28	S	3	52	95	6	1	29	2	49	2	32
98	63,622	11	47,156	28	S	3	34	95	9	2	35	1	43	2	62
99	62,446	6	49,644	30	R	2	23	97	5	0	15	1	49	1	37
100	65,473	8	50,525	31	S	3	28	98	8	1	29	1	38	1	35

Note: U=urban, S=suburban, R=rural, M=mixed, HH=households.

Pennsylvania State House Districts: Demographic Data (cont.)

House District	Population 1997	+/-	Average HH Income ($)	+/-	District Type	Unempl. Rate (%)	College Educ. (%)	White (non-Hispanic) (%)	+/-	African American (%)	+/-	Asian American (%)	+/-	Hispanic American (%)	+/-
Penn.	12,049,031	1	48,834	33	M	6	38	87	0	9	5	1	32	2	26
101	59,209	2	43,735	32	M	4	31	93	0	1	13	1	40	5	33
102	61,442	4	49,141	36	S	4	25	97	4	0	9	1	38	1	39
103	61,558	4	35,976	34	U	10	28	37	-13	51	14	2	22	9	34
104	58,044	0	49,631	35	S	3	37	91	-2	7	20	1	33	1	21
105	63,194	8	62,153	40	S	2	52	93	7	4	30	1	45	1	36
106	61,426	5	54,754	39	S	3	45	93	3	4	35	2	53	1	26
107	57,198	-3	37,041	41	R	7	25	99	-3	0	-5	0	33	0	8
108	60,402	1	40,842	35	R	6	28	98	1	1	6	0	21	1	37
109	59,991	1	39,407	36	R	5	31	98	1	0	6	0	22	1	31
110	59,913	2	38,893	28	R	6	35	98	2	0	-11	1	39	1	46
111	62,376	5	37,683	26	R	6	33	99	5	0	-2	0	16	1	29
112	54,522	-6	37,822	29	U	6	36	96	-7	2	4	1	22	1	24
113	52,903	-6	36,689	29	U	6	30	98	-7	1	13	1	31	1	27
114	57,550	1	53,733	33	S	5	43	98	1	0	16	1	41	0	23
115	59,437	3	37,048	28	S	6	31	98	3	1	22	0	36	1	41
116	56,247	-2	39,735	31	S	6	29	97	-2	1	9	1	39	1	22
117	60,121	3	46,570	32	S	6	33	95	3	3	9	1	33	1	45
118	66,142	15	39,902	25	S	6	33	96	13	1	69	1	66	2	89
119	56,530	-3	32,535	29	S	7	24	99	-3	0	6	0	17	1	28
120	55,659	-2	47,122	32	S	5	43	99	-3	0	6	1	30	0	4
121	51,666	-9	32,508	28	U	7	29	95	-10	3	6	1	23	1	15
122	60,056	4	37,954	26	R	6	26	98	3	0	-17	0	43	1	36
123	57,325	-2	32,124	28	R	7	20	98	-3	1	39	0	23	1	42
124	62,633	8	41,506	30	R	5	27	98	7	0	5	0	52	2	91
125	58,789	1	38,274	27	R	4	26	98	1	0	-30	1	39	0	13
126	59,722	2	45,310	25	S	5	31	87	-1	4	12	1	37	8	38
127	58,110	0	31,799	24	U	8	19	63	-10	10	15	1	-8	26	29
128	58,209	1	60,191	31	S	3	45	96	0	1	24	1	41	1	39
129	62,584	8	54,666	29	S	3	41	96	7	1	38	1	48	2	54
130	61,762	6	53,728	30	R	4	34	97	5	1	30	0	48	1	33
131	57,181	-1	37,809	24	U	6	27	77	-8	5	11	2	24	16	34
132	54,955	-3	44,242	31	U	6	41	81	-7	4	6	1	26	13	27
133	58,073	0	42,979	26	M	5	35	84	-4	2	15	2	32	11	28
134	63,858	5	72,364	32	S	4	54	96	4	0	18	3	46	1	38
135	58,172	2	56,125	32	U	4	45	84	-1	2	9	2	38	12	31
136	59,487	4	44,809	31	S	5	31	88	1	6	22	1	32	5	54
137	61,106	5	56,863	32	S	3	41	97	4	1	11	1	37	1	43
138	68,640	18	49,539	26	S	4	33	98	17	0	20	0	47	1	61
139	72,065	25	38,554	17	R	5	35	97	24	1	45	1	76	2	76
140	61,315	4	48,209	23	S	5	33	87	1	7	27	2	45	5	37
141	57,796	0	47,286	22	R	5	27	88	-2	7	15	2	35	3	40
142	59,744	2	62,907	25	S	3	50	94	0	2	20	2	45	2	39
143	65,529	10	80,677	32	R	3	56	96	9	1	24	1	50	1	33
144	67,877	14	63,443	26	R	3	50	93	12	2	32	2	57	3	39
145	64,307	9	53,583	25	R	3	38	97	9	1	28	1	51	1	25
146	64,068	12	50,498	29	R	4	36	90	10	7	33	1	52	2	40
147	67,437	14	62,214	30	R	3	46	96	13	1	46	2	56	1	53
148	53,423	1	110,681	34	S	3	66	93	-1	3	29	3	43	1	33
149	60,662	0	107,638	33	S	3	69	88	-3	6	18	4	38	2	21
150	60,524	4	65,628	30	S	3	51	88	3	8	6	2	44	3	36

Note: U=urban, S=suburban, R=rural, M=mixed, HH=households.

Pennsylvania State House Districts: Demographic Data (cont.)

House District	Population 1997	+/-	Average HH Income ($)	+/-	District Type	Unempl. Rate (%)	College Educ. (%)	White (non-Hispanic) (%)	+/-	African American (%)	+/-	Asian American (%)	+/-	Hispanic American (%)	+/-
Penn.	12,049,031	1	48,834	33	M	6	38	87	0	9	5	1	32	2	26
151	60,653	6	81,560	33	S	3	61	90	4	5	27	4	54	1	34
152	56,419	-2	72,688	30	S	3	52	95	-3	2	19	2	40	1	24
153	56,516	-2	78,798	31	S	3	55	87	-5	9	13	3	36	1	35
154	56,350	-2	79,360	28	S	3	63	82	-5	12	9	4	20	1	30
155	64,288	11	79,532	46	R	2	58	93	10	4	30	2	54	1	59
156	64,467	11	76,963	46	R	4	64	85	9	9	27	2	49	4	23
157	60,083	5	97,603	46	R	3	65	92	3	5	24	2	44	1	25
158	64,767	12	93,840	45	R	2	60	87	9	5	24	1	52	7	42
159	52,917	-8	34,660	30	R	11	20	38	-21	57	0	0	-7	4	25
160	63,739	11	63,558	34	S	3	44	94	9	4	64	1	55	1	52
161	59,401	1	59,142	30	S	4	46	91	-1	6	40	2	43	1	30
162	56,518	-3	46,047	32	S	6	25	88	-6	10	21	1	31	1	25
163	55,955	-1	52,592	33	S	4	43	94	-3	4	43	1	37	1	22
164	57,702	-2	49,185	31	S	5	42	87	-6	5	30	7	26	1	25
165	57,602	0	84,161	35	S	3	60	93	-2	1	51	5	46	1	28
166	57,333	-1	78,274	36	S	3	63	93	-3	3	42	3	45	1	18
167	63,230	6	109,583	43	R	3	69	92	4	4	31	2	48	2	34
168	56,580	0	89,759	39	S	3	63	86	-3	10	32	2	40	1	37
169	53,432	-7	51,444	28	U	5	28	92	-9	3	34	3	35	2	17
170	59,012	-4	51,336	28	U	5	36	91	-7	2	35	4	45	2	36
171	63,746	6	40,792	31	R	5	41	98	6	0	10	0	40	1	29
172	52,663	-10	41,331	24	U	5	24	96	-11	1	44	1	33	2	29
173	54,332	-8	39,383	23	U	7	19	84	-11	11	1	2	32	4	33
174	51,312	-9	40,902	25	U	6	32	90	-12	1	32	5	35	3	34
175	55,957	-6	39,937	32	U	9	21	81	-11	11	19	2	32	6	22
176	54,424	-10	47,121	27	U	5	32	93	-12	2	33	3	34	2	36
177	52,929	-11	33,706	24	U	10	13	92	-14	2	35	2	27	4	38
178	63,546	8	81,395	30	S	3	57	96	7	1	25	2	52	1	41
179	52,353	-10	28,675	17	U	14	16	14	-52	37	-5	9	3	39	17
180	53,618	-11	19,987	15	U	20	4	11	-52	15	-13	1	-22	72	3
181	51,857	-9	38,178	34	U	17	29	17	-18	72	-8	4	10	7	1
182	56,566	-5	53,436	31	U	6	61	68	-14	22	23	5	37	4	15
183	60,120	5	46,482	28	S	4	32	97	4	1	32	1	48	1	45
184	51,587	-11	34,402	26	U	9	14	80	-16	11	17	6	26	3	8
185	54,595	-9	37,754	27	U	9	20	62	-16	34	4	2	16	2	15
186	54,800	-7	28,179	26	U	15	15	26	-25	65	0	6	16	3	12
187	67,865	12	55,425	30	S	4	40	97	12	1	32	1	49	1	47
188	54,846	-5	34,624	25	U	12	38	14	-29	79	0	5	10	2	1
189	67,830	16	44,027	15	R	6	41	94	15	2	33	1	64	2	46
190	55,588	-8	27,692	26	U	15	26	9	-31	84	-5	4	2	2	5
191	57,395	-4	37,281	27	U	9	26	22	-23	74	3	3	12	1	16
192	54,661	-9	37,565	25	U	9	29	28	-22	68	-4	2	15	2	15
193	63,788	8	45,473	27	R	4	27	97	8	0	11	1	49	2	26
194	55,787	-4	46,507	30	U	7	37	62	-11	34	7	2	27	1	25
195	57,033	-7	35,723	33	U	13	36	26	-18	68	-2	3	15	3	-6
196	63,638	6	54,703	27	S	3	37	97	5	1	21	1	48	1	39
197	54,789	-8	26,354	25	U	20	10	0	-45	98	-8	0	-23	1	-8
198	55,771	-7	49,862	28	U	8	45	31	-23	66	2	1	9	2	9
199	61,270	3	45,653	29	S	3	38	96	2	2	16	1	38	1	22
200	56,183	-7	52,535	28	U	7	47	26	-20	71	-1	1	11	1	5

Note: U=urban, S=suburban, R=rural, M=mixed, HH=households.

Pennsylvania State House Districts: Demographic Data (cont.)

House District	Population		Average HH Income		District Type	Unempl. Rate	College Educ.	White (non-Hispanic)		African American		Asian American		Hispanic American	
	1997	+/-	($)	+/-		(%)	(%)	(%)	+/-	(%)	+/-	(%)	+/-	(%)	+/-
Penn.	12,049,031	1	48,834	33	M	6	38	87	0	9	5	1	32	2	26
201	55,522	-6	35,096	24	U	14	27	7	-39	91	-2	1	-8	2	9
202	55,567	-9	36,241	22	U	10	25	39	-24	43	0	9	11	9	26
203	54,351	-6	42,811	27	U	8	30	16	-33	74	0	5	11	5	33

Note: U=urban, S=suburban, R=rural, M=mixed, HH=households.

RHODE ISLAND

Rhode Island packs a lot of diversity into a small package. As everyone knows, it is the smallest state geographically and could fit into Texas 250 times with room to spare. Yet only New Jersey crams in more people per square mile. Founded by people disgusted with Massachusetts Puritanism, it became a wide open colony known scornfully as "Rogues' Island," and later a wide open state. "Rhode Island," as one writer put it, "is separatism personified."

Ethnically, it is a hodgepodge of old-family Yankees, Irish, Portuguese, and eastern and southern Europeans. Only three state house districts in the country are at least half Italian, all of them in Providence. Today, Rhode Island is the fourth-most-popular destination for immigrants from the Dominican Republic. It is also perhaps the most Catholic state.

The state can be divided into three broad regions. There are two urban pockets, one around Providence and Pawtucket along I-95 and a second around Woonsocket. The lower half of the state along the ocean from Newport to the Connecticut border is rural. The rest, a broad band reaching from the Massachusetts border to Warwick, with a tongue pointing down to Narragansett, is suburban. Rhode Island is the third-most-suburban state, after Maryland and Connecticut.

The recession in the early 1990s hurt Rhode Island's manufacturing plants, and it is much less wrenching in a state so small to move a few miles elsewhere, to Connecticut or Massachusetts, in search of work. Hence, having grown by almost 6 percent during the 1980s, it has in this decade been the only state to lose population. That population loss has been most severe in Newport, with its high taxes and crowded neighborhoods; the two house districts that comprise the western end of the island have each shrunk by about 30 percent.

Growth has been fastest outside of Providence, both in Rhode Island and across the state line near Foxboro, Massachusetts. The rural Fifty-second District, beyond the I-295 beltway, has grown by 23 percent, while the suburban Thirty-first District just to the east has grown by 19 percent (as has the Sixty-ninth District between Providence and Woonsocket).

The state has areas of great wealth and great poverty. Its two wealthiest districts, the Eighty-eighth, around Barington (average income, $96,000), and the Fourth, on the Providence waterfront (average income, $85,000), sit a few miles from each other on opposite banks of the Providence and Seekonk River Channels. The poorest districts are all in downtown Providence. Income in the Seventeenth House District, in the southwest corner of the city, has grown by just 4 percent during the decade, making it the slowest-growing district in the United States.

Rhode Island's diversity is more ethnic than racial. It is 87 percent white, a higher percentage than that in either Massachusetts or Connecticut. The largest black neighborhoods are in the south side of Providence and in Cranston—the Nineteenth (34 percent), Fifth (26 percent), Twentieth (23 percent), and Eighteenth (22 percent) Districts. The state also boasts nine house districts that are more than 30 percent Hispanic; many of the Hispanics are Dominican immigrants who are concentrated around Cranston and in the suburbs between Providence and Woonsocket. Downtown Providence also has four districts that are more than 10 percent Asian.

Almost one person in four here is age fifty-five or older, and the state has more senior citizens by percentage than any state except Florida and Pennsylvania. As jobs have left, Rhode Island has grown older. From 1990 to 1996, while the state's overall population declined by more than 1 percent, the number of persons over age sixty-five grew by 4.3 percent. An older population may be expected to demand more in social services, perhaps increasing the tax burden in an already heavily taxed state and making it that much harder to attract new businesses.

Politically, Rhode Island is one of the most Democratic states in the country, one of six to support Jimmy Carter's reelection bid in 1980. Even its Republicans, such as long-time U.S. senator John Chafee, are liberals. The legislature is overwhelmingly Democratic—84–16 in the house, 41–9 in the senate—and is likely to remain that way.

RHODE ISLAND
State Senate Districts

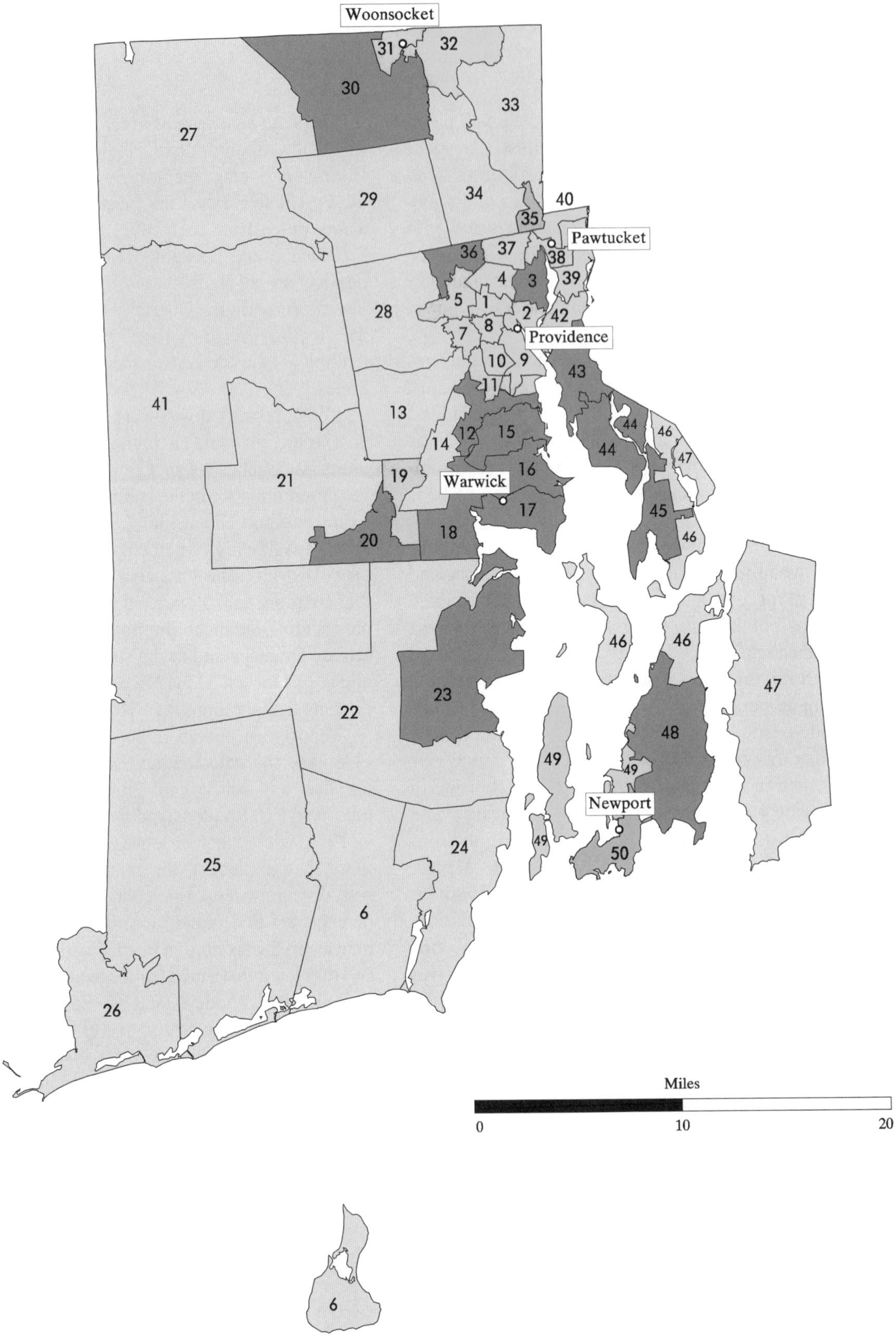

Woonsocket

31 32

30 33

27

29 34

40

35

Pawtucket

36 37 38

4 3 39

5 1 42

28 2

8 7 Providence

10 9

11 43

13 44 46

47

12 15 44

14

16

19 Warwick

20 18 17 45

46

23 46 46

47

22

48

24 49 49

Newport

6 25 50

26

6

Miles

0   10   20

Population Growth   ▨ -27% to -19%   ▨ -14% to -5%   ▨ -4% to 3%   ▨ 5% to 15%

Rhode Island State Senate Districts: Demographic Data

Senate District	Population		Average HH Income		District Type	Unempl. Rate	College Educ.	White (non-Hispanic)		African American		Asian American		Hispanic American	
	1997	+/-	($)	+/-		(%)	(%)	(%)	+/-	(%)	+/-	(%)	+/-	(%)	+/-
Rhode Island	987,999	-1	48,921	25	S	7	40	87	-4	4	5	2	9	7	45
1	17,192	-13	34,805	17	U	8	35	65	-25	7	9	7	-2	20	52
2	18,182	-6	46,778	25	U	7	64	75	-14	8	28	9	22	7	55
3	20,337	-4	64,016	24	U	6	67	71	-13	15	13	3	21	8	65
4	17,762	-11	36,153	24	U	8	29	75	-21	10	14	1	11	13	71
5	18,473	-7	43,671	21	S	5	35	92	-10	2	48	1	22	5	66
6	22,179	9	57,602	23	R	5	61	91	7	2	17	3	24	2	67
7	18,044	-9	33,776	21	U	10	19	69	-21	6	19	4	9	19	55
8	17,483	-13	23,552	17	U	10	16	34	-42	13	-15	7	-13	44	41
9	17,155	-13	28,320	16	U	15	19	23	-45	29	-14	6	-18	38	32
10	17,241	-12	30,032	12	U	12	20	14	-53	20	-23	12	-17	51	29
11	17,664	-7	40,396	21	S	7	37	88	-11	3	22	3	26	5	64
12	21,728	0	47,470	22	S	6	38	88	-4	5	23	2	37	5	76
13	22,790	12	58,350	31	S	5	41	96	10	1	55	1	54	2	106
14	18,961	11	55,751	18	S	6	45	93	8	2	50	2	54	2	115
15	19,712	-4	46,479	20	S	5	39	96	-5	1	11	1	8	2	64
16	19,424	-3	48,118	21	S	6	40	96	-3	1	15	1	17	2	60
17	19,493	0	51,269	19	S	7	38	96	-1	1	12	1	17	2	58
18	20,294	1	54,377	23	S	4	51	96	0	1	22	1	28	2	63
19	19,032	-8	43,526	19	S	8	33	94	-9	1	10	1	10	3	47
20	19,866	0	45,722	23	S	6	33	97	-1	0	10	1	14	2	52
21	21,538	6	52,672	24	S	5	38	98	6	0	20	0	29	1	45
22	21,592	5	80,209	27	S	4	61	97	5	1	15	1	26	1	41
23	20,353	1	60,650	26	S	5	53	95	0	2	25	1	13	2	63
24	21,747	9	53,064	25	S	5	59	95	7	1	29	1	29	1	73
25	22,506	14	54,110	31	R	6	44	97	14	0	30	1	22	1	83
26	21,778	6	51,817	24	R	7	42	97	5	1	25	1	21	1	51
27	21,977	7	51,303	28	S	7	38	99	7	0	48	0	-10	1	41
28	22,681	8	47,474	25	S	5	30	97	7	1	49	1	46	1	99
29	21,884	8	58,351	27	S	5	48	97	7	1	42	1	47	1	84
30	19,332	-3	50,560	28	S	7	34	96	-4	1	32	1	26	1	56
31	17,150	-14	33,817	24	U	10	18	81	-21	5	19	6	11	7	60
32	17,734	-8	44,090	27	U	7	30	93	-11	2	31	1	15	3	67
33	23,281	12	59,748	26	S	6	45	97	10	0	43	0	39	2	82
34	21,753	6	61,413	29	S	5	45	96	5	0	32	1	36	2	77
35	16,138	-19	29,606	23	S	9	15	54	-36	3	-15	0	-23	40	24
36	20,528	3	53,686	30	S	6	40	94	0	1	44	2	41	3	94
37	18,834	-5	39,569	24	U	8	24	76	-11	5	17	1	17	12	46
38	17,463	-10	35,820	23	U	8	23	72	-19	6	13	1	1	15	44
39	19,026	-6	45,198	23	U	6	36	95	-8	1	26	1	5	3	61
40	18,904	-9	35,051	24	U	10	23	83	-15	3	23	1	13	12	54
41	23,272	15	60,744	28	S	6	45	98	14	0	36	0	46	1	61
42	17,674	-7	42,444	24	S	6	23	85	-10	7	19	1	3	3	22
43	23,112	3	43,630	23	S	6	34	89	1	6	37	1	15	2	49
44	19,230	1	80,509	24	S	4	63	97	0	1	18	1	25	1	79
45	18,470	-2	43,705	20	R	6	32	96	-3	0	-10	0	13	3	52
46	22,490	6	50,322	21	R	7	39	97	6	1	34	1	36	2	47
47	21,781	8	53,433	16	S	6	41	98	7	0	26	0	42	2	68
48	22,677	2	53,631	17	R	6	55	91	-1	3	34	2	32	3	58
49	15,629	-9	49,033	23	R	7	53	83	-12	9	-2	1	-11	5	41
50	14,068	-27	46,899	13	R	7	56	88	-30	7	2	1	-6	3	24

Note: U=urban, S=suburban, R=rural, M=mixed, HH=households.

RHODE ISLAND
State House Districts

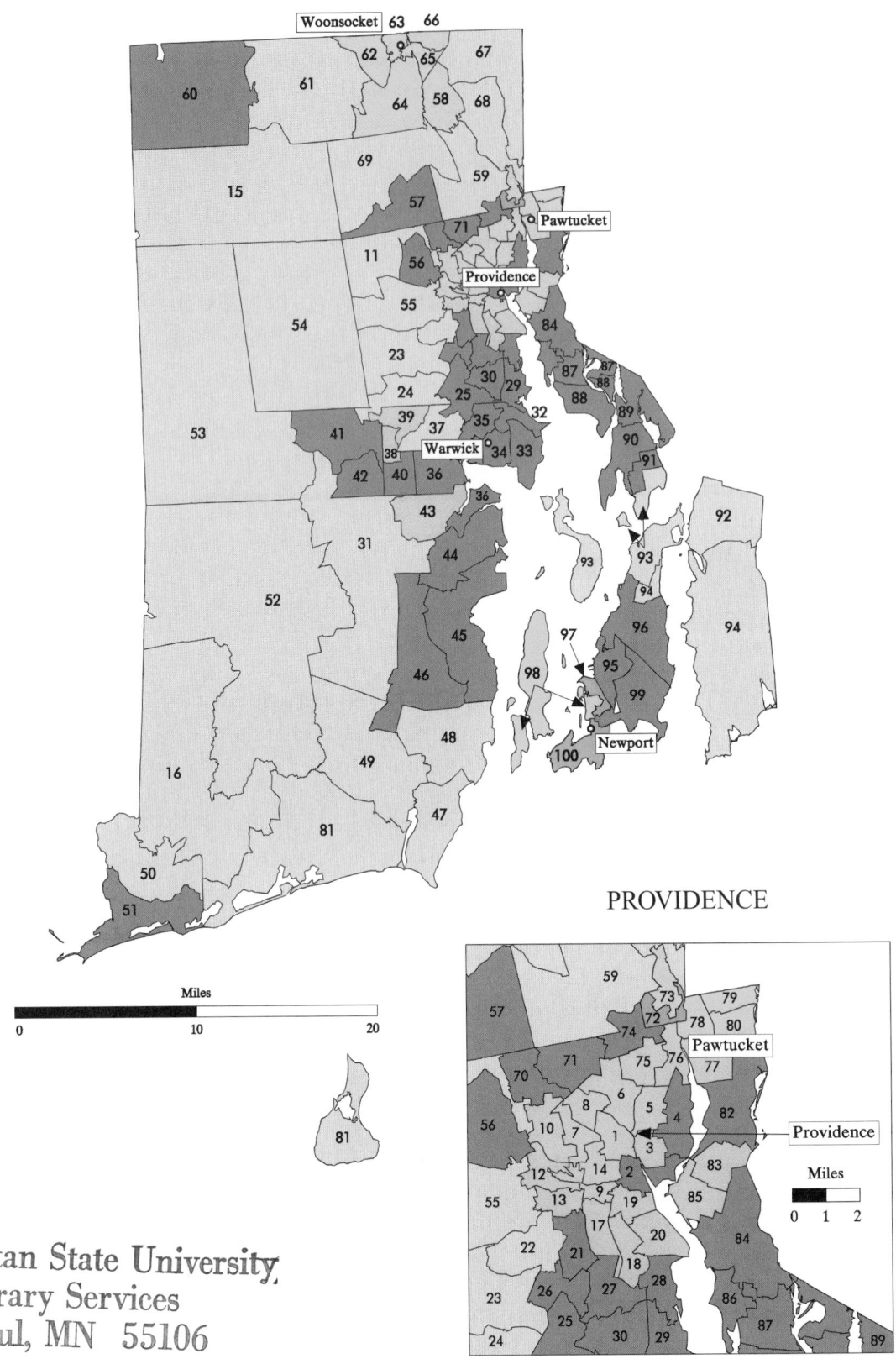

PROVIDENCE

Miles
0   10   20

Population Growth   ▢ -30% to -22%   ▢ -18% to -6%   ▢ -5% to 5%   ▢ 6% to 23%

Rhode Island State House Districts: Demographic Data

House District	Population		Average HH Income		District Type	Unempl. Rate	College Educ.	White (non-Hispanic)		African American		Asian American		Hispanic American	
	1997	+/-	($)	+/-		(%)	(%)	(%)	+/-	(%)	+/-	(%)	+/-	(%)	+/-
Rhode Island	987,999	-1	48,921	25	S	7	40	87	-4	4	5	2	9	7	45
1	9,060	-12	29,997	15	U	11	27	38	-39	17	2	12	-3	32	51
2	9,051	-5	34,455	19	U	9	48	72	-14	11	23	5	27	9	60
3	9,485	-6	61,793	36	U	5	79	66	-17	12	31	13	19	8	62
4	9,142	-3	85,109	21	U	4	83	89	-6	3	39	4	32	3	60
5	8,418	-6	43,417	22	U	7	57	57	-18	26	7	2	17	9	62
6	9,709	-9	31,203	17	U	9	21	82	-16	6	27	1	2	10	75
7	8,603	-14	42,065	28	U	7	43	84	-20	2	13	1	2	12	58
8	9,094	-13	43,270	27	U	5	41	86	-18	6	29	2	21	6	64
9	9,421	-11	23,871	17	U	10	12	18	-55	17	-13	11	-9	51	38
10	9,727	-8	40,461	18	U	7	35	87	-13	2	42	2	17	9	75
11	11,306	13	49,488	28	S	7	36	96	11	1	43	1	55	3	117
12	7,811	-11	30,994	19	U	11	17	56	-29	11	19	5	6	27	43
13	9,150	-11	35,263	22	U	9	21	82	-18	2	12	3	15	12	79
14	8,344	-14	25,056	17	U	10	23	59	-32	6	14	2	-2	32	56
15	10,826	9	54,727	27	S	6	46	98	8	0	47	0	31	1	64
16	11,220	14	50,686	32	R	8	39	97	13	0	33	0	16	1	60
17	9,022	-13	30,424	4	U	10	20	20	-46	18	-23	14	-15	45	30
18	10,075	-9	31,015	18	U	14	22	12	-58	22	-18	9	-16	54	33
19	8,384	-12	23,183	19	U	17	14	8	-62	34	-20	7	-27	47	28
20	7,790	-18	32,906	20	U	15	18	32	-43	23	-17	7	-18	34	30
21	9,407	-4	38,252	21	S	7	26	91	-7	1	9	4	29	4	77
22	10,869	11	44,945	29	S	7	30	95	9	1	48	1	52	3	110
23	12,706	10	66,277	29	S	5	51	97	9	0	53	1	55	1	93
24	9,042	7	63,619	26	S	4	47	94	3	2	167	2	58	2	221
25	11,312	-3	41,276	15	S	7	29	80	-9	10	18	2	16	8	75
26	9,717	1	51,377	16	S	5	46	93	-1	1	44	4	42	2	63
27	9,885	-5	38,982	16	S	8	36	93	-7	2	30	2	35	3	65
28	9,558	-2	55,073	30	S	6	52	87	-6	5	29	2	23	5	63
29	9,911	-1	50,611	19	S	5	48	97	-1	1	9	1	21	1	75
30	9,255	-4	44,377	21	S	5	31	95	-5	1	15	1	9	2	67
31	12,257	19	69,346	20	S	5	50	97	18	0	32	1	44	1	61
32	9,425	-3	46,089	21	S	6	39	97	-4	1	12	1	20	1	49
33	10,497	0	53,293	22	S	8	40	96	-1	1	18	1	18	2	61
34	9,697	0	46,878	18	S	6	34	96	-2	1	13	1	9	2	60
35	10,890	-2	48,672	22	S	4	40	96	-3	1	11	1	17	2	65
36	10,484	4	63,388	24	S	4	60	96	3	1	19	2	33	2	60
37	9,794	13	50,043	21	S	6	43	97	12	1	41	1	55	1	70
38	8,442	-12	36,189	23	S	7	25	95	-13	1	7	1	2	3	29
39	9,240	-9	41,470	17	S	9	28	95	-10	1	10	1	6	3	45
40	10,398	1	53,756	24	S	6	46	95	0	1	15	2	17	3	61
41	11,365	0	47,511	22	S	5	33	98	0	0	10	0	20	1	24
42	9,653	3	44,488	18	S	6	30	97	2	0	14	0	8	2	73
43	8,217	-8	83,150	29	S	4	65	97	-9	0	-3	1	15	1	34
44	9,538	-3	58,139	25	S	5	50	94	-4	2	18	1	8	2	62
45	10,135	5	63,477	29	S	5	57	95	4	2	30	1	20	1	66
46	9,771	-2	70,396	30	R	5	61	93	-4	2	5	3	14	3	60
47	10,318	7	50,941	24	R	5	54	95	6	1	34	1	29	2	77
48	11,081	10	54,865	26	S	5	64	95	9	1	25	1	30	1	66
49	11,447	14	57,550	22	R	5	63	88	12	2	28	5	30	2	70
50	12,261	8	46,322	26	R	7	38	96	7	1	30	1	25	1	54

Note: U=urban, S=suburban, R=rural, M=mixed, HH=households.

Rhode Island State House Districts: Demographic Data (cont.)

House District	Population		Average HH Income		District Type	Unempl. Rate	College Educ.	White (non-Hispanic)		African American		Asian American		Hispanic American	
	1997	+/-	($)	+/-		(%)	(%)	(%)	+/-	(%)	+/-	(%)	+/-	(%)	+/-
Rhode Island	987,999	-1	48,921	25	S	7	40	87	-4	4	5	2	9	7	45
51	9,517	3	58,252	23	R	8	48	97	2	1	17	1	14	1	46
52	12,412	23	62,202	32	R	5	43	97	22	1	32	1	29	1	75
53	11,436	14	55,630	23	S	6	42	98	13	0	36	0	36	1	81
54	10,477	7	69,194	31	S	6	50	98	6	0	47	1	45	1	81
55	11,401	7	41,634	24	S	5	25	97	6	1	49	1	42	1	86
56	9,331	1	46,846	23	S	5	26	97	0	1	46	1	36	1	51
57	10,177	-1	56,540	33	S	4	44	98	-1	0	30	1	36	0	26
58	8,110	-14	59,223	29	S	4	44	97	-15	0	8	1	13	1	32
59	12,649	17	61,528	27	S	5	45	97	16	0	71	1	50	2	98
60	10,114	2	47,446	28	S	6	36	99	2	0	-33	0	-17	1	27
61	10,182	8	56,317	25	S	6	37	99	8	0	53	0	12	1	41
62	9,948	-6	46,512	33	U	9	29	87	-10	4	20	3	11	6	68
63	8,596	-15	32,442	24	U	11	20	82	-20	5	19	8	12	5	49
64	8,970	-10	45,521	27	U	9	28	96	-11	1	31	2	25	1	60
65	8,674	-12	35,792	24	U	11	19	92	-14	2	28	2	11	4	70
66	9,308	-10	39,491	24	U	5	25	89	-14	3	32	2	15	6	66
67	11,890	15	70,968	28	S	6	55	97	14	0	50	1	47	2	103
68	12,365	9	51,225	24	S	6	37	96	8	0	38	0	32	3	71
69	12,445	19	65,338	20	S	5	52	96	18	1	49	1	56	2	101
70	10,852	-2	48,222	23	S	6	41	94	-4	1	48	2	32	3	82
71	10,689	4	62,186	32	S	5	41	92	1	2	52	2	40	3	93
72	7,757	-22	27,736	21	S	10	15	44	-45	4	-15	1	-27	47	24
73	8,341	-16	31,296	25	S	9	14	63	-29	2	-15	0	-18	34	24
74	9,200	-3	40,688	24	U	7	25	80	-9	4	13	1	12	12	49
75	8,787	-12	37,684	28	U	9	20	61	-24	8	10	1	10	18	42
76	9,818	-10	36,331	27	U	8	31	67	-21	8	18	1	2	18	49
77	9,164	-7	38,729	22	U	6	26	86	-11	3	26	1	13	9	37
78	9,154	-10	30,698	19	U	11	24	76	-19	4	23	1	21	16	55
79	9,585	-8	41,476	26	U	8	24	92	-10	1	19	0	0	6	60
80	9,606	-8	40,291	22	U	7	29	95	-10	1	22	0	9	3	60
81	11,144	16	55,754	27	R	4	54	97	16	1	33	1	21	1	78
82	10,588	-4	53,845	25	S	5	45	95	-5	2	26	1	8	2	57
83	7,718	-6	40,050	22	S	5	21	82	-9	9	17	0	0	3	14
84	11,895	4	46,385	22	S	6	34	87	1	8	40	1	5	1	5
85	9,336	-8	39,408	24	S	7	18	86	-11	5	20	1	1	4	28
86	10,150	4	40,921	23	S	6	33	92	1	3	40	1	28	3	94
87	9,606	1	64,470	25	S	4	54	96	0	1	22	1	23	2	90
88	9,625	0	96,032	23	S	4	70	98	0	0	-6	1	28	1	63
89	9,788	-3	44,427	21	S	5	31	97	-3	0	-7	0	10	2	45
90	11,508	4	54,240	23	S	6	39	97	4	0	3	1	27	2	45
91	7,846	-2	41,948	24	R	9	23	95	-3	0	-5	0	26	4	51
92	11,010	8	44,568	16	S	6	32	97	7	0	42	0	47	2	67
93	12,108	6	47,140	16	R	7	44	97	5	1	37	1	26	2	57
94	10,519	11	61,478	15	S	5	53	97	11	0	44	1	51	1	75
95	8,557	4	42,333	7	R	8	47	86	-2	7	47	2	31	5	89
96	10,688	2	58,475	21	R	5	61	90	0	3	29	2	25	4	65
97	6,626	-30	35,564	16	R	9	47	72	-36	17	-12	2	-25	6	12
98	9,710	-7	56,499	24	R	6	56	90	-8	5	-3	1	-17	3	28
99	9,705	-3	51,739	15	R	5	57	91	-6	4	27	2	40	3	56
100	7,091	-29	51,514	14	R	7	56	92	-31	4	3	1	-5	3	15

Note: U=urban, S=suburban, R=rural, M=mixed, HH=households.

SOUTH CAROLINA

The English planters who first settled South Carolina, it has been written, thought of themselves as inhabiting not the southern edge of America but the northern edge of the West Indies. They came from Barbados and imported West Indian traditions, in particular an economy built on rice, indigo, and slaves. They built their society around Charleston ("where the Ashley and Cooper Rivers meet to form the Atlantic Ocean," in the marvelous old boast), never ventured far inland, and left the mountains to be explored not by South Carolinians moving west but by North Carolinians pushing south.

Theirs was the first of an unfortunate series of economic choices the state made. South Carolina produced turpentine for sailing ships until the age of steam, indigo until the development of synthetic dyes, cotton until the boll weevils came, and, in our own time, textiles until the mills moved overseas. South Carolina's newest economic base is tourism and recreation, and in this it has done quite well. Charleston remains one of the most charming cities in the United States, and the coastal golf courses and tennis resorts from Myrtle Beach to Hilton Head draw business conferences and vacationers year-round.

The resorts have energized the state's economy and helped South Carolina join the other growing states of the South. But South Carolina started at a disadvantage and is still more like Alabama, Mississippi, and Louisiana than Florida, Georgia, and North Carolina, the booming states of the southern eastern seaboard. South Carolina's population grew by 11.7 percent during the 1980s, a good pace yet slowest among the southeastern states. During the 1990s, it has grown another 7 percent—a boom if it had occurred in Iowa. But Virginia has grown by 9 percent, North Carolina by 12 percent, Florida by 13 percent, and Georgia by 15 percent.

Growth is scattered around the state. It has been fastest in Myrtle Beach, but fast also in Greenville in the western mountains, in Aiken near the Savannah River, and in the Columbia suburbs. Charleston has been hardest hit, chiefly because the naval base closed, a decision that cost the One Hundred Eighteenth House District 35

percent of its population. In all, South Carolina's growth is distinctly suburban: of the twenty fastest-growing house districts, only one was urban, twelve were suburban, and seven were rural, most of those lying just beyond the more established suburbs.

Long one of the nation's poorest states, South Carolina has much ground to make up. Despite the mill closures, it has one of the lowest rates of unemployment, but average household income is $1,900 behind North Carolina and $5,200 behind Georgia. The poorest districts are also sprinkled around the state—parts of downtown Charleston, Spartanburg, Greenville, and Columbia, as well as rural Florence and Sumter—but they share one characteristic in common. All are populated primarily by African Americans. Though South Carolina, once the most immovable proponent of slavery, has made great strides in matters of race, its legacy of a poor and ill-educated black underclass is not so quickly remedied.

South Carolina is 68 percent white, but in only ten districts, all in the northwestern mountains, do whites constitute 90 percent of the population. Unlike that of most other states, South Carolina's black population is primarily rural; of thirty-two black-majority districts, eighteen are classified as rural, six as suburban, four as mixed, and only four as urban. Yet in only two of those districts is household income above the state average, and of the twenty house districts with the highest rates of unemployment, every one has a black majority.

When Strom Thurmond left the Democratic for the Republican Party in 1964, he did what many in the state were growing inclined to do, and South Carolina has been a reliably Republican state in presidential contests ever since. In the 1990s, Republicans caught up in the state legislature as well. A 73–50 Democratic majority in the state house (with one independent) after the 1992 elections shrank to a 61–60 majority (with three independents) after the 1994 elections; after 1996, the Republicans held a 67–55 majority (with 2 independents). Democrats still control the senate, but their twenty-seat majority in 1990 had slipped to just six seats by 1996.

SOUTH CAROLINA
State Senate Districts

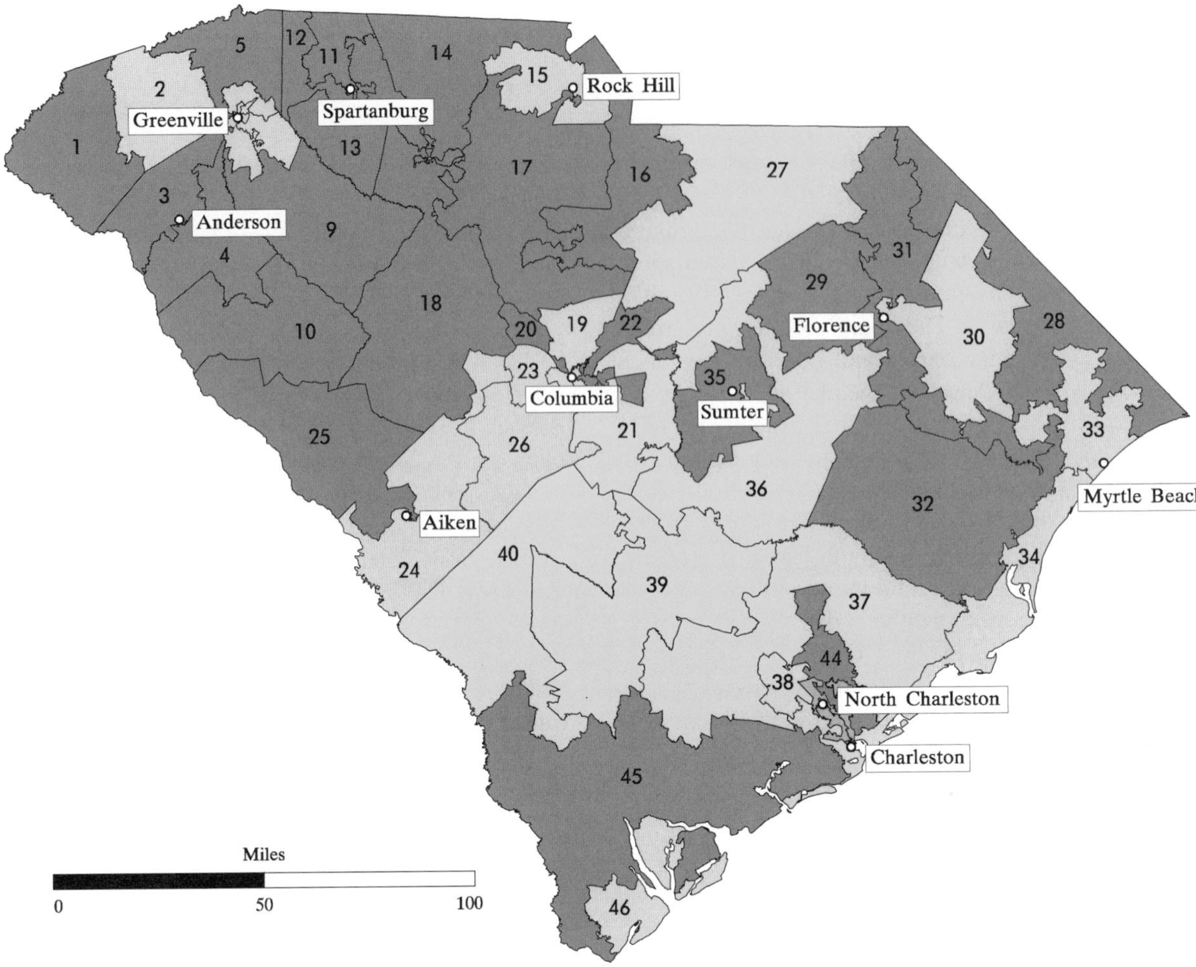

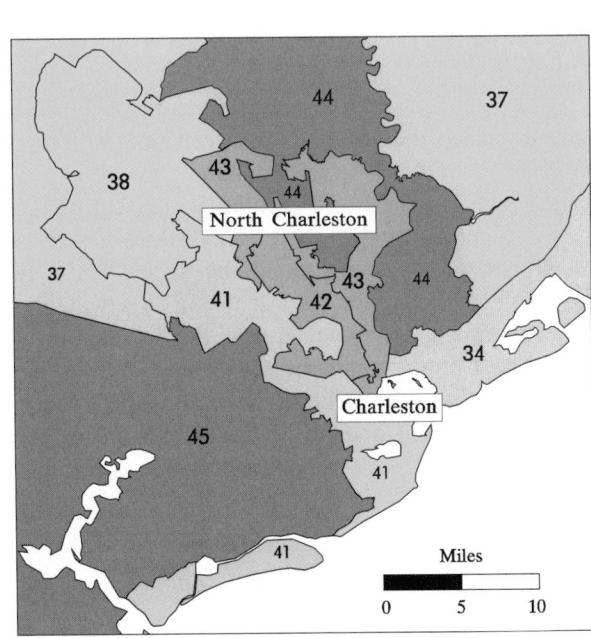

CHARLESTON

Population Growth   ▦ -20% to -17%   ▦ -4% to 4%   ▦ 5% to 12%   ▦ 14% to 23%

GREENVILLE

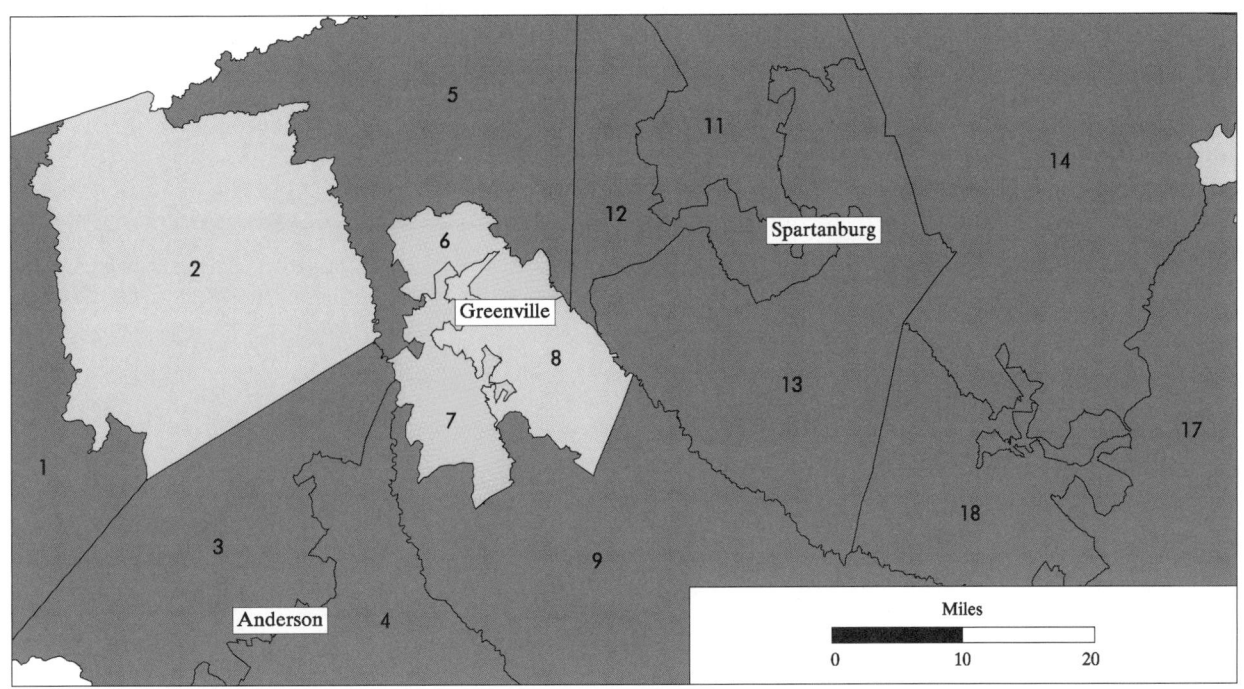

COLUMBIA

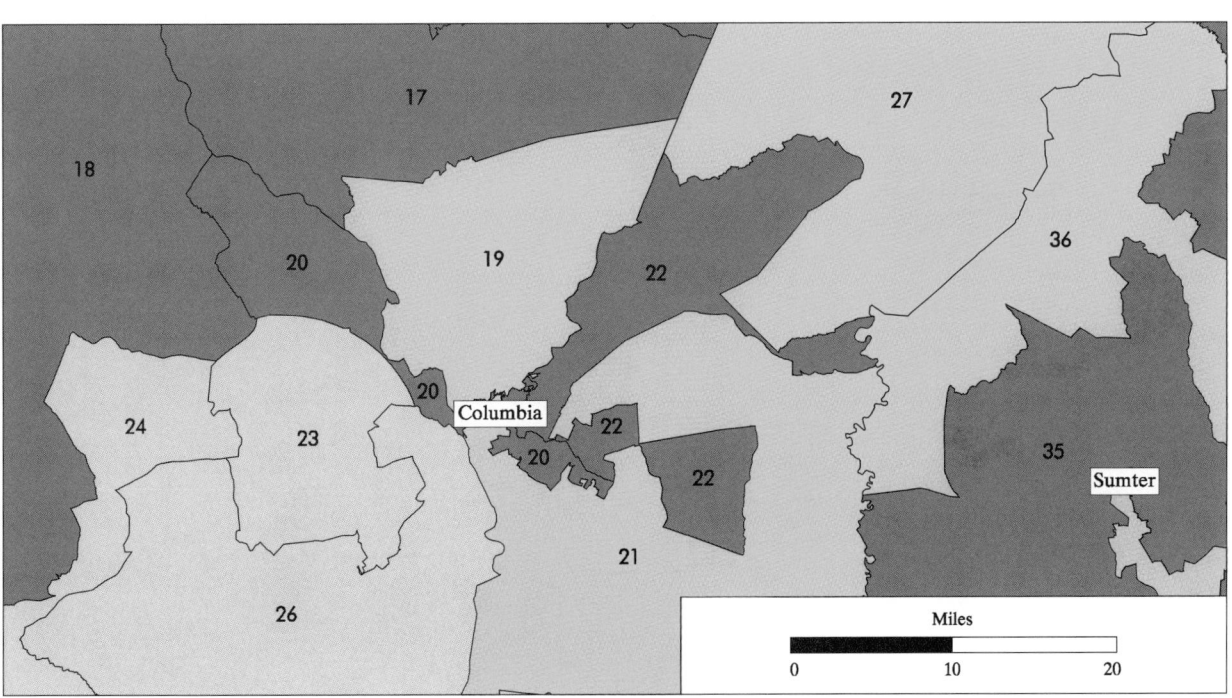

Population Growth   -4% to 4%   5% to 12%   14% to 23%

South Carolina State Senate Districts: Demographic Data

Senate District	Population 1997	+/-	Average HH Income ($)	+/-	District Type	Unempl. Rate (%)	College Educ. (%)	White (non-Hispanic) (%)	+/-	African American (%)	+/-	Asian American (%)	+/-	Hispanic American (%)	+/-
S. Carolina	3,721,715	7	43,673	35	R	5	33	68	6	30	7	1	25	1	26
1	80,495	8	40,316	27	R	6	33	88	7	10	10	1	26	1	32
2	87,900	15	40,658	29	R	5	29	92	14	7	24	0	37	1	36
3	83,140	11	46,350	31	S	4	38	86	10	13	16	0	32	1	47
4	82,593	6	34,581	29	S	6	19	77	6	22	10	0	11	0	22
5	82,804	8	38,783	28	S	5	25	88	7	11	16	0	4	1	37
6	76,460	1	56,522	35	S	3	52	91	0	6	14	1	26	1	31
7	75,563	2	35,587	31	S	7	24	46	-3	52	6	0	3	1	15
8	89,595	19	61,757	39	S	3	55	87	18	10	29	1	40	1	55
9	86,010	12	40,208	31	R	6	26	75	12	24	12	0	28	1	53
10	79,987	5	39,151	34	R	6	29	67	4	32	7	0	24	0	20
11	79,575	7	37,246	36	S	6	20	65	6	33	8	1	31	1	32
12	81,153	9	48,224	36	S	4	34	82	8	17	15	1	28	1	29
13	84,121	8	45,858	36	S	5	29	84	7	14	12	1	28	1	38
14	82,111	8	40,519	30	R	6	24	80	7	19	12	0	18	1	21
15	88,601	15	50,358	37	S	5	36	82	14	16	22	1	38	1	31
16	79,627	7	43,951	35	R	6	27	75	6	24	8	0	-2	1	30
17	76,274	5	35,295	34	R	8	20	47	3	53	6	0	31	0	10
18	80,849	8	41,632	39	R	6	29	69	9	30	8	0	-3	0	21
19	77,007	3	37,699	27	S	7	34	30	-1	68	4	1	17	1	11
20	83,506	7	47,016	27	S	3	59	74	4	23	14	1	36	2	41
21	70,188	-4	31,283	28	N.A.	8	30	35	-12	61	1	2	7	2	-5
22	84,600	10	58,822	25	S	3	56	74	7	20	17	2	33	3	36
23	90,729	20	56,958	28	S	3	52	90	19	7	26	1	49	1	50
24	88,244	16	51,650	32	R	4	43	81	17	17	12	1	38	1	47
25	78,308	5	37,215	25	R	7	24	60	1	39	11	0	10	1	24
26	84,592	14	42,019	32	S	4	29	82	12	16	17	1	36	1	53
27	80,056	4	37,637	31	R	6	22	68	2	31	7	0	-7	1	23
28	83,536	5	39,116	41	R	5	24	70	4	28	8	0	-2	1	19
29	79,639	7	37,186	32	R	6	26	54	5	45	9	0	-7	0	3
30	74,511	2	30,477	31	R	8	18	38	-1	61	4	0	-3	0	4
31	83,733	9	46,520	40	N.A.	5	35	69	8	30	9	0	22	1	35
32	81,052	5	33,612	40	R	7	20	39	3	60	7	0	-24	0	-7
33	87,853	20	43,900	40	R	5	35	81	18	16	26	1	41	1	43
34	90,368	17	59,354	55	R	5	47	78	16	20	17	1	43	1	50
35	83,112	8	41,581	37	R	6	36	65	4	32	13	1	26	2	26
36	75,833	1	32,528	41	R	9	19	36	-2	63	2	0	-14	1	5
37	76,897	0	36,453	32	R	7	22	51	-3	48	4	0	10	0	-7
38	75,231	2	45,088	25	S	5	38	82	1	14	5	1	26	2	29
39	77,559	2	31,031	29	R	10	24	34	0	65	3	0	-8	0	8
40	78,310	4	37,825	35	R	8	28	53	3	45	6	0	19	1	10
41	74,304	-3	60,735	47	S	3	51	82	-5	15	6	1	24	1	26
42	61,891	-20	32,266	38	M	8	27	33	-32	64	-13	1	-6	1	-10
43	56,790	-17	50,415	57	S	6	37	66	-19	28	-15	2	9	3	1
44	90,237	8	51,859	40	N.A.	4	40	79	6	15	17	3	28	3	29
45	82,354	5	39,003	47	R	7	22	37	0	62	7	0	1	1	11
46	94,403	23	56,430	33	R	5	49	71	20	24	32	1	52	3	39

Note: U=urban, S=suburban, R=rural, M=mixed, HH=households.

SOUTH CAROLINA
State House Districts

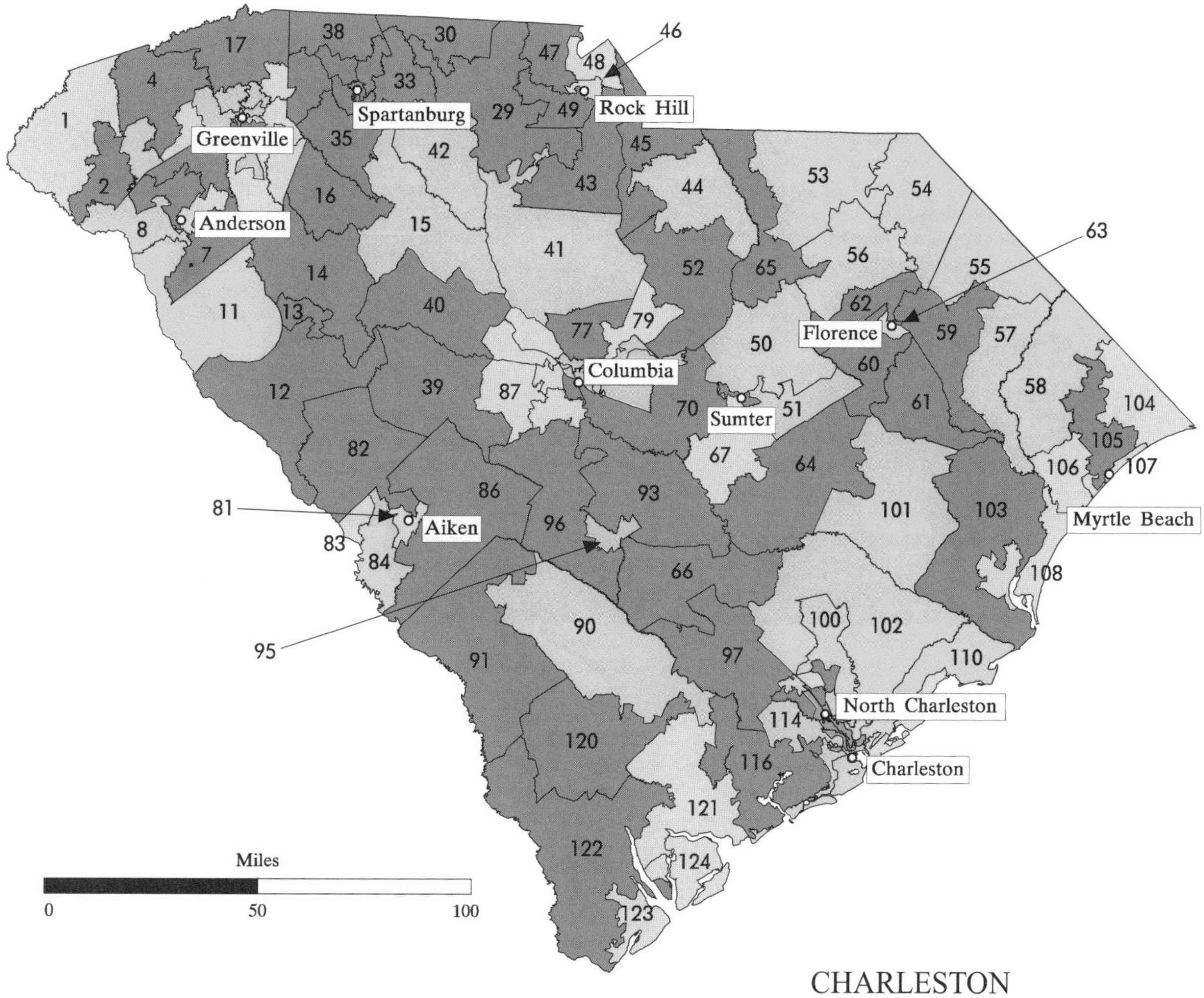

1 4 17 38 30 47 46 48
Greenville 33 Spartanburg 29 49 Rock Hill
2 35 42 45
Anderson 16 43 44 53 54
8 15 41 52 65 56 55 63
7 14 77 79 50 62 Florence 59 57
11 13 40 Columbia 60 58 104
12 39 87 70 51 61 105
82 Sumter 67 64 106 107
86 93 101 103 Myrtle Beach
81 96 108
Aiken 66 102
83 84 90 100 110
95 91 97
120 North Charleston
114 116
121
122 124
123

CHARLESTON

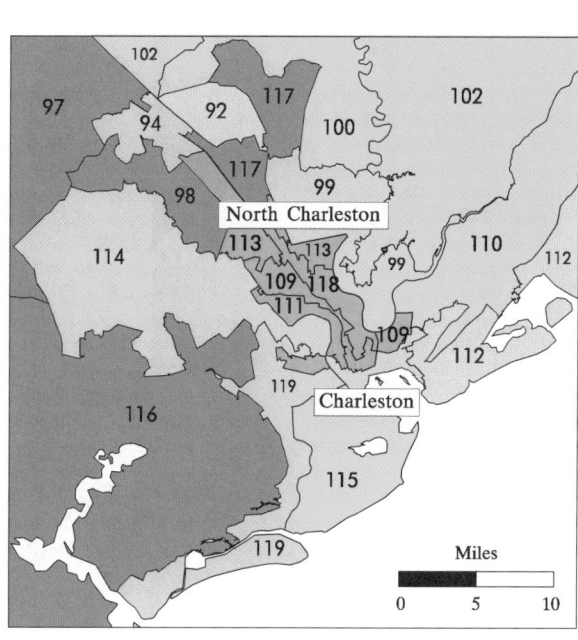

Miles
0   50   100

Miles
0   5   10

Population Growth   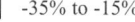 -35% to -15%   ☐ -7% to 3%   ■ 4% to 13%   ☐ 14% to 34%

GREENVILLE

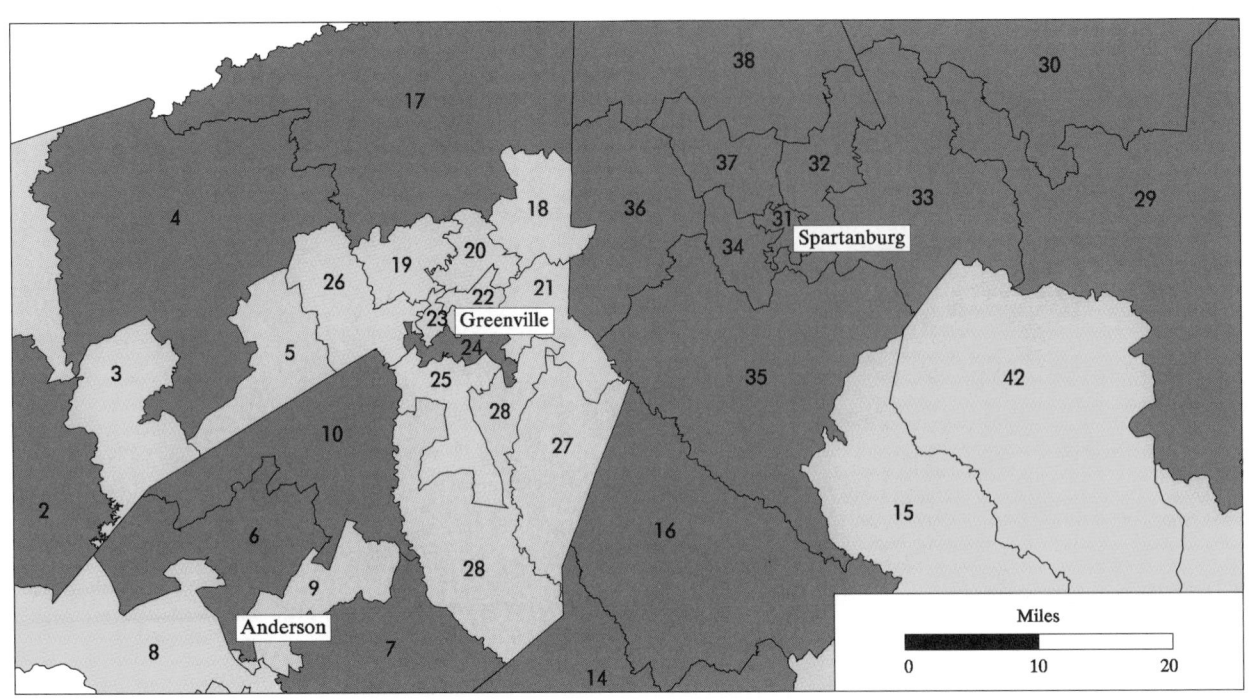

COLUMBIA

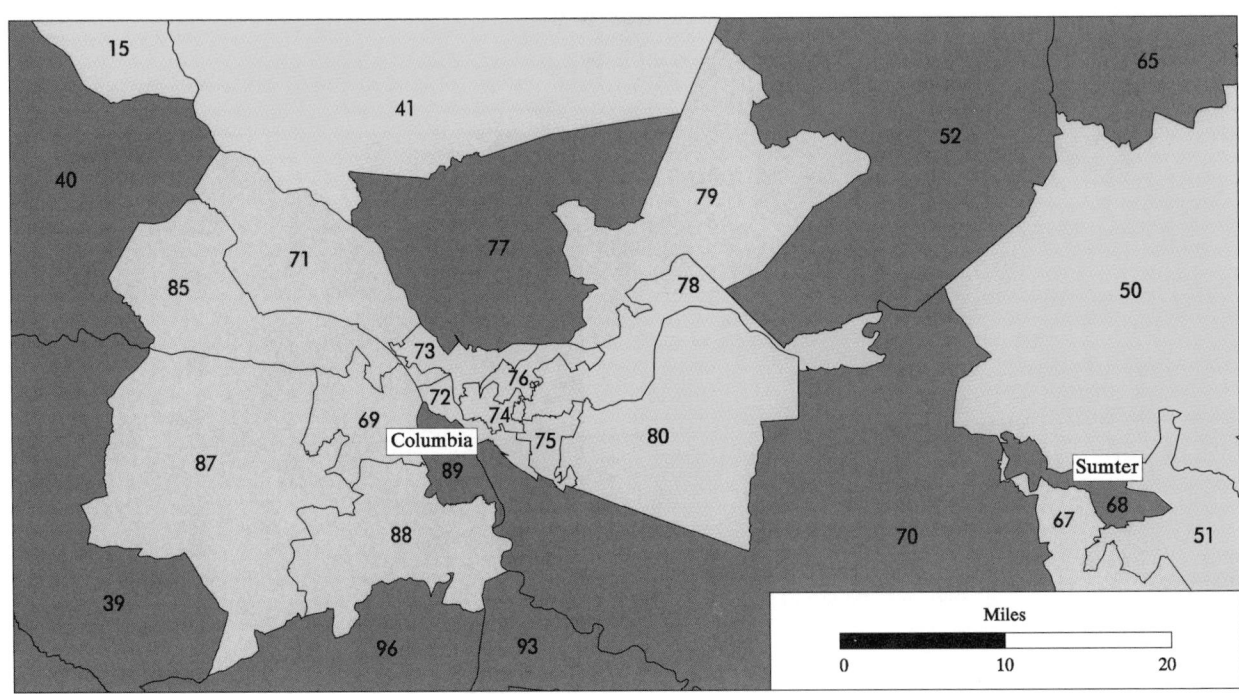

Population Growth   ☐ -4% to 4%   ■ 5% to 12%   ☐ 14% to 23%

South Carolina State House Districts: Demographic Data

House District	Population		Average HH Income		District Type	Unempl. Rate	College Educ.	White (non-Hispanic)		African American		Asian American		Hispanic American	
	1997	+/-	($)	+/-		(%)	(%)	(%)	+/-	(%)	+/-	(%)	+/-	(%)	+/-
S. Carolina	3,721,715	7	43,673	35	R	5	33	68	6	30	7	1	25	1	26
1	33,928	16	42,202	33	R	4	24	94	15	5	36	0	38	2	51
2	27,673	4	38,701	20	R	6	30	84	4	15	7	0	17	1	10
3	28,898	3	40,380	29	R	5	56	86	2	10	8	3	28	1	13
4	30,199	9	35,080	23	R	5	22	94	9	5	21	0	26	0	17
5	34,805	23	43,251	32	S	5	29	90	22	9	25	0	42	1	60
6	30,193	10	40,624	27	M	6	33	76	9	23	13	1	37	1	49
7	30,310	11	36,981	28	S	5	21	80	10	19	14	0	14	0	14
8	27,244	0	42,111	30	S	5	28	88	0	11	2	0	4	0	17
9	31,683	15	39,688	31	U	6	35	75	15	24	12	0	30	0	70
10	32,045	10	45,816	35	S	4	30	91	9	8	21	0	29	1	40
11	29,952	0	36,009	33	R	6	21	72	-1	28	4	0	3	0	11
12	31,561	11	31,752	29	R	8	18	49	9	50	13	0	18	0	7
13	27,144	4	48,058	41	R	5	41	78	3	20	6	1	29	1	40
14	33,377	7	37,515	34	R	5	24	76	8	24	4	0	8	0	5
15	28,678	2	37,025	25	R	6	23	70	1	29	5	0	-14	0	13
16	28,838	7	37,857	29	R	6	22	67	4	32	11	0	6	1	42
17	32,319	12	39,495	26	S	4	23	92	11	7	22	0	-8	1	47
18	30,837	17	38,276	29	S	5	25	79	14	19	27	0	22	1	30
19	27,247	-2	37,135	25	S	5	28	91	-4	7	11	0	13	2	28
20	27,270	-1	51,823	33	S	3	49	88	-2	10	5	1	12	1	27
21	34,323	19	76,115	39	S	3	63	92	17	5	35	2	37	1	45
22	28,867	3	49,912	30	U	3	59	88	1	8	24	2	27	2	37
23	27,955	1	27,923	28	U	10	21	33	-7	66	5	0	3	1	13
24	29,265	6	63,953	42	U	3	50	87	5	11	13	1	31	1	37
25	28,002	3	37,312	26	S	6	25	40	-2	58	6	0	-8	1	16
26	29,169	3	37,153	31	S	5	21	86	1	12	6	0	1	2	38
27	34,736	30	58,731	41	S	4	45	85	28	12	39	1	62	1	80
28	36,743	22	51,515	34	S	3	40	85	21	13	27	1	54	1	55
29	31,302	6	41,430	32	R	6	25	79	5	20	6	0	14	1	30
30	30,518	11	30,510	19	R	8	16	73	10	26	12	0	14	1	15
31	29,197	5	26,349	30	U	10	16	32	1	67	8	0	22	1	7
32	28,748	5	49,506	33	S	4	42	86	4	12	12	1	33	1	49
33	28,579	4	50,480	39	S	5	34	85	3	13	9	2	24	1	32
34	29,864	6	51,552	39	S	4	43	79	5	18	9	2	30	1	38
35	31,696	10	46,065	37	S	4	25	85	9	14	14	0	15	0	9
36	31,701	11	42,990	36	S	5	21	86	10	13	15	0	31	1	31
37	29,536	6	41,111	34	S	5	24	81	5	16	7	1	32	1	46
38	29,890	8	44,664	40	S	5	23	88	7	11	12	1	37	1	26
39	31,296	9	38,514	35	R	6	22	70	8	30	11	0	-31	1	15
40	28,838	4	36,694	30	R	6	31	62	3	37	6	0	14	1	21
41	28,765	1	34,430	31	R	8	20	40	-1	60	2	0	-33	0	-6
42	28,642	2	35,067	38	R	7	19	69	1	30	4	0	-23	0	-8
43	29,154	5	40,409	31	R	7	23	72	4	26	8	0	-4	0	2
44	28,641	1	38,152	32	R	6	17	75	0	25	3	0	-48	1	31
45	31,085	10	42,550	37	R	6	26	72	9	27	12	0	5	0	13
46	32,693	17	49,662	39	U	5	40	85	16	12	25	1	41	1	53
47	31,711	13	48,745	32	S	4	30	83	11	15	23	0	24	1	20
48	33,330	18	63,617	41	S	4	45	92	17	6	26	1	40	1	45
49	31,275	13	40,377	35	U	8	23	43	12	56	14	0	70	0	20
50	28,733	3	33,518	41	R	9	18	38	0	61	6	1	21	1	-3

Note: U=urban, S=suburban, R=rural, M=mixed, HH=households.

South Carolina State House Districts: Demographic Data (cont.)

House District	Population 1997	+/-	Average HH Income ($)	+/-	District Type	Unempl. Rate (%)	College Educ. (%)	White (non-Hispanic) (%)	+/-	African American (%)	+/-	Asian American (%)	+/-	Hispanic American (%)	+/-
S. Carolina	3,721,715	7	43,673	35	R	5	33	68	6	30	7	1	25	1	26
51	26,064	-2	29,672	33	R	11	22	31	-8	68	1	0	10	1	-4
52	29,353	4	38,902	20	R	6	30	65	2	34	8	0	17	1	47
53	28,857	2	37,409	43	R	7	19	65	1	35	5	0	-36	0	2
54	28,461	1	29,738	31	R	10	16	47	0	50	3	0	-33	0	0
55	28,431	2	31,063	31	R	7	18	55	1	43	3	0	-2	0	13
56	29,522	2	39,203	29	R	5	24	66	2	34	1	0	-31	0	20
57	29,511	2	30,191	31	R	8	19	43	1	56	3	0	0	0	9
58	29,230	3	32,802	35	R	6	23	69	-1	30	10	0	17	1	20
59	28,706	5	33,713	28	M	7	21	41	0	58	8	0	0	0	4
60	30,882	12	43,877	43	S	5	30	64	9	36	18	0	10	0	-3
61	29,634	6	36,120	39	R	6	20	58	2	41	12	0	-16	0	-14
62	30,083	5	29,281	25	R	8	20	36	3	64	6	0	-10	0	-8
63	32,431	14	58,922	42	U	3	49	84	13	14	17	1	32	1	83
64	28,512	4	36,423	50	R	8	21	44	2	56	5	0	-19	1	1
65	30,975	10	39,311	39	R	6	27	64	7	36	14	0	-22	0	-1
66	29,840	6	28,483	29	R	10	20	34	4	65	7	0	-16	0	-8
67	27,474	14	42,970	34	R	5	33	66	12	32	17	1	32	1	32
68	34,277	4	39,954	35	R	7	41	64	1	32	7	2	24	2	24
69	32,128	15	53,492	29	S	3	53	88	14	9	21	1	47	2	64
70	29,955	6	34,953	32	M	7	24	29	-1	69	9	1	14	1	19
71	32,550	16	49,746	25	S	2	59	76	13	22	23	1	49	1	65
72	27,875	-2	39,246	28	U	4	57	72	-4	23	-1	2	23	2	23
73	26,599	-3	33,006	22	S	7	33	24	-12	74	0	1	8	1	17
74	26,194	-4	28,444	28	U	11	34	30	-12	68	-1	1	11	1	-4
75	22,221	1	60,822	31	U	2	69	83	-1	14	9	1	27	1	14
76	27,190	-2	34,971	18	S	7	38	33	-10	63	1	2	18	2	27
77	31,809	11	45,776	27	S	6	38	41	10	57	11	1	30	1	18
78	30,139	3	56,356	23	S	3	60	74	0	20	7	3	31	3	12
79	34,457	24	60,743	26	S	3	51	78	21	18	32	2	47	2	61
80	30,480	-6	45,435	26	S	3	43	59	-9	34	-1	2	6	5	8
81	34,218	24	54,629	27	N.A.	4	56	84	23	14	26	1	39	1	94
82	31,186	8	34,714	25	N.A.	7	24	46	6	54	11	0	-7	1	11
83	32,645	16	52,647	32	S	4	44	78	14	20	21	1	39	1	19
84	26,662	-6	36,598	23	R	7	16	78	-8	21	-1	0	-38	1	16
85	36,700	27	68,574	29	S	3	63	92	26	7	30	1	49	1	48
86	29,336	7	39,280	29	R	6	24	68	6	31	9	0	4	1	13
87	35,708	29	55,204	35	S	3	38	91	28	7	36	0	49	1	65
88	33,772	16	46,048	30	S	4	31	89	15	9	20	1	40	1	55
89	28,662	6	41,083	31	S	4	35	79	4	18	11	1	33	1	46
90	33,263	2	36,098	37	R	8	23	50	1	49	2	0	-27	1	15
91	26,632	4	37,032	41	R	10	23	42	3	57	4	0	-19	1	7
92	31,268	18	52,713	33	S	4	39	85	15	10	29	2	41	3	51
93	30,281	8	37,899	30	R	8	31	46	5	53	9	0	28	0	17
94	26,441	-6	45,289	25	R	5	40	79	-7	17	-5	1	11	2	17
95	27,936	1	35,455	29	R	9	37	35	0	64	1	1	21	1	19
96	32,023	11	36,377	32	R	6	19	73	12	27	10	0	12	0	17
97	27,685	5	35,970	25	R	6	18	56	4	42	6	0	24	0	-3
98	31,056	6	47,235	25	S	4	46	84	4	11	12	2	31	2	37
99	28,966	-3	43,405	30	S	5	34	75	-8	15	8	5	19	5	29
100	23,486	-2	40,925	34	R	6	30	68	-6	29	7	1	13	2	14

Note: U=urban, S=suburban, R=rural, M=mixed, HH=households.

South Carolina State House Districts: Demographic Data (cont.)

House District	Population		Average HH Income		District Type	Unempl. Rate	College Educ.	White (non-Hispanic)		African American		Asian American		Hispanic American	
	1997	+/-	($)	+/-		(%)	(%)	(%)	+/-	(%)	+/-	(%)	+/-	(%)	+/-
S. Carolina	3,721,715	7	43,673	35	R	5	33	68	6	30	7	1	25	1	26
101	28,461	2	33,686	48	R	8	20	32	0	68	3	0	-31	0	-21
102	28,311	-7	36,489	35	R	7	18	46	-12	53	-3	0	13	1	-12
103	28,860	6	32,978	38	R	7	12	41	1	59	9	0	-53	0	9
104	33,703	18	42,484	40	R	6	31	72	15	27	27	0	-2	1	24
105	28,955	5	39,702	34	R	5	30	77	2	19	13	1	26	2	18
106	33,340	18	45,387	42	R	4	38	89	18	9	12	1	48	1	52
107	37,682	34	51,948	41	R	5	43	89	32	8	37	2	54	1	83
108	33,831	16	55,958	57	R	5	40	70	15	29	17	0	-28	1	37
109	25,216	-16	39,124	47	M	7	26	36	-20	62	-14	1	4	1	-3
110	29,698	-3	70,826	62	U	4	58	73	-7	25	7	1	5	1	9
111	22,158	-17	35,162	34	S	7	30	31	-27	68	-11	1	-2	1	-6
112	31,763	21	75,524	61	N.A.	3	58	83	19	15	31	1	59	1	53
113	23,979	-15	39,811	47	S	6	25	69	-19	24	-8	2	5	4	13
114	26,425	-5	60,630	50	U	3	51	77	-8	19	7	2	21	2	18
115	27,872	-1	59,471	51	S	4	45	74	-4	24	8	1	18	1	20
116	28,551	5	47,300	60	M	6	27	41	-3	57	11	0	12	2	31
117	33,475	8	47,370	41	S	5	32	78	6	17	17	3	35	2	16
118	18,141	-35	22,513	31	S	12	13	26	-53	71	-22	1	-48	1	-56
119	28,620	-5	54,637	45	N.A.	4	48	75	-8	22	3	1	19	2	28
120	29,404	6	34,736	31	R	6	24	56	4	44	8	0	-3	0	-7
121	34,725	20	32,379	23	R	8	24	44	15	52	24	1	51	3	34
122	30,118	7	32,609	32	R	7	18	44	3	52	9	0	8	3	46
123	34,615	23	73,600	34	R	3	58	86	21	12	28	1	49	2	61
124	33,604	20	47,504	40	R	5	44	65	23	32	15	1	63	2	6

Note: U=urban, S=suburban, R=rural, M=mixed, HH=households.

SOUTH DAKOTA

North and South Dakota entered the Union on the same day, November 2, 1889. Because it was impossible for President Benjamin Harrison to sign both statehood bills simultaneously, one of them was going to enter the Union first, albeit by a few seconds, creating a permanent source of pride for one and disgrace for the other. In order to avoid the problem, both bills were covered, leaving only the signature lines showing. They were shuffled and then reshuffled after Harrison signed, so that no one would ever know which was rightfully the thirty-ninth and which the fortieth state.

Those who have never ventured west of the Alleghenies or east of the Sierras may joke that the two states remain indistinguishable, but they are not. North Dakota grows wheat. South Dakota mines gold. North Dakota had the Nonpartisan League and socialist farmers. South Dakota had Sitting Bull. North Dakota is in many ways an extension of the Minnesota grain fields; South Dakota is, too, but includes the Black Hills and the Badlands, which George Armstrong Custer once described as "a part of hell with the fires burnt out." South Dakota has bigger cities, more Native Americans, and a more diversified economy, which includes meat packing. Most of Citicorp's credit card business is headquartered here, as is Gateway Computers.

South Dakota is still a big state with few people, the forty-fifth most populous. Imagine the population of Delaware spread across a land area almost forty times bigger, and you have South Dakota. But after having grown by less than 1 percent during the 1980s, when the farm crisis drove thousands of families out of state, the population has grown by a robust 6 percent in this decade. City work is becoming the basis of its economy. Almost all the rapidly growing house districts are located in Sioux Falls, the largest city, while the farm districts continue to lose people.

Given its reliance on agriculture and the large number of dependent tribes, South Dakota has traditionally been a poor state. But with the birth of a service economy and a recovery in farm prices, household income has grown 48 percent since 1990, giving South Dakota the fastest rate of growth of any state and one of the lowest rates of unemployment (4 percent). That has been enough to boost income here from forty-seventh among the states in 1990 to forty-first just six years later. As might be expected, income has grown fastest in and around Sioux Falls, as well as Rapid City, South Dakota's other city. Growth has been slowest in the farm districts and on the reservations, the only districts in the state with double-digit unemployment.

It is impossible to write about South Dakota without writing about the Indians, who make up only 7 percent of its population. The Sioux ruled the Plains until Custer, who discovered gold here and brought the settlers, drove them into Montana, where they would have their revenge. Later, South Dakota saw the Ghost Dances, the tribes' late, futile turn toward mysticism. South Dakota also saw the massacre at Wounded Knee, the last shots fired (at unarmed Indian civilians) in the War for the West.

Whites fanned out across the state after the Sioux were conquered, so evenly that the Twenty-seventh House District, where two of the large reservations are located, is the only one in which whites are not a majority. Whites are thickest along the Minnesota border but predominate throughout. In no district do blacks, Asians, or Hispanics account for more than 4 percent of the population.

For a heavily Republican state, South Dakota has produced two very prominent Democrats in former presidential nominee George McGovern and current Senate minority leader Tom Daschle. Both chambers of the legislature are securely in Republican hands. Democrats briefly controlled the senate after 1992, but the GOP regained control two years later. South Dakota lost its second congressional district in 1982 and despite the recent growth is not expected to get it back.

SOUTH DAKOTA
State Legislative Districts

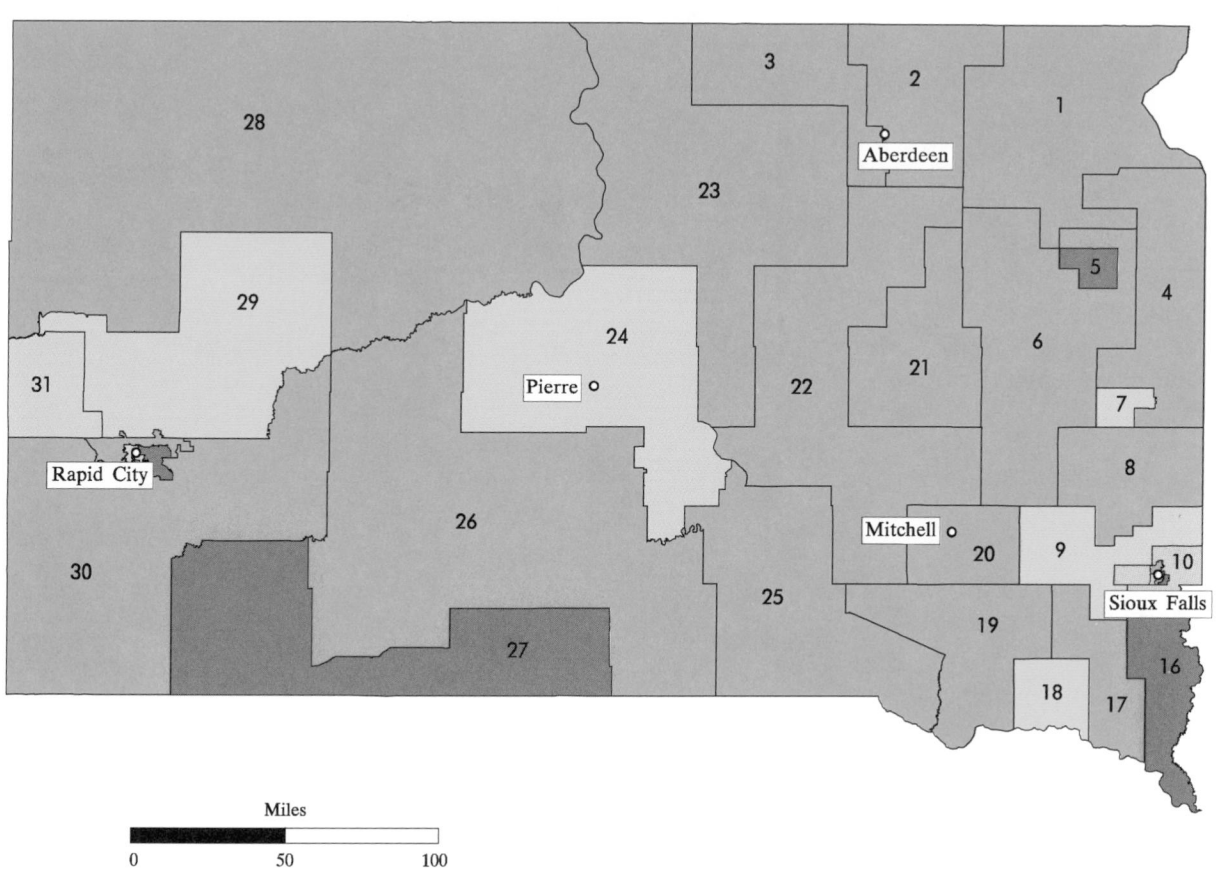

RAPID CITY

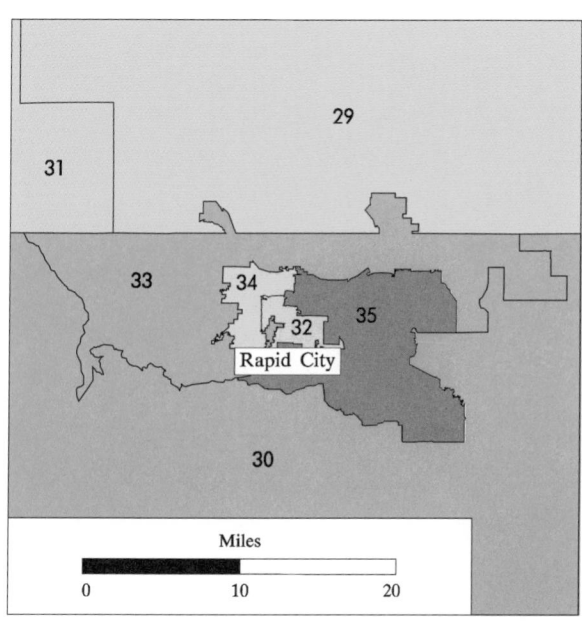

SIOUX FALLS

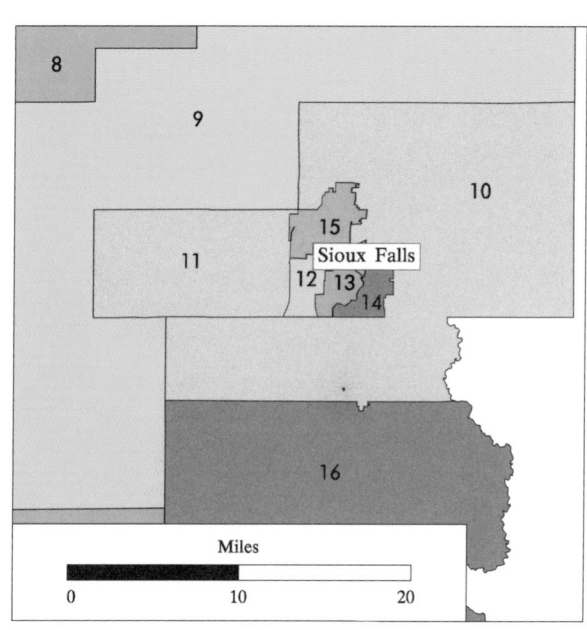

Population Growth ▨ -4% to 3% ☐ 6% to 10% ▨ 13% to 18% ☐ 26% to 28%

South Dakota State Legislative Districts: Demographic Data

Legis. District	Population		Average HH Income		District Type	Unempl. Rate	College Educ.	White (non-Hispanic)		African American		Asian American		Hispanic American	
	1997	+/-	($)	+/-		(%)	(%)	(%)	+/-	(%)	+/-	(%)	+/-	(%)	+/-
S. Dakota	736,679	6	41,574	48	R	4	38	91	5	0	3	1	34	1	33
1	21,063	-2	30,935	38	R	6	27	86	-3	0	-75	0	-69	0	-6
2	20,532	1	38,004	40	R	4	38	97	1	0	-64	0	29	0	46
3	19,603	-2	40,056	36	R	3	39	96	-2	0	0	1	42	0	35
4	20,754	0	40,243	50	R	4	35	99	0	0	-90	0	-22	0	41
5	21,941	13	40,057	51	R	5	35	98	13	0	0	0	51	0	48
6	20,775	1	38,581	57	R	2	29	99	1	0	-9	0	-61	0	13
7	18,338	6	39,692	52	R	4	50	97	5	0	6	2	34	0	42
8	19,224	1	43,720	52	R	3	37	96	1	0	-42	0	-27	0	16
9	21,310	10	43,407	52	R	2	34	99	10	0	-8	0	-41	0	14
10	26,017	26	60,305	52	M	2	45	98	26	1	31	0	45	1	50
11	23,207	28	53,795	47	U	3	48	98	28	0	30	1	81	1	93
12	20,941	7	47,840	50	U	3	48	96	6	1	16	1	58	1	53
13	20,563	2	51,436	45	U	3	51	96	2	1	9	1	47	1	48
14	20,759	18	68,667	53	U	2	58	98	18	0	20	1	74	0	67
15	19,865	3	33,783	39	U	4	27	93	2	1	6	1	49	1	41
16	24,242	16	44,817	60	R	3	32	99	16	0	0	0	29	0	47
17	20,002	2	39,436	61	R	5	47	96	2	0	-13	1	13	1	22
18	21,024	9	39,950	50	R	2	39	96	9	1	6	0	58	1	40
19	18,725	-2	34,386	53	R	2	28	98	-2	0	-18	0	-82	0	18
20	20,748	1	38,089	50	R	4	38	98	1	0	-32	0	3	0	13
21	19,679	-1	36,798	43	R	4	34	98	-1	0	-18	0	-19	0	22
22	20,223	-3	35,212	50	R	4	32	92	-3	0	-80	0	-52	0	-2
23	19,232	-4	32,987	37	R	3	32	97	-4	0	-40	0	-37	0	13
24	22,259	8	44,051	46	R	3	43	89	8	0	-5	0	23	1	29
25	20,823	1	35,716	56	R	5	28	85	0	0	-64	0	-30	1	21
26	18,936	-1	34,859	36	R	6	29	77	-2	0	-43	0	-31	0	-4
27	22,505	17	26,357	48	R	25	26	13	12	0	69	0	-25	1	-20
28	21,866	2	31,057	31	R	10	25	64	1	0	-21	0	-17	1	15
29	23,408	10	37,975	39	R	4	34	96	9	0	20	0	65	2	55
30	21,633	3	39,318	35	R	5	36	94	3	0	19	0	5	2	41
31	22,561	9	41,942	43	R	4	38	95	8	0	-34	0	29	2	54
32	18,573	6	42,532	40	U	5	46	91	5	1	9	1	52	2	27
33	24,434	3	52,513	47	U	7	48	84	1	4	-3	2	36	4	35
34	16,663	6	52,890	47	U	5	48	88	5	1	5	1	51	3	35
35	24,251	13	35,904	41	U	7	31	84	12	1	13	2	55	3	41

Note: U=urban, S=suburban, R=rural, M=mixed, HH=households.

TENNESSEE

Few states span such a great distance, psychologically as well as geographically, as Tennessee. Kingsport, at its eastern tip, is closer to Washington, D.C., than to Memphis, and Memphis is itself more a part of the Mississippi Delta than of the broad farms and tobacco fields in the middle of the state. Rather like Ohio (which it resembles in no other way), Tennessee is three states, each with its representative city. The mountainous east, predominantly white and staunchly Unionist during the Civil War, is centered around Knoxville. (Early in the country's history, some proposed to break Tennessee into two states and name the eastern half after Benjamin Franklin.) The middle of the state is bluegrass country (with four times as much actual bluegrass as Kentucky), centered around Nashville, one of the country's rising cities. On the western edge is Memphis, more heavily black than the others and still Tennessee's largest city, but one being rapidly overtaken by Nashville. Each region may also be said to have its distinctive style of music: bluegrass in the hills, country at the Grand Ol' Opry in Nashville, and the blues on Beale Street (as well as rock 'n roll at Graceland) in Memphis.

Tennessee is the seventeenth-most-populous state but is projected to rise to sixteenth by 2000 and to fifteenth by 2025. Growth has been fastest in and around Nashville, particularly on its southern edge: the Sixty-first District has grown by 40 percent; the Forty-ninth, which lies between Nashville and Murfreesboro, by 38 percent. The Nashville area's economic base is now remarkably diverse: country music, research at Vanderbilt University, book publishing and distribution, and even automobile assembly at the Nissan and Saturn plants not far from the city.

Memphis, on the other hand, which serves as the focal point for the poorest parts of two of the poorest states—the cotton-growing regions of Mississippi and Arkansas—has been losing population. Three downtown districts, the Eighty-eighth, Ninetieth, and Ninety-first, have each shrunk by at least 5 percent. The Ninety-fourth District, on the other hand, in the predominantly white suburbs of Shelby County (where the wealthy mob lawyers in John Grisham's novel *The Firm* lived), has grown by 41 percent, the largest gain in the state.

The suburbanization of Tennessee can be seen in the following figures: of the twenty fastest-growing state house districts, twelve are suburban, four are rural, and four are urban (two in Clarksville, one in Murfreesboro, one in Nashville). Every district that is losing population is urban.

Income is rising quickly in Tennessee. The wealthiest districts are in downtown Nashville (average income is $107,000 in the Fifty-sixth District), the southern Nashville suburbs ($98,000 in the Sixty-first District), and the southeast Memphis suburbs ($97,000 in the Ninety-fourth District). The poorest districts and the ones with the highest rates of unemployment are in the big cities, as well. In Memphis's Eighty-eighth District, average income is just $23,000 and the unemployment rate is 14 percent, which are the worst in the state.

Although Tennessee borders several states with large black populations—Mississippi, Alabama, Georgia, and North Carolina—it does not border heavily black sections of those states; hence, the percentage of Tennessee residents who are African American is not particularly high. The districts with the greatest share of African Americans are located in Nashville and in Memphis, the one part of the state that does lie next to predominantly black areas, in the Mississippi Delta and in Arkansas.

No state suffered a greater political transformation in 1994 than Tennessee, which replaced a Democratic governor and two Democratic U.S. senators with Republicans. Those gains did not filter down to the legislature, which the Democrats still control. Their margins have been trimmed in both chambers, enough to put control of the senate (18–15 in 1996) in jeopardy but not that of the house (61–38).

Finally, it should be noted that Tennessee has been home to three presidents—Andrew Jackson, James Polk, and Andrew Johnson—but birthplace to none. That is not likely to change soon; Vice President Al Gore was born in Washington, D.C.

TENNESSEE
State Senate Districts

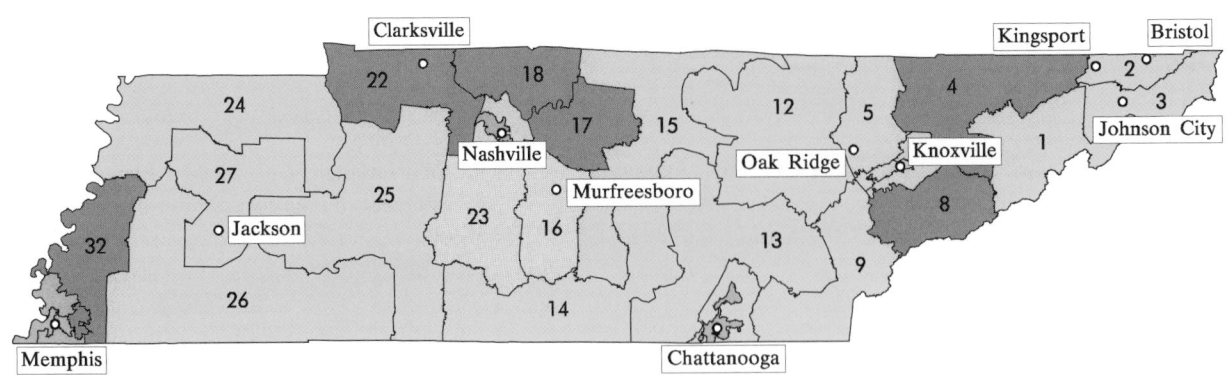

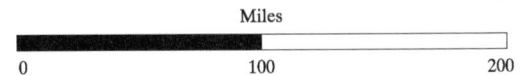

CHATTANOOGA

KNOXVILLE

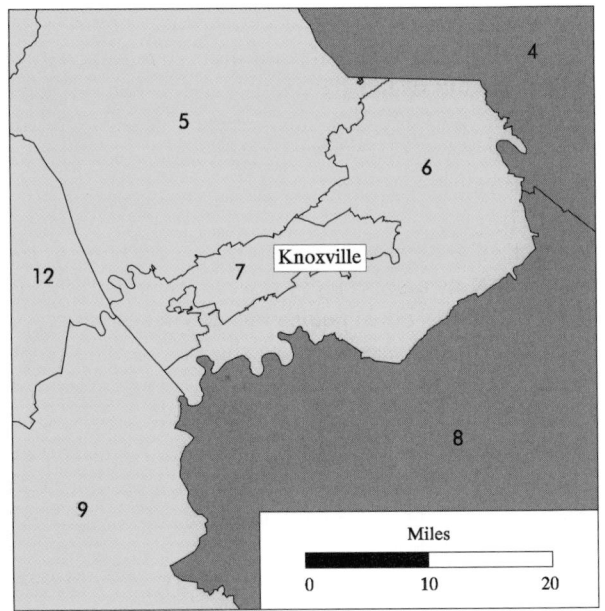

Population Growth   ▨ -5% to 1%   ▢ 5% to 12%   ▨ 14% to 23%   ▢ 29% to 30%

NASHVILLE

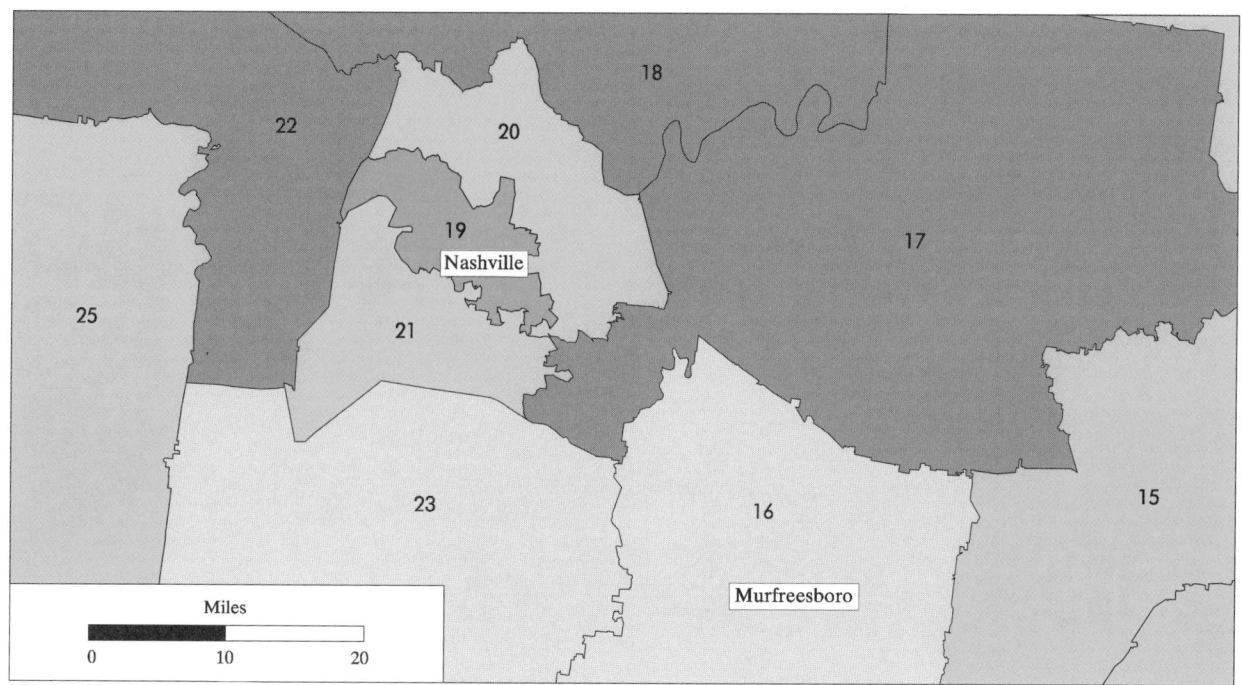

MEMPHIS

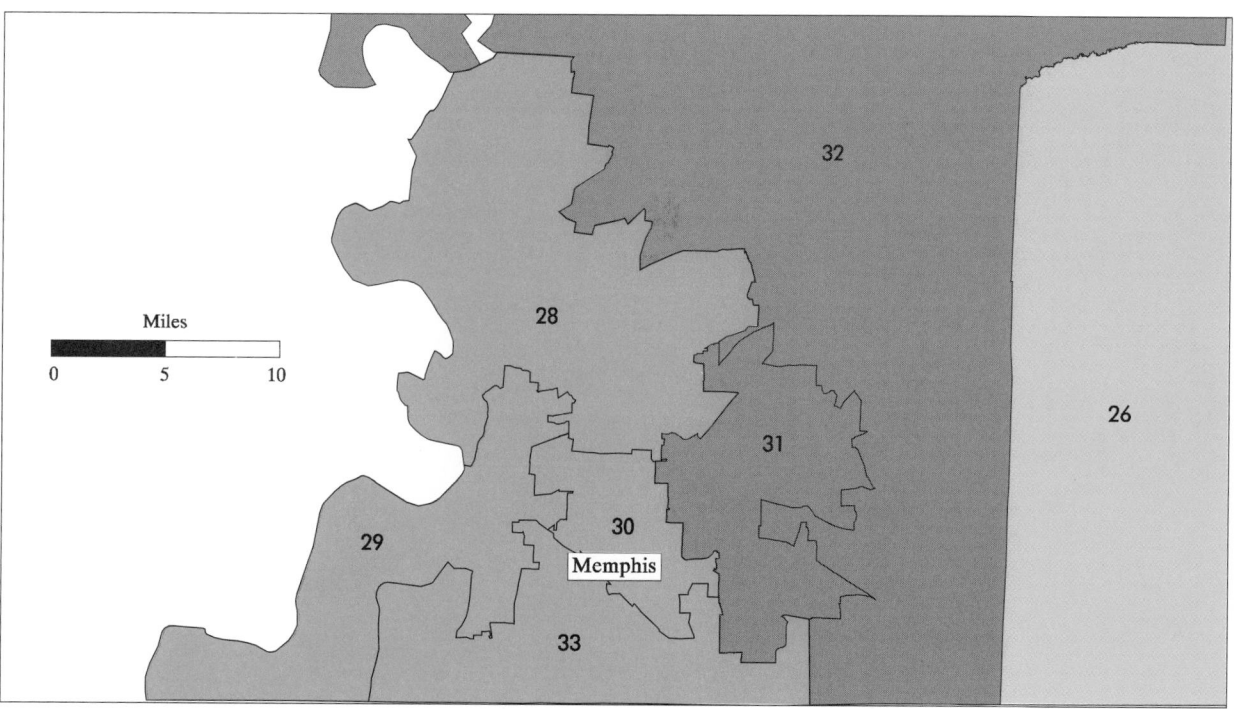

Population Growth ▢ -5% to 1%   ▢ 5% to 12%   ▢ 14% to 23%   ▢ 29% to 30%

Tennessee State Senate Districts: Demographic Data

Senate District	Population 1997	+/-	Average HH Income ($)	+/-	District Type	Unempl. Rate (%)	College Educ. (%)	White (non-Hispanic) (%)	+/-	African American (%)	+/-	Asian American (%)	+/-	Hispanic American (%)	+/-
Tenn.	5,373,120	10	44,611	40	M	6	30	82	9	16	12	1	45	1	55
1	161,602	6	36,077	38	R	8	19	96	6	3	14	0	16	1	58
2	150,541	5	43,008	34	S	6	31	97	4	2	11	0	38	1	53
3	171,315	9	37,546	37	S	7	27	96	8	3	15	0	36	1	60
4	161,295	14	33,494	34	R	7	16	98	14	2	24	0	11	0	57
5	156,317	10	41,681	36	S	6	29	96	9	2	16	1	47	1	62
6	161,087	9	54,283	41	S	5	40	94	8	4	34	1	56	1	53
7	159,878	7	43,771	41	U	7	43	79	5	17	12	2	47	1	62
8	163,110	19	41,327	35	S	8	26	96	18	2	24	1	63	1	80
9	167,052	12	40,039	38	R	6	21	96	11	3	18	0	28	1	60
10	133,869	-1	37,519	35	U	7	29	60	-6	38	6	1	27	1	37
11	162,589	8	56,817	39	S	4	41	92	6	5	35	1	51	1	55
12	165,959	11	34,093	36	R	9	19	98	10	1	12	0	27	1	64
13	157,643	10	32,893	31	R	8	16	96	10	3	16	0	23	1	50
14	149,774	7	37,724	38	R	7	19	92	6	7	15	0	10	1	52
15	170,619	11	37,694	39	R	6	22	96	11	2	19	1	44	1	56
16	193,322	30	47,596	42	M	5	32	87	28	10	37	2	78	1	86
17	171,580	17	53,517	44	M	5	34	87	15	10	34	1	56	1	75
18	172,634	19	51,300	41	S	5	27	91	18	7	27	0	57	1	80
19	136,411	-2	31,958	39	U	9	24	32	-12	65	3	1	26	1	25
20	166,327	5	48,683	43	U	4	34	85	2	12	28	1	41	1	41
21	167,199	8	75,310	51	U	3	57	88	5	8	26	2	48	1	58
22	176,434	22	38,929	30	U	7	29	81	20	13	27	2	63	3	67
23	202,754	29	64,212	49	R	4	39	88	28	11	34	1	76	1	94
24	155,617	5	37,557	41	R	7	17	89	4	10	11	0	8	1	42
25	168,395	11	37,771	43	R	6	16	95	11	4	18	0	7	1	55
26	165,908	8	34,689	41	R	7	15	75	7	24	11	0	3	1	30
27	161,884	7	42,014	50	R	7	24	74	5	25	12	0	27	1	45
28	158,477	1	37,925	28	U	7	27	55	-11	42	21	1	28	1	43
29	131,615	-5	25,447	35	U	15	19	10	-22	89	-2	1	17	0	-3
30	138,256	-3	45,093	34	U	6	38	54	-11	43	8	2	23	1	29
31	169,008	18	69,070	32	S	3	54	86	13	10	62	2	74	2	60
32	195,289	23	62,361	42	S	5	37	77	19	20	40	1	52	1	45
33	149,356	1	40,339	29	U	9	31	23	-11	75	5	0	15	1	29

Note: U=urban, S=suburban, R=rural, M=mixed, HH=households.

TENNESSEE
State House Districts

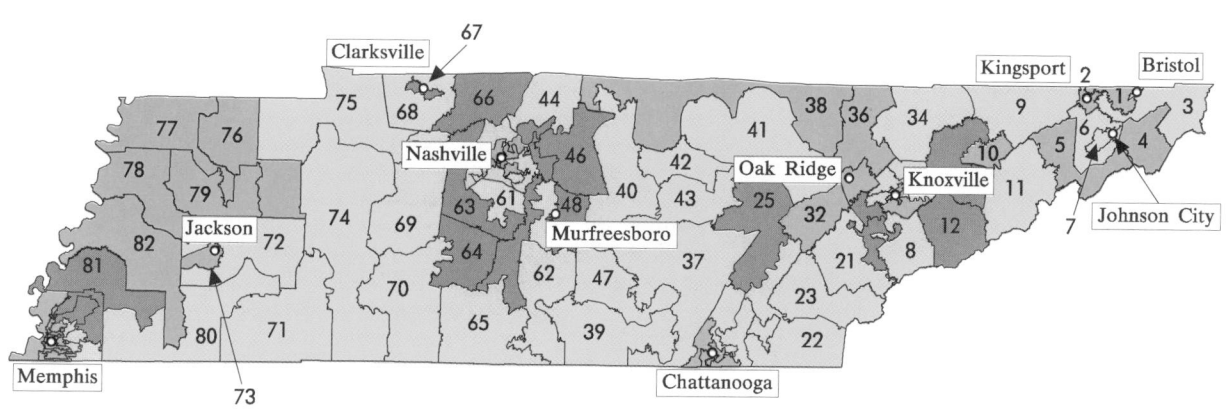

Miles

0   100   200

CHATTANOOGA

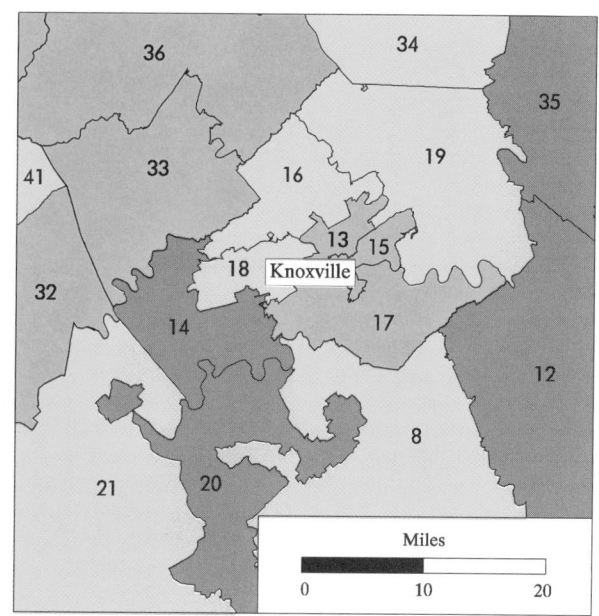

Miles

0   10   20

KNOXVILLE

Miles

0   10   20

Population Growth   ▢ -7% to 6%   ▢ 7% to 17%   ▢ 19% to 29%   ▢ 38% to 41%

NASHVILLE

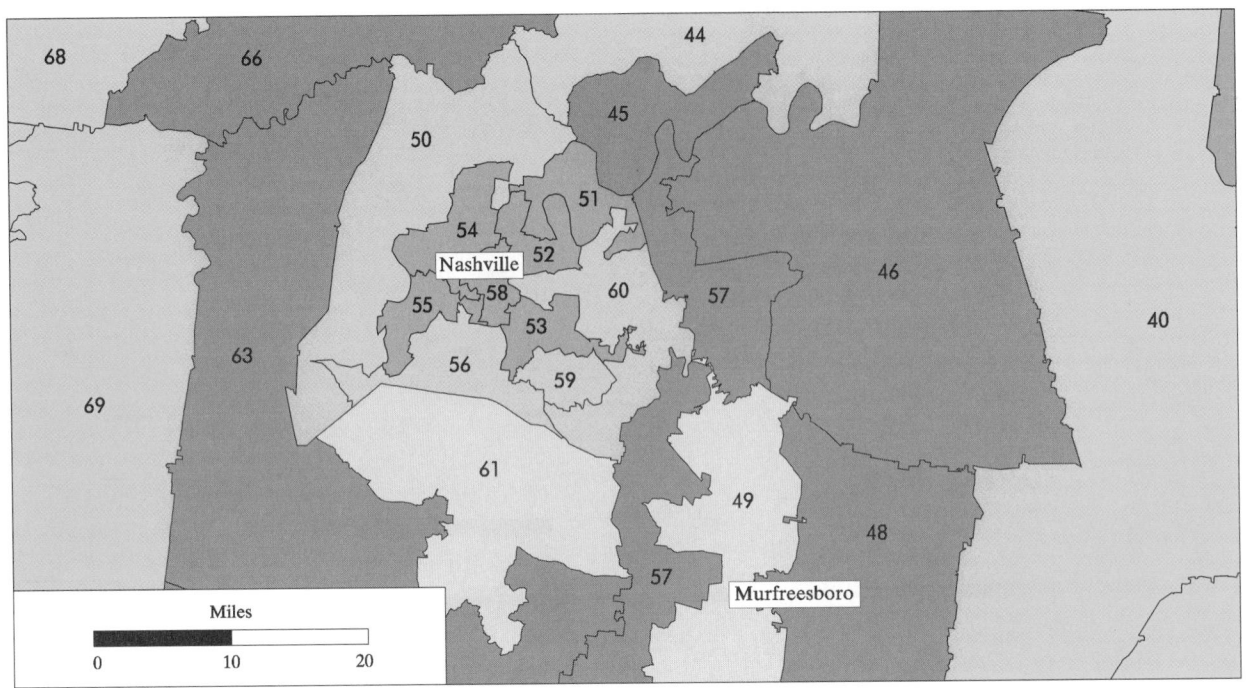

MEMPHIS

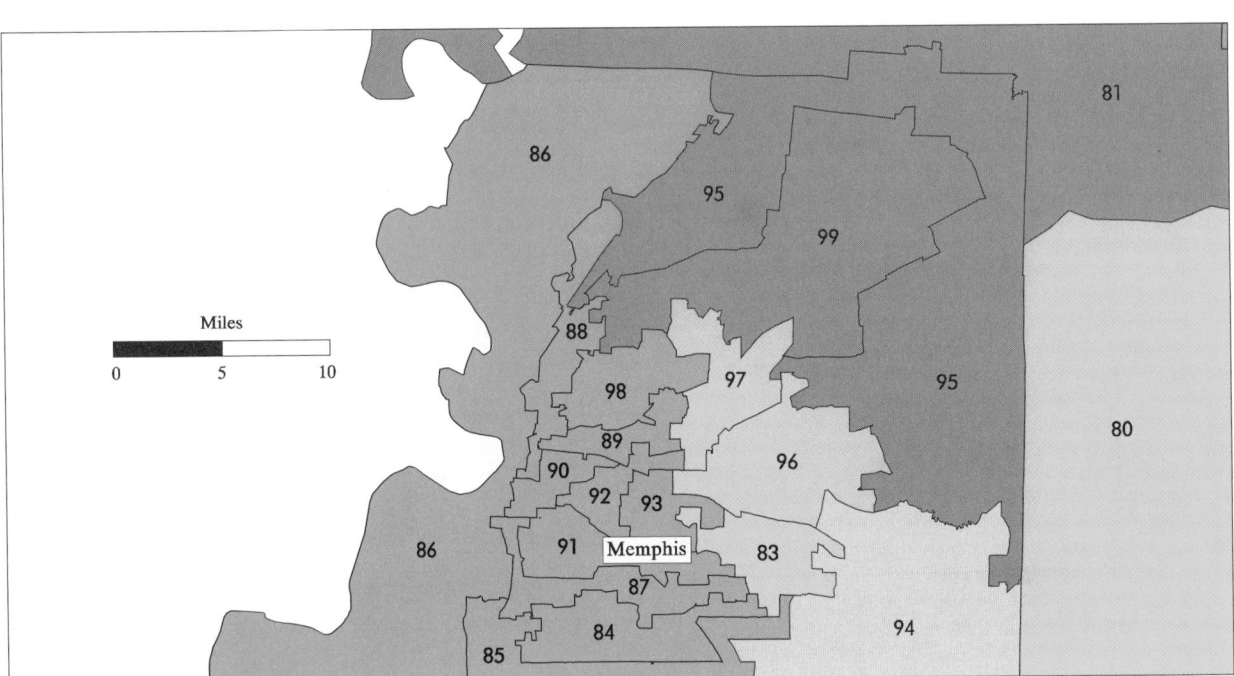

Population Growth   ■ -7% to 6%   ■ 7% to 17%   ■ 19% to 29%   □ 38% to 41%

Tennessee State House Districts: Demographic Data

House District	Population		Average HH Income		District Type	Unempl. Rate	College Educ.	White (non-Hispanic)		African American		Asian American		Hispanic American	
	1997	+/-	($)	+/-		(%)	(%)	(%)	+/-	(%)	+/-	(%)	+/-	(%)	+/-
Tenn.	5,373,120	10	44,611	40	M	6	30	82	9	16	12	1	45	1	55
1	52,884	4	37,142	29	N.A.	6	24	97	3	2	12	0	29	1	54
2	50,677	5	45,251	37	N.A.	6	35	96	5	3	9	1	42	0	48
3	56,072	10	40,420	33	S	6	26	98	10	1	16	0	45	1	63
4	53,379	4	33,077	36	S	8	21	98	3	1	9	0	20	1	50
5	52,275	5	34,167	31	N.A.	8	20	97	5	2	14	0	13	1	52
6	56,403	9	45,449	37	N.A.	5	34	98	8	1	17	0	46	0	39
7	52,443	10	39,052	38	N.A.	7	31	92	9	6	16	1	37	1	75
8	56,040	16	41,628	33	N.A.	7	27	94	15	4	19	0	48	1	68
9	55,704	9	34,922	37	R	8	17	97	8	2	17	0	7	0	58
10	53,679	6	40,631	42	R	6	22	94	6	5	14	0	29	1	57
11	55,643	7	33,457	39	R	9	14	97	7	2	13	0	-10	1	63
12	62,552	23	38,445	36	R	9	22	98	22	0	14	1	72	1	91
13	47,896	2	30,448	35	U	8	24	86	-1	12	23	0	35	1	50
14	61,181	23	75,553	39	S	3	62	93	20	3	50	3	64	1	102
15	44,105	-4	22,973	29	U	10	29	52	-12	44	5	3	31	1	22
16	58,443	16	45,098	34	S	4	34	97	15	2	45	0	49	0	60
17	52,609	4	63,842	47	S	4	46	95	3	3	33	1	47	1	47
18	51,661	16	55,242	39	U	4	54	91	13	6	45	2	59	1	83
19	51,997	10	41,195	33	S	5	22	96	9	3	33	0	44	0	27
20	55,693	23	43,042	34	N.A.	7	29	96	23	2	41	1	68	1	87
21	53,684	13	40,768	43	R	7	20	96	12	3	20	0	9	1	70
22	51,269	7	37,978	35	R	6	16	98	7	1	11	0	17	0	16
23	52,883	8	34,056	29	R	8	19	94	7	4	16	0	42	1	52
24	53,590	13	41,333	33	R	5	29	92	12	5	17	0	43	2	71
25	60,394	19	31,963	29	R	9	19	98	19	1	19	0	27	1	83
26	50,713	13	62,824	40	S	4	40	93	11	4	45	1	55	1	51
27	49,787	5	57,228	37	S	4	48	92	3	5	43	1	47	1	69
28	43,600	-6	27,093	35	U	12	20	29	-14	70	-2	0	10	1	8
29	46,301	-4	37,193	33	U	6	28	57	-15	41	16	1	18	1	38
30	52,459	5	51,517	38	S	4	40	92	2	5	45	2	50	1	54
31	53,601	10	48,769	34	S	6	33	93	8	5	43	1	48	1	53
32	50,199	6	42,381	39	R	9	27	95	6	3	14	1	40	1	59
33	50,997	5	47,754	37	N.A.	6	40	91	4	6	11	1	51	1	64
34	54,128	13	31,597	37	R	8	13	99	13	1	16	0	15	0	65
35	60,662	21	33,656	30	R	7	19	97	21	2	31	0	6	0	52
36	49,202	5	30,242	34	R	9	16	98	5	0	9	0	16	0	43
37	57,220	9	33,184	36	R	8	14	96	9	3	16	0	10	1	40
38	51,038	5	33,577	41	R	8	12	99	5	0	-1	0	-20	0	22
39	54,390	7	38,302	37	R	7	23	93	6	5	14	0	12	1	56
40	51,062	12	36,492	42	R	6	13	97	12	2	17	0	-21	0	30
41	53,015	7	29,354	39	R	9	12	99	7	1	7	0	-20	0	48
42	58,753	14	38,141	36	R	6	29	96	14	2	21	1	52	1	65
43	54,737	12	34,602	36	R	7	15	97	11	2	15	0	13	1	56
44	58,905	14	43,215	38	R	6	20	91	13	8	22	0	44	0	52
45	62,955	22	61,046	40	S	4	37	94	20	3	33	1	73	1	93
46	63,195	22	47,256	39	S	6	24	89	20	9	29	0	64	1	50
47	55,956	11	37,317	35	R	6	25	95	10	3	19	1	41	1	60
48	61,430	25	41,957	39	U	6	34	80	22	16	36	3	75	1	69
49	65,100	38	57,985	49	S	4	41	91	36	6	51	2	92	1	95
50	57,751	10	55,526	47	U	4	41	80	7	18	19	1	56	1	51

Note: U=urban, S=suburban, R=rural, M=mixed, HH=households.

Tennessee State House Districts: Demographic Data (cont.)

House District	Population 1997	+/-	Average HH Income ($)	+/-	District Type	Unempl. Rate (%)	College Educ. (%)	White (non-Hispanic) (%)	+/-	African American (%)	+/-	Asian American (%)	+/-	Hispanic American (%)	+/-
Tenn.	5,373,120	10	44,611	40	M	6	30	82	9	16	12	1	45	1	55
51	54,936	5	44,781	42	U	5	29	87	2	10	30	1	45	1	34
52	51,488	0	39,856	38	U	7	26	62	-7	36	14	1	30	1	20
53	52,405	2	50,518	47	U	4	38	82	-3	13	25	3	36	2	64
54	49,894	-2	34,105	39	U	9	27	27	-13	71	2	1	29	1	16
55	51,624	3	67,938	58	U	4	56	88	0	7	20	4	45	1	43
56	60,030	14	107,219	48	U	2	69	94	12	3	54	2	65	1	76
57	68,197	27	54,260	40	S	4	29	93	25	5	35	0	59	1	109
58	45,555	-3	26,856	42	U	11	21	24	-13	73	0	1	18	1	18
59	51,515	8	44,808	41	U	4	38	76	1	18	29	3	44	2	69
60	62,691	16	55,051	48	U	3	42	86	12	11	41	1	55	2	61
61	69,321	40	98,192	43	S	3	62	93	38	4	50	1	87	1	118
62	51,892	11	36,674	30	R	6	19	87	10	12	16	0	39	1	46
63	66,058	28	49,334	38	S	4	29	91	27	8	39	0	63	1	85
64	63,545	26	47,453	50	R	6	25	82	24	17	32	0	59	1	99
65	54,391	11	42,033	46	R	5	18	88	10	11	20	0	9	1	65
66	58,548	21	47,699	41	S	5	22	89	19	10	29	0	-19	1	79
67	64,534	29	38,488	29	U	9	35	69	24	22	31	3	72	5	83
68	58,875	17	38,030	26	U	7	31	81	15	14	20	1	50	3	43
69	57,251	16	39,981	39	R	7	18	93	16	5	23	0	13	1	74
70	57,515	12	38,409	50	R	6	14	97	12	2	7	0	20	1	54
71	54,516	7	32,456	37	R	6	13	93	7	6	14	0	-5	1	45
72	62,297	15	47,675	52	R	4	28	86	13	13	31	0	64	1	54
73	46,465	2	39,122	48	U	7	29	52	-4	46	9	0	23	1	40
74	58,371	10	34,148	38	R	6	15	97	10	2	15	0	-9	1	44
75	51,760	10	36,249	44	R	8	16	92	10	7	13	0	6	1	40
76	52,142	3	36,901	42	R	6	18	90	2	8	8	1	15	1	29
77	48,265	3	38,498	42	R	7	16	87	2	12	11	0	-3	1	30
78	50,124	4	40,914	45	R	7	18	85	3	14	10	0	-5	0	34
79	49,463	5	36,362	44	R	9	15	78	3	22	9	0	-18	1	43
80	53,472	9	36,458	38	R	8	17	68	7	31	15	0	11	1	29
81	54,598	20	38,664	41	R	8	16	70	19	29	23	0	22	1	58
82	49,109	2	32,348	38	R	10	14	56	0	43	5	0	-21	1	24
83	57,399	11	64,332	31	U	3	55	85	5	11	81	2	61	2	66
84	45,156	-4	37,482	18	U	8	33	23	-30	75	7	0	-14	1	45
85	49,289	2	47,098	26	U	8	33	29	-8	70	7	0	21	0	13
86	49,546	1	35,821	42	U	10	19	28	-12	71	6	0	22	1	14
87	43,436	-5	36,277	23	U	8	30	26	-26	72	4	1	2	1	31
88	43,454	-7	22,675	21	U	14	15	24	-28	74	3	1	8	1	5
89	44,709	-3	33,734	33	U	7	30	60	-10	38	8	1	21	1	29
90	44,642	-5	32,142	39	U	12	32	30	-7	67	-5	2	22	1	30
91	45,199	-6	32,158	27	U	10	23	24	-19	74	-1	1	15	1	29
92	44,771	-2	41,562	35	U	10	29	27	-16	72	4	1	15	0	-11
93	48,242	-3	40,161	31	U	6	35	56	-11	41	10	2	31	1	27
94	71,168	41	97,215	35	S	3	58	87	35	10	100	2	80	1	87
95	67,096	25	61,717	38	S	4	43	77	17	19	62	2	52	2	35
96	56,736	16	82,617	N.A.	S	3	57	84	12	11	34	2	77	3	50
97	55,044	9	53,392	N.A.	U	3	42	88	4	9	68	2	54	1	39
98	48,807	-1	30,396	27	N.A.	11	23	26	-20	73	8	0	18	1	43
99	57,270	20	51,687	35	N.A.	5	35	63	12	34	34	1	45	1	66

Note: U=urban, S=suburban, R=rural, M=mixed, HH=households.

TEXAS

As John Gunther observed more than a half century ago in *Inside USA,* Texas does not properly belong to the West, the South, or even the Southwest, although it spans all three regions. It is a region unto itself. The land area of Texas is bigger than that of New York, Pennsylvania, Massachusetts, Illinois, Ohio, and Wisconsin combined. Fifty-nine Texas *counties* are larger than the state of Rhode Island. Germany and Great Britain could fit inside it with room to spare.

One dominating factor in state life, then, is distance. It takes two days to drive from Amarillo to Houston or from El Paso to Dallas. The town of Perryton, at the top of the Panhandle, is closer to Madison, Wisconsin, than it is to Brownsville on the Mexican border. Most towns in the Panhandle, in fact, are closer to six other state capitals than they are to Austin, fostering in them a sense of isolation and hostility to state government, as well as to federal. Yet people there *think* of themselves as Texans in a way difficult for non-Texans to appreciate. People in Ohio do not take strictly Ohio vacations, in which they set off not for a specific destination but to see the wonders of their state. Texans do.

The statute admitting Texas to the Union gave it the right, by simple act of the legislature, to divide itself into as many as five separate states, but it is inconceivable that Texans would ever do so—if only, someone has suggested, because they could never agree on which of the new states got to keep the Alamo.

The second-largest state is also the second-most-populous. Texas has twenty cities of more than 100,000 people and three of the country's ten most populous: Houston (fourth), Dallas (eighth), and San Antonio (ninth). Here, as in many places around the country, the slowest-growing areas are the inner cities, while those growing fastest are the suburbs of those cities or even the rural areas beyond them. To take Dallas as an example, the One Hundredth House District, downtown, has grown by just 1 percent since 1990. The One Hundred Twelfth District, slightly farther out, has grown by 7 percent; the One Hundred Thirteenth District, just beyond that, by 26 percent; and the Sixty-Third District, which reaches perhaps thirty miles from Dallas and borders the city of Sherman, by 32 percent.

Of the state's twenty fastest-growing districts, fourteen are suburban, four are urban, one is rural, and one is of mixed use. Of the twenty slowest-growing districts, fifteen are urban and five are rural, most of them in the oil-, cattle-, and wheat-dependent counties of North and West Texas.

Texas is one of only a few states that has large numbers of both African Americans and Hispanics. Hispanics are more numerous, accounting for 28 percent of the population, while blacks make up only 12 percent. Fifty-seven percent of Texans are white, and they are expected to become a minority here by 2025.

Areas dominated by minorities are very likely to be poor. In none of the thirty-one Hispanic-majority districts in the state house of representatives is household income above the state average, and it is above the average in only one of the eleven black-majority districts—the One Hundred Eleventh District in downtown Dallas. By comparison, income is above average in forty-five of the ninety-six white-majority districts.

Hispanic districts are concentrated most heavily, but not exclusively, along the Mexican border. Blacks and Hispanics live in close proximity to each other in major cities, such as Houston, but are divided politically by gerrymandering; politicians now use computers to sort neighborhoods down to the street level, placing Hispanics in one district and blacks in another. As a consequence, Dallas, Houston, and San Antonio have some of the most tortuously drawn district boundaries in the country. The effort to create two new black-majority congressional districts and one new Hispanic-majority district was so clumsy that the U.S. Supreme Court ordered the map redrawn.

Those tortuous districts have helped Democrats increase their majority in the state house of representatives, though Republicans have captured the senate. Texas gained three new congressional seats in the last round of reapportionment and stands to gain two more in the next.

TEXAS
State Senate Districts

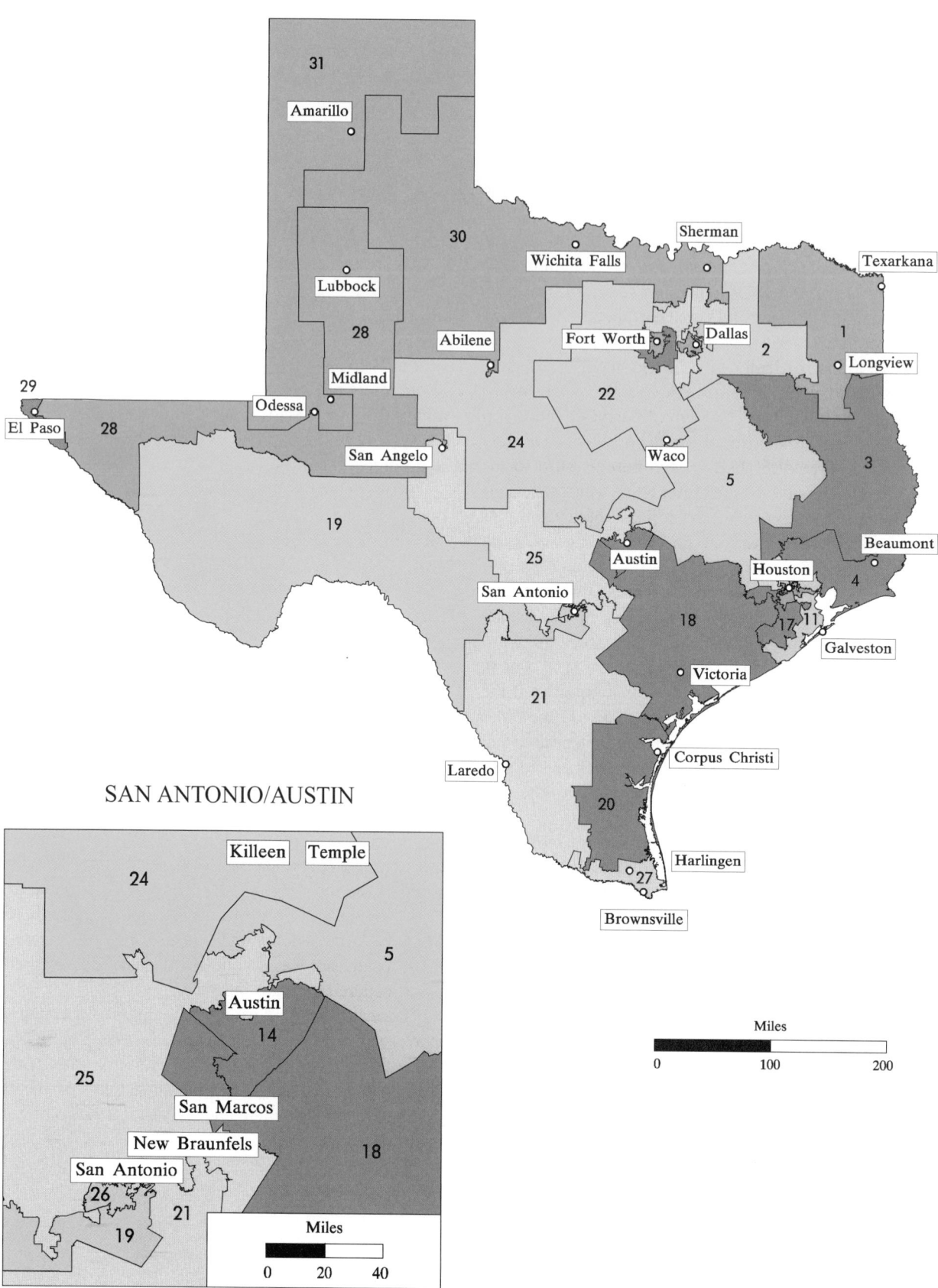

SAN ANTONIO/AUSTIN

Population Growth   ▨ 2% to 8%   ▨ 10% to 13%   ▨ 15% to 20%   ▨ 22% to 30%

DALLAS/FORT WORTH

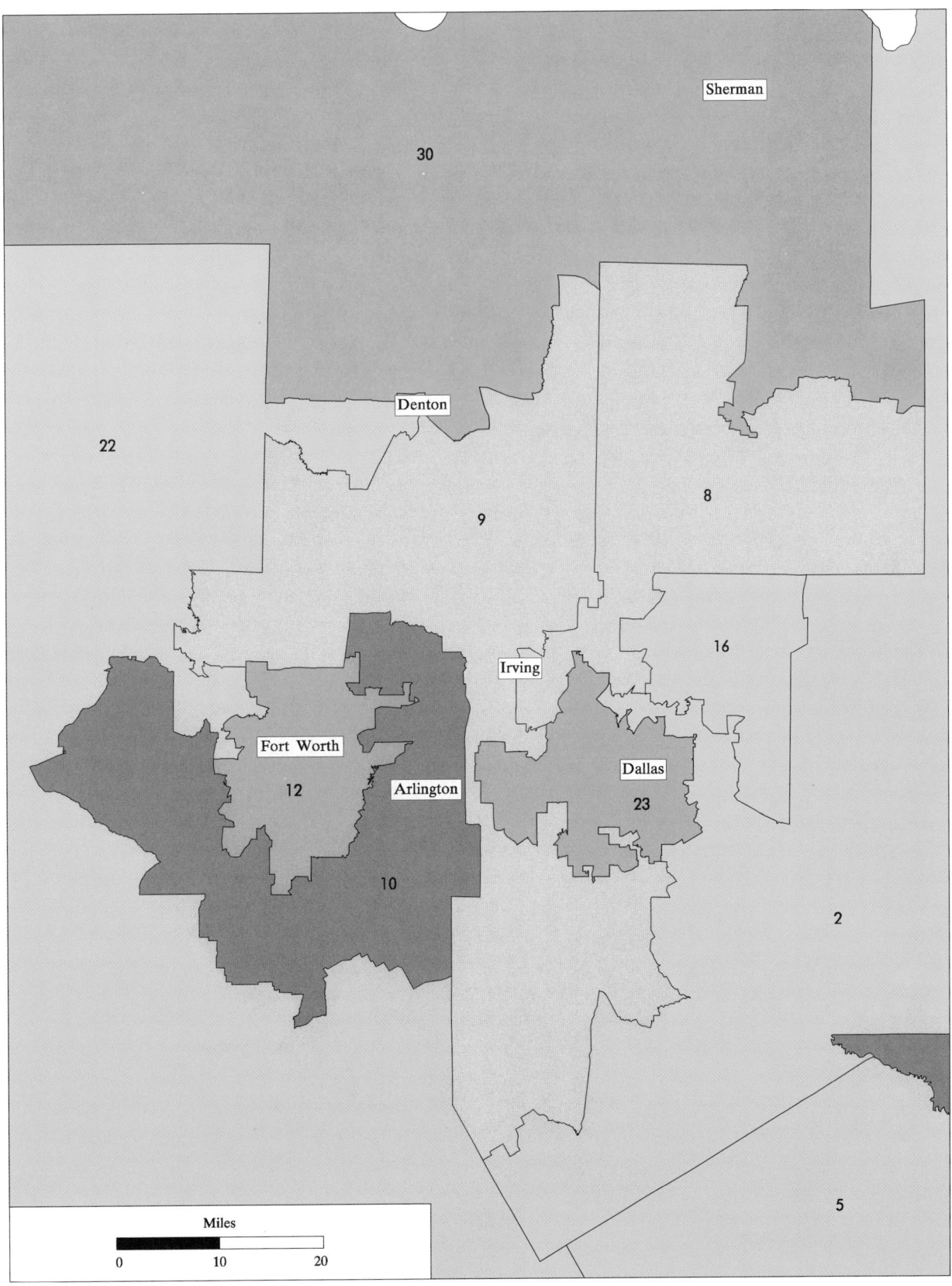

Sherman

30

Denton

22

9

8

16

Irving

Fort Worth

12

Arlington

Dallas

23

10

2

5

Miles

0   10   20

Population Growth   ■ 2% to 8%   □ 10% to 13%   ■ 15% to 20%   □ 22% to 30%

HOUSTON

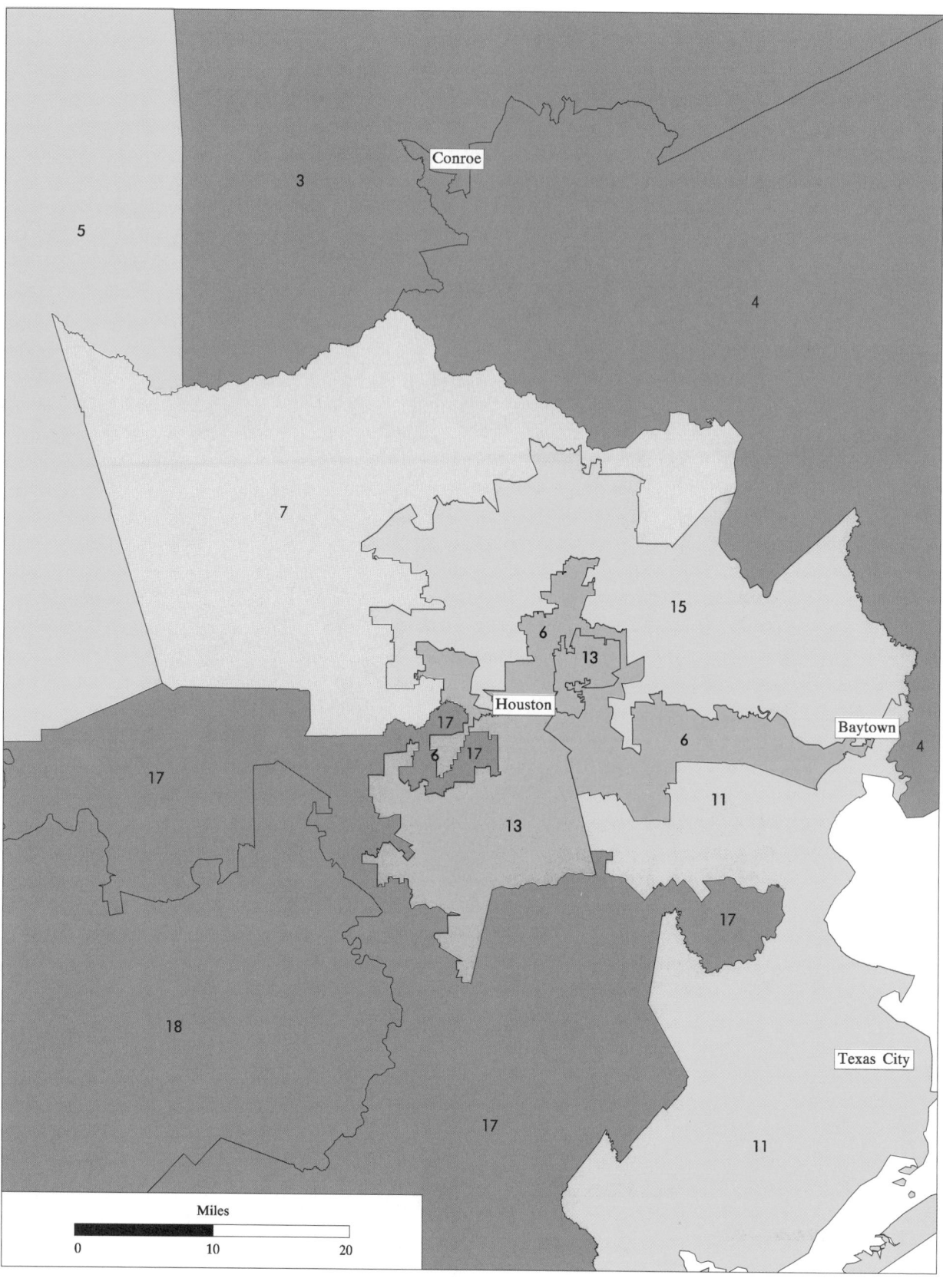

Conroe

3

5

4

7

15

6

13

Houston

17

6   17

6

Baytown

4

17

13

11

18

17

17

Texas City

11

Miles

0   10   20

Population Growth   2% to 8%   10% to 13%   15% to 20%   22% to 30%

Texas State Senate Districts: Demographic Data

Senate District	Population		Average HH Income		District Type	Unempl. Rate	College Educ.	White (non-Hispanic)		African American		Asian American		Hispanic American	
	1997	+/-	($)	+/-		(%)	(%)	(%)	+/-	(%)	+/-	(%)	+/-	(%)	+/-
Texas	19,384,303	14	48,030	35	M	7	35	57	8	12	15	2	49	28	26
1	604,979	7	39,188	31	R	7	30	77	5	19	12	0	29	3	23
2	624,827	10	39,841	30	M	7	27	64	5	17	17	1	24	17	21
3	653,626	15	38,063	32	R	7	24	79	14	14	18	0	32	6	34
4	635,475	15	48,341	37	M	7	32	75	14	16	10	2	44	6	38
5	617,990	13	38,843	36	R	6	32	68	8	17	14	1	37	13	34
6	525,304	4	35,368	28	U	10	18	21	-23	10	6	2	20	66	16
7	695,188	22	81,991	41	S	4	55	77	17	6	42	5	63	12	45
8	701,163	24	77,549	30	M	4	59	78	19	5	36	4	62	12	43
9	744,185	30	60,911	33	S	4	49	78	25	7	46	4	72	11	48
10	666,327	19	60,281	35	U	4	46	80	14	7	40	4	53	9	52
11	633,103	11	51,370	34	M	6	35	63	5	13	16	3	47	21	27
12	550,940	3	45,316	31	U	7	33	57	-4	20	9	3	40	20	19
13	563,114	8	49,443	37	U	10	41	25	-9	52	11	5	35	17	26
14	675,649	20	49,096	39	U	6	48	59	11	11	26	3	51	26	39
15	644,536	13	43,225	29	U	8	27	43	-2	28	19	4	48	24	37
16	640,484	13	61,988	38	S	4	48	74	8	10	31	5	46	11	33
17	677,179	19	71,050	39	M	4	53	67	11	8	32	9	57	16	39
18	656,358	17	44,091	36	R	6	30	60	10	9	18	3	72	28	29
19	566,433	11	31,258	28	U	12	18	24	-7	7	7	1	20	68	20
20	614,717	16	39,756	34	U	10	25	31	1	2	7	1	32	66	24
21	631,715	24	37,872	35	R	10	23	29	8	2	19	1	45	68	32
22	592,873	10	38,582	32	R	7	27	80	7	7	12	1	37	11	26
23	525,894	2	38,244	29	U	10	24	23	-13	46	3	1	31	29	16
24	601,897	12	36,325	30	R	8	30	70	7	11	18	2	53	16	28
25	736,300	26	59,393	32	M	5	49	77	21	2	32	2	66	19	47
26	560,476	11	34,237	26	U	10	28	24	-8	6	9	1	39	69	19
27	676,034	25	33,113	32	U	14	19	14	11	0	19	0	49	85	28
28	584,692	4	39,448	31	U	7	29	55	-3	6	3	1	27	38	18
29	638,526	17	36,199	22	U	11	26	22	3	3	19	1	48	74	22
30	571,336	7	39,270	31	M	6	30	81	4	6	13	1	40	11	20
31	573,012	6	46,725	37	U	6	32	72	2	4	11	1	39	22	18

Note: U=urban, S=suburban, R=rural, M=mixed, HH=households.

TEXAS
State House Districts

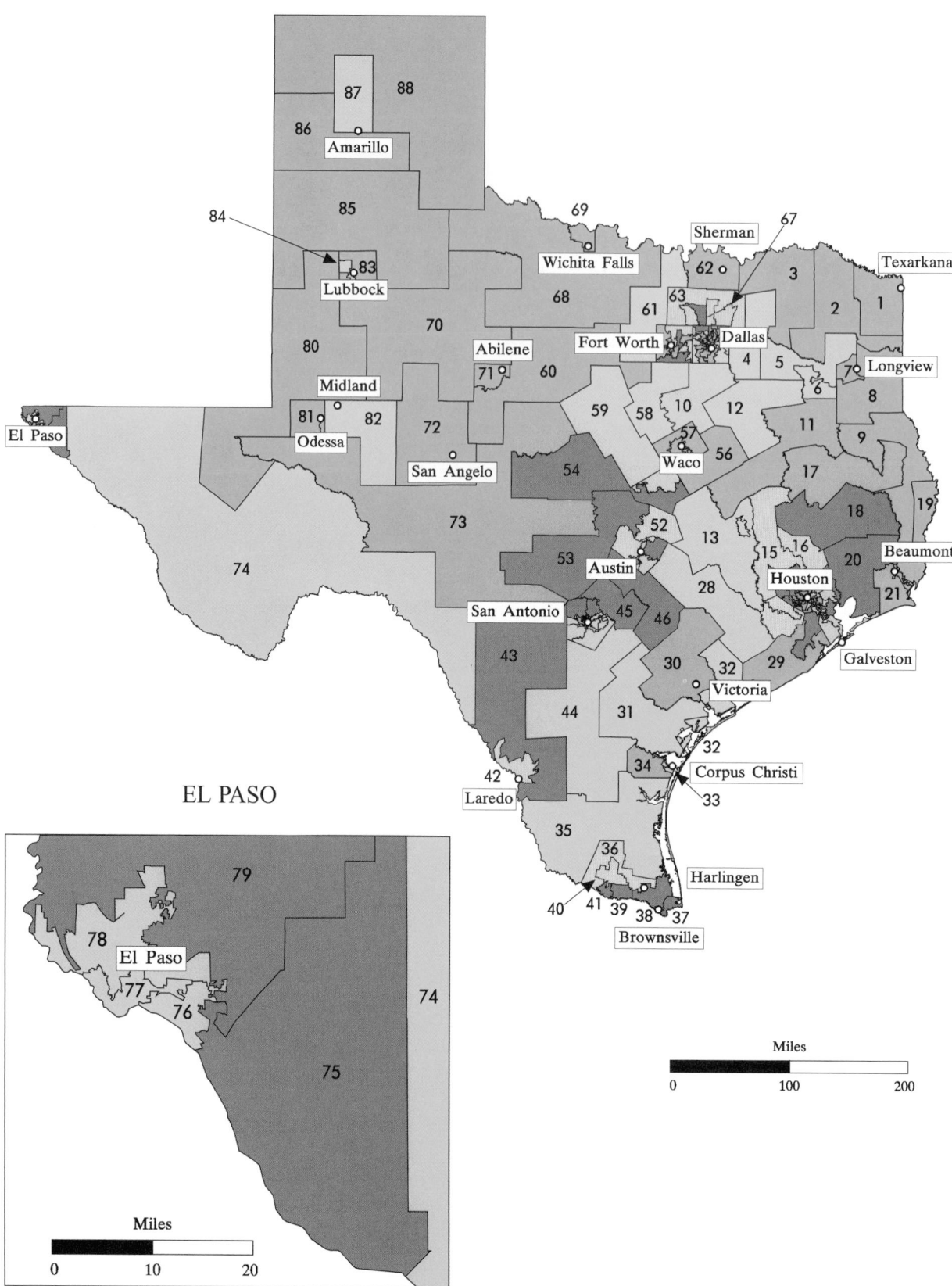

EL PASO

Population Growth   ▢ -4% to 8%   ▢ 9% to 18%   ▢ 19% to 30%   ▢ 32% to 50%

DALLAS/FORT WORTH

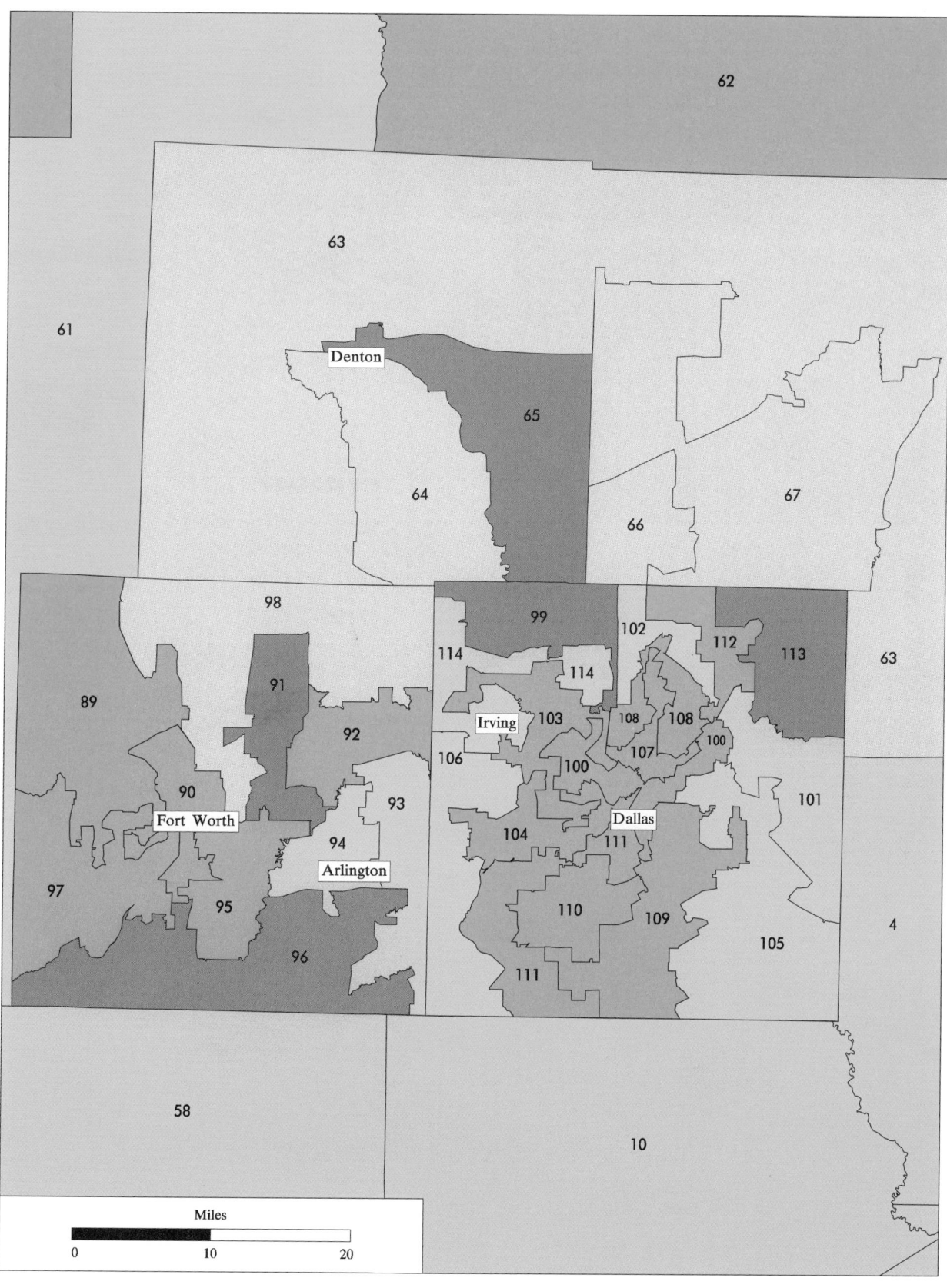

Denton

Fort Worth

Arlington

Irving

Dallas

Population Growth   ▨ -4% to 8%   ▢ 9% to 18%   ▨ 19% to 30%   ▢ 32% to 50%

Miles
0   10   20

HOUSTON 1

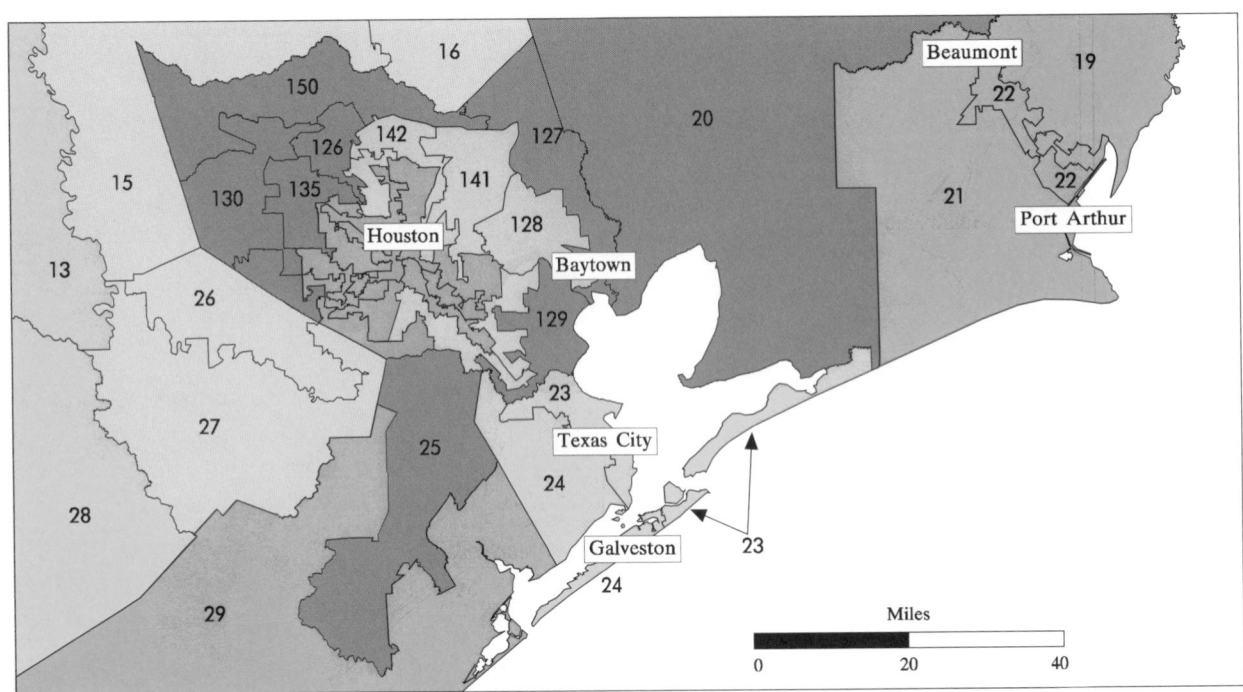

HOUSTON 2

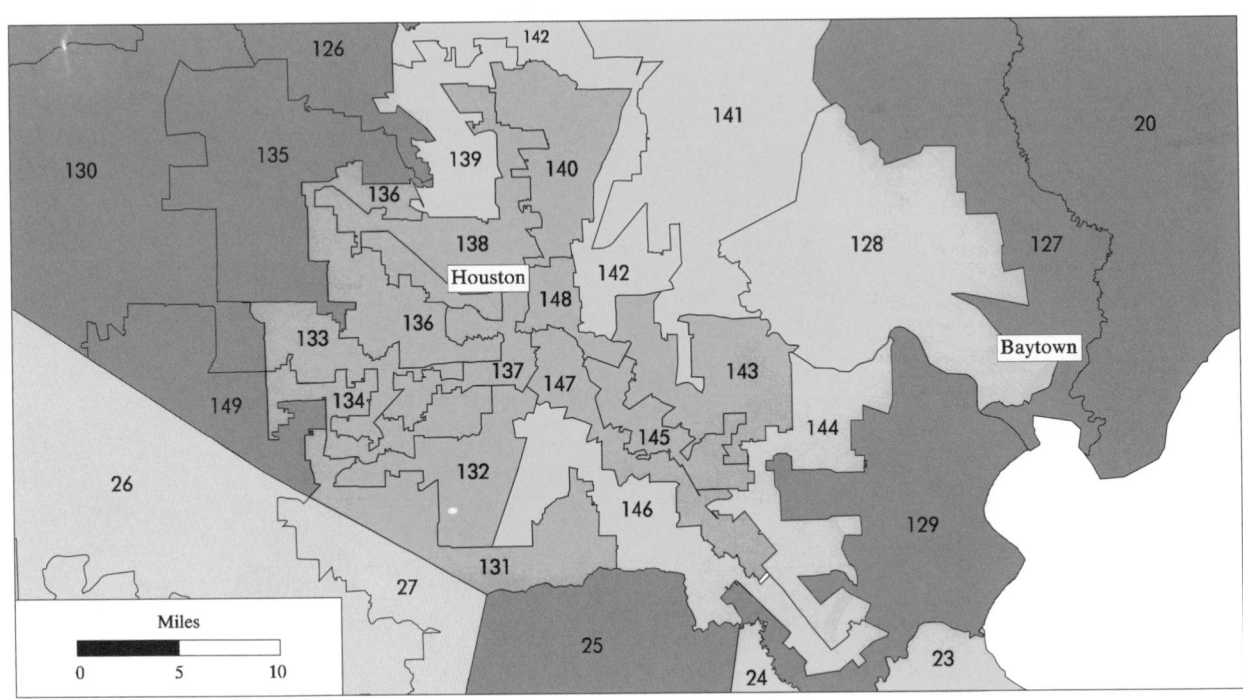

Population Growth ▢ -4% to 8%   ▢ 9% to 18%   ▢ 19% to 30%   ▢ 32% to 50%

AUSTIN

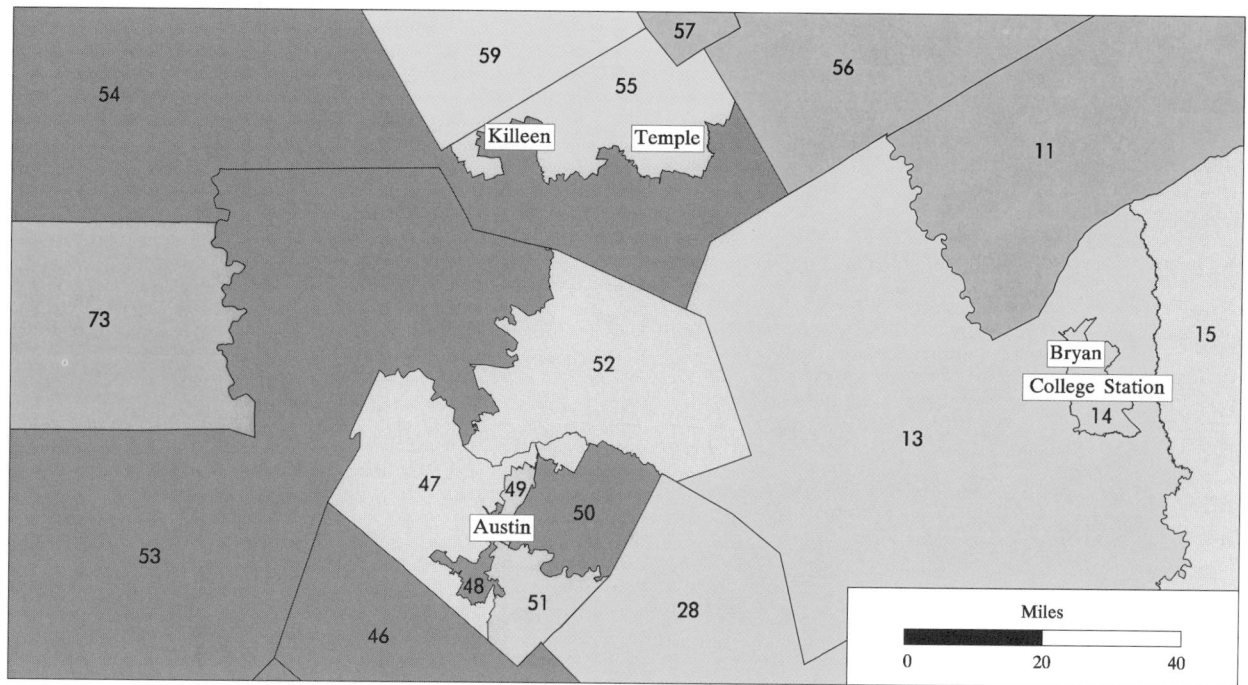

SAN ANTONIO

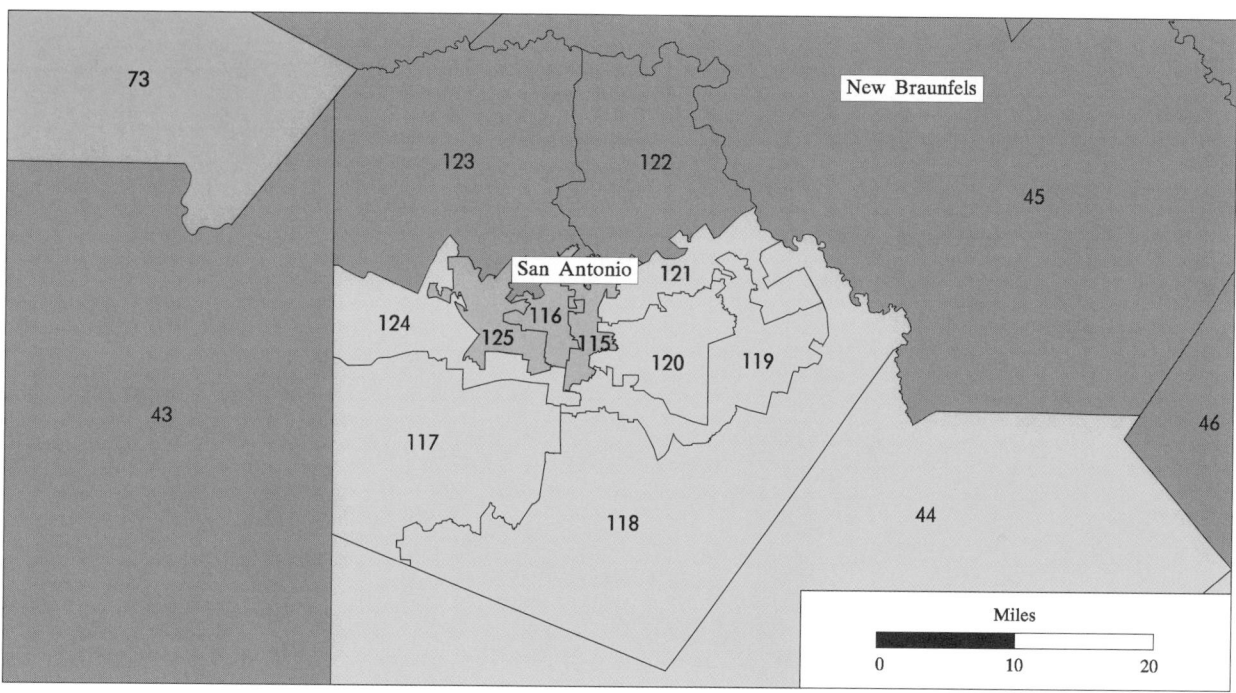

Population Growth   ☐ -4% to 8%   ☐ 9% to 18%   ☐ 19% to 30%   ☐ 32% to 50%

Texas State House Districts: Demographic Data

House District	Population 1997	+/-	Average HH Income ($)	+/-	District Type	Unempl. Rate (%)	College Educ. (%)	White (non-Hispanic) (%)	+/-	African American (%)	+/-	Asian American (%)	+/-	Hispanic American (%)	+/-
Texas	19,384,303	14	48,030	35	M	7	35	57	8	12	15	2	49	28	26
1	116,076	4	35,722	23	M	7	28	75	2	22	9	0	26	2	24
2	117,246	8	35,249	30	R	8	21	78	7	16	10	0	-22	5	20
3	117,283	7	36,471	34	R	7	23	86	7	11	11	0	7	3	22
4	131,925	13	40,617	26	R	7	26	80	11	13	19	1	42	6	31
5	120,747	9	34,108	30	R	9	21	70	8	22	8	0	-7	7	26
6	124,605	14	49,146	34	M	5	43	82	10	12	32	1	50	4	30
7	118,027	7	41,828	30	U	7	35	75	5	19	13	1	39	4	24
8	123,854	5	35,747	29	R	8	25	71	2	25	10	0	-4	3	22
9	123,343	5	34,940	36	R	7	25	77	3	18	11	0	16	4	21
10	128,742	15	45,383	34	R	6	26	75	11	10	20	0	23	14	32
11	125,354	7	35,605	37	R	7	21	70	4	21	10	0	22	9	21
12	125,711	10	36,097	31	R	8	22	80	9	14	12	0	25	6	24
13	121,688	9	39,653	33	R	6	27	73	6	15	14	0	20	11	25
14	117,738	11	40,224	42	U	6	54	66	6	12	17	5	37	17	28
15	155,424	32	56,737	39	S	5	38	76	32	13	20	1	93	10	47
16	159,698	36	44,497	24	S	6	25	84	33	6	43	1	74	9	56
17	119,346	8	36,745	28	R	7	23	72	5	19	11	0	25	8	26
18	142,633	24	33,248	25	R	8	24	73	22	18	26	0	31	8	40
19	114,552	5	41,658	33	S	8	26	87	4	10	12	1	39	3	24
20	136,141	19	42,111	38	R	8	20	82	17	12	27	0	18	5	41
21	119,501	5	54,488	36	U	5	41	81	1	12	27	1	52	5	28
22	108,503	-2	29,077	26	U	12	22	30	-14	58	1	4	27	8	15
23	120,604	12	45,834	30	U	7	37	61	6	18	13	3	48	18	26
24	122,372	12	49,996	29	S	6	36	65	6	18	19	1	43	15	32
25	143,192	21	54,433	27	S	5	37	74	16	5	27	2	60	19	38
26	168,464	43	84,719	33	S	4	59	65	34	9	48	13	86	13	57
27	148,018	37	47,973	29	S	6	32	31	17	34	42	3	80	31	55
28	128,536	10	39,363	37	R	6	23	65	6	13	13	0	6	21	24
29	118,907	8	39,908	21	R	7	22	60	1	15	14	1	30	24	23
30	127,823	8	43,744	40	M	6	25	60	2	7	11	0	17	32	23
31	128,165	13	37,215	36	R	9	23	45	3	2	5	0	21	53	22
32	139,877	17	48,123	35	U	6	38	64	9	3	20	2	48	29	38
33	120,785	9	42,117	34	U	8	31	29	-9	3	22	1	35	67	18
34	114,686	3	38,227	35	U	10	21	29	-8	6	-6	0	0	65	10
35	130,837	17	29,781	38	R	15	15	12	-6	1	-7	0	0	86	22
36	149,784	38	30,303	27	S	14	16	16	19	0	29	0	30	84	43
37	130,471	21	28,410	25	U	16	18	8	-9	0	2	0	28	92	24
38	137,628	28	36,962	42	S	12	21	18	17	0	18	0	47	81	30
39	138,957	30	27,840	31	S	17	14	12	17	0	-6	0	47	88	33
40	138,984	33	31,539	27	U	12	21	11	7	0	23	0	62	88	37
41	134,616	25	36,793	31	U	13	21	15	14	0	36	0	61	84	27
42	145,303	33	41,949	53	U	10	23	5	18	0	47	0	64	94	34
43	137,246	24	31,403	35	R	12	16	25	10	0	-6	0	-2	74	29
44	125,799	15	35,640	37	R	9	18	36	8	0	0	0	-3	63	18
45	146,778	26	43,459	29	R	6	31	66	20	3	23	1	51	30	40
46	132,917	22	42,156	41	R	7	32	58	15	6	19	1	44	35	35
47	158,897	32	85,660	44	S	4	63	85	28	3	49	3	71	9	54
48	136,243	19	56,898	39	U	5	54	68	10	5	39	3	49	24	43
49	134,532	14	41,095	35	U	6	55	69	6	7	31	6	48	17	37
50	135,091	22	38,220	38	U	8	35	40	10	31	22	2	53	26	43

Note: U=urban, S=suburban, R=rural, M=mixed, HH=households.

Texas State House Districts: Demographic Data (cont.)

House District	Population		Average HH Income		District Type	Unempl. Rate	College Educ.	White (non-Hispanic)		African American		Asian American		Hispanic American	
	1997	+/-	($)	+/-		(%)	(%)	(%)	+/-	(%)	+/-	(%)	+/-	(%)	+/-
Texas	19,384,303	14	48,030	35	M	7	35	57	8	12	15	2	49	28	26
51	132,013	18	31,023	30	U	8	33	38	2	10	24	3	46	49	31
52	174,774	47	54,216	41	S	4	44	75	42	6	57	2	101	17	69
53	153,116	30	42,476	32	R	5	32	83	27	1	32	0	41	16	48
54	139,484	24	35,384	32	M	10	31	61	15	18	37	4	72	17	42
55	124,080	12	43,297	37	U	7	39	68	9	15	3	2	40	14	30
56	121,468	7	44,031	35	M	5	38	77	5	13	13	1	39	9	21
57	120,274	5	33,933	37	U	8	23	59	-1	22	8	0	26	18	23
58	135,307	15	41,972	25	S	7	25	87	13	2	21	0	32	9	33
59	128,129	13	34,633	29	R	8	28	73	9	13	19	2	54	12	32
60	121,038	7	38,907	35	R	7	24	88	6	1	1	0	29	9	19
61	134,466	17	45,071	32	R	6	26	92	16	1	19	0	48	6	36
62	118,429	7	38,877	25	U	7	29	88	6	7	12	1	36	4	23
63	152,586	32	51,040	17	M	4	39	84	28	5	45	1	79	9	57
64	154,963	37	51,216	24	S	4	49	83	34	5	33	3	72	8	61
65	141,986	28	54,213	24	S	4	55	80	23	6	42	5	79	9	47
66	162,358	48	85,492	25	S	2	70	86	44	3	59	6	98	5	79
67	169,543	50	59,108	17	S	4	51	84	46	4	57	3	103	9	73
68	112,046	0	37,563	37	R	6	23	89	-1	3	0	0	8	8	8
69	113,716	5	40,414	33	U	7	32	76	1	10	10	2	41	11	24
70	110,127	0	37,721	38	R	7	22	68	-4	4	3	0	8	27	12
71	118,102	3	41,003	29	U	7	38	74	-1	7	7	2	35	17	19
72	118,777	5	40,371	33	U	8	29	66	0	4	8	1	30	29	19
73	128,144	8	34,441	29	R	6	25	74	5	2	2	0	-6	23	17
74	138,711	18	29,836	27	R	14	19	21	0	1	7	0	12	77	24
75	143,191	21	30,923	16	U	12	15	11	-4	1	10	0	38	88	25
76	134,529	14	32,621	23	U	12	19	13	-3	2	13	0	41	84	17
77	135,164	17	27,800	27	U	13	19	12	-1	2	16	1	46	85	19
78	139,071	13	53,075	24	U	7	48	50	7	7	6	3	47	40	21
79	142,773	23	32,011	12	U	10	28	25	1	5	18	2	45	68	33
80	117,177	-1	42,692	45	R	8	18	53	-7	3	-4	0	-7	44	7
81	122,145	4	36,734	21	U	8	23	60	-2	5	5	1	27	34	16
82	122,507	9	57,695	38	U	6	40	66	4	8	13	1	42	25	22
83	107,674	0	31,470	26	U	9	24	44	-10	13	5	1	21	41	12
84	125,487	9	51,202	32	U	4	50	81	4	3	23	2	40	14	42
85	111,290	1	38,519	44	R	7	20	53	-5	4	-2	0	-3	42	10
86	122,356	8	49,407	31	U	5	41	82	6	1	9	1	40	15	16
87	129,626	12	39,260	44	U	8	25	64	6	8	15	3	44	24	26
88	114,722	1	43,146	43	R	5	26	83	-1	2	2	0	-3	13	13
89	124,018	5	41,748	26	S	7	29	78	-1	4	24	2	43	15	30
90	109,403	-4	29,008	24	U	11	15	26	-28	17	6	2	16	54	10
91	144,927	25	55,347	34	S	4	41	81	21	9	34	2	69	7	58
92	126,827	7	57,420	33	S	4	47	83	2	5	34	4	45	8	43
93	133,660	12	46,327	29	U	5	43	63	0	14	32	5	46	17	48
94	130,541	11	61,304	31	U	5	52	80	5	7	38	5	44	8	43
95	112,719	-1	31,991	25	U	11	18	26	-19	60	4	1	13	13	22
96	151,075	28	61,769	35	U	4	47	78	20	9	56	3	73	9	69
97	125,546	7	68,718	34	U	4	57	83	3	6	35	3	51	7	29
98	162,142	38	72,641	47	S	4	45	86	35	2	51	3	66	8	60
99	145,006	22	69,584	39	S	4	56	70	14	7	40	6	65	17	43
100	107,515	1	35,895	28	U	12	26	32	-7	49	3	2	25	17	11

Note: U=urban, S=suburban, R=rural, M=mixed, HH=households.

Texas State House Districts: Demographic Data (cont.)

House District	Population 1997	+/-	Average HH Income ($)	+/-	District Type	Unempl. Rate (%)	College Educ. (%)	White (non-Hispanic) (%)	+/-	African American (%)	+/-	Asian American (%)	+/-	Hispanic American (%)	+/-
Texas	19,384,303	14	48,030	35	M	7	35	57	8	12	15	2	49	28	26
101	138,947	18	58,051	41	S	4	40	78	12	7	42	4	55	11	40
102	126,511	11	80,484	35	U	4	62	70	2	12	30	7	42	11	42
103	120,733	2	41,877	28	U	8	32	33	-22	17	15	4	22	45	22
104	107,426	-1	31,864	18	N.A.	10	11	17	-34	13	4	1	14	68	12
105	133,335	9	39,518	29	U	7	21	60	-2	18	26	1	39	20	36
106	137,193	16	52,506	36	S	5	35	67	7	9	39	4	52	19	34
107	117,110	1	45,745	35	U	7	44	46	-11	16	17	3	19	35	13
108	125,606	3	91,033	41	U	3	69	83	-1	8	28	3	40	6	29
109	119,728	5	41,422	33	U	10	25	33	-4	53	7	1	30	14	24
110	116,551	5	47,034	32	U	8	37	32	-5	58	8	1	37	9	22
111	112,631	5	48,918	39	U	8	33	33	6	51	-1	2	48	13	24
112	127,202	7	67,153	42	S	4	50	76	1	5	22	7	35	11	32
113	150,972	26	66,790	43	S	4	46	75	23	10	36	4	63	10	30
114	130,388	9	78,590	37	U	5	54	74	2	6	33	5	48	15	29
115	113,536	8	30,487	24	U	11	24	24	-8	2	8	1	35	72	15
116	112,452	7	31,511	24	U	9	26	20	-20	3	3	1	29	75	17
117	116,181	9	34,784	31	U	11	20	22	-16	6	5	1	23	70	22
118	116,384	10	30,429	26	U	11	12	26	-5	2	6	0	12	71	16
119	122,407	13	33,889	29	U	11	21	27	-1	7	19	1	56	65	19
120	120,935	13	33,849	33	U	12	25	26	-7	33	9	2	31	39	36
121	119,585	10	60,669	30	U	6	51	68	2	7	16	3	42	23	35
122	140,466	28	63,353	29	U	4	57	73	21	3	22	2	64	22	51
123	131,701	20	59,347	22	U	5	57	64	8	2	26	3	57	31	54
124	122,379	14	39,160	28	U	9	29	25	1	5	12	1	44	68	19
125	118,944	7	39,033	23	U	8	34	28	-6	4	6	1	35	67	14
126	152,249	25	90,335	47	S	4	58	76	19	7	37	6	63	11	50
127	137,349	22	78,086	46	N.A.	4	50	83	18	6	35	2	69	9	40
128	136,604	16	45,515	30	S	8	22	56	6	17	27	2	44	25	33
129	136,488	20	76,726	46	S	4	49	81	16	4	36	4	63	10	30
130	134,129	20	75,744	40	S	3	54	79	15	4	38	4	62	12	38
131	114,366	8	44,175	29	U	9	42	25	-8	53	10	6	37	16	21
132	112,441	4	68,788	44	U	6	57	47	-7	32	12	6	34	16	20
133	125,796	5	82,228	45	U	4	63	68	-4	5	21	8	39	18	32
134	128,786	8	57,775	39	U	6	53	49	-6	17	17	7	35	25	32
135	160,141	29	67,124	36	S	4	51	71	21	7	48	7	71	14	48
136	131,369	6	110,153	46	U	4	57	66	-4	7	20	6	47	21	34
137	112,936	3	49,643	42	U	7	46	41	-13	9	4	4	20	45	20
138	121,035	7	41,042	31	U	8	24	43	-9	22	15	2	38	32	30
139	111,676	16	39,293	25	U	9	31	24	-8	50	20	8	49	18	40
140	118,234	8	30,727	20	U	10	9	27	-20	13	16	2	33	57	26
141	117,137	9	38,119	32	U	11	20	29	1	51	8	1	46	18	27
142	126,684	13	33,308	35	U	11	22	23	5	51	7	3	54	23	35
143	113,505	4	32,082	25	U	10	9	24	-16	4	4	1	21	71	13
144	125,021	9	57,297	43	S	5	41	71	3	3	18	4	49	21	28
145	109,372	2	31,468	21	U	10	14	18	-31	5	3	3	16	73	14
146	118,098	9	42,566	35	U	11	33	28	0	54	9	6	44	12	22
147	110,267	2	33,853	28	U	11	27	24	-15	50	3	4	31	22	20
148	111,267	2	36,102	34	U	9	17	21	-19	9	5	2	29	67	10
149	143,781	24	56,613	28	U	5	52	49	6	13	34	21	54	17	48
150	147,862	24	61,791	35	S	5	42	81	20	7	42	2	67	10	47

Note: U=urban, S=suburban, R=rural, M=mixed, HH=households.

UTAH

Legend has it that in 1846, when Mormon settlers first looked over the crest of the Wasatch Mountains into the Valley of the Great Salt Lake, Brigham Young struck his cane on the ground and declared, "This is the place." Having endured a thousand-mile march across plains and mountains, Young and his band were nothing if not people who knew where they were going and who recognized when they got there.

The Mormons raised orchards on the thin strip of land between the mountains and the lake, possibly the deadest body of water on the continent. Young wanted to name his state Deseret, the word from the Book of Mormon meaning "Land of the Honeybee," thus revealing much about his conception of the role his Latter-day Saints would play in their new society. The beehive symbol remains ubiquitous on state road signs and even the Salt Lake sidewalks.

Although Young sought safety in Utah, he did not seek isolation. Mormons were great traders and built their Zion as a distribution point for the vast territory beyond. Salt Lake City is not large (about the same size as Arlington, Virginia), but it is strategically placed, almost exactly equidistant from Seattle, Portland, San Francisco, Los Angeles, and San Diego. In 2002, it will host the Winter Olympics.

Mormonism may be a fundamentalist religion, but it is a peculiarly American kind of fundamentalism, embracing rather than resisting technology. The Golden Spike completing the Transcontinental Railroad was driven at Promontory Point, about fifty miles north of the Mormon Temple. Eventually, 70 percent of all east-west railroad traffic went through the state. Today, Utah is one of the great high-tech areas of the West, home to Novell and WordPerfect, as well as Morton Thiokol, maker of rocket engines. In the rotunda of the state capitol is a statue of Philo T. Farnsworth, the "Father of Television."

Utah has grown by 18 percent in each of the past two decades, giving it the fourth-fastest rate of growth in the 1990s. The state is entirely rural except for a strip running along the edge of the Wasatch from Ogden to Provo, where more than three-quarters of the state's population lives. That strip is filling up, pushing development northeast toward the Wyoming border, although the fastest growth has occurred around Cedar City and St. George, in the far southwest, miles from anywhere. A house district in downtown Provo is the only one to have lost population during the decade.

Utah's population is mostly white, but there is a mix of minority groups: a few African Americans, some Asians, some Hispanics, some Indians. It has the highest literacy rate and, owing to the number of young Mormons who perform church service on foreign missions, one of the most multilingual.

About two-thirds of Utahns are Mormons, and Mormons believe in big families, giving Utah the largest average household size in the country. It is also the youngest state, with the lowest median age (26.8 years old, versus 34.3 for the rest of the country), and the state with the greater share of its population under age five, sparking the old joke that the most popular means of transportation here is the baby carriage. In two house districts, one outside of Salt Lake and the other in Provo, only 5 percent of the population is over age fifty-five, making them, by that measure, the two youngest districts in the country.

Even though the percentage of elderly in Utah is small, when combined with the number of children it gives Utah the highest "dependency ratio" in the country—that is, the highest ratio of working people to persons either too young or too old to work. In a state like Pennsylvania, this might provoke intergenerational warfare, but Utah seems to bear it happily.

The legislature is overwhelmingly Republican and has remained so throughout the decade. Utah has voted for a Democratic presidential candidate just once since 1948. In 1992, Bill Clinton finished third here, behind Ross Perot.

UTAH
State Senate Districts

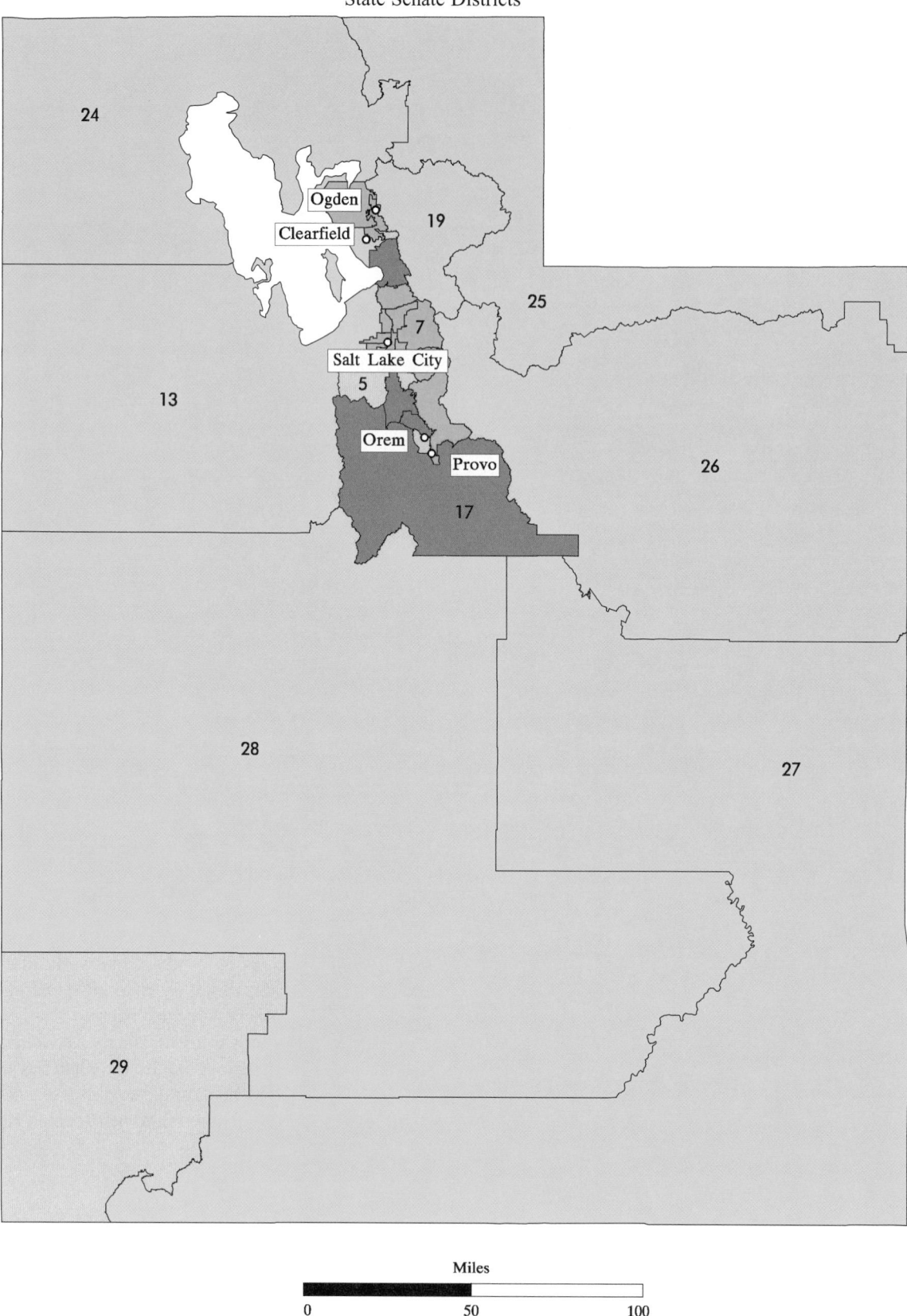

Miles

0   50   100

Population Growth   ■ 4% to 13%   □ 14% to 23%   ■ 28% to 35%   □ 42% to 48%

SALT LAKE CITY

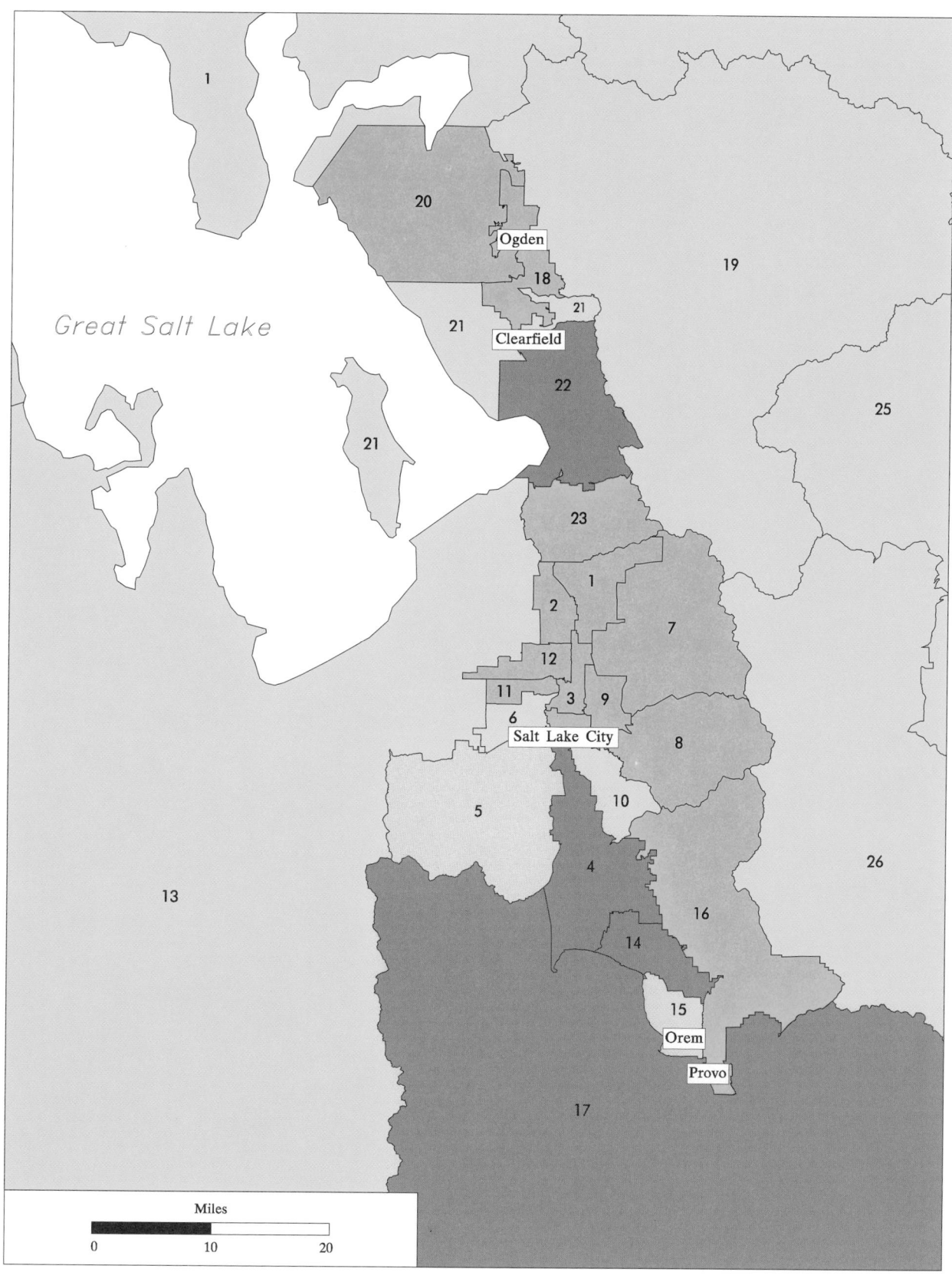

Great Salt Lake

Population Growth | 4% to 13% | 14% to 23% | 28% to 35% | 42% to 48%

Utah State Senate Districts: Demographic Data

Senate District	Population 1997	+/-	Average HH Income ($)	+/-	District Type	Unempl. Rate (%)	College Educ. (%)	White (non-Hispanic) (%)	+/-	African American (%)	+/-	Asian American (%)	+/-	Hispanic American (%)	+/-
Utah	2,034,380	18	49,457	41	S	5	42	90	16	1	39	2	45	6	40
1	64,114	12	49,477	49	U	5	58	83	7	2	51	6	41	7	40
2	64,127	11	33,669	36	U	7	29	65	1	4	46	8	41	21	37
3	66,786	10	38,462	37	S	5	34	85	5	1	51	3	41	9	48
4	74,769	35	54,088	45	S	4	39	92	33	0	48	2	59	5	45
5	88,877	42	55,516	48	S	4	38	92	41	0	63	2	74	5	52
6	70,002	18	52,372	41	S	4	36	89	16	0	47	3	51	7	43
7	64,399	7	69,617	41	U	3	60	95	6	0	37	2	43	3	39
8	66,545	10	65,638	50	S	4	47	93	8	0	40	2	45	5	35
9	65,236	11	60,287	39	S	4	52	94	9	0	38	2	46	3	47
10	72,780	20	77,697	51	S	4	51	95	19	0	51	2	51	3	28
11	62,910	6	43,344	37	S	6	32	85	2	1	45	4	35	9	40
12	63,406	13	41,504	42	S	7	27	83	9	1	53	5	45	9	37
13	69,258	15	41,315	28	S	6	28	85	12	1	34	2	43	11	38
14	78,855	32	55,285	53	S	5	47	95	31	0	36	1	73	3	52
15	70,148	16	54,824	59	U	5	48	92	14	0	32	2	58	5	50
16	68,118	6	47,656	54	U	6	54	91	5	0	23	3	35	4	23
17	83,532	32	47,834	50	S	5	38	94	31	0	19	1	63	4	58
18	68,195	10	41,128	32	U	7	34	80	6	3	29	3	37	13	30
19	66,908	15	47,030	32	U	5	41	92	13	1	35	1	37	5	42
20	63,645	13	49,689	37	S	4	33	91	11	1	42	2	41	6	51
21	68,096	18	45,002	33	S	5	35	86	15	3	26	3	45	8	40
22	77,579	28	60,858	33	S	4	49	95	27	1	40	1	66	3	47
23	59,481	4	59,179	35	S	4	48	95	3	0	-8	1	38	3	58
24	64,692	14	49,125	33	R	5	38	93	12	0	0	1	42	4	32
25	69,663	22	42,954	45	R	6	48	92	21	0	42	4	47	3	41
26	72,179	23	49,767	44	R	8	39	91	23	0	-18	0	29	4	36
27	66,914	14	36,231	30	R	9	30	82	14	0	26	0	7	5	27
28	70,740	16	33,293	26	R	6	35	95	15	0	-11	1	22	3	31
29	92,347	48	42,511	44	R	5	39	95	48	0	38	1	74	2	80

Note: U=urban, S=suburban, R=rural, M=mixed, HH=households.

UTAH
State House Districts

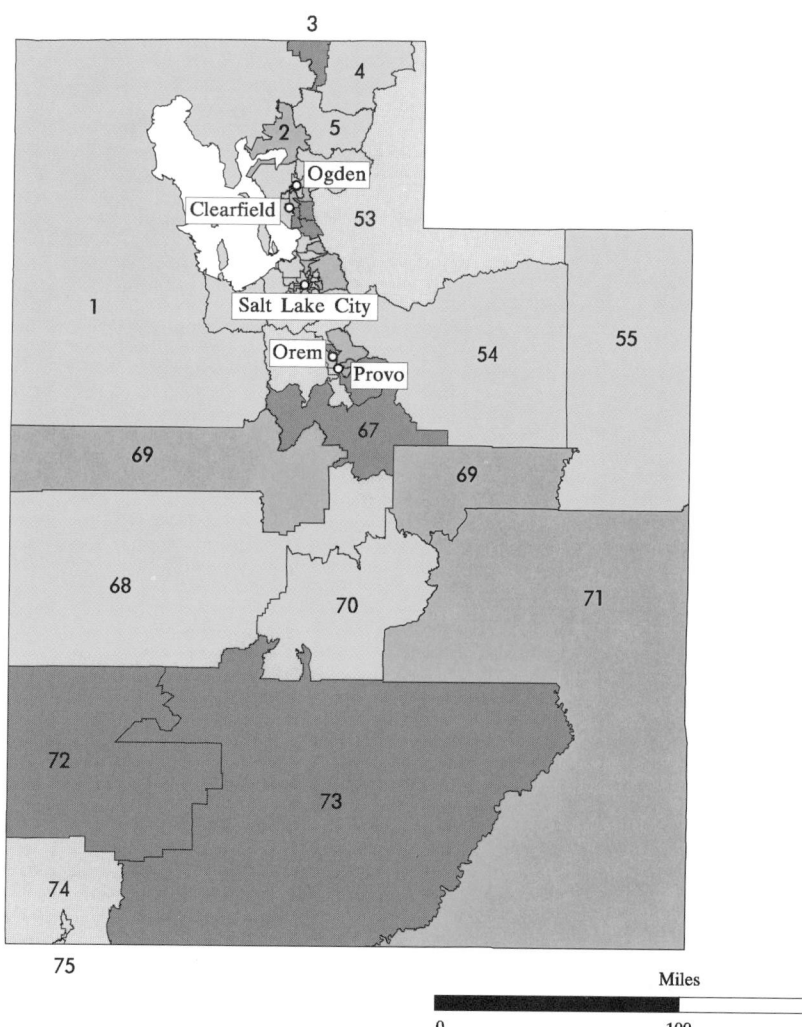

3

4

2

5

Ogden

Clearfield

53

1

Salt Lake City

55

Orem

Provo

54

67

69

69

68

70

71

72

73

74

75

Miles

0   100   200

SALT LAKE CITY 1

23

25

27

28

30

26

31

29

Salt Lake City

36

33

32

35

37

22

34

38

40

41

39

44

42

43

45

52

47

46

48   49

50

51

Miles

0   5   10

PROVO/OREM

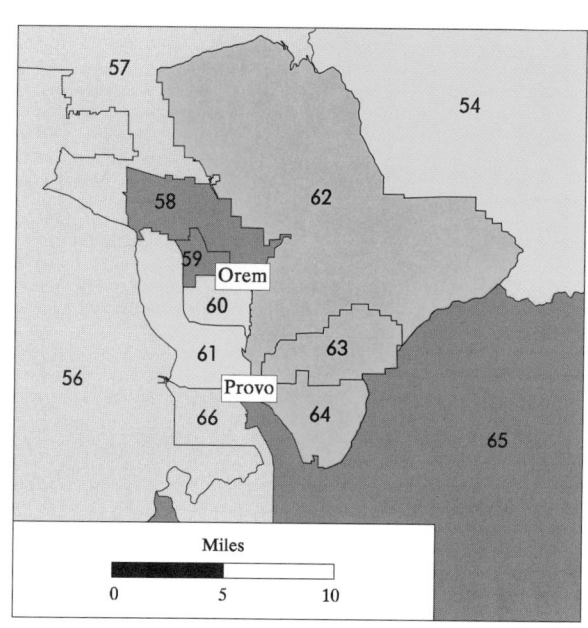

57

54

62

58

59

Orem

60

56

61

63

66

Provo

64

65

Miles

0   5   10

Population Growth   ☐ -4% to 10%   ☐ 11% to 20%   ☐ 22% to 35%   ☐ 38% to 57%

SALT LAKE CITY 2

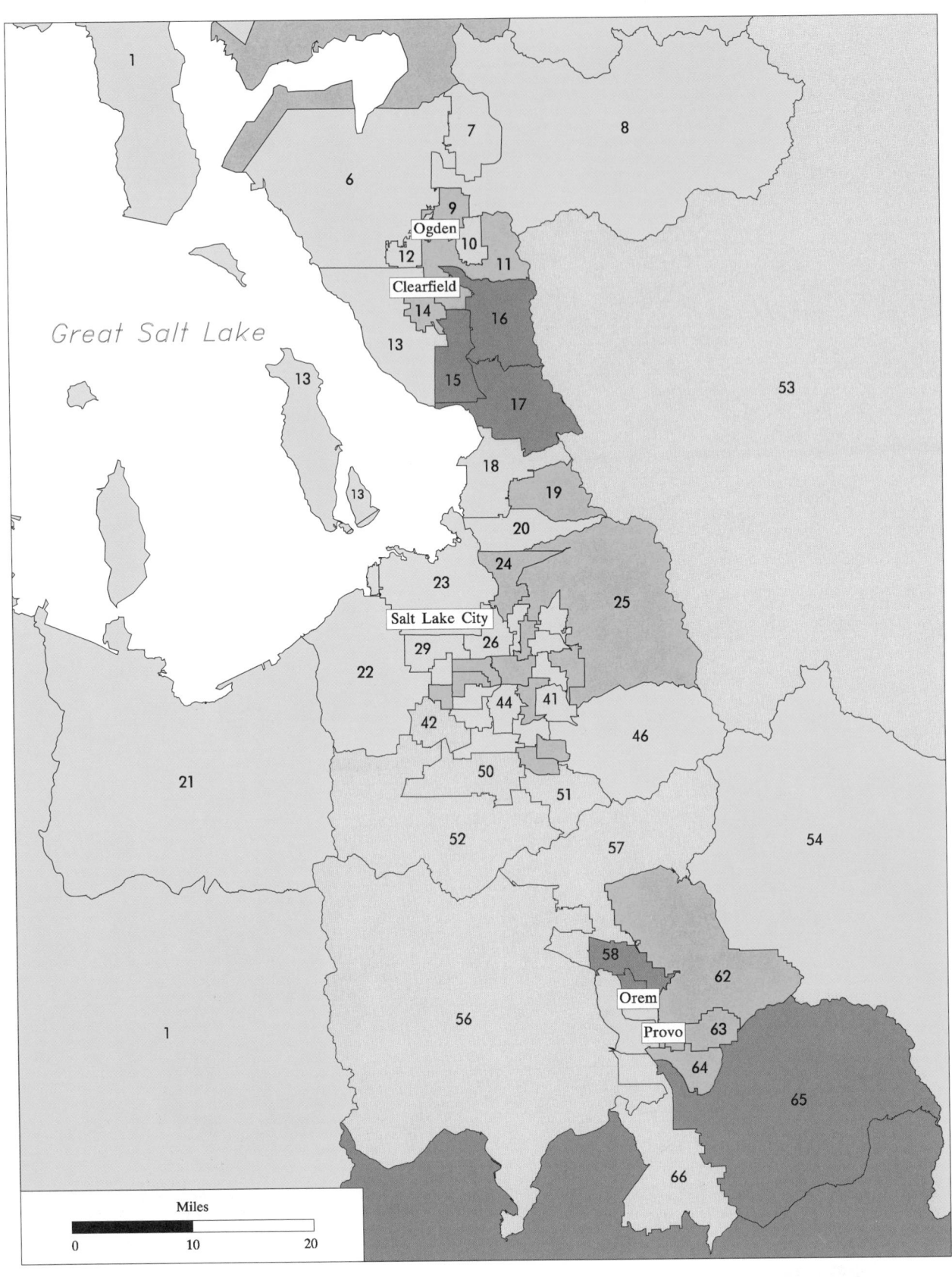

Great Salt Lake

Population Growth   ▨ -4% to 10%   ▢ 11% to 20%   ▨ 22% to 35%   ▢ 38% to 57%

Utah State House Districts: Demographic Data

House District	Population		Average HH Income		District Type	Unempl. Rate	College Educ.	White (non-Hispanic)		African American		Asian American		Hispanic American	
	1997	+/-	($)	+/-		(%)	(%)	(%)	+/-	(%)	+/-	(%)	+/-	(%)	+/-
Utah	2,034,380	18	49,457	41	S	5	42	90	16	1	39	2	45	6	40
1	28,845	15	45,751	33	R	4	33	89	12	1	23	1	46	9	47
2	23,865	9	46,266	23	R	6	38	92	8	0	-33	1	44	5	24
3	26,449	26	45,019	47	R	5	45	94	25	0	53	2	65	3	44
4	24,024	12	42,268	49	R	7	60	87	9	1	43	7	43	3	37
5	26,370	20	50,595	44	R	5	41	94	19	0	6	2	37	3	44
6	27,228	14	51,565	38	S	5	34	94	13	0	18	1	43	4	57
7	26,358	16	51,597	35	S	5	40	92	14	2	36	1	42	5	36
8	27,168	13	41,671	32	U	5	36	90	10	1	41	1	31	7	43
9	24,624	4	24,511	17	U	12	21	63	-5	5	27	3	31	27	28
10	24,350	13	54,193	36	U	5	50	91	11	1	40	3	45	5	39
11	29,196	8	50,159	35	S	4	37	88	6	3	30	3	35	5	32
12	24,143	17	51,034	35	S	4	33	89	14	1	48	2	42	7	53
13	31,852	17	47,767	32	S	5	35	89	14	1	31	2	46	7	54
14	19,581	7	38,536	29	S	7	27	79	3	5	15	4	32	10	31
15	28,177	23	40,464	31	S	6	32	86	21	3	40	3	52	8	34
16	33,846	35	67,536	34	S	4	48	93	34	1	60	2	77	3	53
17	26,804	24	61,586	33	S	3	54	97	24	0	22	1	64	2	41
18	25,307	14	56,550	34	S	4	49	96	13	0	26	1	52	2	54
19	22,989	0	60,534	37	S	4	50	96	-1	0	-36	1	31	3	45
20	25,487	11	61,989	34	S	4	47	95	9	0	16	2	44	3	81
21	25,491	14	40,750	25	R	8	29	88	13	0	30	1	41	9	21
22	28,505	14	41,955	31	S	5	29	87	11	1	49	2	50	9	43
23	27,393	14	37,035	37	U	7	26	65	4	4	51	7	45	21	42
24	26,869	10	41,535	53	U	6	48	80	6	2	46	6	42	11	26
25	30,072	10	62,263	50	U	4	68	86	7	1	50	7	42	5	33
26	27,675	14	30,554	31	U	8	17	66	4	3	44	10	42	19	40
27	24,900	11	27,593	32	U	10	27	68	1	3	45	5	39	20	46
28	22,459	11	78,003	47	U	3	68	91	9	0	36	5	38	3	44
29	27,173	13	44,222	38	S	5	28	85	10	1	49	5	40	8	34
30	25,865	9	35,174	36	U	5	38	84	5	1	49	4	39	10	45
31	25,370	13	52,033	38	U	4	52	94	11	1	53	2	51	3	47
32	26,347	15	47,416	40	S	6	33	86	11	1	58	4	47	9	47
33	25,468	8	41,381	44	S	6	31	84	3	2	48	4	36	9	40
34	25,858	8	47,864	38	S	5	37	85	4	1	51	4	38	9	44
35	25,311	4	34,229	28	S	5	33	86	0	2	49	3	33	8	34
36	20,886	2	77,204	43	S	3	60	96	1	0	6	2	35	2	25
37	24,995	11	56,059	31	S	4	53	94	10	0	46	2	49	3	56
38	25,199	7	36,699	25	S	7	26	86	4	1	43	3	40	10	34
39	26,715	12	55,606	40	S	4	39	89	9	1	37	4	44	7	41
40	23,686	6	49,244	39	S	4	48	94	4	0	48	2	40	4	35
41	26,659	15	72,290	44	S	4	54	94	13	0	35	2	52	3	54
42	31,319	38	47,095	36	S	4	35	89	36	0	82	2	78	8	63
43	25,232	13	57,988	53	S	4	36	90	11	0	43	2	43	7	28
44	27,340	13	51,162	51	S	4	35	89	11	1	49	2	48	7	37
45	26,395	12	55,674	51	S	4	44	93	11	0	44	2	46	4	35
46	25,202	12	88,433	48	S	3	54	95	11	0	41	2	53	3	46
47	29,015	19	46,796	52	S	5	33	86	17	0	39	4	44	10	31
48	24,582	9	63,312	45	S	4	47	94	8	0	49	2	42	3	23
49	24,589	9	88,841	47	S	4	57	96	9	0	38	2	42	2	23
50	36,063	51	62,276	49	S	3	41	94	50	0	67	2	82	4	62

Note: U=urban, S=suburban, R=rural, M=mixed, HH=households.

Utah State House Districts: Demographic Data (cont.)

House District	Population		Average HH Income		District Type	Unempl. Rate	College Educ.	White (non-Hispanic)		African American		Asian American		Hispanic American	
	1997	+/-	($)	+/-		(%)	(%)	(%)	+/-	(%)	+/-	(%)	+/-	(%)	+/-
Utah	2,034,380	18	49,457	41	S	5	42	90	16	1	39	2	45	6	40
51	34,672	45	85,355	55	S	3	51	96	44	0	71	1	87	2	51
52	36,263	44	54,625	39	S	3	37	93	42	1	56	1	80	5	79
53	33,255	49	63,392	39	R	6	50	97	48	0	-27	1	76	2	73
54	26,363	16	43,988	41	R	7	33	94	15	0	55	0	-2	3	36
55	25,568	12	35,600	28	R	10	26	86	10	0	-89	0	-8	4	32
56	31,052	44	51,862	49	S	6	38	96	42	0	18	1	101	2	75
57	29,263	42	56,118	50	S	5	46	97	42	0	6	1	79	2	46
58	32,220	34	63,917	55	U	5	51	96	33	0	50	1	75	2	48
59	27,242	22	51,365	52	U	4	46	92	20	0	43	2	68	4	50
60	26,734	19	60,714	61	U	4	52	93	17	0	21	2	65	4	59
61	25,845	17	54,838	61	U	5	47	91	15	0	42	2	60	5	50
62	27,410	8	72,712	66	U	5	59	94	7	0	21	3	40	3	22
63	22,084	-4	33,381	35	U	7	55	91	-6	0	19	4	25	4	9
64	22,994	7	27,262	32	U	7	42	87	4	0	27	4	41	7	33
65	25,498	27	46,639	52	S	5	39	95	26	0	31	1	63	3	44
66	34,999	39	48,716	50	S	5	38	95	38	0	0	1	73	4	71
67	21,692	32	45,856	47	S	4	36	93	30	0	-60	0	46	6	61
68	26,673	14	33,101	22	R	7	38	93	13	0	8	2	30	4	33
69	29,735	6	37,014	26	R	8	31	89	4	0	39	0	3	10	22
70	25,792	14	34,773	23	R	6	34	96	14	0	-50	0	0	2	27
71	24,209	9	33,719	37	R	13	28	64	9	0	-19	0	-42	5	31
72	29,268	32	39,474	42	R	7	40	94	31	0	35	0	31	2	50
73	26,432	23	33,203	32	R	6	32	97	23	0	-36	0	15	2	31
74	38,744	57	45,697	47	R	4	36	96	57	0	38	1	87	2	80
75	31,155	57	40,578	41	R	5	39	94	56	0	43	1	93	3	101

Note: U=urban, S=suburban, R=rural, M=mixed, HH=households.

VERMONT

The physical attributes of a state are immutable, but the characteristics, manners, and values of the people who live there change. So it is that Vermont, birthplace of Calvin Coolidge and long a state whose Republican support was as solid as its granite hills, is now one of the most Democratic.

As John Gunther points out in *Inside USA,* Vermont was also once one of the most belligerent states. It was a sovereign nation from 1777 until 1791, one of only three states ever to be so (Texas and Hawaii are the others), a place where Ethan Allen and the Green Mountain Boys vowed to "make war on all mankind" rather than compromise their independence. (It became the first "new" state, the first to be admitted after the original thirteen.) Vermont sent more troops per capita to fight in the Civil War than any other Northern state and had the highest percentage of volunteers in the army before World War II. The state legislature also did its part, passing a resolution two months before Pearl Harbor in which it declared its own "state of belligerency with Germany." During the 1980s, as it attracted more new residents from out of state, Vermont became a headquarters for Greenpeace and the nuclear freeze movement—belligerency of another kind, perhaps.

The state has grown faster over the last three decades than it ever had before. From 1880 until 1970, it gained fewer than 60,000 people, and twice during that period actually lost population. The state was appreciated anew for its clean environment during the 1970s, much as Oregon was, and population leapt by more than 15 percent, the biggest boom since the 1830s. It jumped another 10 percent during the 1980s.

Growth has slowed during the 1990s, as it has throughout New England, and Vermont slipped from being the forty-eighth most populous state at the start of the decade to forty-ninth at the end. The state is entirely rural except for a small niche in the northwest corner around Burlington. But in what is almost a parody of a trend occurring across the country, Burlington is developing its own tiny metropolitan doughnut; districts in the center of town are losing population while those on the outer edge of the suburbs, including a few rural districts, are growing fastest.

Vermont is usually regarded as quaint rather than poor, but average household income here is the same as it is in South Carolina. The inevitable comparison between Vermont and its neighbor, New Hampshire, is revealing. New Hampshire is considerably more populous (it ranks thirty-eighth in size) and considerably wealthier. Lacking the mills or proximity to the growing Boston suburbs, Vermont has average household income almost 20 percent lower than that across the Connecticut River.

The Burlington suburbs include the wealthiest districts in the state (average income peaks at about $73,000), while the poorest districts are in the center of that city (average income, $25,000), as well as the smaller towns, including St. Johnsbury, in the rural northeast corner of the state.

Vermont has a higher percentage of white residents (more than 98 percent) and fewer African Americans than any other state. It also has the second-fewest Asians, by percentage, and the third-fewest Hispanics. Every one of its 150 house districts is at least 93 percent white.

Montpelier is the least populous state capital (and the only one, it is said, without a McDonald's), yet Vermont has one of the largest legislatures (a 150-member house of representatives) and is one of two that still elects its governor for a two-year term (New Hampshire is the other). Republicans held the state house as recently as 1990 and the senate as recently as 1994, but Democrats made large gains and now hold both chambers of the legislature handily. Vermont was John Anderson's best state in the 1980 presidential election and Ronald Reagan's worst, and it was one of only a handful of states to give Bill Clinton an absolute majority in 1996. Its transformation from 1936, when it was one of only two states to support Alf Landon against Franklin Roosevelt, seems complete.

VERMONT
State Senate Districts

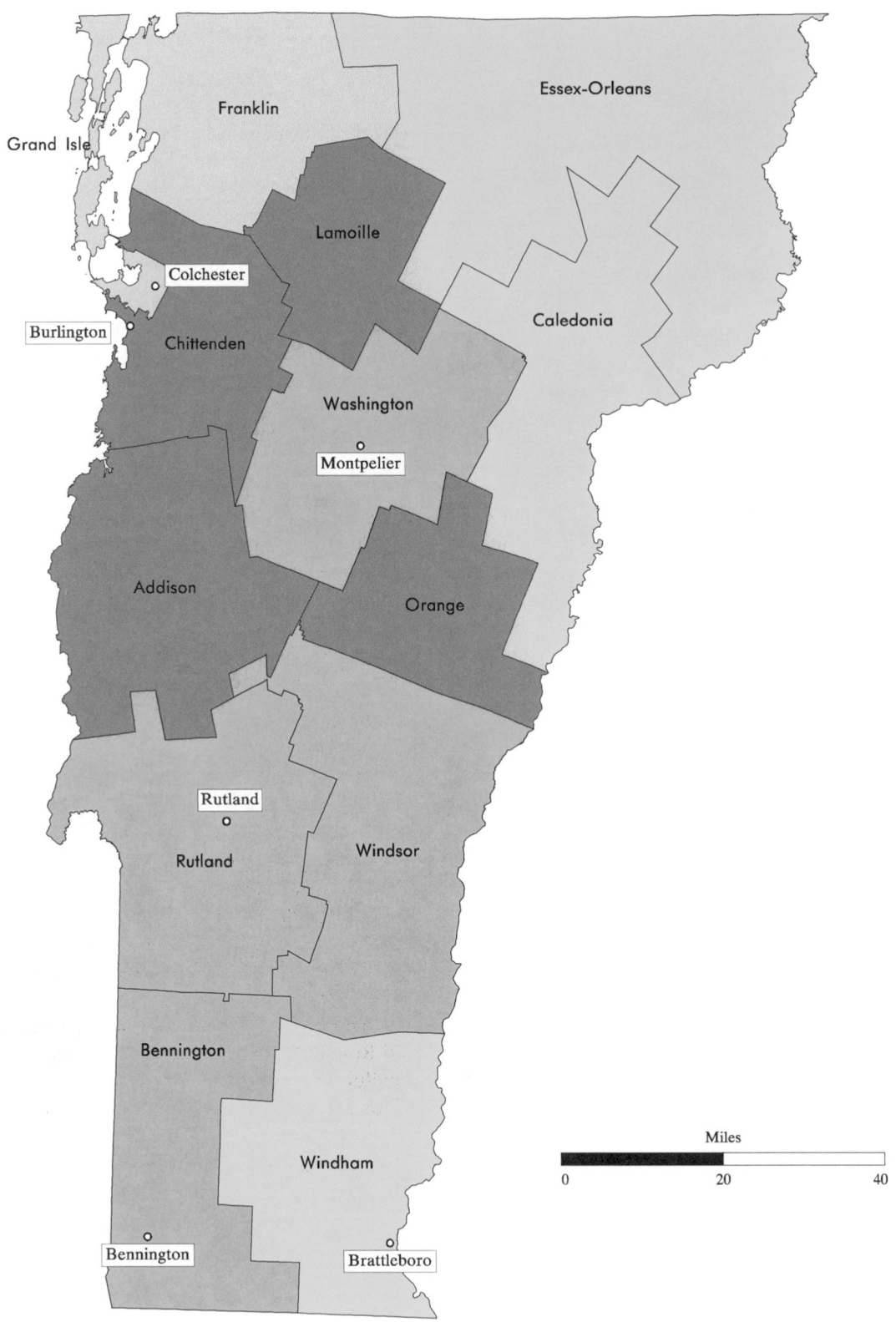

Grand Isle

Franklin

Essex-Orleans

Lamoille

Colchester

Caledonia

Burlington

Chittenden

Washington

Montpelier

Addison

Orange

Rutland

Rutland

Windsor

Bennington

Miles

0   20   40

Windham

Bennington

Brattleboro

Population Growth   ▨ 1% to 3%   ▢ 4% to 5%   ▨ 6% to 8%   ▢ 10% to 12%

Vermont State Senate Districts: Demographic Data

Senate District	Population		Average HH Income		District Type	Unempl. Rate	College Educ.	White (non-Hispanic)		African American		Asian American		Hispanic American	
	1997	+/-	($)	+/-		(%)	(%)	(%)	+/-	(%)	+/-	(%)	+/-	(%)	+/-
Vermont	591,909	5	43,842	24	R	6	49	98	5	0	33	1	49	1	12
Ad	39,549	6	43,771	24	R	4	47	98	6	0	9	1	24	1	5
Be	37,643	2	42,891	22	R	8	46	98	1	0	17	1	29	1	5
Ca	35,585	4	36,540	22	R	7	42	99	3	0	29	0	32	0	26
Ch	125,841	8	52,059	22	S	4	60	96	7	1	46	2	58	1	19
EsOl	36,054	5	34,874	28	R	9	30	99	5	0	3	0	38	0	10
Fr	41,504	10	39,439	20	R	6	36	98	10	0	26	0	51	0	16
Gl	22,512	12	49,257	19	S	5	55	97	11	1	57	1	67	1	-18
La	20,021	8	41,866	25	R	8	47	99	8	0	-15	0	44	0	11
Og	20,570	7	40,064	21	R	6	48	99	7	0	55	0	49	0	-11
Ru	58,556	1	40,845	24	R	6	43	99	1	0	27	0	42	1	15
Wa	56,616	3	43,173	24	R	6	49	98	3	0	21	1	32	1	11
Wm	41,952	4	42,227	28	R	7	48	98	3	0	34	1	50	1	9
Wr	55,318	2	44,454	26	R	6	49	98	2	0	25	1	57	1	15

Note: U=urban, S=suburban, R=rural, M=mixed, HH=households.

VERMONT
State House Districts

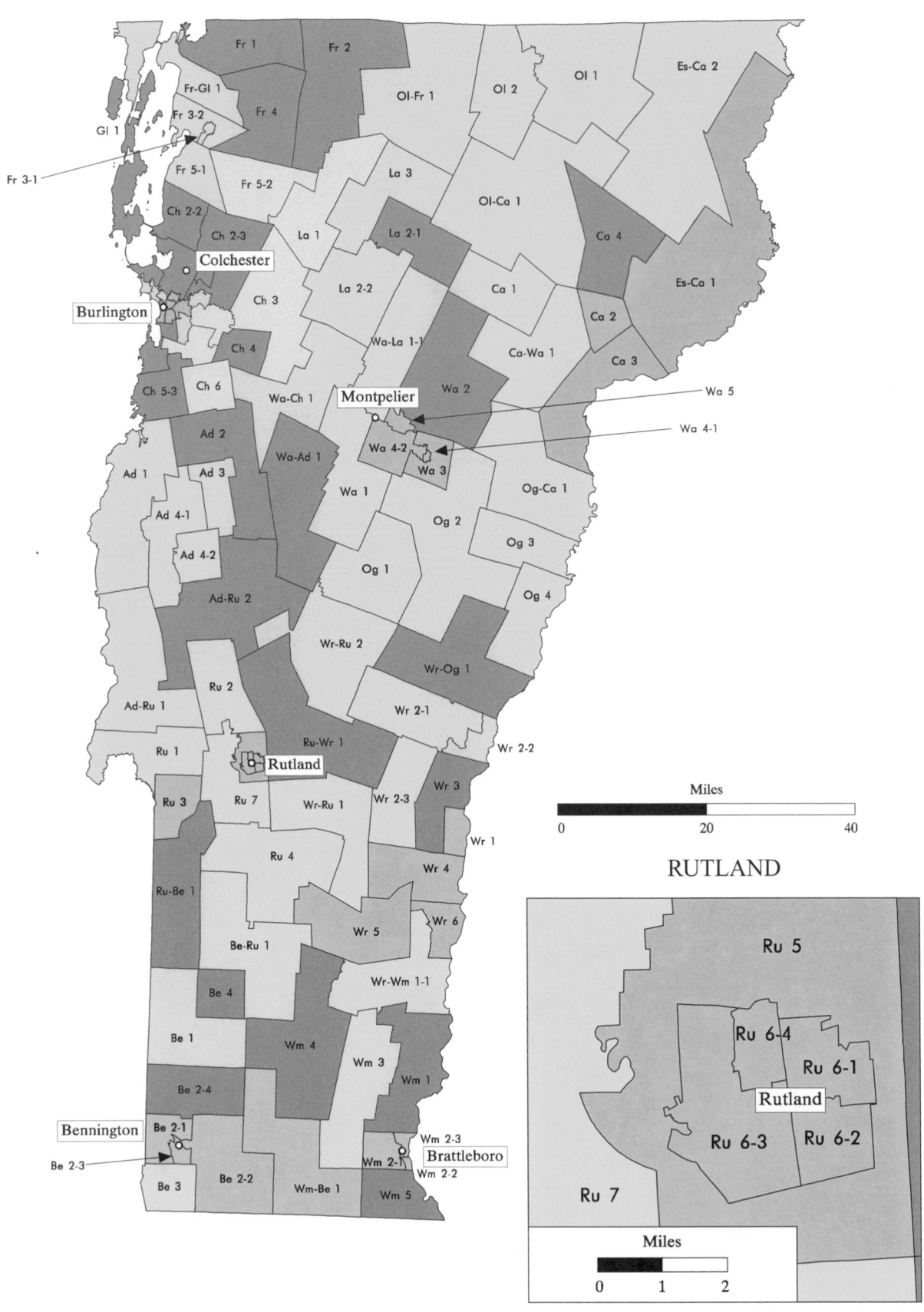

Fr 1

Fr 2

Fr-Gl 1

Ol-Fr 1

Ol 2

Ol 1

Es-Ca 2

Fr 4

Fr 3-2

Gl 1

Fr 3-1

Fr 5-1

La 3

Ol-Ca 1

Ch 2-2

Ch 2-3

La 1

La 2-1

Ca 4

Es-Ca 1

Colchester

Ch 3

La 2-2

Ca 1

Ca 2

Burlington

Ch 4

Wa-La 1-1

Ca-Wa 1

Ca 3

Ch 5-3

Ch 6

Wa-Ch 1

Montpelier

Wa 2

Wa 5

Ad 2

Wa 4-1

Wa 4-2

Wa 3

Og-Ca 1

Ad 1

Ad 3

Wa-Ad 1

Ad 4-1

Wa 1

Og 2

Og 3

Ad 4-2

Og 1

Og 4

Ad-Ru 2

Wr-Ru 2

Wr-Og 1

Ru 2

Wr 2-1

Ad-Ru 1

Ru-Wr 1

Wr 2-2

Ru 1

Rutland

Wr 3

Ru 3

Ru 7

Wr-Ru 1

Wr 2-3

Wr 1

Ru 4

Wr 4

Ru-Be 1

Wr 6

Be-Ru 1

Wr 5

Be 4

Wr-Wm 1-1

Be 1

Wm 4

Wm 3

Wm 1

Be 2-4

Bennington

Be 2-1

Wm 2-3

Be 2-3

Wm 2-1

Brattleboro

Be 3

Be 2-2

Wm-Be 1

Wm 5

Wm 2-2

Miles
0   20   40

RUTLAND

Ru 5

Ru 6-4

Ru 6-1

Rutland

Ru 6-3

Ru 6-2

Ru 7

Miles
0   1   2

Population Growth   ☐ -9% to 0%   ☐ 1% to 8%   ☐ 9% to 18%   ☐ 22% to 45%

BURLINGTON

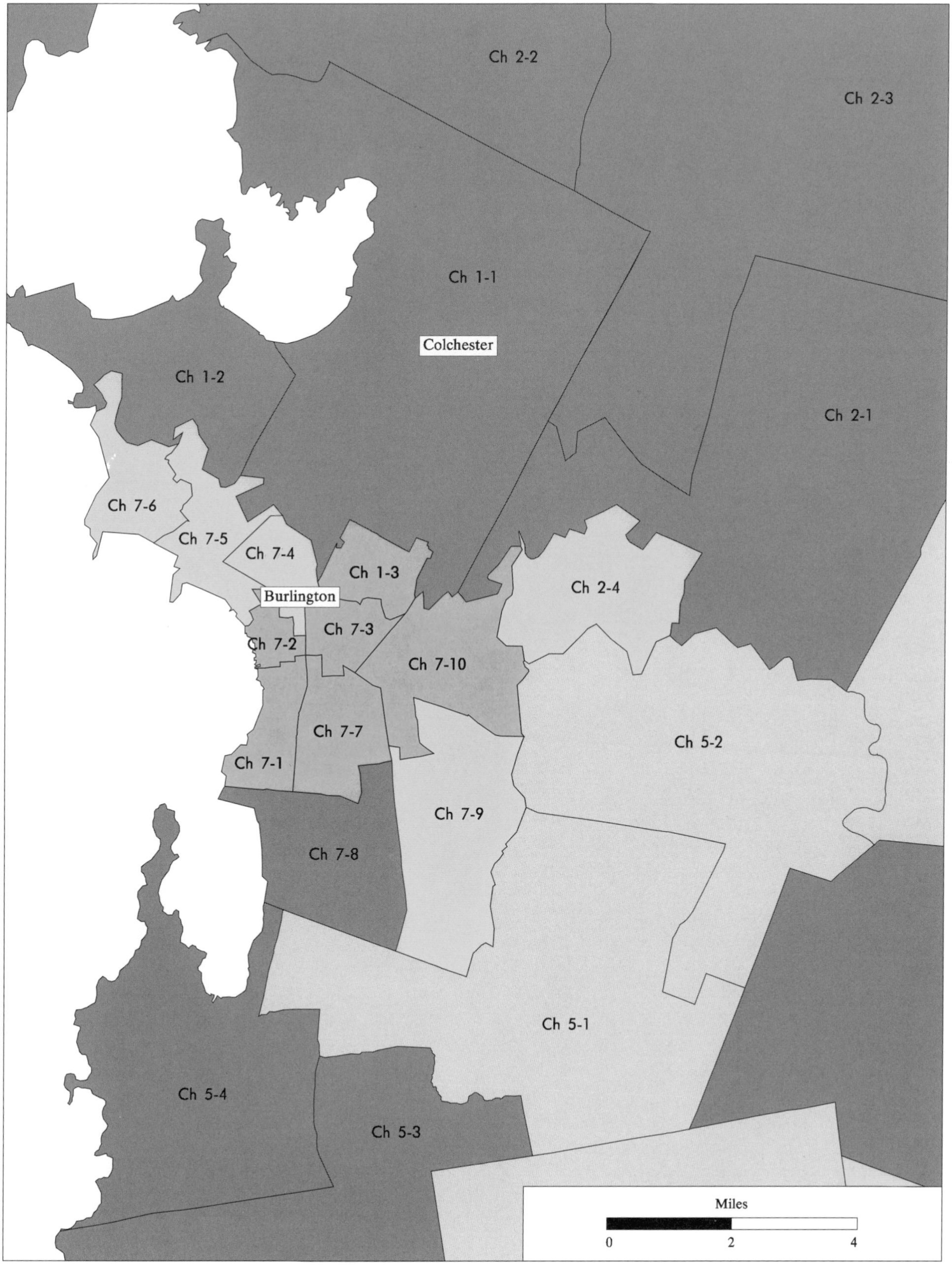

Ch 2-2

Ch 2-3

Ch 1-1

Colchester

Ch 1-2

Ch 2-1

Ch 7-6

Ch 7-5

Ch 7-4

Ch 1-3

Ch 2-4

Burlington

Ch 7-3

Ch 7-2

Ch 7-10

Ch 5-2

Ch 7-7

Ch 7-1

Ch 7-9

Ch 7-8

Ch 5-1

Ch 5-4

Ch 5-3

Miles

0   2   4

Population Growth   ☐ -9% to 0%   ☐ 1% to 8%   ☐ 9% to 18%   ☐ 22% to 45%

Vermont State House Districts: Demographic Data

House District	Population		Average HH Income		District Type	Unempl. Rate	College Educ.	White (non-Hispanic)		African American		Asian American		Hispanic American	
	1997	+/-	($)	+/-		(%)	(%)	(%)	+/-	(%)	+/-	(%)	+/-	(%)	+/-
Vermont	591,909	5	43,842	24	R	6	49	98	5	0	33	1	49	1	12
Ad 1	8,367	3	43,506	23	R	4	44	98	3	0	0	1	23	1	0
Ad 2	4,662	18	43,394	27	R	4	49	99	18	0	40	0	29	0	-36
Ad 3	3,861	3	39,290	25	R	4	42	99	3	0	11	0	-11	0	-53
Ad 4-1	3,573	5	49,591	26	R	3	54	98	5	0	0	1	33	1	16
Ad 4-2	8,338	7	44,805	20	R	4	63	96	7	1	11	2	26	1	29
Ad-Ru 1	3,718	7	42,316	24	R	5	42	99	7	0	13	0	50	0	0
Ad-Ru 2	4,269	9	45,274	26	R	6	47	99	9	0	20	0	23	0	-18
Be 1	3,731	8	41,216	22	R	6	46	99	8	1	38	0	29	0	-30
Be 2-1	7,303	-4	40,769	19	R	8	40	97	-5	1	7	1	26	1	10
Be 2-2	2,879	-4	43,056	21	R	8	37	99	-4	0	0	0	43	1	6
Be 2-3	7,063	-4	37,269	21	R	7	41	98	-4	0	8	1	30	0	-19
Be 2-4	4,183	13	47,605	22	R	7	53	98	13	0	40	0	50	1	52
Be 3	3,652	5	39,484	26	R	11	40	99	5	0	33	0	42	0	25
Be 4	3,992	10	47,307	22	R	6	55	99	10	0	38	1	41	0	-6
Be-Ru 1	3,932	4	51,698	24	R	9	57	99	4	0	25	0	0	0	19
Ca 1	4,045	5	36,639	28	R	9	33	98	5	0	100	0	0	1	53
Ca 2	7,413	-3	31,727	19	R	7	37	99	-3	0	13	0	24	1	14
Ca 3	3,675	0	41,807	26	R	3	45	99	0	0	22	0	56	0	14
Ca 4	8,131	9	36,074	21	R	8	43	99	9	0	38	0	52	0	-10
Ca-Wa 1	3,874	8	42,153	20	R	3	54	99	8	0	20	0	10	0	40
Ch 1-1	10,780	12	48,513	21	S	4	57	97	12	1	68	2	72	1	-35
Ch 1-2	5,698	9	56,634	17	S	4	63	98	9	0	50	1	67	1	23
Ch 1-3	5,984	-9	36,785	19	S	5	35	96	-11	1	35	2	34	1	32
Ch 2-1	8,923	10	61,382	19	S	4	66	96	9	1	60	2	63	1	13
Ch 2-2	6,735	10	46,948	22	S	5	41	99	10	0	29	0	35	0	-8
Ch 2-3	5,207	11	52,764	21	S	3	56	99	11	0	36	0	31	0	5
Ch 2-4	8,301	7	49,130	17	S	4	59	95	6	1	57	2	62	1	7
Ch 3	9,889	23	63,913	22	R	2	68	98	22	0	58	1	84	0	12
Ch 4	4,218	13	54,480	21	S	4	61	98	13	0	0	0	50	1	35
Ch 5-1	4,885	30	69,128	18	S	2	73	97	29	1	93	1	76	1	59
Ch 5-2	5,485	45	57,823	20	S	3	70	97	44	1	75	1	121	1	56
Ch 5-3	3,992	11	73,309	21	S	1	74	98	11	0	57	1	67	1	10
Ch 5-4	4,011	15	73,529	25	S	3	66	98	15	0	9	1	68	1	67
Ch 6	4,889	29	53,079	20	S	7	59	99	29	0	78	0	73	0	15
Ch 7-1	7,491	-3	42,633	21	U	6	61	95	-4	1	44	1	41	2	19
Ch 7-2	6,492	-6	25,236	13	U	11	41	93	-8	2	36	3	49	2	13
Ch 7-3	5,411	-2	38,896	20	U	6	74	94	-4	1	47	3	50	2	13
Ch 7-4	4,949	3	30,411	15	U	8	49	94	1	2	44	3	53	1	22
Ch 7-5	4,135	1	48,918	20	U	3	56	97	0	1	53	2	57	1	18
Ch 7-6	6,142	1	52,978	19	U	3	53	96	0	1	49	2	56	1	39
Ch 7-7	5,771	-5	71,290	16	U	4	71	93	-7	1	27	3	49	2	23
Ch 7-8	3,835	12	65,308	22	S	4	68	96	11	1	55	3	82	0	0
Ch 7-9	3,786	4	61,640	22	S	1	71	95	3	1	50	3	64	1	2
Ch 7-10	4,062	0	50,981	17	S	2	56	95	-1	1	56	3	53	1	3
Es-Ca 1	3,609	0	36,019	31	R	9	30	99	0	0	-43	0	-13	1	25
Es-Ca 2	3,789	4	32,448	31	R	16	20	99	4	0	-17	0	0	0	-7
Fr 1	4,461	9	41,377	23	R	7	28	97	9	0	-100	0	-71	0	40
Fr 2	7,701	12	33,343	22	R	7	26	99	12	0	-43	0	75	0	-12
Fr 3-1	7,976	5	34,210	18	R	7	34	98	5	0	18	1	54	1	24
Fr 3-2	4,559	4	47,553	19	R	4	38	98	4	0	58	0	50	1	35

Note: U=urban, S=suburban, R=rural, M=mixed, HH=households.

Vermont State House Districts: Demographic Data (cont.)

House District	Population		Average HH Income		District Type	Unempl. Rate	College Educ.	White (non-Hispanic)		African American		Asian American		Hispanic American	
	1997	+/-	($)	+/-		(%)	(%)	(%)	+/-	(%)	+/-	(%)	+/-	(%)	+/-
Vermont	591,909	5	43,842	24	R	6	49	98	5	0	33	1	49	1	12
Fr 4	3,980	16	38,445	22	R	4	33	99	16	0	50	0	70	0	0
Fr 5-1	4,027	7	52,080	25	S	4	53	99	7	0	38	1	60	0	-30
Fr 5-2	4,248	24	43,733	18	R	4	55	99	24	0	50	0	88	1	59
Fr-GI 1	7,507	7	33,759	15	R	8	25	96	8	0	0	0	56	0	-33
GI 1	4,502	14	49,463	20	S	6	52	98	14	0	14	0	20	0	0
La 1	4,161	22	41,340	23	R	5	52	99	22	0	-14	0	71	0	-17
La 2-1	4,194	17	37,997	28	R	11	42	99	18	0	0	0	33	0	0
La 2-2	8,219	1	45,586	28	R	7	50	99	1	0	-18	1	41	0	-33
La 3	4,265	7	34,164	20	R	11	38	97	6	0	-20	1	43	1	57
Og 1	7,368	5	37,547	21	R	6	46	99	5	0	67	1	44	0	-39
Og 2	7,988	6	38,241	21	R	7	37	99	6	0	45	0	58	0	-13
Og 3	4,029	7	36,019	18	R	5	45	99	7	0	60	0	33	1	23
Og 4	4,243	7	47,823	23	R	6	61	98	7	0	54	0	33	1	78
Og-Ca 1	3,918	3	35,376	21	R	7	38	99	3	0	0	0	29	0	-29
Ol 1	7,435	7	37,668	26	R	7	33	98	7	0	32	0	50	0	19
Ol 2	7,660	2	34,835	25	R	10	27	99	2	0	-7	0	47	1	11
Ol-Ca 1	7,973	5	34,928	29	R	8	38	99	5	0	29	0	28	0	17
Ol-Fr 1	4,080	7	33,862	26	R	9	29	99	7	0	0	0	71	0	-13
Ru 1	7,661	1	39,194	27	R	5	45	98	0	0	18	0	53	1	50
Ru 2	7,437	4	41,847	27	R	6	36	99	4	0	-50	0	40	0	0
Ru 3	3,472	-1	35,077	22	R	3	44	99	-1	0	-50	1	36	0	30
Ru 4	4,288	2	39,978	24	R	6	40	99	2	0	25	0	0	0	27
Ru 5	3,789	0	53,838	25	R	6	56	98	0	0	36	1	47	1	46
Ru 6-1	3,449	-6	55,902	33	R	3	53	98	-7	0	0	1	38	0	-21
Ru 6-2	3,322	-6	37,258	16	R	4	39	99	-6	0	38	0	36	0	-25
Ru 6-3	6,822	-6	28,307	18	R	9	26	98	-7	1	37	0	48	0	-21
Ru 6-4	3,498	-6	34,930	16	R	7	43	98	-7	0	14	1	24	1	-7
Ru 7	8,017	3	39,772	22	R	5	40	99	3	0	33	0	43	0	-22
Ru-Be 1	3,759	9	40,966	30	R	5	41	99	9	0	0	0	60	0	7
Ru-Wr 1	4,402	16	52,511	25	R	6	53	98	16	1	59	1	57	0	50
Wa 1	7,785	2	41,064	23	R	6	47	97	2	1	57	1	41	2	27
Wa 2	8,198	15	43,178	24	R	6	56	98	14	1	28	0	44	1	23
Wa 3	6,993	-6	48,395	21	R	5	45	98	-6	0	-38	0	5	1	-6
Wa 4-1	3,845	-1	38,833	23	R	6	40	97	-1	0	-14	0	13	2	-7
Wa 4-2	8,291	0	33,997	21	R	10	25	98	0	0	20	0	44	2	5
Wa 5	6,744	-4	41,611	21	R	6	61	96	-4	1	21	1	33	1	-8
Wa-Ad 1	4,359	16	51,812	26	R	7	58	97	16	0	15	0	43	2	66
Wa-Ch 1	7,565	5	49,157	25	R	4	49	99	5	0	6	0	37	1	60
Wa-La 1-1	4,492	6	47,161	29	R	7	61	98	6	0	0	1	33	1	0
Wm 1	8,283	9	45,325	29	R	5	53	98	8	0	48	1	61	1	24
Wm 2-1	5,472	-4	40,285	23	R	5	46	97	-4	1	35	1	43	1	-10
Wm 2-2	2,958	-3	34,889	15	R	11	42	96	-4	2	47	1	54	1	5
Wm 2-3	3,392	-3	42,731	36	R	5	53	93	-5	2	33	3	53	2	14
Wm 3	4,038	5	47,508	29	R	9	54	98	4	0	25	1	56	1	24
Wm 4	4,438	11	41,813	27	R	11	44	99	11	0	20	0	22	0	13
Wm 5	4,337	14	49,161	28	R	6	46	99	15	0	67	0	0	1	0
Wm-Be 1	3,806	-1	43,120	31	R	8	44	99	-1	0	0	0	33	0	-25
Wr 1	3,483	-6	42,175	27	R	6	41	99	-6	0	14	0	40	0	-13
Wr 2-1	3,980	5	54,895	26	R	5	60	99	4	0	0	0	50	0	17
Wr 2-2	7,608	4	41,595	22	R	6	49	96	3	1	30	2	63	1	48

Note: U=urban, S=suburban, R=rural, M=mixed, HH=households.

Vermont State House Districts: Demographic Data (cont.)

House District	Population		Average HH Income		District Type	Unempl. Rate	College Educ.	White (non-Hispanic)		African American		Asian American		Hispanic American	
	1997	+/-	($)	+/-		(%)	(%)	(%)	+/-	(%)	+/-	(%)	+/-	(%)	+/-
Vermont	591,909	5	43,842	24	R	6	49	98	5	0	33	1	49	1	12
Wr 2-3	3,856	1	50,172	27	R	4	58	99	1	0	25	0	0	0	8
Wr 3	4,398	13	60,248	29	R	4	51	98	12	0	17	1	73	0	-11
Wr 4	4,024	0	41,803	26	R	9	33	99	0	0	0	1	40	0	13
Wr 5	3,773	-2	40,451	28	R	7	48	99	-2	0	0	0	50	0	-36
Wr 6	7,217	-3	33,174	15	R	6	39	98	-3	0	40	1	51	1	24
Wr-Wm 1-1	8,572	1	35,536	22	R	4	44	98	1	0	-40	1	44	1	18
Wr-Og 1	8,436	11	51,625	27	R	3	62	98	11	1	36	1	71	0	32
Wr-Ru 1	3,934	2	42,643	27	R	6	41	99	2	0	-50	0	33	1	41
Wr-Ru 2	4,279	6	40,946	26	R	7	45	98	5	0	20	1	53	1	-3

Note: U=urban, S=suburban, R=rural, M=mixed, HH=households.

VIRGINIA

Though it left the Union reluctantly in 1861, no state suffered more during the Civil War than Virginia. Its capital was burned, its farms looted, and a generation of its young men killed. When the war ended, wrote historian Douglas Southall Freeman, Virginia "went straight from Appomattox to the old house that typified the civilization that had perished. She climbed to the second-story bedroom; she pulled down the blinds and through the darkness of reconstruction sat in her mourning."

There is great irony in the fact that Virginia owes much of its economic recovery in this century to the same federal government it once lost so much in fighting—to the branch of the Federal Reserve that made Richmond a banking center; to the naval bases at Norfolk and Newport News, which revitalized the Tidewater region; and to the swelling federal bureaucracy, which has made the Northern Virginia suburbs across the river from Washington the wealthiest part of the Commonwealth.

Virginia has ridden these developments back into a place of national prominence. It was the nineteenth-largest state as recently as the 1940s, and fourteenth in 1980, but it has since jumped over Indiana and Massachusetts (two very Yankee states) to twelfth. Its 9 percent growth rate since 1990 is fast if one considers Virginia the southern edge of the northeast corridor; slow if one considers Virginia the northern edge of the rising South. Virginians often seem to think of the state both ways.

Nowhere has growth been faster than in the Washington suburbs. Few areas in the country demonstrate that phenomenon of suburban growth called the "metropolitan doughnut" better than Northern Virginia. Taking Washington, D.C., as the declining city center, one finds that population growth surges the farther one pushes into the countryside, across the Beltway and out I-66 past the last Metrorail stop. Development has turned into a flood around Vienna, at the edge of Fairfax County, which has grown by 43 percent since 1990. Beyond Fairfax, in Prince William County, development threatened to engulf the Bull Run battlefield a few years ago. Loudoun County, still farther out, has grown by 47 percent.

A similar phenomenon has occurred around Norfolk. With cutbacks in shipbuilding, it has lost almost 8 percent of its population since 1990 and is the third-fastest-shrinking city in the United States, after Hartford and New Haven. But Virginia Beach has become one of the faster-growing areas of the country, filling with young, white, often military families. It is now listed as the nation's thirty-fifth-biggest city, with almost as many people as Tucson.

Growth has shifted the balance of economic power to the north. Virginia's wealthiest districts are now all clustered around Washington, in the older suburbs of McLean and Falls Church. Virginia Beach is prosperous but more middle class. The old Richmond aristocracy has fallen from prominence, and the touted West End ranks only eighth in average household income. Poverty is greatest, and unemployment highest, in the western mountains and in the heavily black neighborhoods on either side of Hampton Roads.

Almost three of every four Virginians are white, which is close to the ratio for the nation as a whole, but the races are unevenly distributed geographically. The western districts along the Shenandoah are almost entirely white; the eastern districts in the Tidewater are much less so. Urban house districts in Norfolk and Newport News are heavily African American, as are those in central Richmond.

An interesting comparison can be made between the Maryland and Virginia suburbs of Washington. One house district in Prince George's County, Maryland, southeast of Washington, is 74 percent black. But none of the districts on the Virginia side southwest of the city is even 20 percent black. The Potomac River has become the true dividing line between the Democratic Northeast and the Republican South.

The battle for control of Virginia's legislature has been fierce. Despite Republican gains, Democrats still control the house of delegates, the lower chamber, though by a narrow margin. In the senate, Democrats held a 22–18 edge through three election cycles, but in 1996 the Republicans were able to force a tie, and now they control it by a single seat.

VIRGINIA
State Senate Districts

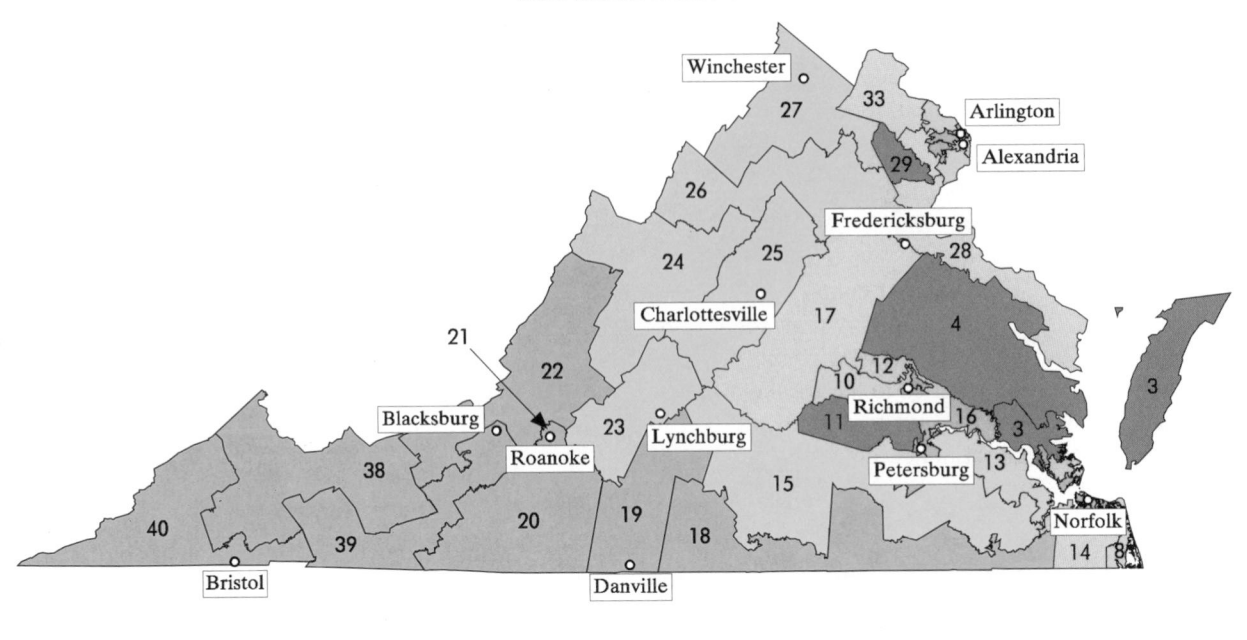

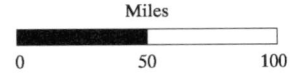

NORTHERN VIRGINIA

RICHMOND

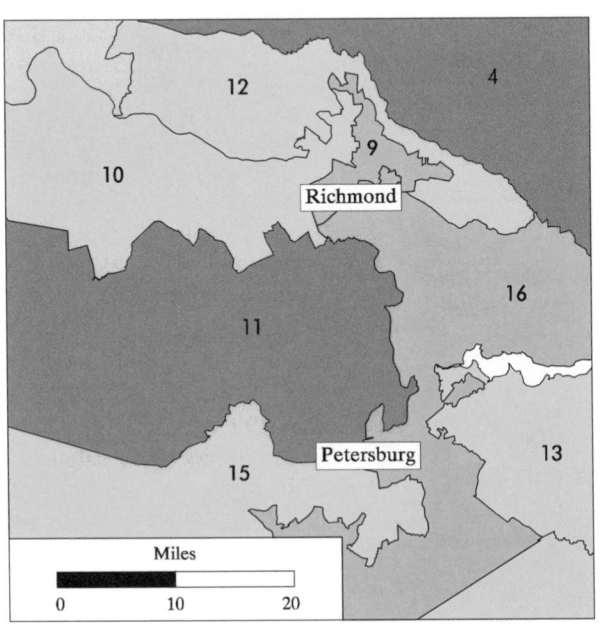

Population Growth   ▢ -8% to 4%   ▢ 6% to 12%   ▢ 13% to 18%   ▢ 24% to 33%

NORFOLK

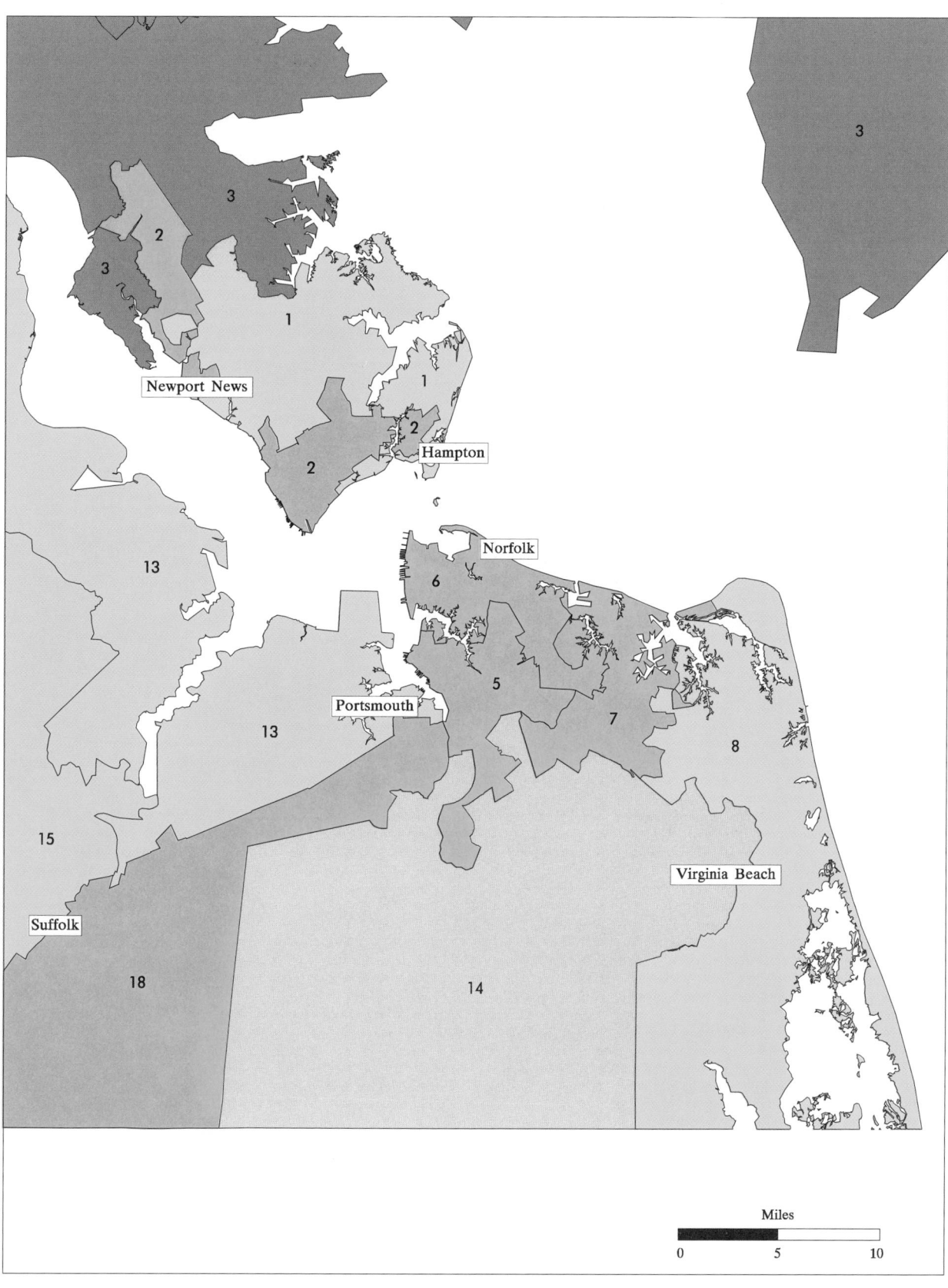

Population Growth
-8% to 4%   6% to 12%   13% to 18%   24% to 33%

Virginia State Senate Districts: Demographic Data

Senate District	Population 1997	+/-	Average HH Income ($)	+/-	District Type	Unempl. Rate (%)	College Educ. (%)	White (non-Hispanic) (%)	+/-	African American (%)	+/-	Asian American (%)	+/-	Hispanic American (%)	+/-
Virginia	6,720,147	9	52,740	26	M	4	42	74	5	20	14	3	38	3	38
1	176,065	9	46,340	18	U	5	44	74	3	20	28	3	40	3	39
2	147,308	1	34,156	19	U	8	31	40	-6	55	5	2	27	3	30
3	174,616	13	49,251	30	M	5	41	71	9	24	21	2	42	2	35
4	187,200	17	46,769	20	R	3	30	76	15	22	25	0	31	1	35
5	143,965	-3	35,534	28	U	9	28	33	-12	63	1	2	14	1	8
6	119,892	-8	42,229	29	U	7	35	68	-14	23	6	4	18	5	14
7	159,990	4	51,876	19	U	5	45	77	0	14	14	4	31	4	34
8	171,192	9	50,357	19	U	5	45	79	5	14	19	3	37	4	40
9	138,545	-2	34,267	20	U	6	32	31	-12	66	3	1	15	1	19
10	165,006	9	64,437	26	S	3	55	84	6	13	32	2	42	1	42
11	180,297	18	54,794	24	S	3	40	81	15	15	35	2	49	2	60
12	172,762	11	60,583	24	S	3	52	82	7	13	33	3	39	1	44
13	157,556	9	45,474	24	U	5	31	67	2	29	26	2	38	2	40
14	209,466	30	53,115	21	S	4	42	74	24	17	47	6	55	3	69
15	156,758	7	37,125	27	R	5	21	61	2	38	16	0	4	0	11
16	153,645	2	35,557	24	U	7	22	36	-4	61	5	1	18	2	21
17	188,294	24	47,587	25	R	4	31	75	21	22	32	1	54	1	60
18	172,847	3	31,278	21	R	8	17	38	-3	61	7	0	8	1	9
19	157,999	1	36,871	24	M	6	23	70	-2	28	10	0	18	1	23
20	160,479	4	34,613	17	R	4	20	82	2	17	11	0	-7	1	26
21	155,968	0	44,908	32	U	4	36	81	-2	17	9	1	28	1	32
22	160,448	3	42,223	29	R	5	31	94	2	5	14	1	12	1	20
23	157,836	8	42,037	25	M	5	32	78	6	20	16	1	28	1	29
24	166,142	6	41,187	26	R	4	30	92	6	6	17	0	1	1	27
25	164,115	8	52,576	36	M	3	47	81	6	15	19	2	32	1	34
26	173,865	12	49,026	27	R	4	31	89	10	8	27	1	39	1	42
27	176,198	10	47,561	23	R	4	30	92	9	6	20	1	28	1	46
28	202,023	25	52,275	18	R	4	39	77	22	17	30	2	57	4	66
29	182,954	16	65,452	19	R	3	46	79	12	11	26	4	51	5	46
30	165,578	7	69,523	30	S	3	63	61	-1	20	13	6	34	12	33
31	161,519	4	71,015	31	U	3	67	65	-4	10	6	8	29	16	27
32	172,907	11	120,284	34	S	2	74	81	6	4	31	9	46	5	38
33	208,772	32	73,212	18	R	2	59	81	28	8	43	5	56	5	74
34	158,663	2	71,785	23	S	3	63	64	-7	7	7	13	27	16	31
35	155,428	0	81,866	20	S	2	70	76	-6	5	14	12	31	6	32
36	174,269	9	73,851	26	S	3	58	65	1	17	11	9	39	8	47
37	207,251	33	97,702	36	S	2	68	81	27	6	49	8	80	5	80
38	162,244	2	32,620	24	R	8	20	97	1	2	16	0	5	0	29
39	159,521	2	34,832	28	R	6	32	93	1	4	13	2	27	1	17
40	151,871	0	32,223	32	R	9	18	97	0	2	10	0	1	0	18

Note: U=urban, S=suburban, R=rural, M=mixed, HH=households.

VIRGINIA
State House Districts

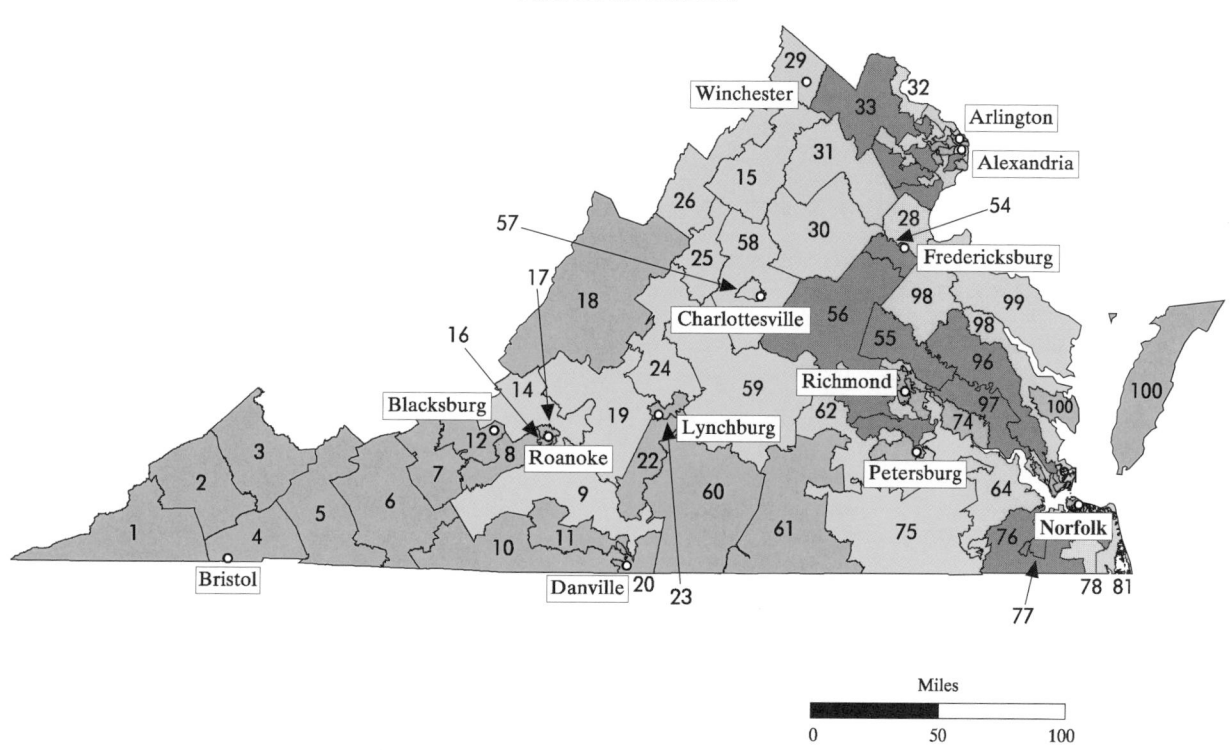

Miles

0   50   100

NORTHERN VIRGINIA

RICHMOND

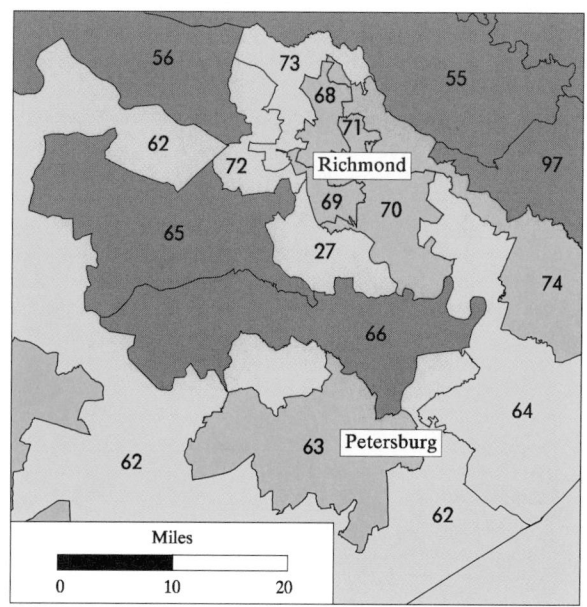

Miles

0   20   40

Miles

0   10   20

Population Growth   -17% to 4%   5% to 15%   18% to 31%   38% to 47%

NORFOLK

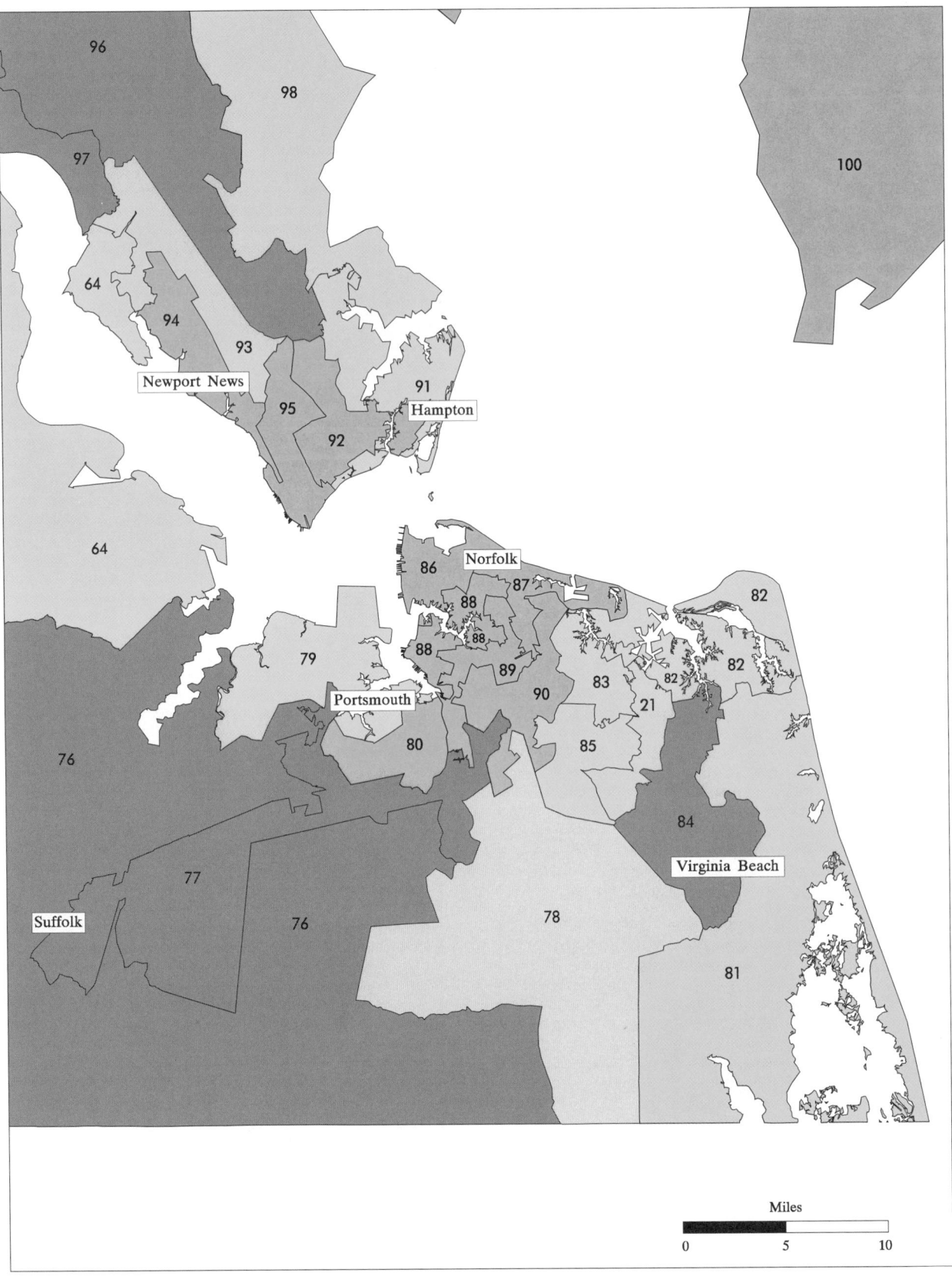

Population Growth   ▨ -17% to 4%   ▢ 5% to 15%   ▨ 18% to 31%   ▢ 38% to 47%

Virginia State House Districts: Demographic Data

House District	Population		Average HH Income		District Type	Unempl. Rate	College Educ.	White (non-Hispanic)		African American		Asian American		Hispanic American	
	1997	+/-	($)	+/-		(%)	(%)	(%)	+/-	(%)	+/-	(%)	+/-	(%)	+/-
Virginia	6,720,147	9	52,740	26	M	4	42	74	5	20	14	3	38	3	38
1	61,741	-1	30,264	33	R	10	15	98	-1	1	8	0	-9	0	25
2	64,359	0	31,623	31	R	11	16	98	0	2	10	0	0	0	11
3	62,161	-2	30,512	19	R	10	13	99	-2	0	0	0	7	1	24
4	66,671	4	35,709	30	M	6	27	96	3	3	13	0	4	0	36
5	65,609	3	33,083	30	R	7	21	96	2	3	15	0	13	0	25
6	64,500	4	32,235	28	R	5	20	96	3	3	14	0	-20	0	13
7	61,376	0	34,041	21	R	7	29	93	-1	6	14	1	12	1	17
8	61,354	2	49,692	28	S	3	39	95	1	3	16	1	27	1	21
9	67,629	8	37,075	21	R	4	22	85	7	15	15	0	-9	1	27
10	61,881	3	33,717	21	R	3	16	83	1	16	10	0	-9	1	31
11	62,200	-1	34,924	15	R	4	20	74	-4	26	9	0	-4	0	17
12	62,159	3	37,172	27	R	6	54	88	1	5	15	6	29	1	22
13	77,913	26	72,225	20	S	3	56	85	21	8	52	3	70	3	56
14	65,505	9	46,814	26	S	3	31	96	9	3	23	0	31	1	36
15	67,456	6	39,381	23	R	5	21	96	6	2	25	0	7	1	35
16	60,913	0	48,302	36	U	5	44	74	-1	24	2	1	29	1	21
17	61,244	-2	38,125	30	U	5	23	79	-6	19	18	1	22	1	34
18	64,367	2	38,785	31	R	6	27	91	1	8	24	0	-3	0	6
19	71,116	12	44,593	28	R	4	30	89	10	10	25	0	20	1	39
20	64,591	1	35,304	26	U	8	24	61	-3	37	8	1	20	1	16
21	71,154	10	46,014	16	U	5	43	69	3	17	23	8	41	5	44
22	66,347	3	38,811	22	M	5	28	83	1	16	15	1	28	1	37
23	63,839	2	39,610	25	U	6	33	66	-3	32	11	1	23	1	21
24	67,091	6	39,709	24	R	3	30	87	5	12	15	0	1	1	28
25	63,758	8	44,953	26	R	3	33	94	7	5	8	0	-5	1	45
26	73,581	10	42,846	29	R	4	33	93	9	4	19	1	36	2	39
27	70,665	9	50,382	19	S	3	37	75	3	20	29	3	40	2	54
28	84,764	38	55,687	13	R	3	41	88	36	8	54	1	74	3	84
29	72,618	13	45,277	24	R	4	32	93	12	5	24	1	39	1	46
30	73,391	15	44,186	21	R	4	29	81	12	17	28	1	36	1	48
31	69,834	10	59,927	23	R	3	36	87	8	11	21	1	28	2	45
32	88,457	47	67,998	15	R	2	55	83	42	8	66	5	85	4	96
33	76,117	29	73,526	24	R	2	51	88	27	8	43	2	53	2	72
34	69,300	13	135,357	34	S	2	73	78	6	5	23	10	47	7	53
35	65,140	6	99,427	25	S	2	71	80	1	4	21	10	41	6	39
36	77,001	18	95,587	32	S	3	73	78	14	9	27	6	45	6	51
37	66,873	1	83,537	24	S	2	68	75	-5	5	12	13	30	7	30
38	60,806	-1	73,092	26	S	3	61	63	-8	6	-1	13	20	18	18
39	62,512	2	76,751	22	S	2	64	69	-6	7	12	14	34	10	39
40	80,757	31	108,741	36	S	2	72	81	25	5	60	9	72	5	81
41	57,768	-2	80,246	15	S	2	73	76	-8	5	9	12	26	6	24
42	70,653	9	79,479	24	S	3	59	65	2	16	11	11	41	7	50
43	71,419	18	75,178	31	S	3	61	70	9	12	30	10	52	8	63
44	62,127	-1	69,327	22	S	3	59	64	-7	20	5	7	20	8	34
45	63,183	7	80,475	38	S	4	63	64	2	24	10	2	33	10	31
46	66,279	9	60,642	24	S	3	64	60	0	20	17	7	37	12	30
47	59,889	-2	65,897	26	U	3	62	58	-13	9	6	11	18	21	27
48	68,316	10	88,049	34	U	2	72	73	4	6	11	7	47	13	32
49	62,133	1	59,853	24	U	3	63	56	-9	16	4	8	24	20	25
50	71,880	12	62,125	18	R	3	42	81	8	9	24	3	47	6	48

Note: U=urban, S=suburban, R=rural, M=mixed, HH=households.

Virginia State House Districts: Demographic Data (cont.)

House District	Population 1997	+/-	Average HH Income ($)	+/-	District Type	Unempl. Rate (%)	College Educ. (%)	White (non-Hispanic) (%)	+/-	African American (%)	+/-	Asian American (%)	+/-	Hispanic American (%)	+/-
Virginia	6,720,147	9	52,740	26	M	4	42	74	5	20	14	3	38	3	38
51	68,227	10	61,947	14	S	3	47	72	5	16	17	5	41	7	46
52	76,371	23	55,883	17	S	4	44	71	16	16	35	4	53	8	62
53	69,454	9	81,176	29	S	3	68	69	-1	5	15	13	40	12	49
54	76,377	30	54,753	27	R	3	42	82	27	14	43	1	66	2	66
55	78,444	24	52,234	14	S	3	37	87	22	11	39	1	57	1	63
56	80,867	25	48,790	23	R	4	27	73	21	25	37	0	40	1	53
57	67,421	5	56,163	44	U	4	59	75	2	19	16	4	34	2	27
58	71,720	11	55,376	35	R	3	42	89	10	9	22	1	33	1	43
59	65,876	8	36,679	29	R	5	22	66	3	34	18	0	-14	1	9
60	64,034	3	32,350	23	R	6	17	60	-2	39	12	0	-9	1	15
61	62,555	4	32,398	23	R	5	18	57	-1	42	12	0	-23	1	12
62	70,923	7	45,824	31	R	5	23	64	2	33	15	1	16	2	21
63	61,653	4	34,553	18	U	7	26	36	-1	61	6	1	20	1	23
64	67,920	10	44,292	25	R	5	28	61	4	34	23	1	27	3	32
65	80,525	23	70,474	25	S	2	58	88	20	8	44	2	62	1	76
66	79,701	24	55,056	24	S	3	39	87	20	9	49	2	55	1	52
67	84,729	43	98,388	41	S	2	67	81	36	5	61	9	87	4	94
68	64,171	-2	52,854	23	S	3	50	83	-6	14	23	2	23	1	27
69	63,006	2	32,847	17	U	6	32	32	-15	65	12	1	12	1	32
70	61,144	-1	32,205	23	U	8	20	35	-8	64	3	0	9	1	13
71	54,923	-6	39,716	29	U	6	39	38	-12	59	-3	1	20	1	14
72	69,998	14	83,331	28	S	2	67	91	12	5	39	3	49	1	45
73	74,232	12	60,708	22	S	3	56	84	8	11	39	4	41	1	48
74	58,851	-1	37,239	16	S	5	26	36	-11	62	5	1	7	1	17
75	64,109	6	34,772	29	R	6	19	41	-1	58	11	0	5	0	8
76	71,141	20	48,328	24	M	5	30	70	14	28	37	1	49	1	54
77	75,555	19	33,668	12	S	8	21	36	7	62	27	1	48	1	21
78	83,195	41	58,953	31	S	3	40	82	36	15	62	2	80	2	90
79	63,556	6	42,144	20	U	5	31	65	-1	31	19	2	40	2	53
80	56,554	-4	30,367	17	U	9	18	33	-13	65	1	0	10	1	7
81	68,021	14	44,054	19	U	5	42	77	10	16	21	2	50	4	47
82	64,818	10	69,679	22	U	3	60	91	8	5	17	2	43	2	36
83	69,939	9	46,653	18	U	6	40	71	3	20	19	4	39	4	47
84	70,995	19	46,582	24	U	5	40	72	13	17	29	6	53	5	55
85	67,414	7	58,252	18	U	4	51	75	1	11	21	10	37	3	33
86	49,295	-17	45,668	34	U	9	38	65	-22	24	-7	3	11	6	-4
87	52,427	-11	40,020	29	U	8	30	70	-16	21	1	4	13	4	4
88	54,027	-10	44,650	31	U	6	45	66	-15	27	-1	3	14	3	16
89	51,349	-11	31,486	25	U	10	19	32	-16	63	-9	2	10	2	4
90	59,256	-3	35,904	19	U	8	27	38	-8	57	-1	2	18	2	25
91	65,158	5	45,993	17	U	5	43	70	0	24	18	3	32	3	35
92	59,102	1	33,447	13	U	8	31	34	-8	62	6	2	24	2	23
93	70,730	15	42,266	22	U	5	42	69	5	24	48	3	40	4	43
94	58,865	2	49,915	22	U	5	45	70	-6	23	27	3	25	3	30
95	55,400	-6	30,943	20	U	9	26	37	-8	60	-6	1	29	1	14
96	79,629	25	48,625	22	S	4	40	73	22	22	32	2	65	2	61
97	76,928	18	58,193	33	R	4	46	76	14	20	33	2	47	1	49
98	68,748	11	46,612	22	R	4	32	75	8	23	23	1	24	1	34
99	66,797	12	44,067	24	R	7	27	67	8	31	19	0	22	1	27
100	60,313	3	33,381	22	R	6	24	64	0	34	8	0	-1	2	20

Note: U=urban, S=suburban, R=rural, M=mixed, HH=households.

WASHINGTON

To the American pantheon of great inventors—from Thomas Edison at Menlo Park, New Jersey; to Henry Ford in Dearborn, Michigan; to the Wright Brothers at Kitty Hawk, North Carolina—future generations will surely add Bill Gates and the birth of computer software in Redmond, Washington.

More accurately, the credit should be to Albuquerque, New Mexico, for that is where Micro-soft (it once had a hyphen) was founded in 1975 with three employees and $16,005 in revenues. But the company moved to Bellevue, Washington, in 1978 and up the road to Redmond in 1986, and it will forever be associated with the Pacific Northwest. Like San Francisco thirty years ago, the Seattle area in the 1990s—from Microsoft to Kurt Cobain and salmon to Starbucks—has become America's Happening Place To Be.

San Francisco is an apt comparison. The Seattle-Tacoma metropolitan area has about the same population. Both Seattle and San Francisco are hemmed in by water on two sides, giving them little room to expand and exorbitant real estate prices. Both were built almost overnight on gold; Seattle burst into prominence in 1896 as the gateway to the Klondike. Both now have large aerospace industries. Both have seen radical politics. The Seattle area was the scene of some of the country's worst labor confrontations in the years around World War I, as the Industrial Workers of the World (the I.W.W., or "Wobblies," as they were known) staged a massive general strike in Seattle in 1919 and had violent clashes with police at Everett and Centralia.

Surely not by coincidence, the two decades since Microsoft's move have been a period of rapid growth for the state. Washington grew by almost 18 percent during the 1980s and by another 15 percent during the 1990s, leaping from being the twentieth-largest state in 1980 to fifteenth-largest today. Only Arizona has made a bigger jump.

For all the high-tech explosion around Seattle, the fastest-growing part of the state is actually the city of Vancouver, across the Columbia River from Portland, Oregon. Seattle's suburban growth is occurring both in Snohomish County, along the Cascades east of Everett, and in previously rural districts on the Olympic Peninsula. No state house district has lost population during the decade (Arizona and Oregon are the only other states that can make such a claim). The districts experiencing the slowest growth are all in downtown Seattle and Bellevue.

Household income in Washington is almost exactly at the national average. The wealthiest districts, surprisingly, are nowhere near the town of Medina, on Lake Washington, where Bill Gates is building his mansion. Instead, they are all east of Bellevue, roughly on either side of I-90, skirting the Wenatchee Mountains, where many other "Microsoft millionaires" have moved. The poorest district is located in Spokane, the self-proclaimed capital of the wheat-growing "Inland Empire."

Although Washington is 84 percent white and has almost exactly the same racial composition as Massachusetts, it has much more cultural harmony than Massachusetts does. Only 3 percent of Washingtonians are African American, for example, yet Seattle has elected a popular black mayor, Norm Rice. In 1986, the state rechristened King County, which includes Seattle, to honor Martin Luther King, Jr.; it is the only county in the country named for an African American. Only 5 percent of the state is of Asian ancestry (still one of the highest percentages in the country; Washington does sit on the Pacific Rim), yet in 1996 the state elected the nation's first Chinese-American governor, Gary Locke.

Washington has ridden a political roller coaster during the 1990s. Its congressional delegation was 8–1 Democratic in 1992 and 7–2 Republican in 1994, and the casualties included Speaker of the House Thomas Foley. In the state house, the Democrats, who had gained seven seats in 1992 (for a 65–33 majority), lost twenty-seven seats in 1994, gained seven back in 1996, and now trail 53–45. Republicans held the senate in 1990, lost it in 1994, and regained it in 1996. It would be foolish to try to predict what will happen next.

WASHINGTON
State Legislative Districts

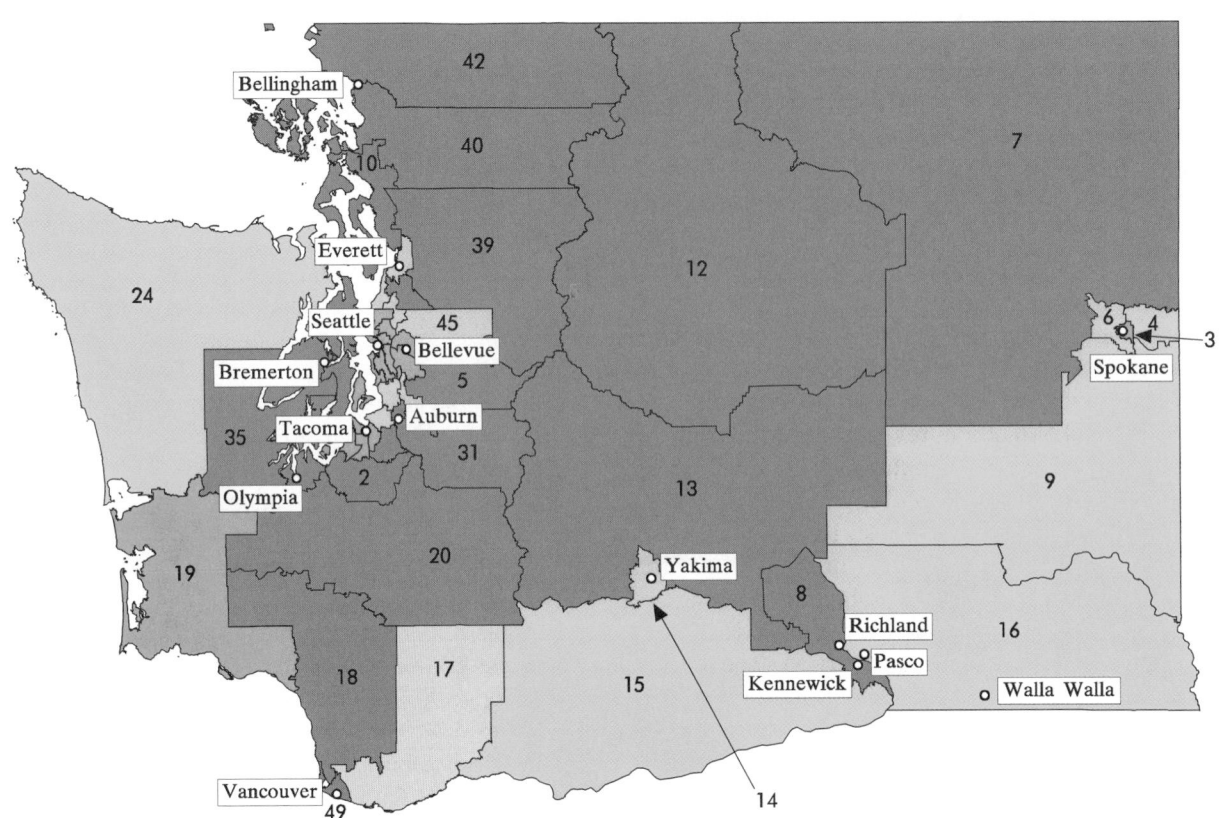

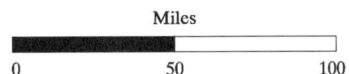

Miles

0   50   100

Population Growth   ☐ 0% to 9%   ☐ 10% to 18%   ■ 19% to 29%   ☐ 43%

SEATTLE

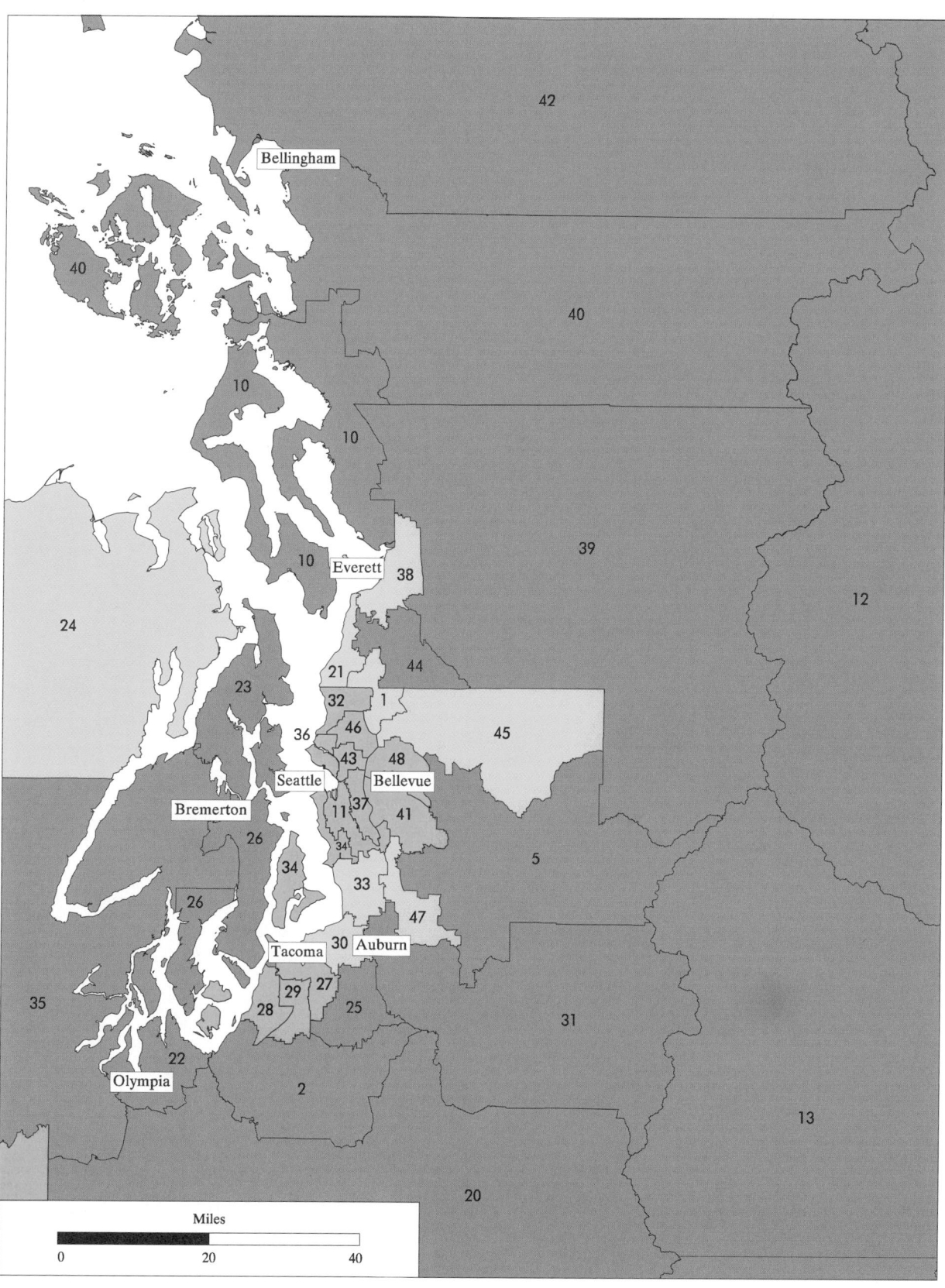

Bellingham

42

40

40

10

10

10

Everett 38

24

39

12

21

23 32 1 44

36 46 45

43 48

Seattle 37 Bellevue

Bremerton 11 41

26 34 5

34

33

26 47

30 Auburn

Tacoma

29 27

28 25

35

22

Olympia 31

2

20 13

Miles

0   20   40

Population Growth   ☐ 0% to 9%   ☐ 10% to 18%   ☐ 19% to 29%

Washington State Legislative Districts: Demographic Data

Legis. District	Population 1997	+/-	Average HH Income ($)	+/-	District Type	Unempl. Rate (%)	College Educ. (%)	White (non-Hispanic) (%)	+/-	African American (%)	+/-	Asian American (%)	+/-	Hispanic American (%)	+/-
Wash.	5,600,590	15	51,384	34	M	6	43	84	12	3	23	5	43	5	43
1	109,943	11	63,737	38	S	3	49	89	8	1	28	6	50	3	36
2	123,709	21	47,061	37	S	7	32	79	18	9	19	5	49	5	40
3	108,361	9	30,670	32	U	10	36	88	7	3	23	3	39	3	41
4	111,920	13	45,642	35	S	7	41	95	12	1	23	2	45	2	41
5	117,250	19	77,637	42	S	3	54	91	17	1	38	5	64	2	45
6	111,361	14	52,329	38	U	6	51	94	12	1	30	2	51	2	41
7	121,679	21	38,939	30	R	10	33	92	20	0	5	1	34	3	45
8	120,370	22	55,623	49	U	6	46	88	19	1	31	3	56	8	57
9	109,985	11	41,091	34	R	6	47	86	9	1	15	4	34	8	34
10	118,198	20	51,282	33	R	5	40	88	17	2	16	3	52	4	43
11	102,080	5	40,062	28	U	6	34	56	-6	13	18	22	26	7	37
12	117,081	19	42,236	36	R	8	33	85	16	0	7	1	38	11	43
13	122,871	21	39,626	34	R	7	31	82	17	1	27	1	43	15	48
14	114,814	16	41,746	36	U	9	31	79	11	2	33	1	21	16	44
15	115,821	17	39,474	35	R	12	22	54	9	0	6	1	14	39	35
16	115,830	16	42,105	36	R	8	35	75	10	2	29	2	33	20	42
17	145,376	43	49,051	25	S	5	35	92	41	1	68	3	83	3	74
18	119,109	22	47,108	29	R	7	32	94	21	0	24	1	50	3	59
19	105,558	8	37,583	25	R	8	29	93	7	0	-6	2	40	2	28
20	120,193	20	42,698	36	R	8	33	92	18	1	40	2	60	3	51
21	107,328	10	60,796	32	S	3	48	87	7	1	25	7	47	3	44
22	123,363	25	49,070	35	S	7	49	87	22	2	40	6	58	4	59
23	123,348	25	52,668	27	S	6	44	86	22	2	34	6	59	4	53
24	116,623	16	38,191	25	R	8	35	92	15	0	20	1	44	2	38
25	113,283	19	52,752	37	S	5	37	91	16	1	45	3	70	3	65
26	117,886	23	54,442	35	S	5	42	90	21	2	34	3	57	4	60
27	103,288	4	41,364	35	U	7	36	72	-2	13	16	8	30	5	42
28	107,026	7	49,866	29	S	7	47	74	0	11	27	9	42	5	36
29	101,834	5	34,684	28	U	8	26	71	-3	12	24	9	41	6	39
30	115,284	17	62,802	37	S	4	48	83	12	4	44	9	61	4	48
31	121,411	22	56,207	39	S	5	35	90	20	1	46	3	65	3	64
32	103,818	4	62,728	33	S	4	52	83	-1	2	30	11	46	3	36
33	112,138	11	53,468	32	S	4	41	83	6	5	40	7	53	4	46
34	103,395	4	54,036	32	S	4	46	86	0	2	33	6	47	4	38
35	127,309	26	42,331	26	R	7	35	90	25	2	40	3	63	3	54
36	100,386	1	56,497	38	U	4	60	87	-2	2	35	6	44	3	26
37	99,996	1	46,811	33	U	8	40	31	-17	37	8	26	17	5	22
38	115,823	16	46,686	31	U	5	33	90	13	1	37	4	59	3	51
39	128,487	29	55,101	35	S	5	33	95	28	1	38	1	69	2	57
40	122,325	21	48,713	33	R	6	41	91	19	0	23	2	53	5	55
41	105,805	5	90,652	41	S	3	63	84	1	2	31	11	44	2	27
42	119,815	22	48,666	39	M	5	38	90	20	0	26	2	57	4	54
43	100,729	2	52,055	39	U	5	68	78	-4	6	27	10	34	4	23
44	125,040	23	61,734	31	S	4	45	90	20	1	43	5	64	3	65
45	117,084	17	74,517	42	S	3	57	90	14	1	43	5	59	3	49
46	100,151	0	56,537	34	U	4	63	79	-6	3	26	13	40	4	28
47	118,085	18	61,661	38	S	4	45	86	14	3	42	7	58	3	44
48	99,774	2	83,510	40	S	3	63	84	-3	2	25	11	40	3	27
49	118,247	19	47,913	43	S	7	35	89	16	2	40	4	62	4	63

Note: U=urban, S=suburban, R=rural, M=mixed, HH=households.

WEST VIRGINIA

Born in war and the scene of crushing poverty and brutal labor disputes, West Virginia has witnessed its share of trouble and lawlessness. It has been called, unfairly, the "Afghanistan of America," a place of fierce tribal loyalties and impenetrable communities hidden amid the mountains: in short, a state as wild as it is wonderful. Yet after a generation or more of decline, West Virginia may at last have righted itself.

Communication here has always been frustrated by topography (the mountains) and geography (the state's unusual shape). It has two panhandles and no direct, in-state route between Wheeling to the north and Harper's Ferry to the east. Although it never enjoyed the wealth its labor created, West Virginia took on some of the dirtiest, most hazardous work in industrial America—mining coal, forging steel, and developing a petrochemical industry along the Kanawha River, which for a time produced almost all of the nation's nylon and antifreeze.

No state fared worse during the 1980s, when declining oil prices hurt the chemical industry and the Clean Air Act made the state's bituminous coal uneconomical to mine. West Virginia lost 8 percent of its population during the 1980s—a cataclysm. (By contrast, the state with the worst economy in this decade, Rhode Island, has lost just 1 percent of its population.) Since 1990, however, the state has grown by 2 percent—the eighth-slowest rate in the country but nevertheless faster than Massachusetts, New York, or Pennsylvania. West Virginia takes its good news where it can get it.

As in other states, the few urban areas here are losing population, while the suburban districts are growing. Two-thirds of the population, though, lives in rural areas, and here prosperity depends on location. Rural areas on the outer edge of the suburbs or those that cater to recreation are doing well. Seven of the eight West Virginia house districts that have enjoyed double-digit growth are located around Harper's Ferry, an area that has received much of U.S. senator Robert Byrd's federal largesse and has become a distant commuting suburb of Washington, D.C., and popular weekend getaway destination.

Rural areas that are still dependent on extractive industry are faring poorly. The districts losing population fastest are still in coal country, around the Kentucky and Virginia borders. The Twenty-second District, which includes McDowell County, has lost 12 percent of its population since 1990, double the rate anywhere else in the state, and its unemployment rate is 22 percent. West Virginia has the highest unemployment in the country, 9 percent, but that masks sharp geographic divisions. Twenty-six state house districts still have double-digit unemployment, but in the eastern panhandle the rate is below the national average.

Although West Virginia remains the second-poorest state (average household income is just $258 more than in Mississippi, which ranks last), it has the seventh-fastest rate of income growth. Its lumber and poultry-processing industries are doing well, and Byrd has made good on his pledge to make himself "West Virginia's billion dollar industry" by forcing numerous federal agencies to move offices there. But because the state has attracted so few new jobs, most of its young people continue to move away. More than a quarter of West Virginians are now age fifty-five or older, a percentage second only to Florida's. That seems unlikely to improve; the Census Bureau projects the state to have by far the slowest rate of population growth over the next twenty-five years, less than 1 percent.

Statistically, West Virginia is one of the least racially diverse states in the Union; all but four of its state house districts are at least 90 percent white. Two districts along the Ohio River have no black residents at all, according to 1997 Census Bureau estimates. It has fewer Hispanics and Asians by percentage than any other state.

It is also one of the least-diverse states politically. With the exception of a few wealthy enclaves and corners that have Republican allegiances going back to the Civil War, West Virginia is as Democratic a state as any. Three-quarters of the members of the state house are Democrats, and they controlled the senate by a margin of 33–1 as recently as 1990.

WEST VIRGINIA
State Senate Districts

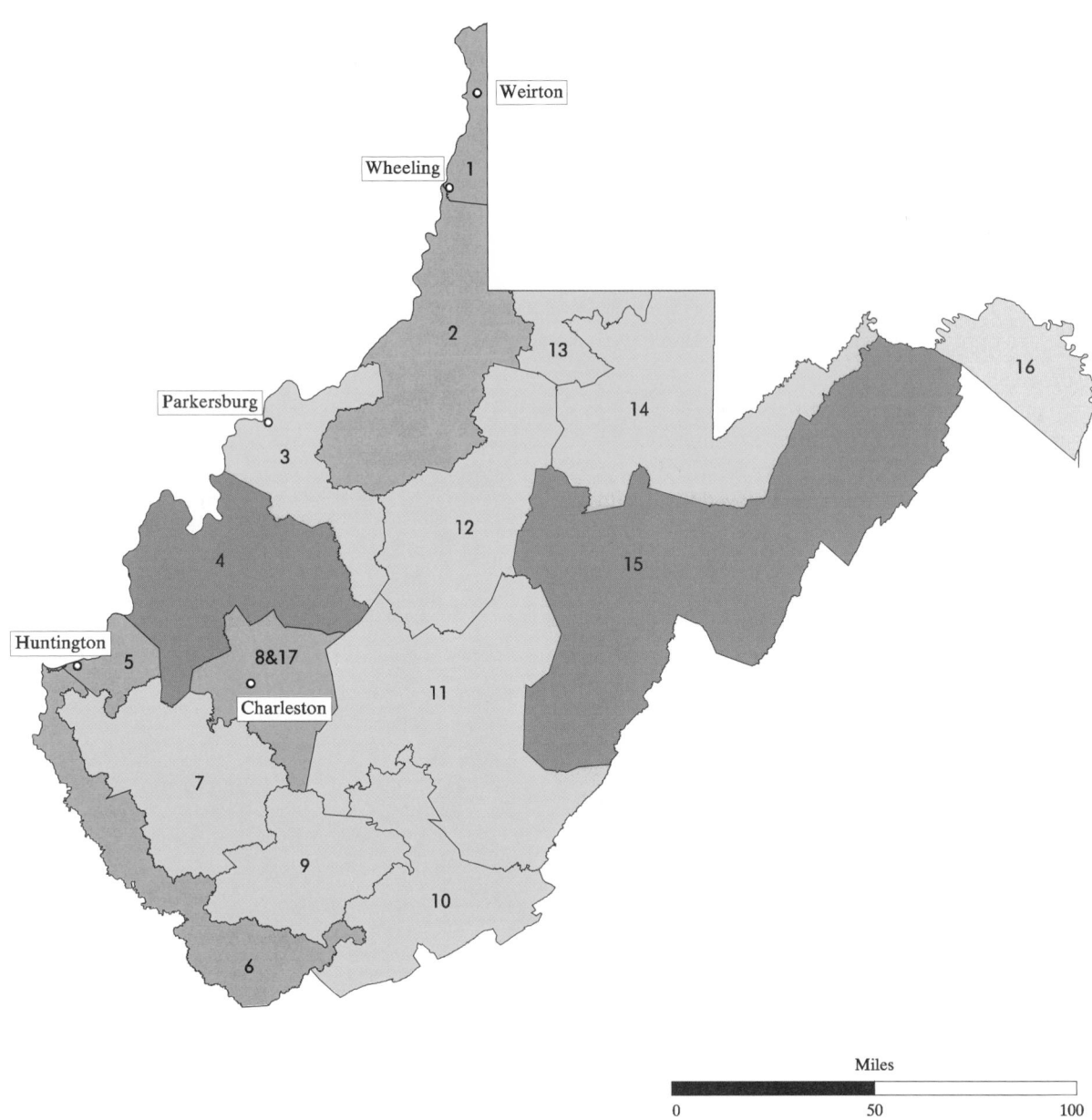

Population Growth   ▨ -5% to -1%   ▨ 0% to 4%   ▨ 7% to 9%   ▨ 15%

West Virginia State Senate Districts: Demographic Data

Senate District	Population 1997	+/-	Average HH Income ($)	+/-	District Type	Unempl. Rate (%)	College Educ. (%)	White (non-Hispanic) (%)	+/-	African American (%)	+/-	Asian American (%)	+/-	Hispanic American (%)	+/-
W. Virginia	1,931,105	2	38,495	41	R	9	26	95	2	3	2	0	16	1	19
1	98,490	-2	43,547	36	M	6	34	97	-2	2	2	1	18	0	19
2	98,932	-2	35,237	37	R	11	22	98	-2	1	-4	0	-1	0	10
3	108,835	1	41,566	44	M	7	28	98	1	1	-2	0	12	0	10
4	119,434	9	41,386	51	R	10	23	99	9	0	-13	0	29	0	17
5	98,429	-1	42,048	43	U	9	34	95	-1	4	0	1	15	1	18
6	96,676	-5	32,579	44	R	15	14	94	-4	5	-9	0	18	0	14
7	100,734	0	32,115	38	R	15	13	98	0	2	-3	0	15	0	6
8	204,447	-2	44,796	43	S	7	33	92	-2	7	2	1	20	1	17
9	107,109	1	35,224	38	R	12	21	93	1	6	5	1	25	0	26
10	106,555	1	32,883	34	R	11	22	93	0	6	2	0	15	1	24
11	115,303	3	31,304	36	R	13	19	96	2	3	5	0	-19	0	13
12	109,674	2	35,110	42	R	11	26	97	2	1	2	0	2	1	22
13	110,747	2	41,033	49	R	9	41	94	1	3	5	2	13	1	12
14	114,869	4	35,082	35	R	9	24	98	4	1	4	0	-3	0	14
15	115,256	7	34,600	40	R	9	22	98	6	1	1	0	3	1	20
16	123,374	15	43,307	33	R	6	27	94	14	5	19	1	49	1	35
17	204,447	-2	44,796	43	M	7	33	92	-2	7	2	1	20	1	17

Note: U=urban, S=suburban, R=rural, M=mixed, HH=households.

WEST VIRGINIA
State House Districts

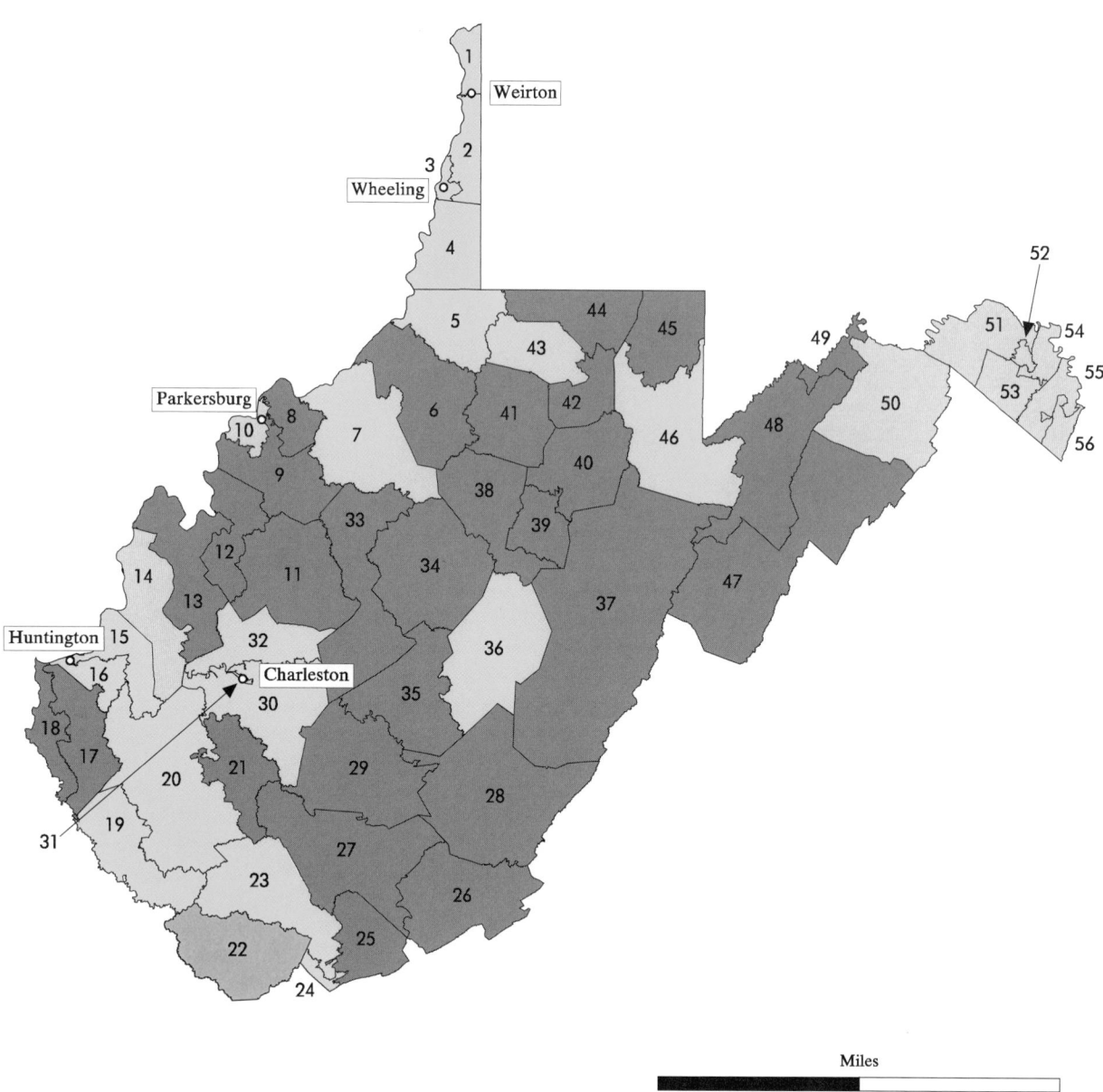

Population Growth   ▨ -12%   ▢ -6% to 0%   ▨ 1% to 9%   ▢ 10% to 19%

West Virginia State House Districts: Demographic Data

House District	Population		Average HH Income		District Type	Unempl. Rate	College Educ.	White (non-Hispanic)		African American		Asian American		Hispanic American	
	1997	+/-	($)	+/-		(%)	(%)	(%)	+/-	(%)	+/-	(%)	+/-	(%)	+/-
W. Virginia	1,931,105	2	38,495	41	R	9	26	95	2	3	2	0	16	1	19
1	35,736	-2	41,574	31	U	7	27	96	-2	3	2	0	9	1	15
2	38,090	-1	41,072	35	S	7	31	98	-1	1	2	0	29	0	28
3	36,434	-4	42,474	44	U	7	37	94	-4	4	-2	1	17	0	13
4	36,311	-3	38,581	34	S	9	25	98	-4	1	1	0	13	1	16
5	18,574	-3	38,296	40	R	14	26	99	-3	0	-38	0	-3	0	-11
6	17,312	3	33,675	39	R	11	23	99	3	0	-67	0	-27	0	0
7	18,884	0	35,505	43	R	11	20	100	0	0	-24	0	-71	0	5
8	22,430	9	50,436	45	S	7	35	98	9	0	-6	1	21	0	45
9	18,082	3	39,473	42	R	8	25	99	3	0	-12	0	-5	0	-7
10	52,807	-2	41,689	45	U	7	29	98	-2	1	0	0	11	0	-5
11	19,645	4	29,974	44	R	16	13	99	4	0	-80	0	-6	0	-3
12	18,549	4	38,592	45	R	9	23	99	4	0	-54	0	22	0	20
13	40,206	7	42,760	49	R	9	22	99	7	0	-23	0	22	0	23
14	41,011	18	46,789	56	R	8	29	99	18	0	-1	1	42	0	19
15	53,585	-1	36,540	42	U	11	30	93	-1	6	-1	0	13	0	10
16	49,781	0	46,636	43	S	7	36	97	-1	2	5	1	16	1	29
17	20,794	2	34,724	39	S	12	19	99	2	0	-38	0	15	0	14
18	18,371	3	35,313	44	S	9	18	100	3	0	-44	0	18	0	-40
19	34,311	-3	34,220	44	R	15	13	96	-3	3	-1	0	47	0	26
20	68,522	-1	33,153	41	R	16	13	97	-1	2	-3	0	17	1	8
21	16,441	2	30,419	27	R	13	13	99	2	1	-1	0	0	0	10
22	31,051	-12	26,955	43	R	22	9	86	-12	14	-11	0	-62	1	2
23	36,696	-4	31,454	37	R	15	12	98	-4	1	-6	0	-31	0	8
24	16,946	-4	38,613	33	R	7	27	83	-5	16	-2	0	11	0	7
25	38,674	2	34,287	34	R	10	25	95	1	3	8	1	15	1	22
26	18,044	2	29,768	30	R	11	18	94	2	4	0	0	21	2	43
27	87,105	3	35,495	37	R	11	23	91	2	7	5	1	30	1	27
28	35,549	3	34,927	38	R	9	24	95	3	4	7	0	-71	0	13
29	51,281	2	31,595	41	R	14	18	92	2	6	5	0	11	1	12
30	119,415	-1	48,004	43	S	6	36	92	-1	6	4	1	23	0	13
31	18,102	-6	29,285	34	U	12	30	68	-9	30	-2	1	8	1	40
32	66,332	-1	44,327	45	S	6	30	97	-1	2	3	0	15	0	13
33	20,029	2	26,673	40	R	16	14	99	2	0	-19	0	-9	0	0
34	17,968	1	28,921	35	R	15	19	99	1	0	-38	0	0	0	4
35	19,882	6	30,339	27	R	13	19	99	6	0	-100	0	-7	0	18
36	17,997	-3	25,273	28	R	18	12	99	-3	0	-60	0	-39	0	0
37	38,186	4	32,359	40	R	13	24	98	4	1	-1	0	-3	1	17
38	18,848	3	31,111	41	R	14	19	99	2	0	-21	0	14	1	45
39	18,164	4	31,705	32	R	9	26	98	4	1	2	0	16	0	18
40	20,857	5	28,395	31	R	12	20	98	5	1	1	0	0	1	17
41	71,329	3	37,598	44	R	9	29	97	2	1	7	0	1	1	21
42	18,447	3	35,572	46	R	11	22	99	3	1	-5	0	7	1	19
43	56,584	0	34,582	34	R	11	29	95	0	3	4	0	12	1	13
44	76,399	4	46,351	56	R	7	46	94	3	3	7	2	13	1	11
45	18,191	6	33,245	32	R	9	21	99	6	0	-10	0	-43	0	8
46	19,582	0	30,389	27	R	11	18	99	0	0	-31	0	-42	0	15
47	19,591	5	41,348	63	R	5	18	97	5	2	3	0	-53	1	20
48	19,536	5	36,051	36	R	6	21	97	5	2	-3	0	25	0	0
49	17,741	5	35,504	27	R	7	30	96	4	3	13	0	10	0	21
50	21,077	15	35,569	32	R	8	21	99	15	1	-1	0	-12	1	38

Note: U=urban, S=suburban, R=rural, M=mixed, HH=households.

West Virginia State House Districts: Demographic Data (cont.)

House District	Population		Average HH Income		District Type	Unempl. Rate	College Educ.	White (non-Hispanic)		African American		Asian American		Hispanic American	
	1997	+/-	($)	+/-		(%)	(%)	(%)	+/-	(%)	+/-	(%)	+/-	(%)	+/-
W. Virginia	1,931,105	2	38,495	41	R	9	26	95	2	3	2	0	16	1	19
51	20,420	19	37,601	28	R	8	24	98	19	1	17	0	53	0	25
52	17,198	12	38,004	31	R	8	30	89	9	8	24	1	64	2	72
53	21,810	17	45,727	35	R	5	22	97	17	2	23	1	64	1	18
54	23,479	17	40,821	33	R	6	25	95	16	4	20	1	66	1	37
55	19,988	10	54,579	37	R	5	35	90	9	8	16	0	22	1	30
56	20,524	15	44,501	33	R	5	24	91	15	7	18	0	12	1	23

Note: U=urban, S=suburban, R=rural, M=mixed, HH=households.

WISCONSIN

Blessed with a pleasant climate, rolling hills, orderly farms, and shores on two Great Lakes, Wisconsin ends the century still possessing many of the natural advantages with which it began it. Little apology need ever be made in behalf of a state best known for cheese and beer.

In the nineteenth and early twentieth centuries, Wisconsin managed to balance the grasping capitalism of Chicago against the sometimes messianic collectivism of the upper plains. Among the state's gifts to national politics have been Lincoln Republicanism (the GOP was born in Ripon in 1854) and the La Follette family's clear-eyed Progressivism, both of which shared a faith in the fundamental reasonableness of people. Wisconsin believed in innovation and participation—the direct primary, the referendum, and the recall. For many years, all state income tax returns were open for public inspection.

At times, Wisconsin politics has slid more toward the ridiculous, like pro-German apologist Victor Berger, Milwaukee's avowedly Socialist U.S. representative (who served 1911–1913 and 1923–1929), or toward the dangerous, like Joe McCarthy in the 1950s. But a better representative might be former U.S. senator William Proxmire, who spent next to nothing on his campaigns, preferring to work the crowd at Green Bay Packers games. There have been (and still are) bitter strikes against the meat-packing and automobile plants in Racine and Kenosha, but the huge government employees union, AFSCME, was also founded in Wisconsin, in 1935.

The state has steered a fairly steady course over the last several decades. Its 4 percent growth rate during the 1980s, a bad time for farmers, was unspectacular but best among the states in the region. Its 6 percent growth rate since 1990 is about at the national average.

Milwaukee remains a center for skilled engineering, although its downtown has been losing population as its suburbs have been growing. Five urban house districts have lost at least 7 percent of their population since 1990, while the Eighty-third District, which spans the suburbs between Milwaukee and Waukesha, has grown by 21 percent. The suburbs around Madison, home of state government and the state university, have also enjoyed strong growth. Fitting a pattern seen nationwide, most of Wisconsin's fastest-growing house districts (sixteen of the top twenty) are either suburban or rural, while three are urban (in smaller Kenosha, Waukesha, and Janesville) and one is of mixed use. Thirteen of the twenty slowest-growing, and all those that have lost population, are in downtown Milwaukee.

Mansions overlook Lake Michigan just north of the city, but only a few miles away poverty reaches its national nadir. The Sixteenth House District, on the north side of Milwaukee, is the poorest state house district in America, poorer than anything in the South Bronx or the Mississippi Delta. Average household income there is just $19,003, and the unemployment rate is 20 percent. The majority of its residents are black, but not an overwhelming majority; almost 20 percent are white, 3 percent are Asian, and 5 percent are Hispanic, among the larger concentrations of the latter two groups in the state. Average income in the Eighteenth District, just to the west, is barely $21,000, making it the tenth-poorest district in the country, and the unemployment rate is 21 percent, highest in the state.

Wisconsin as a whole is 90 percent white, slightly less than Minnesota but considerably higher than Illinois. Concentrations are greatest outside the cities, especially around Sturgeon Bay, along Lake Michigan, and in the southwest corner bordering Iowa. The state has five heavily black house districts, all in Milwaukee. A district in Madison is 9 percent Asian. The Eighth District, south of the Menomonee River, is almost half Hispanic.

Wisconsin has experienced more political volatility recently than either Illinois or Minnesota, as both chambers of its legislature have changed hands, the senate more than once. Democrats began the decade in control of the house and the senate but lost the senate in 1992 and the house in 1994, as Republican candidates rode the coattails of the popular governor, Tommy Thompson, who was up for reelection. Democrats retook the senate in 1996 after one Republican member was successfully recalled by his constituents after voting for a tax increase to pay for a new Milwaukee baseball stadium. La Follette traditions are at work again.

WISCONSIN
State Senate Districts

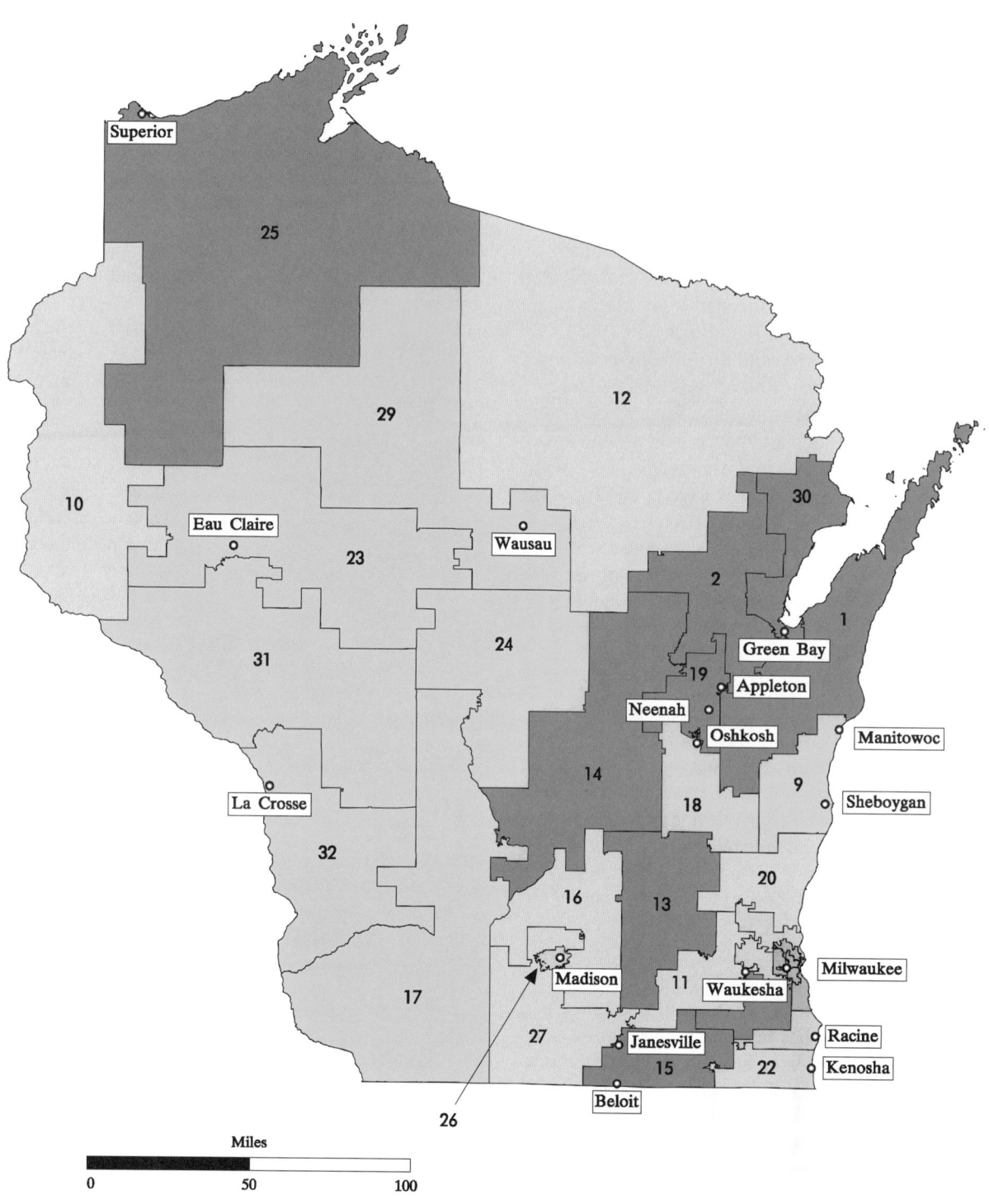

Population Growth ☐ -7% to -2%   ☐ 2% to 6%   ☐ 7% to 10%   ☐ 11% to 15%

MILWAUKEE

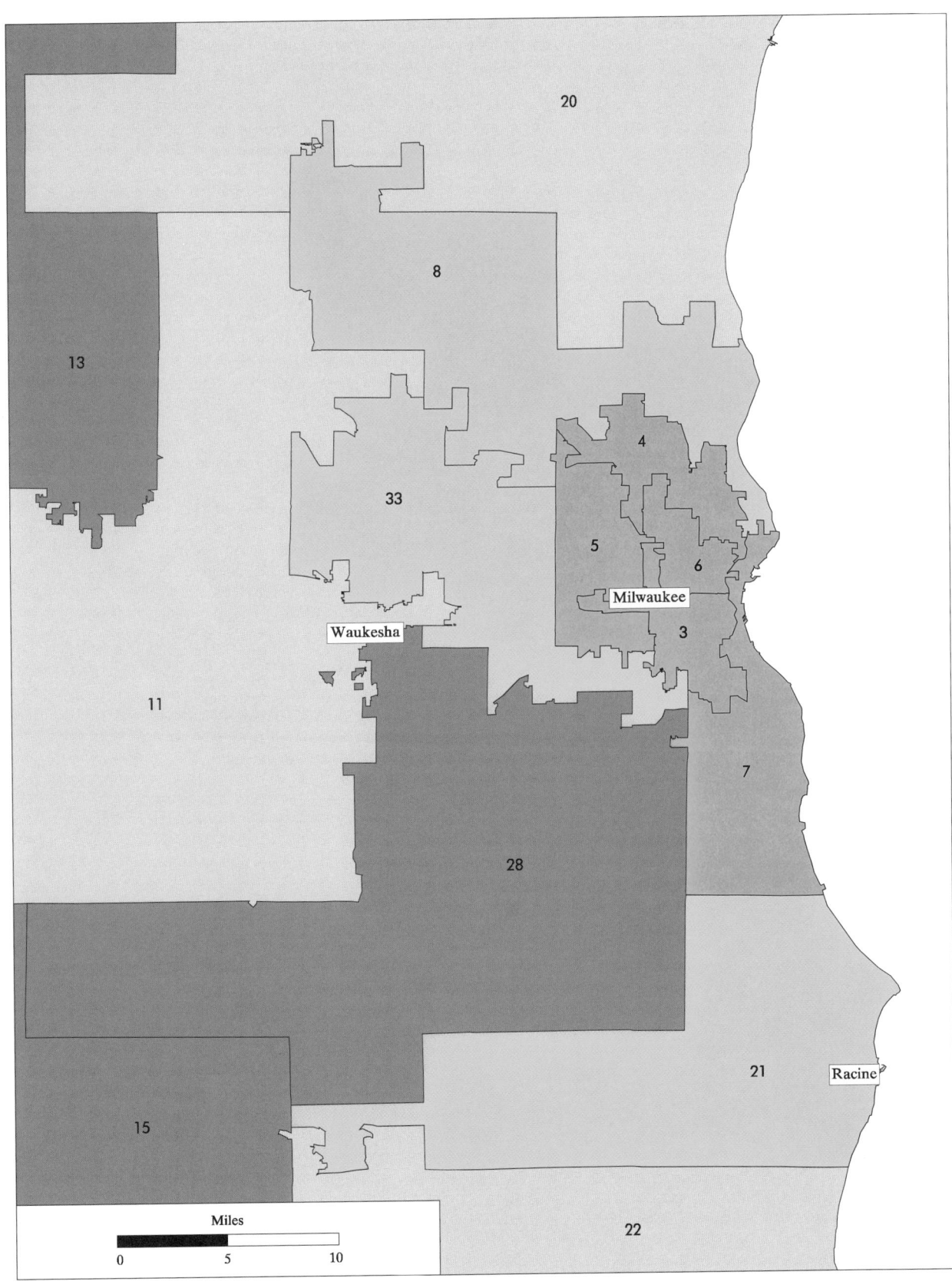

Population Growth   ▢ -7% to -2%   ▢ 2% to 6%   ▢ 7% to 10%   ▢ 11% to 15%

Wisconsin State Senate Districts: Demographic Data

Senate District	Population 1997	+/-	Average HH Income ($)	+/-	District Type	Unempl. Rate (%)	College Educ. (%)	White (non-Hispanic) (%)	+/-	African American (%)	+/-	Asian American (%)	+/-	Hispanic American (%)	+/-
Wisconsin	5,189,832	6	48,831	39	M	5	40	90	4	5	18	1	41	2	34
1	163,949	8	48,473	36	R	4	38	98	8	0	-8	1	43	1	37
2	162,714	9	52,446	40	S	4	40	95	8	0	28	1	41	1	37
3	142,845	-4	35,457	30	U	8	25	68	-13	5	42	3	31	21	25
4	139,780	-6	36,165	29	U	10	25	34	-29	61	12	1	6	4	20
5	136,923	-7	51,158	38	S	3	44	92	-10	4	54	1	41	2	28
6	141,631	-4	24,345	21	U	17	22	17	-36	76	8	3	-1	4	6
7	145,727	-2	49,643	43	U	5	41	90	-5	3	85	2	54	4	26
8	154,464	3	73,603	38	S	3	56	89	-1	7	60	2	46	1	30
9	153,489	5	47,610	39	M	4	36	95	3	0	20	3	48	2	42
10	163,951	11	46,892	36	R	6	41	98	11	0	11	1	42	1	38
11	166,631	15	64,200	38	S	3	49	95	13	1	34	1	59	3	46
12	165,692	12	37,188	38	R	7	28	94	11	0	13	0	3	0	30
13	156,198	9	49,121	39	R	4	35	97	8	0	14	0	42	2	45
14	163,531	10	40,359	36	R	6	30	98	10	0	8	0	18	1	44
15	163,531	10	50,291	41	U	5	36	91	7	5	36	1	45	3	45
16	168,245	12	56,740	48	M	3	47	96	11	1	35	1	53	2	52
17	157,288	6	38,816	31	R	5	34	99	6	0	-22	0	11	0	34
18	156,423	6	45,326	39	R	4	37	96	5	1	34	1	49	1	45
19	162,116	10	56,804	42	U	4	47	96	9	0	27	2	58	1	49
20	167,420	14	62,002	36	R	3	44	98	13	0	36	1	54	1	53
21	152,691	3	50,404	35	U	6	35	77	-3	14	30	1	41	8	38
22	164,588	12	49,391	37	U	6	33	89	9	4	38	1	48	5	47
23	156,487	4	39,481	33	R	6	32	97	3	0	4	2	39	0	31
24	157,186	6	46,218	38	R	6	38	96	5	0	29	1	41	1	49
25	158,000	7	35,058	36	R	9	33	94	6	0	-5	0	14	1	23
26	150,019	2	55,909	47	U	4	71	84	-3	6	33	7	44	3	44
27	172,321	12	57,007	44	M	3	48	95	11	2	41	1	53	1	44
28	161,640	9	63,944	40	S	3	46	95	8	1	64	1	56	2	46
29	155,332	5	44,652	37	M	5	35	97	4	0	-9	2	43	1	33
30	156,522	7	42,269	36	U	6	37	95	5	0	35	2	54	1	42
31	155,709	6	40,633	36	R	6	38	97	5	0	16	1	37	1	37
32	156,328	5	41,782	39	M	5	41	96	4	0	19	2	44	1	43
33	159,939	6	69,212	38	S	3	49	96	5	0	55	2	60	2	51

Note: U=urban, S=suburban, R=rural, M=mixed, HH=households.

WISCONSIN
State Assembly Districts

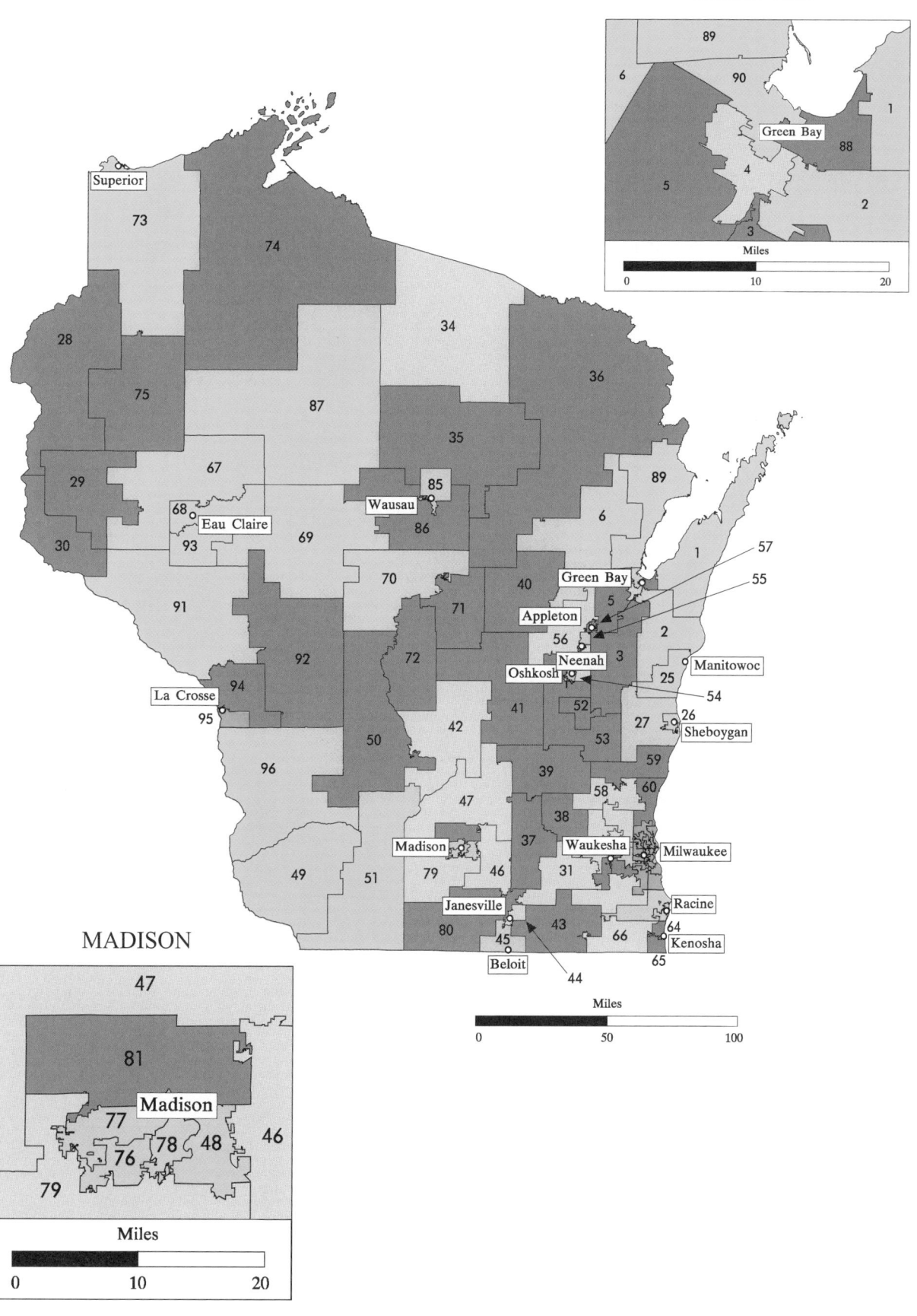

GREEN BAY

MADISON

Population Growth ▨ -10% to -1%   ▨ 0% to 6%   ▨ 7% to 13%   ▨ 14% to 21%

MILWAUKEE

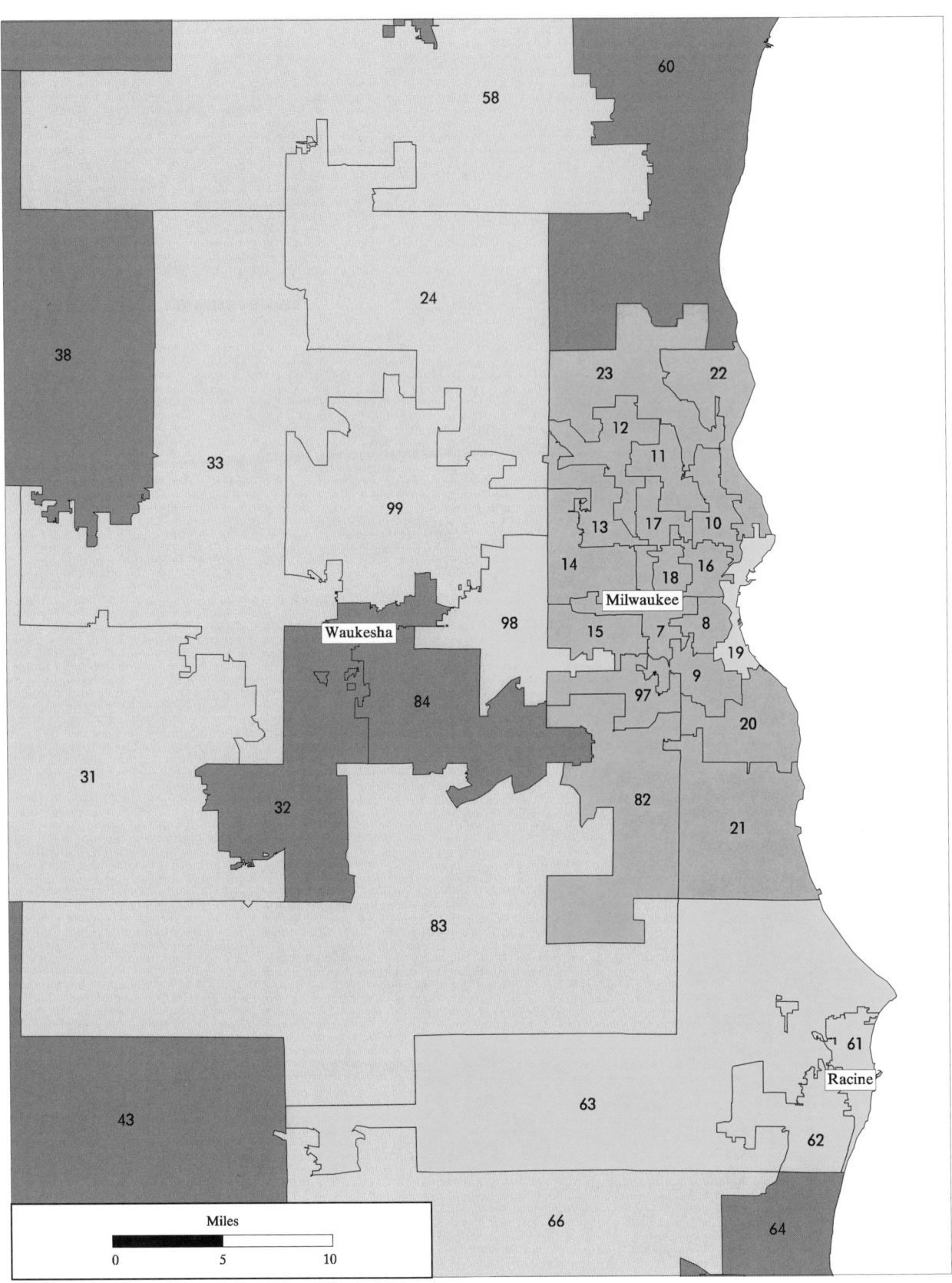

Population Growth ▨ -10% to -1% ▨ 0% to 6% ▨ 7% to 13% ▨ 14% to 21%

Wisconsin State Assembly Districts: Demographic Data

Assembly District	Population		Average HH Income		District Type	Unempl. Rate	College Educ.	White (non-Hispanic)		African American		Asian American		Hispanic American	
	1997	+/-	($)	+/-		(%)	(%)	(%)	+/-	(%)	+/-	(%)	+/-	(%)	+/-
Wisconsin	5,189,832	6	48,831	39	M	5	40	90	4	5	18	1	41	2	34
1	52,242	6	41,883	28	R	5	35	99	5	0	-28	0	-13	1	32
2	53,817	6	49,997	41	R	4	37	98	6	0	4	1	44	0	23
3	57,590	12	53,292	38	M	3	43	98	12	0	-4	1	59	1	52
4	57,127	16	62,666	39	S	4	53	96	15	1	32	1	62	1	41
5	53,757	7	54,902	44	S	4	37	93	6	0	21	1	39	1	40
6	52,357	5	39,541	34	R	6	27	97	4	0	-34	0	-8	1	29
7	46,638	-7	39,232	33	U	6	35	79	-13	10	30	3	25	7	27
8	47,854	-2	24,407	19	U	14	12	38	-27	4	68	6	30	48	23
9	48,486	-2	40,775	35	U	6	26	88	-6	1	79	1	48	8	39
10	49,543	-2	30,648	28	U	15	25	20	-25	73	6	1	6	6	20
11	45,813	-6	32,078	25	U	11	20	21	-40	76	10	1	-9	2	13
12	44,887	-10	45,646	35	U	6	31	63	-25	32	43	1	14	3	24
13	45,034	-8	45,089	34	U	4	39	85	-13	10	54	1	32	2	29
14	46,020	-6	65,974	41	S	2	58	95	-8	2	58	2	49	1	28
15	45,948	-7	43,159	37	S	4	30	96	-8	0	60	1	38	2	26
16	48,023	-2	19,003	25	U	20	18	19	-23	72	4	3	16	5	17
17	45,946	-8	32,676	22	U	11	27	20	-40	77	8	1	-14	2	10
18	47,801	-2	21,186	19	U	21	20	12	-44	78	12	4	-8	5	-5
19	51,602	4	49,096	48	U	5	53	84	-2	7	88	3	59	5	26
20	48,034	-5	45,809	37	S	4	31	93	-7	1	71	1	47	4	30
21	46,210	-3	54,624	42	S	4	35	94	-5	1	75	1	49	3	20
22	47,447	-4	97,236	45	S	3	70	91	-7	3	75	3	50	2	23
23	48,494	-4	62,784	40	S	4	51	77	-13	18	58	2	33	2	25
24	58,374	17	62,511	33	S	3	44	98	16	0	50	1	71	1	63
25	49,827	4	43,838	37	R	5	36	96	2	0	-6	2	44	1	42
26	49,521	6	50,589	41	U	4	38	93	4	0	21	4	51	2	41
27	54,102	4	48,404	37	M	4	33	96	3	1	25	1	42	2	43
28	54,809	11	39,038	35	R	7	32	97	10	0	-33	0	-16	0	29
29	54,895	11	44,598	35	R	6	41	97	11	0	22	2	49	1	35
30	54,250	11	58,186	38	R	4	50	98	11	0	11	1	41	1	47
31	55,453	14	55,147	37	R	4	45	96	13	1	34	1	52	2	48
32	52,186	12	58,688	36	U	3	50	91	9	1	37	2	63	7	45
33	58,976	18	77,546	39	S	3	52	97	17	1	32	1	60	1	46
34	57,106	16	38,951	40	R	7	33	95	15	0	0	0	14	0	22
35	53,265	8	40,020	40	R	6	27	98	8	0	8	0	-1	1	34
36	55,289	12	32,427	33	R	9	22	88	11	0	22	0	-5	1	31
37	50,367	9	47,962	36	R	4	38	97	8	0	3	0	39	2	40
38	52,704	10	52,186	37	R	3	38	98	9	0	7	0	48	1	55
39	53,245	8	47,245	42	R	4	30	97	8	1	17	0	41	2	46
40	54,970	9	43,917	44	R	6	30	98	9	0	-48	0	7	1	37
41	52,240	7	39,476	32	R	6	30	98	6	0	-21	0	22	2	38
42	56,324	15	37,879	31	R	6	31	97	14	1	20	0	23	1	60
43	56,046	10	51,883	40	R	4	35	95	9	0	28	1	42	4	46
44	54,541	16	52,450	42	U	5	42	96	15	1	54	1	57	1	54
45	52,958	3	46,293	41	U	7	29	80	-2	16	36	1	37	2	39
46	55,733	20	54,510	47	S	4	46	97	19	0	45	0	61	2	70
47	63,828	16	58,244	47	R	3	42	98	15	0	41	0	43	1	47
48	48,672	0	57,316	49	U	3	53	93	-2	3	34	1	53	2	40
49	49,742	1	36,673	25	R	5	38	99	1	0	-5	1	26	0	24
50	54,732	10	39,324	39	R	6	28	98	10	0	-42	0	-11	1	43

Note: U=urban, S=suburban, R=rural, M=mixed, HH=households.

Wisconsin State Assembly Districts: Demographic Data (cont.)

Assembly District	Population 1997	+/-	Average HH Income ($)	+/-	District Type	Unempl. Rate (%)	College Educ. (%)	White (non-Hispanic) (%)	+/-	African American (%)	+/-	Asian American (%)	+/-	Hispanic American (%)	+/-
Wisconsin	5,189,832	6	48,831	39	M	5	40	90	4	5	18	1	41	2	34
51	52,773	6	40,265	29	R	4	36	99	6	0	-32	0	0	0	29
52	53,618	8	44,787	37	R	5	38	96	7	0	24	1	47	2	42
53	53,739	10	52,625	42	R	4	35	96	9	2	39	0	65	1	53
54	49,045	1	38,951	36	U	5	38	94	0	1	28	3	48	1	38
55	49,162	6	51,749	39	S	4	43	97	5	0	26	1	51	1	43
56	60,816	17	64,156	45	S	3	47	97	16	1	28	1	61	1	49
57	52,275	7	54,097	41	U	4	50	94	5	0	24	4	59	1	55
58	58,267	17	55,470	32	R	3	40	98	16	0	-16	0	57	1	54
59	53,993	13	51,739	33	R	3	35	98	12	0	-15	0	49	1	39
60	55,164	12	78,787	42	S	2	55	97	11	1	48	1	56	1	71
61	48,745	2	37,954	28	U	10	28	54	-13	32	24	0	18	14	31
62	49,387	1	48,121	33	U	5	36	83	-4	9	49	1	40	6	37
63	54,593	6	64,467	39	S	4	41	92	3	3	54	1	51	4	63
64	53,098	7	40,881	31	U	8	31	82	2	9	39	1	43	8	41
65	54,963	12	51,391	35	U	7	34	89	9	4	36	1	58	6	47
66	56,456	17	55,847	42	R	5	32	96	16	0	40	0	36	3	71
67	53,125	6	38,972	33	R	6	33	99	5	0	-14	0	27	0	32
68	50,506	1	41,762	35	U	6	39	94	-1	0	25	5	42	1	33
69	52,875	4	37,737	32	R	5	25	99	4	0	-24	0	13	0	26
70	54,225	2	48,279	40	R	5	37	97	2	0	2	1	39	1	42
71	52,080	9	45,329	40	R	5	44	96	8	0	15	2	38	2	46
72	50,879	7	44,982	35	R	8	32	95	6	1	41	1	47	2	56
73	53,236	5	35,961	36	U	9	34	96	4	0	4	1	26	1	26
74	52,676	7	34,248	43	R	10	33	89	6	0	-20	0	-9	1	14
75	52,084	7	34,957	30	R	7	32	98	7	0	-21	0	-1	0	33
76	50,747	3	64,802	48	U	3	73	88	-1	5	40	5	59	2	46
77	50,555	2	67,809	50	U	3	77	84	-2	3	35	9	33	3	47
78	48,837	1	36,043	41	U	5	63	80	-5	10	29	6	52	4	39
79	60,413	20	66,327	49	S	2	57	96	19	2	58	1	80	1	61
80	56,825	8	48,012	34	R	5	35	98	8	0	37	0	12	1	40
81	54,936	8	56,520	46	U	3	51	91	6	4	36	2	50	2	38
82	46,851	-4	63,800	42	S	3	47	92	-6	3	67	2	51	2	31
83	59,928	21	62,802	40	S	4	40	97	20	0	60	1	61	2	55
84	54,858	10	65,245	39	S	3	53	95	8	0	45	1	63	3	52
85	50,747	5	47,896	40	U	4	40	92	3	0	6	6	46	1	42
86	53,805	8	52,560	42	S	4	38	98	8	0	-22	1	51	0	41
87	50,728	2	33,679	25	R	7	28	99	2	0	-15	0	3	0	12
88	53,491	11	44,776	42	U	6	41	91	9	1	42	4	55	2	45
89	51,772	6	40,582	32	R	7	30	99	6	0	-38	0	19	1	34
90	51,332	3	41,228	32	U	5	39	94	2	0	37	2	54	1	42
91	51,005	4	37,381	32	R	5	30	99	4	0	-52	0	-36	0	13
92	53,273	7	37,558	34	R	6	29	96	7	0	17	0	19	1	42
93	51,411	6	47,104	41	U	6	53	96	5	0	25	2	51	1	42
94	55,296	11	48,743	43	S	4	45	97	10	0	25	2	42	1	50
95	48,362	-1	42,222	41	U	5	48	91	-3	1	23	6	47	1	51
96	52,696	6	34,253	30	R	5	29	99	6	0	-8	0	-2	0	16
97	47,977	-3	49,905	38	U	4	34	94	-5	1	73	1	53	3	40
98	50,890	4	76,818	36	S	3	56	96	3	1	58	2	59	1	52
99	61,014	17	79,854	34	S	3	55	96	16	0	32	2	66	1	76

Note: U=urban, S=suburban, R=rural, M=mixed, HH=households.

WYOMING

Wyoming is the least-populous state and one of the emptiest in the nation. Population density is 5 people per square mile, as compared with the District of Columbia, where it is 8,847. Just 481,000 people lived here in 1997, in a land area seventy-eight times as big as Rhode Island. The least populous of California's forty state senate districts, to make another comparison, contains 637,000 people.

One can drive for hundreds of miles across the middle of Wyoming without finding a gas station or picking up either an AM or FM radio station. Although real cowboys continue to work the cattle ranches (riding pickups instead of horses), eastern vacationers still flock to the many dude ranches to experience the life they have read about in novels. The past is not far away. A visitor to the state fifty years ago could have met living delegates to the statehood convention of 1889. (Like Nevada, Wyoming was admitted illegally, when it lacked the requisite number of residents for statehood.) A person who stops by the side of the road to walk through the sagebrush can still see ruts made by covered wagons.

Wyoming is more complicated than the old westerns suggest. Until recently, men still outnumbered women, yet Wyoming approved women's suffrage when it was a territory, and in 1925 it became the first state to elect a woman governor. Much of the land now included in Grand Teton National Park once belonged to John D. Rockefeller Jr. and was given to the United States in 1943. Although much of the land is devoted to sheep and cattle grazing (the two sets of ranchers once fought violently), Wyoming also grows sugar beets and alfalfa and is the nation's leading coal-mining state, thanks to the Clean Air Act, which made its cleaner-burning, low-sulfur coal more economical.

Wyoming also sits atop vast oil reserves. Seventy-five years ago, the nation shook with scandal when it was discovered that Interior Secretary Albert Fall had made sweetheart leases for cronies at the Naval Petroleum Reserve Number 3, better known for the name of a nearby rock formation: Teapot Dome.

An oil-, gas-, coal-, and ranch-based economy was bound to suffer during the 1980s, when Wyoming lost more than 3 percent of its population. Its 7 percent growth rate during the 1990s is a sharp improvement but still the slowest in what is again the fastest-growing region of the country. The fastest-growing, and wealthiest, district in the state is Jackson Hole, now a ritzy ski resort and as dissimilar from the rest of Wyoming as can be imagined. Part of Cheyenne and the town of Riverton have also grown by close to 20 percent.

The Casper suburbs and Carbon County (coal mining territory) are among the areas that have lost people. Yet Wyoming is not an especially poor state; household income here is the same as in Oregon and Florida. Unemployment is now at the national average, though it peaks at 15 percent on the Wind River Indian reservation.

No state was the destination of fewer immigrants in 1995, the most recent year for which figures are available, than Wyoming—252, to be exact. (California, much bigger of course, received more than 166,000 immigrants.) Ninety-one percent of Wyoming's citizens are white, with the highest percentages in the isolated northern corners of the state. Most of the few African Americans (only 1 percent of the population) live in Cheyenne. Another house district across town, however, is 20 percent Hispanic. Two percent of the population is Native American.

The smallest of Wyoming's state house districts has fewer than 5,000 people, making it possible for representatives to know many of their constituents personally, though they must travel great distances to see them. The GOP controls both chambers of the legislature by better than two-to-one majorities, which have gotten bigger during the decade. Wyoming, finally, has one at-large U.S. representative, and in one hundred years of statehood has never had a second district.

WYOMING
State Senate Districts

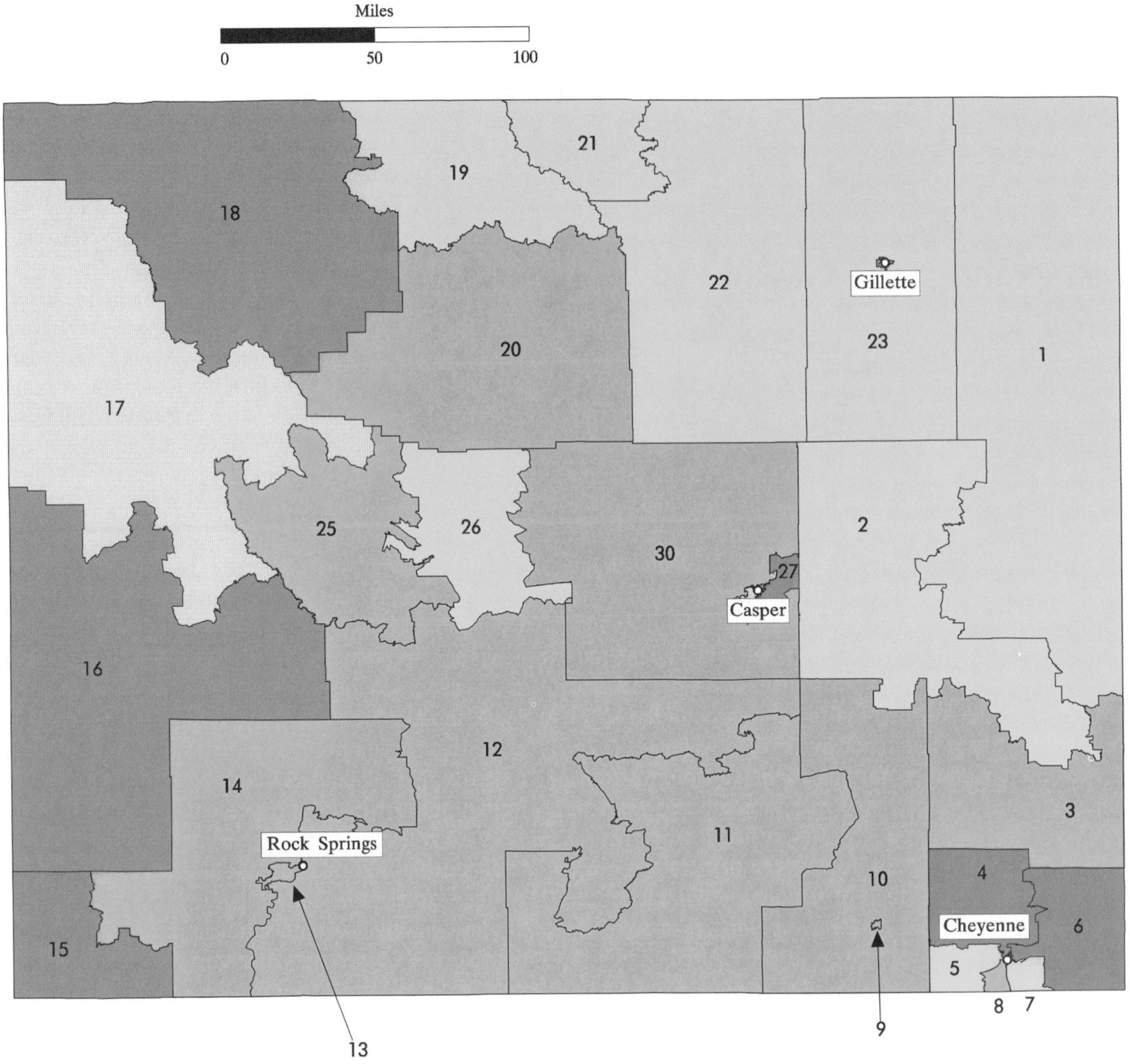

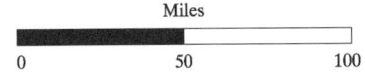

Miles

0   50   100

18

19

21

17

20

22

Gillette

23

1

25

26

30

27

Casper

2

16

12

14

11

3

Rock Springs

10

4

Cheyenne

6

15

5

8   7

9

13

CASPER

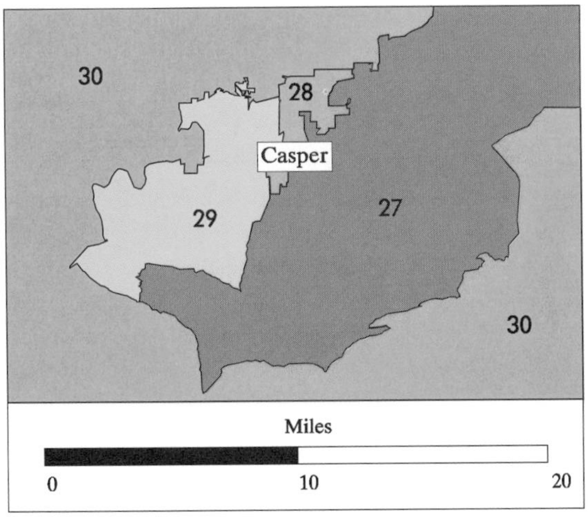

30

28

Casper

29

27

30

Miles

0   10   20

GILLETTE

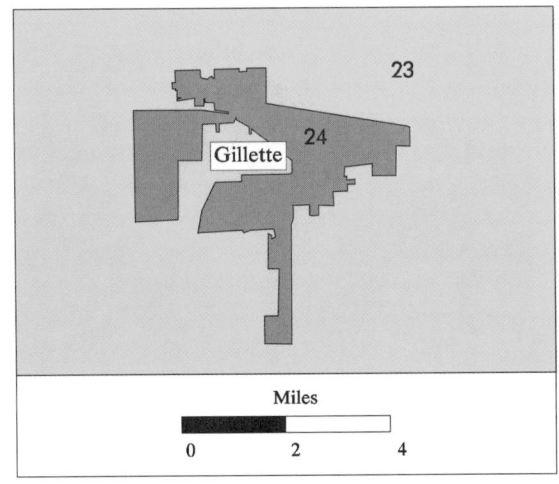

23

24

Gillette

Miles

0   2   4

Population Growth   ☐ -5% to 4%   ☐ 5% to 10%   ☐ 11% to 13%   ☐ 23%

Wyoming State Senate Districts: Demographic Data

Senate District	Population		Average HH Income		District Type	Unempl. Rate	College Educ.	White (non-Hispanic)		African American		Asian American		Hispanic American	
	1997	+/-	($)	+/-		(%)	(%)	(%)	+/-	(%)	+/-	(%)	+/-	(%)	+/-
Wyoming	484,723	7	46,404	42	R	6	39	91	7	1	-9	1	18	6	8
1	15,663	5	40,563	37	R	5	33	98	5	0	22	0	-47	1	5
2	17,596	7	39,368	29	R	8	29	92	7	0	-17	0	-16	7	5
3	15,191	4	39,220	43	R	6	33	93	4	0	-8	0	-11	6	2
4	21,692	13	54,521	39	U	5	46	90	11	1	1	1	36	7	27
5	13,979	9	55,010	43	U	7	50	88	9	4	-5	2	30	5	15
6	13,836	13	48,093	41	U	5	41	90	13	2	5	1	17	7	24
7	15,170	8	39,038	38	U	5	33	85	6	2	-5	1	25	12	23
8	15,255	3	36,265	45	U	12	29	71	4	4	-14	1	23	23	5
9	12,983	2	32,852	37	R	5	52	88	1	1	-8	2	6	9	12
10	17,716	-1	50,927	46	R	5	59	91	-1	1	-10	2	6	5	-10
11	13,295	-5	42,924	41	R	5	36	86	-6	0	-7	0	25	12	-3
12	17,934	2	54,216	47	R	6	33	87	2	1	-16	1	22	10	2
13	11,891	4	59,688	52	R	5	33	88	4	1	-23	1	17	11	7
14	17,795	3	60,785	52	R	5	36	91	3	0	-33	0	20	7	1
15	16,742	12	49,852	30	R	6	33	94	11	0	-40	0	21	5	11
16	17,166	13	43,116	33	R	5	35	97	13	0	-45	0	7	2	14
17	18,508	23	59,207	51	R	3	49	97	23	0	5	0	32	1	20
18	19,179	12	45,250	37	R	5	40	96	12	0	-56	0	20	2	12
19	15,360	8	35,428	33	R	7	33	93	8	0	0	0	16	6	7
20	15,741	2	38,586	34	R	5	35	92	2	0	-27	0	-2	6	1
21	15,774	8	43,647	41	R	6	37	97	8	0	-36	1	18	2	10
22	16,573	9	40,034	34	R	5	37	97	10	0	-68	0	16	1	-2
23	19,382	9	63,578	48	R	5	37	96	9	0	-7	0	28	3	10
24	12,974	13	53,430	47	R	6	39	95	12	0	20	0	45	3	21
25	15,311	4	37,097	40	R	11	35	71	4	0	-58	0	-6	3	-5
26	17,960	10	38,195	39	R	8	32	82	10	0	-13	0	0	5	13
27	16,488	11	50,024	40	U	6	48	95	10	1	10	1	31	3	22
28	15,209	0	45,253	51	U	8	42	92	0	1	-7	1	24	5	7
29	16,287	7	50,347	41	U	6	45	95	7	0	4	0	31	3	6
30	16,025	0	45,728	46	M	6	31	95	0	0	-20	0	6	4	-8

Note: U=urban, S=suburban, R=rural, M=mixed, HH=households.

WYOMING
State House Districts

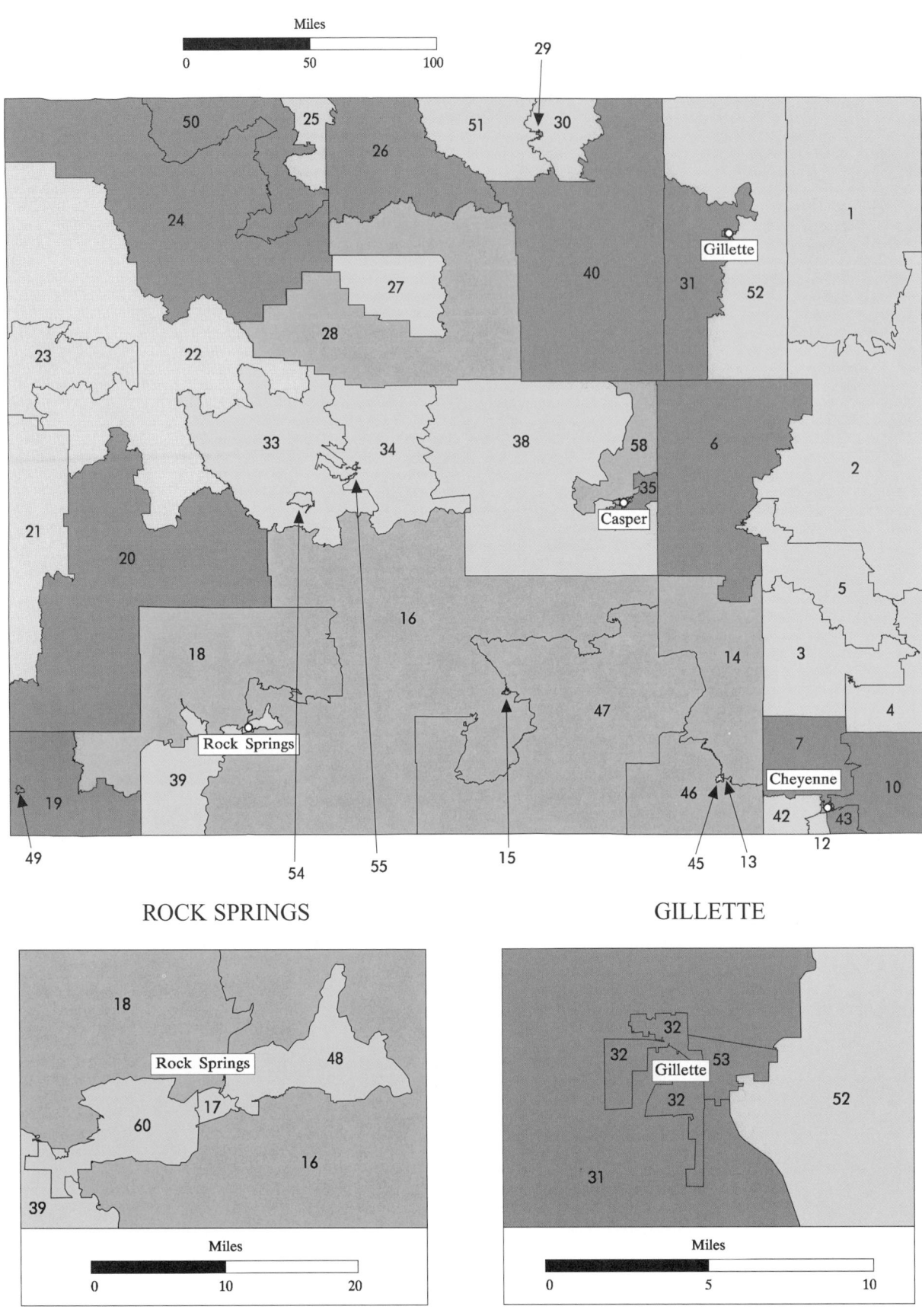

ROCK SPRINGS

GILLETTE

Population Growth   ▢ -8% to 0%   ▢ 3% to 8%   ▢ 9% to 15%   ▢ 17% to 25%

CASPER

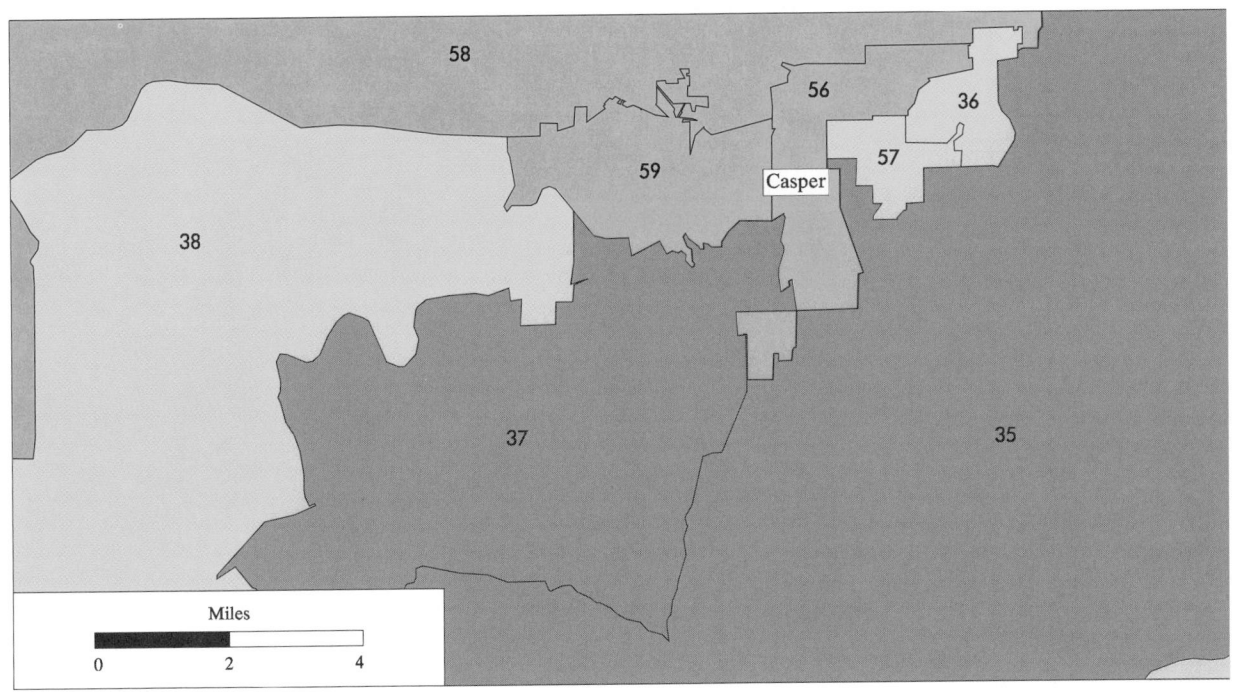

CHEYENNE

Population Growth   ▢ -8% to 0%   ▢ 3% to 8%   ▢ 9% to 15%   ▢ 17% to 25%

Wyoming State House Districts: Demographic Data

House District	Population		Average HH Income		District Type	Unempl. Rate	College Educ.	White (non-Hispanic)		African American		Asian American		Hispanic American	
	1997	+/-	($)	+/-		(%)	(%)	(%)	+/-	(%)	+/-	(%)	+/-	(%)	+/-
Wyoming	484,723	7	46,404	42	R	6	39	91	7	1	-9	1	18	6	8
1	8,704	6	40,689	44	R	5	36	99	6	0	0	0	-44	1	0
2	6,959	4	40,421	31	R	4	30	97	4	0	22	0	-50	2	8
3	8,264	4	38,813	40	R	5	31	91	3	0	0	0	-20	8	15
4	6,926	3	39,683	46	R	7	35	96	4	0	-8	0	0	3	-24
5	9,433	4	39,720	32	R	8	27	91	4	0	-27	0	-20	8	0
6	8,125	12	39,026	25	R	7	32	93	12	0	13	0	-15	6	14
7	12,895	14	61,247	38	U	4	50	91	13	1	4	1	35	6	27
8	7,041	10	55,781	43	U	6	53	90	9	2	0	1	33	6	32
9	4,982	19	45,722	42	U	6	43	87	19	3	6	1	45	8	29
10	8,874	10	49,397	41	M	5	39	92	10	1	0	0	-4	6	20
11	8,222	6	38,015	37	U	5	35	85	4	2	-6	1	25	12	25
12	7,941	8	40,337	38	S	9	32	78	8	3	-10	1	22	17	14
13	6,110	-2	36,581	39	R	5	60	92	-1	1	-10	2	6	5	-12
14	9,071	0	46,656	46	R	5	69	91	1	1	-11	3	6	3	-20
15	5,718	-3	40,760	38	R	5	33	77	-5	0	-19	0	44	22	3
16	11,869	0	51,383	46	R	7	32	86	0	1	-17	1	17	11	1
17	6,388	5	61,458	55	R	4	37	90	5	1	-15	1	19	8	9
18	8,364	0	59,523	48	R	6	30	93	0	0	-32	0	10	5	0
19	10,411	10	48,380	38	R	6	31	94	10	0	-29	1	17	5	10
20	8,263	9	44,310	23	R	5	35	96	9	0	-75	0	14	2	8
21	8,903	17	41,834	49	R	6	35	98	17	0	33	0	-22	1	25
22	9,026	21	50,614	44	R	4	47	97	21	0	-50	0	5	1	18
23	9,485	25	67,302	56	R	3	50	97	25	0	21	1	50	2	22
24	8,788	15	50,529	40	R	4	43	98	15	0	-100	0	11	2	30
25	6,978	7	37,455	37	R	8	36	93	7	0	0	1	24	6	0
26	8,382	9	33,825	31	R	6	30	93	8	0	0	0	-9	6	14
27	7,897	4	40,266	34	R	5	37	89	4	0	80	0	3	10	2
28	7,844	0	36,968	34	R	5	34	96	0	0	-59	0	-15	2	-5
29	7,884	11	36,242	39	R	7	30	96	10	0	-43	1	17	2	17
30	8,529	8	42,201	35	R	7	36	97	9	0	-67	0	21	2	-2
31	10,257	11	61,275	47	R	5	39	95	11	0	0	0	52	3	15
32	4,617	13	65,444	46	R	3	43	95	13	0	10	0	47	3	18
33	8,407	3	37,067	46	R	15	28	55	3	0	-67	0	-31	3	-10
34	11,304	7	41,391	46	R	9	31	79	7	0	-19	0	2	5	6
35	9,290	13	57,490	46	U	6	52	95	13	1	13	1	36	3	29
36	7,198	7	40,733	29	U	7	42	95	7	1	4	1	23	4	16
37	9,054	13	64,949	43	U	5	53	96	13	0	14	1	33	2	12
38	9,169	6	52,398	46	U	4	38	97	6	0	-21	0	21	2	11
39	9,430	5	61,941	56	R	5	40	89	5	0	-29	1	26	9	2
40	8,044	11	37,788	32	R	3	38	98	11	0	-100	0	0	1	-1
41	8,855	11	45,534	40	U	5	39	88	9	2	-3	2	36	8	26
42	6,939	8	53,770	43	S	7	46	86	9	7	-7	3	30	4	-3
43	6,948	10	40,475	39	M	6	31	85	9	1	-4	1	22	12	22
44	7,314	-2	32,793	50	U	15	27	63	-1	5	-17	1	24	29	0
45	6,893	5	29,589	35	R	5	45	84	3	1	-6	2	7	13	23
46	8,640	-2	54,296	47	R	5	52	92	-2	0	-5	1	6	6	-2
47	7,560	-7	44,666	43	R	6	37	93	-6	0	9	1	21	5	-18
48	6,065	5	59,108	48	R	5	35	89	5	1	-16	1	26	8	7
49	6,315	14	52,253	20	R	5	37	95	15	0	-67	0	25	4	13
50	10,361	9	40,661	34	R	6	37	96	9	0	-43	1	26	3	5

Note: U=urban, S=suburban, R=rural, M=mixed, HH=households.

Wyoming State House Districts: Demographic Data (cont.)

House District	Population		Average HH Income		District Type	Unempl. Rate	College Educ.	White (non-Hispanic)		African American		Asian American		Hispanic American	
	1997	+/-	($)	+/-		(%)	(%)	(%)	+/-	(%)	+/-	(%)	+/-	(%)	+/-
Wyoming	484,723	7	46,404	42	R	6	39	91	7	1	-9	1	18	6	8
51	7,902	6	51,576	43	R	5	44	97	6	0	-29	0	24	2	3
52	9,124	6	66,232	50	R	5	33	96	6	0	-17	0	8	3	6
53	8,357	12	48,013	47	R	7	36	95	12	0	30	0	44	4	23
54	6,906	5	37,143	34	R	7	42	90	5	0	-33	0	9	2	3
55	6,678	17	33,698	29	R	6	34	85	15	0	0	0	-4	7	24
56	8,219	-5	42,946	54	U	9	40	92	-5	1	-14	0	10	5	-5
57	7,047	8	48,262	45	U	6	44	93	7	1	7	1	33	5	27
58	6,856	-8	37,501	42	S	9	21	93	-7	1	-20	0	-9	5	-18
59	7,242	0	35,388	31	U	6	33	94	0	0	-17	0	22	4	2
60	5,503	4	57,566	49	R	5	28	85	4	0	-31	0	8	13	6

Note: U=urban, S=suburban, R=rural, M=mixed, HH=households.